Bill & Hillary

So This Is That Thing Called Love

Award-Winning Entertainment
About How America Interprets its Celebrities

www.BloodMoonProductions.com

Was There a Vast, Right-Wing Conspiracy?

Reactions to Bonnie & Clyde's Invasion of Washington

"It became well known during the Clinton years that while the president was a 'certified' sleazeball, the most evil partner of this Bonnie and Clyde duo was Hillary. She is the *consigliore* of the couple, the one who executes (pun intended) their dastardly plans and deeds."

—Larry Klayman

"When Hillary Clinton spoke of a vast right-wing conspiracy determined to bring down the president, many people dismissed the idea. Yet, if the First Lady's accusation was exaggerated, the facts that have since emerged point toward a covert and often concerted effort by Bill Clinton's enemies—abetted by his own reckless behavior—which led inexorably to impeachment. Clinton's foes launched a cascade of well-financed attacks that undermined American democracy and nearly destroyed the Clinton presidency."

—Joe Conaston & Gene Lyons

"I saw it all—the violent arguments, the back-hall scheming, the empire-building, the backstabbing, the cynical posturing, the raw ambition, and the last-minute flip-flops that somehow produced real accomplishments, but also set in motion an almost tragic series of events that placed the president's fate in the hands of the Senate."

—George Stephanopoulos

"Who is Hillary? High-powered lawyer or re-invented cookie-baking wife and mother? Trusted helpmate to her hubby, or the one who pulls the strings? Human computer or warm, caring person? Proud spirit or suffering wife, betrayed by Bill's marital infidelities?"

—Judith Warner

"When it comes to lipstick, I say the brighter. Besides, being the mother of Bill and Roger, I'm known for my weird hair, heavy makeup and colors, and my penchant for playing the horses."

—Virginia Clinton Kelley

"We were the only game in town. A Southern babe, a Rhodes scholar presidential candidate, a compelling wife, tabloid sex, lies, an audiotape—how could you care about another candidate?"

—James Carville on the 1992 presidential race

"The story of the Clinton presidency has always been the story of a marriage. Their relationship is both supportive and destructive. Hillary is addicted to Bill, and he desperately depends on her to bring him back again from the political dead."

—Gail Sheehy

"The Clinton years might seem like a long national nightmare of scandal, sleaze, and ruthless acquisition of power. Hillary herself is the link from the excesses of the Watergate staff to the Whitewater fiasco to abuses of executive power and obstruction of justice. But now it is her turn. The Clinton era is far from over, and Hillary's ambitions are far from satisfied."

—Clinton hater Barbara Olson,
whose hijacked plane crashed into the Pentagon

"That stain on Monica Lewinsky's blue dress distracted the FBI and other security forces from recognizing the imminent attack of 9/11."

—Hillary Clinton

"The Clinton family had long-standing ties to the notorious Dixie Mafia. Billions of dollars of cocaine, cash, and weapons passed through Arkansas in the 1980s with the full knowledge of Bill and Hillary. During their reign, Arkansas was nothing less than a narco-state, with tiny banks in backwoods Arkansas laundering more cash than the big banks of New York City."

—Victor Thorn

"No public figure in contemporary life has elicited more polarized reactions than Hillary Rodham Clinton, the first presidential spouse who pursued a major policy-making role. The beleaguered First Lady has been a heroine and a role model for her feminist allies—and, to her conservative foes, a malevolent, power-mad shrew. Is she Bill Clinton's greatest asset, or his greatest liability?"

—David Brock

"In spite of Paula Jones' allegations about a peculiar bend in President Clinton's penis, in terms of size, shape, direction, whatever the devious mind wants to concoct, he is a normal man."

—Clinton Attorney Bob Bennett on CBS

"Hillary Clinton directs a coven of brutally correct women who want to rule over us. Her regiment of hardened militant feminists include lesbians, sex perverts, child molester advocates, Christian haters, and the most doctrinaire of communists. If she becomes president, will she go on to usher in a frightening new Millennium?"

—Texe Marrs

"I worked for both Bill Clinton and George W. Bush on the White House staff. President Clinton had his faults, but Bush wasn't perfect. During the worst nights, he used to chase imaginary flies with a fly swatter, running up and down the corridors of the White House until Laura restrained him."

—an anonymous White House aide

"Bill and Hillary Clinton left the White House under a cloud, dogged by sordid sexual scandals, a series of highly compromising investigations, and last-minute pardons that won bipartisan condemnation. Even many Democrats were glad to see them go. Yet within just a few years, Bill had secured a reputation as a global humanitarian and Democratic Party Elder Statesman, and Hillary was running for president."

—Daniel Halper

"I was singing in nightclubs, wearing very sexy outfits and gowns, a very independent and liberated woman. I was the Madonna of my day in Little Rock. Bill Clinton was the love of my life."

—Gennifer Flowers

"Bill Clinton is a womanizing, Elvis-loving, non-inhaling, truth-shading, war-protesting, draft-dodging, abortion protecting, gay-promoting, gun-hating Baby Boomer from hell."

—George H.W. Bush

"Brad Pitt is too good looking to play me in a movie of my life. George Clooney is at least more my size. He's good looking, you know. You could put bulbous things on his nose and could do makeup with him."

—Bill Clinton

"I don't think you should conclude that Bill Clinton has done anything to merit this hatred, other than be a symbol of everything some people fear and despise about the modern world. These are tales from the fundamentalist apocrypha. He's been accused of everything but devil worship."

—Gene Lyons, The Arkansas Democrat-Gazette

"In America now, paranoia runs deep, and the Clinton crazies' influence taps into that climate. Nearly half the population believes that the C.I.A. was involved in the assassination of President Kennedy; one in ten adults thinks the moon landing was a hoax. People seem to want to believe the worst about the Clintons. They don't trust the networks, the newspapers, or the government."

—Philip Weiss, The New York Times

Bill & Hillary
So This Is That Thing Called Love

Darwin Porter and Danforth Prince

www.BloodMoonProductions.com

Manufactured in the United States of America

ISBN 978-1-936003-47-1

Special thanks to the Stanley Mills Haggart Collection, Shutterstock.com, APImages.com, the Library of Congress, The Clinton Library, the White House Press Office, and Wikimedia Commons

Front cover design by Richard Leeds (Bigwigdesign.com)
Videography and Publicity Trailers by Piotr Kajstura

Distributed worldwide through National Book Network
(www.NBNbooks.com)

1 2 3 4 5 6 7 8 9 10

BILL & HILLARY

So This Is That Thing Called Love

Darwin Porter &
Danforth Prince

New And Coming Soon!

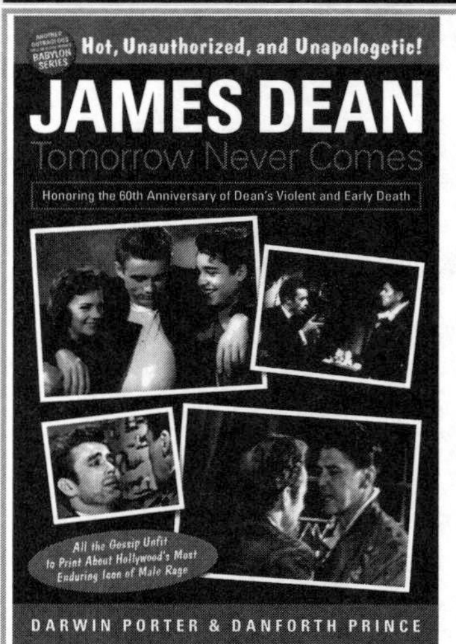

On the 60th anniversary of the death of James Dean, Blood Moon will explode some Hollywood myths with a fresh, often shocking new look at an enigmatic cult icon who defined male rage and a new generation of actors.

Immortalized as the brooding archetype of adolescence, he was a handsome and charismatic boy/man determined not to love or be loved, but to live faster than his Porsche and to achieve conquest of both women and men.

He lives again in this, the most insightful and unvarnished overview to emerge from the wreckage of the car crash that killed him. James Dean, the first true pop star victim of the American Dream Machine. Or, in his words, "the male Marilyn Monroe."

JAMES DEAN, TOMORROW NEVER COMES

Darwin Porter & Danforth Prince
Softcover, 528 pages, with photos
ISBN 978-1-936003-49-5
Available online and in bookstores everywhere in March, 2016

And in time for the Elections, from the same biographers who crafted this love story about Bill & Hillary, a breathlessly irreverent overview of the Republican Party's most controversial candidate since John McCain joined forces with roguish Sarah Palin:

DONALD TRUMP

THE MAN WHO WOULD BE KING

Softcover, 500 pages, with photos, available everywhere in August, 2016, another proud and presidential addition to Blood Moon's Babylon Series. ISBN 978-1-936003-51-8

Other Works by Darwin Porter
Produced In Collaboration with Blood Moon

Biographies

Peter O'Toole, *Hellraiser, Sexual Outlaw, Irish Rebel*

Love Triangle, *Ronald Reagan, Jane Wyman, & Nancy Davis*

Jacqueline Kennedy Onassis, *A Life Beyond Her Wildest Dreams*

Pink Triangle, *The Feuds and Private Lives of Tennessee Williams, Gore Vidal, Truman Capote, and Famous Members of their Entourages.*

Those Glamorous Gabors, *Bombshells from Budapest*

Inside Linda Lovelace's Deep Throat, *Degradation, Porno Chic, and the Rise of Feminism*

Elizabeth Taylor, *There is Nothing Like a Dame*

Marilyn at Rainbow's End, *Sex, Lies, Murder, and the Great Cover-up*

J. Edgar Hoover & Clyde Tolson
Investigating the Sexual Secrets of America's Most Famous Men and Women

Frank Sinatra*, The Boudoir Singer. All the Gossip Unfit to Print*

The Kennedys*, All the Gossip Unfit to Print*

Humphrey Bogart, The Making of a Legend *(2010) , and*
The Secret Life of Humphrey Bogart *(2003)*

Howard Hughes, *Hell's Angel*

Steve McQueen, *King of Cool, Tales of a Lurid Life*

Paul Newman, *The Man Behind the Baby Blues*

Merv Griffin, *A Life in the Closet*

Brando Unzipped

Katharine the Great, *Hepburn, Secrets of a Lifetime Revealed*

Jacko, His Rise and Fall, *The Social and Sexual History of Michael Jackson*

Damn You, Scarlett O'Hara, *The Private Lives of Vivien Leigh and Laurence Olivier*
(co-authored with Roy Moseley)

Film Criticism

Blood Moon's 2005 Guide to the Glitter Awards
Blood Moon's 2006 Guide to Film
Blood Moon's 2007 Guide to Film, *and*
50 Years of Queer Cinema, *500 of the Best GLBTQ Films Ever Made*

Non-Fiction

Hollywood Babylon—It's Back! *and* ***Hollywood Babylon Strikes Again!***

Novels

Blood Moon,
Hollywood's Silent Closet,
Rhinestone Country,
Razzle Dazzle
Midnight in Savannah

Other Publications by Darwin Porter

Not Directly Associated with Blood Moon

Novels

The Delinquent Heart
The Taste of Steak Tartare
Butterflies in Heat
Marika *(a roman à clef based on the life of Marlene Dietrich)*
Venus *(a roman à clef based on the life of Anaïs Nin)*
Bitter Orange
Sister Rose

TRAVEL GUIDES

Many Editions and Many Variations of ***The Frommer Guides, The American Express Guides,*** *and/or* ***TWA Guides, et alia*** to:

Andalusia, Andorra, Anguilla, Aruba, Atlanta, Austria, the Azores, The Bahamas, Barbados, the Bavarian Alps, Berlin, Bermuda, Bonaire and Curaçao, Boston, the British Virgin Islands, Budapest, Bulgaria, California, the Canary Islands, the Caribbean and its "Ports of Call," the Cayman Islands, Ceuta, the Channel Islands (UK), Charleston (SC), Corsica, Costa del Sol (Spain), Denmark, Dominica, the Dominican Republic, Edinburgh, England, Estonia, Europe, "Europe by Rail," the Faroe Islands, Finland, Florence, France, Frankfurt, the French Riviera, Geneva, Georgia (USA), Germany, Gibraltar, Glasgow, Granada (Spain), Great Britain, Greenland, Grenada (West Indies), Haiti, Hungary, Iceland, Ireland, Isle of Man, Italy, Jamaica, Key West & the Florida Keys, Las Vegas, Liechtenstein, Lisbon, London, Los Angeles, Madrid, Maine, Malta, Martinique & Guadeloupe, Massachusetts, Morocco, Munich, New England, New Orleans, North Carolina, Norway, Paris, Poland, Portugal, Provence, Puerto Rico, Romania, Rome, Salzburg, San Diego, San Francisco, San Marino, Sardinia, Savannah, Scandinavia, Scotland, Seville, the Shetland Islands, Sicily, St. Martin & Sint Maartin, St. Vincent & the Grenadines, South Carolina, Spain, St. Kitts & Nevis, Sweden, Switzerland, the Turks & Caicos, the U.S.A., the U.S. Virgin Islands, Venice, Vienna and the Danube, Wales, and Zurich.

BIOGRAPHIES

From Diaghilev to Balanchine, *The Saga of Ballerina Tamara Geva*

Lucille Lortel, *The Queen of Off-Broadway*

Greta Keller, *Germany's Other Lili Marlene*

Sophie Tucker, *The Last of the Red Hot Mamas*

Anne Bancroft, *Where Have You Gone, Mrs. Robinson?*
(co-authored with Stanley Mills Haggart)

Veronica Lake, *The Peek-a-Boo Girl*

Running Wild in Babylon, *Confessions of a Hollywood Press Agent*

HISTORIES

Thurlow Weed, *Whig Kingpin*

Chester A. Arthur, *Gilded Age Coxcomb in the White House*

Discover Old America, *What's Left of It*

CUISINE

Food For Love, *Hussar Recipes from the Austro-Hungarian Empire*

AND COMING SOON, FROM BLOOD MOON

James Dean, *Tomorrow Never Comes*

Donald Trump, *The Man Who Would Be King*

WITH ACKNOWLEDGMENTS TO A CAST OF HUNDREDS OF OTHER PLAYERS,
THIS BOOK IS DEDICATED TO

ANITA FINLEY

RADIO HOST, ZEITGEIST COMMENTATOR,
AND PRESIDENT AND PUBLISHER OF SOUTH FLORIDA'S
BOOMER TIMES & SENIOR LIFE MAGAZINE

Contents

A Letter from the Publisher

On the campus of Yale University, in 1970, an "odd couple," Hillary Rodham and Bill Clinton, came together at a Mark Rothko exhibit at the local art museum. Before the end of that rainy afternoon of shared dreams and whispered intimacies, they had formed an intuitive but powerful (and perhaps clairvoyant) bond.

They were from completely different worlds—he an extroverted and folksy populist from a poverty-stricken backwater in Arkansas; she a former "Goldwater Girl" and conservative Republican inexorably moving into the activist liberal camp.

As he sat beside her, holding her hand, she gazed into the eyes of this 210-pound, orange-bearded "Viking," tall and scruffy-looking, with an Elvis drawl. Freshly emerged from Wellesley College, she was a budding feminist—pimply faced, wearing no makeup but with Mr. Magoo eyeglasses, and walking around on chubby legs.

He had all the pretty women he wanted. What he was looking for was a woman with a "sense of strength and self-possession—that afternoon, I knew I'd found my Evita."

He confided to her that since the age of seven, he had had only one abiding, obsessive, ambition. It was to become President of the United States.

Holding out the prospect that she would become the most powerful person on the planet, he promised her that if he got elected, "I will work to make you the country's first woman president. Your administration will follow mine."

As she recalled, "I was giddy with emotion."

And thus began a saga that lured her to Arkansas, which she interpreted as "on the other side of the moon." And the rest is history.

Hillary was at his side as her sex-crazed Bubba became a law professor at the University of Arkansas, then got elected as Attorney General, and then served five terms as governor of his state. Based on a mixture of talent, grit, circumstance, and factors we've tried to define within this book, she promoted and guided him through two scandal-soaked terms as U.S. president, occasionally promoting private agendas of her own. Eventually, through both of their efforts, Bill evolved into the 21st Century's "Greatest Living Elder Statesman."

We've produced a celebrity biography that's not really about politics. It's the story of an intimate and enduring love affair shared by the world's most famous political team. Its revelations derive from hundreds of insiders, each privy to one or more of the private dramas that flourished (or raged) between and around a couple who might once again take over the Free World.

The Clintons had hoped that their reign during the 1990s would be "The Second Coming of Camelot." Camelot—at least as something akin to the giddy, euphoria and national unity that accompanied JFK and his Jacqueline—was never fully achieved for the Clintons. Perhaps they'll get a second chance at it during the 21st Century.

In the pages ahead, from a wide spectrum of witnesses, you'll get a penetration into gossipy insights about the Clintons, some of them more poisonous than a puff adder. It's all here, accumulated into the 600+ pages of this outrageous book—the glitter, the glamor, the glitz, the illicit sex, the blackmail, the enraged vendettas, the lust for power and glory, the heartbreaks, the tragedies, and the triumphs. Through the mess emerges *Bill & Hillary,* a tough, enduring, and spectacularly unconventional love story.

In our pre-publication survey of the dozens of books published over the years about the Clintons, we realized that only a few of them ever portrayed the controversial couple in a favorable light. The vast majority were conceived as diatribes, attacks, and/or denunciations. Some of them paint the Clintons as the son and daughter of Satan. Some authors have even demanded, in conclusion, that they be sentenced to extended terms in jail.

[Few, if any other First Ladies, with the important exception of Eleanor Roosevelt, ever had to endure the venom that has been heaped upon Hillary Clinton. A particularly poisonous remark derives from a former speechwriter for Ronald Reagan, Peggy Noonan: "Hillary doesn't have to prove she's a man. She has to prove she's a woman."]

As equal-opportunity muckrackers confronted with the blurring of lines between show-biz and politics, we emphasize that a persistent odor of sleaze envelops *Clintonistas,* anti-*Clintonistas,* and their respective covens of conspirators. We found ample opportunities in the Clinton saga for overviews on the American Experience as it regards politics, sex, gossip, vendetta, politics, and show-biz. The hotter the sexuality of his scandals, the higher Bill Clinton's poll numbers soared.

This book traces how, from the cauldron of the Clinton's rise and near-destruction, a powerful new incarnation of Hillary has emerged. *[Whether you liken it to a phoenix or a demon depends on your point of view.]*

Whether she can pull off a presidential win in 2016 remains to be seen.

But based on our belief that the past is a preface to the future, we hope that this book illustrates the context from which Hillary might write history once again as the country's first female president.

For an intelligent lawyer, Bill Clinton made a lot of stupid mistakes, many of them, in the words of legal analyst Jeffrey Toobin, "shabby, but not illegal." So did his enemies, who pursued him with dizzying combinations of personal vendetta, ineptitude, hypocrisy, and misguided zealotry. Bill Clinton's stonewalling of the truth, particularly as it applied to his many sexual indiscretions, was spectacularly outmatched by those who wasted millions trying to destroy him.

Extremists of the political right tried to use the legal system to undo an election, and Bill and Hillary responded, perhaps understandably, with something lacking in grace. Only the lawyers got rich, often at the expense of the taxpayer.

What does Presidential Candidate Hillary—a woman who has for years endured, and perhaps thrived, under relentless and obsessive attacks— think of the daily pursuit of wolves hoping to rip her flesh in the months preceding the elections of 2016?

Hillary says, "BRING 'EM ON—the 'legitimate rapists,' the ISIS-like Republican terrorists, the antediluvian bigots, the psychotic misogynists, the transvaginal probers. I may go down in flames, defeated by some Princess Tiny Meat with a case of penis envy, but oh, my friends, and oh, my foes, I will give off a blaze to light the darkest night."

We hope you enjoy this book. Nothing else like it has ever appeared in print before.

Sincerely,

Danforth Prince
President and Founder
Blood Moon Productions

"There are guilty pleasures. Then there is the master of guilty pleasures, Darwin Porter. There is nothing like reading him for passing the hours. He is the Nietzsche of Naughtiness, the Goethe of Gossip, the Proust of Pop Culture. Porter knows all the nasty buzz anyone has ever heard whispered in dark bars, dim alleys, and confessional booths. And lovingly, precisely, and in as straightforward a manner as an oncoming train, his prose whacks you between the eyes with the greatest gossip since Kenneth Anger. Some would say better than Anger."

—Alan W. Petrucelli
The Entertainment Report
Stage and Screen Examiner
Examiner.com

Prologue

It was early in 1974.

The setting was the Old Congressional Hotel on Washington's Capitol Hill. It had been commandeered and retrofitted as the working headquarters of forty-four lawyers. Hillary Rodham was among them, one of only three women assigned to their collective task. It involved reviewing evidence, including tapes recorded in the Oval Office, that might justify the impeachment of then-President Richard M. Nixon.

Tape by tape, hour after hour, she, among others, listened to Nixon's rambling but alarming "Presidential Pearls of Wisdom."

She learned, among other things, that he "hated all fags, especially San Francisco fags."

He didn't care for reporters either, claiming, "I wouldn't give them the sweat on my balls."

He spoke about leadership, too: "You're never going to make it in politics if you don't know how to lie."

About policies associated with Affirmative Action, he claimed, "With blacks, you usually settle for an incompetent, because there are just not enough competent ones. As for Jews, could you please investigate some of these cocksuckers?"

After a grueling week, late one Friday afternoon, Hillary's luck changed. At last, she'd heard "the smoking gun" as it exploded on tape.

Putting down her earphones, she rushed away from her desk into an outer room and yelled at her male colleagues: "By god, we've got the bastard! Come and listen. I just heard him explicitly tell his cronies to cover up the White House involvement in the Watergate break-in. On tape, he even boasts that he can raise the hush money that's needed."

It wasn't until late that evening, around 10PM, that Bernard Nussbaum, a pugnacious Assistant U.S. Attorney in New York, allowed the staff to go home for much needed weekend rest. Although he was only eleven years older than Hillary, she viewed him both as a father figure and as her mentor, affectionately addressing him as "Bernie."

Since it was late, he offered to drive Hillary back to her lodgings within the townhouse of Sara Ehrman, who had become her friend in San Antonio when they'd worked together on the unsuccessful presidential campaign of George McGovern. Ehrman, known for coke-bottle glasses, long, stringy hair, and outsize brown corduroy pants, was a middle-aged Jewish housewife from Brooklyn who looked like a hippie version of an Ivy Leaguer.

Emerging from the foxhole mentality of the coven of lawyers laboring inside, Hillary got into the front passenger's seat of Nussbaum's aging Oldsmobile Toronado.

Even as late as it was, she seemed excited. "Almost like a school girl, which was unusual for her," as Nussbaum later described her.

She confessed that her boyfriend had flown in from Arkansas and was shacked up with her at Ehrman's. "All the girls are after him," she said. "They treat him like a rock star—think Elvis. But he claims he prefers a girl with brains and ability over glamor. And he thinks I'm real cute."

She also revealed that "He's running for Congress from Arkansas. Before that, he was a professor at this hillbilly law school somewhere in the Ozarks."

"When Bill wins a seat in Congress, he'll move to Washington, and we'll get an apartment together," she said..

As Nussbaum pulled up in front of Ehrman's townhouse, he complained of fatigue. "It's been a hell of a week."

Nussbaum didn't bother to conceal his impatience with her when she virtually demanded that he get out of his Oldsmobile, and come with her. Then she became vocal and aggressive, beseeching him to come inside to meet her boyfriend. "You'll be shaking the hand of a future president of the United States."

"Hillary, don't be so god damn silly," he answered in a sharp tone. "You're a smart girl, but you're acting really stupid. You expect me to believe that this Ozark hillbilly backwoods boy is going to become President of the United States? Let's talk about the chances of a snowball in hell!"

Years later, Nussbaum ruefully reflected on their confrontation late that long-ago Friday evening. "I didn't realize it at the time, but I had just trampled on her most cherished dream. Her whole life seemed to depend on this kid becoming president. But what chance did a guy like that have? I know she was overworked, her nerves shattered, but she lost control. That wasn't like her. She started screaming and shouting at me."

To Nussbaum's shock, she went ballistic, denouncing him. "Don't be a god damn stupid son-of-a-bitch. A moronic jerk. He is going to become president whether you believe it or not. We'll see that you eat your fucking words!"

Filled with rage and fury, she exited from Nussbaum's car and ran toward the entrance to Ehrman's townhouse.

It took four days before she and Bernie made up and started to speak to each other again.

***

Fast Forward to 1993, Almost 20 Years Later

Nussbaum later recalled, "This guy I viewed as a hillbilly skirt-chaser lost his bid for Congress, but went on to bigger offices. Not only did 'Bubba' become the 42nd president of the United States, with Hillary as First Lady, but I was appointed counsel to the White House."

"Who knows?" he asked. "Perhaps Hillary will go on to achieve her second dream, that of becoming the first woman president of the Republic. I wouldn't put that past her. She's got a pair of *cojones* on her that even a castrator's steel blades can't deball."

BLOOD
MOON
Productions, Ltd.

Chapter One

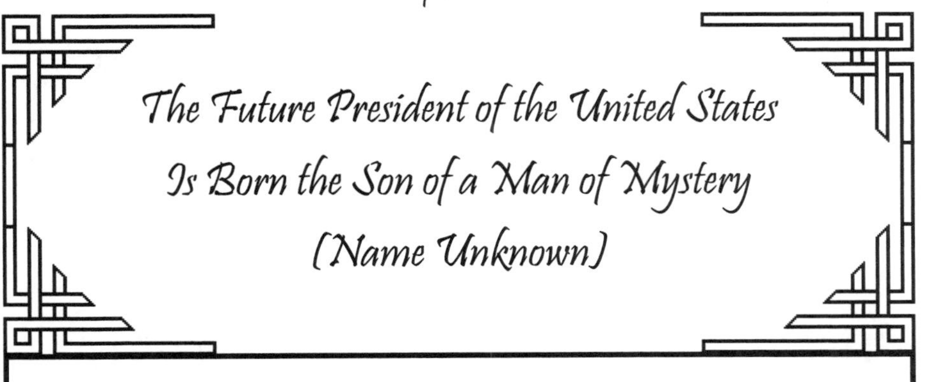

The Future President of the United States Is Born the Son of a Man of Mystery (Name Unknown)

Surrounded by Gamblers, Gangsters, Prostitutes, & Hundreds Desperately Seeking Cures for Sexually Transmitted Diseases, Bill Comes of Age in Arkansas' "Gomorrah of the Ozarks"

One womanizer meets another womanizer as the 42nd President of the United States (Bill Clinton, left) shakes the hand of the 35th President, whose days are numbered.

Young Bill Clinton didn't tell JFK what was really on his mind:

"I want your job—and Jackie, too."

A descendant of Irish farmers and Cherokee Indians, Virginia Dell Cassidy, born in 1923 in the tiny hamlet of Bodcaw, Arkansas, was working the 3-to-11PM shift as a nurse at the Tri-State Hospital in Shreveport, Louisiana. Ever since she was thirteen years old, her motto had been, "The brighter the lipstick, the better."

Despite her stern, dour mother, she was a rebellious young woman, who "overpainted my face and wore bright colors to compete with the rainbow."

Virginia Cassidy with William Blythe II..."To love him is not to know him."

Around town, she had a reputation as a "hey-hey party girl," always ready for a night of fun. She would later say, "It wasn't true that I went for anything in pants. But I did like the boys."

Richard Fenwick, who sold popcorn at the movie theater back in her native Hope, Arkansas, had presented her with a gold ring. He also gave her extra popcorn whenever she came in to see the latest film.

Her life was about to change one night at around 10PM when a handsome, strapping man rushed into the emergency room carrying a young woman in his arms. She was placed on a gurney and wheeled into an examination room, where doctors diagnosed her with acute appendicitis, and with an immediate need for surgery.

Left alone with Virginia, the patient's escort, William Blythe II, trained his eagle eye on her and liked what he saw. She would later admit, "I became weak-kneed. I got this fireball of a feeling."

Blythe immediately spotted Fenwick's ring. "Does that mean anything?" he asked, removing the ring and putting it into her pocket.

"Does that gal you brought in mean anything?" she asked.

"We were just hanging out in a bar," he said, concealing the true depths of their intimacy.

With his girlfriend on the operating table, Blythe invited Virginia for a coke. They didn't have much time, since she had to get back to the nurses' dormitory before its 11PM curfew.

The next day, he arrived with a bouquet of red roses for his girlfriend, who was recovering from her emergency appendectomy. When Virginia spotted him, she said, "So you're bringing flowers to someone you met in a bar?"

"I always bring flowers to a gal right before I dump her. How about a date

Tanked Up on Rotgut Whiskey, Bill's Redneck Mother Dances the Night Away in Bowjack Honky-Tonks

tonight?"

"You're on, big boy," she said. "Let the good times roll!"

She would always remember their first date. He liked action movies and his favorite actor was Ronald Reagan, especially in films where he played Secret Service Agent Brass Bancroft. She didn't like Reagan movies, preferring romantic pictures with Cary Grant, instead, but she didn't let him know that.

Virginia Cassidy...
the Hey-Hey Party Girl

[She would always remember the last movie they saw together, before the Army sent Blythe overseas. It was Casablanca, *co-starring Humphrey Bogart. According to Virginia, "At the end of the picture, when Bogie has to tell Ingrid Bergman goodbye, I couldn't stop crying. I'm such a romantic. Soon, I'd have to be saying goodbye to William."]*

After their first date, which she followed by returning to his hotel with him to spend the night, they dated regularly. After only two weeks, she wanted to marry him, but he held her off because of his uncertain future in the Army during wartime. As it turned out, he would be shipped out within two months, ending up in Egypt, where he repaired engines and heavy equipment for the Allied Armies fighting "The Desert Fox" (Field Marshal Rommel) on the sands of North Africa.

She finally persuaded him to marry her on September 3, 1943, in Texarkana, Arkansas. During their honeymoon, although she talked about her upbringing with a very strict mother and an indulgent father, he remained a man of mystery. "To love him is not to know him," she said, years later to a local reporter.

[Years would pass before the secrets of Blythe's former life would emerge. In the beginning, all that Virginia knew was that he was one of nine children born to dirt-poor farmers in Sherman, Texas, on family acreage that would later be seized by the bank.]

In his late teens, Blythe became a traveling salesman hawking auto parts for tractors. According to rumor, many a bored housewife found him irresistible until their husbands came in from the fields. On a few occasions, he was chased off a farmstead by a jealous husband armed with a shotgun.

His marital record and his role as a father have never been fully revealed. At one point, someone said, "Bill may have fathered twenty children either in or out of the bonds of his four (known) marriages." What is known is that in December of 1935, in Medill, Oklahoma, he married the seventeen-year-old daughter of the owner of a seedy bar in Sherman. Her name was Virginia Adele Gash, and she would divorce him a year later. But the couple must have linked up again after the divorce, because on January 17, 1938, they gave birth to a baby boy. He was named Henry Leon Blythe (later changed to Ritzenthaler), who would later claim that he was Bill Clinton's half-brother.

Less than eight months later, in Ardmore, Texas, on August 11, 1938, Blythe married Maxine Hamilton, age twenty, though she filed for divorce nine months later.

In a bizarre twist, in 1940, he went on to marry Faye Gash, the younger sister of his first wife, Adele. The couple separated three months later, and later, she divorced him.

In 1941, in Kansas City, Missouri, he married his fourth wife, Wanneta Alexander, only eight days before the birth of her daughter, Sharon Lee Blythe (later Pettijohn), who later identified herself as Bill Clinton's half-sister.

Bill mentions Sharon in his first memoir, *My Life.* Although he doesn't specifically name the girl's mother, he stated that she eventually divorced his father. Actually, there is no record of such a divorce. Lack of any formal divorce proceeding would, if one never occurred, thereby render Virginia's marriage to Blythe invalid and Bill technically illegitimate, if indeed, Blythe had been his father.

While Blythe was far away, in North Africa, Virginia resumed her former heavy dating schedule, often taking the train from Hope to the French Quarter of New Orleans. There, she listened to Dixieland jazz—Al Hirt was her favorite—with various "beaux," as she called them. On mornings after some of her many hellraising nights, she ended up at the Morning Call Café, ordering black coffee and beignets with her boyfriend *du jour.*

She told friends, "For all I knew, my Billy Boy husband is making out with half the belly dancers in Cairo. I'm young and I want to have fun. Already, I've developed a gray streak in my hair. *Time's a' wastin'.*"

Blythe didn't return home from the war effort until December 7, 1945, about three months after the Japanese surrender.

When at last he came marching home, Virginia was already pregnant with her first child, William Jefferson Blythe III, who, under another name, in 1992, would eventually be elected President of the United States.

To conceal the fact that Blythe wasn't his real father, Virginia announced that her son, Bill, was a premature baby. Actually, at the time of Bill's conception, Blythe was still overseas in the Army.

It is not known if Blythe ever accused Virginia of infidelity. All that is known for certain is that he told friends that his wife was pregnant and that he was about to become the proud father of a "baby in the oven."

He didn't want to live in Arkansas, but preferred to return to Chicago where, before the war, he had a job selling farm equipment, which meant he had to travel all over the state. His former company was eager to rehire him because his charm and affability had made him popular with buyers. He was known for not only relating to the farmers, but to their wives, many of whom invited him in for lunch.

In an attempt to relocate to better pastures, he drove his pregnant wife north to Chicago, where they temporarily lived in a seedy hotel. He was low on funds until he started to sell some farm equipment. Because he had found employment, he managed, like many other returning veterans, to secure a bank loan for the construction of a small tract house for himself and his family. At its construction site, he had purchased a small piece of land in Forest Park, a western suburb of Chicago.

As the weeks when by, Virginia felt isolated and alone in this hotel, because Bill would be on the road sometimes for weeks at a time. Also, she didn't want her child born into a hotel frequented by alcoholics and prostitutes.

Despite his objections, she decided to travel back south to Hope and put herself under the care of her mother, who was a nurse skilled at providing care to pregnant women.

Although Virginia was nervous about having a baby, once she was back in Arkansas, she continued to drink in spite of dire warnings from her mother that the infant might be born deformed or retarded.

By May 17, 1946, Bill inspected their newly built house in Forest Park and decided it was ready for her to move in. After a phone call to his wife, he decided to drive to Hope to pick her up and bring her back to the Chicago area where her baby could be born in one of the local hospitals. Reluctantly, she agreed to pack up her bags and return with him to the big, Windy City, even though her mother objected, wanting her daughter to deliver the baby in Hope.

As part of his plan to retrieve her, Blythe got two extra days off, plus the weekend, and set out on a Friday from Chicago for Arkansas, driving at breakneck speed behind the wheel of his maroon-colored Buick.

The flat farmlands of Illinois passed before him. He knew the territory well because he'd often come this way, selling farm equipment. He zoomed through the towns of Effingham and Salem, allowing himself a "pit stop" in Cairo, Illinois. Set at the southernmost tip of the state, at the junction of the Mississippi and Ohio Rivers, it had been named after the city in Egypt, close to which he'd been stationed during the war.

Veering west across the Mississippi River, he entered Missouri. Low on gas, he spotted a filling station in the town of Silkeston.

Although it was already late in the evening, he planned to continue driving throughout the night, with the goal of reaching Hope before dawn for a reunion with his pregnant wife. It had rained heavily throughout most of the day, and the pavements of Route 60 were slippery. Blythe was impatient, recklessly passing other motorists in spite of the bad driving conditions. Three miles from Silkeston, his rear tire blew out, sending his vehicle careening across the highway. It flipped over twice before landing, upside down, in an open field.

Somehow, he managed to extricate himself from the wreckage. He was dazed, weak, and dizzy, but except for a blow to his head, his body was not severely injured. He staggered back toward the highway, looking for help. Then he stumbled and fell into a drainage ditch containing no more than three feet of stagnant water. Collapsing face down into the ditch, he could not push himself up from its depths.

Within a few minutes, spotting the wreckage, a motorist named Elmer Greenlee got out of his car to investigate the ruined, upside-down Buick. There was no sign of its driver, but its car radio was still blaring country music, and its headlights, illuminating a cow pasture, were in working order.

Then other motorists stopped to see what had gone wrong. Soon, Missouri State Troopers appeared, and a search for the missing driver began. An hour or so passed before John Lett and Chester Odum spotted a hand raised from the waters of the drainage ditch. They called for help, and Blythe's dead body was dragged up from the slimy waters and stretched out on the ground. Attendants carried it to an ambulance. When Blythe's wallet was searched, Virginia's phone number and address were found. Within the hour, Edith Cassidy heard her daughter screaming, "BILL—HE'S DEAD!"

***

That summer in Arkansas was long and hot, and Virginia spent most of its duration in her room, mourning the loss of her husband. Without her mother's knowledge, she, on several occasions, considered having an abortion. With no husband, she didn't want to be a single mother living alone with an infant.

A few times, she ventured outside the house alone, wandering to the local movie house. Ironically, the first film she saw was Jane Russell starring in *Young Widow* (1946), which only reminded her of her own predicament. On many mornings, she was sick. For a while, although she tried to hold food down, she sometimes vomited it.

Her mother cared for her, but she sometimes grew impatient with her morbidity. "You're not the only one. Women by the millions, from all over the world, have lost sons or husbands in that dreadful war. You've got to be brave and carry on."

Virginia hadn't slept during the night of August 18, 1946. She sat by a window listening to the sounds of thunder and storms as flashes of lightning streaked the sky.

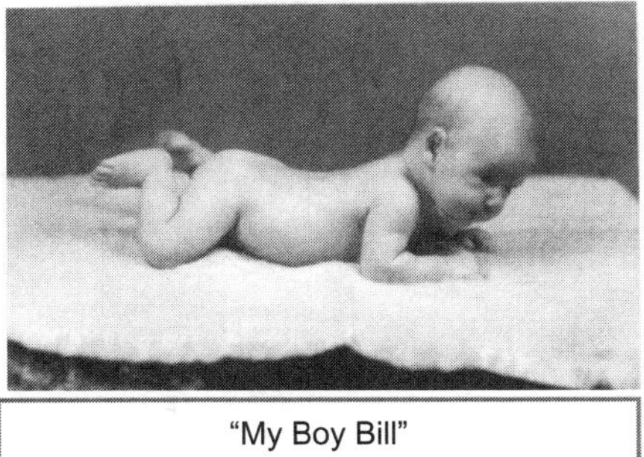

"My Boy Bill"
(Caligula of the Ozarks)

The morning of August 19, 1946, dawned bright and clear. Before her mother left for work, Virginia's water broke. She began screaming for Edith.

In thirty minutes, she'd been transferred to the Julia Chester Hospital in Hope. Within the hour, William Jefferson Blythe III was born. He weighed six and a half pounds.

Eventually, after the infant morphed into a world class politician, his enemies regretted the day he was born. As one author would proclaim, "His mother gave birth to Caligula of the Ozarks."

***

When she recovered from childbirth, Virginia, with her infant son, went to live with her parents, Eldridge and Edith Cassidy, in a large white-painted house in Hope.

From the beginning, there was trouble in the household, as Edith—a respected private nurse— did not view Virginia as a proper mother who knew how to rear a child. Making things worse, Bill's grandmother was frequently overwhelmed with sudden and sometimes violent mood swings.

As Bill grew up, he remembered the "torrents of rage" that his grandmother, Edith, sometimes directed at both her daughter, Virginia, and at her husband, the rather kind and generous Eldridge. His appearance would later remind Bill of the movie action hero, Randolph Scott. On the wall hung a whip which Edith had used, and on occasion, continued to use, to beat her daughter after the slightest infraction.

Every morning, Edith would leave for work wearing a crisp white nurse's uniform and cap with a billowing navy blue cape around her shoulders.

She took obsessive care of her young grandson, dictating when he was to go to bed, what he was to wear, and what he could or could not eat. He called her "Mammaw." Eldridge was "Pappaw."

Her husband, a small but wiry man, would deliver ice from the back of a refrigerated truck, carrying the heavy, dripping blocks into various homes.

When Eldridge's back gave out, he opened a small general store in the center of Hope, supplying foodstuff and supplies to the mostly impoverished people of the town.

From his more tolerant grandfather, Bill learned about racial equality, or the lack thereof. Although many establishments did not welcome African American customers, Eldridge invited them to trade at his general store. Bill visited most afternoons, having developed an addiction to chocolate chip cookies.

He noticed that Eldridge allowed many of his customers to charge food and supplies on credit. Regrettably, because so many people owed him money and didn't have the cash to pay him back, his generosity later led to his losing the business.

In the latest local election, the people of Hempstead County had voted to go dry. To fulfill the need for liquor, Eldridge began to sell Mason canning jars, each filled with "white lightning moonshine" from under the counter of his store.

When her son turned one year old, Virginia "with a sad heart" left him in Hope as she journeyed south to Louisiana for training as a nurse anesthetist at New Orleans' Charity Hospital. Once she got there, far from the prying and judgmental eyes of her mother and the demands of her infant son, she resumed a heavy dating agenda.

As a result, Bill spent the first four years of his life living with, and being supervised by, his grandparents, adapting to their diet of Southern cooking. Dishes that appeared frequently included cornbread, collards cooked with "fatback," and salty country ham. He learned to work the crank of an ice cream freezer, making homemade ice cream, peach being his favorite.

As he grew older, his grandfather bought him a black Hopalong Cassidy outfit with silver buttons, which he wore to attend Miss Marie's School for Little Folk in Hope.

After an accident on the playground in which he broke his leg, he was confined to his bed for two months. It was then that he met his favorite playmate, Mack McLarty, whose father ran the Ford dealership in Hope. Ironically, in 1993, newly installed in the Oval Office, Bill Clinton would name McLarty as his first Chief of Staff.

THE PROGRESSIVE AND THE HAYSEED

HOPE, ARKANSAS
Home of President Bill Clinton *(left)*, Governor Mike Huckabee *(center)*, and the world's largest watermelons

By the early '50s, Bill had become a

movie fan, his alltime favorite picture being *High Noon* (1952), starring Gary Cooper with the much younger Grace Kelly. Over the years, Bill would see that film many times. When he faced his own daunting challenges as president, Cooper became a role model for him. "I often thought of the look in Gary Cooper's eyes as he stares into the face of almost certain defeat, and how he keeps walking through his fears toward his duty. It works pretty well in real life, too."

William Jefferson Blythe III, in Hope in 1950.

"My mother was dating a lot of men. She told me to call each of them uncle."

***

"Husband Number Two" was looming in Virginia's future. Early in 1948, Roger Clinton entered her life. He was likable but a bit of a braggart. He was the director of a Buick dealership in Hope, an enterprise owned by his more prosperous brother, Raymond, who had another, larger, dealership in Hot Springs.

Flamboyant, party-loving, womanizing, and a heavy drinker, Roger was a hellraiser. He dressed like a "river gambler on the Mississippi," Virginia said. "In some ways, I thought he looked like my poor dead first husband."

He stood just under six feet tall, and she described him as "hair dark and curly, with twinkling eyes when he talked because he was always about to say something funny. He was the life of the party, and he partied a lot. He absolutely loved to gamble." She also liked the fact that he was kind to her young son.

Thirteen years her senior, he was married at the time he started dating Virginia to Ina Mae Clinton, but the couple were in the process of getting a divorce. In Ina Mae's petition before the court, she accused him of "violent spousal abuse," a warning Virginia chose not to heed.

On June 19, 1950, despite the strident protests of Edith, Virginia married Roger Clinton. Edith saw to it that Bill and Eldridge boycotted the wedding.

On the day of their wedding, Roger received notice from the court that he owed $2,000 in overdue child support. At the time, he was making $10,000 a year.

At some point, tiring of Hope, Roger moved Virginia and her little boy to Hot Springs, then known as "The Most Sinful City in Arkansas," because of its gambling joints, hot-bed motels, striptease joints, and bordellos. In the past, visitors had included every gangster from Bugsy Siegel to Al Capone. Its spas and bathhouses, flowing with hot water from the local springs, were said to provide possible cures for syphilis and gonorrhea.

As Virginia once claimed, "I think one out of five people walking the streets *[of Hot Springs]* had VD."

Author Joe Klein referred to Hot Springs as "the Bible Belt Gomorrah." Researcher Pat Matrisciana defined it as "a place like the corner of every barnyard where the manure is piled." Reporter Michael Isikoff characterized Hot Springs as "a mingling of bizarre characters, Southern folklore, and a strange mix of rumor, fact, and tabloid fantasy."

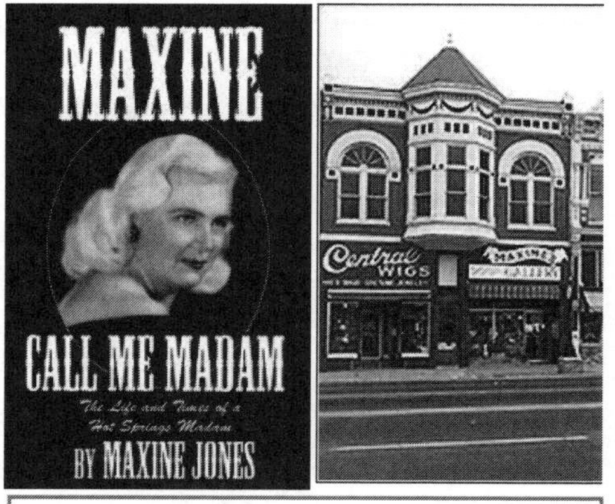

Maxine Jones, the leading whorehouse madam of Hot Springs, where Bill grew up, and *(right)* the entrance to her brothel:

"I did everything but remove my bra to the underworld figures and hired killers who turned up at my bordello. Little Billy Clinton came by when he was twelve, but I kicked his ass out the door."

After their marriage vows, Virginia began to know her husband better. Even with a wedding ring on his finger *[he would remove it whenever it was convenient and necessary],* Roger was still the irrepressible carouser he'd always been. On most nights, he returned home drunk. On other nights, Virginia joined him on his rounds of the city's honky-tonks, matching him drink for drink of rotgut whiskey, while Bill was put to bed by a kindly nanny.

As a means of making a living, Roger worked for his brother, Raymond, at his Buick dealership, while Virginia was employed as a nurse at the local hospital.

Although Roger had always been belligerent when he drank, three months into their marriage, the Mr. Hyde part of his split personality emerged.

In the beginning, the fights between Roger and Virginia had erupted within various taverns after they'd been drinking heavily. Usually, they began as a result of her flirting with other men. As she admitted herself, "I was one awful flirt. Every time I saw a good-looking man, I began to bat my long, fake eyelashes."

Even so, in spite of almost nightly denunciations of each other, delivered loudly while young Billy cowered in his room, Virginia and Roger usually recovered before the debut of the following night's round of partying. Sometimes it began on Friday night and continued until Monday morning.

In 1955, after Bill's grandmother, Edith, suffered a stroke, he and his mother went to visit her. "It was a big one and in its aftermath, Edith began to scream hysterically," Bill said. "Her doctor gave her morphine. Soon, she became an addict, I mean really hooked. We hated to do it, but we had to have her committed to this mental asylum at Benton, Arkansas. We visited her every Sunday. The conditions were awful, reminding me of this Hollywood movie I'd seen, starring Olivia de Havilland. It was called *The Snake Pit* (1948), and that's where Mammaw was lodged. She was in that hellhole for a few months before she was allowed to come home."

Somewhere along the way, Virginia became pregnant with Roger Clinton, who was born July 25, 1956. He was destined to develop into Virginia's "problem child," a source of future embarrassment to Bill and Hillary.

At this point, Bill decided to legally change his name to William Jefferson Clinton. As he explained it, he didn't do it for any love for his stepfather, but because he wanted to have the same name as his little brother "so I wouldn't have to explain to people why we had different last names."

It was a sad day for Bill in 1957 when his beloved grandfather, at the age of fifty-six, died in Arkansas' Ouachita Hospital, the same medical facility where Virginia had worked as a nurse. "He'd had a hard life and was always short of cash. Also, Mammaw, though kind to me, constantly attacked him, citing his failures and always making him seem unworthy. At one point, I think he couldn't take it anymore."

One night, when Roger was about five years old, he walked into the laundry room after hearing his mother screaming. There, he saw his father with a pair of scissors, threatening to plunge them into his mother's throat.

"Bubba! Bubba!" he screamed, running into Bill's bedroom. "Daddy's killing Dado!" *[His pet name for Virginia.]*

At that point, Bill stood an inch taller than his stepfather, and he rushed into the laundry room and forcibly removed the scissors from Roger's hand. Seeing an escape route, Virginia fled upstairs and locked herself in their bedroom, not coming out until morning.

On some nights, while Roger sat alone in his room, "drunk and wallowing in morbidity" *[Bill's words],* Virginia began to "date" her son. Unlike the dynamic that existed between Bill's hero—Elvis Presley and Elvis' mother, Gladys—incest was never suggested.

Virginia ask him to escort her to some of the clubs of Hot Springs, providing he would order a coke and let her drink the rotgut. "He was a good dancer," she recalled. "We just wanted to have fun. Roger was ceasing to be any fun at all."

Vapors was one of her favorite clubs. She took Bill—her "date"— there one night to hear Liberace. She whispered to her son that the entertainer at the piano, dressed in a suit of sequins, was a homosexual.

"And what is that?" he asked.

"It's a man who likes to get fucked in the ass by another man," she bluntly told him.

Bill seemed embarrassed and didn't ask for any more details.

At Vapors, after Virginia had had too much to drink, she sometimes stumbled onto the stage and attempted to sing with the star entertainer that night. Once, she joined Frankie Laine in a rendition of "Ghost Riders in the Sky." She once was tempted to join Patti Page in her rendition of "Tennessee Waltz," but decided it was too much of a challenge.

Bill *(left)* started "dating" his mother when her husband was too drunk to walk. Little Roger, Bill's half-brother, would grow up to become "the problem child."

In addition to his school work, Bill began to read newspapers and magazines. In a straw poll conducted around the time of the National Elections of 1960 *[Senator John F. Kennedy vs Richard M. Nixon],* Bill was the only one in his class who voted for Kennedy.

Bill was not just awed by Kennedy, the handsome young senator, but he developed a long-lasting "crush" on his wife, Jacqueline, as well.

One evening, Virginia received news that her grandmother *[Bill's great-grandmother],* was dying at a local hospital, and that she should come at once. She told Bill she wanted him to go with her "to see your Granny for the last time."

But when Roger—at the time drunk and belligerent—learned what they were doing, he demanded that neither of them was to leave the house.

Defiantly, and despite his objections, she headed out the door with Bill anyway.

Suddenly, Roger removed a gun from a drawer, firing it at her, narrowly missing her by less than a foot. The bullet lodged in the wall.

Bill and Virginia fled across the street to a neighbor's house, where he called the police. With dome lights flashing, a squad car with two cops arrived to haul Roger off to jail where he spent the night. He was released the following morning after he had sobered up.

At long last, in April of 1962, Virginia filed for a divorce, charging spousal abuse. Bill testified on her behalf, citing violent incidents from Roger's recent past.

During their divorce proceedings, Virginia was granted custody of her two sons, and Roger Sr., was ordered to pay child support of $50 a month, but only for his biological son, Roger Jr., not for Bill. Roger had refused to adopt him, in spite of Bill having changed his name to Clinton.

In the weeks ahead, a sometimes sober Roger began arriving on Virginia's doorstep, urging her to take him back. Finally, she relented, and brought him back into her bedroom. After a two-week reunion, she told Bill that she and Roger were set to get remarried.

"Mother, you're making a mistake," Bill said. "A big mistake."

Predictably, her son was right.

Although Bill referred to Roger as "Daddy," during the years ahead, he was always uncertain who his father really was. He once said, "It's hard for a boy to grow up without knowing who his Daddy was. Maybe my real name is William Jefferson Blythe III. But maybe not."

In later years, chroniclers of Bill's life would label Blythe as "a wanderer, a roustabout, an adulterer, and a bigamist."

***

Professor William J. Chaffe, in his book, *Bill and Hillary, The Politics of the Personal,* wrote: "It is unlikely that Blythe was the father of Bill."

Bill himself more or less echoed that belief when he said, "I made a promise to myself a long, long time ago that if I was ever lucky enough to have a child, he or she would never grow up wondering who the father was."

Over the years, there has been wild speculation about the identity of Bill's real father, and claims that Bill's refusal to turn over his medical records is based on his reluctance to reveal his identity. Improbable candidates for that honor have ranged from Arkansas Governor Winthrop Rockefeller to, of all people, John F. Kennedy. Of course, there is no evidence whatsoever that these allegations of fatherhood can be associated with either of those prominent political figures.

In Arkansas, especially after Bill became president, locals claimed, "He's the first bastard ever to be elected President of the United States."

In both Hot Springs and in Hope, most of the speculation about Bill's father centered on Raymond Clinton, the car dealer with links to the co-called "Dixie Mafia." He was the brother of Roger Clinton, Sr., Virginia's second husband.

She had been known to date him before her marriage to Roger. They were seen together getting drunk in the honky tonks, and he was said to have given her expensive gifts.

As he was growing up, Bill referred to him as "Uncle Raymond, the father I wished I'd had." Raymond was also known to have supplied Bill with money when he was a boy, and Bill referred to him as "my mentor."

Although Bill always talked affectionately about Raymond, he omitted at least one important detail. Like many Southerners of his day, Raymond was an ardent segregationist. Whenever another staunch segregationist, Governor George Wallace of Alabama, came to visit Arkansas, Raymond usually volunteered as his chauffeur, driving him anywhere in the state the governor wanted to go.

Whatever faults Roger Sr. had before his divorce seemed magnified when he came back into Virginia's life. In her autobiography, *Leading With My Heart,* she presented a horrific story of abuse, violent confrontations, and domestic conflict as she struggled to rear two boys in a household falling apart, largely because of Roger's alcoholism.

In 1965, he developed a virulent form of oral cancer. Fearing disfigurement, he refused to submit to surgery. He did, however, acquiesce to radiation treatments.

On weekends, during his enrollment as an undergraduate at Georgetown University in Washington, D.C., Bill, whenever he could, drove down to visit Roger at Duke University Medical Center in Durham, North Carolina.

By Thanksgiving of 1967, Bill was back in Hot Springs, forced to carry his stepfather to and from the bathroom because he was too weak to walk or even crawl. His weight had dropped to a hundred pounds, and at the age of fifty-seven, he was dying.

Virginia didn't want to be in the same room with him. Little Roger told her that, "I hope he dies...and soon. I hate him!"

As the days went on, and as Roger Sr.'s life dragged on, despite his weakened condition, she said, "He's hanging on as an act of terrorism against us."

When death came, Bill was relieved. He had been the only member of his family who had witnessed up close and personal the agonizing pain he was enduring.

"At last, Little Roger's prayers were answered," she said. "His father died. We buried him. I was ready to move on with my life."

On January 17, 1968, two months after Roger's death, Edith Cassidy, 66, suffered yet another devastating stroke, this one fatal. Since its transformation into a nursing home, she'd been living at the old Julia Chester Hospital, occupying the same room in which her grandson Bill had been born.

Both Bill and Virginia wept openly at her funeral.

***

In the summer of 1963, Bill attended Boys Nation. It was an annual conference, run by the American Legion and formatted something like a summer camp, devoted to civic training, leadership, and ethics. At the camp, young men campaigned in simulated elections for offices that included both Governor and Senator of their respective states. Whereas Hope's football hero Mack McLarty, Bill's friend, won a "governorship," Bill was elected as "Senator" from Arkansas. As part of the summer's curriculum, they were invited, along with a "sea of Republicans," on a field trip to Washington, D.C. The highlight of their trip included an invitation to the Rose Garden of the White House.

On July 24, 1963, as a means of better hearing JFK's speech to the young men, Bill positioned himself as close to the podium as he could. Standing more than six feet, two inches, and weighing 180 pounds, he was a figure not to be missed. In fact, he was the first to shake the president's hand. It was a historic moment, and he knew it. A photographer from Reuters snapped a picture. Bill later described it as "a present President of the United States meeting a future President of the United States."

Back in Arkansas, Bill went around "glad-handing," proclaiming, "Do you want to shake the hand of the man who shook the hand of President Kennedy?"

As part of the "Senators" brigade from Boys Nation, Bill, along with his classmate, Larry Taunton, was invited to the Senate Dining Room to meet "the real thing," the influential Southern Democrat J. William Fulbright. The long-time Senator from Arkansas (1945-1974), he had become known for tangling with President Lyndon B. Johnson over his Vietnam policy, and for his status as the powerful chairman of the Senate Foreign Relations Committee,

The night before his encounter with Fulbright, Bill stayed up almost until dawn, reading everything he could about the Senator's policies. At the lunch, Taunton was no doubt jealous that Bill monopolized the Senator's time as both of them engaged in a lively dialogue.

Fulbright later said how impressed he was with Bill. "In a few years, that young man with the crew cut and the good looks will probably be the Senator from Arkansas himself."

After the luncheon, Bill told Taunton, "Fulbright is the cat's meow. From now on, he's my political role model."

By 1966, Bill would be working in Fulbright's Senate office in Washington.

In November of 1963, back in Hot Springs, Bill was in his high school classroom when the news arrived that President John F. Kennedy had been assassinated in Dallas. Bill almost went into mourning, later telling one of his teachers, "It is said that almost every boy growing up in America dreams of becoming president. But as the slaying of JFK has shown, it often involves getting killed on the job."

***

During the closing months of his school term ('63-'64), Bill was known as "The Golden Boy" of Hot Springs High, although that title was usually bestowed on the football captain.

Bill had become very popular with teenage girls. As tenor saxophone player for "The Stardusters," and as a key player in the award-winning high school band, he also had his groupies.

One such teenager, Carolyn Yeldell (later Staley), lived in the parsonage next door to Bill's house. Her father, the Rev. Walter Yeldell, preached at a local church. Harboring a crush on Bill, she became involved with him in a relationship that lasted over a period of many years.

"At first I didn't think I had much chance," she recalled. "So many girls were chasing after him. Stories were spread about him. When the band went on a tour of other towns in the state, I was told that Bill often handed girls the key to his hotel room."

At his high school graduation ceremony, Bill placed fourth, scholastically, from among 363 classmates. Although he was not the class valedictorian, he was invited to deliver the benediction, with Carolyn's father giving the sermon.

Called "The Golden Boy of Hot Springs," Bill, a tenor saxophone player for The Stardusters, poses in his uniform.

"All the girls were chasing after me like I was a rock star. I felt it impolite to turn them down."

Bill urged his fellow classmates "to keep a high sense of values while wandering through the complex maze which is our society."

But it was not Carolyn he invited to go out with him after the ceremony. Instead, he asked a girl he'd long known, Dolly Kyle (later Browning). He drove her to the drive-in movie theater. That weekend, it featured a film about invaders from Outer Space.

Reportedly, they didn't watch the movie. Like the young couples in other cars, they got involved in a lengthy bout of post-graduate heavy necking.

That night, he told Dolly that he had been accepted for the semester beginning that autumn at Georgetown University, and he spoke of his dreams for a political future.

"My goal is to become President of the United States, running no later than 1988."

Assuming much more than she should have, his date seemed ecstatic. "Imagine! Me! The First Lady of the United States. I'll be Jackie to your Jack."

"We'll create the Second Coming of Camelot," he promised her.

Chapter Two

"I'm Not a Sandra Dee Slut, & I'm Not a Lesbian," Hillary Protests to Fellow Students

She and Her Two Brothers Survive a "Boot Camp Life" With a Brute of a Tobacco-Chewing Father

"No one ever accused Hillary of being a pretty girl," said Doria Hannah, who dropped out of Wellesley after only two and a half months to get married. "When I first met her, she was an ardent Republican, but by the time she graduated, or so I heard, she was a liberated Democrat from Hell."

"Okay, I admit it, I looked like a god damn drowned rat when this picture was taken for the yearbook by some jerk," Hillary later said.

"I always hated appearing camera ready. At Wellesley, I was trapped between an outdated past and an uncharted future."

In her book, *It Takes a Village* (1996), Hillary Rodham Clinton, the First Lady, wrote, "I grew up in a family that looked like it was straight out of a 1950s television sitcom, *Father Knows Best."*

That was the idyllic view she wanted to share with the world. The actual circumstances of her girlhood were far more brutal than she admitted.

Dorothy and Hugh Rodham were all smiles in this blissful 1942 photo.

Actually, their faces masked a household that was icy cold and a marriage that was often in the deep freeze.

William H. Chafe, a professor of history at Duke University, stated the case more accurately: "Far from nurturing an environment of love and mutual support, the Rodham family was often dominated by hostility and authoritarianism. Rather than providing a model of mutual affection, it frequently degenerated into a brittle verbal battle among avowed combatants. Her family experience witnessed psychological abuse."

Much of the latent hostility derived from her stern father, Hugh E. Rodham, not from her loving, God-fearing mother, Dorothy Howell Rodham.

Hugh frequently tested his daughter and his two sons, Hugh Rodham, Jr. ("Hughie") and Anthony (Tony) Dean Rodham, with condescension bordering on contempt.

Author Carl Bernstein characterized Hillary's father as a man who "seemed to push through adulthood in a fog of melancholia."

He was hard on Hillary. When she came home one afternoon with her report card, showing all A's except for one B, he told her "to try harder next

At Her College Graduation, a Classmate Predicts That Hillary Will Become the First Woman President of the United States

time."

Later in life, Hughie defined his father as, "gruff, confrontational, completely and utterly so. Growing up with Hillary and Tony was like boot camp, with father, the drill instructor, ordering yet another round of push-ups."

Historian Roger Morris claimed that Hugh's treatment of his children "amounted to a kind of psychological abuse that might have cursed some children."

The son of English and Welsh immigrants, Hugh had been the by-product of a raw-boned, rough childhood. As a very young man, he was sent to work deep within the coal mines of Scranton, Pennsylvania. Throughout his life, Hugh was noted for his sullen, even sour, disposition, never mixing amicably with his neighbors in the staunchly Republican middle class suburb of Park Ridge, 35 miles northwest of downtown Chicago. His political hero had been Red-baiting Joseph McCarthy, the senator from Wisconsin who seemed perpetually obsessed with a witch hunt search for communists in both government and the entertainment industry.

Hugh had paid cash for a two-story brick house that opened onto a front-yard shaded by trees.

He chewed tobacco and usually didn't care where he spat the juice. He was tight-fisted with a dollar, his children having to beg him for money for new shoes. When Dorothy complained that she could take it no more, he always told her, "Don't let the doorknob hit you in the ass on your way out."

With a certain melancholy loveliness, Hillary claimed, "I inherited my father's laugh, the same big guffaw that can turn heads and send cats running from the room."

[Born in Scranton, Pennsylvania in 1911, Hugh Rodham went to Pennsylvania State University, where he played football, graduating during the depths of the Depression. He found work selling drapery fabrics around the Midwest, sending money home to help his cash-strapped parents.

In 1937, he met his future wife, Dorothy, and married her early in 1942 after a long courtship. That year, he enlisted in the U.S. Navy in the wake of the Japanese attack on Pearl Harbor. In the Great Lakes, he trained sailors heading for the Pacific theater of war.

Once he returned from the Navy, he opened his own drapery fabric business in

Chicago's Merchandise Mart and it was relatively successful, moving his family up to middle class status.

On October 27, 1947, Hillary was born, a healthy, eight-pounder. Dorothy said, "She was, from the beginning, mature." Her brother Hughie followed in 1950. Her younger brother Tony, born in 1954, was the couple's last and final child. Growing up, whereas Tony shared a bedroom with his older brother, Hillary was assigned to a room of her own next door.

[Dorothy's background was Dickensian and gloomy. Her mother, Della Murray, was from French Canadian stock, with a touch of Native American blood. At the time she gave birth to Dorothy, Della was a child herself, only fifteen years old and illiterate. Her father, Edwin Howell, was a seventeen-year-old fireman-in-training.

By the time Dorothy turned eight, her parents separated, and she was sent on a cross-country train ride to the town of Alhambra, California. With her was her three-year-old sister, both of them traveling alone.

The two little girls found themselves in an unwanted, brutal household, where Dorothy was treated like a slave. Her sister was forced to work at the age of five. Their grandparents, both of them recent immigrants from Britain, were almost sadistic. For an alleged infraction, Dorothy was confined to her room for one year, being allowed outside only for transits to either school or work. Sometimes, a meager supper was sent to her room; on many a night, nothing at all.

When she turned fourteen, Dorothy fled to Chicago, where she was employed as a $3-a-week nanny with a family that allowed her to finish high school.

After graduation, she managed to find work in a fabrics factory as a low-paid secretary. There, she met Hugh, whom she married after a five-year courtship. Even though she knew after the first year that the marriage was a disaster, she stuck it out, not believing in divorce.

As Hillary revealed, "Mother was a staunch Methodist and a secret Democrat married to a rabid Republican. She went to bed with God, woke up with God, ate with God, and, on occasion, had serious arguments with God."

Dorothy tried for a reconciliation with her mother, who had remarried to Max Rosenberg, but was rejected. She later said, "I'd hoped so hard that my mother would love me. But she didn't."

In later life, Hillary claimed that her mother's brutal childhood interested her in the welfare of other kids, with the belief that caring adults outside the family can fill a child's emotional voids.

That philosophy of hers was best expressed in her book, It Takes a Village, *perhaps with the loveliest photograph of Hillary ever taken displayed on the cover, along with some snaggle-toothed children.]*

Park Ridge, where the Rodhams lived, was almost rigorously white and all Republican, typical of the Baby Boomer Eisenhower years. People listened to Pat Boon's "Love Letters in the Sand" and watched *I Love Lucy* on TV. In summer, some of the children sold lemonade on the sidewalk and learned to play checkers or Monopoly.

Unlike Bill Clinton's brutal background, growing up in Arkansas into a dysfunctional family, Hillary's girlhood was typical except for her father. First, she was a Brownie, then a merit-winning Girl Scout, proudly showing up at school in her uniform. Her life was a series of football games, bake sales, marching in parades, and attending the carnival whenever it pulled into Park Ridge.

In contrast to her father, Dorothy always believed in her daughter's ability and encouraged her. She told friends, "One day, Hillary is going to become the first woman justice on the Supreme Court."

She later said, "I was brainwashed by Father. He turned me into a card-carrying Republican, back when the GOP was a kinder, gentler party that still tolerated a liberal wing, if you could imagine such a thing."

***

From the moment Hillary entered high school, she made it clear to her female classmates that she didn't accept Sandra Dee as a role model. The perky blonde actress, rather virginal looking, seemed to represent the prevailing values of the Hollywood film industry as the 1950s came to a thundering end.

Hillary almost never wore makeup. Her best friend, Betsy Ebeling, said, "Her hair had a life of its own. She tied it in the back with a mock tortoiseshell Revlon comb. Her eyes were hidden behind 'Coke-bottle glasses,' and she wore pants and sandals when the weather was warm; otherwise, she placed her feet and thick ankles into boots. She also had a rather large butt."

Perky and permed, Sandra Dee, America's sweetheart, was pointedly NOT adopted as a role model during the increasingly radicalized adolescence of Hillary Rodham.

She was not popular with the boys, although one or two asked her out to a dance. "She was a bit of a turn-off," Jim Van Schpyck said to a fellow classmate. Reportedly, he once said, "I figured she might be love-starved and that would make for an intriguing evening. I was wrong. I found her very smart. She wanted to talk politics—not love. Frankly, I think she was a bit of a nerd, but rather a nice person."

"I certainly wasn't the school slut," Hillary said. "That honor went to two or three other girls who used Mamie Van Doren as their role model." To her embarrassment, the school paper mockingly referred to her as "Miss Frigidaire," suggesting that she'd be well-advised to enter a nunnery after graduation.

She wasn't, however, as staid as the school paper made her out to be—in fact, she became President of the local Fabian Fan club, *[in ironic contrast to her future husband, an Elvis Presley devotee]*. She also liked Paul McCartney. Later in life, after she got to meet her idol, she wrote: "I didn't know whether I should shake his hand or jump up and down squealing."

Whereas Elvis Presley was Bill Clinton's singing idol, Hillary was president of the local Fabian fan club. She idolized the wavy-haired pop singer and endlessly replayed "Turn Me Loose" and "Tiger."

Actually, Hillary had another profession in mind: She wanted to become the first female astronaut. To that effect, she sent NASA a letter to sign her up when she became of age. "Instead of the man in the moon, I want to be the woman in the moon." In response, NASA sent her a brief note: "SPACE IS THE PROVINCE OF THE MALE GENDER." She was furious at such discrimination.

Before graduation, Hillary did manage to snare a boyfriend, Jim Yrigoyen, a fellow classmate who later became a high school guidance counselor.

Their so-called romance got off to a rocky start. She was raising rabbits and confined eight of them in cages in her backyard. She had to protect them from boys who threatened to let them out to run wild through the neighborhood.

Long before she dreamed of wanting to be the first woman president of the United States, Hillary longed to be the first female astronaut to walk on the moon.

When she had to go away for something, she instructed Yrigoyen to guard her rabbits "with your life." However, when a local housewife, a former farm girl, came over and begged for a fat rabbit to skin and cook for dinner, Yrigoyen acquiesced.

When Hillary returned an hour later, she knew that one of her rabbits—her favorite, the one she'd named "Peter"—was missing. She became furious, calling him a "rotten jerk" and punched him in the nose, from which he bled a lot.

Eventually, they made up, for the rest of the school term, at least, and he often came to her house after school to do homework. "But it was not a serious romance," he said.

More violence was to come. When the first big snow of winter fell, Hillary and Yrigoyen joined in a snowball fight with several other schoolmates. "I landed a bull's eye at least twice in her face. But instead of joining in the fun again, she got real angry, like she did with the rabbit. She started to punch me real hard in both my face and chest. I mean *real* hard. Presto, a nosebleed again. That ended our high school romance. Too bad. If she ever becomes president, I might have become America's First Man."

***

During her escape from her father's Republican dogma, Hillary came under the influence of other opinions. Eventually, she encountered two men who each had a big influence on her thought. One pulled her opinions to the Left, another to the Right.

The more charismatic of the two, Don Jones, was a Methodist Youth Minister who drove her around in his "fire engine red" Chevy Impala convertible. He was twenty-six years old. In his white bucks and sports outfits, she found him better looking than either Robert Wagner or Tab Hunter.

Hillary developed a crush on Don Jones, a handsome Methodist youth minister, who introduced her to the "University of Life" after he moved to Park Ridge in 1961.

She became enthralled with his dreamy blue eyes, fashionable 1950s crew cut, his Pat Boone white bucks, and his fiery red Chevy Impala convertible.

During one of his field trips, he took her as part of his youth ministry, along with some other church members, to the South Side of Chicago "to see how the other half lives." For the first time, she was exposed to massive displays of chronic poverty, especially within the African-American community.

Jones began to take her to museums and to suggest books and poetry for her to read, exposing her to J.D. Salinger's *Catcher in the Rye,* which she did not understand; and to the poems of T.S. Eliot and e. e. Cummings.

He also introduced her to the works of the Beat poet Allen Ginsberg, whose writings she interpreted as pornographic.

Jones described himself as an Existentialist. Her most memorable event with him was when he took her to Chicago's Orchestra Hall, where he heard a speech delivered by Dr. Martin Luther King, Jr. She was most impressed. She didn't tell her father where she was going, because he considered King "a womanizer, rabble-rouser, and all around troublemaker, stirring up black people."

After his speech, Jones accompanied her backstage, where she got to shake King's hand. It was a major moment in her life, although nothing compared to 1963, when Bill Clinton, as a teenager, got to shake the hand of President John F. Kennedy in the Rose Garden of the White House only months before his assassination. Hillary was always a campaigner for civil rights, paying particular attention to the needs of the black community.

In contrast to Jones, she also came under the influence of Paul Carson, her high school history teacher. In fact, she was his "teacher's pet." He was very right wing, preaching against the communist menace and praising political heroes on the Right, one of whom was General Douglas MacArthur. Carson often lectured on the horrors of the Soviet system.

"Carson and Jones were locked in a battle for Hillary's mind and soul," said Betsy Ebeling.

The teacher also was working behind the scenes to undermine Jones, convincing the hierarchy in the Methodist Church that, because of his radical political views, they must relieve him of his duties. Jones was eventually let go, although Hillary stayed in touch with him for years to come.

In the autumn of 1959, Hillary came under the spell of Paul Carson, her charismatic history teacher. As an extreme right winger, he was almost violently anti-communist.

Years later, writer Gail Sheehy found him "a character out of Charles Dickens, a tall, burly man with milky blue pop-eyes resting on deep pouches and white muttonchop sideburns crawling across his full jowls."

When Kennedy narrowly beat out Richard Nixon for the presidency in the national elections of 1960, Hillary, on her own, and in her then-capacity as a Republican, canvassed the South Side of Chicago in an attempt to find evidence of voter fraud. She was often chased off many a stoop by irate homeowners, who told her, "Go back to where you came from."

She discovered that some listings for what voter records described as "home addresses" were, in reality, either vacant lots or, in one case, a seedy tavern.

Hugh Rodham, Sr. wasn't pleased, warning her, "A white gal like you could have been raped...or worse."

Four years later, he also participated in the 1964 election when President Lyndon B. Johnson, who had replaced Kennedy in office after he was assassinated, was pitted against Senator Barry Goldwater on the Republican ticket. During the campaign, Hillary became one of the "Goldwater Girls," going from door-to-door throughout her neighborhood, handing out campaign literature for her candidate, "who lost big time to LBJ," Hillary recalled. "Big Time."

[Years later, Goldwater learned that she had supported him in 1964. In 1996, when she was in Arizona, she went to visit him at his home in Phoenix, later saying: "He was a true conservative and an outspoken supporter of individual rights, not the creatures calling themselves Republicans in the 1990s. He noted all that fuss the Republicans stirred up about gays in the military. 'Hell,' he said to me, 'A guy in the Army doesn't have to be straight. He only has to shoot straight!'"]

High School Hillary, "Goldwater Girl" and President of her Junior Class, as she appeared in her yearbook.

***

In Chicago, Hillary became familiar with the work and philosophy of the avant-garde radical philosopher and community organizer, Saul Alinsky, although she was never his disciple to the degree that Barack Obama was. She was so impressed with him, however, that at Wellesley, she wrote her college thesis on his confrontations of those in power with sit-ins, strikes, and marches. Alinsky, who, like Hillary, was from Chicago, knew that she was far more conservative in her political views than he was, but, even so, he offered her a chance to come and work for him after her graduation from college. Unsure of how she wanted to play her immediate post-graduate months, she re-

Arizona "Conservative Republican with compassion," Barry Goldwater, who favored gays in the military.

jected his offer, turning down two other offers too.

Nonetheless, Alinski invited Hillary to participate in a "fart-in," an event conceived to disrupt Chicago's power elite during one of their gathering at a concert by the Rochester, New York, Philharmonic. She was asked to consume a large can of baked beans before her arrival at the protest. As expressed by author Nicholas Von Hoffman, "Alinsky's gaseous music-lover members would hie themselves to the concert hall, where they would sit expelling gaseous vapors with such noisy velocity as to compete with the woodwinds."

Saul Alinski adopted Hillary as an acolyte.

Barack Obama later became Alinski's disciple. As a tool in his arsenal of tools for social change, he developed the "fart-in."

Alinsky also asked her to attend a roughly equivalent event, in this case, a "piss-in" at O'Hare Airport. In a (successful) attempt to draw attention to one of his liberal causes, he instructed mainly African Americans to occupy all the urinals and toilets in the airport until city officials could be brought to the bargaining table.

During the contentious presidential campaigns of both Barack Obama and Hillary, Republicans attacked their respective links to Alinsky, who is credited today as the father of modern community organizing and noted for his authorship of the controversial book, *Rules for Radicals.* He described his book as "A manual for 'Have-Nots.'"

At one point, after she was elected president of the Wellesley Republican Club, she wrote to Jones: "Is it possible to be a mind conservative but a heart liberal?"

In a Speech to Her Graduating Class at Wellesley, Hillary Blasts Barbara Walters' Black Lover, & Then Loses Her Virginity to Bill's Classmate at Georgetown

Throughout her senior year in high school, Hillary had her heart set on attending Wellesley. Founded in 1870 as one of the original "Seven Sisters" colleges, it was an elite liberal arts institution in the town of Wellesley, west of Boston. The college was known for the beauty of its 500-acre campus, views from which encompassed Lake Waban.

"I thought it was the best choice for me, a place that celebrates womanhood, where one could be surrounded with bright, independent women. It gave me a sense of empowerment. Everything from student government to college publications will be run by women."

The autumnal winds were blowing across its manicured grounds as Hillary began her walk across campus, heading for her assigned dormitory. The leaves were beginning to change, as was her life.

The year was 1965.

She didn't look like a future First Lady, and certainly not like a future President of the United States. Her outfit was a bit bizarre, mixing a fire engine red woolen sweater with a pair of striped, rainbow-hued pants, and a pair of scuffed and serviceable brown lace-up boots. Her eyes were visible from behind a pair of red plastic-framed glasses, and her hair was unruly.

Arriving on campus, she carried two suitcases. One contained a copy of Goldwater's *Conscience of a Conservative,* along with penny loafers, blouses with Peter Pan collars, white knee socks, and pleated skirts.

At Wellesley, unlike at Park Ridge, she was no longer the smartest girl on campus. Within her new digs, she met young women who were better educated than she was, better financed, and better-traveled, many with a knowledge of foreign languages.

She often was confronted with "a bevy of liberals," who ridiculed men like Goldwater. Some of the more liberated women wore frayed jeans and tie-dyed shirts. But, in a letter to her mother, she assured her, "I will not become a scruffy pothead or shaggy-maned radical. Please tell father that!"

Since she didn't date during her first months, rumors spread that she was a lesbian. Those same ru-

After Hillary made her notorious commencement speech in 1969 at Wellesley, reporters from *Life magazine* interviewed her for a feature story. The editors ran it, but found her looks "almost too dowdy."

Years later, she said, "What did they expect for a future First Lady? That I would look all dolled up like Nancy Davis in college before she married Ronnie?"

mors would still be dogging her in 2015, when she announced her bid for the U.S. Presidency.

Lesbianism had long been a tradition among the young women of Wellesley. The charge that the college was "crawling" with lesbians actually dated from the early 20th Century, when only one woman on the faculty out of more than fifty got married. Back then, of the young graduates, less than half of them would get married after graduation. In the greater Boston area, two women living together as partners were known as participants in a "Wellesley marriage," or, in some cases, "a Boston marriage."

During the early years of Wellesley's existence, at school dances, men were barred. Two women went together to school dances, one of them attired in a gown, the other in a tuxedo with black tie. *[After World War II, that policy was rescinded.]*

Two of Hillary's closest friends at college, Nancy Wanderer and Eldie Acheson, were said to be lesbians. A friend who knew Hillary said, "It wasn't lesbianism that attracted Hillary as much as the fact that she saw it as a political statement of a greater goal: Women's liberation as it emerged in the 1960s."

Rumors that Hillary experimented with lesbianism have never been proven. By the same token, rumors were spread that Bill Clinton at Georgetown University "experimented" with gay sex, but only as a recipient of fellatio.

One of Hillary's foremost biographers, Carl Bernstein, found absolutely no proof of lesbianism in Hillary's past.

"Hillary was also for civil rights, but that didn't go so far as her sleeping with Black Panthers in the way Jane Fonda or Jean Seberg were said to have done," claimed a friend.

On weekends, young men from other colleges arrived to date Wellesley women. On one such occasion, Hillary was introduced to Geoffrey Shields, who was at Harvard studying Pre-law. Like her, he was from the Chicago area. A jock, he had been a star football player in high school.

He began to date her, driving from Cambridge to Wellesley on weekends. Sometimes, they'd go dancing, often to her favorite—music by the Supremes.

At first, he noted that Hillary listened more than she talked. But as time went by, she became more outspoken in her beliefs, taking strong positions on civil rights and social issues. He, too, was an advocate of civil rights and had a black roommate at Harvard.

Shields was good-looking but not devastatingly handsome, and their relationship may never have gone beyond the heavy necking stage. Whenever they were separated for any length of time, they exchanged letters. Carl Bernstein was privileged to read some of those which have survived. He found them "soft, thoughtful, dreamy, romantic, and passionate."

She did not confine her dating just to Shields, and he often dated other women in the Boston area. One friend of Hillary's said she specialized in men who were "poli-sci, earnest idealists, and good government types instead of wild-eyed hippie radicals."

In time, Shields' interest in Hillary waned, perhaps because he fell for a more glamorous woman closer to his locale at Harvard.

She followed her broken romance with him by becoming more intimately involved with David Rupert, a "Black Irishman" who had attended Georgetown University with Bill Clinton. At the time, she met him, he was working as an intern for the Republican Party, and she was president of the Wellesley Republican Club. He later claimed, "When Hillary and I met up, I was 150 pounds of pulsing hormones."

It seemed that Hillary at Wellesley became intimate with an intern long before Bill got intimate with his years later in the White House. She has remained mum on the subject, but Rupert later said that their relationship was sexual. He, in fact, may have taken her virginity.

Hillary's friend, Nancy ("Peach") Pietrafesa, claimed, "She was always drawn to arrogant, opinionated, hard-to-please guys who reminded her of her father."

"David became my significant other," Hillary admitted. "I even took him to meet my father. The more David got to know me, the more he challenged me. One night, he shouted at me, 'You're not a real Republican. To say you are is bullshit...and you know it!'"

He recalled that he did not find her especially attractive, although "I was drawn to her in a physical sense in spite of those big, ugly glasses and that pulled-back hair. Not a touch of mascara. I admired her character and intellect."

Rupert was darkly handsome, and he and Hillary seemed rather passionate with each other. He later admitted, "It was an intense love affair, but she was very cautious, not wanting to get pregnant. Even in the heat of passion, she was always careful using protection."

150 pounds of pulsing hormones: "Black Irishman" David Rupert

They were often seen at parties together smoking marijuana. Unlike Bill, she inhaled.

Her affair with Rupert would last on and off for three years until her graduation from Wellesley. The lovers shared much in common, marching against the Vietnam War, as did millions of other students at the time.

A natural athlete, Rupert liked to go skiing,

especially as part of long, cross-country jaunts, but he found her rather clumsy. "I tried to teach her to ski, but it was obvious that she had absolutely no interest in it. I regretted that, because it was a way of bonding. She was afraid of falling down, perhaps of injuring herself."

"One thing that amazed me was how sensitive she was to criticism," he said. "I warned her that if she ever wanted to go into politics, she'd have to learn to take a lot of abuse and attacks, far worse than what her father had subjected her to. She was offended even at the slightest casual remark. She'd retreat and not speak to me if I slighted her. That seems ironical now, as she was to become, by the 1990s and beyond, one of the most criticized women on the planet."

After he graduated from Georgetown, Rupert became a conscientious objector and moved to a commune in Vermont. On at least three occasions, Hillary visited him there, but the idea of becoming a hippie did not appeal to her. "I remember many a Vermont moonbath with her under a starry night during Vermont's ridiculously short summer," Rupert later recalled. "On occasion, we talked about religion. I was born a Catholic, but had long ago left the church. I did not consider myself a spiritual person. She told me she was agnostic."

"She had such a steely drive, unbounded ambition, yet she was a perfectionist, too. I told her such a thing was impossible, because we lived in an imperfect world."

"Perhaps if I had had more ambition, Hillary and I might have made it. But along came my buddy, Bill Clinton. At long last, she found a man whose ambition matched hers."

"Ours was certainly a love affair, but one without commitment," he recalled. "There was no talk of any future together, getting married, or even living together in the months ahead—nothing like that."

Eventually, like many relationships from college, the pair drifted apart. When a reporter traced Rupert down, years later, he reflected on his romance with Hillary. "Had I expressed a desire to become President of the United States, I think Hillary and I would still be together today. Besides, I'm better-looking than Bill, and from what I saw in the showers in college, better somewhere else, too."

"Because we'd spent so much time together, been so close, breaking up was so hard to do. But I didn't plan to challenge Bill to a duel or any shit like that. For a while, I was a bit hurt and I missed her. But I've always believed in moving on after a chapter in your life ends. After my hippie days, I became a successful businessman. As for Bill Clinton, who in hell knows what happened to that fucker?"

Hillary Changes Her Political Stripes & Joins the Democrats, Frank Sinatra Attacks "First Ladies With Thick Ankles"

Somewhere along the way at Wellesley, Hillary shifted her party affiliations, abandoning the Republicans and joining the Democrats. In fact, when Senator Eugene McCarthy announced that he was going to compete with Lyndon B. Johnson for the Democratic nomination for president, she went with friends from Wellesley to help promote his campaign, handing out pamphlets and helping with mail-outs.

By the time she became president of her junior class, she had resigned from the Republican Party.

The year 1968 had been tragic for America. It had included the assassination of both Robert F. Kennedy, who was running at the time for president, and of Martin Luther King, Jr., setting off riots across the landscapes of America.

Hillary Who?

Hillary flew to Miami Beach to attend the Republican nominating convention, supporting a last-minute draft of Rockefeller to counter the rising political ambitions of Nixon.

With schoolmates, she checked into Miami Beach's Fontainebleau Hotel. At one point, a campaign aide invited the students to visit Frank Sinatra in his hotel suite for some party-line boosterism and a short "hello."

John Wayne, ultra-conservative action hero.

Along with her school friends, Hillary was ushered into the singer's suite. She would later record in her memoir, "Sinatra feigned how much he enjoyed meeting us."

Afterwards, in the corridor, Hillary told a friend, "Sinatra's not really a Republican. He's just supporting Nixon because Robert Kennedy once made him *persona non grata* at the Kennedy White House."

[Years later, when Sinatra learned that he had met the then-unknown future First Lady, Hillary Clinton, he told Dean Martin and others, "I don't remember her. So, I've met three First Ladies and fucked two of them. Did you know that Nancy (Reagan) has thick ankles? And Hillary looks like she has the same affliction. Frankly, I prefer a dancer's angle on a woman. Take Juliet Prowse, for example."]

After leaving Sinatra's suite at the Fontainebleau, Hillary found herself riding in an elevator with John Wayne. "The Duke looked a fright, like he was recovering from a hangover," Hillary said. "He spent all our time together in the elevator complaining about the lousy food at the hotel."

Back in Chicago, later in 1968, Hillary also attended the now-notorious Democratic National Convention. She later said that she was horrified that Mayor Richard Daly had "allowed the police to crack the skulls of demonstrators protesting the war in Vietnam. "It was a bloody battlefield. Fires were started and tear gas filled the air."

In spite of the widespread protests and violence, she lent her support to the Vice President, Hubert Humphrey, even though he was hardly her favorite candidate. "I'd prefer almost anybody more than Nixon," she proclaimed.

***

The sun rose bright on May 31, 1969, the day Hillary was scheduled to graduate from Wellesley. Although her mother could not attend the ceremony, Hugh flew in from Chicago, arriving late in the evening before the event.

It is customary for colleges to invite a prominent speaker to address their audiences at graduations. In this case, it was Senator Edward W. Brooke of Massachusetts. Running as a liberal Republican, Brooke, the only African American in the U.S. Senate at the time, had won the support of Hillary two years before when she campaigned for him.

Senator Edward Brooke

There was talk that he might become the first African American to run for President of the United States.

Unusual for such events, the President of Wellesley, Ruth Adams, asked Hillary to deliver a speech following Brooke. She had carefully prepared one. Having shown up in granny glasses, wearing no makeup, she was introduced to the audience by Brooke.

On that fateful day, she had waited peacefully through his speech, covering up the horror she felt inside as she listened to his words. He seemed "too much of a pussy footer," she later said.

In 1973, newscaster Barbara Walters launched a clandestine affair with Brooke, whom she termed "a black married man."

"He was simply the most attractive, sexiest, funniest, charming, and impossible man. I was excited, fascinated, intrigued, and infatuated."

Brooke, who at the time was having an affair with newscaster Barbara Walters, said that although he had "empathy" for student concerns over Vietnam and civil rights, that he found the nationwide protests tearing apart Chicago and other cities at the time "repugnant to American politics."

Departing from her prepared speech, Hillary stood before the lectern and began her attack on Brooke. The senator sat near her in stunned silence. She didn't exactly call him an Uncle Tom, but, tearing into the senator, she attacked Brooke's relevance.

"Part of the problem with empathy with professed goals is that empathy doesn't accomplish anything," she said to the hushed and suddenly breathless audience.

As Hugh would later say, with an utter lack of chivalry: "That was my daughter up there on that stage, and I wanted to crawl under my seat and die!"

From the audience, during the final moments of her speech, Hillary's picture *["I looked awful"]* was taken by a photographer and her words were printed in *Life* magazine with the explanation that she was part of a new generation speaking out on the day's most pressing issues.

Hillary addressing her fellow graduates at Wellesley, during which she attacked Senator Edward W. Brooke.

"Michelle and Barack never forgave me for that," Hillary reportedly told Bill. "The Obamas believe that Brooke's shit doesn't stink."

After her speech, she rushed out to the campus lake and tossed off her black gown. Underneath, she wore a bathing suit. She jumped into the water, even though swimming was forbidden to students.

Ruth Adams, Wellesley's president, was alerted by campus security, and she ordered that a guard remove Hillary's clothing and glasses from where she had left them on the shoreline.

As Hillary remembered it, "Like a blind person, with my nearsighted vision, I had to find my way back to the dormitory."

On that graduation day, a prophetic announcement was made by classmate Marge Wanderer. She tuned to her mother, "That Hillary Rodham one day will become the first woman president of the United States. Mark my words!"

In the 21st century, during her recollection of the event, Hillary said, "Michelle and Barack never forgave me for my attack on Brooke. He was a great hero to them, the first African American elected to the U.S. Senate. A black pioneer and a war hero, even though he was a Republican. To Michelle, it was like I was attacking Martin Luther King or, God forbid, Rosa Parks."

Post-Graduation, Hillary Heads North to Alaska for the "Psychic Revenge" of Right-Wing Zealot, Sarah Palin

After her graduation, wherein she had denounced Brooke, Hillary fled north to Alaska, where she got a job at a salmon processing plant at Valdez. Working on an assembly line, she found herself removing the guts from salmon with a spoon and standing in high boots in up to a foot of bloody water.

On her first day, she complained to her boss that some of the fish smelled bad, and that some of it had actually turned rancid and black. She doubted if it was fit for human consumption.

He fired her on the spot, telling her to return the following day to pick up her paycheck.

When she got there, at around 10AM, she found that the plant had been abruptly closed and all of its employees dismissed.

"It's back to the summer streets of Chicago for me," she said.

By the 21st Century, Hillary was referring to "that bloody, salmon-canning ordeal" as "Sarah Palin's revenge."

Hillary's Double Whammy—The Brothers Rodham

Whereas then-President Bill Clinton's brother, indeed, caused administrative embarrassment, issues with his in-laws (Hillary's brothers) might have been even worse.

As one reporter claimed, "While Roger Clinton *[Bill's brother]* was pretty much a run-of-the-mill troublemaker, Hillary's brothers, Hughie and Tony, were bumbling power-grabbers who kept making almost comical attempts to capitalize on their sister's high station."

Hughie, now a lawyer, had moved to Miami to practice criminal law. After around 1980, he functioned as a public defender in Dade County. There, he married Maria Victoria Arias, a Cuba-born lawyer specializing in immigration issues.

Although Hughie had earned good marks for his role as a public defender, in 1993, both he and his brother, Tony, ignited a controversy when they tried to solicit corporate donations for the Clintons' inaugural galas. After a public outcry, they abandoned their campaign.

As president, Bill often played golf with Hughie. When the president ran into trouble with his appointment for U.S. Attorney General, (Zoë Baird, who had employed illegal immigrants) Hughie suggested Janet Reno, who was eventually confirmed.

In 1994, Hughie won the Democratic Nomination for a Florida Senate seat, but lost the general election to the Republican incumbent, Connie Mack III.

At around the same time, both Hughie and Tony were involved in "Hazelnut Gate," a scandal centering around the Republic of Georgia, a former Soviet satellite. Hillary's brothers joined together in a $118 million plan to process and import hazelnuts from that small country. Regrettably, their dealings were with Aslan Abashidze, the most prominent political enemy of Eduard Shevardnadze, the president of Georgia at the time and a major U.S. ally in that troubled region. Hughie claimed that he was acting only as a lawyer for the ill-conceived business venture, and that he had not invested in it personally.

The association of the two Rodham brothers with Abashidze caused great embarrassment to both Bill and Hillary, straining their relationship with Shevardnadze. "He's our ally," Hillary shouted at Hughie over the phone. "You're fucking up our deal with a key ally in a part of the world where the United States needs any friend we can get. Shove those hazelnuts up your ass and cut your ties with Abashidze. He's an enemy of America!"

Most of the Clintons' White House staffers agreed with George Stephanopoulos, who said, "You never wanted to hear the Brothers Rodham names get mentioned in any context other than playing golf."

Living large: Hughie Rodham

During the waning days of the Clinton presidency, Hughie's name was linked with the "Cocaine Kingpin," Carlos Anibal Vignali, who had been convicted of shipping nearly half a ton of the drug to Minneapolis. It was first revealed in the tabloids that Hughie had charged the Vignali family $200,000 for "Carlos" ticket to freedom," meaning that he had arranged for him to be pardoned.

Hughie also received a subsequent $200,000 for seeking a presidential pardon for Almon Glenn Braswell, who had been convicted of mail fraud, peddling a cure for baldness, and other dubious products, including a prostate remedy. During one deposition in the autumn of 2000, he pleaded the Fifth Amendment nearly two hundred times.

When these revelations were exposed, Hillary, then the U.S. Senator from New York, said, "Hughie is my brother, and I love him. I'm just extremely disappointed in this terrible misjudgment that he made. I knew nothing about my brother's involvement in these pardons. I knew nothing about his taking money for his involvement." She went on to claim that she asked him to return the $400,000.

It is not clear if he acquiesced.

Often called Hillary's "Brobdingnagian older brother," Hughie, during the 21st Century, was sometimes photographed on some of Florida's golf courses. His weight has ballooned, one reporter from *The Miami Herald* asserting, "He would make ten Jackie Gleasons." He's also known for his slovenly dress, one paper naming him "the worst dressed man in Florida," where competition for that title is fierce.

***

Tony, Hillary's younger brother, today a heavyset man in his 60s who walks with a cane, is a consultant and a businessman.

Before that, he's had a varied career: Once employed at a metal equipment company in Texas, he later was an insurance man in Chicago, acting as a repo agent for the repossession of cars for non-payment of monthly payments. According to reports, shots have been fired at him from within Chicago's infamously oversized Cabrini-Green housing projects.

For a time, Tony worked as a prison guard before moving to South Florida in 1983. There, he lived for a while with his brother, Hughie, working as a process server and private detective until 1992, when his brother-in-law ran for the presidency.

During the second year of the Clinton presidency, Tony married Nicole Boxer (daughter of California Senator Barbara Boxer) in the Rose Garden of the White House. Together, they produced a son, Zachory, in 1995.

As a consultant, Tony said, "I bring different peoples together. I negotiate deals for them. I solve problems."

Many of his deals have been controversial, including meetings with the President of Paraguay, the Mayor of Moscow, and the Prime Minister of Cambodia. He has been accused of influence-peddling.

In March of 2001, it was revealed in the press that he had helped gain a presidential pardon for Edgar and Vonna Jo Gregory, a Tennessee couple working in the carnival business who had been accused of bank fraud. By 2000, a court ordered Tony to repay $100,000 in loans to the estate of the since-deceased Edgar Gregory.

Tony's dispute and scandals continued into the 21st Century, making unwanted headlines for Hillary. In August, 2011, at Lake Winola in Pennsylvania, he charged a man with assault. He broke into a cottage, where Tony was having sex with the man's girlfriend. Tony was badly injured in the attack. The man pled guilty to trespassing assault and making terroristic threats.

The following year, Boxer's daughter, now divorced, charged that Tony owed her $168,000 in unpaid child support payments. In 2005, he remarried, this time wedding Began Madden of Vienna, Virginia.

In May of 2015, as part of a front-page article in *The New York Times,* it was revealed that Tony's calling card was a handshake and a promise: "If there's anything I can ever do for any of you people, let me know. I'll be more than happy to do it."

Since many of these people are convinced that Hillary will become president in 2016, that calling card is highly prized. *The New York Times* also pointed out that Tony, for more than two decades, has used connections with his sister and brother-in-law to further a string of business ventures that have met with more failure than success. These enterprises have included collaboration with Chinese business interests, and an attempt to mine for gold in Haiti. He also tried to make a deal through his brother-in-law for the acquisition of $22 million for the rebuilding of homes in Haiti after the ravages of that country's many earthquakes, hoping to raise the funding through the Clinton Foundation.

When he has run out of money, Tony has turned to the Clintons for help, such as in 2010, when Bill arranged for him to be hired by an electric car company owned by family friend, Terry McAuliffe, a Democrat who has, since 2014, been the governor of Virginia.

As Hillary runs for President, the subject of her brothers frequently comes up. Her aide, Nick Merrill, said, "Her brothers have always been there for her, and she will always be there for them. Both men, though, have their own lives, their own jobs, and their own ups and down."

Today, with his second wife, Tony lives in a big house on a hill in Vienna, Virginia, a suburb of Washington, D.C. At one point, in court in 2012, he admitted to being ten months behind in his mortgage, and that he was facing foreclosure.

It seemed that Hillary's purse strings were tied. He thanked her by saying, "Hillary and Bill are done for now. But in the past, they've given me money all the time. But $6,000 a month is not enough."

Former Clinton aide, Rahm Emanuel, Mayor of Chicago, said, "The Brothers Rodham are colorful. They're all living large."

Chapter Three

Bill Surveys a Nude Photo of Elvis Snapped During His Induction into the Army and Says, "The King & I Have Something in Common—Hillbilly Peckers"

In High School, Bill Had Two Role Models: John F. Kennedy & Elvis Presley. "They Had a Way With Women"

Bill looked like the poor man's Elvis Presley in this picture from his early teens. At least he copied Elvis' famous "ducktail" hairdo. But Bill never mustered those few strands that would fall over Elvis' forehead, completing "The Look."

"I loved Elvis," Bill said. "I could sing all of his songs. Unlike most parents, who thought his gyrations obscene, Mother loved Elvis, too, maybe even more than I did. Beyond his music, I identified with his small-town Southern roots, and I thought he had a good heart."

In the 1950s, when Elvis Presley burst onto the scene, he garnered two of his most dedicated and devoted fans from deep within the bowels of Arkansas. They were Virginia Kelley and her son, Bill Clinton, who later wrote, "I loved Elvis. Mom and I didn't think his movements were obscene. In fact, I not only loved Elvis, I wanted to be Elvis."

Bill had originally been "knocked off my block" when he first heard an obscure country singer by the name of Elvis Presley on a hillbilly radio station broadcasting from nearby Shreveport, Louisiana. "His name sounds like a Presbyterian deacon," Bill told his mother.

When Elvis started to sing, Bill became glued to the radio. He'd never heard a voice quite like that. She felt the same way. From that day forth, both of them became devoted Elvis fans.

Bill went so far as to try to dress like Elvis, beginning with his hairdo. He remembered sitting with Virginia in 1956 to watch *The Ed Sullivan Show*. Before that, the popular TV variety show host had loudly asserted, "I will not allow this rabble-rouser onto my show." But in 1956, when he saw that huge audiences were tuning in to his rivals whenever Elvis appeared, he became more accommodating.

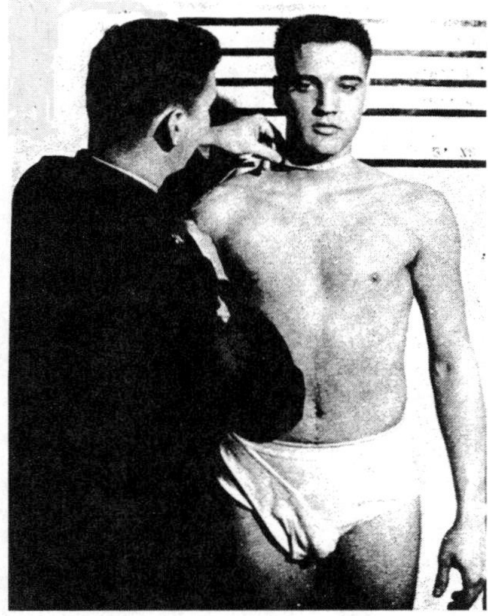

This picture of Elvis in his jockey shorts —taken when he was being inducted into the Army—made the underground rounds of his fans in the 1950s.

In the Army, Elvis was mercilessly kidded and called a stripper. His co-workers begged him to do "bumps and grinds" for them. These soldiers had a point, as Elvis had borrowed some of the moves from burlesque dancers, including his former lover, Tempest Storm.

According to one of his biographers, Albert Goldman, "He would shoot out his legs in a series of hot shots that were the pimp-walkin' daddy's equivalent of a bump. But his erotic pantomime suggested not so much the coitus of the burlesque dancer or the masturbation of the go-go girl so much as the aggressive and brutal motions of rape."

Bill Is Shocked at the F.B.I.'s Dossier on Elvis— Reports Allege Everything from Homosexuality to Incest

"Mom and I laughed when Sullivan ordered his cameramen to photograph Elvis only from the waist up."

"Like Elvis, Bill's favorite sandwich was made with a banana and peanut butter," Virginia wrote in her memoirs. "I acquired this bust of Elvis and placed it in a position of honor in our dining room. I also bought a puka-shell necklace that had once belonged to Elvis. Sometimes, I could still smell his Brut cologne coming from its porous shell."

When Elvis began to make movies, Bill was the first to show up at the local movie house, and the last to leave at night, living off popcorn and candy bars from the theater's refreshment stand.

In spite of all of Elvis' future movies and future songs, "Love Me Tender" remained Bill's eternal favorite, both as a song and as the black and white film *[Elvis' first]* it subsequently inspired in 1956.

[Bill learned in a movie magazine that Elvis had been assigned as the film's romantic lead after both Robert Wagner and Jeffrey Hunter each rejected the role. Originally entitled The Reno Brothers, *its name was changed as a means of capitalizing off Elvis' hit song.*

It was set in the aftermath of the Civil War, focusing on the robbery of military payrolls from a Union train by two Confederate brothers (Richard Egan played Elvis' older brother). Elvis didn't like the script.]

As a movie fan, Bill remained loyal to Elvis as he went on to make such films as *Jailhouse Rock* (1957). In that film, Elvis kills a man and is sent to jail.

Right before he went into the Army, Elvis also made *King Creole* (1958), which also thrilled Bill. In it, Elvis was cast as a nightclub singer who is

Bill Clinton, in a biography, once evaluated some of Elvis' movies:

"Elvis' first movie, *Love Me Tender,* was my favorite and remains so. I also liked *Loving You, Jailhouse Rock, King Creole*, and *Blue Hawaii.* After that, his movies got more saccharine and predictable."

"The interesting thing about *Love Me Tender,* a post-Civil War western, is that Elvis, already a national sex symbol, got the girl, Debra Paget. But only because she thought his older brother, whom she really loved, had been killed in the war. At the end of the film, Elvis gets shot and dies, leaving his brother with his wife. I never quite escaped Elvis."

"In *Jailhouse Rock* (1957), Elvis is sent to prison when he accidentally kills a man in a barroom brawl. The prison guards hear him singing "Treat Me Nice" and "I Wanna Be Free."

unwillingly dragged into the criminal world. But after Elvis' return from Germany, he starred in a movies that Bill found disappointing. Consequently, although the King of Rock 'n' Roll lost Bill as a movie fan, he never wavered in his devotion to Elvis as a singer.

For years, Bill kept this picture of the Presley family (Gladys, Elvis, and Vernon) in his bedroom on his dresser. "It showed that even if a Southern boy were born into poverty, he could grow up to be a King," Bill said.

Three days after this picture was taken, Vernon was convicted of forgery for cashing a $5 check, and sentenced to eight months in the notorious Parchment Farm Prison in Mississippi. During his incarceration, for lack of money, Gladys and Elvis were evicted from their humble home.

Hillary later claimed in a memoir that when she started dating Bill, during some of their long walks, he would suddenly break into an Elvis song. As late as his campaign for the presidency in 1992, his staff sometimes referred to him as "Elvis."

As he was growing up, Bill couldn't seem to make up his mind: Did he want to become President of the United States or the next Elvis Presley?

On the political front, John F. Kennedy was his role model, and he wanted to emulate him. He'd actually met the soon-to-be assassinated president and had shaken his hand.

During high school, the singer/musician in Bill prevailed, at least temporarily. At first, he played the saxophone for a group called "The Stardusters," and he was a member of the Hot Springs High School Dance Band. Later, he formed his own Jazz Trio, "The Kingsmen."

At gatherings of his extended family, "The Clan," which included Bill, he always entertained with Elvis songs, complete with the churning hips and upcurled lip.

On August 16, 1977, Bill, in his capacity as the Attorney General of Arkansas, was in Fort Smith to make a speech. Heading for the hall where he was to speak, he heard over his car radio that Elvis had been found dead in his bathroom at Graceland. "I went into such a state of shock, I could hardly deliver my talk. I forgot what my subject was going to be and ended up talking about Elvis and what a wonderful legacy he'd left the South, and the world at large, with his music."

After his speech, he went to the home of Marilyn Speed, a longtime supporter, to watch the TV coverage of the death of the King of Rock 'n' Roll. He also placed a call to Virginia, whom he found crying. She told him, "I feel the loss like one of my own sons. " He told his mother that he'd be home soon to comfort her.

Traveling with him later that night was a fellow lawyer, Terry Kirkpatrick. "On the airplane back to Little Rock, all Bill could talk about was Elvis, how he'd died, the life he'd lived. I felt he was mourning more than the death of Elvis, but the death of a whole era of his life."

"Bill told me that Elvis could have been a great movie star had it not been for Colonel Parker, who kept signing him to cheap exploitation films and kept turning down really dramatic roles where the singer could have 'shown his god-given talent.'"

Bill cited role after role that could have been played by Elvis: Marilyn Monroe's co-star in *Bus Stop,* the Oscar-nominated role that went to Jon Voight for his role as the sex-industry anti-hero in *Midnight Cowboy*; and the Kris Kristofferson role opposite Barbra Streisand in the third remake of *A Star Is Born.*_

***

As the years went by, and as Bill—as governor—became more embroiled in Arkansas politics, Virginia faithfully kept the Elvis home fires burning, a loyalty that had found a niche within her heart ever since she'd heard him sing "Hound Dog" and "Don't Be Cruel."

"I had never heard such a spiritual sound coming from anyone; it was the sweetest, most beautiful singing in the world. And of course, you can't discount the man's sex appeal. If I hadn't children and a job, I'd have to spend the rest of my days traveling around from Elvis concert to Elvis concert."

Later in life, she carried her devotion to Elvis so ardently that she visited his former manager, Col. Tom Parker, at his home in Nevada.

[In 1993, Virginia told the press, "I still love Elvis, but I don't listen to his music much anymore. I'm not an Elvis nut like people think. I also don't believe that Elvis is still alive, and I firmly deny that Bill has stashed Elvis in the attic of the White House."]

***

In spite of the firestorm that had rained down on his head, Bill, from all reports, continued his obsession with Elvis even when he became President of the United States.

He soon learned one of the "delicious quirks: of being president was that "you could request almost anything—and get it. I was surrounded by some of the top talent in the world, who could carry out almost any order."

[It was not just Elvis' music that intrigued Bill, but his reputation as a se-

ducer. Elvis once told his stepmother, Dee Presley, that he'd slept with some 1,000 women before his marriage to Priscilla Ann Beaulieu. Apparently, he didn't boast about how many women he'd seduced after his marriage.]

On a whim, in his capacity as U.S. President, Bill ordered two of his staff members to compile a list of the "name" women who Elvis had seduced. "Forget the carhops, starlets, groupies, or hairdressers."

Elvis seduced many women, but his heart always belonged to one, his beloved mother, Gladys.

When he saw this picture of the two of them together, he said, "My momma looks like the saddest woman who ever lived."

Within ten days, he was presented with the list, which contained some predictable names, but some real surprises too.

The president expected the usual list of actresses, led by Marilyn Monroe, but it also included Natalie Wood, Tuesday Weld, Deborah Walleys, Barbra Streisand, Mamie Van Doren, Connie Stevens, Nancy Sinatra, Rita Moreno, Cybill Shepherd, Joanna Moore, Jayne Mansfield, Peggy Lipton, Anne Helm, Ginger Alden, and Ann-Margret, the latter his co-star in *Viva Las Vegas* (1964).

The list also included singers and songwriters Carol Connors, Jackie De-Shannon, and Phyllis McGuire. Coming as a real surprise was America's most famous stripper, Tempest Storm.

The roster also contained some surprises: singer Ricky Nelson and actor Nick Adams. Elvis had also been seduced by Doris Duke, the tobacco heiress considered at the time as the richest woman in the world.

After witnessing the presence of two men on the list, Bill reportedly said, "I didn't know Elvis went that route. Maybe it was a 'Long Lonely Highway' for him one night."

The most genuinely shocking name on the F.B.I's list of Elvis sexual liaisons included Gladys Presley, Elvis' beloved mother. "I knew he was close to his mother, but not *that* close," Bill said.

He wasn't satisfied with just a list of Elvis' conquests. He demanded the complete FBI file that J. Edgar Hoover had assembled on Presley. He knew that the former F.B.I. director began having his agents compile a dossier on Elvis that began in the late 1950s.

Bill would not be satisfied with just the stuff that could be released under the Freedom of Information Act, preferring the "real lowdown" that Hoover kept in a private file.

The F.B.I. files that were made public dealt mainly with death threats against the singer; complaints about his "obscene public appearances"; extortion attempts; mentions, here and there, of various paternity suits; theft by white-collar larceny, of an executive jet Elvis had owned; and insights into how Hoover had responded to various "citizen complaints."

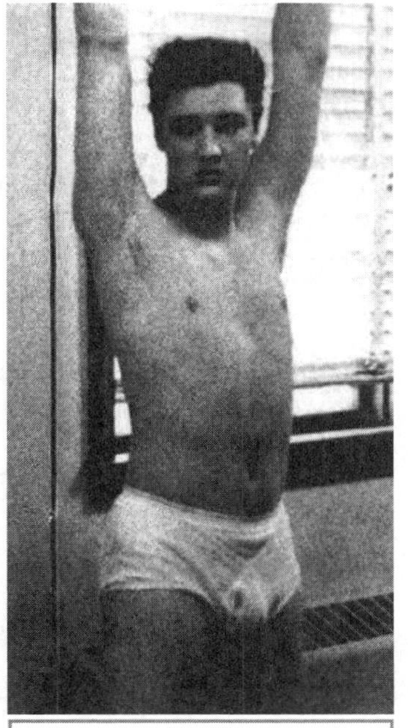

Before he doffed his Navy blue trousers, gray and white-checked sports coat, and blue and red-striped shirt, even his pink-and-black socks, Elvis told an Army recruiter, "I'm nervous as a whore with twenty sailors lined up outside her door, guys who had been at sea for three months."

Almost as a hobby *[and according to some, an obsession]* Hoover had spent a great deal of his time at the F.B.I. prying into the secret lives not only of Elvis, but also into those of John and Robert Kennedy and Marilyn Monroe. He compiled and reviewed F.B.I. dossiers on the sex lives of, among others, Jane Fonda, Martin Luther King, Jr., Albert Einstein, Frank Sinatra, Errol Flynn, Katharine Hepburn, Marlon Brando, Joseph McCarthy, and his alltime least favorite person, Eleanor Roosevelt. *[Infuriated by her outspoken criticism of his invasion of American liberties, Hoover had compiled extensive documentation of her lesbian activities and partners.]*

During Hoover's tenure as the F.B.I. chief, despite his frantic compilation of dossiers on gender preferences of his self-defined enemies, Hoover was locked into a longtime romance with his chief aide, Clyde Tolson, who, partly because of his taciturn confidentiality and good looks, had been nicknamed "the Gary Cooper of the F.B.I."

As president, Bill even pursued information about Elvis' most intimate boudoir secrets, learning that he wasn't all that addicted to penetration, as he had a delicate foreskin that would sometimes tear under friction, causing him to bleed and risking infection.

According to the report, Elvis maintained a fetish for women in white panties. One F.B.I. investigator learned that the sight of pubic hairs peeping and curling under white panties drove him wild. "According to the FBI reports, Elvis loathed making love to a woman who had already borne a child. After Priscilla gave birth to their only child *[Lisa Marie Presley, born in Memphis in 1968]*, she "turned him off, the report claimed, and she had to "find love elsewhere."

***

Bill was especially intrigued with the photographs in the F.B.I.'s Elvis file. It contained about a hundred candid shots of the singer, many of them snapped when Elvis was not aware that he was being photographed. Some of them were shot in Las Vegas, depicting him in sexually compromising positions with showgirls, snapped with cameras and recording devices hidden inside his suites.

When Elvis was inducted into the Army, a picture of him in his white jockey shorts was taken and disseminated around the world.

Every man who has ever been examined by an Army doctor knows that at some point, those jockey shorts have to be dropped. As Ronald Reagan once said, "A doctor orders you to cough as he fondles the family jewels."

When Elvis showed "his full monty" someone snapped a full frontal nude.

A copy of that photograph was included in the files Bill had requested. He studied it for a moment and then told one of his staffers, "Elvis and I have more in common than our music. We practically have identical hillbilly peckers."

Reportedly, Bill didn't believe some of what he read in the F.B.I.'s Elvis dossier, dismissing much of it as "Hoover's fantasy."

One can only speculate how Bill Clinton absorbed the implications of the FBI file on his hero, Elvis Presley. Perhaps the most horrifying aspect involved the realization that the agency's power to spy, as it had on Elvis, might one day be directed onto him, too.

Bill's Brother, Roger (Codenamed "Headache" by The Secret Service) Generates Scandals as "The Other Clinton Who Wants to Be Elvis"

As boys growing up in Arkansas, Roger Clinton referred to Bill as his "Big Brother."

"Bill was almost obsessive about wanting to be near me, and he was my best friend, my guardian, my father, and my role model."

There was a big difference, however, between the two brothers: Whereas Bill was skilled at avoiding trouble, Roger, in the words of his Big Brother, "always managed to step into the next pile of shit."

Like his older brother and his mother, Roger, as he grew up, became addicted to the music of Elvis Presley. He developed and maintained a vague dream about evolving into "the Second Coming of Elvis."

Virginia, by now a familiar presence on Arkansas' honky-tonk circuits, encouraged Roger's musical aspirations. According to Virginia, whenever her boy found a little gig in some smoke-filled tavern filled with Arkansas boozers, "I spent many a night in these clubs, watching Roger trying to get his career launched. He was so handsome."

Like Bill, Roger, too, formed a small band. He named it "Dealer's Choice" after a brand of pinball machine. There was a certain irony in his selection of the band's name, as he'd later be arrested for dealing cocaine.

He not only sold coke, but he became addicted to it, based partly on the influence of an immigrant drug kingpin from Colombia who had recently arrived in Little Rock. "I'd get hammered," Roger later confessed. "Just stoned out of my head."

In the 1970s, when Bill hooked up with Hillary Rodham and became embroiled in state politics, he had less and less time for his little brother. Since Roger had no father to turn to, and with Big Brother involved elsewhere, Roger, throughout the course of his adolescence and teen years, operated more or less on his own.

Both Bill and Virginia later blamed themselves for not paying enough attention to Roger, and for not having noticed the clues to his oncoming fall. "Sometimes, he was dead broke," his mother said. "At other times, he seemed rolling in dough. I never once asked him how he made so much money. I guess I really didn't want to know."

After 1979, when Bill became the youngest governor in the history of Arkansas, Roger bragged to a wide circle of acquaintances about the "wild cocaine binges" being conducted within the Governor's Mansion. Although he vaguely implied that Bill was a participant in recreational use of the drug, he didn't quite come out and say so.

Ironically, it was Bill himself, as governor, who launched a sting operation that eventually led to his brother's arrest. Based on new directives defined by Bill, "Cocaine Cowboys" were secretly videotaped at various locations in Little Rock, both indoor and outdoor, selling drugs.

The dragnet that Bill had established caught Roger selling cocaine in a hotel room. In 1985, he was arrested, later pleading guilty to conspiring to distribute cocaine. An Arkansas judge sentenced him to two years in prison.

Both Bill and Virginia were devastated, as each of them loved Roger very much. As governor of the state, Bill was also deeply humiliated.

Following his arrest, during a meeting with Bill, Roger threatened suicide. In an immediate reaction, Bill revealed his anger. "Don't you dare do such a god damn thing! You know that to mother and me you are the most precious thing in the world. Be a man. Face up to your trouble. Go to prison and get off on good behavior. Get out and rebuild your life. I know you can do it."

"For the first time in my life, I saw Big Brother burst into tears," Roger recalled.

Bill shared his grief over Roger with his long-time friend, Carolyn Yeldell *(aka Carolyn Staley)*. "Some people are addicted to drugs. Some to power. Some to food. Some to sex. We're all addicted to something."

Two views of Roger Clinton—one, "mugging" for the camera, the other a publicity picture, where he's singing his heart out like Elvis.

Before his incarceration, Hillary, Bill, and Virginia gathered to wish Roger a sad (but temporary) farewell.

Reportedly, it was Roger's arrest that prompted Hillary to confront Bill's particular form of addiction, which, apparently, was to sex. At one point, after she discussed a possible divorce from her husband with her brother, Hugh Rodham, he recommended family therapy as a means of saving their highly visible marriage.

Searching for an alternative to divorce, Hillary turned to religion, joining a Methodist congregation. Bill did likewise, becoming a member of Little Rock's Immanuel Baptist Church, where he sang in the choir.

Roger served only a year of his sentence, first at a low-security federal prison for male inmates in Fort Worth, Texas, and then at a Halfway House in Dallas.

[Other embarrassing implications arose from Roger's trial in 1985. In it, he had delivered testimony that implicated Bill's friend and supporter Dan R. Lasater, an Arkansas financier with investments in everything from bond funds to hamburger joints to racehorses. Lasater, it was charged, had been Roger's main source for the inventories of cocaine he had distributed. Based partly on Roger's testimony, Lasater was tried and convicted, eventually serving a six-month prison sentence.

Bill was embarrassed by this, as Lasater had been one of his major contributors during his campaign for governor, and the subject of some of his largesse in the awarding of state-funded contracts.

In 1990, Bill used his authority as governor to pardon him, an act that allowed for the drug-related conviction to be expunged from Lasater's police record.]

***

Virginia was waiting outside the Texas Corrections Facility to meet her errant son after his release, later recalling it in a memoir. "The day he got out of prison was one of the happiest days of my life."

After his stint as a convict, Roger landed a job with a construction company building bridges. "Even I recognized the symbolism of that," Virginia said.

In 1991, Roger began a brief relationship with Martha Spivey, which led to the birth of a daughter, Macy Clinton.

During the course of her childhood and adolescence, Macy saw very little of her "Deadbeat Dad." Her mother would later sue for unpaid child support.

When the girl turned eighteen, she told an interviewer at *Inside Edition* that she was living on food stamps. "It's hard, because I'm a Clinton, too, but I have to depend on government assistance to make it from day to day."

"My father told me that when I turned eighteen, I'd come into a trust fund he'd set up for me. To date, I never saw any of the money."

In 1994, Roger entered officially into a marriage (his first) with Molly D'Ann Martin. On May 12, 1994, during the second year of Bill Clinton's presidency, she gave birth to a son, Tyler Cassidy Clinton.

During the eight years Bill was president, the Secret Service assigned to Roger the codename "Headache," because he always seemed to be getting into trouble and causing Bill embarrassment.

In January of 2001, during his final days in office, the president granted his brother a pardon for his 1985 cocaine arrest.

Roger, however, wasn't satisfied with that, and complained bitterly. In prison, he'd made some friends, and he wanted six of them pardoned for various crimes, too. Bill promised his little brother that he'd think about it, but—probably because of the intense scrutiny the affair had attracted—never granted pardons for the members of Roger's prison entourage.

A month after his pardon, Roger was arrested in California on a drunk-driving charge.

Years later, Roger was overheard telling a friend, "It's not been easy living in the shadow of a world-famous brother and perhaps a future sister-in-law set to make more history than she already has."

***

In January of 2001, during one of Bill's final nights in the White House, his friend, the Hollywood producer, Harry Thomason, said, "Bill surveyed the private apartment for the last time, but perhaps not forever. He looked around nostalgically. When he spoke he meant to sound like General Douglas MacArthur saying:

But he sounded like Elvis Presley."

When Elvis Came to the White House
was one of the few moments when Bill Clinton might have envied Richard Nixon.

Chapter Four

Bill's Hot Pursuit of Beauty Queens

From the "Bowels of Dogpatch" to Washington (D.C.), Oxford (England), and Beyond

Bill Shows a Talent for Skirtchasing

Dodging the Draft, Protesting the Vietnam War, and Early Commie Controversies

It was New Year's Eve, 1969. A bearded and disheveled young foreigner, Bill Clinton, a student at Oxford, was transiting across the heavily guarded frontier of the Soviet Union. A burly guard was about to let him pass, but when two of his superiors spotted Bill, they suspected him of being "one of those foreign hippies" trying to smuggle drugs into Russia.

He was arrested and sent to a back room, where he was ordered to strip by a fat Soviet woman for a search over every inch of his body. He was even forced to bend over to touch his feet with his hands.

Whereas Bill Clinton confessed to Monica Lewinsky and several other confidantes that before he met Hillary at Yale Law School, there were "hundreds upon hundreds of other women," there is no record of his ever confessing about how many affairs he had after his marriage to Hillary.

An irresistible campaigner with, to women at least, an irresistible charm

Many of his pre-marital flings involved one-night stands with women he picked up in the taverns or honky-tonks of Arkansas. Others were from the parade of women he dated when he attended Georgetown University in Washington, D.C. He also was known as "a seducer from the major leagues" at Oxford when was in residence as a Rhodes Scholar there in 1968.

At Georgetown, Bill schmoozes, perfecting a style that would later get him elected President of the United States.

Many of his sexual interludes with these women flew undetected under the radar screen. A former aide, Dick Morris, reportedly said, "If a biographer wanted to document all the affairs Bill Clinton had before and after marriage he would need at least a thousand pages, but it would get monotonous. At the very least, he far exceeded Don Juan's legendary 1,000 or so conquests. And he ran state and Federal governments as well. Truly amazing!"

Some of these affairs were more significant than others. Before Hillary, nearly all of these women were beautiful or at least attractive.

Each of them noticed that Bill had one rather obvious trait. In his memoirs, *My Life,* he confessed it, describing it as "my inability to have anything other than brief relationships with women."

It has been said that whenever Bill became obsessed with sex, his brain was not the organ that controlled his actions. As his own brother, Roger, ex-

Bill's Lament: "What's a Guy Gonna Do? Women Just Throw Themselves at Me!"

plained it, "Anyone who watches an addiction develop has seen how predictably stupid behavior follows."

Rover Boy, as an Early Teenager, Meets a Pert Eleven-Year-Old Blonde. Will He Still Love Her When She's 44?

Bill's most enduring affair began when he was in junior high school in Arkansas. It would last, on or off, for some thirty-three years. The pert blonde beauty was Dolly Kyle (later, Browning).

When they met in Hot Springs, she was only eleven at the time, and he was a studly boy of thirteen, rather tall for his age.

Like most such school romances, in the beginning, it was just "kid stuff," and included stolen kisses behind the gym. He called her "Pretty Girl," and she referred to him affectionately as "Billy," or "Billy Boy."

By the time Dolly turned thirteen (if that), she was seen riding around town in Bill's black Buick sedan. On the surface, it seemed like a typical school romance, centered around creamy milkshakes at the corner drugstore, movie dates at the Bijou, and hand-holding at teen parties and at school dances.

But as Dolly testified on March 8, 1998, at some point, their relationship turned sexual. Her sworn statement was released five days later, on March 13, by Paula Jones' lawyers as part of their opposition to the Clinton legal team's motion for a summary judgment.

"We had a bond that included sexual relations," Dolly testified. "The frequency of our contact with each other, and the frequency of our sexual encounters, varied over that time period, but we did have many contacts over the years. "

Arkansas beauty, Bill's early squeeze, Dolly Kyle Browning.

Among their friends, many high school romances ultimately led to marriage and children. Not so with Dolly and Bill. At some point, as Dolly revealed, she realized that he was never going to marry her. She also became aware that he was slipping around, dating other girls.

In her testimony, Dolly recalled key moments when they came together for reunions in various cities. One of their encounters occurred in 1968, when they were each in Washington during his enrollment at Georgetown University. During that turbulent year, cities across America were burning in the wake of the assassination of Dr. Martin Luther King, Jr.

Presidential candidate George McGovern, depicted above with his wife, Eleanor, were in the next room when Bill did more than sing "Hello, Dolly!"

Dolly remembered Bill driving with her past burning tenements and past stores that had been barricaded to protect against looters. He piloted her to the Mayflower Hotel, where John F. Kennedy had arranged many of his sexual trysts. In her testimony, she asserted that she and Bill spent the night there together, and that he made love to her even though she was eight months pregnant at the time.

Tough, calculating, conservative, and pro-Bill: J. William Fulbright

Dolly also asserted that in 1972, in Little Rock, Bill was campaigning for Democratic Senator George McGovern during his bid for president against the Republican candidate, Richard Nixon. Within the home of two McGovern supporters, Dolly claimed that "Bill grabbed me and kissed me with real passion when McGovern and his wife, Eleanor, were in an adjoining room."

Later, when the hosts and Mr. and Mrs. McGovern were due elsewhere, Dolly and Bill agreed to babysit for the family. That left them four hours together, as they retreated upstairs while their kids played together on the ground floor, in the living room.

After Dolly returned to Washington, she found Bill working in the office of Arkansas Senator J. William Fulbright. Fulbright, who was away on business, had lent Bill his suite at the Mayflower.

Dolly and Bill returned together for a tryst within the same hotel they'd made love in a year before.

By then, Bill had met Hillary. After their sexual reunion, he informed Dolly that he didn't know when he could hook up with her again "because 'The Warden' keeps me on a tight leash." That marked the first of many times that he'd refer to Hillary to a third party as "The Warden."

In March of 1974, when Bill was running for the post of Congressman from Arkansas, Dolly toured the state with him in his attempt to garner votes. They spent many a night together in roadside motels. She recalled celebrating July 4 of that year with him in Little Rock.

The primary for the Congressional race in Arkansas was on May 28 of that year. It was then that Dolly met Hillary for the first time, as part of her arrival at Adams Field outside Little Rock, in a donor's private twin-engine Aero Commander. Dolly had joined friends and supporters who were there to greet Bill. Looking at first embarrassed, Bill introduced Dolly to Hillary, who pointedly ignored her outstretched hand.

Dolly was not impressed. "Hillary looked a mess," she said. "Unkempt hair that was greasy. There was a heat wave, and she was sweating a lot. It was obvious that she didn't use deodorant. If you stood next to her, I'd recommend you not get caught in a downwind. It was hard for me to believe that Bill would fall for a gal like that."

Three years later, during the summer of 1977, Dolly phoned Bill to tell him that she'd be passing (alone) through Little Rock during her transit from Dallas to New Orleans for an upcoming anniversary celebration with her second husband, a Texas lawyer. Bill made arrangements to meet her.

Arriving in town in a new spring-green Cadillac El Dorado, she was greeted by him. He took the wheel, heading for some secluded spot down a back road. She remembered his dangerous driving and his tailgating of other cars, wanting to pass. In a little grove, they made love in the front seat, not once, but twice. "Bill seemed to have this sense of danger, taking the risk of getting caught."

Two years after that, in 1979, after his election as Governor of Arkansas, she received another call from Bill. He told her that "The Warden" was away as part of an invitation for her as his guest at the Governor's Mansion.

Arriving once again in a Cadillac convertible, she was amazed at how open he was about their relationship, taking her around and introducing her, without hesitation, to his friends. "He didn't seem to be concealing our affair—in fact, was quite upfront about it in the presence of his aides. I asked myself, 'What in hell is going on here?' I just hoped he knew what he was doing."

After that, as the years went by, Dolly and Bill saw each other less frequently. Early in 1984, when they got together after five years of separation, he told her that his sex life with Hillary was more or less over. "Perhaps we'll sleep together once a year," he claimed.

"It was obvious to me that he wasn't looking forward to that occasion," Dolly said.

In 1988, he told her that he was not sure when they would meet again. "I'm planning to run for President of the United States on the Democratic ticket against George H.W. Bush," he revealed.

She cautioned against it, telling him, "With your boudoir record, honey, they'll come after you, digging up all sorts of dirt. You'll be disgraced."

He took her advice, which mirrored the counsel of others.

In 1990, he shared a rendezvous with Dolly in a hotel in San Antonio, Texas. She asked him about all the rumors she'd heard about his affairs with various women.

"You know, Pretty Girl," he told her, "although I'm away from you a lot, you're the only one I've ever loved."

She noticed that he didn't mention Hillary.

He left early the next morning, but before she had departed from their suite, a call came in from a reporter for *The San Antonio Star.* He was crude and blunt: "Are you having an affair with Bill Clinton?"

She slammed down the phone and immediately tried to get in touch with Bill. When an aide informed her that he was not available to speak to her, Dolly asked what she should do.

According to Dolly, the aide responded, "If he calls again, deny it. If you claim an affair, *we will destroy you!"*

Four days later, a call came in from Roger Clinton in Los Angeles at around one or two o'clock in the morning. From the direction and tone of his questions, she knew he was fully aware of her affair with his brother, and she sensed that he was taping their conversation.

Roger warned her to keep a tight lip if questioned by the press "for the good of all of us, and especially for your own good."

She interpreted that as yet another threat.

During his 1992 run for the presidency, Dolly expressed some comments about Bill's sex life. By then, their relationship was over. "He's a sex addict," she told friends. "When he's not getting enough, be becomes a food junkie. You can always tell the nature of his sex life by his weight. You'll know that when he's photographed lean and mean, he's being satisfied between the sheets."

The last time she met Bill was at the high school reunion in Little Rock in 1994. With Secret Service agents hovering nearby, they talked together for forty-five minutes.

"Up until around midnight, I had avoided him until he approached me," she said.

He greeted her, saying, "How are you?"

"You are such an asshole," she said. "I can't believe you'd even bother to ask."

When she said that, a Secret Service agent reached to grab her, but Bill instructed him not to interfere.

As they talked, their voices were mostly drowned out by loud dance music. She chastised him for having an aide who had threatened to destroy her, and he apologized. According to Dolly, "We talked of many things, including his affair with Gennifer Flowers."

At the end of their talk, he invited her to Washington, where he promised to get her a job.

She did come to Washington, in March of 1998, but it was to answer a subpoena in the lawsuit of Paula Jones *vs.* William Jefferson Clinton. During cross-examination, she admitted to her long-enduring affair with the President of the United States.

Later, on a TV show, she confessed once again to the affair, but added, "Yes, it was not appropriate, but fortunately, I have at least repented and changed my life, while he, unfortunately, has not."

Romance in Bloom on the Georgetown Campus

Southern Fireball Meets Jersey Girl

In September of 1964, Virginia, along with her son Bill, arrived in Washington to enroll him in Georgetown University. He would be there until 1968, the year he received his Bachelor of Science degree from Georgetown's Edmund A. Walsh School of Foreign Service.

Bill never bothered to apply to such prestigious Ivy League colleges as Harvard. From the beginning, he wanted to attend Georgetown—a college founded in 1789—because he was impressed with its reputation for political science.

His family would be saddled with $1,200 per semester in tuition, plus $700 for room and other fees. Bill would have $25 a week to live on, a sum that included his expenditures on food.

During their time together in Washington, Bill and Virginia set out to see the sights and visit the museums. At night, they were seen drinking in the taverns of Georgetown.

When she returned to Little Rock, he allocated himself a budget of a dollar a day for food. Both lunch and dinner were accompanied by a Royal Crown Cola, his favorite drink. Years later, he would mourn the "demise of my beloved RC. Pepsi and Coca Cola just didn't hit the spot for me like an RC did."

Bill's roommate was Tom Campbell, an Irish Catholic from Huntington, Long Island, who had tacked a poster of Barry Goldwater for President onto the door of their dorm room.

Bill introduced himself "as a diehard Democrat from Arkansas," warning him that there would soon be a change of poster art on the door. "I'm an LBJ man myself."

In spite of their differences, the two men, each from widely diverse backgrounds, would bond for years to come. "Bill hit campus like a fireball," Campbell recalled. "From the first week on, he appeared like a candidate running for president of his class. He insisted on shaking the hand of every freshman. As for his professors, he was a regular suck-up. Call it 'brown-nosing.'"

He also bonded with another close friend, Tommy Caplan, the son of a jeweler from Baltimore. "I liked him a lot, but I wasn't fooled by all that *'Aw, Shucks,'* Southern charm of his. I knew it masked a steely determination to succeed. That hick from Arkansas was going places—that was for damn sure."

Bill confided to both of his classmates that he found Georgetown "brimming over with beauties, with more blondes than they have in Norway. I'm partial to blondes. My only regret is that Marilyn Monroe passed on before I got my chance at her."

He dated casually until one cold February day in 1965 when he spotted a beautiful blonde entering a class on British literature. He stationed himself outside the door, through which he could hear a woman professor lecturing on Chaucer.

His "prey" was Denise Hyland of Upper Montclair, New Jersey, the daughter of a surgeon.

When a bell sounded, signifying the end of the class, the tall, statuesque blonde emerged. finding Bill ready to pounce.

She would recall their introduction. "There he was, introducing himself and wooing me with Dixie charm, me, a Yankee girl. After only two or three minutes of chit-chat, he asked me for a date, although apologizing for sounding too forward. I was drawn to him."

"By eight o'clock that night, we were in an Italian trattoria called Victor's. I knew he didn't have a lot of money, so both of us settled on meatless spaghetti, the cheapest *entrée* on the menu. After that, he took my hand as we strolled leisurely, very leisurely, back to my dorm at St. Mary's Hall."

When they got to the entrance, he abruptly asked her to be his date for the Diplomats Ball which was months away. She found herself accepting, but asked him, "Why are you so sure we'll still be dating that far into the future?"

"We will," he predicted, giving her a brief little peck on the cheek. "I'll pick you up tomorrow night here at seven, and we'll go out for a Coke and a hamburger, maybe a movie."

"It's a date," she said. "After I watched as he slowly walked away, it sounded like he was singing Elvis' 'Love Me Tender.'"

He showed up that following night and again and again, for many months to come. During summer separations, they corresponded through the mails.

"As Bogie told Claude Rains in the closing reel of *Casablanca* (1942), it was the beginning of a beautiful friendship, but a lot more than that, too, a hell of a lot more than that," she said.

He would slip around and date other young women, usually government workers, not on the Georgetown campus, but in the city of Washington itself.

Despite the allure of those other women, Denise would remain his number one college sweetheart. They were seen holding hands as they walked to class, or sitting close to each other, discussing politics on the steps of the Capitol. She was as smart as she was attractive.

Many of their debates centered on the Vietnam War, an issue he had not yet settled within himself. As Denise remembered, Bill's most pressing fear was that he might get drafted.

At times, he seemed homesick for Hope, where, as he told her, "the watermelons grow as big as a Volkswagen Beetle." When he ran successfully for president of Georgetown's sophomore class, she campaigned actively for him.

On one of two occasions, he discussed marriage with her, telling her that he wanted to wed an independent woman who had a life of her own. "I don't expect the little woman to be sitting home at night darning my socks when I come back from the office. I want her to have her own goals, her own career."

"What about children?" she asked.

"Perhaps a daughter," he said. "Based on my own experience, I'm not impressed with father-son relationships."

At one point, she invited him home to New Jersey to meet her parents and family. He fitted smoothly into their middle class life, wrestling with her brothers in the living room; teaching her little sister how to make peanut butter and banana sandwiches; listening to her mother, a dietician, tell him how to eat cheaply on healthy food, and finally, helping her dry the dishes in the kitchen.

By the time he and Denise entered their junior year, she realized that there was little chance that he'd ever ask her to marry him. "He had too much living to do and seemed very uncertain of his future. Several options were available to him, and that dreaded draft loomed over his head."

Eventually, she enrolled in an academic program at the Sorbonne in Paris.

He was there to see her off, and shortly before her departure for Europe, she presented him with a blank diary, urging him to make regular entries within it. She told him, "Write down what's going on in your life. One day, when you become president, it will be a valuable document for historians."

Their promise to write to each other was faithfully carried out. For years ahead, he regularly wrote to her, pouring out his feelings, even though they would each move on to other relationships.

"Every man needs a college sweetheart," he said. "It doesn't mean you have to marry her."

"Bill Always Had This Sense About Him That He Collected Girls"

—Carolyn Yeldell Staley

More than any other girlfriend, Carolyn Yeldell (later Staley) represented Bill's amazing talent for retrieving a friendship out of an affair that had cooled.

Carolyn lived across the street from the Clintons in Hot Springs. She was the daughter of a Baptist preacher, Walter Yeldell. As a little girl going to Brookwood Elementary School in Hot Springs, she developed a crush on Bill that would last for years.

As Virginia remembered it, "She was always in and out of our house with a tongue hanging out, panting for Bill. Once, when watching TV at night with him, she fell asleep on the sofa in our living room. At around eleven that night, her father was pounding on the door like he was going to break in. All I heard were his screams in the night, denouncing the poor little girl as a Jezebel. It had been a completely harmless evening."

Carolyn found Virginia "an exotic. Never had I met such a painted woman. She must have spent at least one fourth of her salary on makeup. She was painted up more than a clown. My father didn't approve. He wouldn't even let me wear lipstick."

"Bill pretended to me that he was leading a normal family life, but I knew better. We could hear the Clintons screaming and fighting, especially on a summer night when the windows were open."

Carolyn became such a fixture in Bill's life that he devotes some space to her in his memoirs, the first volume of *My Life.* His time with Carolyn became a series of card games, walks home from school hand in hand, school dances, and sporting events.

What really drew them together was their joint love of music. She was an accomplished piano player, and she'd accompany him on his saxophone.

That musical instrument almost ended their relationship. Virginia saved up the money and had purchased him a new saxophone. As Carolyn was emerging from his Buick, with the instrument, she dropped it and broke it. "I've never been cursed so much in my life," she recalled. "I fear that the saxophone meant more to him than I did."

But he finally forgave her.

Her pursuit of Bill often got Carolyn into trouble with her parents. In the summer of 1965, she took money she'd saved and purchased party supplies and liquor, with the intention of hosting a party for Bill's friends. She'd read in a column by Emily Post about how the wife of a future politician should entertain.

When her mother found out what she'd done, she was furious. The money her daughter spent was supposed to have paid for an operation Carolyn needed for surgery on her infected tonsils.

It took Bill a long time to get around to treating Carolyn as a romantic object of passion. It perhaps happened that Christmas oF 1965 when he flew into the Little Rock airport. Seeing him from afar, she rushed up and kissed him passionately.

When he backed away, he asked her in astonishment, "Carolyn, where did you learn to kiss like that?"

"Bill Clinton, you're not the only boy in Little Rock!"

From that day forth, he pursued her, wanting to make their relationship sexual. Presumably, he did, although neither ever came clean with a full explanation.

Carolyn's hopes and dreams about becoming the skilled hostess wife of an on-the-rise politician were dashed one afternoon when she walked across the street in Hot Springs. Through the window of his house, she spotted him passionately kissing the local beauty queen. She burst into tears and ran back across the street into her own house.

"In time, our friendship survived," she said, "lasting for years and years. But I knew I would never marry Bill Clinton. I knew he would never be faithful to just one woman. I wanted a monogamous relationship with a man. Bill was not that man."

She later attended Indiana University, where she studied music, hoping to become an opera singer. There, she met Jerry Staley, a photographer, and married him.

Her friendship with Bill continued. When he became governor of Arkansas, she and her husband lived in a house only three blocks from the Governor's Mansion. Bill put her in charge of the state's Adult Literacy Program. Later, when he became U.S. President, he put her in charge of the National Institute for Literacy in Washington. After her association with that post ended, she entered the ministry, following in the footsteps of her Baptist father.

"Bill, If You Want to Idolize Jack Kennedy for His Womanizing, You're Gonna End Up That Way Yourself!"

—Arkansas Senator J. William Fulbright

When Bill returned from Georgetown to Hot Springs for the sultry summer of 1966, he was eager to get into politics. He was very impressed with Judge Frank Holt, who at the time was seeking the Democratic nomination for governor of Arkansas.

Holt's main opponent for the Democratic party's nomination for governor was challenger Jim Jackson. Thanks partly to his endorsement by the KKK, Jackson was known as "The razorback version *[i.e., the Arkansas version]* of Alabama's George Wallace."

Both Holt and Jackson were running against the sitting Republican governor, Winthrop Rockefeller, a member of the famous Gilded Age dynasty that included his brother, Nelson Rockefeller.

The Jackson camp was already smearing the sitting governor. Although they never printed any damaging material, they ordered their staff to spread via the grapevine that Rockefeller was gay "with a preference for Mandingo blacks with monstrous appendages."

Judge Holt was tremendously impressed with young Bill and give him the key assignment of driving his wife, Mary, and their two daughters, Lyda and Melissa, to hamlets too small, or too isolated, for the judge himself to conveniently visit.

With the female members of the Holt family crammed into his car, Bill, as chauffeur and trip coordinator, crisscrossed the highways and secondary roads of Arkansas, attending and speaking at hoedowns, barbecues, and chicken fries in hamlets with such names as "Evening Shade" or "Fifty-Six."

The itinerary and its stopovers were rough and brutalizing. Bill and the Holts often received hostile receptions, especially in towns where "Justice Jim" was a formidable candidate among those sympathetic to the KKK. More than once, Bill was denounced as a "nigger lover," based on his calls for tolerance. In retrospect, he remembered "the blood-sucking mosquitoes that must have drained a quart of my blood."

In the Arkansas primary, Johnson won 25% of Democratic vote, Holt garnering 22%. The rest of the vote went to minor candidates.

[In the election that fall, Rockefeller retained his governorship. That caused Bill to vow: "One day, I will win for the Democrats, and I'll be sleeping in the Governor's Mansion."]

Despite the loss in the gubernatorial elections of his preferred candidate, Bill appealed to Judge Holt to use his influence with Senator J. William Fulbright to get him a job on his staff in Washington. Holt was so impressed with the way Bill had handled his wife and daughters in guiding them across Arkansas, that he contacted Senator Fulbright and got a position for Bill almost immediately.

Despite his new position, Bill still had to complete his studies at Georgetown. Complicating matters was that in addition to classes and his endless womanizing, he also had to put in long hours, as one of the "backroom boys" within Fulbright's political network. In that capacity, he was virtually obligated to fulfill any assignment that arose, including answering letters, sorting mail, manning the phones, running errands, or making bicycle deliveries across the city.

It was grueling work, but Bill enjoyed it, "because I felt at the center of power in Washington."

Despite his status as an ardent Democrat, Fulbright was strenuously opposed to Johnson and the Vietnam War. From 1959 to 1975, he functioned as chairman of the powerful Senate Foreign Relations Committee.

As it happened, Bill soon emerged as the most dedicated and ardent member of the Fulbright entourage. As the Senator recalled. "There was no task, however awful, that he would not volunteer for. I was the one who recommended him for a Rhodes scholarship at Oxford. Of all the young men from Arkansas, I felt he deserved it the most."

"One thing I noticed about our new boy is that he sure was attracted to the girls, and they were sure attracted to him. I don't know how he keeps up. I suspect he eats an extra bowl of Wheaties for breakfast."

The Arkansas Beauty Queen Meets "The Horndog from Hot Springs"

One summer day, while still working for Fulbright, Bill was entrusted with a "juicy" assignment. He was asked to drive Sharon Ann Evans, the newly crowned Miss Arkansas, around Washington, D.C., showing her the sights.

[Winner of the Miss Arkansas Contest in 1967, Sharon Ann Evans, then 20 years old, from North Little Rock and at the time, a student at Ouachita Baptist University, was preliminary winner in the swimsuit award, showed particular talent for vocals and dance, and tied with another contestant for the designation of "Miss Congeniality."]

That afternoon, as they viewed the monuments, he seemed to win her affection. Their time together marked the debut of a romantic relationship that would stretch over a period of years, on and off, of course.

He recalled, "I got the job of showing Sharon Ann around, because of all the backroom boys *[on Fulbright's staff]*, I was the tallest. That southern beauty was almost six feet tall herself."

After her visit to Washington, Bill continued to see Sharon whenever both of them happened to be in Arkansas at the same time.

For Bill, the tall, statuesque beauty depicted above was "The Rose of Arkansas."

He told his male friends, "After Sharon, my goal was to seduce every Miss Arkansas contest winner. Needless to say, I fell far short of that desire."

He proudly introduced her to Virginia. "I was really pleased that Bill followed my advice about dating beauty queens. She was one looker. I thought they might get married. What beautiful grandchildren I might have had if they did."

The highlight of his affair with Sharon occurred when she designated him as her escort to Winrock, the sprawling estate of Winthrop Rockefeller.

[Site of a cattle farm in central Arkansas near the town of Morrilton, it was the elegant home of Winthrop Rockefeller for the final 20 years of his life. Positioned atop Petit Jean Mountain (pronounced "petty gene," by Arkansas locals), a flat-topped plateau rising above the floodplains of the south bank of the Arkansas River, it functions today as the flagship of the Arkansas State Parks System, and home base of the Winthrop Rockefeller Foundation.]

During the festivities, Sharon introduced him to the event's host, Republican Governor Rockefeller, with whom Bill got on fabulously, failing to mention that he'd worked on the campaign of one of his most outspoken rivals, Judge Holt, who had for a while hoped to unseat him.

Bill couldn't help but notice that the governor had exceptionally handsome young men on his staff, and he learned that he also maintained a cottage in The Pines, a mostly gay and male district of New York's Fire Island. He began to wonder if all those rumors about the governor being a homosexual were true after all.

After his departure from Winrock, Bill told Sharon, "One day, I'll be governor of Arkansas. Sooner than later."

"You're far too young," she responded.

Even during his enrollment at Oxford as a Rhodes scholar, he continued to see Sharon. She flew into London for a whirlwind visit, and he acted as her tour guide, meeting her at Heathrow. It was a passionate reunion.

When he introduced Sharon to his classmates at Oxford, he told them, "I have fallen madly in love with this Rose of Arkansas."

Their relationship was sorely tested when, back in Little Rock, a silly feud developed between Virginia and Honey Evans, Sharon's mother.

Honey and her daughter had appeared at some political rally, the details of which were later misrepresented to Virginia. She was told that Honey had announced that Sharon was going to become "Mrs. Bill Clinton."

New York-born Winthrop Rockefeller *(aka "the Arkansas Rockefeller; depicted in both views, above)* championed the state's industrial growth.

He eventually became the first Republican Governor of Arkansas since Reconstruction

Both Sharon and her mother denied that they had leaked anything to the press, but Virginia remained convinced that that they had. Words were exchanged and Virginia turned against her prospective daughter-in-law. She later used her influence with her son to break off the liaison.

By that time, Bill had moved on to so many other women that he acquiesced, not wanting to antagonize his mother, who still asserted a powerful role over his decisions.

So Many Women, So Little Time
"How Can I Get Around To Them All?" Bill Laments

In 1967, with Denise Hyland stashed away in a garret in Paris, pursuing her studies at the Sorbonne, and with longtime girlfriend Carolyn Yeldell Staley happily married, Bill was free to roam the Georgetown campus with a gleam in his eye.

Young people all over America, especially the hippies, were heading to San Francisco to experience that year's "Summer of Love."

Bill was not among them. He remained mostly in Hot Springs or in Washington "where I had more women than I could take care of."

"It seemed that our Billy Goat had a different girl every night," said Tom Campbell. "That was no big accomplishment. Young people were a bit crazy that summer. Even a nerd could get laid."

"I went girl crazy," Bill said "Well, that's not quite true. I think I was always girl crazy. I started playing the field...and how! Well, that's not quite true either. I've always played the field."

He became a "social artist," skilled at juggling competing and conflicting commitments to women. Campbell noted that at one time, he maintained at least three "permanent girlfriends, and god knows how many others he was stringing along."

Some of his women complained that he didn't like to use a condom. Bill told his male friends, "A condom dullens the sensation. I like skin meeting skin, like rubber hitting the road."

In the midst of all this philandering, along came Ann Markesun, a tall, attractive blonde with an avid interest in politics. At Georgetown, she was majoring in economics and was the captain of the women's sailing team. Bill met this Minnesota native at the Washington campaign headquarters of Senator Eugene McCarthy, a key member of that state's liberal Democratic/ Farmer/Labor party who was avidly opposed to Lyndon Johnson's war in Vietnam. Ann joined in that opposition, and soon, Bill was seen escorting her to peace rallies.

Bill's schoolmates at Oxford remembered him as "majoring" in women, fish & chips, parties, cards, Guinness stout, and letting the good times roll in such pubs as The Bear and Turf Tavern.

Fellow student Robert Reich called his Arkansas accent "syrupy," and remembered his favorite drink as a "Shandy," (Guinness with lemonade). "He was the classic example of a glad-handing Dixieboy politico on the rise who wanted your vote even if he weren't running for anything."

As Bill later confessed, "She was brainy but beautiful, and she satisfied my lust for blondes."

Throughout his senior year at Georgetown, she became the most important woman on his love calendar. Their relationship would continue on and off throughout the course of his first year (1968) at Oxford (England), where he was a Rhodes Scholar.

"From the beginning, Bill was not faithful to Ann," said his friend, Tommy Caplan. "She would be in the next room talking to girlfriends, and Bill would be in an adjoining room, flirting with some girl he'd just met."

Late one summer, as Bill became more involved with Ann, he invited her to Hot Springs. He was proud to introduce this statuesque, regal woman to Virginia. When Ann donned a very skimpy bikini and went water skiing on Lake Hamilton, she practically caused a riot among the local Peeping Toms, who gossiped about the event and her appearance for weeks to come.

By December of 1968, Bill was on the plane to join her briefly in Minnesota, when she'd returned to her native state. At the time, she was on Christmas break from Michigan State, where she'd been pursuing a doctorate.

Just before Bill departed for his studies at Oxford in 1968, he agreed to a reunion with her during spring break in March of 1969. She had arranged a trip for herself to Germany at that time, and they enjoyed a reunion in the Cathedral City of Cologne.

That was followed by a joint tour of the Bavarian Alps, when they heard the news that President Eisenhower had died. Both of them agreed that there would come a time when America would no longer be electing a president who'd actively served in the military during World War II. "One day, the postwar Baby Boomers will run this country," he predicted.

Although their holiday together went well, somewhere high in the Alps, their romantic relationship came to an end. He gave the reason why. "I was too uncertain of myself at that point in my life to make a commitment to anyone else."

He would later say, "A lot of time would go by before Ann and I re-established our relationship. This time, it was a friendship."

A Southern Rebel Boy Invades Oxford to Chase the "Dollybirds"

Motivated by the urging of Senator Fulbright, Bill applied for and ultimately won a Rhodes scholarship to Oxford, a two-year commitment for higher academic training.

[The Rhodes scholarships are named after the vastly wealthy and ferociously imperialistic Cecil John Rhodes (1853-1902) a British politician and mining magnate. One of the early prime ministers of the then-British colony of South Africa, Rhodes was the founder and namesake of the southern African territory formerly known as Rhodesia (now Zimbabwe).

The international postgraduate awards, often cited as the most prestigious scholarships in the world, are funded by his estate and available only to selected "foreign" (i.e., non-British) candidates. Scholarships include payment of most Oxford University and college fees, a monthly stipend for living ex-

penses and accommodation, and access to Rhodes House, an early 20th-century mansion inhabited during part of its existence by Cecil Rhodes himself.]

Usually, they were awarded to scholar athletes. Bill was a scholar, but hardly an athlete. He had never played a varsity sport, either during high school in Little Rock or at college in Georgetown.

Even Virginia called him "gawky and lacking in coordination." He tried his hand at basketball, but his coach asked him, "Why are your feet glued to the floor?"

As a golfer, he was a "mid-handicap hacker." And, like many "Bubba Boys" of Arkansas, he could bowl. But Rhodes scholarships were not handed out to bowlers.

Despite of his lack of accomplishment in sports, Bill revealed what a clever political animal he was through a series of maneuvers that put him in the forefront of those applying for the Rhodes grant. Of course, he was aided greatly by his origins in Arkansas, which, of the eight Rhodes regions in the United States, was the least competitive. Had he applied from New York State, he would have faced hundreds of other eager applicants.

When it was announced, with fanfare, that he'd won the scholarship, he later said, "Up to that point, it was the proudest day of my life."

[One of Bill's favorite movies was A Yank at Oxford (1938), starring Robert Taylor. He'd gone to see it in a revival movie house. He later said, "I should star in the remake, and it should be entitled, Johnny Reb Invades Oxford.*"]*

At Oxford, he opted to study politics, philosophy, and economics.

He joined the rugby team, but "majored in women," as he bragged when he wrote back to his male pals in Little Rock.

His overseas romantic life actually had begun in 1968 when he'd sailed to England from the Port of New York aboard the SS *United States.* At sea, he developed a shipboard romance with an attractive young woman, Martha Saxon, and also tasted Scotch for the first time, eventually deciding that he preferred bourbon. "I'm a Southern boy and we're known for liking bourbon and branch water."

[In the late 1970s, he would develop an allergy to all liquor except vodka.]

En route to England during those troubled years, he was fleeing an America in turmoil in the wake of the assassination of Martin Luther King, Jr. Enraged African Americans had rioted, setting major fires in the centers of 200 American cities.

During his time at sea, he engaged in long talks with fellow Rhodes Scholarship recipient, Robert Reich, who was seasick throughout most of the crossing, When Bill became president, he would name Reich as his Secretary of Labor.

At Oxford, Bill "broadened" his experience, or, as he put it, "With an emphasis on 'broad.'"

He plunged into the late 1960s, an era of parties, one-night stands, endless mugs of lager, and political protests giving way to love-ins.

In a letter he wrote to Virginia, he said, "These beautiful, rosy-cheeked English lassies are turned on by my Elvis drawl."

One of his classmates warned his fellow males, "Don't introduce your girlfriend to this Southern hillbilly. While you're pissing away some lager, he'll be getting your bird's phone number."

A young and durable visionary at Oxford: Robert Reich, eventually designated by Bill as his Secretary of Labor

As evidenced by some of the entries within his date book, Bill dipped into what he labeled "exotica." That included a princess from India, a Malaysian beauty queen, and a lovely, tall, and statuesque black woman from Senegal.

As a friend noted, "Bill definitely crossed the color line, something I bet he couldn't do back in redneck Arkansas. He told me he liked "black poontang' on occasion. I had to ask for a definition. But a lot of guys—girls, too—were switching colors back then, with white girls singing, 'Black boys are so delicious,' and black girls singing 'White boys are so sexy,' based on the lyrics of that song from the American Tribal Love-Rock Musical, *Hair* (1967)."

Of course, Bill paid special attention to those beautiful English girls, especially the blondes, "whose complexions evoked Devonshire cream."

For a while, his "main squeeze" was a fellow student named Tamara Eccles-Williams, a young woman he introduced only as "Mara".

"He was my cuddly bear," she told a reporter years later, when Bill was running for president. "Good for a winter's night but a bit sweaty in summer."

At one point, he dated two women, each named Katherine. One was Katherine Vereker, the beautiful daughter of a professor of philosophy at Oxford. She lived in an attic apartment, where she invited him for tea, and, from reports, maybe a lot more.

Another was Katherine Gieve, bright, progressive, and good-looking. They often discussed politics, and she found him "well-informed on almost everything—Richard Nixon, the Vietnam War, marijuana, and free love."

With the growing visibility of the feminist movement, it became inevitable that some of his dates became advocates of women's rights. Mandy Merck found him sensitive to women's issues. In discussing her years later, Bill said "I never really moved in on her, fearing she batted for the other team, but I'm not sure about that."

She didn't seem attracted to him physically, finding him overweight and poorly dressed, with an unkempt beard that looked as if it contained a nest of insects.

She remembered that in July of 1969, he became very upset after reading about Senator Teddy Kennedy going off that bridge in Chappaquiddick, a misfortune that led to the death, by drowning, of Mary Jo Kopechne.

Merck reported that Bill became indignant, telling her that "politicians should not use their position to seduce unsuspecting women. Guys who have great power also have big egos. If I become a bigtime politician, I will never do that. I will never take advantage of a woman in that way."

He also made a friend in the novelist, accomplished writer, and feminist Sara Maitland, known as "Lady Sara." She was described as "very open and very noisy."

He interpreted her as "most challenging. You expanded your mind just by talking to her."

Maitland was also an amateur theologian. In 1966, she scandalized her brothers by winning a foot race in a flimsy, very short, and very revealing cotton dress. During Bill's residency at 46 Leckford Road in Oxford, she was a frequent visitor, meeting his "roomies," Frank Aller, Jana Brenning, and Strobe Talbot.

One night, Bill invited both Maitland and Merck to a lecture given by author Germaine Greer, who was on the dawn of publishing her feminist manifesto, *The Female Eunuch.* He described her as "standing tall, with great legs."

Radical feminist Germaine Greer in 1972.

At one of her lectures, in front of an audience, pink-suited Bill, the Rhodes Scholar, suggested that he might give her "the ultimate orgasm."

Wearing a pink poplin suit, he had arrived at the lecture hall escorted by his duet of female guests. When Greer finished her speech, she encouraged questions from the audience.

He stood up and, referring to a key point she had made within her speech, said, "About the overrated orgasm. In case you decide to give a bourgeois man another chance, can I have your phone number?"

"NO WAY IN HELL!" she shouted at him.

Throughout his time at Oxford, he continued to pursue young women, yet amazingly, and based on his quick intellect, also found time for study and for reading the works of everyone from Dylan Thomas to Jean-Jacques Rousseau. He even managed to read Carl Sandberg's six-volume biography of Abraham Lincoln.

More than any other, he preferred two specific hangouts at Oxford. One of them was The Bear Inn on Alfred Street. Dating from the 13th Century, it had been frequented by the Earls of Warwick and by most of the luminaries who had attended or visited Oxford down through the centuries, many of whom had cited it in their novels and memoirs.

His other favorite watering hole was the Turf Tavern, a 13th Century pub on Bath Place. It had been featured as a setting within the Thomas Hardy novel, *Jude the Obscure.* When Elizabeth Taylor and Richard Burton were in Oxford, they made it their "local."

When Bill ran for President in 1992, reporters swarmed over both pubs, swilling drinks and hoping to "dig up dirt" on the presidential candidate.

But all they got was a confession from Bill that he had tried marijuana once, but that "I didn't like it, and I didn't inhale."

"Mother's Marrying a Jailbird —and a Hairdresser at That!"

In 1968, Virginia, only six months after the death of her previous husband, Roger Clinton, Sr., received a phone call from Jeff Dwire, her hairdresser, a man who had served nine months in prison in 1962 for issues associated with stock fraud. He wanted to come over. Although she was tired, she invited him to join her for drinks at her home.

She would later tell Bill in faraway Oxford, "Jeff treated me like a queen after all the abuse I'd suffered from Roger. He was still handsome, close to six feet tall, with dark hair, a project of his Cajun genes. He reminded me of *Gone With the Wind's* Rhett Butler, with sideburns down to the bottom of his ears."

When Virginia mentioned the prison term he'd served, Bill wanted to know the charge. His mother answered, "Oh, some silly thing. Along with others, he got some people to invest in a movie about Pretty Boy Floyd, a real gangster. That was back in 1962. As it turned out, the producers were running a scam with no intention of ever making a film. Jeff, along with others, was tried and convicted on two counts of embezzlement. He was innocent, his investors the guilty party. He entered a plea bargain and went to the Federal pen in Texarkana."

After their first evening together, Virginia and Dwire began to date almost nightly. He loved music and dancing, and so did she. Somewhere along the way, he admitted that he suffered from a severe case of diabetes, and that he had to be careful if he wanted to stay alive and healthy.

While he was at Oxford, Virginia called Bill, telling him that she wanted to marry Jeff. She told him he'd had three previous marriages. Bill was very skeptical of her choice.

"At least if I marry him, you'll get free haircuts," she told her son.

When Dwire arranged to send him an airline ticket for round-trip transit between London and Little Rock, Bill agreed to fly home for the wedding.

Arriving in Little Rock, Bill suspected that Dwire might be just "a slick Southern charmer," but Virginia assured him that she had "fallen head over heels in love with him."

Bill was introduced to the 48-year-old groom-to-be and found him very compatible, and very much in love with Virginia. The two men bonded and seemed to respect each other, enough so that Dwire asked Bill to be "Best Man" at his upcoming wedding.

Bill soon surmised that most of Virginia's friends were adamantly opposed to the marriage. Defending his mother's choice, he interpreted them as "really pernicious ill-wishers. If Jeff is nothing more than a con man, then consider me conned."

Bill defended Dwire to their friends and to the rest of the world at large, defining him as "hard-working, smart, good with my brother, Roger, and clearly in love with Virginia."

Virginia and Dwire were married in January of 1969, at which time, Bill flew back to London, transferring to a train for his return to Oxford for resumption of his studies and his nocturnal pursuits.

From all reports, until Dwire's death in 1974, his marriage to Bill's mother was successful, although he inevitably brought some "baggage" to it.

Virginia's marriage to Dwire meant that Bill had acquired a new step-sister, Dianne Welch, who had at the time had served six years of a 45-year sentence at Mountain View Maximum Security Prison in Gatesville, Texas. She had been convicted in 1985 on a charge of bank robbery and drug dealing.

NATIONAL ENQUIRER

HILLARY'S 'STEPSISTER': DRUG-DEALING, BANK-ROBBING PSYCHO!

Clinton family secret that could derail her 2016 White House run!

Jessie McClure, the bank teller during the robbery of the Gold Coast Savings & Loan Bank in Sugarland, Texas, claimed that Dianne ordered him to "Get the cash register opened or you get a bullet in the head."

Soon after her release from prison, she was arrested again during a drug raid when she and her 16-year-old son were caught in possession of fifty pounds of marijuana. Her lawyer told the court that he was resigning from her case because she had threatened him with bodily harm. While behind bars, she was accused of ordering a murder contract on a policeman who had nabbed her on the marijuana charge.

Finally, after two appeals, charges against her were thrown out of court, based on a technicality, in 1992.

That was the year that Bill won the presidency. She had met him before. "I saw him when he came home from college," she recalled. "He was very polite and very serious. He never came over to our house for dinner with the rest of the Dwire family. He stayed home studying. As my brother, he was a bit of a bore."

She also said she had not been invited to the inauguration.

"His campaign workers spirited me away to a Holiday Inn and gave me orders not to speak to anyone, hoping that my arrests and prison record would not surface."

At the time, it was also suppressed that her son, Jeff Welch, had also been convicted of drug dealing and forgery. The lid was also kept on a darker secret: He had been a member of the Ku Klux Klan.

In 1992, Dianne died at the age of 52. As reported by her family, her last words were, "It's been a rough ride for this country gal."

The Curse of Vietnam / Dodging the Draft:
Those G.I. Blues "Keep Me Out of the Trenches of Vietnam"

As a presidential candidate in 1992, Bill Clinton came under heavy fire from Republicans. He was widely dismissed as a "draft dodger."

His record of military service (or lack thereof) is complicated. During his eligibility for the draft, a controversial and unpopular war was echoing throughout America. It had torn the country apart. Bill himself had adamantly opposed the war.

By 1992, his participation in anti-war demonstrations on foreign soil (i.e., the U.K.) during the Vietnam War had led to charges that he was a "traitor to his country."

In accordance with laws prevailing at the time, Clinton registered for the draft in August of 1964, shortly after his eighteenth birthday. The following month, he enrolled as a freshman at Georgetown University.

Before the end of November of that year, he had been classified as 2-S (beneficiary of a student deferment), a status that would shield him from induction into military service until the end of his undergraduate years.

Three and a half years later, in February of 1968, then-President Lyndon B. Johnson's administration unexpectedly abolished student deferments. Within three weeks, Bill, now age 21, was abruptly reclassified as 1-A, making him immediately eligible, especially as he neared graduation from Georgetown, for induction.

Bill's uncle, Raymond Clinton, was able to use some political influence in Hot Springs. As a local who knew virtually every politician in the county and state, he maneuvered behind the scenes to obtain a deferment for his nephew. Opal Ellis, the Executive Secretary of the local draft board, later said that Bill's status as a Rhodes Scholar provided the most obvious justification for his deferment. "We were so proud of our hometown boy going off to Oxford."

Ultimately, Bill stood out as the only man of draftable age within his jurisdiction for whom the Selective Service Board significantly delayed a pre-induction physical—in his case a delay that lasted for nearly eleven months, more than twice as long as anyone else's and more than five times longer than the time allotted to most other young men of comparable eligibility within the district.

Robert Corrado, one of the three members on Bill's draft board, later admitted that "political and family influence kept Clinton out of the immediate draft. He did receive some form of preferential treatment. We held back his file so he wouldn't be called up and possibly sent to Vietnam."

Corrado admitted that government bureaucrats reporting directly to Senator J. William Fulbright had exerted considerable influence to keep Bill from being drafted.

Pressure was also exerted on Commander Trice Ellis, Jr., Commanding Officer of the local Naval Reserve unit, to obtain a slot for Bill. To that effect, he secured a standard enlisted man's billet, not an officer's slot, which would have required him to commit two years of his life to active duty, beginning with the year of acceptance. This Navy Reserve assignment was created especially for Bill at a time in 1968 when no existing reserve slots were open in the Hot Springs area.

After a delay of two weeks, impatient to begin Bill's inaugural interview and the scheduling of an physical examination, Ellis called Raymond Clinton and asked, "What happened to your nephew? He hasn't shown up."

Raymond responded, "Don't worry about it. He won't be coming down. *It's all been taken care of.*"

Because of this continuing postponement, Bill was able to enroll at Oxford in the fall of 1968

In February of 1969, while at Oxford, he received notice that he must submit to a long-delayed, Army-approved physical examination. He did so.

His doctor delivered a verdict. "You are one of the healthiest specimens in the Western world, suitable for display at medical schools, exhibitions, zoos, carnivals, and base-training camps."

That April, Bill received his induction notice from the Hot Springs draft board. He was advised, however, to ignore it, the notice had been mailed after what had been defined as the deadline for induction. By then, his draft status entered the realm of the bizarre. At this point, a second induction notice arrived, establishing July 28 as the date he'd be compelled to enter the Army.

He reacted with something akin to panic, unclear about what to do. He contacted a friend, Cliff Jackson (later, his political enemy), based on his perceived influence with state bureaucrats and members of the local Republican Party. Recalling their previous meeting at Winrock, Bill asked Cliff to intercede on his behalf with Governor Rockefeller.

He also debated the value of joining the ROTC, but concluded that an affiliation would be a "dead end." He also debated joining the National Guard, but its quota of new recruits for that year had already been filled.

Jackson, working behind the scenes, came through for him, eventually informing Bill that he had been accepted into the ROTC unit associated with the University of Arkansas, an institution he had rejected (and continued to reject) as a future venue for his law studies, much preferring the Yale Law School instead.

Bill not only avoided getting drafted to fight in the Vietnam War, but he joined protests in both Washington and London against the war itself.

His friend, Sara Maitland, recalled that during his time at Oxford, Bill was sure he'd be drafted that summer. "We even threw a going-away party for him to see this young soldier-to-be off to battle the Vietcong in those rice paddies."

It was also reported that many of his girlfriends gave him "a farewell fuck" when he told them that he never expected to come out of the war alive.

Then, in a surprise move, one that had obviously resulted from political pressure, the commander of the University of Arkansas' ROTC deferred Bill's service for an additional year.

As Jackson later admitted, "I had several of my friends in influential positions, each trying to pull strings on Bill's behalf."

Back in Arkansas, Bill met

with Col. Williard A. Hawkins, the only military officer who had the authority to rescind a draft notice. Bill prevailed upon Hawkins to allow him to finish his first year as a Rhodes scholar at Oxford.

Later, as a presidential candidate, Bill would claim that he received no special treatment in avoiding military service.

By August of 1969, he was once again reclassified, this time as 1-D, a ranking that carried the provision that after he finished his Rhodes program at Oxford, he would enter the ROTC program at the University of Arkansas.

Jackson later claimed, "Clinton used the ROTC program to avoid the draft. He promised to join the University of Arkansas's ROTC program, with the understanding that it would inevitably result in military service. But after that, he never enrolled, never appearing for registration at either ROTC or at the University, either."

In the autumn of 1969, Bill returned to Oxford for his second year's association with the Rhodes Scholarship program. This was in direct opposition to the commitment he'd made to register—at least according to Jackson—at both ROTC and as a student at the University of Arkansas' Law School.

After that, both nationally and as it applied to the life of young Bill Clinton, there began a period of turmoil and confusion.

On September 19, 1969, then-President Richard Nixon, facing insurrection on many college campuses, nationwide, suspended the draft, halting military inductions during the months of November and December.

In an act of political brinksmanship, Nixon also made it clear that if Congress did not act to establish a fair and equitable lottery system for the drafting of Americans into the country's armed forces, he would remove, by Executive Order, the vulnerability to the draft of all men aged 20 to 26. Bill was 23 at the time. On October 1, 1969, Nixon announced that anyone then enrolled in graduate school at the time would be allowed to complete up to a full year of their present curriculum.

Because of these many stopgap regulations and compromises, Bill developed a belief that he'd be safe from a military draft, at least until June of 1970.

With his freedom from military service secured, at least momentarily, he finally relented to the urging of his friends and participated in anti-war demonstrations in London. He had not joined their ranks before, because he'd heard that Lt. Gen. Lewis B. Hershey, then-head of the nation's Selective Service administration, was striking blows specifically aimed at anyone protesting either the war or the draft, moving them systematically to the top of the government's list of potential draftees.

At the time, Bill announced, "I oppose the war in Vietnam. It leaves me with the same depth of feeling that I reserve for racism."

In London, in October of 1969, Bill helped organized an anti-war demonstration in front of the American Embassy in London on Grosvenor Square. He was joined by the highly visible, highly newsworthy movie stars, Paul Newman and Joanne Woodward.

As reported in the London press, the anti-war demonstrators benefitted from the support of British Peace organizations that included the British Peace Council, a subdivision of the KGB-backed World Peace Council.

That same month, to Bill's horror, perhaps as a result of his anti-war demonstrations, his draft board reclassified him as 1-A, making him eligible for immediate induction. It was also noted that, contrary to what had been clearly understood, he had failed to enroll in the University of Arkansas's ROTC program.

In November, still in London, and not to be deterred, Bill joined in yet another anti-war demonstration, protesting in front of the American Embassy on Grosvenor Square once again.

He was joined at the rally by folk singers Judy Collins and Peggy Seeger *[the songwriting sister of the better-known folk singer and activist, Pete Seeger].* As it happened, the high-visibility star of the rally was the British actress Vanessa Redgrave, daughter of the celebrated British actor, Michael Redgrave. In advance of the rally, a black coffin was moved to a position directly in front of the embassy, and Redgrave dropped cards with the names of war victims into it.

On December 1, 1969, Bill was notified that his number, as determined by the then-newly inaugurated lottery, was 311 out of a possible total of 365. *[With the understanding that the first draftees would be culled from the lower numbers, it was, therefore, virtually certain that Bill would not be drafted based on the number he had drawn.]*

Two days later, in a communication inspired by his political hopes and dreams, Bill wrote to Lt. Col. Eugene Holmes, Commander or the ROTC Program at the University of Arkansas. "From my work," Bill later reminisced, "I came to believe that the draft system is illegitimate. I decided to accept the draft in spite of my beliefs for one reason—to maintain my political viability."

Holmes did not immediately respond. Instead, he avoided comment altogether until nearly twenty-three years later. In September of 1992, a few weeks before the presidential elections pitting Bill Clinton against President George H.W. Bush, in a delayed response heavily motivated by partisan politics, Holmes wrote, "There is the imminent danger to our country of a draft-dodger becoming Commander-in-Chief of the Armed Forces of the United States. I believe that Bill Clinton purposefully deceived me, using the possibility of joining the ROTC as a play to work with the draft board to delay his induction and *[to thereby]* get a new draft reclassification."

Was Bill Brainwashed in Moscow, and Subsequently Enrolled as a KGB Agent?

During the winter break from his studies at Oxford, late in 1969 and early 1970, Bill, the antiwar activist, took the longest and most controversial trip of his life. It has since been labeled "The Future President's Road to Moscow."

His trip would take him through the Netherlands, followed by visits to the Scandinavia capitals of Copenhagen, Oslo, and Stockholm. After that, he continued his trip to what was then known as the Soviet Union.,

For the Holland part of his trip, he was accompanied by his artist friend, Aimee Gautier. At the Rijksmuseum in Amsterdam, when he went to retrieve their coats, he encountered the Russian dancer, Rudolf Nureyev, who had defected to the West from the Soviet Union in 1961.

The homosexual dancer made a pass at Bill. But before Bill could turn him down, he noticed a handsome but obviously angry young man urging Nureyev to hurry up.

As Bill later wrote, "Rudi and I finally got to sit down for tea years later, but it was in Taipei, Taiwan. We had tea and chatted...nothing else."

After that, Bill continued on to Oslo, where he was seen meeting with representatives from various "peace" organizations, including the Institute for Peace Research.

Leaving Oslo, he headed by train to Stockholm before taking the overnight ferry to Helsinki, the capital of Finland. There, he spent the Christmas holidays with Richard Shullaw, a former classmate at Georgetown.

After a few days in Helsinki, he boarded a train to Russia, traveling via Leningrad (St. Petersburg) to Moscow. Arriving there on New Year's Eve in bitter cold, he checked into the Hotel National.

What he did during his five days in Moscow eventually morphed into a political bombshell during the 1992 presidential elections. His most severe critics asserted that he had been "brainwashed" by the KGB and that, ever since, he had operated as an agent of the Soviet Union, sent back to America to do its dirty work. Such a charge might have been inspired by the 1962 Cold War Frank Sinatra thriller, *The Manchurian Candidate.*

Bill remembered clearing Russian customs and his encounter with a "pudgy, cherubic border guard," obviously wanting to see if I had any dirty books he could confiscate." But all that the guard found were English translations of novels by Tolstoy and Dostoevsky.

In Moscow, Bill claimed that "relations between Russia and the United

States are pretty good." He called Moscow "a friendly place, a good atmosphere."

Perhaps that was too optimistic an appraisal. The city lived under a reign of terror, and, far from enjoying a *détente* with America, the Soviets were supplying the North Vietnamese with anti-aircraft weapons.

As a student at Oxford, Bill Clinton was on his way to Moscow when, during a stopover in Amsterdam, he encountered the fabled Russian dancer, Rudolf Nureyev. On June 17, 1961, the homosexual dancer had fled from Soviet guards at Le Bourget Airport in Paris.

Nureyev was never subtle with his propositions. He assured Bill that as a dancer, he had developed pelvic movements that "could drive a man wild" if he went to bed with him.

Nureyev's pass was not intercepted by Bill.

In the scene above, Rudolf Nureyev appears as another Rudolf (Valentino) opposite Michelle Phillips, cast as his wife, Natacha Rambova. The controversial film, *Valentino,* was released in 1977 and directed by Ken Russell.

In his memoirs, Clinton said that the only person he knew in Moscow was Anik Alexis, the daughter of a French diplomat studying at the Patrice Lumumba Peoples' Friendship University, a KGB-training ground whose alumni had included the terrorist "Carlos the Jackal." Alexis was the girlfriend of his former classmate, Tom Williamson.

After dinner with her and her friends, he took the bus back into Moscow, where he met another passenger, Oleg Rakito, who—in English—drilled him with many questions. He later wrote, "He told me he worked for the government, virtually admitting he was assigned to keep an eye on me."

In his autobiography, Bill did reveal that at his hotel, he befriended some fellow Americans. At first, they thought he was Russian because of "my long hair and beard, rawhide boots, and Navy pea jacket."

They were in Moscow to see if the North Vietnamese stationed there would give them information about a missing American pilot, Henry Fors, who was missing after his plane crash-landed over North Vietnam. One of the Americans, an older man, wanted to know if his son were still alive. (He wasn't).

One of the members of the delegation, Charles Daniels, remembered the future American President as "out of money and hungry. We fed him."

Bill headed back to Oxford, but only after a stopover in Prague. He arrived at Oxford on January 19, 1970, to begin one of the most important years of his life.

In late May of 1970, he received news that his life was about to change, and that soon he'd be returning to America. He'd been accepted into Yale Law School.

During his final days at Oxford, he made the rounds, telling everyone goodbye, especially his string of girlfriends, many of whom were rewarded with kisses and tight embraces.

Before he left, he told his roommates, "I've decided to take the advice of the Beatles as expressed in 'Hey Jude': *Take a sad song and make it better."*

Chapter Five

Bill & Hillary, San Francisco, and Their Postgraduate "Summer of Love"

Her Association With a "Commie Law Firm."

Hillary's "Black Panthermania"

Invading Texas: Tales from the Lone Star State: "Cowgirl Hillary," Butch Cassidy, & The Sundance Kid

With his shaggy mane and scraggly orange beard, Bill Clinton reminded Hillary of one of those ancient Vikings invading England to pillage its villages and rape its women. He later introduced her to his friend, Paul Fray, who appraised Hillary to Bill.

"You mother-fucking son-of-a-bitch. You could have any god damn woman on the face of God's earth, and you take up with this kook. She looks like the south end of a mule going north. What's got into you? Were you drunk?"

But by October 11, 1975, both of them had "cleaned up our acts," in Bill's words. "She was my beautiful, curly-haired bride, and I even cut my hair—well, not that much. I wore a suit and tie to make myself presentable to her, so she wouldn't kick me out of bed on my honeymoon night."

"In our wedding bed, I promised to be true to her forever—no other gals for me. My tomcatting days were over, and I meant that!"

"I thought I would fall in love with her, and I didn't want to fall in love."

—Bill Clinton

"Hillary loves Bill. And Bill Loves Bill. That gives them something in common."

—Dick Morris

One enchanted evening, across a crowded room, Bill spotted Hillary, and history was made.

In this case, it was the reading room *(depicted above)* of the Yale Law Library, modeled after the King's College Chapel at Cambridge (UK).

"Here I am back in New Haven, going to Yale," Bill wrote his mother, Virginia, back in Arkansas. "My friend, Bob Reich, calls it 'the vile crotch of Connecticut.'"

Reich later claimed, "I was the first person who introduced Bill to Hillary in the school cafeteria. But I guess neither of them remembered that. In each of their memoirs, they preferred to give a more melodramatic account."

It was November of 1970, and a cold wind was blowing down from Canada, as Bill Clinton strolled into the Yale Law Library. He was reasonably good looking and rather tall, with a wild shrub of hair. He wore what he called "high-water pants and a pair of Arkansas clodhoppers."

In a library Illuminated with light flooding in through arched windows, Bill talked to a friend, Jeff Glekel, an editor at the *Yale Law Journal.* He was urging Bill to join the staff.

Bill wasn't really paying attention, his eyes glued to a woman who sat at the far end of the room. As he remembered her, "She had thick, dark blonde hair, and wore these Mr. Magoo eyeglasses with no makeup. But she conveyed a sense of strength and self-possession I had rarely seen in anyone, man or woman."

Finally, when Glekel realized that Bill was not paying attention, he wandered off.

Surrounded by law books, Hillary rose from her table and headed toward Bill. Approaching him, she said, "Look, I'm not blind. You've been following me around campus. It's very disturbing. What do you want? You should at

"What Do Marilyn Monroe & Hillary Clinton Have in Common? Lesbianism."

—Anna Freud

least introduce yourself." Then she extended her hand. "I'm Hillary Rodham."

He later claimed something that's hard to believe: "I must have seemed like the dumbest hillbilly. For I moment, I forgot my own name." Finally, he was able to mutter, "Hi, I'm Bill Clinton from Arkansas."

"I figured you must be from some hick state like that," she said, before suggesting, "Well, let's not stand here looking like dumbasses. How about going over to the cafeteria for a cup of coffee?"

"It'd be an honor," he said.

"By the way," she said, as they exited from the library. "Are those Elvis sideburns for real, or just glued on?"

She would later claim that she was impressed by his next action in the cafeteria. He ordered two cups of coffee for them, placed them on a tray, and carried them over to a table where African American students usually sat at mealtimes.

"He might be from a state devoted to segregation, but I saw at once that he was not your typical bigoted Southern Boy," she recalled. "That act of sitting at that table told me a bit about his politics. His display of tolerance impressed me."

Later, she learned that at the time of their meeting, he was dating a beautiful, statuesque African American student studying at Yale to become a psychiatrist.

Opposite him, sipping her coffee, she asked, "So, what's your goal? Like every other student in law school, you probably want to go to Wall Street and become a high-priced attorney getting rich off stocks."

"Not at all," he answered. "I don't even want to be a lawyer, but feel I need a legal background. I want to be a politician."

"An even more horrible breed than a Wall Street lawyer," she said.

"Well, not just a politician," he said. "My ultimate goal is to become the President of the United States."

"In that case, I must warn you to get in line. I plan to become President of the United States before you."

"A woman president!" he said. "What a novel idea. You won't carry the South."

"As LBJ predicted, the South is lost to the Democrats for at least the next forty years," she said. "What's your more immediate goal?"

"After Yale, I plan to return to Arkansas. Run for Congress when I qualify. I want to sit in the Governor's Mansion in Little Rock directing the show. After I serve maybe two terms, then I'll run for president."

That's a damn big jump," she said. "Perhaps I'll first pick you as my vice presidential running mate. That way, you'll have eight years as an intern in the White House. I'll show you how it's done before you sit in the Oval Office yourself."

"Touché!" he said.

Even though the specific day of their first meeting remains a matter of debate, historians might conclude that it was as significant a date as Stanley meeting Livingston in colonial Africa: Roosevelt meeting Stalin at Yalta; a middle-aged Humphrey Bogart meeting teenager Lauren Bacall; or, more maliciously, Senator John F. Kennedy being introduced to Marilyn Monroe.

Apparently, if accounts are to be believed, Bill and Hillary did not become a couple until March of 1971. During the winter of 1970 and '71, Hillary was still romantically involved with David Rupert, who was living like a hippie in Vermont. One Monday, after she'd returned from a visit with him there, Bill encountered her roommate. She told him that Hillary had returned from a visit with an awful cold she'd caught up there in the snowfields.

Rather gallantly, he ordered a bowl of takeaway chicken soup and some orange juice and arrived at her dorm to deliver them. She later said, "That gesture touched my heart."

When she recovered, he asked her out on a date, and she accepted. They wandered over to the Yale Art Gallery to see an exhibit of works by Mark Rothko. But they found the service employees there had gone on strike. At the door, a security guard turned them away.

"Bill didn't take 'no' for an answer, and I admired him for that," she said. "He told the guard we'd pick up litter in front of the museum if he'd let us go in. The guard agreed, and we were admitted.

Afterward, in the courtyard, she sat in the lap of a bronze and bulky Henry Moore sculpture, *Draped Seated Woman.* At one point, Bill leaned down, resting his head on her shoulder.

Later that night, she invited him to a party hosted by her roommate, Kwan Kwan Tan, a student from Burma studying law at Yale.

The next evening, he invited

Henry Moore's *Draped Seated Woman* was one of only six modelings of it ever cast. The one depicted here stands on the outdoor terrace of the Yale Art Gallery in New Haven, Connecticut.

A plaque near this sculpture should read: "Bill Clinton Courted Hillary Rodham Here."

After she plopped down in the ample seat of this woman with the tiny head and the big body, Bill leaned in, whispering "sweet nothings" in her ear.

One of history's most notorious romantic liaisons had begun.

her for a plate of meatless spaghetti at an Italian *trattoria*, as he'd done with so many girls before. "It was Bill's hands that first attracted me, not his Afro. His wrists are narrow and his fingers tapered and deft, like those of a pianist or surgeon."

"We kept talking and talking and found that politically, in spite of certain differences, we were on the same side," she said. "By then, I was a full-fledged Democrat. We'd later joke that our first date had actually begun at the Yale Museum, where we were scab labor, picking up trash on the lawn."

Beginning with that date, he saw her for the next ten nights in a row. By that time, she'd broken off from Rupert in Vermont, and Bill had ended his romantic liaisons with three other women, one of whom had returned to her original boyfriend. Previously, his African American beauty had attached herself to one of the Black Panthers.

The third woman he'd been involved with had informed him that she'd decided that she didn't like the male appendage, comparing it to a "string of guts hanging out." She preferred, she said, "the beautiful, breasty contours of a woman with a lovely vagina."

He told her he also preferred a vagina, and that they, even though they were parting, still had something in common to talk about.

It soon became apparent across campus that Bill and Hillary were a couple, an alliance that drew mixed reactions. Betty Stevens, who worked at the local drugstore, said, "I made creamy milkshakes for Bill and his gal, Hillary. He seemed to have forgotten that he had already picked me up and seduced me one night in the back seat of his car. With Hillary, he pretended he didn't know me. I lost out with him. By the way, the two of them carried on, I was convinced he was fucking her brains out every night."

A classmate of Hillary's, who didn't want to reveal her name, claimed that, "Most people liked Hillary. Of course, many did not, secretly calling her 'Dragon Lady' behind her back. That spring, a rumor spread that she was a dominatrix and that Bill liked to be 'punished.' I don't know if that was true or not, but it sure traveled along the grapevine."

Soon, Hillary was seen riding around as a passenger in Bill's 1970 Halloween orange Opel station wagon, which she called "one of the ugliest cars ever manufactured."

Classmate David Masselli likened Hillary to "that serious, intense, long-haired girl who appears as Woody Allen's first girlfriend in all those 1970s movies of his. Her uniform consisted of white socks and sandals, and she wore loose-fitting flowing pants favored by the Vietcong, for which she was teased by her classmates."

A law student, Richard Grande, remarked, "She was among those coven of young women at Yale who believed in a 'look-like-shit' brand of feminism."

A fellow classmate, Michael Medved, who later developed a following as a movie critic, said, "When I saw them on campus, I felt they were definitely a couple in love. They reminded me of Katharine Hepburn and Spencer Tracy in the movies, combative but in love. She took strong positions with him. When he got too long-winded, she'd tell him 'to cut the bullshit.' Sometimes, she called it 'mental masturbation.'"

"I was not immediately taken by his deep roots in Arkansas," Hillary said. "Most of us at Yale were trying to break from our boring middle-class backgrounds. I was not bamboozled by his downhome palaver. I told him to quit talking about how big those god damn watermelons grow back in Hope, Arkansas."

Yet at other times, she expressed this great belief in Bill, telling friends, "This young man is going to change the world."

Another classmate, Kris Rogers, said, "We predicted that Hillary and Bill would either end up running in some political race against each other, or working together as a powerful team—in fact, we jokingly referred to them as the 'Dynamic Duo.' He was intuitive, she was more rational. Often, they arrived at the same political conclusion, but reached it through different brain processes."

Law student Alan Bersin said, "Bill was more free-floating than Hillary, more of a dreamer. She was more direct, rather intense in expressing her likes and dislikes. He was more diplomatic. She was smarter than he was. She got better marks in a class they took together. In fact, she was viewed as the smartest woman enrolled in Yale's Law School. A real straight shooter. Bill was destined to charm his way through life. He could sell iceboxes to an Eskimo."

Hillary later wrote about Bill's shaggy mane and scraggly orange beard.

"At first, I found her frightening, intimidating, a real challenge to a man," he wrote in a memoir. "She was a star on the rise, and I was actually afraid of her. No woman had ever scared me like that. Yet I was powerfully attracted to her, finding her a formidable presence."

She didn't seem to realize that Bill, at first, had been afraid to approach her. She told friends, "He's the only man I've met who's not afraid of me. I had this well-ordered cerebral existence planned for myself, until this wild card came along."

Sometimes, their political arguments became confrontational, as when they debated against one another during mock trials in class.

One professor said, "As trial lawyers, whereas Bill was diplomatic, soft-spoken, self-deprecating, and polite like Atticus Finch in *To Kill a Mockingbird,* Hillary displayed more masculine traits."

Years later, Bill would express his feelings at the time to a reporter from *Vanity Fair.* "As I got involved with Hillary, I feared falling too deeply in love with her. I knew she was a great person and could lead a great life. If she ran for public office, I thought she might win. But I was who I am. I wanted to go back to Arkansas and run for public office. But could I really ask her to join me when she clearly belonged in Washington, perhaps becoming mayor of Chicago? She didn't seem destined for traveling the backroads of Arkansas or slopping the hogs."

***

During his first term at Yale Law School, Bill rented a four-bedroom house in Milford, Connecticut, along the beach of Long Island Sound. Technically, it was an inadequately insulated house at its best in summer, and it tended to be uncomfortably cold during frigid New England winters.

Bill's three housemates included Doug Eakeley, a fellow Rhodes scholar who had originally located the sprawling antique house. Bill second roomie was Don Pogue, described as very blue collar and "more Left Wing than all of us."

"Don was like a concrete block and strong as an ox, riding a motorcycle to law school where he engaged all comers in intense political debates," Bill said.

Bill's third housemate was an African American, William T. Coleman III. Coleman's father, a Republican Lawyer, William T. Coleman, Jr., would serve as Secretary of Transportation during the Administration of Gerald Ford, who would succeed the much-disgraced Richard Nixon after his resignation from office in August of 1974.

In 1995, Bill, as president, would present Coleman Jr., with the Presidential Medal of Freedom.

From their big, rented house, the roomies would bring girlfriends in for sleepovers. Each of the building's four occupants had his own room. One attractive female student boasted, "I had three of them, including Bill, before the spring term ended."

Carolyn Ellis, a mutual friend, remembered visiting their house for potluck suppers. "Everybody had to bring something, perhaps a casserole. We'd sit on the front porch and engage in endless debates while the music of Jefferson Airplane, Janis Joplin, or the Rolling Stones blared through the house."

All the classmates recalled the era as a pre-AIDS sexual revolution punctuated with easy availability of marijuana and an emphasis on letting the good times roll.

At one point, Virginia arrived on campus for a reunion with Bill. The night before, Hillary had tried to cut her own hair in an attempt to save money. When Bill saw the result, he said, "You look like a punk rocker."

Strolling around campus, Virginia showed off her coiffed hairdo, which included a "skunk strip" in the middle, a creation of her hairdresser husband, Jeff Dwire.

As Bill later commented, "Mother looked stunned a she came face to face with this young feminist who wore no makeup and Coke bottle glasses, in contrast to Mother, who had the most overpainted face in Arkansas, with lipstick so red it challenged the rays of the sun. She was attired in the finest dress sold at the local department store. Hillary wore blue jeans and a man's work shirt. She'd been walking on the beach at Milford and had tar on her shoes."

"I hear you're from Chicago," Virginia said to her, noticing Hillary's feet. "I thought only people from North Carolina are tarheels."

As Virginia recalled in her memoirs, "Meeting Hillary was a growth experience on my part. When we first came together, it was a case of an old immovable object running up against irresistible force."

The true story of Virginia vs. Hillary would not unfold, of course, until later.

Hillary & the Black Panthers Invade Yale

In the late spring of 1971, Hillary and Bill faced a tough choice: Should they split up for the summer, or stay together?

She was the first to make up her mind by accepting a position in the Oakland, California law firm of Treuhaft, Walker, & Burnstein

In contrast, Bill wavered as to how he wanted to spend his summer, vacillating between accompanying Hillary to the San Francisco area, or accepting a role as a campaign worker for Senator George McGovern, who had announced his bid for President of the United States in the upcoming election of 1972.

Hillary's links to Robert Treuhaft, a senior partner at the law firm who wanted her, dated back to the infamous Black Panther trials in New Haven, details of which drew nationwide attention in 1970.

It had all begun on May 19, 1969, when members of the Black Panthers kidnapped, tortured, and murdered Alex Rackley, suspecting that he had "ratted" on them to the FBI.

After two days and nights of torture, including cigarette burns on his body and pouring scalding water on him, he was forcibly carried and dragged to the Coginchaug River, where he was executed with gunshot wounds, his corpse thrown into the water. His battered and lacerated body was discovered a day later.

Police immediately raided the Panther headquarters and arrested nine men, who became collectively known as the "New Haven Nine," a *cause-céle-bre* evoking the infamous "Chicago Seven."

Of those arrested, George Sams, Jr., and Warren Klimbro later confessed to their roles in the murder. In exchange for a plea deal, they agreed to testify that Lonnie McLucas had fired the second shot into Rackley's chest.

The arrest and subsequent trials attracted hundreds of Panther supporters to New Haven and to the Yale Campus. At one point, during a riot, the Yale Law School Library, whose façade had been inspired by that of the Parthenon in Athens, was set on fire. Hillary was part of the fire brigade trying to rescue rare volumes from its interior.

Protesters claimed that the Panthers would not get a fair trial, charging—even before its members had been selected— that the jury itself was "racist."

The arrival into the stewpot of emotions and politics of a notorious married couple, Robert Treuhaft and his wife, author Jessica Mitford, would change Hillary's life. One of the infamous and supremely controversial Mitford sisters of England, she had written *The American Way of Death* in 1963, a bestselling (and scathing) indictment of the funeral industry.

Over the course of many years, Treuhaft and (Jessica) Mitford had been repeatedly investigated by the FBI. During Joseph McCarthy's "Red Scare" of the 1950s, they had been forced to answer questions about their alleged association with the Soviets before the dreaded HUAC (House Un-American Activities Committee).

Shortly after her arrival from Oakland, Jessica hosted a large fund-raising party for the Panthers that was attended by Hillary. The women met together the following day and Jessica introduced her to Treuhaft. During the course of their luncheon, he became so impressed with Hillary's sharp mind that he offered her a summer internship at his leftist law firm in Oakland, California.

A friend, Kristine Olson Rogers, asserted that "Hillary was the ballast that spring at organized rallies that kept the ship from leaning too far right, too far left. She was always the one who saw the need for balance between the two warring fac-

Jessica Mitford *(depicted above on one of the covers of her bestselling exposé of the funeral industry)* and her activist husband, attorney Robert Treuhaft, were accused by conservatives of taking their marching orders directly from Nikita Khrushchev.

Both were deeply impressed with "the potential" of Hillary Rodham.

tions."

Another friend, Carolyn Ellis, weighed in on Hillary's role during the Black Panther controversies. "She allowed both sides to express themselves and air their grievances at meetings she chaired. She wanted to break the stalemate between the Yale administrators and the University's angry students. Unusual for a woman at that time, she became a sort of bridge between the protesters and the establishment. She didn't join either side; the administration defining the looters, rioters, and arsonists as 'thugs.' *[In contrast,]* many of the white students viewed the protesting African Americans as 'Black Robin Hoods.'"

Author Gail Sheehy claimed that "Hillary's choice was grim: Those in the middle stood between the reactionary forces of J. Edgar Hoover—the cross-dressing white supremacist director of the F.B.I., who branded Black Panthers as 'the greatest threat to the internal security of the United States' and threatened to rescind civil rights freedoms so recently granted—and the stoned radical forces led by Huey P. Newton, the black son of a New Orleans sharecropper and the white anarchist Abbie Hoffman, who called for 'revolutionary suicide.'"

Caught in the crossfire, Hillary had attended the May Day rally of 1970 that drew hundreds of protesters. There, she heard Hoffman deliver his "paeans to pot" as he gave a fiery speech filled with rants. "FUCK RATIONALITY! FUCK LAW AND ORDER! WE'VE GOT ADULTS AFRAID TO FUCK ANY MORE, 'CAUSE THEY KNOW THEY'RE GONNA RAISE LONG-HAIRED BABIES LIKE US!"

In spite of many dire forecasts, the trial judge and jury seemed fair, even lenient. McLucas was acquitted of the most severe murder charges, and convicted only on a lesser charge of conspiracy to commit murder. He was sentenced to twelve to fifteen years in prison. His two collaborators, pleading guilty to second degree murder, were sentenced but released after four years.

Bobby Seale, co-founder of the Black Panthers, had also been accused of murder by a fellow member testifying for the police. But the jury hearing his case deadlocked eleven to one. The charges against him were later dropped.

Years later, in 2000, when Hillary ran for her Senate seat from New York, her involvement with the Black Panther trials resurfaced through the efforts of anti-Clinton activists. She was also attacked for her internship with Treuhaft's left-leaning law firm in Oakland, her enemies charging that was "a commie front."

Specifically, Hillary's role at the Black Panther trials in New Haven was that of a monitor looking for civil rights violations, with the understanding that if she found any, she'd report them to the American Civil Liberties Union. Although she was later falsely accused of playing a greater leadership role than that, she had no direct involvement with the legal defense team defending the Black Panthers.

Then and in the years that followed, Bill never appeared unduly concerned that her role would harm either her future political career or his own.

In weighing his options that spring, Bill had been offered a position in Florida as a coordinator during the political campaign of Senator George McGovern for the U.S. Presidency. But when he heard of Hillary's upcoming internship with Treuhaft's firm in Oakland, he changed his mind, despite being sorely tempted by the McGovern campaign.

Evaluating it later, Bill said, in a memoir, "I screwed up my courage and asked Hillary if I could spend the summer with her. She was incredulous at first, because she knew how much I loved politics and how deeply I felt about the Vietnam War."

***

Leaving New Haven, they hit the road, heading west Park Ridge, near Chicago, to meet her family, especially Dorothy and Hugh Rodham, along with her two brothers.

When they got there, Dorothy, although warmly embracing her daughter, was at first rather chilly to Bill. She had not been informed about the depth of their involvement, only that Hillary was bringing home a "young law student driving her across the country to Oakland."

Dorothy would later candidly confess to a writer from *Paris Match,* "My introduction to Bill was a bit cold because I just knew this was the man who would take my daughter away from me."

In the Rodham family's living room, Bill was introduced to Hugh, Hillary's father. "He was a no-nonsense, tobacco-chewing Republican Right-Winger," Bill said. "In time, Archie Bunker on the TV sitcom, *All in the Family,* would share Hugh's political philosophy. He was very gruff talking, actually rude to me."

In time, Bill would win Dorothy over with his Southern charm. He would later claim in a memoir that "the more I talked to Hugh, the more I liked him." That was far too diplomatic, and far too optimistic.

Based on models defined by *All in the Family,* whereas Hugh Rodham would represent Archie; Dorothy might be compared to Edith, Archie's long-suffering, dignified wife. Bill might have been compared to "Meathead," Archie's liberal, well-meaning son-in-law.

"We were at loggerheads when it came to politics," Bill said, "and to his dying day, Hugh wanted me to switch from the Democrats to the GOP."

Bill got on better with Hillary's brothers, Hughie and Tony, who seemed to welcome him. In fact, Tony invited him to share his bedroom, warning him, "If

Dad catches you slipping out in the middle of the night for visits with Hillary, you're in for it."

After a few somewhat strained days, Hillary and Bill would tell the Rodhams goodbye before heading out on the long drive to Berkeley. There, he helped her move into an apartment near the Treuhaft's law firm in Oakland. It was within a house owned by Dorothy Rodham's half-sister, Adeline. When he got her to Berkeley, Bill told Hillary, "I put everything else aside to be with the one I love."

On a visit to the Rodham family, Bill was introduced to his future father-in-law. He soon learned that Hugh Rodham shared the same views as Archie Bunker *(lower center)* on the sociologically daring TV sitcom, *All in the Family.*

***

Ironically, after their long westward trek, Bill spent only three nights in Oakland. For some reason, shortly after his arrival, even though Hillary had advised him that it would be easier to phone, Bill opted to return (alone) to Washington for a meeting with Gary Hart, who was directing McGovern's presidential campaign. Hart had invited him to Florida to organize the McGovern's campaign in that crucial state.

Although he turned down the Florida job, he told Hart that he'd make himself available for one of McGovern's future campaign, in some Southern state.

This time, as he headed back to Oakland, he took the southern route, stopping off for a visit with Virginia, Roger, and his friends in Arkansas.

After that, he drove west again, taking the bleak route through Death Valley, the hottest place in the United States. "I was sweating like a pig on castration day."

As a symbolic recognition of his Southern origins, and as a celebration of his return to Oakland, Hillary had learned how to bake a peach pie. "That pie disappeared pretty quickly," he said.

Together, they set up housekeeping in the small, inadequately furnished apartment. Its location was near the Berkeley campus, then one of the most potent bastions of liberalism and free speech in the world.

In her capacity as an intern with a firm that was revered for fighting for social justice, Hillary got to know its director, Treuhaft. David Brock, in his book, *The Seduction of Hillary Clinton,* charged that "Treuhaft was a man who dedicated his entire career to advancing the agenda of the Soviet communists and the KGB."

In the meantime, Bill toured San Francisco, Oakland, and the Bay area. At home, both he and Hillary learned to make chicken curry with rice, which they served to their newly minted friends. After dinner, Bill entertained them either with renditions of Elvis songs or saxophone concerts.

He was most intrigued wandering through Oakland, the hotbed of urban radicals and the birthplace of the Black Panthers.

During their inaugural meeting in New Haven, Hillary's time with Jessica Mitford, Treuhaft's wife, another dedicated communist, had been brief. But Hillary got to know her better in San Francisco, where she found her "one of the most fascinating women I've ever met."

[Jessica, born to the 2nd Baron Redesdale of the English peerage, was the most left-leaning of the otherwise über-right wing Mitford sisters, who included Nancy, Pamela, Diana, Deborah, and the notorious Unity Mitford. These sisters had a brother, Tom.

As the girls were growing up, Unity and Jessica shared a bedroom. Sleeping within ten feet of each other, they were miles apart, politically. A line was drawn in the middle of the room, Jessica painting a hammer and sickle on her side of the floor, with Unity decorating her space with a swastika and a portrait of Adolf Hitler.

As she grew into a beautiful young woman, Unity went to Berlin where she managed to ingratiate herself into the Führer's inner circle. He pronounced her "the perfect specimen of womanhood."

Unity became some close to Hitler that he used her to make his mistress, Eva Braun, jealous. However, when England declared war on Germany in 1939, Unity went to Munich's English Garden. There, using a pearl-encrusted pistol that Hitler had given her, she shot herself in the head. The bullet lodged in her brain, but she survived.

When he heard the news, Hitler flew to Munich to be by her side. When he discovered her condition, he paid her hospital bill and arranged for her eventual transport to England, where she arrived with the bullet still lodged in her head. Doctors defined it as inoperable.

Living in disgrace, and in horrible physical and mental shape, she survived until 1948, when she died of meningitis caused by the swelling of her brain in the area surrounding the deeply embedded bullet.

Hillary found the story horrible but fascinating.

Another of the Mitford sisters, Diana, married Oswald Mosley, leader of the British Fascist Party. The wedding took place in the home of Joseph

Goebbels, with Hitler in attendance. Of all the sisters, Diana was viewed as the most beautiful, and compared to Botticelli's Venus.

Whereas Nancy became a popular novelist; her sister, Deborah, became the Duchess of Devonshire. The most unobtrusive sister, Pamela, was the least political, although she was a rabid anti-Semite. After a divorce from the millionaire physicist, Derek Jackson, she went to live with the love of her life, the Italian horsewoman, Giuditta Tommasi.]

In Oakland that summer, at the law firm, Hillary worked mainly not with Treuhaft, but with his partner, Mal Burnstein.

She performed research for him and wrote legal motions and briefs in child custody cases. On weekends, she shopped with Bill for what she called "student décor," picking up heavily discounted pieces of furniture at the Goodwill or at Salvation Army stores.

"The wind howled through cracks in the walls, which we stuffed with newspapers," she said.

"We paid Hillary almost nothing, but she worked like she was getting a hundred dollars an hour," Burnstein claimed. Their most controversial case that summer involved members of the Black Panthers. They had marched on Sacramento where Ronald Reagan was governor. It was reported that Ronald and Nancy had fled from the State's capitol.

Eventually, several of the Panthers were arrested. Burstein and Hillary defended them, and most of the charges against them were eventually dropped. The few who did go to jail received only light sentences.

In spite of a spirited defense, spearheaded by Hillary herself, Treuhaft later said, "She had no real commitment to the Panthers. Her heart wasn't in it. But she did her job of defending them admirably. Frankly, Hillary was far, far, more centrist than the rest of us."

***

After Oakland, Bill and Hillary agreed to migrate to Texas as volunteers in Senator McGovern's presidential campaign. he later said, "Finding a vote for McGovern in Texas was like discovering a baby rattlesnake in your soup."

During their campaign for McGovern in the Lone Star State, the loving couple didn't always find themselves in the same city. Whereas Bill was mostly centered in Austin within McGovern's campaign headquarters. Hillary was assigned to register Democratic voters, most of them Hispanic, in and around San Antonio.

In Austin, Bill got to know Gary Hart, who, in 1988, would eventually run for President himself.

"Gary was a bad role model for Bill," Amanda Smith, a campaign volunteer, said. "Gary had a real Don Juan complex."

As another attractive female campaign aide later charged, "I thought I was the love of Gary's life one Saturday night when he made love to me. But on Monday morning at campaign headquarters, he walked right by me, and didn't even speak after whispering all those sweet nothings into my ear two nights before."

California Governor Reagan with his wife, the former actress Nancy Davis, posing together in their swimming pool in Pacific Palisades in early 1970s

Reagan later predicted that Hillary's work for the Black Panthers in Oakland would doom her chance of ever winning a political office.

Larry Feldman, another campaign volunteer, said, "Bill should have learned from Hart not to get caught with your pants down if you want to be a successful politician."

Feldman was referring to the notorious 1987 incident in which Hart, the Democratic Senator from Colorado running at the time for president, was photographed with the beautiful Donna Rice sitting on his lap aboard a yacht *[Monkey Business]* sailing around The Bahamas.

[Monkey Business was an 83-foot motor yacht custom built and owned by the developers of South Florida's luxurious Turnberry Isle resort. Other famous guests associated with the yacht had included Elizabeth Taylor, Jack Nicholson, Julio Iglesias, and Elton John. The yacht was used by Colorado Senator Gary Hart during his presidential campaign in 1987 at around the time that Hart challenged the press to provide evidence of his sexual infidelities. Consequently, after a stakeout of Hart's lodgings, reporters associated with The Miami Herald *snapped photos of Hart aboard the vessel with Miami-based model Donna Rice. The media frenzy that followed destroyed Hart's bid for the presidency.]*

During the Texas campaign, Hillary and Bill would often meet, usually on weekends. Arriving in Austin, she was proud to announce to Bill that she had lured Shirley MacLaine to San Antonio for a political rally for McGovern.

They were seen enjoying barbecue at Scholz's Beer Garden while listening to a mariachi band. Here, she tasted barbecued goat's head *(cabrito)* for the first and last time.

When they became too depressed about McGovern's chances of carrying Texas, they retreated for a romantic vacation in the little Mexican town of Zihuatanejo on the Pacific Coast.

After her return, Hillary showed up at one point in cowgirl drag. An aide recalled, "If Roy Rogers had seen her in this garb, he would have dumped Dale Evans for Hillary."

Back in Texas and on the campaign trail, Bill worked with the Georgia-born journalist Taylor Branch, a fellow Southerner, who at the time was writing for *The Washington Monthly.* In time, he would win a Pulitzer Prize for his three-volume biography of Martin Luther King, Jr. In Texas, based on their carousings and lusty, devil-may-care similarities, Branch and Bill became collectively known as "Butch Cassidy and the Sundance Kid."

Texas is known for its long distances and oversized personalities. One of them was Billie Carr, the "Godmother of Texas Liberals." When she first met Bill and Branch, she phoned Hart. "You told me you were sending down some young men. But Bill looks ten, Branch maybe twelve."

But after two weeks, she came to appreciate both men for their effectiveness as campaign workers. "Bill was the good cop, sweet and friendly, most accommodating," she said. "Branch worked harder, but was a bit stiff and not at all hip. When I told him I had gotten Linda Ronstadt to agree to fly in for a fund-raising concert, Branch asked me, 'Who is Linda Ronstadt?'"

Billie Carr was a rugged woman, about twenty years older than Bill Clinton. "She reminded him of Virginia," he said. "I adored her. One time, she asked me if I really knew how to fuck. 'So few men do, you know,' she said."

One night in Dallas, over a Tex-Mex plate, he told her, "One day I want to become President of the United States."

"I've heard that line before," she said. "One night, when a young Texas politician rose from my bed and put Jumbo back in his pants, he told me he, too, planned to run for president. You guessed it. Lyndon himself. Then he went home to Lady Bird."

Bill came to love Billie, who wore a badge over her left breast, reading "BILLIE CARR—BITCH."

She was heavyset, bombastic, and known as "The Boss" among the grassroots Democrats of Texas. She was a hard-charger, challenging the *status quo*, opposing the Vietnam War, and fighting for civil rights. Later in life, she took up the causes of gay rights and environmental protection.

She became a political mentor to Bill. Called "The Eleanor Roosevelt of Texas," she visited Bill at the White House during the Monica Lewinsky scandal. When he received her in the reception line, she shook her finger at him. "Hillary should knock you over the head with a two-by-four. What a stupid son of a bitch you were."

"I expected that from her," Bill said. "She was fearless in her opinions, and she was right about me."

When she died in September of 2002, Bill praised Billie's accomplishments and mourned her passage. "I loved my rawhide mother. She's probably up in Heaven right now, swilling down a few beers."

She had left instructions that at her funeral, her open casket was to be carried by a delegation of pallbearers who were "black, brown, gay, and an equal number of women."

Bill spent a lot of time in Dallas, where he visited the Texas School Book Depository at Dealey Plaza, where John F. Kennedy had been assassinated in November of 1963. One evening, as reflected in one of his memoirs, as the sun set over the city, Bill stood for a long time wondering if someone would try to assassinate him when he became president one day.

During the McGovern campaign, Bill worked with Ron Kirk, the future mayor of Dallas, and with Ann Richards, a charming, dynamic, hard-drinking political celebrity. In 1994, when she ran unsuccessfully for a second term as Governor of Texas, her defeat was to a large extent the result of Karl Rove *[The ultra-conservative Republican strategist who's usually credited with the 1994 and 1998 Texas gubernatorial victories of George W. Bush, as well as Bush's 2000 and 2004 successful presidential campaigns]* having discredited her as a lesbian.

When Bill heard this, he said, "Ann is anything but a lesbian. I can assure you of that."

That led to rumors that he and Richards had had an affair.

Bill also met and worked with a then-unknown television director, Steven Spielberg.

Taylor Branch in the Oval Office with Bill.

Both men went on to greater glory, but back in their hellraising days together in Texas, they were known as "Butch Cassidy and the Sundance Kid."

Bill Gavin, a campaign aide who worked with Bill, remembered that "Billy the Goat had at least three women a week when Hillary was in another town. One little Texas wildflower told me that one night, he locked campaign headquarters at eight o'clock and took her right on his desk top. I don't know for sure, but the prospect of getting caught seemed to add to his excitement."

In late August of 1972, Hillary arrived in Austin, and someone decided to transmit recent details of

Bill's womanizing to her. This led to a big blow-up right in the office in front of volunteers.

That evening, in the aftermath of their fight, Hillary was packing her bags, heading back East, Franklin Garcia, a Latino labor leader from San Antonio, interceded and brokered a reconciliation.

Bill credited him with "saving our relationship," but later said, "God damn, I don't know who that blabbermouth was."

While in Texas, Bill bonded with Betsey Wright, an activist from the University of Texas, who always had a Lucky Strike dangling from the corner of her mouth. As tough talker, she could relate "to the reddest of the rednecks."

Bill admired Wright's ability to organize. When he became governor of Arkansas, he designated her as his Chief of Staff.

When Wright met Hillary, she found her "brilliant, both her drive and her determination." She told Bill, "I think this gal is going to become the first woman President of the United States."

Wright approved of Bill's burgeoning relationship with Hillary, although noting the tension. "He tapped into a part of Hillary's psyche that no one else had. She had a fun side to her, believe it or not. She wasn't always serious. She had a hearty laugh, real guttural, nothing held back. Her public rarely saw that side of her. Bill had never met anyone like her before. Let me say that differently. *Nobody* had ever met anyone like Hillary before."

Wright also concluded, "Both Hillary and Bill—note that I named the woman first—passionately share one firm commitment. Each of them thinks it's their duty to change the world and to leave it a better place before they go on. They each had that firm determination before they met each other."

One aide, Johnny Ville, differed: "Hillary could never have made it in politics, in spite of Betsey's ringing endorsement, had she not hooked her skirttails to Bill. She would go through life hanging onto him. Politically, if she ever makes it to the finish line, it'll be because he carried her over it."

As was inevitable, all of Bill's, Hillary's, and their team's efforts to win for McGovern proved in vain. Yet, as Hillary recalled, "We learned much in the 1972 race against Nixon. It was our first rite of political passage. Looking back on our time in Texas, both of us knew we still had much to learn about campaigning as we headed East to Yale."

On reflection about his time in Texas, Bill said, "Although McGovern didn't win, at least something good came out of it. I discovered my alltime favorite treat: mango ice cream, which I first devoured at Menger's Hotel in San Antonio."

***

Back in New Haven, Hillary had enrolled in her third year at Yale, and Bill in his second. They found a Victorian, New England-style house with a pillared front porch, just off the campus, and subsequently they moved in together. Often, they sat there, enjoying the final rays of the breezes of a dying summer.

She made a strong commitment to Bill. Although she had graduated in 1972, she remained behind at Yale for another extra year until he could finish Law School in the spring of 1973.

Anna Freud, a gossipy psychoanalyst with a superb pedigree, was known for revealing too many secrets of her former patients.

As a fiery activist at Yale, Hillary took many positions. She began to champion a crusade for the installation of tampon dispensers in women's toilets across the Yale campus.

At the Yale Child Study Center, she began clinical work in child development, always a special concern of hers, both in her past and in her future. She sat in on diagnostic assessments with the center's nursery school teachers.

The center's director, Albert J. Solnit, defined Hillary as "The best pupil I ever had from the Law School."

She developed a controversial platform—that of the "child citizen"—a position that asserted that a kid should possess" all the procedural rights granted adults under the Constitution."

When she later became a politician, her critics attacked her work at the center, falsely claiming that her main goal involved "breaking up families and allowing them to sue their parents."

Young Anna, touring through the Dolomites with her famous father, Sigmund Freud. Marilyn Monroe and Hillary Rodham would one day lie on her couch.

Through the center, she came into contact with Anna Freud, the sixth and final child of Sigmund Freud, who had followed in her father's footsteps into the field of psychoanalysis. The distinguished psychiatrist regularly visited America to lecture and to teach.

During the 1970s, Anna had become involved with the problems unique to emotionally deprived and socially disadvantaged children. She taught seminars on crime and the family at the Yale Law School.

As such, she met Hillary, who found her fascinating and became a disciple of her teachings. Reportedly, although this has never been proven, Anna analyzed Hillary.

Amazing for a psychiatrist, Anna had a major, and in retrospect, highly embarrassing flaw: She often revealed the secrets of her clients. She told certain faculty members that "I am convinced that Miss Rodham is a lesbian, although she probably doesn't know it yet."

In another indiscreet revelation, she had revealed that Marilyn Monroe was a bisexual when she'd analyzed her in London during her filming of *The Prince and the Showgirl* (1957) with Laurence Olivier.

Bill and Hillary paid $754 a month rent at 21 Edgewood Avenue in New Haven. At night, they slept in a very small bedroom—"and did a lot of cuddling," as Bill remembered it. In front of the fireplace, they read, talked, read, and read some more before making love.

Since Hillary wasn't much of a cook, they were often seen eating on a modest budget at the Elm Street Diner, which had a Blue Plate special and was open all night. At the local Y, they took yoga classes together. Often, they were seen watching a movie at the Lincoln Theater, holding hands.

A classmate, William Reed, who knew both Bill and Hillary, casually said, "Theirs was a union of sex appeal coupled with brains: She had the brains, and he had the sex appeal, to judge from the way the girls clustered around him."

Since they had little money to live on, Bill took several part-time jobs. One was as a teacher of law enforcement at a nearby community college; the other was that of a researcher for an attorney in New Haven. Often, they shared their experiences at the Blue Bell Café, near the Law School, where they devoured the 88¢ breakfast special.

Like Hillary with Anna Freud, Bill, too, had a soon-to-be-famous instructor, Robert Bork, who would later become his political enemy. Rather defiantly, student Clinton often argued with Professor Bork over legal points of the Constitution.

He was horrified in 1987, when President Ronald Reagan, in one of his most controversial, almost reckless, decisions, designated Bork as a candidate for the U.S.

Then-President Ronald Reagan attempted to appoint Robert Bork *(depicted above)* to the Supreme Court. "Fortunately for America," Bill Clinton said, "Reagan did not succeed."

Bork had been one of Bill's law professors at Yale. "This guy was to the right of Attila the Hun."

Supreme Court.

When Bill heard that, he said, "Too bad Joseph Goebbels is no longer with us. Otherwise, Ronnie Boy would have nominated him. If Bork makes it to the Supreme Court, he'll bring back the Salem Witch Trials."

Bill avidly followed his future friend, Massachusetts Democratic Senator, Ted Kennedy, who denounced Bork from the podium of the Senate Floor: "His America is a land in which women would be forced into back-alley abortions: Blacks would sit at segregated lunch counters; rough police could break down a citizen's door in midnight raids; and schoolchildren could not be taught about evolution. Writers and artists could be censored at the whim of government, and the doors of Federal courts would be shut on the fingers of millions of citizens. No justice would be better than this injustice."

On October 23, 1987, the Senate denied Bork's confirmation with 58 voting against him.

Since then, in American speech patterns and word usage, the term "to Bork" *[i.e., "to savage and vilify and ultimately, to nullify any possibility of candidate getting elevated to a position of influence,"]* entered English usage as a verb.

Another of Bill's classmates, although he didn't really get to know him, was the even more controversial Clarence Thomas, who would become the second African American to serve on the Supreme Court, succeeding the much more liberal Thurgood Marshall, known for his success in Brown Vs. Board of Education, a decision that eventually desegregated the nation's public schools.

In 1990, President H.W. Bush nominated the controversial, relentlessly right-wing Clarence Thomas for a seat on the U.S. Supreme Court, which caused outrage among the Democrats in the Senate. The subsequently televised Senate hearing became the most contentious and disputed nomination process in the history of the Supreme Court. Anita Hill came forward, accusing Thomas of sexually harassing her.

Thomas denied Hill's allegations, angrily defining the hearing as "a circus, a national disgrace, As a black American, it is a high-tech lynching for uppity Blacks. I'll be lynched, destroyed, caricatured by a committee of the U.S. Senate rather than hung from a tree."

Even so, the U.S. Senate ultimately confirmed Thomas by a vote of 52 to 48.

As Bill told friends, "Leave it to Daddy Bush to nominate an Uncle Tom. My god, in 2003, the fucker even upheld Texas' anti-gay sodomy laws."

Bill Proposes Marriage Four Times to Hillary: She Rejects Him Every Time

After graduation from the Yale Law School in 1973, Bill took Hillary on her first trip to Europe, stopping off in England to visit the venues he'd known beginning in 1968 as a Rhodes Scholar.

They drove together across England, beginning at his former stamping ground of Oxford, before he took her to the West Country, where they visited the cathedral city of Salisbury and the ancient ruins of Stonehenge.

Then, following in the footsteps of the poet Wordsworth, they drove north to the Lake District, one of the most romantic spots in the U.K.

As he sat holding her hand on the beautiful shores of Lake Ennderdale, he asked her to marry him.

"Not now, Bill," she told him, rejecting his proposal, which seemed to shock him. "I want my marriage to last. I don't want to make the mistake my mother did. I haven't really decided what I want to do in life."

Before he left England, he proposed three more times to her. Each time, she gracefully rejected his proposal.

Finally, exasperated, he told her, "I'm not going to ask you to marry me again. If you decide to marry me, you'll have to propose to me next time."

Although she had rejected each of his four of his previous proposals, she did accept one final request. He asked, when she returned to the States, to go with him for a visit to Arkansas.

To his surprise, she accepted his offer.

The rest is history.

Chapter Six

Head vs. Heart—Hillary's Dilemma: Pursue Her Own Hot Career in Washington DC? or Barge into the Sleepy Deep South as "Ma Kettle of the Ozarks"

Campaigning for a Boyfriend with a Wandering Eye, Hillary Hits the Backroads of Rural Arkansas

Hillary Works Behind the Scenes to Impeach Nixon

As the autumn winds blew over Fayetteville on October 11, 1975, Hillary Rodham married Bill Clinton. In this wedding photo *(left to right)*, Hillary is linked to Bill; his mother, Virginia; and his brother Roger.

At breakfast at the local Holiday Inn, Bill told his mother, "Hillary's keeping her own name."

"When he told me this, his actual words began to fade," Virginia said. "All I could focus on was the roar that filled my head. My tears started to flow."

"Probably more has been written or said about my marriage to Hillary than any other in America. I've always been amazed at the people who felt free to analyze, criticize, and pontificate about it. I've learned that marriage, with all its magic and misery, its contentments and disappointments, remains a mystery, not easy for those in it to understand and largely inaccessible to outsiders.

"I was thrilled to be in a relationship that might never be perfect, but would certainly never be boring."

—Bill Clinton

"Suppose I sat down to map out my life. Do you suppose I would have said I'd be married to the governor of Arkansas and practicing law in Little Rock? There is no way. I think life presents opportunities."

—Hillary Rodham Clinton

Whereas Hillary as a law professor was rigorous and demanding, Bill was more lenient.

He flirted with his female students, but many of his male students avoided him. Rumors were rife on campus that he was gay.

With Hillary in Washington and Bill teaching law at the University of Arkansas in Fayetteville, most of their romance was conducted by telephone, with an occasional short rendezvous in the nation's capital.

Although, during their time together in England, she had already rejected four separate marriage proposals, and despite his promises to stop insisting, he kept beseeching her to marry him and settle down with him in Arkansas.

Sometimes, as she reported to friends, their phone calls became bitter. One night, she bluntly told him. "It is not my desire to become a sacrificial political spouse, another Pat Nixon. I'm also not ready to be a doormat to a man who chases anything in skirts." Then she slammed down the phone, although she reconciled with him during his call the following morning.

Eventually, after much persuasion, she traveled to Arkansas for a visit. Before her arrival, Bill described her to his friends: "She has the biggest, most generous, the kindest heart, not to mention the most beautiful eyes. Her middle name is Diane. You know, that loving, gorgeous goddess."

Later, when he introduced her to his male friends, none of them seemed to agree that his initial description actually corresponded to the young woman who stood before them wearing jeans, a work shirt, large glasses, and not a trace of makeup.

Arkansas Voters Want To Know:

"Is Bill Clinton a Womanizer or a Homosexual?"

Hillary had driven to Arkansas with friends, who repeatedly warned her that settling in the backwoods of the South would mean giving up a great career. She was hearing that a lot.

Shortly after her arrival, instead of immediately hauling her off to meet Virginia and Roger, Bill took her on a scenic tour of Arkansas, meandering into the mountains and stopping at scenic lookouts. She called him "a one-man Chamber of Commerce promoting Arkansas."

Years later, she told a reporter from *Newsweek,* "We drove around for eight hours. He took me to all the places he considered beautiful, including the state parks. For food, we stopped in one of his favorite barbecue places. Then we drove down the road until he came to a place that specialized in fried pies. Yes, fried. My head was reeling because I didn't know what I was going to see or what to expect in this land where people fried pies."

Finally, after all that motoring—and presumably, all that courting—he drove her home to meet Virginia, who had already been briefly introduced to her at Yale.

Wearing tailored red silk men's pajamas and mules, with a cigarette dangling from the corner of her mouth, Bill's overpainted mother greeted Hillary.

She was even less impressed with Hillary on their second meeting than she had been on the first. She would later spread the word, "I could grind my teeth and wish I could sit Hillary on the edge of my tub and teach her a lesson in makeup."

As part of his campaign to lure Hillary to his home state, Bill aggressively promoted the scenic wonders of Arkansas. She was struggling at the time with her hopes, dreams, and conflicting emotions about her career.

A rumor persisted for years that Bill had been hostile to then-president Richard Nixon when he visited Fayetteville in 1969 for the Texas vs. Arkansas football game.

Protesting the Vietnam War, a young man in a tree shouted obscenities at him. Rumor had it that it was Bill in that tree.

Actually, he had been in Oxford, England, at the time.

In *Gentlemen Prefer Blondes*, the 1953 Hollywood musical, Marilyn Monroe and Jane Russell pretended, unconvincingly, that they were "just two little girls from Little Rock."

When word reached Hillary about what Virginia had said, she responded in anger. "I have no desire to make myself up like a clown. Virginia learned about penciled eyebrows from watching Joan Crawford movies. She seems to have learned makeup from Tammy Lee Baker. She must wear at least a half inch of pancake makeup and enough powder to spray half of Arkansas' fields from a cropduster."

After Roger met Hillary, he told Virginia, "I didn't know that Big Brother made passes at girls who wear glasses. She isn't the usual dance hall floozie he brings home. She looks tough, the kind of gal you want working for you—not against you."

"Bill usually dated Barbie Doll types," said Little Brother. "Hillary was different...and how! Rather brilliant. I was jealous of her. I also felt intimidated by her straightforward manner and female independence. I grew up in a culture where women were subservient to men."

During her first visit to Bill's home state, Hillary and Bill had many arguments about Arkansas. The future First Lady of the state asked, "What is it known for? Its Ozark culture and backwoods poverty. Don't forget racism."

She was referring to the notorious 1957 attempt by nine black students to enroll at the all-white Little Rock Central High School. Although then-governor Orval Faubus summoned the National Guard to block their entrance, they stood down when President Eisenhower summoned military forces from the U.S. Army's 101st Airborne Division to oppose them.

Bill was eloquent in the defense of his home state and of the political opportunities that awaited him here. As she left Arkansas, heading back to her job and her life in Washington, she was still unsure about how to play their futures, separately or together.

Her friend, Carolyn Ellis, said, "Bill's inviting her to come and to settle in Arkansas was like inviting her to come and live on the moon."

He was asking that she immerse herself in the politics and lifestyles of the second poorest state in the Union, and to abandon a spectacularly promising career as either a lawyer or as a politician in Washington or possibly in New York, each a

Little Rock Central High School
Architectural grandeur that belied its contentious past.

It was here that Governor Orval Faubus proclaimed, "Segregation yesterday, segregation today, and segregation tomorrow."

focal point of world power. Instead, he was proposing that she move to Little Rock, the sleepy backwater hometown of characters played by Marilyn Monroe and Jane Russell in the 1953 musical, *Gentlemen Prefer Blondes.*

After a night of lovemaking with Bill, she drove back to Washington to fulfill an important commitment she had made: To work with an investigating committee whose aim involved justifying impeachment proceedings against then-President Richard Nixon, a man she'd already defined as "evil."

Was Nixon a Vicious Homophobe? An Enraged Anti-Semite? A Dyed-in-the-Wool Woman Hater? Hillary Wants to Know!

After her graduation from Yale Law School in 1974, Hillary worked as an attorney for Marian Wright Edelman's fledging Children's Defense Fund in Cambridge. But in January, she was lured away by John Doar to serve on the House Judiciary Committee preparing for the impeachment of President Richard Nixon.

[In integration and liberal circles, Doar had already evolved into something of a cult celebrity for having spearheaded the government's response to the admission and bodily protection of James Meredith as the first black student at the University of Mississipi. He continued playing a key role in the civil rights movement as it applied to the promotion of voter registration and racial integration in the South.]

Doar had previously invited Bill Clinton to work on his panel, but was turned down, Bill explaining that he wanted to concentrate instead on seeking political office in Arkansas. He recommended Hillary instead. Apparently, even without Bill's recommendation, Doar had already planned to invite her to join his panel.

He was a stern taskmaster, warning Hillary not to discuss the impeachment proceedings with the press. He reminded her of a "Gary Cooper" type, a quiet lanky lawyer from Wisconsin." He had previously worked for then-Attorney General Robert F. Kennedy, during his administration (1961-1964) of the Justice Department.

Soon, Hillary found herself analyzing documents pertinent to Nixon's impeachment proceedings, including diaries and tapes sent to the Doar Committee by Senator Sam Ervin's Senate Committee to investigate the Watergate break-ins.

For very little pay, she pored over documents within dank, rigorously guarded, and makeshift offices in the Old Congressional Hotel on Capitol Hill. Behind prison-like bars, she labored during sessions lasting between twelve and eighteen hours. Some of them caused her eyes to turn red and to ache from the strain.

After her graduation in 1974 from Yale Law School, Hillary worked for the Children's Defense Fund, supervised by Marian Wright Edelman *(depicted above)*. She was the first black woman admitted to the bar in Mississippi.

Edelman assigned Hillary to conduct research on the education and health of migrant children. "They led harsh lives, yet they were bright, hopeful, and loved by their poverty-stricken parents," Hillary said.

Much of the language she came across in documents pertinent to Nixon she found "vulgar, often obscene. Nixon and the men around him didn't speak the Queen's English," she said. "They were vile, sometimes sounding like a caricature of Mafia bosses, with whom Nixon had dark ties."

Long before her work was finished, she had already concluded that Nixon should be impeached for a number of reasons, not just the burglary he had sanctioned at Democratic offices at Watergate, but because of his secret bombings of Cambodia. "It was not only immoral but criminal," she claimed.

She later recalled that her most fascinating moments arrived during the playing of "the tape of tapes," that is, Nixon listening to what he had said on previous tapes and trying to cover up his statements. Time and time again, she heard him utter "What I meant to say is this..."

"If you say I hate Jews and homosexuals," Hillary said, "how can you justify that with a later revision of your words? The only group he left off his hate list were gypsies."

When "inside the Beltway" Washington learned about the Doar committee's findings, Hillary noticed a vast increase in the amounts of mail she received from named and unnamed sources associated with Nixon's White House. Many of them loathed the president and wanted to contribute to his destruction through revelations of his darkest secrets.

During Hillary's investigation, she became familiar with details associated with Nixon's serious, even dangerous problem with alcohol. This was especially alarming since "the football" was always near him, the control box that would allow him to launch a nuclear attack against any target in the world.

Even one of Nixon's closest and highest-ranking associates, Secretary of State Henry Kissinger, became immune to his calls at two or three o'clock in the morning. According to evidence she unearthed, one of Nixon's most chilling commands, issued to Kissinger before he talked him out of it, was to "Nuke 'em!"

She learned that Nixon was "quite drunk—raging and raving" in the immediate aftermath of North Korea's shootdown of a U.S. Navy reconnaissance plane over the Sea of Japan. He suggested that Kissinger consider the use of B-52 bombing raids, perhaps using nuclear weapons, of the North Korean mainland.

Kissinger later informed his aides, "I was the one who kept that drunken lunatic from blowing up the world."

As an ardent feminist, Hillary was appalled to learn about Nixon's oft-disguised attitude toward women. He was said to have despised women in general, declaring at one point, "I don't think women should be educated." One of Nixon's aides, Jim Bassett, claimed, "Nixon has a total scorn for the female mentality."

Nixon did most of his drinking with his best friend and longtime companion—some say male lover—Bebe Rebozo, a rich banker and real estate speculator with ties to the Mafia. Throughout the course of his presidency, Nixon was with Rebozo one out of every ten days. The Cuban-born American had full access to his own bedroom and his own office within the White House, out of which he came and went as if it were his home.

During her time on the Doar committee, Hillary also read reports that Nixon was a "vociferous homophobe," asserting in one document that he would not shake the hand of anyone who lived in San Francisco. He was constantly claiming that "Aristotle and Socrates were homos, and homosexuality destroyed the glory that was Greece."

Nixon biographer, Don Fulsom, a longtime White House reporter, suggested that Nixon's expressed antagonism toward gays was a cover for his own repressed homosexuality or bisexuality, especially as it manifested itself with Rebozo, who was known for hosting notorious, all-gay pool parties in South Florida.

At Key Biscayne, Nixon and Rebozo would go out together at night, patronizing local restaurants. One diner, who happened to be a reporter for *The Miami Herald,* noticed them at a corner table together getting drunk. As they left, he saw Nixon "schmoozing the room, doing some glad-handing in spite of his condition. "He had one arm wrapped around Rebozo like he was his senior prom date," the reporter claimed.

Bobby Baker, a scandal-soaked former aide to Lyndon B. Johnson, said, "Bebe loved Nixon more than he loved anybody. He worshipped him, in fact. Nixon was his God, his Little Jesus."

According to LBJ, "I don't know how anyone could make love to Nixon, even Pat, but if there's one person on earth who can stomach the fucker, it's that Cubano faggot, Bebe Rebozo, down there in Miami."

General Alexander Haig *[Nixon's last and final Chief of Staff, and later, Supreme Commander of Allied Forces in Europe (1974-79) and Secretary of State (1981-82) under Ronald Reagan]* was overheard mocking "Nixon's limp-wristed friend" and joking about his gay relationship with Nixon.

[On the death of Richard Nixon in 1994, Rebozo told The Miami Herald, *"For forty-five years, he enriched my life."*

Rebozo himself died four years later, willing $19 million to the Nixon Library in Yorba Linda, California.]

The New York Times

NIXON RESIGNS

HE URGES A TIME OF 'HEALING'; FORD WILL TAKE OFFICE TODAY

'Sacrifice' Is Praised; Kissinger to Remain

The 37th President Is First to Quit Post

When Hillary picked up a copy of *The New York Times*, she was relieved but disappointed to read the heading—NIXON RESIGNS.

"Now all the work I did to impeach him has gone to waste," she lamented.

On August 4, 1974, Hillary was stunned that all the time and labor she'd invested in the impeachment proceedings against Nixon would never be applied in a judicial court. Nixon had resigned to escape from the impeachment proceedings she had already, to some degree, orchestrated.

Her work became moot and "historical" on September 8, 1974, when Nixon's replacement, former Vice-President Gerald Ford, stunned the nation by granting his crooked predecessor a blanket pardon for all White House crimes. "The pardon is full, free, and absolute," Ford ordained, thereby dooming his own chances for election as president in the upcoming (1976) elections.

Hillary's work researching the political sins of Richard Nixon later came back to haunt her. During her term with the Doar Committee, she argued for broader and more inclusive legal justifications for the impeachment of a sitting U.S. President. She was painfully reminded of her role in streamlining the process when her own husband faced impeachment proceedings himself in December of 1998.

***

In the month before she left Washington, she seemed hesitant to tell her new friends goodbye, including Fred Altshuler, who had worked with her on the "Impeach Nixon" committee. She shared her misgivings about Arkansas with her boss, John Doar, who warned her that she had probably abandoned a grand career in politics "to bury yourself in some redneck cabbage patch."

Years later, she discussed that time in her life with a reporter from *Vanity Fair.* "I didn't find anything in Washington that provided the challenges that Arkansas did. I decided that I should at least explore marriage to Bill, although I had my doubts. It was a very confused time for me."

When she arrived at Adams Air Field outside Little Rock, Bill was waiting there to pick her up. She had already shipped a lot of her possessions, including her books.

Together, they headed for Arkansas' northwest corner, to Fayetteville, home of the University of Arkansas, a three-to-four-hour drive from Little Rock. Like Bill, she had been hired there as a professor of law.

***

Unlike some of the towns and hamlets she had visited, she found that Fayetteville, lined with trees, had a certain charm, set as it was in the foothills of the Ozark Mountains, close to the border with Missouri.

When they got there, he drove her by a little house that she'd passed by on her first trip, noticing a FOR SALE sign. At the time, she had remarked on its charm.

Bill had a surprise: Without her ever having gone inside, he had purchased the house for $20,000, based on a $3,000 down payment and a mortgage of $174 a month.

Virginia, by now, was adamantly opposed to Bill marrying Hillary. Previously, whenever she'd presented her anti-Hillary case to Bill, he had stormed out of the room, charging that she wanted him to marry some fire-and-ice queen like Grace Kelly or else a sex goddess like Marilyn Monroe. Now, learning that Hillary was once again in Arkansas, Virginia intensified her anti-Hillary lobbying.

Mary Lee Fray, one of Bill's best friends, said, "Virginia loathed Hillary at least for the first years until she came to tolerate her. Anything she could say to pick on Hillary, she did. She once told me that Bill should not bring a woman like Hillary to Arkansas, where she would sabotage his future career in politics."

"The locals will take her for a Yankee hippie," Virginia claimed.

In Fayetteville, for appearance's sake, because they weren't yet married, they opted to live at separate addresses.

"Of course, if you want to become governor of Arkansas with me as your First Lady, we can't live in sin," she said. "I understand that."

He promised, however, to slip over to her place every night, retreating back to his own apartment during the pre-dawn hours.

In Fayetteville, with the understanding that the newly purchased house would be occupied by Bill, she rented a big-windowed, three-bedroom house that evoked a Frank Lloyd Wright design, bow-shaped and glassy, with an interior divided into oddly shaped rooms. It belonged to a friends of hers, Rafael Guzman. In the backyard was a large swimming pool, in which they would frolic at night. There were rumors of nude, after-midnight swimming parties.

Before Hillary's arrival on campus, a student, Betsy Beyer, said, "Bill was a walking streak of sex on campus. He wore his hair, a deep auburn, long like one of his students. He preferred corduroy jackets with leather sewn on the elbows. He always wore bright plaid shirts, often red. In all, I met at least five girls who had gone to bed with him, even though teachers and students were not supposed to have sex with each other. Bill always seemed to have the attitude that rules were not made for him."

With a certain embarrassment, Hillary confided to him that she'd failed the bar exam in Washington, a confession that shocked him. "The cards must have been stacked against you," he said. "You have a brilliant legal mind." Then he urged her to take the bar exam again, this time for the practice of law in Arkansas.

She did, and she passed. "At least I can practice law here," she said, still embarrassed at her failure, and its subsequent blow to her ego, in Washington.

At the university, Bill and Hillary, as professors, maintained very different styles. Bill was easy-going and an "easy grader," whereas Hillary was very strict, very formal, and a harsh grader.

One of her male students, who didn't want to be named, said, "Frankly, I resented being taught by a female. Also, Hillary didn't dress sexy like the other girls in school. I wanted to take her to some cowfield and give her a really good fuck with my Southern pecker. Maybe that would have taught her how to be more of a woman and not try to boss men around."

In contrast to Hillary's rigorously disciplined teaching style, students found Bill rather sloppy. "He didn't teach from notes," said Mary Hemphill. "But he had oodles of charm. Often, we'd skip the lesson for the day and talk about Nixon, the Supreme Court, abortion, stuff like that. It was rather enjoyable."

At the end of the semester, he accidentally lost all of our exams," Hemphill said. "In lieu of that, he gave all of us a passing grade. Even the dumbest in the class got a C. He paid a lot of attention to the black students."

[Bill was not admired by all of his students, an example of whom was Susan Webber Wright. Before the end of the 1990s, she'd become a judge in Arkansas. When Bill was held in contempt of court for "giving false testimony and being evasive in the Paula Jones sexual harassment case," she fined him $90,000, even though he'd given her an A in his course.]

Deep in the heart of the Ozarks, this lovely home in Fayetteville was the setting, on October 11, 1975, of one of the most famous marriages in America. Two law professors at the local university were united—Bill Clinton taking Hillary Rodham for his bride.

Depending on how the election of 2016 turns out, their union might represent the only time in the history of the Republic when a future President of the United States has married another future President of the United States.

Today, their former abode, cramped and with only one bedroom, is a museum, with a focus on Clinton memorabilia.

For Hillary's introduction to the charms of Arkansas, Fayetteville was a worthy choice. Since it was a college community, she met better-educated people and found it easier to make friends.

As she confessed in a memoir, Hillary soon found herself cheering the Arkansas Razorbacks at football games and yelling the hog call, *"Suuuuu-eeee, suuuuu-eeeee!"*

In Fayetteville, Diane Blair, a professor of political science at the university, became Hillary's best friend. To some degree, she understood Hillary's dilemma, since she, too, had moved from Washington, D.C., to be with her husband. Blair recalled her first discussion with Bill about Hillary. It took place at the Student Union.

"Hillary is a paragon, the smartest woman I've ever known," he said. "I want to marry her and bring her here, but I have guilt about it. It's my state and my political career. Staying where she is in the northeast could mean a brilliant career of her own, perhaps a run for governor or a U.S. Senate seat from Illinois."

A student, Lorena Leddy, was surprised that even with Hillary on staff at the university, Bill continued with his rather brazen approach to girls. He always put his arm around a girl, and in a few cases, his hand landed on a breast. "Amazingly none of the little sluts in my class objected. He made very suggestive remarks to many of the girls, but he never pulled that shit with me.

Even though he was my professor, I would have hauled off and smacked him one to teach him some manners. I was going steady. One afternoon, Bill asked me if my boyfriend was 'delivering anything good.'"

Student Dale Donovan later said, "Actually, rumors arose on campus that Bill was a homosexual. A lot of guys were warned to stay clear of him, fearing he might put the make on us. I know he had a reputation for flirting with all the gals, but a lot of us thought that was just a coverup to conceal his homosexuality. After all, he was almost thirty years old, and unmarried. In Arkansas back then, that meant you were gay. When Hillary showed up, a lot of us were still not convinced. Again, we thought that was just for show because she looked like a lesbian. We thought they were pretending a love affair to conceal their true sexual preferences."

During a break in the curriculum, Hillary scheduled time out of the state for visits to family members and friends. The time had come for her to agree to either marry Bill or else to end their relationship.

In Washington, Carolyn Ellis, who was still one of her best friends, urged her to return to Arkansas and marry Bill. "She seemed in love with him, and he was obviously in love with her. She knew that if she didn't return and marry him, and stayed in Washington and took another job, it would soon be all over for them."

At Park Ridge, outside Chicago, both Dorothy and Hugh—still a staunch Republican—shared grave reservations about Hillary's migration to Arkansas and the implications it carried about marrying Bill.

After leaving her parents, she seemed more confused than ever. Hugh had almost convinced her that she'd be sabotaging the career for which she had labored so hard and for which he had paid so much for her education.

Dorothy's maternal advice to her was, "Bill's not the man for you. You deserve much better."

Shortly thereafter, in Washington, Dorothy's words seemed to ring true after Hillary received a phone call from someone in Fayetteville. It is not known if the person were male or female, or whether it was a friend of hers or else an enemy of Bill's.

Stern and difficult to impress: Susan Webber Wright was a student—and later, a judge—that Professor Clinton did NOT successfully charm.

The information delivered to her during the course of the phone conversation was that Bill was deep into a torrid affair with Marla Crider, a 20-year-old political science student at the University of Arkansas.

Enraged, Hillary phoned Bill and informed him

that she had launched an affair (perhaps based on getting even) with a young attorney in Washington that she refused to name.

Paul Fray, who was on the dawn of getting designated as Bill's campaign manager in his first Congressional race, overheard Bill talking to Hillary.

"At one point, Bill broke down and cried over the phone," Fray reported. "He asked her why she wanted to make his life miserable."

Using all his personal charm, warmth, and charisma, Bill managed to persuade Hillary to return to Arkansas and to forgive him for his transgression. He did not deny it.

"For the sake of love," as she told Carolyn Ellis in the aftermath of their reconciliation, "I will return to Arkansas. But not for one minute do I believe that Bill will keep his promise and be faithful to me, even or especially if I marry him. I don't even believe that he will give up this college girl infatuation until it's run its course, as I'm sure it will. He's a love 'em and leave 'em type of guy."

"I may even marry the cad," she went on to say. "After all, Eleanor forgave Franklin. I don't think sexual fidelity should be the test of every marriage or the tie that binds. I think it's sharing a common goal like traveling the road to political power in America, as tortuous as that damn highway might be for both of us."

"I'm told that the Queen of England doesn't expect fidelity from Prince Philip. But she does expect loyalty, and at the end of a long marriage, it's loyalty that counts more than anything else in a marriage. Not where Bill puts his wee-wee from time to time."

***

Newly returned to Fayetteville, Hillary experienced what she'd later define as "The most carefree and happiest time in my romance with Bill. Although trouble, more than we ever dreamed, lay ahead, we had some halcyon weeks in Fayetteville as members of the faculty. It was a college town where you could make new friends and really get to know people. At my house, with its swimming pool, we often had friends in for dinner and spent long hours sitting out on moonlit nights talking till very very late—and not just about politics."

One night, he drove her south along Highway 71 to Alma, Arkansas *[a town that bills itself as "Spinach capital of the world" because of the approximately 60 million pounds which are canned there annually by the Allen Canning Company]*, to attend a concert by Dolly Parton. "Next to Elvis," Bill said, "Dolly was my favorite. How can I say this? She was in good form that night—in fact, she was busting out all over."

As a professor of law at the University of Arkansas, Hillary pursued an aggressive campaign for liberalization within a conservative, mostly male bastion. She launched a Rape Crisis Center in Fayetteville, based on complaints from co-eds and local residents about sexual and physical violence against women. "It was fairly common back then for men to beat up their wives at the slightest provocation."

She appeared before the Arkansas Law Association, urging its mostly male members to establish Legal Aid programs to benefit poor African Americans who face trouble with the law.

In this campaign photograph, Paul Fray *(left)* ran Bill Clinton's unsuccessful race for Congress in 1974. From Washington, where she was serving at the time on the "Impeach Nixon" committee, Hillary telephoned daily, telling Fray how to run the campaign.

Finally, Fray, in disgust, yelled to his staff: "What in the fuck does this gal know about how a guy gets elected in Arkansas?"

Their tranquility would not last for long. One night, sitting in her backyard beside the pool, Bill told Hillary that, "I want to be one of the Democratic Watergate babies swept into power as payback to the Republicans for giving the nation Richard Nixon."

That occurred the same night he told her that he had decided to run for Congress. At the age of twenty-eight, he was going to take a big chance and challenge a popular congressman from his district, John Paul Hammerschmidt, who had carried 72 percent of the vote in the 1972 election.

When Virginia was informed of his decision, she purchased a blue and white seersucker suit for him. "Who ever heard of a Southern politician worth his salt who didn't own a seersucker suit?" she asked.

Bill's friend, Paul Fray, was named as his campaign manager, though before long, Hillary was trying to take over running the show herself. She viewed Fray as a "sticky-fingered white trash political hack."

Fray's wife, Mary Lee, claimed that "Hillary had to learn the Southern way of politics. Down here, we feed you a slice of peach pie before throwing acid in your face."

As his campaign manager, from the onset of the campaign, Fray had to deal with Bill's womanizing."Whenever I saw Hillary pull into the parking lot, I had to hustle Marla Crider out the back door just in the nick of time."

Fray said that Bill launched his campaign with just $10,000 his uncle Raymond Clinton had given them. "Bill was broke, busted, and begging for some cash."

After announcing his candidacy, Bill set out in his little green Gremlin to tour the counties in his district, collecting business cards and making friends for the day he would run for governor. "He related to people very well," Fray said, "Although he encountered the eventual hostility—he was called 'nigger lover,' and shit like that."

Whenever possible, Hillary joined him on the campaign trail. She was introduced to Arkansas style campaigning—potluck suppers, chicken fries, livestock auctions, political rallies, apple pie bake-offs, and fund raising where she learned the meaning of the saying that "all politics are local."

Even when she wasn't at campaign headquarters, she was on the phone at least three times a day, advising Fray about what to do. "Who told her she knew how to run a congressional campaign in the Ozarks?" he asked. "Her advice often wasn't that germane."

A campaign aide, Hal McDonald, said, "Bill ended up with a girlfriend in every county of his district."

Bill's future campaign aide, Dick Morris, didn't quite understand Bill's physical attraction to women. "He looked like a mama's boy. He didn't control his junk food diet, and he was a bit pudgy around the hips, with a potbelly that was emerging. He was rather gangly in his legs, but the kid had charisma, and that went a long way."

Betsey Wright, who had worked with Bill in Texas, campaigning for Senator McGovern, said, "Gals were falling all over him. They treated him like a rock star. Sometimes, when he walked into our headquarters, some of the staff would say, 'Here comes Elvis!'"

Arthur David Brock wrote, "Arkansas politics are notoriously rumor-charged, and it was only a matter of time before Hillary felt the sting of unfounded stories about herself. The rumors emanated from the Gaslite Bar in Little Rock, where political cronies caroused. Hillary was labeled a lesbian and that reflected a deep-dyed cultural prejudice against a woman who didn't wear panty hose, sexy high heels, or fit the Southern male's image of how a woman should look and behave."

Without going into detail, Hillary in her first memoir wrote of "a barrage of personal attacks and dirty tricks the Republicans were pulling."

The homosexual rumors that had risen to the surface at the University of Arkansas somehow seeped into the campaign. "Clinton is a homosexual," was heard frequently. There were even rumors that he'd been having a torrid affair with one of the football players for the Razorbacks. These were false charges.

However, in total contrast to the gay rumors, there were more serious—

and more accurate—charges that he was a womanizer. Some fire-breathing Baptist pastors even attacked him from the pulpit, alleging "a series of affairs with underage gals." He was also accused of "living in sin with a Yankee woman."

At a labor union rally in Fort Smith, a stronghold of Bill's Republican opponent, he was publicly attacked as a "left-wing dope and sex addict."

One labor leader yelled out, "I wouldn't piss in your brain even if it was on fire."

Hillary urged Bill to fight back and attack these rumors. Fray was riding in the front seat of a car, with Hillary "the back seat driver."

She was urging a counterattack. "For God's sake, Bill, for once in your life, don't be an asshole. If you want to lose this election because you're chickenshit, then count me out!"

When John Paul Hammerschmidt had run for Congress in 1972, rumors had circulated that he was a womanizer, too. Then, the Democrats had launched a counter offensive, claiming, "SEND JOHN PAUL TO WASHINGTON, THE WIFE YOU SAVE MAY BE YOUR OWN."

Although Hillary had initially demanded an offensive assault, she ultimately vetoed the idea of such a campaign strategy against their opponent, perhaps fearing that it might backfire.

The lovely Clinton congressional campaign aide, Marla Crider *(depicted above)* was the beauty Bill's mother, Virginia, wanted her son to marry instead of Hillary.

While working in Washington, Hillary learned that Bill had developed a "serious romance" with Crider and that he was shacked up with her back in Little Rock.

Bill's campaign manager, Paul Fray, claimed that Marla was "just Bill's type. Brown hair the color of bark, green cat eyes that were bewitching, a smile to brighten a gray day, olive skin smooth as a baby's ass, and a piquant face that held out such promise. I never understood why Bill married Hillary, when he could have had this lovely, bewitching Arkansas belle."

An aide, Douglas Wallace, said, "Paul wanted to play hardball, cut and slash. Miss Rodham did not want to go there."

A Clinton campaign aide, who didn't want to be named, claimed, "Hillary always arrived at campaign headquarters ready to kick ass. She ordered people around. She didn't have our laidback Southern way of doing things. She was a real dictator, not friendly at all. Our loyalty was to Bill, not to her. She didn't even want us to take coffee breaks. She'd bust us up and tell us to get back to work. After a few days, I quit. I wasn't going to take that Yankee shit. The day I left, the Rodhams arrived from Chicago."

Hillary had decided to rally what her detractors at the time defined as "her personal troops, and subsequently, "The Rodham Yankees arrived in a Cadillac with Illinois license plates." Fray said.

He was referring to Hillary's father, Hugh, and to her two brothers, Hughie and Tony. Both had accepted her invitation to campaign in Arkansas for Bill. Fray speculated that Hillary also needed family members to keep Bill's womanizing in check.

It was suggested that Hugh rub his Illinois license plates with mud during his rounds though the Congressional district nailing up VOTE FOR CLINTON signs wherever they could.

One Clinton campaign aide telephoned Fray and said, "There are some Yankee boys up here driving around in a Cadillac with Illinois plates urging us to vote for your boy, Bill. What in hell should we do?"

To these rural people, Illinois meant Chicago, and Chicago meant gangsters. Rumors soon spread the Bill had "fat members of the Mafia" coming to Arkansas to campaign for him. There was speculation that the mob—the same organization that had once attracted Al Capone and other Chicago-based gangsters—wanted to rejuvenate gambling in Hot Springs.

Although a confirmed Republican, Hugh was often seen chatting with the good old boys, chewing tobacco, and spitting the juice. He may have been of some vague, unfocused help to Bill, but aides said that on most days, he was "gone fishing."

Hillary became reliant not only her own "Rodham police force," but on other spies as well for reports about Bill's sexual transgressions as he traveled around the state without her. She was acutely aware, even back then, that his sexual dalliances were a threat both to his own political career and to her future plans.

A news story appeared in the Hope *Star* with Bill's take on the current fad of streaking. "It's a little extreme for my taste," he told a reporter for the Associated Press. "And I find it offensive. It, too, will pass. It's somewhat like the popular habit of mooning when I was in high school. You drop your drawers and stick your fat ass out of the window to a passing car."

Finally, election night came. As a Democrat, Bill had scored an impressive record, attracting 48 percent of the vote. Hammerschmidt's percentage of the vote, however, had shot up to 52 percent after the labor-oriented vote was tallied from Fort Smith.

After the results were announced at Bill's campaign headquarters, Hillary picked up a ringing telephone, thinking the call-in might be a supporter. Instead, it was an anonymous caller with a thick Southern accent, who shouted into the phone, "I'm so glad that nigger-loving commie fag, Bill Clinton, lost." Then he slammed down the receiver.

Tensions burst out that election night between Hillary and Paul Fray. "You're the guy who found a bedmate for Bill when I was up in Washington trying to get rid of Nixon! You're nothing but a god damn Jew bastard!"

"Bill Is Making an Honest Woman Out of that Yankee Girl."

—Talk from the Local Yokels

After Bill's loss of a congressional seat, Hillary flew North to huddle with family and friends. She met with her friend, Bernard Nussbaum, who later would be designated as President Clinton's Chief of Staff.

She was filled with despair. "I fear I've backed a loser. I don't think Bill will ever become President."

As she told Nussbaum goodbye and headed for the airport in advance of her return to Arkansas, she mourned, "It's like I'm going back to Australia in 1956, where Jell-O is not only served for dessert, but can take over one's brain. But I love the guy in spite of everything."

"Who knows, I might find a handsome Arkansas lover boy myself," she continued.

When, after months of indecision, she finally decided to marry Bill. Then, she even managed to persuade the Rodhams to move to Arkansas with her. She told Hugh and Dorothy, "Perhaps with the Rodham police, all of us can watch over Bill, curbing his Rabelaisian appetite for sex."

Dorothy arrived in Arkansas in time to help Hillary prepare for her wedding. She accompanied her daughter to Dillard's Department Store in Fayetteville, where the bride-to-be purchased an off-the-rack white wedding dress trimmed in Victorian lace.

Hillary also went out and bought some furnishings, linens, and dishes for their sparsely furnished new home. She even got Hugh to repair their screened-in porch, which had gaping holes that let in the flies and mosquitoes.

Their new home in Fayetteville was so small that only family and a few friends could fit into its living room for the wedding. The ceremony was conducted by Victor Nixon, a Methodist minister. "He would be named Nixon!" Hillary quipped.

Roger Clinton was Bill's Best Man. The groom had not quite reached his 30th birthday, and Hillary was 27. The date was October 11, 1975.

Years later, Bill said, "No marriage in the history of the Republic has ever been more debated, dished, dissected and ravaged than our union."

Paul Fray weighed in with his opinion. "There was one good reason Bill married Hillary. It was his attempt to show the world he wasn't white trash."

After their vows had been exchanged, the wedding party adjourned to a large reception at the home of their friends, Ann and Morriss Henry, who opened their house and gardens to more than 200 guests. Morriss was the chairman of the local branch of the Democratic Party.

Bill turned the event into a rally for a future campaign.

As he told Morriss, "JFK married for beauty. As you can plainly see—emphasis on plain—I married for brains."

In a surprise move, Dorothy arranged the honeymoon, paying for discounted airfare to Acapulco *[site of JFK'S honeymoon with Jackie in 1953]* on the West Coast of Mexico, for more than just the bride and groom. After booking one of the largest family suites she could find through a travel agent, she planned a holiday not only for the honeymooners, but for Hugh, Hughdie, Tony, and herself, as well.

As diversion during his honeymoon, in case he tired of making love to Hillary with her family sitting outside in the living room, Bill brought along one book. It was Ernest Becker's *The Denial of Death.*

At the end of their (communal and family-centered) honeymoon, Dorothy delivered her opinion to her family. "Bill supplies the passion for a political life, and Hillary comes in to put everything in focus."

As Bill Becomes Attorney General of Arkansas
The Clintons Campaign for Jimmy Carter

Soon after his wedding, Bill firmly positioned himself to run for Attorney General of Arkansas, which, if he won, would mean moving from Fayetteville to Little Rock. They would have to give up their positions as professors of law at the University of Arkansas.

The current attorney general, Guy Tucker, had called Bill and told him that he would not seek re-election. He had aimed his sights on the congressional seat formerly held by the Arkansas Congressman, the disgraced Wilbur Mills, who had been the powerful chairman of the House Ways and Means Committee.

An alcoholic, Mills been involved in several widely publicized scandals, one of which had focused on the stripper, Fanne Foxe, nicknamed "the Argentine Firecracker." They were photographed together in a drunken romp jumping into the Tidal Basin in Washington, D.C.

After announcing his candidacy, Bill found himself running in the primary against two other politicians, each seeking the Democratic nomination.

In Little Rock, in January of 1975, Bill opened his campaign headquarters. During the first months of the campaign, Hillary saw little of him, as she continued her role as a professor in Fayetteville.

For the next six months, Bill, along with the Rodham brothers, crisscrossed the state for votes.

He won the Democratic primary, garnering slightly less than 56 percent of the vote, and beating out two opponents. He faced the November election with no competition from the Republicans.

Representing Arkansas, both Bill and Hillary attended the Democratic National Convention in July of 1976 in New York City, the event that would nominate Jimmy Carter as the Democratic Party's candidate for president, with Walter Mondale as his VP. While there, Bill signed on as Chairman for the Arkansas Committee to elect Carter.

That November election was vital for the Democrats. A peanut farmer from Georgia, Jimmy Carter, governor of that state, was planning to run for president against Gerald Ford, who had taken over the Oval Office after the resignation, midterm, of Richard Nixon.

Later, when Carter announced his plan to campaign in Arkansas, both of them were there to greet him. Although later, the president-to-be remembered meeting Bill, he did not recall having been introduced to Hillary.

In Arkansas, he approached her and said, "Hi, I'm Jimmy Carter. I'm gonna be the next president."

"Well, governor," she answered. "I wouldn't go around telling people that. It might be off-putting to them."

"But I'm going to be president," he protested. "I just talked to Bill Clinton. He told me that after I become president for eight years, he's going to run for president himself."

"I know that upstart kid," she said. "He's my husband."

Before he left Arkansas, Carter and Bill mulled over his campaign in Arkansas. Then, in a surprise move, Carter asked Hillary to go to Indiana to become a field coordinator for him, even though that meant a separation between herself and the husband she had recently married. She agreed to do it.

In 2015, when Bill learned that Jimmy Carter had been diagnosed with cancer, he expressed his deep sorrow.

However, when Carter was president, the two men often conflicted, Bill calling him "That god damn peanut farmer from Georgia."

In Indiana, she regretted her decision when it became clear that she probably would never get along with the male-dominated local Democrats. In one tense meeting, one of the campaign directors grabbed her by her Peter Pan collar and told her, "Now listen, girlie, here in Indiana, bitches rattle those pots and pans in the kitchen and don't tell us men how to run a political campaign."

She slapped his face and stormed out of the room. She might have even been secretly pleased that these men, who refused to adhere to her campaign strategy, eventually lost the Indiana vote for Carter.

On election night, November 2, 1976, Bill, in Arkansas, swept to victory as that state's newest Attorney General.

Hillary, however, referencing her performance in Indiana, lamented "We lost Indiana for Carter. He got only 46 percent of the vote, but nobody, not even Carter, ever expected him to carry this Republican stronghold. But god damn it, I sure put up the good fight, and I learned a lot about campaigning."

When Virginia heard that her son had been elected as the next Attorney General of Arkansas, she told friends, "I hope he won't throw me in jail for all those speeding tickets I've gotten."

Before moving from Fayetteville to Little Rock, and before abandoning her teaching job, Hillary told friends, "During the congressional race, Bill and I were accused of living in sin. We still are. The sin of adultery. That's my Bill. Marriage hasn't changed him. He'll never change.

Hillary is seen shortly after moving to Arkansas to join her lover, the aspiring young politician, Bill Clinton. She defined his previous affairs as “short, sexual, casual, and one-dimensional.”

Before her move to the Ozarks, she had had several romances and nurtured dreams that were distinctly different from those of her husband.

Those dreams had included bumming around Europe and Africa; working at a crafts center in the Carolinas, at a theater in Los Angeles, or in the TV indusry in New York; exploring Mount McKinley, or perhaps occupying a cave in Nevada “where all the real hippies are going.”

There was also, of course, that lingering fantasy about becoming a high-priced lawyer on Wall Street.

Chapter Seven

"The Nation's Youngest Governor"

is Described, in Headlines as

"The Horniest of Horndogs"

Two of Arkansas' Hottest Lawyers Get It On: Vince Foster Moves In on Hillary

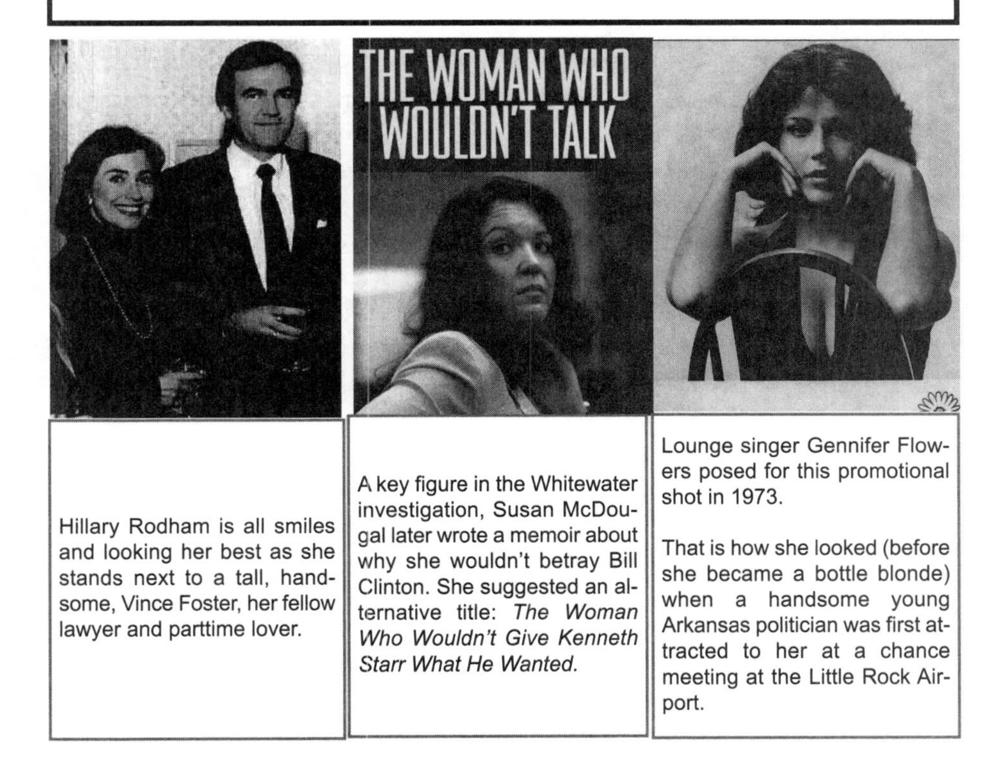

Hillary Rodham is all smiles and looking her best as she stands next to a tall, handsome, Vince Foster, her fellow lawyer and parttime lover.

A key figure in the Whitewater investigation, Susan McDougal later wrote a memoir about why she wouldn't betray Bill Clinton. She suggested an alternative title: *The Woman Who Wouldn't Give Kenneth Starr What He Wanted.*

Lounge singer Gennifer Flowers posed for this promotional shot in 1973.

That is how she looked (before she became a bottle blonde) when a handsome young Arkansas politician was first attracted to her at a chance meeting at the Little Rock Airport.

"You Know Why Men Go into Politics, Don't You? It's Because of an Unsatisfied Sexual Desire."

—Bill Clinton

In Hillcrest, a Little Rock neighborhood of yuppies, a young couple, Bill and Hillary Clinton, arrived and moved into the house depicted above. He had become Attorney General of Arkansas.

As newlyweds in 1975 the Clintons moved to Little Rock, Arkansas' state capital, their home for the next sixteen years. Twelve of those years would be spent in the Governor's Mansion.

Together, they found a small house, about the same size as their little home in Fayetteville, for a purchase price of $34,000. In all, their living space totaled about a thousand square feet. The house was located in Hillcrest, an upscale, largely residential section of the city.

Hillcrest was quite "yuppyish." They settled on L Street at the foot of a tree-studded hill. Mostly, their neighbors were young professionals, doctors, and lawyers. A number of boutiques and antique shops had recently also opened, along with a few restaurants.

"We hardly had time to move in," Hillary said. "Bill's salary was only $26,500 a year, which meant I had to find a job—and be quick about it."

At first, the challenge was daunting for her. Bill could have arranged a position for her in state government, but she rejected the idea so as to avoid the appearance of a conflict of interest. She decided instead to enter private practice, seeking a job in a Little Rock law firm, if she could find one that would accept a woman.

She did not make a formidable appearance, driving around Little Rock in frumpy clothes behind the wheel of a modest Fiat. Her lack of concern for her appearance earned a mention in the local newspaper. A society writer wrote, perhaps with a sniff, "The wife of the new Attorney General, Hillary Rodham

Before Things Get Ugly, Whitewater Real Estate Brings a Fringe Benefit to "Hizzoner, the Gov.": She Wears Cowboy Boots, She Rides a White Arabian Stud Horse, and Her Name Is "Hot Pants."

(she kept her maiden name after marrying Bill Clinton) is an intellectual, we are told. She does not seem overly concerned with her appearance. Her petticoat is often showing—that is, when she wears a dress. Mostly, she puts on a pair of pants. She is seen about Little Rock in a favorite pair of orange pants, the same color prisoners are forced to wear."

It was at this time that "my shining knight" arrived to rescue his damsel in distress. He didn't appear before her on a white horse. Nor did he wear a suit of armor. His name was Vince Foster, a partner in the Rose Law Firm.

In contrast to Hillary's sloppy appearance, he was perhaps the best-dressed man in Little Rock, wearing tailored suits, custom-made shoes, white Arrow shirts, and designer neckties.

At the time Hillary met Vince, she seemed to be floundering around, trying to find a place beneath a sun that seemed to shine down only on men.

Once she met Vince, however, her world changed.

A secretary at the Rose Law Firm claimed she had a one-night stand with lawyer Vince Foster.

"He was a dreamboat, a fantasy man in bed. He had fabulous equipment and knew how to make all the right moves. Lucky Hillary!"

***

Once upon a time in Arkansas, two boys growing up in Hope, Vince Foster and "Billy-Boy" Clinton, used to play cowboys and Indians. "I lived with my grandparents in a modest little house across from Vince's nice, big, white brick house," Bill said.

A bond was formed between the two men that would ultimately carry them to the pinnacle of power in America.

In high school, Foster was a top athlete and student, graduating in 1963 as president of the senior class. Although his father wanted him to join the family's real estate business, he chose to study law at Vanderbilt University and joined the National Guard to avoid getting drafted into the Vietnam War.

He later transferred to the University of Arkansas' Law School, graduating in 1971 after scor-

The entrance to the Rose Law Firm, founded in 1820, sixteen years before Arkansas became a state.

Its lawyers knew how to operate in the local business and political climate of "backslapping and backscratching."

ing the highest in his class on the Arkansas Bar exam.

That same year, he joined the Rose Law Firm in Little Rock, becoming a full partner three years later. Along the way, he met Hillary when they worked together on the Arkansas Bar Association's Committee overseeing the dispensation of legal aid to the poor.

Webb Hubbell was one of the partners in the Rose Law Firm with Hillary and Vince Foster. In time, he followed the Clintons to Washington, where he became the third-ranking member of the Justice Department. He would later spend eighteen months in prison.

Vince was acknowledged as "the soul of the Rose Law Firm," since he had many liberal views about aiding the underprivileged.

He was so impressed with Hillary that he became instrumental in bringing her into the Rose firm, where she became its first female associate. To do that, he had to strong-arm some of the older, more conservative members of the firm, who objected to having any woman becoming an insider within their operation.

In style and substance, she compared Foster to Atticus Finch, the Oscar-winning role that Gregory Peck played in Harper Lee's *To Kill a Mockingbird.* She once compared Bill to the same character. She would also compare Vince to Clint Eastwood, "without any of that actor's political baggage,"

She saw him "as a campaigner fighting the good and just fight for what was right."

In Hillary's view, Vince had "princely manners." He was rather formal and brought a sense of taste and dignity to a meeting or a court appearance. It was reported that women serving on a jury were often influenced by his "male flash and charm," in spite of the merits of any particular case. At times, he was soft-spoken to the point of taciturnity.

"Vince was a real gentleman," Bill said. "Not a good ol' boy Bubba type. He made me feel country crude, but I love the man, who was one of my first supporters."

Three years before working with Hillary, he'd married Elizabeth ("Lisa") Braden, the daughter of a Nashville insurance broker who was Catholic. He was not. In time, they would have three children, Vince III, Laura, and John (nicknamed "Brugh").

From the beginning, Lisa reportedly was jealous of all the time Vince spent with Hillary, lunching with her every Monday to Friday at The Villa, their favorite *trattoria* in Little Rock. Sometimes, they were joined by another lawyer in the firm, Webb Hubbell. He was a whale of a man, a pasta lover who devoured his favorite dish, a "half-a-cow" steak. He had been a quarterback in college and weighed some 300 pounds.

At The Villa, Hillary would sometimes order pasta, although for the most part, "I starved myself to keep my weight down." At the Rose Firm, the three of them became collectively known as "The Unholy Trio."

With Hillary, Vince appeared fun loving, often laughing and telling jokes. But when he went home, he was more reserved, not indulging in excessive displays of affection to either his wife or his kids.

Lisa claimed, "He was driven, always sweating over his next case, fretting that he might lose, which he almost never did."

In him, she spotted early signs of depression. Somehow, Hillary was able to help him get over the dark moods that frequently descended.

Eventually, Vince and Hillary began to dine together without any attempt to include Hubbell, and as a consequence, Vince often "missed supper" with his family. Hillary poured out her political ambitions to him, defining him as "a good listener."

She was brought into the Rose Law Firm in 1977, at a salary of $25,000 a year. *[By 1979, she became its first female partner, the* National Law Journal *listing her as one of the 100 most influential attorneys in America.]*

Her first trial was nicknamed "The Rat's Ass Case" at the Rose Firm. She represented a canning company being sued by an irate consumer who had opened a tin of pork and beans to discover "a rat's ass staring me in the face." The plaintiff maintained in his suit that after witnessing the disgusting sight, he had not been able to kiss his fiancée.

In the company's defense, Hillary argued that rat was considered an edible food in some parts of the world. She also suggested that there was no danger of the rat being diseased because the canning and packaging process had sterilized it. Somehow, she managed to convince the jury, which awarded the consumer only a small percentage of the damages he sought, not the millions he had demanded.

As a highly vocal champion of women's rights, her second case raised many eyebrows. She successfully defended a big bruiser of a man, weighing some 300 pounds, who was charged with brutally assaulting his girlfriend, attacks that later required her hospitalization. In this suit involving her defense of a battery and assault case, based on a technicality, Hillary managed to convince an Arkansas judge to throw the case out.

Law cases aside, the romance of Vince and Hillary advanced, as was clearly evident to other members of the law firm. He had nicknamed her "Hillary Sue," and she called him Vincenzo Fosterini because "he resembled a suave Mafia *consigliere* from *The Godfather.*"

In the beginning, news about Vince's burgeoning romance with Hillary was confined mainly to the office, but after she became First Lady of Arkansas, it mushroomed into widespread gossip. As Hillary herself, noted, "Back then in Little Rock, a woman didn't dine alone with a man who was not her husband. But times are a-changing', my friends and my foes."

A reporter for the *Arkansas Democrat* claimed, "All of us in the newsroom knew about the Hillary/Vince Foster affair, but we didn't report it."

When he stepped from a voting booth, Bill Clinton told a reporter for *The Arkansas Democrat*, "I cast my vote for this rising young politician named Bill Clinton."

In 1978, then-President Jimmy Carter appointed Hillary to the board of directors of the Legal Services Corp., an organization providing federal funds to legal-aid bureaus throughout the United States. To fulfill some of the demands associated with that position, she often traveled without Bill to Washington, D.C. On some of those trips, she was accompanied by Vince.

In those days, illicit lovers could slip into the U.S. capital under the radar. "People didn't really know what Bill Clinton looked like," said one restaurateur in Georgetown where they liked to dine. "At first, I thought Vince was the Governor of Arkansas."

Hillary and Vince would share a suite at the Hay-Adams Hotel, known for its discretion, having catered to many off-the-record couplings in Washington.

One room service waiter, Harold Woode, later claimed, "I served them breakfast in bed one morning. Foster got up and let me in. He had a towel wrapped around his waist. But he dropped it when he crawled back in bed, jaybird naked, with Hillary. I served them breakfast in bed and got a dollar tip for it."

Looking rather geeky, Hillary is all smiles listening to the new Attorney General of Arkansas.

"I was a very big fish in a small pond," he claimed.

Bill, in gossipy Little Rock, knew of Hillary's affair with Vince, but apparently, he never confronted her with the evidence. If anything, news of her affair provided an excuse for him to continue his womanizing.

Jimmy Carter, as president,

often invited both Hillary and Bill to White House galas, as a way of paying them back for the hard work they'd performed during his presidential race in both Arkansas and Indiana.

During their first visit to the White House, Bill escorted Hillary around the public rooms. He told her, "Here is where you're going to live for sixteen years, first during my two terms as president, with you as First Lady, and then your own two terms as president, with me as your First Man. Not a god damn bad record waiting for us, wouldn't you agree?"

Artfully redneck and utterly charming: Dolly Parton

***

On his first day as his state's newest Attorney General, Bill walked into a bleak, badly furnished office in Little Rock. Responding to its bureaucratic blandness, he decided to add some personal touches. His first decorative adornment involved affixing a photographic portrait to the wall of his bathroom. It was of Dolly Parton, "busting" out of a red-and-while polka dot bikini. His behavior evoked that of JFK, who had pinned a cheesecake photograph of Marilyn Monroe to the wall of his hospital room after he'd survived a life-threatening operation in 1954.

Bill didn't plan to remain Attorney General for long. Almost every day, he discussed options for his political future with his cronies. His most obvious choices included either running for governor of Arkansas, or else for a seat in the U.S. Senate, representing his home state. Hillary wanted him to take the option that would allow them the most time in Washington.

As he grew more experienced in his new job, Bill became the most consumer-friendly Attorney General in Arkansas' history. He even fought to keep pay phone calls priced at a dime each, and he sued dairy companies when they tried to raise the price of milk. He also championed improvements in nursing home care and tried to upgrade the state's health-care system.

He failed, however, in his attempts to regulate lobbyists who flocked to Little Rock with their pet projects, and he seemed unaware that many of the state's legislators were on the take.

During his tenure as Attorney General, he faced two thorny issues, both having to do with sex, fortunately not his own. To the horror of liberals, some Arkansas-based right-wingers proposed a bill that would tax "every unmarried couple living in sin in Arkansas $1,500 a year."

Bill worked behind the scenes to kill that silly proposed legislation, persuading lawmakers to add a rider that would interpret any Arkansas State legislator caught committing adultery as a Class D felony. *[Bill was fully aware that many of the State's lawmakers—far removed from wives and families in remote parts of the state—were carrying on adulterous relationships in Little Rock.]*

Thanks partly to the rider Bill had attached to the proposed legislation, it died a very discreet death.

The next bill was more sensitive. It was a proposal for law that would criminalize homosexuality within the state of Arkansas. In his talks with Hillary, he discussed his dilemma. If he criticized the bill, his political enemies would use it against him, charging that he was "promoting the homosexual lifestyle." He wavered on the subject, afraid to oppose it. Instead, he stood on the sidelines, allowing the bill to pass.

[The Arkansas bill faced a painful death in 2003 when the Supreme Court ruled that consensual homosexual acts were protected by the right of privacy.]

As Attorney General, it wasn't all work and no play for Bill.

Two of his aides later charged that during Hillary's involvement with Vince Foster, "Bill chalked up two, maybe three, one-night stands a week. He was the horniest of the horndogs," one office worker said, "and he was rather blatant about it as if not expecting any kickback from his wife."

However, his involvements with two attractive young women would eventually have far-reaching consequences.

Their names one day would become notorious—Gennifer Flowers and Susan McDougal.

Gennifer Flowers: Stolen Moments with "Mr. Kinky"

A sexual relationship between Bill Clinton and Gennifer Flowers began one summer evening in Little Rock in 1977 and would last on and off until 1989, leading to a scandal that almost derailed his presidential campaign. In the 1990s, Gennifer became the most famous former mistress in America.

An attractive, shapely young woman with black hair, she was a TV news reporter who joined other journalists waiting for the state's new Attorney General to arrive at the Little Rock Airport in the aftermath of his involvement at a conference in Washington. This was Gennifer's first assignment for the TV station, KARK, and she was nervous.

Once his feet hit the ground, he talked for about five minutes with reporters before singling her out. He walked over to her, looking deeply and seductively into her eyes. "*Where* did they get you?"

She would later say, "I couldn't believe that the Attorney General was coming on to me." She stared into his pale blue eyes, feeling that he was undressing her. What she would remember most clearly was that he had "the sexiest mouth I had ever seen."

During the next few weeks, as she covered him as a news reporter, "He circled me like Commanches surrounding a wagon train of helpless frontier women." She admitted, "I found him incredibly sexy."

After weeks of occasional public encounters that involved more intense eye contacts, she accidentally ran into him in the lobby of the Little Rock Justice Building. It was then that he asked for, and got, her phone number.

The next day he called and she invited him to her apartment for a drink. "We talked for hours and hours. Other than holding my hand, he made no moves to seduce me."

The "deflowering" of Miss Flowers would have to wait until the following afternoon.

She would later write about the experience, calling it "The greatest sex of my life. As a lover, Bill was great! Though not particularly well endowed, his desire to please was astounding. He was determined to satisfy me and, boy, did he. His stamina amazed me. We made love over and over that night."

Although he had to return to Hillary, he left her his sweaty T-shirt so she could go to sleep with the scent of him.

"What he lacked in dimension, he more than made up in passion and technique," she claimed.

Thus, their stormy affair began with visits two or three times a week. "It was much easier for him to visit me for love in the afternoon when he was Attorney General. When he became governor, he had security guards to deal with."

After a few weeks, he was calling her "Baby," with her nicknaming him "Pookie." He also labeled his testicles "The Boys," referring to her breasts as "The Girls." He rarely spoke of Hillary, but when he did, he referred to her as "Hilla the Hun."

He usually arrived with marijuana for them to smoke. "He most certainly *did* inhale," she said.

He admitted that although he snorted cocaine on occasion, "It has a bad effect on me." One afternoon, he told her that he'd snorted a lot of cocaine at a party the night before, "and I got really fucked up like my little brother, Roger."

He conjured up sex games for them to play, and she found him a very inventive lover. "I remembered the first time he climaxed in my mouth," she said. "He'd never done that before, and I was shocked. "Sometimes, we'd have food fests, and we'd end up heading for the shower with lots of catsup and cream on our bodies."

A publicity show-biz photo of then-brunette Gennifer Flowers, bar room singer and entertainer. Photo is from 1980, and associated with her lounge gigs in Dallas.

At one point, he lit a candle and asked her to drip hot wax onto his chest. She also claimed that he liked to be tied up, at which time she used a dildo-shaped vibrator on him. "It was exciting to see him get so aroused." However, she turned down his offer for a three-way when he wanted to bring another woman to her apartment.

She claimed that she once painted his face with makeup like a drag queen. Although he bought lingerie for her, including a little black nightie, it is not clear from her confessions whether he dressed up in it himself. Other girlfriends claimed he liked to model women's lingerie for them as part of foreplay.

***

Gennifer had always wanted to be a singer, and to an increasing degree, she became known as a cabaret-style bar and lounge singer at some of the watering holes of Little Rock. As she made her rounds, she heard rumors that Bill was indulging in affairs with other women. "I don't know how he did it. He'd leave my apartment pretty drained."

She had also heard rumors that Hillary was having affairs not only with her male friend, Vince Foster, but with other women, too. Gennifer decided to confront Bill with these rumors.

When she did, according to Gennifer, he burst out laughing. "I was stunned at how casually he treated these accusations," she said.

"Honey," he said to her, "Hilla the Hun probably eats more pussy than I do."

As other women have also reported, Bill did not like to use condoms, usually telling his conquest of the moment that he was sterile.

One day, to her dismay, Gennifer realized that she had missed her period.

She visited her gynecologist, Dr. K.M. Kreth, who examined her. He sent her urine test to the Clinical Laboratory of Little Rock which confirmed that she was, indeed, pregnant.

The next afternoon, she revealed those realities to Bill. "I thought that at this point, he might be willing to divorce Hillary and marry me and become the father of our newborn baby. But that was not to happen. He gave me $200 for an abortion."

Ironically, weeks before, she had interviewed a woman for KARK, who ran one of the most frequented abortion clinics in Little Rock. Now she found herself calling that same woman to seek an abortion herself. Reluctantly, she went through with the procedure, finding it extremely painful.

The abortion was performed during January of 1978, just two months before Bill held a press conference to announce that he was running for election as the next Governor of Arkansas.

Soon after her abortion, Gennifer attended a fund-raiser for Bill. This was the first time she spotted Hillary, who was pointed out to her from across the room. "I was shocked. She looked like a fat frump with her hair hanging down curly and wavy. She wore big, thick glasses, an ugly dress, and had a big fat butt. My first thought was, 'What in hell does Bill see in her?'"

Gennifer got a singing gig in the Lounge of the Camelot Inn in Little Rock. Bill often came to hear her sing, but to conceal his affair, he usually showed up with friends. The first time he appeared there as a patron, she sang, "Since I Fell in Love With You," looking directly at him.

As she later testified during the course of her emotional delivery of the lyrics, the governor's face began to heat up, and she feared that reporters would unearth the details of their affair. She, with encouragement from Bill, decided it might be discreet to leave town, and was lucky enough to eventually find a gig as a backup singer for the entertainer Roy Clark. That meant a move to Tulsa.

The night before her departure for Oklahoma, Bill dropped into her apartment for what was termed "a farewell fuck." Neither of them knew whether their relationship might be resumed at some future date.

She had other affairs on the road as a lounge singer, but she claimed that Bill still occupied a special place in her heart. She found that touring on the road with Clark was exhausting and grueling, but that she liked performing as a singer at various nightclub venues throughout the Southwest.

She eventually managed to spend a night with Bill when he visited Tulsa during a period when she wasn't on the road. She recalled that visit with him as "a rare treat."

Months would pass before she hooked up with him again, this time in Fort Worth. He'd had business in Dallas and drove to nearby Fort Worth to spend the night with her. In the future, he would make at least two more trips to Dallas for business. As part of his itinerary, he would include secret rendezvous with her.

Sometimes, as governor, he would buy her a round-trip ticket to Little Rock, where he would arrange and pay for a hotel suite for her. As a high-profile and closely watched figure, he had to take elaborate precautions during the arrangement of their lovefests.

It was shortly after one of her visits to Little Rock that she heard the news that Hillary had given birth to a daughter and that she had named her Chelsea. "If I had any hope that Bill would ever leave Hillary and marry me, that wish was dashed with the news."

She later told reporters that if Hillary had not become pregnant with Chelsea, "Bill might have married me after the divorce dust had settled. After all, he was the love of my life."

In the mid-1980s, Gennifer decided to return to live in Little Rock. Bill arranged to rent an apartment for her at the Quapaw Tower, which was only a short distance from the Governor's Mansion. Once installed there, she resumed their affair, and she found that his stamina as a lover had not slackened. "If anything, our passion was stronger than ever, and he slipped over to my apartment two or even four times a week in the beginning."

It is believed that Hillary learned about the abortion and about Bill's affair with Gennifer at the same time. Whatever confrontations ensued between Bill and her are not known. In Hillary's memoirs, she ignores any of the details associated with his race for governor, a strange omission on her part. Reportedly, she viewed this as a troubled time in her life, and didn't want to provide details.

During her time on the road as a singer, Gennifer had met a number of men, but none who appealed to her like Bill. However, that changed in 1989, when she met Finis Shelnutt, the recently divorced Vice President of the South Trust Investment Bank of Alabama. "He had the bluest eyes of any man I'd ever seen—and was real cute," she said.

When Bill visited to make love to her, she went through the act for a final time, even though by then, she had fallen in love with Shelnutt. At the end of their love-in-the-afternoon session, she delivered the news to Bill: "It's our last time," she said to him. "He cried and I felt awful, but the time had come for us to move on."

"In many ways, I felt our story, our love affair, was over, but it was only the beginning. Our former romance would be played out before the eyes of the world."

Bill Clinton: The Lip-Biting Rapist

It wasn't until near the end of Bill Clinton's presidency that the sordid details of one incident in Bill's life as Attorney General emerged. This time, it was not associated with a bimbo, but with a respected, well-to-do businesswoman, a former nursing home administrator, who charged that Bill had raped her in 1978 during his tenure as Attorney General of Arkansas.

The then-President's lawyer, David Kendall, denied the allegations on Bill's behalf.

***

In 1978, when he was campaigning for governor for the first time, Bill visited the town of Van Buren, Arkansas, a 150-mile drive northwest from Little Rock, where he encountered an attractive blonde, Juanita Hickey (later Broaddrick). She ran Brownwood Manor, one of the best nursing homes in Arkansas.

She was very impressed with Bill, finding him "charismatic and very smart. He'd make a great governor."

He invited her to drop into his campaign headquarters during her next visit to Little Rock. That opportunity came only a week later, when she arrived there to attend a conference of the American College of Nursing Home Administrators.

Together with her friend and fellow nurse, Norma Kelsey, the two women rented a room at the Camelot Hotel in Little Rock, where Gennifer Flowers was the featured singer in the hotel's cocktail lounge.

Juanita put through a call to a Clinton campaign aide and was surprised when he told her, "Bill has been expecting your call. I'll give you his home phone number."

When she spoke to Bill, he agreed to meet her in the coffee shop of the Camelot Hotel. But when he arrived at the hotel, he telephoned her room, telling her that the coffee shop was swimming with reporters, and asking to come instead to her room, where they'd be able to talk about the campaign.

She later admitted to having a slightly uneasy feeling about inviting him to her room, since Kelsey wasn't there at the time, and she was alone.

After he knocked and entered the room, she offered him a cup of coffee, but he settled for looking out at the view. "He then came over to me, put his arm around my waist, and began to kiss me passionately." She broke away, telling him, "I'm married. You're married, too."

He did not listen to her and continued to kiss her, this time biting down on her upper lip. Again, she tried to pull away, but he forced her back onto the bed, piling on top of her, never releasing the grip of his teeth from her lip. She had started to bleed.

"He had seemed so nice," she claimed. "But this was a different side of him, mean and vicious."

He unzipped his pants, pulled up her skirt, and tore the crotch out of her panty hose. He then raped her, all the time holding her down captive, still biting her upper lip.

She claimed she was crying when he rose from the bed and adjusted his clothing. At the door, he put on a pair of very dark sunglasses and advised her to put some ice on her lip, which had already started to throb and soon after swelled to twice its normal size.

Juanita Broaddrick, *right*, with a resident *(center)* of her Arkansas retirement home in Van Buren, Arkansas, and Bill Clinton in April 1978, during a campaign stop when he was running for governor.

She alleged that Clinton assaulted her the same month.

"Bill Clinton was just a vicious, awful person. At some point I stopped resisting. It was a real panicky situation. I was even to the point where I was getting very noisy, you know, yelling to 'please stop.' And that's when he pressed down on my right shoulder and bit my lip."

She had become aware at that point that he had not used a condom. He told her, however, not to worry, since he'd had the mumps as a kid and was sterile.

When Kelsey returned to the room, she found Juanita lying in bed, weeping and nursing her upper lip. She confessed to everything that had happened, and asked her friend to drive her back to Van Buren immediately, thereby skipping the remainder of the nurses' convention.

At home, she told her husband, Gary, that she'd injured herself in an accident involving a revolving door at the Camelot. Two days later, she met her lover, David Broaddrick *[the man she married after her divorce from Gary]* and confessed the whole story to him.

Two weeks later, she appeared at one of Bill's political fund raisers in Little Rock. "I was still blaming myself for the rape, since I had let him come up to my bedroom."

Although she did not meet with him for any private dialogue at the fund raiser, she was shocked to see Hillary seeking her out. "She forcefully took hold of my arm in a very strong grip, even though her words to me were kind as she thanked me for all I was doing for Bill in the campaign."

Juanita would later tell Sean Hannity on *Fox News*, "I felt almost nauseous when she came over to me. I understood her hidden message in spite of her kind words. In her subtle way, she was warning me not to make trouble. Bill must have told her about me."

Years later, Juanita was asked why she hadn't reported anything to the police. "My God, who would believe me? After all, Clinton was more or less set to become the next governor. It would be his word against mine!"

Ironically, it was Hillary who had previously established the first Rape Crisis Center in Arkansas.

Juanita didn't encounter Bill again until 1991, when he was campaigning for U.S. President in Little Rock. "I accidentally ran into him in the hallway of a hotel. He recognized me and apologized to me for what he'd done."

"I'm sorry," he said. "I'm not that man I used to be."

"Go to hell!" she told him, running from his presence.

In 1997, Juanita was drawn into the Paula Jones sexual harassment lawsuit against Bill. Her lawyers were trying to round up various women with whom the president supposedly had had affairs. The attorneys wanted to show that Bill had a long record of sexual harassment of other women, not just Jones.

In response to a subpoena issued by Jones' lawyers, Juanita filed an affidavit, claiming that rumors circulating about Bill's assault on her were unfounded. "Clinton did not make unwelcome sexual advances to me," she falsely stated.

However, in November of 1998, in an interview with *Dateline NBC,* Juanita reversed herself, claiming that she'd lied in her affidavit and that, indeed, she had been forcibly raped by Bill.

To back up her story, three women testified that Juanita had told them about the rape back in 1978, shortly after it had allegedly happened. They included Lousie Maw, Jean Darden, and Susan Lewis.

When Dolly Kyle Browning, Bill's longtime girlfriend, saw Juanita's appearance on television, she told a reporter, "I absolutely believe that Billy was capable of rape back then, perhaps not now. He has a cruel streak in him. He's capable of destroying anyone, and that includes a woman who might stand in his way. I think that was part of his nature, although it was not obvious to me in the beginning."

Finally, in April of 1998, Juanita agreed to testify before Kenneth Starr's investigative committee, providing details of the assault because she feared lying to a Federal Grand Jury. Starr had already agreed to grant her immunity from prosecution for perjury.

NewsMax investigated a specialist in sexual violence who claimed, "The reason rapists bite is, even with the full weight of her attacker on top of her, the woman is often able to resist the parting of her legs by locking her ankles. The rapist's arms are busy keeping her pinned down. The only weapon the rapist has is his teeth, which he uses to bite while demanding that she open her legs."

Candice E. Jackson, in her book *Their Lives: The Women Targeted by the Clinton Machine,* wrote: "What does it mean that we may have permitted a rapist to run the Free World for eight years? Juanita Broaddrick isn't the only woman ever rumored to accuse Bill Clinton of rape. But she is the only woman who has confirmed her claims publicly."

Lisa Myers of NBC, during her interview with Juanita Broaddrick:

MEYERS: "You're saying that Bill Clinton sexually assaulted you, that he raped you?"

BROADDRICK: "Yes."

Juanita also went on TV giving an interview to NBC's Lisa Myers, although she feared that she'd be dismissed as "just another one of Clinton's bimbos."

Broaddrick's account, though dismissed by Clinton loyalists, did have one major significance. Several Republicans who had been "fence straddling" read her material in the Starr Report and saw her appearance on TV and decided to vote to impeach Clinton.

Representative Chris Shays (R-CT) said, "I believe Ms. Broaddrick. It's hard for me to imagine she would make this claim if it were not true."

No charges leveled against the Clintons were more scalding than those that appeared in *Hillary (and Bill) The Sex Volume,* written by Victor Thorn, an investigative journalist for the American Free Press.

In that book, Thorn asserted, "Bill and Hillary Clinton are two of the most criminal political figures to ever exist in this country, and they should either be facing imprisonment or capital punishment."

If that weren't enough, the aptly named Thorn also stated: "Hillary has misled the public about her family, the origin of her name, her sexual orientation, her potty mouth, and how she engaged in violent spousal abuse directed at her cheating husband. Practically every aspect of her life is a contrived, well-calculated charade; and by selling her soul to enter into a prearranged marriage, her life is marred by a downward spiral of deviance and deceit."

Thorn chose not to be discreet in his lacerations of Bill, charging that he hated his wife. "Their union most certainly wasn't based on love. On the contrary, the marriage was conceived for the sole purpose of pushing Slick Willie to national prominence and, as a result, it reeked of subterfuge, skullduggery, and perfidy."

He also called Bill "an immature, sex-crazed, spoiled, rotten child. Party Boy Bill vociferously indulged his every hedonistic desire and intentionally created turmoil when boredom set in."

Hillary, The Cattle Queen of Arkansas

During her association with the Rose Law Firm in Little Rock, Hillary decided to try to raise some much needed cash. She was jealously aware that many commodities and futures brokers in Little Rock were hauling in $50,000 a month and were seen driving around in Mercedes, Porsches, or Cadillacs. She had heard of one gas jockey who had become a millionaire from trades in Tyson and Walmart stocks.

She was befriended by a local investment adviser, Jim Blair, who at the time was making millions in the tricky cattle futures market. She had only $1,000 to invest, but based on references and encouragement from Blair, she opened a trading account with an investment company named Refco, Inc.

Her involvement in the futures market evolved into a ride on an emotional and financial roller-coaster, with many sometimes terrifying twists and turns. During the course of one trading day, she made $26,000 in one trade, then lost $16,000 in another. At one point she owed Refco, her broker, $100,000.

[A New York based financial services company, Refco, founded in 1969, was the largest broker on the Chicago Mercantile Exchange. By 2005, the company entered a crisis when it was discovered that its chairman, Philip R. Bennett, had hidden $430 million in bad debts. Bennett was later sentenced to sixteen years in a Federal prison on twenty charges of securities fraud and the company was plunged into bankruptcy.

Significantly, Hillary was not asked to cough up hard cash for "margin calls" (i.e., money due from a client when a speculative investment turns sour) on her trades. This astonishing leniency did not apply to most of the firm's other investors.]

As someone later wrote in *The New York Post*, "There is no way that the commodity exchange or a broker would permit a novice speculator to control $280,000 worth of cattle with a skimpy investment of $1,000. Not, that is, unless a friend, a guardian, or a partner guaranteed her investment."

Her "angel" was no doubt Blair himself, who, as their general counsel, was deeply immersed in the inner workings of the gigantic poultry producer, Tyson Foods, the largest employer in the state of Arkansas. He was also a major player within Arkansas' Democratic Party.

Bill described Blair as a "six-foot-five-inch idiosyncratic genius who would become one of my closest friends."

Blair had introduced Hillary to Robert Bone, nicknamed "Red Bone," who worked at Refco, the futures and commodities trader. As a flashy, high-profile, high-stakes gambler, he was well-known to the pit bosses of Las Vegas. For him, cattle futures were just another form of gambling.

Hillary did not stay in the cattle futures markets for a long time. At one point, Blair warned her that a dip in the market was coming, and advised her to sell short, which she did, pocketing a $40,000 profit in just one afternoon.

Nervous about risks, she decided during the coming weeks to close her account, but before her exit, she was able to pocket a bonanza of $100,000 on her minor $1,000 investment. Had an equivalent bonanza been awarded as part of a state lottery, the odds of winning would be calculated at 24:1,000,000.

She later said, "I didn't have the nerve to go on gambling. By July of 1978, she was out of the market. As an explanation of her success, she said "I was lucky." She could have added, "Lucky and with a little help from friends in high places."

One of those friends turned out to be Don Tyson himself. From his headquarters in northwest Arkansas (Springdale), he was called "Big Daddy" by his associates in the poultry business. He wore the same khaki uniform with red stitching on the shirt pocket that his employees did. One of his quirks involved an ongoing demand that each of the doorknobs in his vast plant be shaped like an egg, from which stemmed the source of his millions.

Don Tyson, the Poultry King of Arkansas, looked and dressed like a downhome Bubba, but he was, in fact, a multi-millionaire and the largest employer in the state.

Politically and personally, he became an FOB (Friend of Bill).

As the major polluter of Arkansas, he was the scourge of environmentalists who labeled him "Mr. Chicken Shit."

When Bill first ran for governor, Tyson became his largest financial contributor. Once Bill obtained the office, Tyson's chicken empire benefitted from millions of dollars in tax breaks, state loans, and a general relaxation of environmental regulation.

At one point, chicken feces from a Tyson meatpacking plant were dumped into "Dry Creek," a nearby river, and from there, they seeped into the local drinking water supply, forcing then-governor Bill Clinton to declare the locality a disaster area.

Tyson was pointedly not impressed with Hillary, telling Bill, "The best you can do with your wife is to keep her mouth shut." When Bill was first elected governor, Tyson called on him at the Governor's Mansion for a private chat. Hillary reportedly used that opportunity to investigate the contents of Bill's desk drawers, tearing up all the telephone numbers of potential girlfriends he'd met on the campaign trail.

Tyson's support of Bill would continue during his first campaign for president. He commissioned music and lyrics for what became a popular song, which was subsequently played over and over again on the radio.

Bill's a lot like me,
A lot like you.
Bill Clinton's gonna get things done,
And we're gonna send him to Washington."

When Bill finally moved into the White House, Tyson ordered that his own office be reconstructed as an exact replica of the Oval Office at 1600 Pennsylvania Avenue.

***

By the 1990s, the names of James B. McDougal, nicknamed Jim, and his wife, Susan McDougal, would live in infamy as key figures in what came to be known as "The Whitewater Controversy" or "The Whitewater Scandal."

What had begun as a failed real estate development in 1978 and the early 80s mushroomed with an intensity that would eventually evolve into jail terms for the McDougals. Later, it threatened the president himself, even his First Lady, after Hillary was drawn into the controversy.

According to Susan McDougal, "Whenever Bill was with my husband, (*Jim McDougal, depicted above*), he always had a gleam of fun in his eyes. Bill loved Jim, and because he was six years younger, he was always asking Jim's advice."

Jim McDougal's advice lured the Clintons into the notorious Whitewater real estate investment.

Whitewater began with a certain innocence, a deal to make money from a speculative real estate development. Its purpose involved buying a tract of unspoiled land in the Ozark Mountains for the construction of either vacation homes and/or retirement homes. At the time, many retired persons were settling into the scenic Ozarks where taxes and the cost of living were among the lowest in America; social unrest was rare if not unknown, and the scenery was beautiful.

Jim McDougal, who later surfaced at the center of the controversy, had known Bill since 1968, when they worked together at the campaign headquarters of Arkansas' Senator J. William Fulbright. Bill called Jim "an old-fashioned populist who told great stories in colorful language."

One reporter described Jim as "having a bland Lex Luther dome and a dandyish preference for ice cream white suits and watch fobs."

When Hillary met him, she interpreted him as "charming, witty, and eccentric, driving around in a baby blue Bentley and looking as if he'd just stepped out of a Tennessee Williams' play."

Jim met his future wife, Susan Henley, when he was her professor at Ouachita Baptist University in Arkadelphia, Arkanasa. She would remember him as resembling an absent-minded professor with holes in his Bally shoes and frayed shirts. "Even then, he was a very political creature," she said.

Susan had been born in Germany, in the university city of Heidelberg, famous for its associations with *The Student Prince.* She was the daughter of an American G.I. married to a Belgian wife.

The professor and his student, despite the fifteen-year difference in their ages, would soon fall in love. In 1976, they were married. As Susan would soon discover, her husband was no mere professor, but a flamboyant real estate speculator with dreams of getting rich sooner than later.

She helped promote his schemes by appearing in TV ads for his land development deals. Wearing boots, astride a white Arabian stallion, with her long hair streaming in the breeze against a scenic Ozark backdrop made her look like a cowgirl. But unlike Roy Rogers' wife, Dale Evans, Susan wore shorty-short shorts to show off her shapely legs. The press soon dubbed her "Hot Pants."

Although Susan had met Bill briefly when he'd arrived at her college to deliver a speech, she didn't get to know him until much later, when Jim arranged for the three of them to have dinner together.

The McDougals agreed to meet on a street corner, where at the designated time, Bill kept them waiting for nearly an hour. Suddenly, a dark blue convertible driven by a beautiful redhead came to a screeching stop, let Bill out at the curb, and then sped off into the night.

Over dinner, Jim quizzed Bill about the girl, who resembled "a budding young Rita Hayworth type."

Bill dismissed her, claiming, "She's just a friend of a friend giving me a lift."

"Bubba, you always go for the big-breasted, big hair types," Jim said.

Bill shifted the talk from the redhead to a blonde he'd been dating named Hillary Rodham from the Chicago area.

"I can't get Hillary out of my mind," he told Jim and Susan. "I've never met a gal like her before. She's smart—in fact, the smartest gal I know. She would be a great support for my political career. She's a lawyer like I am. All these other gals I date can only flash a beauty smile and look pretty, like they'd just won the Miss Dairies crown."

Later, after Hillary's arrival in Little Rock, a dinner was arranged for the two couples at the Black Pea Restaurant, a Southern-style eatery with red-and-white checkered tablecloths. "Its motto was to fry anything that moves and to slap some gravy over it," Susan said.

For the first time, Susan came face to face with Hillary, whose appearance shocked her. "She wore huge owl-like glasses and had a mane of frizzy hair. She used no makeup and looked like she'd just gotten off the boat as a refugee from Greenwich Village."

It was at the Black Pea that night, as they devoured thick juicy Arkansas steaks, that Jim proposed the Whitewater land deal that would evolve into a disaster for all of them, especially the McDougals.

The proposal was based on the understanding that all four of them would go in on a deal to purchase 230 acres of scenic undeveloped land on the south bank of the White River near Flippin, Arkansas. Jim even suggested that Hillary and Bill might want to build their own second home as a retreat by annexing one of the subdivided parcels of land for themselves.

Priced at $203,000, the land grab was defined at the time as a steal. Initially, Bill and Hillary needed to borrow only $20,000 from a bank.

Jim marketed Whitewater as "an Ozark Valhalla for the retired set," defining it as "a sweetheart deal."

Before the end of the meal, when a high-calorie version of pecan pie was served, a deal was struck that all of them would later regret. Later, the substance of the conversation of that evening evolved into The Whitewater Development Fund. Jim's vision involved selling each of the building plots for prices, depending on the view, that began at about $10,000 each.

Amazingly, Bill and Hillary never visited the property, even after it became the origin of a nationwide scandal and Whitewater a household word. They were satisfied with Jim's assessment.

The remainder of the money needed for the Whitewater deal was financed by the Citizens Bank and Trust of Flippin. Ironically, the president of the bank, James Patterson, was the owner of the land being sold.

As time moved on, Susan's seductive beauty didn't escape Bill's roving eye, even though he'd only recently been married to Hillary. One journalist described Susan as "having big luscious eyes, a demure but coquettish look, and a sexy face over a steely ambitious interior."

Reportedly, his attraction for her was first made evident at a Democratic fund-raiser at Justine's, a landmark restaurant in Memphis, Tennessee, a city with many Elvis Presley associations.

As author Christopher Andersen described it, "She was wearing a slinky black gown with a provocative flesh-colored top with rhinestones around the bodice. He crept up behind her, slipping his arm around her waist. Her surprise turned to adoration. You could feel the electricity between them."

If reports, many of them unverified, are to be believed, the evening at Justine's marked the beginning of an on-again, off-again affair that would last until 1990, even though she was married to one of Bill's best friends. Of course, there were problems associated with the fact that the governor had a wife, too, although that had never stopped him from pursuing other women.

One witness to Bill's affair with Susan was Larry Douglass Brown, an officer with the Arkansas State Police assigned to the security detail at the Governor's Mansion. As such, Brown had an up-close and personal overview of many of then-Governor Clinton's dalliances.

Once, Bill commented on Susan's TV commercials, particularly one which depicted her on horseback wearing form-fitting riding pants: "She looks good in those riding pants, doesn't she?" he asked Brown, before continuing with, "And she looks even better out of them!"

According to Brown, "Bill would brag many times about his victories on the sexual playing field, and Susan was one of the first in a long line of them. He would always make comments about poor Jim, since he didn't see what Susan saw in him. 'He's one goofy son-of-a-bitch,' Bill would say about Jim. 'But he sure is a cash cow!'"

It is believed that Jim learned about the affair of his wife with the governor in 1982 because of a crossed phone line. He overheard his wife arranging details of a rendezvous with Bill.

Brown said that Susan was not the only woman the governor seduced. Brown made the amazing charge that during his term of em-

Larry Douglass Brown (right) was a member of Governor Clinton's security detail.

In his tell-all memoir, Brown claimed to have been a witness to "almost all the alleged offenses circling around Bill Clinton in Arkansas—misuse of state funds for sexual liaisons, Whitewater, illegal campaign fundraising and bribery, cocaine use, and drug smuggling."

Brown later testified, "Bill and I had a stormy relationship at the Governor's Mansion *(depicted above)* in Little Rock. To say that Bill and Hillary had an open marriage would be an unfair characterization."

"They had an 'understanding.'"

ployment, he brought "at least a hundred women to Bill for the purposes of seduction. The governor rated each woman on a scale of one to ten, and he alluringly referred to them as 'ripe peaches.'"

Susan heard about Bill's other affairs, but in her memoirs was rather dismissive of them. "I'm sure these sessions consisted of five minutes of actual sex, then thirty minutes of Bill talking about how good he was in the saddle."

***

Eventually, the Whitewater dream burst, as Bill noted in his memoirs. Interest rates soared and money became tight during the waning years of Jimmy Carter's presidency. Many people were trying to hold onto their principal residence, and didn't have the cash to buy land and erect a second home.

When Ronald Reagan became president in the early 1980s, land values plummeted. Whitewater ultimately ended up costing the Clintons some $60,000. Despite the hopes and dreams inspired by its original concept, it eventually devolved into a shabby trailer park, a looming menace in the future of both the McDougals and the Clintons.

"The Boy Whiz Kid" With "That Yankee Gal" Hit the Campaign Trail, Running for Governor

As Attorney General, Bill plotted his next political move. Should he run for the Senate seat from Arkansas, a six-year-term, or else pursue the easier goal of becoming governor, which at that time was only a two-year term.

He needed advice, so he hired a New Yorker, Dick Morris, who had a reputation as a savvy political consultant and an expert on polling.

John McClellan, Arkansas' aging Democratic Senator, had announced his retirement, and consequently, his seat in the U.S. Senate was up for grabs. It was sought by some strong contenders, notably David Pryor, Jim Guy Tucker, and Ray Thornton.

Bill later wrote that Morris was "aggressive, brilliant, and abrasive, brimming with ideas about politics." He had many creative schemes about how to run a hard-fought campaign. "He was so cocksure about everything that a lot of people, especially in a down-home place like Arkansas, found him hard to take, but I was stimulated by him."

Morris concluded that whereas in the race for governor, he would be practically a "shoo-in," winning a seat in the U.S. Senate would be far from certain. Consequently Bill decided to go for the safe option and run for governor.

Friend and foe alike, however, contended that winning even the post of governor would not be easy. Other contenders seeking the nomination for governor included the conservative evangelical Christian, Frank Lady, who was mocked for his last name. Also in the competition was Monroe Schwarzlose, a genial turkey farmer from southeast Arkansas. Although events would show that he wasn't much of a vote-getter, he promised a bird on every platter for Sunday dinners in Arkansas.

This view of Dick Morris dates from when Bill first hired him early in his campaign for governorship of Arkansas.

Later, Morris changed his political allegiance and began addressing Tea Party Republican rallies on Bill's home turf in Little Rock.

After his break with the Clintons, he appeared as a conservative talking head on Fox News, but got the boot, along with Sarah Palin, based on his wildly inaccurate predictions.

At the time, Bill, at the age of thirty-one, was the youngest man seeking any governorship in the United States. *The New York Times* defined him as "the whiz kid of American politics."

For the first time, Bill's unconventional, highly visible wife became the recipient of verbal abuse. Ill treatment would characterize her role in his career—and in her own—throughout the rest of her life. In time, she would even be accused of murder. Her dress, her speech, her opinions, her career as a lawyer, her clothes, and her glasses all received harsh condemnation. The *Arkansas Democrat* even charged that "Miss Rodham doesn't like her husband enough to take his name."

Nothing appeared about it in print, at least not then, but rumors criss-crossed through Arkansas that she was a lesbian. One Republican chairman in one of the state's most backward counties (in this case, in the less-developed eastern part of Arkansas) had to have lesbianism explained to him.

When he was told what the sexual practice involved, he burst into laughter. "There's no such thing. Sex is impossible if you don't have a dick, but I'll vote against Clinton anyway!"

During Bill's campaign, he proved popular with audiences across the state, even among those who "didn't know quite what to make of his Yankee gal."

During Bill's campaign, Hillary was once again horrified at some of the local oddities, quirks, or down-home shenanigans associated with politics in the rural South.

At a country fair during his electoral campaign, as a vote-getting device and as a means of "proving his manhood," Bill, a successful lawyer and former Rhodes Scholar, was asked to engage in a tug-of-war with some "giant log haulers." He was the smallest man on his team, and his side lost. He ended up in a mudhole.

Tomato growers were a strong part of Arkansas' economy, and as such, they played a symbolic role in the election. As a campaign device, Bill enrolled in a tomato-eating contest, competing against rather burly men. Once again, he was the smallest. Each man was given a paper bag brimming with ripe tomatoes, and at the sound of the bell, they were told to begin eating.

Bill ate tomatoes for five minutes, admitting we were "behaving like pigs at the trough." He finished fourth. As the winners were named, he retreated from the scene to a nearby outhouse, where he vomited up the contents of his acidy stomach and vowed privately not to eat anything with tomatoes in it for the duration of the campaign.

Politics in Washington were introduced into the campaign after the U.S. Congress, after years of negotiations and setbacks, passed the Equal Rights Amendment (ERA) to the Constitution in the early 1970s.

It was referred to the individual states for ratification. In Arkansas it became a hot button issue. Both Hillary—of course—and Bill supported the bill, despite the loud recriminations of Frank Lady's Moral Majority, which was "predicting the end of civilization as we know it."

At a campaign rally in Jonesboro, in northeast Arkansas, one woman in a "Lady" T-shirt shouted at Bill, loudly accusing him of "promoting homosexuality."

"Ma'am, in my short life in politics, I've been accused of everything under the sun. But you're the first person who ever accused me of promoting homosexuality."

Bill won the Democratic nomination in the May, 1978 primary with sixty-two percent of the vote within a field of weak candidates.

That autumn, the Republicans nominated a lackluster candidate, Lynn Lowe, a cattleman from Texarkana and the Chairman of Arkansas' Republican Party. He decided to run a dirty campaign, standing on the steps of the Capitol Building in Little Rock and denouncing Bill as a draft dodger.

In spite of having to endure assaults that he was "a sissy coward, afraid to stand up and fight America's enemies," Bill won the general election with 63 percent of the vote, sweeping to victory in seventy-five counties. He'd take office as the youngest governor in America.

His enemies referred to him as "The Boy Governor." The Republican political brass privately talked about "Clinton's zipper problem," referring to his womanizing. They predicted that because of that, he would never be able to campaign for a higher office outside his home state.

After winning, and with something akin to defiance, Bill privately told Hillary and such aides as Dick Morris, "Tonight Arkansas, tomorrow America."

She found herself in a role *[First Lady of Arkansas]* she never expected to play in her wildest dreams. It was a position she would hold from 1979 to 1981, and again from 1983 to 1992, at which time she was "redefined," because of her husband's election as president, as First Lady of the United States.

Bill won the governorship of Arkansas in 1978, lost it in 1980, and regained it in 1982. He would go on to be elected to another two-year term in 1984, and then to two additional terms *[these latest for four year terms, based on changes to Arkansas' election laws]* in 1986 and again in 1990.

Bill's salary was only $35,000 a year, so she would continue her career with the Rose Law Firm. She also sat on the boards of major corporations, including Wal-Mart. Her annual income shot up to at least $180,000 a year, and she chided Bill that he was her "kept boy."

Morris said, "Unlike Bill, Hillary had a taste for the finer things of life, and she craved luxury."

With Hillary holding a Bible, Bill took the oath of office on January 10, 1979, in the State Capitol Building. In spite of criticism, she defiantly wore a pair of super-size glasses, the kind First Lady Jacqueline Kennedy wore when she was photographed in the 1960s.

In addition to their inaugural ball, the Clintons parted with tradition by staging a celebratory gala *["Diamonds and Denim"]*, lasting four hours, a party with several live bands surging out renditions of rock and folk music. The event defined its dress code by stating in advance that guests could show up either in formal wear or in blue jeans, depending on their individual preferences. Name entertainers volunteered to perform, including Al Green, the famous folk singer.

As a rare exception, Hillary showed up elegantly groomed and coiffed, wearing a $20,000 diamond brooch that was defined as rare because its components had actually been mined in Arkansas. Her gown was made from a lustrous *panne* velvet in a shade of dusty rose, created by Arkansas designer Connie Fails, although—according to some arbiters of taste—it looked somewhat old-fashioned.

Chief of Staff Robert Roberts, whom everybody called "Bobby," was set to become Bill's chief legislative liaison. He said, "We were showing our fellow folks we're sorta sophisticated but yet hadn't lost our country ways. Our hope was that the Clintons would bring us a down-home re-creation of 'Camelot comes to Little Rock.'"

Bill performed a saxophone solo that brought a massive ovation.

His friend, Carolyn Yeldell Staley, ended the night by singing directly to the Governor-Elect, "You Light Up My Life," as Hillary looked on, concealing her boiling anger.

If any guests offended the locals, they tended to be those invited from points outside Arkansas. They had arrived as well-wishers for Bill. These included a parade of his friends from his days at Georgetown and Yale Law School. The local revulsion to these out-of-towners was expressed in a country song that was at the time a hit on Arkansas radio. It derided "long-haired hippie-type commie fags who voted for George McGovern."

At his "Diamonds and Denim" Inaugural Gala, Bill entertained on the saxophone.

"This event was less hokey than it sounded," claimed the Arkansas Gazette. "As a sax player, however, Bill had better stick to his day job as governor."

***

Amazingly, despite his recent installation in the Governor's Mansion, Bill continued with one-night stands and a series of affairs, details of which would later be revealed by state troopers assigned to his security detail.

What was not as well known is that while Bill was out "fooling around," Hillary pursued her own affair with the married Vince Foster.

Like clockwork, Foster would show up at the Governor's Mansion in Little Rock whether Bill was out of town or out on late-night carousing in the taverns of Little Rock, not getting back to the mansion until two or three that morning when Hillary was asleep and Vince had long departed to join his own wife and children.

The governor liked to tour the late-night cabarets, the honky-tonks, and the taverns from the Missouri line to Texarkana. Invariably, according to the testimony of state troopers, he always had a bevy of beauties with him, although sometimes with only a favorite girlfriend, according to trooper Larry Douglass Brown, assigned as a bodyguard during many of those nightlife tours.

Webb Hubbell, their colleague at the Rose Firm, remained a favorite friend of both Hillary and Vince. He was keenly aware of their burgeoning romance, but no doubt realized that Bill could not utter one word of protest "because the kettle can't call the pot black."

The troopers later reported that Vince would arrive at around nine at night at the Governor's Mansion when Bill was out of town and not leave until the next morning. One attendant came upon them in one of the private rooms. "They were kissing," Brown claimed. "I don't mean like kissin' cousins. Real deep throat stuff. When he spotted my presence, he just winked at me and resumed his maneuvers while I got the hell out of there."

"To me, Hillary and Vince were two people deeply in love," Brown claimed. "I saw them locked in each other's arms on more than one occasion. He was a neck nuzzler. I liked him. He was a great guy. He seemed devoted to her, something I could hardly say for Bill."

Brown was one of the troopers who drove Hillary and Vince at various times along the 65-mile route between Little Rock and Heber Springs, a community in north-central Arkansas that promotes itself to the tourist trade as "the gateway to the Greer's Ferry Lake and the Little Red River."

There, the Rose Law Firm owned a log cabin used as a vacation retreat for their officers. Provisions, food, drink, and supplies were stockpiled inside for them by a company employee. "They'd disappear inside on a Friday afternoon, and we'd never seem them again until Monday morning, when it was time to head back to Little Rock," Brown claimed.

Hubbell said that "Vince never made the stop at the bus sign marked 'childhood.' He went from little boy to mature adult."

But Hubbell, along with others, noted that Hillary brought out a playful side in Vince. For a birthday celebration, she hired a belly dancer to entertain him.

One of the state troopers assigned to guard Hillary spotted her with Vince "being awfully playful with each other."

On several occasions, a trooper reported that he was "cupping her ass cheeks, and she sure didn't object, laughing and giggling with him. He couldn't keep his hands off that butt of hers. I figured him to be a butt man. Sometimes he'd do it in front of us and just wink. Once at a reception at the Governor's Mansion, when Bill was there, being adored by three beautiful women, Vince couldn't keep from fondling Hillary. He was so god damn attentive. Bill just had to know!"

Another trooper spotted Vince in the library with his arm wrapped around Hillary, feeling her breasts.

Brown recalled a memorable evening in Little Rock when, "I fully expected some marijuana, group sex, and a 'Big Chill' night."

A party of "friendly couples" one night headed for a Chinese restaurant owned by Charlie Yah Lin Trie. It consisted of Bill and Hillary, along with Vince Foster and his wife, Lisa, who were joined by their friends, Mike and Beth Coulson.

At the restaurant, Charlie ushered the couples into a private dining room in the basement. Brown noticed that the couples paired off in unexpected ways: Beth with Bill, Mike with Lisa, and Hillary with Vince.

After most of the party had had too many drinks, Brown witnessed some amorous activities: "Vince and Hillary were acting like they were in the back seat of a '57 Chevy at the drive-in. Hillary was kissing Vince like I've never seen her kiss Bill; and the same thing was going one with Bill and Beth. Mike's and Lisa's oblivion to the escalation of the amorous activity left me bewildered."

The culmination of orgasmic sex anticipated by Brown never happened. At the end of the festive dinner, the couples regrouped back into their original formations and went their separate ways.

As Brown drove Hillary and Bill back to the Governor's Mansion, he witnessed the couple on a hormonal high, as their backseat wrestling began. "This is the only time I have ever seen the two passionate with one another. For fifteen minutes, I struggled to keep the Lincoln Town Car on the road. You would have thought two elephants were doing their best to produce a new Baby Dumbo for the zoo back there. But once at the mansion it was as if someone had thrown cold water onto them."

He later wrote that Hillary adjusted her hair before going inside, and Bill put what he sometimes called "Little Governor" back into his pants and zipped up."

Brown's ultimate conclusion: "Hillary Rodham loved Vince Foster, let's put that issue to rest right here. It has amazed me that the subject has been taboo in 'mainstream media.' She traveled with Vince often, once even to London. They were soul mates."

At one point, Hillary approached Brown and tried to explain her actions. "Some things you can't get in a marriage. It means you have to turn elsewhere for what you're looking for."

[Years later, on television, talk show host Barbara Walters confronted Hillary with rumors of an affair with Vince in the wake of his suicide. She didn't deny the affair, but said, "I miss him very much. And I just wish he could be left in peace, because he was a wonderful man to everyone who knew him."]

Chapter Eight

1980:
A Horrible Year for the Clintons: A Taxpayer Revolt in Arkansas, Violent Assaults from Mother Nature, & (Barely) Avoiding Nuclear Destruction

Into a Cramped Stockade in Western Arkansas, President Carter Dumps 21,000 Cuban Refugees ("Many of them Criminally Insane") from Castro's Asylums & Jails. They Riot, They Menace, They Scream "Liberdade," and They Threaten to Burn Down Fort Smith.

Governor Clinton's Chances for Re-Election to a 2nd Term are Doomed

The birth of Chelsea Clinton was difficult, as she was "in breech" (upside down in the womb). Her birth had to be by cesarean.

"I saw the doctor lift our baby out of Hillary's body," Bill said. "It was the happiest moment of my life. I carried Chelsea out to Mother and anyone else who was available to see the world's most wonderful baby. I talked to her and sang to her. I never wanted the night to end. I knew that being a father was the most important job I'd ever have."

He even taught her how to vote at an early age.

Grand Hall of the Governor's Mansion in Little Rock. We're a long way from Hope (Arkansas) and Bill's days of emulating Elvis.

As Governor and First Lady of Arkansas, Bill and Hillary were somewhat disappointed at their living quarters in Little Rock. Set on six well-manicured acres, the two-story red brick Georgian-style mansion stood in the historic Quapaw Quarters, the neighborhood with the city's oldest and most historic buildings.

Author Carl Bernstein claimed that the Governor's Mansion, constructed in 1950, with Grecian pillars, evoked "a rather grand suburban spec house."

Even though the building was large, most of it was devoted to its public rooms. When Bill and Hillary moved in, they found only five small private rooms and two cramped bathrooms available for their personal use. Even so, they didn't have enough furniture from their little house to adequately furnish their private quarters.

In spite of the crowded apartment set aside for them, there were compensations: housekeepers, cooks, servants, and personal assistants. Many grace notes, including art and expensive carpets, had been donated by the previous occupant, Governor Winthrop Rockefeller.

The Clintons also had drivers to take them wherever they wanted to go, and travel expenses were paid for, including frequent trips to Washington. They also had a sizable entertainment budget.

Still, that wasn't enough. They decided they wanted an outdoor pool on the grounds. Since the state wouldn't pay for it, Hillary solicited friends for donations to install one.

For Bill, the most immediate problem involved being followed around by

Bill Is Replaced With a Bible-Thumping Evangelical Zealot.
Devastated, He Laments: "My Political Career Is Over!"

The Year's Single Bright Spot?
The (Medically Complicated) Arrival of Chelsea

security guards. He had good reasons for wanting privacy, fearing state troopers would learn of his many affairs.

But, in time, he reached an accommodation with them, perhaps naïvely trusting them not to betray his confidence by telling all to the tabloids when he eventually ran for president. Their revelations in the 1990s would become known as "Troopergate."

Young and fresh faced, Bill plastered the state with this poster, hoping to win re-election. Many voters claimed, "The guy needs a haircut."

Bill once asked state trooper Larry Douglass Brown, "Why does a man have to serve in the military to be elected the governor of a state or President of the United States?"

But in 1979, Clinton came to appreciate the troopers who may have saved his life from assassination attempts he faced after his move into the Governor's Mansion.

One escapee from a mental asylum telephoned the mansion and informed the security force that he was on his way to Little Rock "to assassinate Bill Clinton." He'd been confined after decapitating his mother, and he was eventually rounded up and sent back to the institution.

Another "giant of a man," standing six feet tall and weighing more than 300 pounds, arrived on the doorstep of the mansion with a railroad spike that, as he revealed later, he planned to plunge into the governor's heart.

Later, yet another burly man stormed into the mansion, shouting that Bill was the Son of the Devil and that he was going to assassinate him "in the name of Jesus Christ."

Weeks later, a drugged man broke in through the front door in an attempt to get to Bill. The intruder was armed, but a trooper managed to wrestle him to the floor and grab his gun. He was carried out of the mansion in a straitjacket and delivered to the nearest asylum.

For his own protection, Bill, for many weeks, wore a bulletproof vest whenever he left his private quarters, which were kept tightly locked. Some of the troopers observed that sometimes, Bill took reckless chances.

On one occasion, when his mistress, Gennifer Flowers, visited the Governor's Mansion for a gala event, Bill was seen urging her to go with him into the bathroom to make love while a trooper was conspicuously posted outside the door. It was observed that Gennifer refused the invitation because Hillary and some fifty invited guests—*tout* Little Rock so to speak—were partying only fifty feet away.

As stories of womanizing continued to circulate, Flowers worried about getting a disease during the AIDS crisis since Bill still didn't want to use a "scumbag" *[his word]* during intercourse. She suspected that Bill liked the sense of power he had over women now that he'd become governor. In her book, *Their Lives: The Women Targeted by the Clinton Machine,* Attorney Candice E. Jackson charged: "Bill Clinton consistently views and treats women as playthings. He has used his ever-expanding positions of power to seduce, entice, cajole, pressure, abuse, smear, and destroy women unfortunate enough to be caught in his gaze."

As a Southern boy growing up in the Bible Belt, Bill seemed to have been reared with a concept of sex articulated in Suzi Parker's book, *Sex in the South: Unbuckling the Bible Belt.* "The deal in Dixie is that everybody does it, but no one talks about it. Because no one talks about it, sex is encased in a plain brown wrapper making everything about it taboo, taciturn, and twisted."

As reviewer David Humphry put it: "Southern sex is so sinful, but so delicious because of the hellfire-and-damnation guilt that's driven into Southern boys from childhood."

Like John F. Kennedy had done in the White House, Bill on occasion managed to elude troopers assigned to him for security. He developed a habit of slipping out the rear entrance of the Governor's Mansion and going to a movie theater in Little Rock by himself.

There were rumors that he often didn't leave the movie alone, slipping into a nearby motel known for its "hot beds." There was other gossip as well, including that he often took a seat in the relatively unoccupied back row of the balcony, where he was frequently the recipient of fellatio from a young

State troopers at the Governor's Mansion later revealed that when Bill "got that gleam in his eye," he would sometimes disappear with a partner into one of the building's bathrooms. A trooper would be stationed outside the door to keep out anyone in need of a toilet.

Some of the women Bill pursued refused to participate in a "quickie in the john," but any number of them accepted.

According to Arkansas State Trooper Larry Douglass Brown, when Bill was governor, "He sometimes lost out to his main sexual competitor, Steve Clark, the new Arkansas Attorney General."

"Bill told me, 'That son-of-a-bitch is always trying to spoil my fun, getting the gal before I do.'"

woman or, on some occasions, two young women.

Many state troopers felt that Bill and Hillary were engaged in a "loveless marriage" or else a union of convenience. After all, he spent a good part of every week womanizing, and there were all those reports that had surfaced during the campaign that she was a lesbian.

Insights into the sexual landscapes (and lowdowns) of Dixie

But on some occasions, troopers assigned to them noted that they could be fun-loving and cuddlesome with each other.

One trooper riding with a driver remembered Bill and Hillary in the back seat of a limousine devouring Col. Sanders Kentucky Fried Chicken. "They were laughing, talking, and cuddling between taking bites out of those tender white chicken breasts. They were cackling as much as a hen in heat. The driver and I sat in the front seat listening to all this mush and starving to death, wishing they'd offer us a piece, even a wing or a chicken back."

***

The Governor's Mansion was not just a playpen for Bill. As the chief executive of a relatively backward state, he had an ambitious agenda to pursue, and only two years to accomplish his goals.

When he first took office in 1979, Arkansas ranked last in the nation in money spent on education. Potholes, outdated or inadequate infrastructures, and bad roads were costing motorists time and money, even though business was booming for the tire industry.

Bill's sometimes political adviser, Dick Morris, later recalled, "Bill was like a kid in a candy store. He wanted to sample it all, and he became so zealous he made some very serious mistakes that cost him his re-election. Hillary also turned out to be a liability. She was a bit much for the people of Arkansas, not behaving like their concept of a Southern lady."

As a wife, Hillary was supposed to be Melanie in *Gone With the Wind,* but she turned out to be more like Scarlett O'Hara, with a steely will to succeed on her own terms.

From the beginning, Bill's staff learned to operate on "Clinton time." He'd have an appointment at 10AM, but wouldn't show up until noon. He'd set out to go somewhere, but would meet supporters along the way and would stop and "chew the fat" with them, forgetting that he was due somewhere else. If someone had a problem, he'd invite them to drop by the Governor's Mansion and discuss it with him.

One secretary reported that at one time, thirty-two people were waiting in his outer office, each claiming that the governor had invited them to just drop in. Of course, he couldn't live up to all his promises, and made enemies who felt slighted.

The word got out that "The Boy," as he was called by some, was getting too big for his breeches, an oft-repeated Southern putdown. Cartoonists depicted him either in diapers or else a bit more grown up, riding a tricycle.

He didn't have one Chief of Staff, but three young men (Rudy Moore, Jr., Steve Smith, and John Danner) in charge of administering his far-flung influence and commitments. They became derisively known, collectively, as "the Three Beards," "The Diaper Brigade," "The Children's Crusade," or as "Clinton's three hippies trying to run Arkansas." They often showed up for work in ragged cutoffs and T-shirts.

"This trio of hippies Bill brought in as Chiefs of staff had long hair like a woman's," said one of the troopers. "I didn't know whether to fuck 'em or salute 'em. For all I knew, they had vaginas like those bearded ladies in the circus."

Moore, at thirty-five, was the oldest of Clinton's three assistants, handling details associated with lawmaking and legislation, and Smith was in charge of overseeing Bill's dealing with state agencies and economic development.

In contrast, Danner, a former law student in the very liberal environment of the University of California at Berkeley, was charged with dealing with Arkansas' relationship with the Federal government as then administered by President Jimmy Carter. Danner also held educational and public relations seminars, some of which came under fire, especially one devoted to the subject of "What Turns You On?."

Danner was married to an ardent feminist, Nancy (nicknamed "Peach") Pietrefesa, who had been Hillary's closest friend during their senior year together at Wellesley. For a while at least, Hillary seemed to spend more time with Peach than with Bill. Because of that, rumors spread that they were lesbian lovers, especially since they were seen holding hands in the State Legislature during a tense debate on abortion where outrageous, and sometimes poisonous, charges and claims were aired.

As governor, Bill worked for educational reform, and appointed Hillary to a 45-member Arkansas Rural Health Advisory, whose stated intention involved the implementation of adequate health care to poor people living in the backwaters of Arkansas.

As part of her busy schedule, First Lady Hillary also maintained her ties to the Rose Law Firm, which had moved into new quarters in a renovated building that had previously housed a branch of the YWCA. At its swimming pool in the basement, Hillary was often seen going for a dip with Vince Foster, who was impressively packaged in a snug-fitting bathing suit. "His figure is better than mine," Hillary confided to Peach.

Question: Why did Bill Clinton lose his (first) bid for re-election as governor?.

Answer: Escalating fees for Arkansas license plates

The attacks on Hillary's appearance continued, as did her refusal to take her husband's name. From the Governor's Mansion, formal invitations were extended to gatherings and events whose hosts were named as "Hillary Rodham and Governor Bill Clinton."

To improve the horrible road conditions of Arkansas, Bill needed $3.3 billion. To raise funds, he decided to increase license plate fees on all vehicles, both trucks and cars. In some cases, a motorist who had previously paid $15 annually was charged $30.

Two powerful lobbies, the poultry business and the trucking industry, bitterly opposed these new licensing fees, since they would have to pay the lion's share. But in this case, joining the statewide chorus of discontent were the voices of everyday motorists, who objected violently to the increases. Many of them threatened to never vote for Bill again, likening his administration to "the snakebite of a rattler."

After Hours of Childbirthing Agony, The Clintons' "Miracle Child" Arrives Prematurely

For the Clintons, 1980 was one of the worst years of their life, relieved only by the arrival of a "blessed event," a baby daughter. But even that came about in a brutal way, both in the bedroom at conception and in the hospital itself.

It all began with a "rape" while Bill and Hillary were on a vacation in Bermuda during June of 1979. They checked into Horizons and Cottages on Bermuda's South Shore Road in Paget Parish, set on the premises of a former

18th Century plantation estate of 25 acres. They were assigned a suite with an old-fashioned four-poster bed opening onto an ocean-fronting terrace.

On site was an English-inspired pub, where Bill was spotted drinking into the late evening with some advertising executives from Manhattan.

Long after Hillary retired, Bill remained behind, enjoying several pints of lager, drinking far more than he usually did. He wasn't much of a drinker, but enjoyed the company and several games of skittles.

At around 1AM, he rose from the table and stunned his listeners by announcing that he was returning to his suite "to rape my wife." It was just assumed that he was joking.

However, the noise, shouting, and the sound of objects being thrown suggested to those in adjoining rooms that a major fight ensued. Perhaps Hillary was not in the mood for rape. The next morning, the maid cleaned up the broken glass and uprighted the furniture.

As one "Mad Man" from Madison Avenue said, "I guess ol' Bill meant what he said."

Hillary stayed in her suite that day, ordering from room service. Later, Bill showed up, looking worse for wear. He was later seen by one of his drinking companions from the night before, talking intimately with a teenage girl, a guest worker from the Caribbean island of Grenada.

That previous spring, during a visit to San Francisco, Bill and Hillary had gone to a fertility specialist. They were informed that Bill had a low sperm count, and that conceiving a baby might be very difficult.

But after his trip to Bermuda, and after learning that his wife was pregnant, Bill boasted to his cronies in Little Rock, "I guess my 'little boys' did their job that night down in Bermuda."

On February 27, 1980, Bill flew back to the Little Rock Airport after attending the National Governors' Association meeting in Washington. That had been followed by dinner at the White House as guests of Jimmy and Rosalynn Carter.

He'd been in the Governor's Mansion for just fifteen minutes when Hillary's water broke. Both of them had already studied the Lamaze method of natural birth and had attended classes together. He knew exactly what to do and summoned the staff to order an ambulance at once. During their transit to the Arkansas Baptist Hospital, he nestled beside her, holding her hand as she moaned in pain.

At the hospital, over the course of the next four hours, they got nothing but bad news from the medical staff. Not only was the baby about three weeks premature, but it was also "in breech," meaning upside down. *[A breech birth is the birth of a baby from a position in which the baby exits from the birth canal with its feet or buttocks first as opposed to the normal "head-first" exit, a positioning which presents hazards to the baby.]*

After acute suffering by Hillary, the doctors received permission to perform a Caesarian section.

Although Bill was ordered from the room, he stood his ground, informing the doctor that he could watch Hillary "be cut open from head to toe without fainting," which seemed a somewhat callow thing to assert. He held her hand, watching all the "cutting and bleeding" on an image projected onto a screen in the operating room.

When an infant girl emerged, he proclaimed her as "the Miracle Child."

Chelsea Victoria Clinton was born, weighing six pounds, three ounces. The name Chelsea was selected because of her parents' fondness for the Joni Mitchell song, "Chelsea Morning."

After the baby was washed and handed to the eager father, Bill, wearing green scrubs, paraded up and down the hospital corridor, showing off his newborn.

Diane Kincaid Blair, their friend and a political science professor, would later tell *Vanity Fair:* "Bill was carrying on like he invented fatherhood."

His longtime lover, Dolly Kyle Browning, was later quoted as saying, "There goes Bill's cover that he was sterile," as he had told countless women.

Before Hillary left the hospital, her doctors warned her that another pregnancy might result in the loss of her own life and that of her infant's too.

***

"The birth of Chelsea was the only good thing that happened to me in 1980," Bill later said. "That was the year I had to run for re-election. Even Mother Nature conspired against me, and the U.S. Army nearly blew Arkansas off the face of the Earth. Not only that, but Jimmy Carter sent 21,000 Cuban refugees to Arkansas that Fidel Castro had forcibly ejected after defining them as undesirables."

Because of severe winter storms, thousands of the state's residents went for weeks without electricity, causing enormous hardships. State vehicles had to pull hundreds of cars out of ditches. At one point, Bill got President Carter to define Arkansas as a Federal disaster area, so the state could receive badly needed emergency funds.

Truckers vital to the economy went on strike, in the wake of which their perishable cargoes rotted in warehouses.

That year, David Duke, the notorious leader of the Ku Klux Klan, selected Little Rock for the annual gathering of the white-robed and hooded Klansmen. Anticipating riots and violence, Bill called out the National Guard and the State Troopers to keep the peace. The riots that Bill anticipated didn't occur, although personal clashes between Klansmen and those who opposed them, especially African Americans, did lead to some arrests.

During the waning months of the Carter administration, the national economy tanked, and Arkansas was especially hard hit. Anticipated state revenues fell drastically, and schoolteachers were angered that they weren't awarded the raises that Bill, as governor, had promised them.

David Duke, wearing Klan robes, attends a KKK rally in Euless, Texas in June, 1979.

When he went out to address a gathering, he was booed by the locals. This had never happened to him before. Back in the Governor's Mansion, he lamented and raged to his Three Beards, "They used to love me. Now they hate my guts. They're even blaming me for the fucking weather."

As if that weren't enough, tornadoes ripped through the countryside of Arkansas, causing millions of dollars' worth of damages.

To make matters worse, that same year, the state experienced the worst drought in half a century. It got so hot it led to many deaths, especially among senior citizens. Thousands upon thousands of poultry chicks died, practically collapsing one of the state's most vital industries.

David Duke, Imperial Wizard of the KKK, ran for President of the United States in the 1980 election.

According to the Southern Poverty Law Center, he has faced a series of charges over the years--including inciting riots and reckless conduct.

In 2002, he spent two years abroad to avoid arrest. When he returned to the U.S., he pleaded guilty to felony mail and tax fraud charges, serving fifteen months in a Federal prison.

When the heat waves descended, farm fields dried up and turned brown, as thousands upon thousands of crops withered. Fires broke out in the bone-dry forests, taxing the state's fire-fighting equipment as acre after acre was destroyed. "We're experiencing the Great Plague," Bill proclaimed.

On September 19, 1980, when he was visiting his home in Hot Springs and catching up with Virginia, he had told his mother, "I don't think anything else can go wrong in Arkansas."

Then he received an emergency call from a high-ranking officer at The Strategic Air Command (SAC).

[At the time, the Strategic Air Command, jointly maintained by both the Department of Defense and the U.S. Air Force, was responsible for command and control of key operations affecting the U.S. military's nuclear strike force.]

The commander at SAC delivered some terrifying news: There had been an explosion at the Titan II Missile site near Damascus, Arkansas, an isolated hamlet with a population of about 400, positioned about forty miles northwest of Little Rock. While repairing a missile, an Air Force mechanic had dropped a three-pound wrench. It had fallen nearly 75 feet to the bottom of the silo.

"Arkansas had the world's only cow pasture with its very own nuclear warhead," lamented Governor Clinton.

The commander of the Strategic Air Command post in Damascus (Arkansas) had just told him that there had been an explosion inside a Titan II missile silo. As a result of the explosion, Its nuclear warhead had been hurled up into the air, landing, unexploded, in a cow pasture.

"I was beginning to feel snakebite," Bill said, "fearing that the seventeen other Titan II missiles at that site might explode. "If that happened, Arkansas would have been blown into New Mexico."

(left) View of a Titan II InterContinental Ballistic Missile (ICBM) within its underground bunker.

After its descent, it bounced upward, striking and puncturing a tank loaded with highly toxic rocket fuel. When air hit the fuel, a fire broke out, leading to the instant death of the mechanic who had dropped the wrench, engulfing him in flames and seriously injuring about two dozen other Air Force workers. The ensuing explosion destroyed the missile within its silo, and catapulted a nuclear warhead into a nearby cow pasture, where a herd had, till then, been grazing peacefully.

Understandably, Bill became hysterical, fearing that an atomic blast might destroy part of the state, including its capital and biggest city. The commander tried to assure him that the warhead would not detonate. "No radioactive material will be released, so we don't have to evacuate the town," he said.

Before ringing off, Bill demanded assurance from the commander that the remaining seventeen Titan II missiles were not going to explode. "I don't want my state turned into a dozen Hiroshimas," he said.

A few days later, Vice President Walter Mondale arrived and listened to Bill's urgent pleas about how to protect the people of Arkansas in case of a massive missile explosion. Mondale put through a call to Secretary of Defense Harold Brown, who assured him that it was a freak accident, and that it wouldn't happen again.

God damn it, Harold," Mondale said. "I knew we wanted to get rid of that fucking Cuban refugee problem for Bill. But nuclear warheads—that's a bit much, even for you!"

***

The natural and man-made disasters Bill faced during his short, first-term tenure as Governor of Arkansas would have crippled the re-election chances of anyone else. Adding to his problems was the urgent need for him to choreograph and launch a campaign for re-election to a second term, a race he'd lose in 1980 to another candidate.

Once again, his opponent was a 77-year-old turkey farmer, Monroe Schwarzlose of Kingsland in Cleveland County. Although he had previously run against Bill in 1978, he had won only one percent of the vote. But now, in the bid for his re-election in 1980 to a second term, based on Bill's troubles, his opponent was expected to be a more formidable challenger the second time around.

When Bill sat with Hillary, gloomily listening to the tallies coming in from the state's individual precincts, he turned to her and said, "The rural folks are paying me back for those god damn car license plates."

Schwarzlose had based his campaign on the charge that Bill had "lost touch with the good people of Arkansas. Clinton is married to a hippie wife and hires pot-smoking aides. He's not right for the good and decent people of this state, bringing in a lot of foreign riff-raff."

Because of the statewide resentment based on Bill's having raised the price of car tags, his challenger this time, in 1980, garnered 31% of the vote.

Election day's large and unexpected turnout didn't bode well for his November re-election. Bill, who had emerged victorious in the primary, now had to face his Republican challenger, Frank D. White, who had the support of both Christian Evangelicals and the so-called Moral Majority.

"If I'm not careful," he told his aides, "I'm going to become the youngest ex-governor in America's history."

His chance for re-election that November suffered an insurmountable setback after President Carter opted to relocate some 21,000 Cuban refugees, newly arrived in Florida after crossing from Cuba in overcrowded boats, to Fort Chaffee, in western Arkansas. Many of them

Frank D. White, Bible-thumping darling of the Evangelicals.

Vs. Our Boy Bill, "Enduring more afflictions than Job."

were thieves, former inmates of mental asylums, or "undesirables" convicted of sex crimes ranging from garden-variety homosexuality to more serious and aggressive offenses.

At the time, Fort Chaffee was an Army National Guard installation adjacent to the city of Fort Smith. During the mid-1970s, it had been a center for the housing of refugees from Vietnam.

The little town of Barling (population approximately 4,800) bordered the fort. When tensions with Fort Chaffee escalated, it sent waves of fear through this agrarian and very conservative community. In fact, even before the arrival on their doorstep of these thousands of refugees, very few of the residents of Barling had previously ever voted for Bill.

Castro: It was his idea.

"That god damn commie dictator shithead, Fidel Castro, crazed fucker that he is, indirectly caused me to lose my bid for re-election as governor of Arkansas," Bill claimed.

"He made America look foolish, and Carter powerless."

It had all begun with the Mariel boatlift, a mass emigration of Cubans arriving in the United States between April 15 and October 31, 1980. Fidel Castro had announced that anyone who wanted to leave Cuba could do so. An exodus followed, with boat after boat arriving on the shores of Florida.

The dictator saw his chance to get even with America, and he decided to release the worst prisoners in Cuban jails and to empty his country's mental hospitals. In all, it was estimated that as many as 125,000 Cubans arrived in Florida, where they were hardly welcomed. Immigration processing centers in South Florida were almost instantly overwhelmed.

Bill knew at once that the arrival of all those restless refugees meant trouble for his state and threatened his re-election. He also suspected that Carter would go down in defeat, in part because of the gas shortages and the Iran hostage crisis, and in part because of the downturn in the U.S. economy. Ronald Reagan, former movie star and governor of California, looked as if he'd win the 1980 Presidential elections in a landslide. With accuracy, and in a state of frantic anguish, Bill believed that in his own upcoming electoral race for re-election as governor, he'd ride Carter's coattails to defeat.

In June of 1980, he made frantic calls to Washington in an attempt to relocate the refugees to other stockades outside Arkansas, but Carter would not come to the phone. An aide told Bill that the refugees would remain at Fort Chaffee whether the governor liked it or not. Bill was reminded that the fort was Federal property and that Carter had the right to house the refugees there.

Before the arrival in Arkansas of the Cubans, Bill and Hillary maintained a relatively good relationship with then-President Carter. "Jimmy and Rosalynn often invited Hillary and me to the White House for galas," Bill said.

But because of the conflict over the Cubans, "Our friendship went South," Bill later said. "It would never be restored, especially during my own eight years in the White House."

From the moment of their (enforced) arrival, the Cubans, were "young and restless," provoking or organizing sometimes violent disturbances within the stockade. With the passage of time, as fear and frustrations increased, the already tense situation worsened.

Residents of Barling and personnel at Fort Smith feared both full-scale riots and a break-out. It was said that every vendor of guns within a fifty-mile radius of Fort Smith quickly sold all their inventories. Some homeowners posted signs in their front yards: "WE SHOOT TO KILL."

Sheriff Bill Cauthron telephoned Bill in Little Rock, warning him that, "Our people out here are arming themselves for a kind of race war. They're getting daily reports that the Cubans are going to break out and burn Fort Smith."

On May 26, a Monday night, some 200 refugees did just that, fleeing through the unguarded main gate.

Bill was stunned to learn that the gate had had no security, and he immediately rushed sixty-five members of the National Guard to Fort Chaffee to round up the Cubans.

As soon as he and Hillary voted in the primary, he flew to Fort Smith and drove to the stockade to meet with Brigadier General James ("Bulldog") Drummond. He was stunned to hear the officer tell him that, according to Federal statutes, he had no jurisdiction over the Cubans, since the military was not allowed to arrest civilians outside the fort. *[The Cubans had been classified as civilians.]*

Bill immediately telephoned Jimmy Carter, demanding that the president come to the phone this time. This time, Carter picked up the call, and Bill warned that there would be a bloodbath if he didn't grant Bulldog the authority to control and round up the Cubans. This time, Carter got the message and granted the necessary permissions and authority.

From that point onward, the crisis worsened until the evening of June 1, when "all hell broke loose" (Bill's words). This time, 1,000 Cubans stormed past Federal guards and headed in a confrontational protest—armed with sticks and broken bottles with jagged edges—down Highway 22 toward Barling. One of the marchers described the lacerating edge of the broken bottle he carried as "something to cut the throats of the gringos." As they marched, in a style they might have learned in Castro's Revolutionary Cuba, they shouted, *"LIBERDADE! LIBERDADE!"*

The local residents were terrified and heavily armed.

According to Bill, "The Feds did nothing to stop this onslaught of rampaging Cubans, but I did. Once again, I called out the National Guard to bring order from all the chaos. Locals were threatening to shoot the unarmed refugees if they invaded their homes or attacked their businesses."

In the skirmishes that followed, guardsmen fired shotgun blasts over the heads of the rioting Cubans. Many of the subsequent encounters were violent: No one was killed, but some sixty-five people, both locals and refugees, were injured and had to be rushed to nearby hospitals, and three Federal buildings were set on fire.

Once again, Bill flew to Fort Smith on an emergency flight. After disembarking, he engaged in a shouting match with Bulldog Drummond, accusing him of doing nothing to stop the breakout, even though President Carter had given him the authority to do so.

Drummond responded that he would accept orders only from his immediate commander, a two-star general based in San Antonio—and not from President Carter.

Bill called Washington again, threatening to shut down Fort Chaffee unless Federal authorities brought the refugee riots under control, threatening to surround the fort with troops from the National Guard already stationed within Arkansas, barring entrances and exits to everyone except authorized military personnel delivering supplies.

When the riots at Fort Chaffee were finally brought under control, Carter sent word to Bill with the promise that no more refugees from the Cuban immigration crisis would be sent to Arkansas.

That brief and peaceful interlude was shattered, however, that autumn when cold weather descended on other (unheated) refugee stockades in Wisconsin and Pennsylvania.

"Carter called me and gave me the bad news," Bill said. "He told me had had no choice but to go back on his promise to send no more Cubans to Fort Chaffee, which has a warmer climate."

"I protested vehemently, but I was overruled," Bill later stated. "After all, Carter was up for re-election and Wisconsin and Pennsylvania had more electoral votes than poor little Arkansas. I was thrown under the bus. Really fucked by Carter."

Faced with a dilemma, Bill consulted his chief political aides, each of whom urged him to stand on the Capitol steps in Little Rock and denounce Carter for his betrayal of Arkansas.

"I decided not to do that," Bill said. "I didn't want to do anything to help Reagan beat Carter. So I shut my mouth. Carter just turned his back on our state, which had supported him more than any other state in the union, except for his native Georgia."

To better argue his case, he made one final trip to Washington, "'Where I got no satisfaction,' to quote Mick Jagger."

Returning to Little Rock and keenly aware of his humiliation, he was shocked to see TV ads attacking him. His Republican opponent, Frank White, running against him for the post of governor in the upcoming 1980 election, was a Born-Again Evangelical. He was gaining in the voting polls partly because of videotapes depicting refugee riots in and around Fort Smith.

"I couldn't help but notice," Bill commented, "that all the Cubans depicted in White's TV ads were black."

Although their accusations were not directly aired on TV, White's more rabid supporters spread the word that Bill had personally and secretly flown to Havana and selected "only the most violent and depraved convicts and the most criminally insane from Cuban asylums to export to Arkansas."

His aides, including Hillary herself, urged him to fight back: "No one will believe shit like they're spreading," he said. "The charges are so laughable, only an idiot would fall for crap like that."

She warned, "On election night you'll find out just how many idiots go to the polls."

As Bill's grueling gubernatorial campaign against Wright neared its final weeks, hopes for Bill's re-election grew dimmer. "I could have satisfied Arkansas voters if I personally shot every Cuban refugee who escaped from Fort Chaffee," he lamented.

Staffers reported that at times, he seemed strangely removed from his campaign. He spent hours in the basement of the Governor's Mansion, playing a pinball machine which he'd ordered installed.

One aide said, "Bill was counting on his former popularity holding out, hoping it would see him through to victory. His staff didn't think so. Many of us were already looking for jobs in a hard-to-find economy."

One night, Bill and Hillary engaged in a bitter fight over details and strategies associated with his lackluster re-election campaign. "You think you've got friends?" she shouted at him in front of his aides. "I'll tell you what you've got, Pollyanna. You've got political enemies trying to destroy us!"

The next morning, she was seen storming in a barely suppressed rage around the mansion. In an angry voice, she confronted aides: "If I didn't kick ass, nothing would get done in the state of Arkansas!"

Among the many criticisms were some focusing on Bill's relationship with Carter. One columnist wrote, "Our governor would rather please this peanut farmer from Georgia more than he wants to cater to the needs of the people of Arkansas."

Pre-election surveys showed that eight percent of voters were against Bill's re-election because they disapproved of his wife, particularly for her insistence on keeping her maiden name.

"In that so-called marriage, it's obvious who wears the pants," wrote John Robert Starr, managing editor of the *Arkansas Democrat.* "Bill Clinton is a spineless opportunist whose backbone is Hillary."

Later, Starr was credited with coining the label "Slick Willie" that became a nationwide expression during the 1990s.

Sensing a possible loss, Hillary, during the closing weeks of Bill's re-election campaign, became more aggressively involved. Up to then, she'd focused mainly with her newborn child and with her cases, duties, and affair at the Rose Law Firm.

To an increasing degree, she became more frequently irritated by minor infractions that popped up. Bill had launched a highway safety campaign, but once while riding in his Lincoln as a passenger, on his way to a ceremony associated with the dedication of a new library, it was determined that his driver was speeding at 85mph in a 50mph zone. His driver was stopped and given a ticket, an event that Bill's enemies made it a point to have featured as part of that night's news roundup.

Later. although he tried to joke away the bad effects *["We should re-name our daughter, Chelsea, 'Hot Rodham,'"],* voters were not amused.

In advance of Arkansas' 1980 gubernatorial election, many of Bill's campaign aides did not think he was taking the challenge of his opponent, Frank White, for the governor's seat seriously enough. White was a Savings and Loan executive, during an era of notoriety within that particular industry. Originally a Democrat, he had switched to the Republican Party before his run against Bill.

Night after night, White's campaign bombarded Arkansas TV viewers with ads showing the Cuban refugees rioting near Fort Smith and menacing neighboring communities.

As the poison quotient within the gubernatorial campaign slogged on, Bill suffered a ten percent drop in the polls.

To some degree, Hillary blamed the slippage in her husband's approval ratings on herself for having taken four months' maternity leave after the birth of Chelsea. Rallying her energy and her resolve, she went on the offensive. When Bill, after scheduling an appearance at a political rally in Little Rock opted to cancel at the last minute, she showed up in his place.

At that rally, White had gone onto the stage first. But when he saw Hillary enter the auditorium, he quickly finished his speech and headed for the exit, refusing to stand near her on the same stage. "She'd already decimated me in a previous debate, and I didn't plan to become roadkill for her," White later told his aides. "She's a trial lawyer. She wants to remove the flesh from my bones. That's one tough lady. She'd kick the dog shit out of you. I'm a Southern gentleman, and I was taught not to return fire from ladies."

Hillary—acutely aware of the continuing attacks on her personal appearance—occasionally made some counter-attacks of her own: "Take one look at my opponent," she told a reporter about White. "We're up against a homespun banker with a potbelly and bulging eyes."

She had not quite learned that even a casual remark could be overheard and subsequently amplified by a hostile reporter or a political enemy. One morning, she picked up a copy of *The Arkansas Democrat* and read about a remark she thought she had uttered in secret and in confidence: "Arkansas politics is a slimy, sexist sewer."

When Bill read that, he snapped at her: "A real vote getter, wifey dear."

In desperation, Bill and Hillary enticed the politically savvy political consultant and organizer, Betsey Wright, to move to Little Rock. She would remain there as an adviser to the Clintons for eleven years.

They had been impressed with Betsey's skill during their collective campaigning for Senator McGovern in Texas during that politician's attempt to become President in 1972.

After only two or three weeks on the job, Betsey, along with the more deeply entrenched Hillary, became known as "Bill's Two Valkyries."

Betsey became aware that during the waning days of Clinton's sagging campaign, the governor still attracted what she called "bimbos and groupies."

At the National Governors' Association gathering, "women were licking his feet," Betsey observed. "They were always throwing themselves at him. And he was so *naïve* about them. They'd want to take pictures with him, and he'd stand there with his arm around strange women, many of whom would later use them as evidence that they'd had an affair with him. They'd just come up to him and in a Southern drawl, gush, 'Governor Clinton, I've just been dying to meet you.' That was followed by a batting of eyes and a silly gaze as they rubbed up against him, particularly with their often ample Dolly Parton breasts."

"Bill is in politics to be liked," wrote Morris. "His neurotic narcissism demands that he prove his self-worth to a doubting superego by finding more and more people who like him, each a mirror in which he can see a good version of himself. His desperate need to win elections stems not only from his love of the perks and privileges of power—and his genuine desire to use it to help people—but from the psychological balm that public approval rubs on his poorly formed self-image."

November 4, 1980—election night at the Governor's Mansion—was grim. Before midnight, staffers became painfully aware that they would have only two months to find a new job, and there were few openings. When the final results were tallied, Bill had garnered only 48% of the vote, thereby going down in defeat.

White, as the new, two-year governor of Arkansas, triumphantly addressed his supporters, defining the event as "a victory for the Lord Jesus Christ over the forces of the Devil sent to destroy our wonderful state of Arkansas. My campaign will return decency and morality to the Governor's Mansion."

Bill later admitted that he was in such bad shape after his defeat at the polls that he could not bear to face the "avarice of the press."

It was up to Hillary to commute to campaign headquarters to confront its salaried workers and volunteers, many of whom were in despair. She invited her husband's supporters to the rear garden of the Governor's Mansion, an event scheduled for the following day, where Bill appeared to greet them. Though filled "with self-pity and anger," he thanked them as best he could and delivered a bland and innocuous statement about how he planned to cooperate with White, which he had no intention of doing.

Bill later said, "At least I'll go down in Arkansas' State history as the first governor denied a second term in a quarter of a century. Some honor, huh?"

Soon after that, Bill addressed a joint session of the State Legislature, speaking through teary eyes in a choked voice. "Remember me as one who reached for all I could do for Arkansas."

Hillary, cradling Chelsea in her arms, sat in the gallery listening to his *adieu*. As she recalled later, "I tried to look like Madonna and Child."

The following day he called his most trusted aides into his office. "God, I was an idiot. I didn't see it coming."

One aide reported, "Bill was filled with rage and at times purple in the face. In the final weeks, he was a basket case, unable to get anything done. He was filled with self-pity and intense anger, mostly blaming himself, although sometimes attacking 'that asshole in the White House.'"

In his private quarters, Bill kept playing a song over and over again. It was titled, "I Feel So Bad I Don't Know Whether to Kill Myself or Go Bowling."

On his final day as Governor of Arkansas, he assembled the entire staff and shook each hand as he looked deeply into each aide's eyes. At the end of the ceremony, he told them, "You have just shaken the hand of a young governor whose political future is behind him."

Chapter Nine

The Comeback Kid

After His Triumphant Return to the Governor's Mansion, Bill Begins His Ten-Year "Reign" Over Arkansas

Morphing into Superwoman, Hillary Learns to Say "Y'all!" With a Twang

Lookalikes?

Of the many rumors hovering over the Clintons, the most painful involved the premise that Bill was not the father of his beloved daughter Chelsea. That rumor had circulated in Little Rock since the 1980s, but didn't make the national media until the summer of 2015 when Hillary announced her run for the presidency.

Headlines in *The National Enquirer* speculated that Webb Hubbell, Hillary's partner at the Rose Law Firm, had been the "sperm donor." The article also claimed that Bill had "confessed to a close pal" that he was not Chelsea's biological father.

Bill had long reassured his sexual conquests that "I shoot blanks: hence, no condom."

"If Sex Is a Virus that Travels Through the Air, I Hope I Never Get It!"

—Bill Clinton

After being booted out of the Governor's Mansion, Bill and Hillary had to find a place to live that included a nursery for Chelsea. They returned to the Hillcrest section of Little Rock and found a slightly better house than that in which they had lived before.

Their new home had been built in the early 1900s and was painted a bright sunflower yellow with an old-fashioned L-shaped porch with rocking chairs for sitting out on hot nights. Bill's favorite retreat was his little library with its floor-to-ceiling books. In spite of his busy schedule, he was an avid reader.

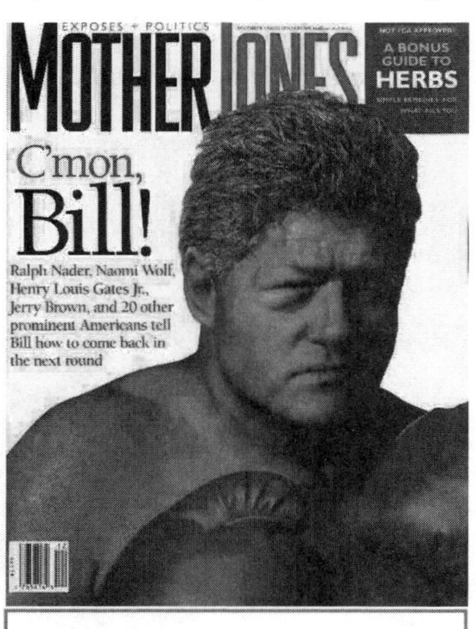

His designation as "The Comeback Kid" originated during Bill Clinton's political career in Arkansas.

Years later, *Mother Jones* hired two dozen prominent Americans to advise him, in print and despite the controversies rolling around him, about how to come back for another round.

One of the first guests to their new home was political adviser Dick Morris, who visited one night for dinner to discuss Bill's plan to run again for the governor's post in the 1982 election. Morris likened the Clinton home "to the lobby of a hotel in an old Gary Cooper western. The glasses and plates in the dining room looked like they were purchased at a discount gas station market, each mismatched and in clashing designs and patterns."

In Bill's library, where they talked about the candidate's future, Morris found him "a very depressed man, wallowing in defeat and fearing he didn't have a political future. I convinced him to pull himself together and begin his campaign for re-

"Men Who Obtain Great Power Become Chick Magnates: Take that Nazi Creep, Adolf Hitler, as an Example"

—Bill Clinton

election as governor, right now."

Morris reportedly told him, "You can be the Comeback Kid." This may have been the first time this expression was used in association with Bill Clinton. Later, of course, it would become a popular saying during the 1992 presidential election.

In the aftermath of their loss of the governor's office, Bill and Hillary experienced some of the greatest tensions in their married lives. This time, it wasn't about his womanizing, but about his losing an election. She called him "a political failure."

When Morris visited the Clintons once again at home, he found Bill on the living room floor, playing with Chelsea and softly singing the Tammy Wynette song, "D.I.V.O.R.C.E."

He was unemployed, and needed a job, soon, to help support his family, although Hillary still had her position at the Rose Law Firm. As a former governor, he had no trouble getting hired by Wright, Lindsey, and Jennings at a salary of $34,000 a year. It was an even larger and more prestigious firm than Rose.

Bill described himself during this period out of political office as "a fish out of water." He was allowed to keep Barbara Kerns, his secretary of four years, and even Betsey Wright was provided with office space in which she could keep his files of voter contacts and volunteer campaign aides up to date. When she wasn't doing that, she was plotting his next campaign for the governor's race in '82.

He was assigned only a few cases, and allocated the smallest office of anyone else in the firm, despite his former status as the Governor of Arkansas.

Hillary not only altered her appearance but began to get rid of some of Bill's political advisers. "I wanted him to be surrounded by real pros, not some guys who looked like they'd just come from a Pink Floyd concert."

Both Bill and Hillary became estranged from former friends, viewing them as "casualties" of the failed election. Paul and Mary Lee Fray were dumped, as were John Danner, one of Clinton's "Three Beards," along with his wife, Peach, who for a time had been one of Hillary's best friends.

A disenchanted Peach later complained "Bill has evolved zero. Albert Einstein's definition of insanity is doing the same thing over and over again and expecting a different result. Hillary thinks everyone needs to understand that she'd engaged in such important business that other people are all expendable. There is no traction in their lives with other human beings."

After she'd been close to the Clintons, Peach claimed, "Bill was fucking a married woman in the summer of 1980 when he went jogging. She'd been a campaign volunteer and wasn't getting on with her husband."

When he began to recover from his loss, Bill launched what Betsey Wright called "an apology tour. He felt like he should be in ashes and sackcloth with the voters flogging him with a horsewhip."

She claimed that Bill viewed these apology jaunts as "more of a masochistic exercise than a depression. He was virtually asking everyone to critique him from the moment he got out of bed in the morning until late at night. Hillary was somewhat disturbed by his excessive self-flagellation, but apart from a few offhand comments, she kept silent as he went about his thing. She seemed to respect how he chose to handle his defeat and rarely interfered. She also doesn't inject herself too much into his bad boy maneuvers. Her tolerance for his apology tour and his constant womanizing has always amazed me."

During extended weekends from his law firm, Bill crisscrossed Arkansas on that apology tour, person to person, contacting voters, especially those who had opposed him. As Hillary told *The Washington Post,* "Bill and I would go out there, and he'd make confessionals in supermarket aisles. People would come up to him and say they had voted against him, but they were sorry he'd lost. He'd say he understood and was sorry for not listening to them with a better ear."

Since Bill was still "hibernating, licking his wounds," Hillary returned to a roster of public events before he did. At her first invitation to a gala at the Governor's Mansion, she encountered the new First Lady of Arkansas, Gay White, wife of the governor, Frank White.

Hillary interpreted her as a "rabid evangelical," who wore raspberry red lipstick and had flaming red hair. Hillary later noted that Gay did not shave her legs, as her dress revealed. Nor did she shave her armpits. Her husband apparently preferred a natural woman.

One of White's aides, Jefferson Smyth, who had campaigned viciously against Bill in the 1980 election, came up to Hillary as soon as Gay had departed to greet other guests. "At last, we've got a First Lady of Arkansas we can be proud of, one who upholds the tradition of Southern womanhood—that is, one who knows how to act like a lady."

Hillary must have taken

RAZORBACK FIRST LADIES AT WAR
Arkansans Kept Score

Hillary *(left)* and Gay White, the wife of Bill Clinton's opponent, during their rivalry to uphold "the traditions of Southern womanhood."

the insult with some consideration. In the coming weeks and months, she began to alter her dress, makeup, hair style, and general appearance. She even hired a fashion consultant.

Soon, the granny dresses and Little Orphan Annie hairdo disappeared. She began to wear lipstick, and sheer nylons encased her rather ample legs instead of her usual black stockings. "She hated her new look," said Betsey, when not smoking what reportedly eventually reached a high of five packages of cigarettes a day. "But the voters loved it."

Peach was also skeptical about Hillary's change in appearance. "The deal was, she'd give up her name and her integrity in exchange for his commitment to take them where she wanted them to go. To the Oval Office, of course."

More and more, Hillary signed her letters, "Hillary Rodham Clinton," not wanting to completely rid the world of her maiden name. Sometimes, if the gathering were conservative enough, she would approach people and say, "Hi, I'm Mrs. Bill Clinton."

She told Betsey and others, "I didn't want my name to interfere with people's perception of the kind of job Bill did. I did not want to adversely affect what he has chosen as his life's work. The only person in Arkansas who has not asked me to change my name is Bill himself."

Arkansas voters began to warm to "the new Hillary," their state's former First Lady. Privately, Vince Foster noted that, "She became more Southern with a lot of hand-shaking and smiles. She'd ask future voters about their children. Many of her new fans found that she wasn't as long-winded as her husband, and that she got down to the real issues more quickly. Some of her most enthusiastic supporters even suggested that she'd make a better governor than Bill, at least one who was more efficient and better organized, and an executive who could stick to schedules and commitments without wandering off to cracker-barrel it."

She even urged Bill to change his own hairstyle. "Get rid of those Elvis sideburns. Show your ears. You keep telling voters you didn't listen to them enough when you were governor. Show the fuckers you actually have ears. When you become governor again, outlaw any aide who shows up with a beard. Surround yourself with clean-shaven men, perhaps men with a doting wife and three adorable children."

In the wake of their loss, Hillary became a take-charge wife, as if asserting command of their political futures. She started by getting rid of the "riff-raff surrounding my husband." She told him, "Many of your campaign aides are nothing but hangers-on, going up in smoke," a reference, of course, to their marijuana use. "They're not successful and they never will be, and they don't have a pot to piss in if you can't get them a job with the state."

On top of everything else, Bill drove from Little Rock to Hot Springs, where he learned that his much-married mother was going to wed for a final time and henceforth would be known in the press as Virginia Kelley. Her husband-to-be was a food broker, a large, pleasant-enough man with a love of the race track, a passion that Bill and he shared. He also became one of Bill's golf partners.

Bill did not oppose the marriage but later expressed his gratitude at the happiness Virginia's latest husband brought to her. "I would come to love Dick Kelley," he wrote. "He liked to travel, and he and Virginia were always going places—and not just to her favorite gambling town, Las Vegas. He even took her to Africa."

Bill and Hillary attended their wedding at Lake Hamilton, at which time Virginia's son, Roger, sang Billy Joel's "Just the Way You Are."

When reports reached Hillary that Bill's womanizing was getting completely out of hand, she telephoned Ivan Duda, the best private detective in Little Rock. She wanted a list of the women with whom her husband was having affairs, admitting that she knew she could not eliminate them. However, she wanted them screened, dividing them into two groups, "the bitches and troublemakers who couldn't shut their fucking traps, and the others who might be discreet, especially those who already had boyfriends or husbands."

During an interview with *Vanity Fair,* Betsey said, "Bill was always very careless out of an unbelievable *naïveté*. He had a defective detector about personal relationships. He just thinks everyone is wonderful. He's careless about keeping up appearances."

She was no doubt referring to his continuing pattern of infidelities in the immediate aftermath of his defeat, which seemed to become even more blatant than before. Vince Foster attributed that to "his trying to resolve his manhood since he felt that his defeat has castrated him."

Did Bill Lie on the "Casting Couch" for Pamela Churchill Harriman?

As Pamela Harriman's biographer, Sally Bedell Smith, wrote in *Reflected Glory:* "With her unwavering, somewhat theatrical gaze, low, chesty voice, and facile manner, Pamela Harriman knew how to beguile men, young and old. Her pale skin retained its translucent glow."

Stuart Eizenstat was President Carter's policy chief. He was awed by Pamela's presence when many women of her generation were settling comfortably into a more sedentary lifestyle, "Pamela radiated a dewy femininity as an older woman, even as she commanded attention with a somewhat masculine mixture of charm, authority, and vigor."

A meeting between Pamela and Bill was arranged in Washington, where the Kingmaker of the Democratic Party could discuss his political future on a national level.

Bill was just thirty-four years old when he met this legendary figure on her sixty-first birthday. She would later take credit for discovering him as a potentially national political figure.

She was flirtatious with him, telling her aides "He's the kind of man I enjoy."

Whether he actually had an affair with her or not is still a subject of debate. "Even if he didn't have an affair with her, Bill wanted people to think he did," said Vince Foster.

Soon, Pamela was comparing Bill's "resilience and inner strength to that of Sir Winston himself."

Three views of one of the world's most worldly and most widely publicized women, Pamela Churchill Harriman,

She was an extraordinary woman who used her beauty, cunning, and hard work to carve out a position for herself in the world of powerful and wealthy men. The English debutante came to world attention when she married Winston Churchill's dissolute son, Randolph.

When Randolph was posted to Egypt in 1941, she launched an affair with Franklin Roosevelt's envoy, Averill Harriman.

Her father-in-law was aware of the affair and appears to have approved of it in his attempt to cement Anglo-American unity during the months leading up to America's entry into World War II.

As an English debutante, Pamela had married Randolph, Sir Winston's son. During World War II, when he was away, she had had an affair with Averell Harriman, son of a railroad baron and America's most famous statesman. He'd been Franklin Roosevelt's special envoy to both Churchill and Josef Stalin. Previously, he'd been the 48th Governor of New York (1955-58).

At the time Bill had his first meeting with Pamela in Washington, she had reinvented herself as the doyenne of the Democratic Party. Before that, she had been hailed as the 20th Century's greatest courtesan, and was described as "having become a world expert on rich men's bedroom ceilings."

Previously, she had been

married to Leland Hayward, the Broadway producer of, among other entertainments, *The Sound of Music.* Later, she'd marry her wartime lover, Harriman, on the occasion of his 80th birthday. At that point, she'd obtained fame and riches through her international affairs with such millionaires and titans of industry as Jock Whitney, Prince Aly Khan, Gianni Agnelli, Elie de Rothschild, and shipping magnate, Stavros Niarchos.

Bill's Republican enemies privately accused him of using the political version of the "Hollywood casting couch" to get ahead in national politics as the "new Golden Boy" of the Democratic Party.

During the Reagan era, Bill was seen coming and going from Pamela's home in Georgetown. Both of them had a single goal in mind, and that involved returning the Democrats to power. As Bill confessed in his memoirs, "Even though Pamela was in her early 60s, she was still an attractive woman."

Rumors spread of an affair between the two. When Bill became President, he appointed her Ambassador to France, where she died "on the job" in 1997.

[During one of her ritual swims in the indoor pool of the Ritz Hotel in Paris, she suffered a heart attack and died instantly.]

In the immediate aftermath of her death, then-President Bill Clinton ordered Air Force One to fly to Paris to retrieve her body. Later, he spoke movingly at her funeral in the Washington National Cathedral.

***

Society orchestra leader Peter Duchin knew both JFK and Bill. He was aware of the differences in the two men. One night, he watched Bill mingling with the "heavy hitters" at a cocktail dance at the Waldorf Astoria in New York.

"Bill is even better than Jack," Duchin claimed. "Clinton wants to fuck everyone in the room. His way is, 'Let's be buddies.' He had more of the common touch than Jack. Jack was more like a prince."

At the party, Duchin teased Hillary about Pamela Harriman. "I know you were responsible for having Bill name her Ambassador to France. That certainly eliminated the competition."

"I'm not stupid," Hillary said, giving him her celebrated "bawdy belly laugh."

***

When Florida Governor Bob Graham invited Bill to address the State Democratic Convention in Miami, near the end of 1981, Bill flew southeast. He was later seen "partying" at a club on Miami Beach. Before that, he delivered a fiery speech to the convention, urging that the Democrats "take a meat ax and cut off the hands of the Republicans."

"A bit melodramatic," he said, "At least I didn't demand a beheading or a castration of the bastards on the Right."

Dick Morris advised him to film a TV ad admitting his mistakes and asking to be given a second chance. It was a risky move. In the ad, he said, "My daddy never had to whip me twice for the same thing."

On February 27, 1982, Chelsea's birthday, Bill announced his bid for another chance at the governorship. Hillary called it "Chelsea's second birthday, Bill's second chance."

He ran on a campaign of improving education and bringing more jobs to Arkansas, and keeping the lid on rising utility rates. "Frank White was vulnerable on all these fronts," Bill said.

His chief competitor for the Democratic nomination was Jim Guy Tucker, who had lost his bid for the U.S. Senate and now wanted to be governor.

On May 25, Democratic voters in Arkansas' Primary delivered Bill 42% of the vote, with Tucker receiving only 23 percent. However, a challenger, Joe Purcell, a low-key man who had been both Attorney General and Lieutenant Governor of Arkansas, got 29 percent of the vote, which meant a runoff with Bill just two weeks later. In that runoff, Bill swept to victory, beating Purcell with 54 percent of the vote, thereby defining himself as the candidate to face White in the November elections. Bill defined that autumn's campaign as "tough but fun."

In looking back to the 1982 governor's race in Arkansas, many "talking heads" on TV later proclaimed that Bill's campaign in Arkansas was a mere rehearsal in his race for the White House ten years later.

Once again, he had challenged White in the governor's race.

As Hillary put it, "Even Lady Gay couldn't save her husband's hide, in spite of her having attended all those country club lunches with fat ladies who doubled up on dessert."

"My daughter Chelsea would win a debate with White," Hillary said.

***

On the road again in 1982, Bill was sometimes joined by Hillary on the campaign trail. They were driven around Arkansas by Jimmy "Red" Jones, and Hillary sometimes took along Chelsea with her diaper bag.

They started in the state's southern tier, where the weather, presumably, was better, often ending up in Fayetteville or Ozark mountain hamlets during snowstorms. Bill had already staked out his favorite barbecue pits in all parts of the state.

They met voters from all walks of life. Hillary was shocked at how browbeaten many of the wives of Arkansas were. Housewife after housewife told her, "My husband makes all the decisions in our family, and he votes for the two of us when he goes to the polls."

A surprising number of African Americans in all parts of the state claimed that the reason they didn't vote was because they could not afford the poll tax. With a sense of urgency, Hillary emphasized that such taxes no longer existed, having been previously defined as illegal, and urged them to go to the polls, preferably without the undue influence of their husbands.

Another driver hauling Bill and Hillary around was Robert (Bobby) Roberts, Bill's Chief of Staff in Little Rock. Mostly, he traveled with Bill alone, stopping in roadside motels where the candidate somehow managed to pick up a bedmate for the night, perhaps a waitress in a café or tavern.

"When Bill and Hillary were riding in the car with me, I noticed they didn't have a lot to say to each other," Roberts said. "When they did talk, it was all about politics, nothing really personal. Even when we stopped to eat together at a roadside joint, Bill always had his head buried in the newspaper as she studied her communications."

From a safe distance, Bill watched Frank White make one blunder after another. One that made him a laughing stock in more educated circles was his push to outlaw the teaching of evolution in classrooms. Thanks to legislation promoted by White, Arkansas became the first state in the Union to embrace "Creation Science," wherein teachers were instructed to present as "scientific fact" the Biblical account of Creation.

George Fisher, a cartoonist at *The Arkansas Gazette,* had ridiculed Bill during his tenure as "the baby governor." But his attack on White was even more vicious, depicting him with a half-peeled banana in his hand to suggest he had not fully evolved and that he was actually "the missing link" between humans and chimpanzees.

Eventually, thanks to intense outrage on the part of politicians not directly allied to the evangelists, White's policies about teaching creation science in the public schools were declared unconstitutional.

When White had beat him for the governorship in 1980, Bill had tried to "rise above that joker's attacks and discuss my political agenda to help the people of Arkansas."

Now, in the 1982 campaign, Bill was a different and a more savvy *politico.* At the urging of Dick Morris and Hillary herself, he became an attack dog. As he so colorfully phrased it, "If some jerk is beating you over your head with a god damn hammer, don't take it. Grab a meat cleaver and cut off the fucker's hand. That's exactly what I did."

Some of his aides went beyond that. As a "God-fearing, Jesus worshipping, devout Christian," White was a teetotaler. His attempts to portray Bill as a heavy drinker backfired. Aides read the word that White, in private, suffered from alcoholism and, in one wild charge made, had the governor running nude down the street until two policemen apprehended him and brought him home.

Morris supervised campaign ads, charging that "White's soft on the utility companies, though tough on the elderly."

During the final days of the campaign, Bill jokingly credited singer Willie Nelson for winning the election for him. At a big rally, Bill walked into a standing ovation as Nelson sang: *"Good morning, America, how are you? Do you know me? I'm your native son."* The crowd cheered wildly for Bill.

Came the election day on November 2. Bill told Hillary, "We're coming back, baby!" He was right, winning 55 percent of the vote for relection to the office of governor. He said, "The black vote for me was staggering."

The next morning, congratulations came in from such leading *politicos* as Ted Kennedy and Walter Mondale.

***

At the inaugural ball at the Excelsior Hotel, some 1,000 supporters showed up to honor Bill and Hillary. He called it "a gathering of my most intimate friends." He was in a bear-hugging mood, and Hillary greeted friends and admirers with her newly acquired Southern accent and her newly polished emulation of Dixie charm.

The *Arkansas Gazette* wrote glowingly of her appearance, calling it "a feminine creation. The dress was soft and wispy, a floor-length gown of Chantilly lace in an overdress (pure innocence) with a satin underdress in that intriguing gray called taupe. Her gown was set off with a Kahn Canary diamond."

She and Bill whirled around the dance floor to the sounds of "You'll Never Know," as interpreted by Betty Fowler's Orchestra.

At the Governor's Mansion, its previous occupants, Frank and Gay White, had moved out the day before.

The morning after the inaugural, a van pulled up, unloading Clinton possessions and furnishings. That afternoon, Hillary arrived cradling Chelsea. "An aide heard her whispering to her little girl, "This is going to be your home until we move into bigger quarters at the White House."

That night, as Hillary and Bill gathered downstairs, a pianist was heard playing "Happy Days Are Here Again."

During the following week, the *Arkansas Gazette* ran a cartoon of its former governor, who was now its governor once more. Previous issues of that paper had depicted him as a boy governor in diapers, or else on a tricycle. After his hard-fought campaign against White, he was portrayed as a conqueror driving a Sherman tank.

He also issued personal orders to his aides, instructing them that at any of his galas, he didn't want to hear gimmick songs. "I'll fire anybody who plays 'Purple People Eater' or 'How Much Is that Doggie in the Window?' I hate goddamn songs like that!"

As governor, Bill faced daunting challenges, as White had left him with a crippling budget deficit of $30 million. Knowing he had only two years to get so very much accomplished, he pitched in right away, telling aides, "Don't quote me, but Arkansas is still living back in the Dark Ages. We've got to drag our people kicking and screaming into the modern world."

He decided to make education one of his chief priorities. "Thank God for Mississippi or else we'd be the worst state in America when it comes to educating our young people."

He decided that the best person to kick off his campaign for better schools and better teachers would be none other than Hillary herself. "She'll get it going and allow me to do other things," he announced. He immediately set about trying to win over senior citizens by removing the sales tax from their medications, and increasing their home property exemptions, a very popular move.

After meeting with Hillary, he decided to take a controversial move to weed out incompetent teachers by giving them mandatory competency tests. That led to statewide protests, especially from the unions. But after much bickering and threatened lawsuits, instructors were forced to take competency tests during March of 1985. The results were horrible. Ten percent of all teachers failed. Since the larger percentage of these were African American teachers, Bill was unfairly accused of being a racist.

"One Stupid Night of Love with Bill Clinton"

—Miss America of 1982

Born in the Ozark Mountains, Elizabeth Ward (later, Gracen), grew up to become a world-class beauty, winning the title of Miss Arkansas and later, Miss America, in 1982.

Her acting career was relatively minor, but not that minor. Her two claims to notoriety were that she had had a one-night stand with then-Governor Bill Clinton, and that she posed nude for Hugh Hefner for a 1992 issue of *Playboy.*

She was twenty-one when she won the Miss Arkansas pageant, which would lead to her being crowned as Miss America

Her family was so poor that for the Little Rock competition, she'd made a gown out of her family's peach-colored tablecloth and had embroidered it with rhinestones.

She hoped that her titles would parlay her into an acting career. The same year she won the crown, she married her high school sweetheart, Jon Birmingham, and moved to Manhattan to test her luck as an actress.

A year later, she flew back to Little Rock for a charity event, and it was there that she met Bill, who had just been re-elected governor. She was staying at the Quapaw Tower, and apartment complex where Bill was a frequent visitor because of his sexual trysts with Gennifer Flowers. He offered to give Gracen a lift back to the apartment where she was staying.

In the back of the chauffeur-driven Lincoln, he flirted outrageously with her, but did not come upstairs with her. However, three nights later, he called her, and she invited him to come over, since her husband was still in New York.

What transpired later, she dismissed as "one stupid night of love—and not that memorable—but it changed my life, and not necessarily for the better."

Years would go by before she finally admitted to having had sex with Bill. She did recall that night: "It was rough going, and at one point, he bit down hard on my lip." In that accusation, she was echoing Juanita Broaddrick, who claimed that Bill had severely bitten her lip when he'd raped her. But Gracen admitted that her sex with Bill had been consensual.

Their sex act had taken place in an apartment owned by an unnamed friend of Bill's. After that night, she never saw him again. However, he did call her one night in New York when her husband was at home with her. "I pretended he had the wrong number and put down the phone."

"Even though I never heard from Bill in the years to come, I experienced a reign of terror as *Clintonistas* waged war against me and scared the hell out of me."

When Bill ran for president in 1992, Gracen was "outed" as having been one of his mistresses, which she never was. When forced to speak out at all, she consistently denied the liaison.

"I believed that if I admitted it, Bill would never have been elected president, not with all those revelations about the Gennifer Flowers scandal."

Before this closeup attention, Gracen had been struggling as an actress, and making television commercials. Suddenly, her career blossomed, and, although it was never proven, there were charges that her boost had come through the influence of Hollywood producer Harry Thomason, one of Bill's closest friends.

"I got an acting job starring in *Sands of Time* in Croatia, of all places," she said. "That was followed by a long-lasting role in Brazil. In other words, I was safely out of the country, and away from reporters."

Back in the States, she landed her biggest break when she was given the sword-wielding role in the long-running TV series, *The Highlander* (1992-1998). *[Gracen would later make her directorial debut in the documentary,* The Damn Deal*, an intimate portrait of three young drag queens from Arkansas who compete in female impersonator beauty pageants.]*

For years, she continued to deny that she'd had sex with Bill, but in 1997, "the shit hit the fan," as she claimed. She was drawn into the notorious Paula Jones sexual harassment lawsuit against the president. Attempts were made to serve her with a subpoena. This came in the wake of testimony from Gracen's former friends, Judy Ann Stokes, who testified under oath that Gracen had admitted to a sexual tryst with the then governor.

Two views of beauty queen and actress, Elizabeth Ward Gracen.

She's depicted *(upper photo)* as Miss America in 1982; and as the cover girl for the May, 1982 edition of Hugh Hefner's *Playboy.*

Tipped off in advance, Gracen stayed out of the country for months, showing up in Canada for work. She was even seen in Paris.

With a boyfriend, she flew to the Caribbean island of St. Martin. It was here that her room was ransacked and thoroughly searched. A maid reported two men in suits had entered her room while another man stood guard at the door. They left behind $2,000 in cash and an expensive Rolex watch.

Gracen claimed that she suspected that they were looking for sex tapes similar to the ones that Flowers had sold when she'd secretly recorded her conversations with Bill in Little Rock.

Finally, in 1998, after years of denial, Gracen appeared on NBC, admitting to her one night of love—"If that's what you call it"—with Bill. During her interview, she apologized to Hillary. "What I did was wrong, and I feel sorry about that," she said. "That's not the way a woman should treat another woman."

In the aftermath of her interview, she

claimed that she received more threatening calls from the *Clintonistas*, warning her to keep her mouth shut. She also received notification that the IRS would move in on her and would seize her wages and personal property. Eventually, that nightmare came true.

To conclude and summarize her tawdry, long-ago encounter with Bill, she told a reporter, "I just wish that the producers of *The Highlander,* in which I played the immortal avenger with my beheading sword, would give me a chance to cut off Bill's head."

More Beauty Queens, More Sexual Trysts, Some Women of Color, & A Coven of "Bimbo Eruptions" Negotiated in Secret

According to many state troopers assigned to guard him, shortly after his return to the Governor's Mansion, Bill not only continued his Rabelaisian lifestyle, but accelerated it.

Many of their revelations about Bill's private life did not surface until his campaign for the presidency in 1992. Four Arkansas state troopers revived allegations about his term as governor in the 1980s. Collectively, these scandals became known as "Troopergate."

Often, these liaisons were with college girls, many aged 19 or, in a few cases, even younger. Sometimes, they were the attractive daughters of some of his most ardent supporters. Many women were flattered to be seduced by a sitting governor of their state.

Sometimes, he managed to turn his morning jogging into a sexual tryst in the bushes, with one of the state troopers standing guard. He called those "quickies." The sexual encounters also occurred in the rear seat of his state-owned limousine, behind darkened windows.

The troopers also alleged that they would slip young women into the Governor's Mansion when Hillary was away or late at night, when she and Chelsea were asleep upstairs.

From 1983 to 1985, Larry Douglass Brown was Clinton's chief of security and a special favorite of his. A native of Pine Bluff, Arkansas, Brown had grown up in a world of segregated bathrooms and segregated schools. He was engaged to Chelsea's nanny, Becky McCoy, whose mother, Ann McCoy, was the administrator and overseer at the Governor's Mansion.

Brown later revealed that one of his main assignments involved retrieving the phone numbers and addresses of young women who had caught Bill's eye.

For convenience's sake, he preferred women who lived in Little Rock. But since he also made frequent trips to other parts of the state, he solicited contacts in towns as diverse as Hot Springs, Fort Smith, and Fayetteville, the latter, because of its status as a university town, a particularly well-inventoried hunting ground for young women.

Brown lost count of the number of women involved, but estimated it to be in the hundreds, most of which were one-night stands. These one-nighters, Brown maintained, were in addition to "mistresses" whose links with Bill continued longer than a one-time single encounter.

Brown later claimed that he and Bill "were really being just good ol' Southern boys, out to have a good time. We would often talk about how 'bad' we really were. Bill had a big problem with women. Women were obviously creatures to be dominated. I rather saw Bill as needing to prove himself, to show that he could overcome the female dominance he'd felt growing up. Marrying Hillary had perpetuated that dominance."

Most of the women Bill seduced returned to their boyfriends or husbands and never again referred to their liaison with the governor. "Those were the ones who kept their mouths shut," Brown said. "The other ones, at least a few of them, turned seducing Bill into a professional career. Gennifer Flowers comes to mind."

Such was the case with most of the dozens of women John F. Kennedy had seduced during his tenures as Congressman, Senator, and President.

However, some of Bill's former seductions while he'd been governor emerged when nosy reporters went to Arkansas and launched intense investigations of their own. Others were revealed in lawsuits and investigative committees.

Troopers later reported that when Hillary and Bill were in the back of the governor's limousine, bitter fights over his womanizing often broke out. However, when they'd arrive at a destination, "They were all smiles," claimed one trooper.

Back at the Governor's Mansion, the troopers also reported that Hillary had a habit of tossing objects at Bill—books, car keys, Styrofoam cups of coffee, whatever. "We grew used to her slamming doors, shattering glasses, plates, anything close at hand."

One night in front of two security guards, she was overheard telling Bill, "I have needs, too! In case it had never occurred to you, I need to get fucked at least twice a year!"

Troopers also alleged that Hillary often took out her frustration on the staff, calling them "shitkickers," "white trash," or "rednecks." At one point, she asked trooper Larry Patterson not to speak when they went out together in public. "You sound like a hick," she charged.

At public events, she could be charming, but Larry Douglass Brown said that in private, she presented a different façade. He remembered her at a state fair, chatting with farmers in bib overalls and women in their feedsack dresses, a sort of Ma and Pa Kettle down on the farm. Later, she'd jump into the car and tell him, "Get me the hell out of here. These people look like refugees from the cast of *Deliverance,"* a reference to the 1972 film starring Burt Reynolds and Jon Voight. It was the story of Atlanta businessmen on a canoe trip in the backwoods of rural Georgia, where they meet two of the most terrifying villains in any movie about the Deep South ever made.

Troopers went with Hillary when she received the "Mother of the Year" award in a ceremony within a Conference Room at the Governor's Mansion. Ralph Parker stood outside, whispering to his fellow troopers, "It should be called Motherfucker of the Year," he said. "That woman terrifies me."

Elizabeth Ward Gracen wasn't the only Miss Arkansas who came under Bill's radar. Before her, was Sally Perdue (sometimes billed as Myra Belle Miller), a beauty queen who had won the state title back in 1958. She went on to become one of the top ten finalists in the Miss America pageant, and later, she reconfigured herself as a radio talk show personality. She was not only beautiful, but articulate.

Her affair with Bill went public in the summer of 1992, after Bill had been designated as the Democratic candidate for president. The next day (July 16), Perdue, by then age 53, appeared on a talk show hosted by Sally Jessie Raphael. On the air, she admitted to having had an affair with Bill in 1983, right after he'd won his second tenure as governor of Arkansas.

The following day, Raphael was subjected to a series of attacks in the media, including from *The Los Angeles Times,* which alleged that, "She'd do anything for ratings." Other media denounced both Perdue and Raphael for "smearing Bill Clinton's character."

Raphael later revealed that she and her producers had serious debates about whether the show, with its revelations, should be aired. "We aired the show with a bit of skepticism and a bit of reluctance. Ms. Perdue told us that she didn't want her story revealed in a 'slimy or bimbo way.'"

Even so, the revelation was the first of what Betsey Wright, one of Bill's chief aides, would later define as "bimbo eruptions." She also denounced some of these women as "gold diggers" and charged that these allegations were "Scud missiles in American politics." She was referring to twenty or so women who came forth with allegations that they, too, had been seduced by Bill during one of his tenures as Governor of Arkansas.

Perdue sold her story to *The National Enquirer,* and provided signed statements from former associates who each asserted that she had told them about the affair at the time it happened.

To counter these charges, *Clintonistas* hired a high-powered private detective in San Francisco, Jack Palladino, who set out to discredit each of the women making these accusations.

Bill denied Perdue's accusation, claiming he had no knowledge of ever having met her. However, some state troopers in Little Rock later corroborated her story.

In a newspaper account, Perdue claimed her affair with Clinton lasted from August to December of 1983. She said that "Clinton came to my home in Little Rock at least twelve times, where we shared our love of music, goofed around, and had sexual relations." He was driven to her house, she asserted, by state troopers as part of his security detail.

She also said, "He had this little boy quality to him that I found most attractive. I still have this image of him wearing my black nightgown, playing the sax badly. It's hard for me to picture him meeting with world leaders. How can they take him seriously?" She was referring to her claim that Bill stripped down and put on her Victoria's Secret *négligée* before performing a saxophone solo.

Their relationship came to an end when she told him that she was going to run for mayor of Pine Bluff. He did not want her to run—in fact, he warned her not to. Eventually, she broke off from him, ran for Mayor of Pine Bluff, and lost.

"Clinton didn't want to think of me as someone who had a brain," she said. "I think he wanted to keep his sexual affairs divorced from politics."

She also said that during her months-long sexual liaison with Bill, he would remove joints from a cigarette case and that he carried cocaine in a plastic bag. "He emptied the coke onto my glass-topped coffee table and snorted."

She later alleged that in August of 1992, she was approached by Ron Tucker, a Democratic Party operative, who told her not to talk any more about an affair with Bill. She was told that if she would be a "good girl," she'd be rewarded with a good-paying Federal job. If she didn't accept that offer, she was warned that "something bad might happen to her pretty legs when she went jogging."

Tucker has denied he did or said any such thing.

Perdue rejected the offer, but was soon fired from her position as a college admissions officer at Linwood College in Missouri. Her car was vandalized, and she received threatening phone calls. She "went into hiding," and moved to St. Louis.

In the 1990s, as Perdue's name kept resurfacing, particularly in the British press, she came in for personal attacks. The *Arkansas Democrat-Gazette,* in a column by Gene Lyons, said, "Sally Perdue's a nut. I wouldn't believe anything she said."

A liberal group, the National Organization for Women, behaved oddly in their blanket defense of Bill. As dozens of women came forward with sexual harassment charges against him, NOW often labeled these women with their allegations as "nuts or sluts."

Lencona Sullivan during her coronation as Miss Arkansas in 1980.

***

Bill's interest in beauty queens continued. In the case of Lencola Sullivan, it was a beauty queen with a difference, at least for the Southern state of Arkansas.

She had won the Miss Arkansas beauty pageant in July of 1980, and went on to represent her state in the Miss America Pageant. Once there, she became the first African American woman to place among the top five contestants, coming in as fourth runner-up.

Her fellow African Americans hailed this as a major step forward in their battle for equal rights, and they were delighted that a woman of color was recognized for her beauty. Arguably, Sullivan was credited with being the inspiration behind the slogan BLACK IS BEAUTIFUL.

Like Gennifer Flowers, Sullivan became a reporter for KARK-TV in Little Rock. Later, when she moved to New York City, she had an affair with Stevie Wonder, who, of course, became one of the most loved musical performers of the late 20th Century. Shortly after he was born in 1950, he became blind.

Bill didn't seem too jealous of Wonder moving in his turf. Two of Wonder's songs were among Bill's favorites: "I Just Called to Say I Love You" and "You Are the Sunshine of My Life."

When Bill ran for governor again in 1984, rumors were rife about his affair with Sullivan. Back then, or even now, gossip about an interracial romance could seriously damage the standing of a Southern politician. However, rumors were widespread about Bill and Sullivan. However, it met with such disbelief it didn't stop him from getting re-elected.

***

Yet another beauty, a blue-eyed brunette, Robyn Dickey, was hired as the new administrator at the Governor's Mansion after Bill's re-election as governor in 1982.

Her job involved overseeing the housekeeping and maintenance staff, as well as the gardeners working on the mansion's sprawling grounds. She also organized galas and special events, including state dinner parties and receptions for distinguished out-of-town visitors.

One reporter defined her job as "taking care of the special needs of the Clintons." A state trooper quipped, "She sure takes care of Bill's every need all right."

At the time she served the governor, she was married to David Dickey, who had been a star football player for the Razorbacks. The couple had three children, and their oldest daughter, Helen Dickey, would later become Chelsea's nanny during the Clinton's White House years.

The security chief in Little Rock, Larry Douglass Brown, later wrote: "Intuitive and understanding to the point of actually claiming she had a second sense, Robyn spent social hours away from the mansion with me whenever time permitted. She also enjoyed spending social time with Bill Clinton."

He would also claim that both Bill and Robyn shared with him "deep conversations" about the details of their sexual liaisons.

When Hillary became suspicious that her husband was having an affair with Robyn, she was dismissed. But Brown alleged that she continued her relationship with Bill, as he sometimes slipped her in through the rear entrance of the mansion when Hillary had retired for the night. He also said that when Hillary was away on business, which was frequent, Bill would more openly receive Robyn.

When Bill became president, Robyn for a while worked as Chief of Protocol. The staff nicknamed her "Thumbs," because of the great massages she allegedly gave to Bill.

"I think Robyn was tired of Hillary, but she needed the job, so she took it," Brown said. However, Hillary booted her once again when she felt the affair had begun anew. Actually, according to Brown, it had never ended.

Bill secured for her the position of Chief of Protocol at the Pentagon. "One had to wonder about the efficacy of the practice of dumping Bill's ex-paramour into top-secret clearance positions," Brown said.

According to author David Brock, the staff once overheard Robyn making a joke about Hillary. "Kentucky Fried Chicken has a new special in honor our First Lady—two large thighs, two small breasts, and a left wing."

On November 10, 1997, Brown was summoned by Paula Jones' lawyers to testify in the sexual harassment suit brought by her against Bill. He gave his sworn testimony at the DoubleTree Hotel in Little Rock. Without being salacious in any way, he admitted that the Clinton/Dickey sexual trysts had taken place beginning at the Governor's Mansion in 1983.

He later summed up the affair. "Clinton's methods of subterfuge, intimidation, and lying have not changed one iota from governor to president. The only difference now and then is that when you leave Clinton's employ, you get a great job that calls for top secret clearance."

"The Al Sharpton of Little Rock" Claims that Bill is the Father of a Black Son

By the 1980s, Bill was known in certain quarters of Little Rock for getting women pregnant and later paying for their abortions. But such was not the case in 1985.

One early evening, he was said to have gone jogging, where he met a prostitute, Bobbie Ann Williams, who allegedly had a drug problem. While a state trooper stood as a lookout guard, Bill was said to have been the recipient of fellatio in the bushes.

His liaison with this prostitute, whom he later impregnated, formed part of the plot of the 1996 novel, *Primary Colors,* published by Random House and written by reporter Joe Klein. It was adapted into a film in 1998, starring John Travolta as a Bill-like politician, with Emma Thompson taking on the role of his domineering wife *[a role inspired by, guess who? Hillary]* trying to "keep the lid on the latest scandal."

It was later alleged that Bill made at least a dozen trips to have sex with Williams, who lived in a low-income housing project only five blocks from the Governor's Mansion. Here, he is said to have snorted cocaine during his interludes with her.

State trooper Buddy Young was cited as having driven Bill to these sexual trysts. He also may have driven him to a hideaway owned by Virginia, his mother, in the hills. One night, or so it was claimed, he drove not only Bill and Williams to his modest retreat, but two other hookers for a four-way. The women were paid $400 each, plus a $50 tip, the most they'd ever been given for "turning a trick."

Williams later told reporters, "I was still walking the streets with Danny, my future son, when I was four months pregnant with my child. I was also still having sex with the governor. He told me that he got extra turned-on by having sex with a pregnant woman. His exact words to me were, 'Pregnancy seems to make a gal hotter.'"

"One night, I told Bill that I was pregnant with his child. He just rubbed my big belly and told me, 'Gal, that can't be my baby, with all the tricks you've turned.'"

She admitted that during their sexual relations, he never wore a condom, continuing to call such an accessory "a scumbag."

This was in contradiction of his future political stand, when he spoke before the Global Initiative, which was broadcast on TV. He claimed that abstinence was not enough, and that young people needed to be educated to use condoms.

After Danny Williams was born in 1985, state trooper Larry Patterson claimed that he was asked to take some of Chelsea's extra Christmas gifts over to Williams' apartment to give to Danny.

Lucille Bolton, Danny's aunt, once arrived at the Governor's Mansion to present Bill with his one-year-old son. Hillary was summoned, and refused to grant them permission to enter.

As early as 1988, one of Little Rock's most flamboyantly visible characters, Robert (nicknamed "Say") McIntosh decided to make the birth of Danny a political issue. He was called "the Al Sharpton of Little Rock." In his memoir, *My Life,* Bill described him as a "volatile black restaurateur, with whom I had an on-again, off-again relationship."

McIntosh was a friend of Williams and saw her with her son Danny on several occasions. "If you see the boy, you can definitely tell that he's Bill's kid. I've met him. Danny is definitely not black."

McIntosh was angered that Bill was not taking responsibility for what he viewed as the governor's boy. He printed handbills and decided to make a political issue of it when rumors spread that Bill was going to run for president. McIntosh distributed these handbills, which claimed, "THE HOTTEST THING GOING! BILL CLINTON'S DICK WILL KEEP HIM FROM RUNNING FOR PRESIDENT." These handbills were distributed all over Little Rock

Bobbie Ann Williams and her son, Danny, hold up a picture of her alleged former lover. When he was younger, Danny sometimes asked, "Why doesn't my daddy come to see me?"

Apparently, a deal was struck between McIntosh and the governor. The restaurant owner's son, Tommy McIntosh, had been given a stiff jail sentence for peddling cocaine. Bill agreed to give the young man a pardon if McIntosh would stop his campaign to expose Bill as the father of "a bastard son."

However, the tabloid *The Star,* in 1999, tried to settle the issue by comparing a blood sample from Danny with a profile of Bill's DNA made public by Independent Counsel Kenneth Starr. The tabloid claimed in an article that DNA samples proved that Danny was Bill's son. However, DNA experts weighed in, claiming that there was insufficient information about Bill's DNA in the *Starr Report* to make any valid comparison. Therefore, the tongues continued to wag about "the so-called 'bastard son.'"

Early in Bill's second term as governor, Hillary hired Ivan Duda, a private detective, to investigate the "extracurricular activities" of her husband. It was damage control," Duda said years later. "She wanted to find out the bimbos he was messing around with. In essence, she was trying to protect him from his own folly."

One woman, whom Duda did not name, was a secretary at the Rose Law Firm, the entity that employed Hillary. "Learning of this liaison really pissed off Hillary," Duda claimed. "She's been working closely with the woman, and didn't have a clue that she was sleeping with her husband."

After Their Move Back Into the Governor's Mansion Bill Continues His Quest for Beauty

When Bill returned to the Governor's Mansion at the beginning of his second term, Hillary noted that he was "a much humbler man, more seasoned, though still determined to get as much done as possible during the next two years."

Both of them were painfully aware that Arkansas remained one of the most backward states in the nation, ranking near the bottom, along with Mississippi, of nearly every list. It was also one of the poorest states in the Union, with educational standards that remained among the lowest.

Bill launched an Educational Standards Committee to institute major reforms. Hillary warned him that this was a politically risky move, since it might lead to an increase in taxes, which had previously, in 1980, doomed his race for the governorship.

Nonetheless, he beseeched her to head the committee to bring about reform. As expected, she ran into strong opposition. At one meeting, a teacher from rural Arkansas, who felt her job was threatened, denounced Hillary as being "lower than the belly of a rattlesnake."

Hillary proved to be a valiant warrior in the field and stood up to her enemies, doing more to improve education in Arkansas than any governor had before her, much less a First Lady, an honorary position where wives mostly hosted ladies' teas.

As a re-elected governor, Bill really had more on his agenda than he could possibly accomplish in such a short time. But he did succeed on many levels, bringing new business to the state and persuading the owners of long-established manufacturing firms from closing down their plants, as that would add to the state's already high unemployment rolls.

He still had his eyes on the presidency, and was often out of state on speaking engagements in an attempt to build up a national profile. His outings to other states gave him a good excuse to continue his womanizing. Often his conquests succeeded, but sometimes he faced a woman who not only rejected him, but was outraged by his flirting and propositions.

Jim McDougal, who was an observer to many of his conquests, once said, "Bill cast quite a net, but didn't always catch something on the hoof." Such was the case with Karen Hinton, whom Bill met in 1984 at a fund raiser in Greenville, Mississippi for the Democratic Party. She was the director of public affairs for the school system in Washington.

As an attractive, statuesque blonde—Bill's favorite hair color for a woman—Hinton was an imposing figure and was very active in the Democratic Party.

When they came together at a dinner with their colleagues, Bill blatantly flirted with her. As she'd later till Michael Isikoff, a reporter for *The Washington Post,* "He looked me up and down like a tasty meal, managing to sit beside me throughout the entire meal."

At the end of dinner, Bill slipped her a napkin on which he'd written his room number at the Holiday Inn. He made it evident that he wanted the twenty-four-

Bubba come-on to Blaz aide in '84

DAILY NEWS

'I'd been talking to him all this time, thinking he was interested in what I had to say, and all he's thinking of is how could he get his hand up my dress.'

As late as the summer of 2015, Karen Hinton—by then, the press secretary to the Mayor of New York, Bill de Blasio— was still making headlines because Bill Clinton one night in 1984, in some backwater in Mississippi, hit on her.

As a spokesperson for Bill said, "Maybe Karen will finally get over it. It's ancient history now—time to move on."

year-old to knock on his door later that evening.

"I thought he'd been interested in my political views," she recalled. "We talked about issues like teen pregnancy. But it seemed that all he wanted to do was get in my pants. I did not accept his invitation."

She did not keep his sexual solicitation a secret, and discussed it with many of her colleagues in the Democratic Party. "Everybody I spoke to seemed aware of his womanizing, and they treated it like a joke. However, they also told me that his reckless behavior would prevent him from ever running for a higher office outside Arkansas."

As the years went by, Hinton continued to be outraged by stories of Bill's seductions. "His reported antics drove me crazy," she said. "When Bill became president, I heard that he was continuing to walk into a room and hit on any beautiful woman he saw."

She accurately predicted that if he continued on his present course, it inevitably would lead to a major political scandal.

Was the Chief Justice of the Arkansas Supreme Court the Biological Father of Chelsea?

Webb Hubbell, a partner with Hillary and Vince Foster at the Rose Law Firm, was seen coming and going at the Governor's Mansion. He was also spotted dining with Hillary, and rumors began to circulate, many locals thinking that he, and not Vince Foster, was having an affair with Hillary. Hubbell sometimes accompanied Foster and Hillary to a rustic cabin in Heber Springs.

Security Chief Larry Douglass Brown said he was often invited to go along, but he always bowed out. "I was afraid I might be asked to participate actively." He was referring to sexual activity. "There were some things I wouldn't do, especially with Hillary."

When the position of Chief Justice of the Arkansas Supreme Court became vacant, Hillary urged Bill to appoint Hubbell to the post. The governor was allowed to fill the vacancy for the remainder of its unexpired term. Bill weighed the options, fearing a conflict of interest since he was one of Hillary's law partners.

Brown overheard Bill and Hillary fighting over the issue. She told him, "God damn it, he's my friend and you have the right by law to name him for the job." Finally, giving in to her, Bill appointed Hubbell as Chief Justice. Hubbell was only thirty-six years old.

[After time as Chief Justice, Hubbell returned to the Rose Law Firm until President Clinton, in January of 1993, made him Associate Attorney General,

the third highest ranking individual in the U.S. Justice Department.]

Because of the editorial coverage that went with his new appointment, rumors arose about Hillary and himself. One day that gossip would be fodder for social media.

Since rumors had it that Hillary no longer slept with her husband, some of Clinton's enemies referred mockingly to Chelsea's birth as "The Immaculate Conception." Although Vince Foster was often cited as the father of the Clinton family's baby daughter, Hubbell came in for his share of the paternity claims.

Robert Morrow, a political researcher and activist, based in Austin, Texas, wrote: "Chelsea Clinton bears a striking resemblance to Webb Hubbell. She has very big lower lips and a weak chin, just like Hubbell. Bill has thin lips and a strong chin. The resemblance of Chelsea to Hubbell is most pronounced in pictures of Chelsea as a teenager."

He claimed that in Hubbell's 1997 memoir, he mentioned Hillary 396 times. Hubbell wrote that "Vince and I were mesmerized by her," and that "Bill wasn't much of a presence in our lives."

That Hubbell is the biological father of Chelsea is pure speculation. It enters the realm of conjecture, often posted on the internet or surmised in the memoirs of their enemies, that Hillary is bisexual "like a string of other politicians (Obama, George H.W. Bush, George W. Bush, probably Lyndon B. Johnson (who also alleged to have screwed his grandmother), John F. Kennedy, and Richard Nixon."

During Bill's Third Term (1984-1986) as Gov. of Arkansas, "Brother Roger" is Jailed for Pushing Cocaine

Bill's second term as governor "went so quickly, it just seemed to flash before my eyes. I couldn't believe it when 1984 rolled around, and I decided to run for governor again."

He was reasonably confident of his chances for re-election to the governorship of Arkansas. Ronald Reagan, who was simultaneously running for re-election as president, was widely popular in the South. Bill was depending on many voters to cross party lines, voting for a Republican for president and a Democrat for governor. As governor, he had scored great victories in the state's educational system, and the economy under his rule had also been vastly improved.

In the May primary, he faced competition from Lonnie Turner, a lawyer from the Ozarks. Bill felt betrayed by Turner, since he always thought they were good friends and that he was a political ally ever since 1975, when they'd worked together on "black lung cases."

Turner had bolted from the Clinton machine because he objected that standards for schools would lead to the closing of many rural schools which did not perform as well as big city or town institutions.

Only weeks after winning the primary, state police held a meeting with Bill and his chief aide, Betsey Wright. The governor was informed that Roger Clinton, Bill's half-brother, was not only a cocaine addict, but a major drug dealer in Little Rock. As previously mentioned, he had been videotaped selling coke.

Bill himself had launched an anti-drug crusade that had led to Roger's eventual entrapment. He made a decision not to alert Roger that he was under surveillance, and he also didn't tell their mother, Virginia. Ultimately, the net came down over Roger's head, and he was arrested, tried, and sent to prison. That decision on Bill's part led to a lot of family conflict, but in time, both Roger and Virginia forgave him.

Roger received a five-year sentence, three years of which were suspended because of his cooperation. In the end, he would spend only fourteen months in jail. At the end of his incarceration, he appeared to have been cured of his addiction.

Bill held a brief press conference, telling reporters that, "I love my brother, but the law must take its course."

That summer, Bill and Hillary flew to San Francisco as leaders of the Arkansas delegation that nominated Walter Mondale as its frontrunner to challenge Reagan in the fall election. Hillary was especially delighted when Mondale chose a woman, Geraldine Ferraro, as his vice presidential running mate. She would later debate Reagan's choice of a Veep, George H.W. Bush.

In San Francisco, both Bill and Hillary became aware of the new health crisis sweeping the city. Many young gay men were coming down with a fatal disease that came to be known as AIDS.

Reagan was heading for a victory in November, calling for "a morning again in America." Bill and Hillary were labeled "San Francisco Democrats," a slur on that city's large gay population. Bill met Bush on the campaign trail. As he later wrote in his memoirs, "Bush fell into the macho mode, telling me he was going to 'kick a little ass.'"

Upon his return to Arkansas, Bill had to accelerate his campaign into high gear before an electoral confrontation with his Republican challenger in November. Woody Freeman, a Republican, was a young businessman from Jonesboro.

Fearing that Roger's arrest might damage his chances for re-election, Bill turned to his friend, Jim McDougal, his partner in the Whitewater real estate deal, as a means of securing a loan to purchase a last-minute flurry of TV ads.

As he told his security chief, Larry Douglass Brown, "Jim is one goofy son-of-a-bitch, but he's sure good for a lot of money."

The ads seemed to work as Bill garnered 63 percent of the vote against Freeman. That November, statewide, Reagan defeated Walter Mondale by a margin of 59 to 41 percent of the vote.

***

After he communicated and articulated his vision and many promises about a get-rich-quick scheme, Jim McDougal was embarrassed by the failure of the Whitewater real estate development. Instead of a windfall, it was creating a morass of taxes and bank interest payments. During the Reagan years, land values had plummeted.

In an almost desperate attempt to recoup his financial standing, he purchased a small Savings and Loan, changing its name to the Madison Guaranty. Through devious means that would later send him to jail, he was able to raise its deposits from $6 million to $123 million in just three years.

He had a hard time disclosing to Bill and Hillary that the Whitewater development deal had morphed into an expensive, embarrassing, politically compromising failure.

Even so, in 1984, Bill jogged over to McDougal's office in Little Rock and suggested that he throw more business to the Rose Law Firm from his S&L. Although in financial trouble, Jim agreed to send them a monthly retainer. He also organized a fundraiser to liquidate Bill's campaign debts from his 1984 race. Bill was $50,000 in the red, and Jim contributed a check from Madison for $12,000 to help lower the balance. He also rallied other supporters to contribute.

In the meantime, Jim was covering some of the losses generated by Whitewater from his S&L accounts. By 1984, Federal investigators became aware of his devious banking practices and issued several warnings. By April of 1985, the First Lady of Arkansas became Jim's legal representative before the Arkansas Securities Commission.

The question never answered was, did Hillary know that Jim had siphoned off some $18 million from his S&L for himself and some of this cronies by engineering a series of fraudulent real estate deals?

Later, in the White House, when Hillary was asked to find her billing records for the Rose Firm, she claimed that they had disappeared. However, later, they showed up on her desk at the White House.

Susan and Jim, along with Hillary and Bill, faced tens of thousands of dollars in interest payments and did not pay their taxes. Both Bill and Hillary were embarrassed to be listed in local newspapers in Little Rock as tax delinquents—not a good political move, of course, for a sitting governor.

Jim later blamed Hillary's greed for wanting to hold onto the Whitewater investment, long after it became obvious that all had been lost. She kept accusing him, "You told me that the investment would finance my daughter's education, and I want to you keep your promise." Bill disagreed, advising her to "abandon ship," but she was determined to hold onto it, hoping it would eventually pay off.

Jim advised her to turn over the Clinton's half interest in Whitewater. In exchange, he would assume its mounting debt and back taxes, a very generous offer, which she rebuffed, throughout both 1985 and '86.

It wasn't until 1992, the year Bill was elected president, that Hillary finally relinquished the investment for $1,000. But by then it was too late. Whitewater would evolve into a national scandal, leaving a black mark on the Clinton presidency and making this obscure tract of Ozark Mountain real estate a household word.

By 1986, Jim could no longer keep Madison afloat, admitting that it was "a House of Cards." He resigned from Madison, and the deal ended up costing U.S. taxpayers a whopping $60 million.

Susan McDougal wrote, "The fall of Madison was every bit as rapid as its ascent. At the beginning of 1986, it was featured as one of the fast-growing financial in institution in the South. Within six months of that article, bank examiners announced that the S&L was close to insolvency. Even if Jim were not a manic depressive, which he was, he still didn't have the business acumen or the temperament to run a multimillion dollar operation."

By the summer of 1985, Susan and Jim had separated, but their divorce would not become final until 1990.

The seeds of disaster were being sown for almost everyone linked to the Whitewater real estate deal. The failed investment would later be used as a tool in an attempt to impeach President Clinton in the 1990s, a goal that the chief investigator, Kenneth Starr, would tirelessly labor to achieve.

Chapter Ten

Bill Falls in Love & Contemplates a Divorce from Hillary
"If JFK Had His Marilyn, Why Can't I?"

Hillary Forces Bill to Be Secretly Tested for AIDS
Reportedly, "It's Only Syphilis I Caught From Some Whore."

At a White House Governors' Dinner, Ronald Reagan, 40th President of the United States, chats with Bill Clinton, the future 42nd President, and with Hillary Rodham Clinton, possibly the 45th President of the United States.

"The Press Ruined Gary Hart. What Will They Do to Me?"

—*Bill Clinton*

Roger Clinton's arrest on August 2, 1984, was a great embarrassment for Bill, but didn't seem to harm Hillary at all, even though he was her brother-in-law. She described him as "a fourteen-year-old boy in the body of a twenty-eight-year-old man.

In spite of the bad publicity, *Esquire* Magazine listed both Bill and Hillary along with 272 other Americans as "the best of the emerging new generation."

She came in for honors of her own by being named "Public Citizen of the Year" by the National Association of Social Workers, and she was also crowned "Woman of the Year" by the *Arkansas Democrat.*

Roger's testimony about his dealings with Dan Lasater implicated Bill. Lasater was a drug kingpin who was later arrested, tried, and sent to jail for a six-month term.

This cocaine trafficker was linked to the so-called "Dixie Mafia." He was also a highly visible supporter of Bill, with a history of contributing heavily to his political campaigns. Bill and Hillary had flown on his private jet. Virginia, mother of both Roger and Bill, sat next to Lasater in a box at the Oakland Horse Racing Track. For a time, Lasater had employed Roger as his chauffeur in Little Rock, and was said to have supplied Bill's half-brother with drugs.

It was further alleged that Lasater had reaped hundreds of thousands of taxpayer dollars in state commissions. His brokerage house handled some $665 million in Arkansas bond issues, which brought in $1.6 million in brokerage fees for Lasater, a setup fully authorized by Bill.

Lasater was also said to have given Roger some $20,000 when Roger perceived that his life was endangered. A thief had stolen a stash of cocaine from Roger's convertible, and drug dealers were holding him responsible, threatening him with death if he did not pay for the stash, which he was supposed to have sold to a Hot Springs attorney. *[It was rumored that the dealers, to emphasize their point, had also threatened the lives of both Bill and Virginia.]*

"Bill, How Would You Like to Switch Roles?" Hillary Asks. "Me, Governor—You, First Gentleman?"

Lasater's lavish parties became notorious, and were said to have evoked those given in F. Scott Fitzgerald's novel *The Great Gatsby.* But whereas the parties in that novel took place in the 1920s and flowed with illegal liquor during the Prohibition Era, at Lasater's parties, cocaine was said to have been passed around in ashtrays.

These revelations came to light in an article by L. J. Davis, published in the April, 1994 issue of *The New Republic*.

Even more damaging were revelations from reporter Jerry Seper, as published in the *Washington Times.* His article quoted some of the transcripts from Roger's interrogation by the FBI after his drug arrest. Before a Grand Jury, Roger was said to have testified that he snorted cocaine at least twelve to eighteen times a day, and that he often supplied the drug and brought women to the Governor's Mansion "for sex during wild cocaine binges."

Later, when a reporter asked Bill if he'd ever snorted cocaine, he denied it.

One of the narcotics officers who had Roger under surveillance before his arrest told investigators that, "The Clinton boys used the Governor's Mansion like a whore hotel."

One officer with the state police claimed, "I don't think Hillary even knew how much coke Bill snorted with Roger or how many girls they'd done together, but we knew she'd tell her husband to feed ol' Roger to the Feds for the sake of Bill's political career, and that's exactly what he ended up doing."

Miraculously, the involvement of the Clintons with the Roger and Lasater link never became the source of any particularly damaging political fallout. For the most part, the scandalous gossip it generated was confined mainly to Little Rock.

***

During his third-term tenure as governor, Bill's time wasn't devoted just to the problems of Arkansas, as plentiful as they were. Whenever possible, he made frequent trips to Washington to build up his name recognition. His biggest exposure on the national stage came when he was selected to deliver the Democrat's response to Reagan's 1985 State of the Union Address.

At that summer's annual Governor's Conference in Idaho, whereas Lamar Alexander of Tennessee was selected as chairman of the National Governor's Association, Bill was elected as its Vice Chairman, thereby allowing him a highly visible platform from which to deliver speeches in other states.

A year later, in 1986, he was elected as that organization's chairman, replacing Alexander. Bill was only forty years old at the time. Chelsea, age seven, answered a question from a reporter who asked her what her father did. "He gives speeches, drinks coffee, and talks on the phone."

Before that, in 1985, he'd also become one of the founding members of the Democratic Leadership Conference (DLC), a group dedicated to moving the party more to the ideological center so that the Democrats would win more state and national elections. The organizers of the DLC, including the Clintons, feared that some members of their party were too liberal to carry the South, the Midwest, and the Rocky Mountain States.

Because of Bill's almost frenzied political involvement on both the state and national levels, the months rolled by so quickly "I hardly had time to fart."

Actually, he did have time to fart, according to the state troopers who'd been assigned to drive him around. As one of them claimed, "I always hated it when he rode in the front seat. He didn't just fart. Those were elephant farts. Real lethal gas. I had to roll down the window to get some fresh air before I passed out."

Soon, it was time to launch his 1986 campaign for re-election to a four-year term as governor. Unlike his 1984 campaign, which had been marred by Roger's arrest for cocaine dealing, Bill's fourth campaign for the governorship would be riddled with other scandals. They would include both personal issues—continued womanizing and his own alleged drug abuse—as well as controversies associated with the questionable business alliances cultivated in league with Hillary. Especially prominent among these was Jim McDougal, whose financial irregularities would later lead to the Whitewater investigation.

In anticipation of the upcoming Democratic primary in May, Bill began his campaign for re-election in February on Valentine's Day. "My heart belongs to Arkansas," he told his supporters.

If he won, he would become the second longest-serving governor in the history of Arkansas, his length in office surpassed only by Orval Faubus. Ironically, it was Faubus himself, the notorious segregationist, who decided to challenge Bill in the May primary that year.

A leaflet addressed to members of Little Rock's School Board, widely distributed throughout the state capital in 1957.

Faubus, the 36th governor

of Arkansas, had served from 1955 to 1967, and had become infamous in 1957 during his stand against integration of the Little Rock School District, in which he defied a ruling of the U.S. Supreme Court. Eisenhower had called out the National Guard when locals tried to prevent black students from attending Little Rock Central High School.

To retaliate against Eisenhower, Faubus shut down every high school in Little Rock for the duration of the 1958-1959 school terms. In retrospect, this period was later defined as the school district's "lost year" for the academic advancement of an entire generation of students.

Amazingly, based on a 1958 Gallup poll, Faubus was among the "Ten Men in the World Most Admired by Americans," although in some quarters, he was the most hated. He had been elected governor for six two-year terms. Hence, he was in office for twelve years, maintaining a defiantly populist image throughout the course of his tenure. Faubus ran for governor again in 1970, 1974, and 1986. *[The 1986 race pitted him against the then-sitting governor, Bill Clinton himself.]*

When Bill had become governor in 1979, he had invited all of Arkansas' former governors, friends and foes, for an event at the Governor's Mansion. Faubus was included on that list, although Bill later confessed, "No good deed ever goes unpunished. I got a lot of whiplash from my more progressive supporters for having invited Faubus."

During his campaign against Faubus, Bill asserted, "His 1957 stance against integration has inflicted lasting damage upon the State of Arkansas. We have moved beyond his backward policies. I will be the governor of all the people, not just a choice few. We have thrown off the dark shackles of segregation and discrimination."

Back in 1974, when Bill ran (unsuccessfully) for the U.S. Congress, he became acutely aware that he'd need Faubus' support. Consequently, with Hillary, he made a social call at the home of the former governor at his home in Huntsville. *[The cost of that home had been partially paid by Faubus' supporters, in the wake of Faubus' departure from the Governor's Mansion with no money.]* There, the Clintons met Faubus' second wife, Elizabeth, a native of Massachusetts who still wore a 1960s beehive hairdo, and who in many ways was even more conservative than her husband. At one point, she asked Bill what he thought about the conspiracy to overthrow the government of the United States.

Bill said he was against it.

During Bill's 1984 gubernatorial campaign, whatever grudges Faubus maintained against Bill bubbled to the surface when he refused to allow the state of Arkansas to buy his beautiful house, designed by Fay Jones, in Huntsville with the intention of incorporating it into the State Park System as a guest house for visiting V.I.P.s. Bill denied his proposal, asserting that the state budget had no "wiggle room" for such a purchase, even though he knew that Faubus, as always, needed the cash.

Thorncrown Chapel, designed by Arkansan architect Fay Jones, and completed in 1980, is one of the best-known modern structures in the state.

*[**Arkansas Esoteria**: Fay Jones (1921-2004) was the most famous architect ever associated with Arkansas, the state where he was born and died. An apprentice of Frank Lloyd Wright and an advocate of his "Prairie Style," Jones is the only one of Wright's disciples to have received a gold medal (in 1990) from the American Institute of Architects, the most prestigious award sponsored by that organization. Jones' most famous work is Thorncrown Chapel. Completed in 1980 near Eureka Springs, it has been critically noted as "one of the finest religious spaces of all time."]*

What Bill feared was that the house might become a memorial and icon to those who still vehemently opposed integration and who continued to define Faubus as their hero.

Furious at Bill's refusal to buy his home, Faubus accelerated his rhetoric against him during his campaign for the governorship, charging that Bill had brought no new jobs to the people of rural Arkansas, and that he had only saddled them with higher taxes and no benefits.

Faubus and Bill continued to campaign vigorously against each other until the Arkansas primary in May.

Bill won that primary with sixty percent of the vote, although Faubus garnered a third of the total, his largest support coming from the more rural and backward parts of the state. Exit polls showed the political sentiments of his more diehard supporters. "He stood up against the niggers," was a frequently repeated racist rant.

After the heat of the campaign had cooled a bit, Faubus met privately with Bill for a drink. Bill needed Faubus' support in the upcoming election in November.

Perhaps having had too much to drink, Faubus became provocative. "I keep hearing all these rumors that you go for black poontang. My campaign aides wanted me to use that against you, but you can thank me for being a Southern gentleman. I would have won the nomination had I aired those charges. So you'll owe me one."

"As for Frank White this autumn," Faubus continued, "I hear his aides are going all out to smear you. They're even going to charge that you're a cocaine addict like your rotgut brother. They don't plan to print anything, but you're also going to be charged with chasing anything in a skirt while your wife is back in the Governor's Mansion licking pussy, the same thing you're doing elsewhere in town."

"Sounds like I'm in for a lot of fun," Bill said flippantly.

"It's no laughing matter," Faubus said. "Your being a pussy hound is going to cost you your chance for the presidency. You can get by in Arkansas, because we are a forgiving people. But wait until you see the damage the Republican power elite—a lot of fat cats—can do to a Democratic candidate. Mark my words."

"Will you support me in the autumn election in spite of everything?" Bill asked.

"I don't know," Faubus answered. "I haven't made up my mind. What in the fuck have you done for me?"

Later, Faubus and his wife, Elizabeth, moved to Houston, where she was brutally murdered in their apartment as part of an unsolved mystery perhaps associated with her stand on race.

***

While campaigning for Bill's re-election as governor in 1986, Hillary was often asked, during her time on the campaign trail, if she planned to seek higher office herself in the future. She told the *Arkansas Gazette,* "I let Bill do that. I value being a private person too much. As for Bill, he is satisfied being the governor of Arkansas. He has no aspiration for higher office."

When White launched repeated attacks against Hillary because of her association with the Rose Law Firm, Bill shot back. "White obviously wants to be First Lady instead of governor." Soon, bumper stickers appeared across the state with the mocking slogan: "Frank for First Lady."

White's accusations against the Rose Law Firm had, indeed, some basis in fact. Even Clinton's aide, George Stephanopoulos, in reference to his first visit to Little Rock, later wrote in his memoirs, "If you've read John Grisham, you've got a pretty good idea what Rose Law was like—Little Rock's version of *The Firm [a novel adapted into a hit movie starring Tom Cruise.]* Not that anyone has ever been murdered there (as far as I know), but its pedigree, power, and aura of buttoned-down mystery had made it *[i.e., the Rose Law Firm]* a force in Arkansas for more than a century. It was also Hillary Rodham Clinton's firm."

As election day neared, White desperately tried to link Bill with recreational cocaine use and challenged him to submit to a drug test. Bill did, and he passed the test. Even so, White continued to make frequent and damaging references to Roger Clinton's drug arrest and imprisonment.

White's campaign workers rounded up witnesses who testified to Bill's having snorted cocaine. One of them was Sharlene Wilson, a bartender in Little Rock, who was later convicted of selling drugs herself. Before a Federal grand jury, she testified, "I sold coke to Roger Clinton. I saw him hand it to Bill for a snort on several occasions."

Janet Parker, who ran the apartment complex where Roger lived, also claimed that "Bill Clinton arrived to snort coke and smoke pot with his little brother."

Roger himself was caught on tape during a police sting operation. During that (taped) conversation, he said that he had to get some of the white powder "for my Big Brother."

At one point, Dr. Sam Houston, a physician in Little Rock, even asserted that Bill had been rushed to the Little Rock Hospital in an ambulance, where he was given emergency treatment for a cocaine overdose.

In an attempt to control the damage, one of Bill's campaign advisers recommended that he answer charges about philandering and his recreational use of marijuana and cocaine. "Issue an apology, say you made a mistake, like so many other Baby Boomers, and that you've reformed, cleaned up your act."

Bill certainly didn't welcome such advice, telling the aide, "I can't open the door to my closet. I'd get crushed by all the skeletons."

Bill & "The Kewpie Doll With Brains"

Near the end of the 1986 race for the governor's seat, new rumors of yet another affair began to surface. Bill had appointed an attractive woman, Beth Coulson, to a state judgeship, despite the fact that she was only thirty-two years old at the time. She was married to Mike Coulson, an executive at an oil company.

Critics claimed that she had been "awarded" with the judgeship in exchange for keeping quiet about an alleged affair with Bill. Both of them vehemently denied that any sexual liaison had ever existed between them, although Bill admitted that he had visited her once when her husband was away. "We did no more than talk politics," Bill claimed.

Coulson's name would later surface in legal proceedings after Paula Jones' lawyers were lining up witnesses against Bill, those willing to testify about previous sexual involvements with the man who had by then became president.

Larry Douglass Brown, Bill's security chief, described Coulson—an attractive woman with sky-blue eyes and a keen intellect—in his memoirs, defining her as "a Kewpie doll with brains" and as Bill's "soul mate."

Although married, Coulson did not have any children and lived with her husband in the fashionable Heights section of Little Rock, about a fifteen-minute drive from the Governor's Mansion.

Brown soon grew used to Bill's command, "Let's go to Beth's."

The route to her house soon became familiar. Sometimes, Brown would be invited inside for a drink, before Coulson and Bill would disappear inside a back room. At other times, Bill would go by himself into the Coulson's house for fifteen or twenty minutes for what Bill would, after his return to the car, define as "a mental or physical fit."

When Hillary was away, Coulson would frequently appear at the Governor's Mansion. "She always entered through the back door," Brown claimed. "I often wondered what her husband thought. He never made any trouble."

In spite of all the negative campaigning, Bill still trounced White in the elections of November, 1986, carrying 64 percent of the vote, statewide. In Little Rock, Bill won with an astounding 75 percent of the vote.

***

For the most part, because of his power, charm, charisma, and good looks, Bill was usually successful with women. But he sometimes struck out. Such was the case with Cyd Dunlop, who might be called "the girl who got away."

At one time, she was married to Daryl Dunlop, one of Bill's campaign contributors. Daryl was the manager of the West Helena Airport, a facility near Arkansas' border with Tennessee. One afternoon, after Bill flew into that airport, he met Cyd, finding her attractive and most appealing.

Years later, Michael Isikoff, a reporter for *The Washington Post,* was credited with breaking the Paula Jones, Monica Lewinsky, and Kathleen Willey scandals.

When Isikoff embarked on an investigation of other behind-the-scenes scandals connected with Bill, the trail led to Cyd. She claimed that Bill had been very flirtatious with her when she and her husband showed up for a victory celebration after he'd won the 1986 governor's race. They checked into the Excelsior Hotel in Little Rock.

At that event, Cyd was a vision in scarlet, based on the color of her dress and her pumps. She danced three times with Bill, who was more flirtatious than ever. "I'm certainly not going to file a sexual harassment lawsuit against Bill, but I found that he was acting like a sex-crazed teenage boy. I thought he was an idiot, possibly having had too much to drink. He sure knew how to party."

After midnight, she and her husband retired to their bedroom. The ringing of their phone awakened her at around 2AM. "I couldn't believe it. My husband was asleep next to me, and the governor was calling me to come and have sex with him. When I refused, he then suggested that I meet him at the Old Statehouse in the park at six the following morning when he went jogging. I agreed to do that, but only to get him off the phone, because my husband was beginning to stir in the bed next to me."

She didn't show up at the Old Statehouse, but at around eight o'clock that morning, as she sat with friends in her hotel's dining room, she shared details of Bill's sexual solicitation of her the night before, and how she had stood him up after agreeing to an early morning rendezvous.

"Up to then, I'd heard a lot of rumors about Bill's womanizing, but didn't quite believe them," Cyd said. "But after that 2AM call to our bedroom, I believed that every rumor about him was based on fact."

***

Bill knew that if he sought the Democratic party's presidential nomination in 1988, he'd face formidable competition from, among many others, his friend, Gary Hart. Polls had revealed Hart as an early frontrunner, in spite of rumors that—like Bill himself—he was a womanizer.

Other names being considered as the Democratic Party's nominee included Mario Cuomo, the governor of New York, and Dale Bumpers, who had previously been a first-rate governor (1971-1975) and Senator (1975-1999) from Arkansas. Previously, within a radically different political environment, Hillary and Bill had once agreed to support Bumpers if he should ever decide to seek the presidency.

Suddenly, a series of fast-moving developments greatly altered the nation's political outlook. Almost overnight, the Democratic nomination for President of the United States seemed available and up for grabs. Bill saw an opening, and some of his advisers told him, "For all you know, this might be your only chance."

The presumed nominee, Hart, had imploded as part of a national scandal after being photographed with a beautiful young woman nestled onto his lap, Donna Rice, during a sailing trip through The Bahamas aboard the aptly named *Monkey Business.*

Mario Cuomo, also viewed for a while as the Democratic Party's national forerunner, also dropped out, as did Bumpers.

The Democratic nomination was, therefore, open to other contenders. Subsequently, Pamela Harriman ("The Kingmaker") summoned Bill to Washington, D.C., for another *tête-à-tête.*

Bill answered her siren call. Accompanied by an Arkansas State Trooper, Larry Douglass Brown, he arrived at her residence in Georgetown, driving up in an old convertible.

As reported in his memoirs, Brown claimed that Bill assured him, "You'll like her, L.D.," giving his security chief what he called "a sex-based wink and a nod."

"She's a little old," Bill told him, "but Pamela is still a looker."

As she greeted Bill and his bodyguard, it was obvious to Brown that Bill adored her. Brown defined her as "a gracious host in her mid-sixties." She was a mesmerizing woman who had sustained affairs with some of the world's most important players. In 1940, during the Nazi *Blitzkrieg* of London, she had slept in a bunk bed near her father-in–law, Sir Winston Churchill.

Brown witnessed a close-up preview of what he called "the chemistry between Pamela and Bill," a heady, sexy atmosphere that prevailed despite the political urgency of the confab.

Bill and Pamela excused themselves for a very private meeting. Bill emerged four hours later, giving Brown that same sex-based wink, but with a difference. "He had a shit-eating grin on his face," Brown recalled.

Back in their convertible, Bill and Brown headed for the airport to catch a plane back to Little Rock. Bill was smiling when he told Brown, "L.D. you're looking at the next President of the United States."

Back in Little Rock, Bill told Hillary, his chief aide, Betsey Wright, and some of his other advisers that he had obtained Pamela's backing to take on Bush during the upcoming presidential election.

***

In 1987, at the age of forty, having been re-elected to a third term as governor of Arkansas, Bill became the subject of much political buzz about how he might be designated as the Democratic nominee in the 1988 race against then-Vice President George H.W. Bush for the White House.

Fallen frontrunner for president, Gary Hart, might have taught Bill Clinton a lesson: Sex and politics make vicious bedfellows.

Drenched in scandals of its own (including the Iran-Contra affair), the Reagan era was coming to an end, and the Republicans were promoting their Veep as the best choice to extend the Reagan legacy, despite Bush's more moderate stance on most issues. Reagan was still popular in spite of the Iran-Contra scandal that, had the circumstances been associated with a less popular president, might have led to an impeachment.

"In spite of what the press did to my friend, Gary Hart, I finally concluded that anyone who believes he has something to offer should just run, deal with whatever charges arise, and trust the American people," Bill said.

"Without a high pain threshold, you can't be a successful president anyway."

During the days and weeks to come, as pressures mounted, Bill was in a quandary. Should he run for president or not?

Hart's scandalous downfall had hugely altered the rule of politics. The private lives of politicians were now accepted as fair game for the mainstream press. *[In vivid contrast, back in the early 1960s, many reporters knew about John F. Kennedy's constant womanizing, but didn't write about it, at least not until after his assassination. Today, they would have, splashing news of the president and any of his indiscretions, especially with Marilyn Monroe, across the front pages.]*

Bill said that he thought Hart had made a serious error in judgment when he challenged the press to "tail me to see if you can find any dirt."

"I felt bad for him," Bill said. "After the Hart exposure, those of us who had not led perfect lives had no way of knowing what the new press standards of disclosures were."

Even Hillary wavered back and forth about Bill seeking the presidency, getting conflicting signals from her own advisers, including her most trusted source, Vince Foster, her lover at the Rose Law Firm.

Other *politicos* in Little Rock disputed claims that Hillary didn't want Bill to run. "She very much wanted him to throw his hat into the ring," said pollster Dick Morris. "It was Bill who was the reluctant bride at the altar."

"Both claims could be true," said Betsey Wright. "One day, Hillary wanted Bill to run; the next day, she feared his running. It depended on her mood, which shifted constantly as she weighed the pros but then contemplated the dangers. She lived in constant fear of what their political enemies would dig up on both of them."

Although Hillary was eager for Bill to occupy the White House, her smartest political judgment involved urging him to finish the work he'd launched in his capacity of governor of Arkansas, and build up more national support before making a run.

She also didn't feel that "the so-called Reagan Revolution had run its course yet." She finally advised Bill against seeking the nomination. She also told him that he had to hold a press conference as a means of publicizing his decision not to run.

It now appears that fifteen minutes before the faced the press, Bill had not completely decided against running. Betsey Wright later speculated that his decision not to run had been finalized only as he was walking toward the microphones to address the press.

"At the last minute, I chickened out," he later confessed. "I feared it wasn't my time."

"All this wavering, going back and forth, meant to me that he had been leaning against running, but really didn't want to close the door," Hillary said. "It was a painful decision for him, and for me, too."

That morning, the *Arkansas Gazette* ran an editorial claiming that "Bill Clinton is not ready to run for president yet." The paper noted, however, that Hillary's parents had purchased a condo in Little Rock where they would be able to look after Chelsea during the long months the Clintons were on the road campaigning.

Of course, that presidential run never happened. Hugh, however, was in very bad health, having suffered a stroke, and could hardly look after himself.

TV crews and news reporters from all over the country showed up in the grand ballroom of the Excelsior Hotel for Bill's announcement. He told his disappointed supporters that he had wanted to seek the presidency in the 1988 race, "but my heart says no." It was obvious that tears were rising in his eyes. He told the audience that his daughter, Chelsea, was seven years old and that she was "the most important person in the world to Hillary and me. To wage a successful campaign, we'd have to be away

Throughout the course of his political career, Bill had to face charges of draft dodging.

In his late teens and early 20s, as a young man, he had toyed with the idea of joining the ROTC, or perhaps the National Guard, as a means to avoid being drafted into active duty in Vietnam.

During his governorship of Arkansas, in an effort to gain credibility for his electoral bid as the Commander in Chief of the United States, he dressed up in National Guard drag. Conspicuously outfitted in this regalia, he participated in military training exercises in the forests and fields of Arkansas.

from her for months, seeing her only during brief visits to Little Rock. That would not be good for her or for us."

Max Brantley, editor of the *Arkansas Times, wrote:* "It was shocking and it was very moving. The room was jammed with network TV crews and people from all over the country. Many were friends of Bill who listened to one of the most moving talks he'd ever given. It went on for a solid hour. He spoke from his heart, a really genuine talk. It was the picture of a politician foregoing a chance to do something that clearly, from the day I met him, I knew he was destined to do. It seemed like a selfless kind of decision he'd made."

After his announcement, Bill spoke to a reporter for *The New York Times,* telling him, "It hurt so bad to walk away from it."

As Bill's rejection of a possible nomination was flashed across America on the nightly news round-up, most *politicos*, including President Ronald Reagan himself, opted not to believe what came to be known as "the Chelsea excuse."

Reagan told a group of future Republican donors, "Clinton didn't run because we know he has a Gary Hart problem more than Hart himself. He is a world class philanderer. He knows that his constant womanizing will prevent him from ever running for president."

A few days later, in Arkansas, Bill and Brantley met as spectators at a softball game in which each of their daughters was playing. Sitting in the bleachers, Bill, in a reflective mood, said, "Doesn't there come a time in a person's life when things you've done in the past are forgotten and not dredged up again? There's nobody in the world who hasn't done things they regret. I read the other day that Frank Sinatra turned down an offer from Jackie (Onassis) to write his memoirs. Apparently, he told her that he'd done a lot of things in his past that he wasn't proud of. Isn't a man at some point in his life forgiven for past actions? Aren't we allowed to move on without the burden of the sins of yesterday coming back to haunt us?"

Bill's announcement rejection of the possible nomination would greatly affect Hillary's own life. Her advisers, including Vince Foster and Betsey Wright, listened to her grapple with her own decisions. Since 1970, one of the most compelling reasons she'd stayed in her marriage to Bill was because she believed he might successfully run for president one day. Now, she was being told that his philandering would make that dream impossible.

Foster advised her to divorce Bill, cut her losses, and pursue her own career. "You'd be free of all the baggage that he brings to you," Foster told her. It was even suggested that if Bill changed his mind and eventually opted to run for the presidency, she should declare herself a candidate for the governor's race in 1990.

Bill once told his aides that his greatest fear was that Hillary might leave him, not because of his many girlfriends, but because their mutual dream of living in the White House might elude them forever.

***

Bill had swallowed a bitter pill by retreating from the 1988 presidential race. However, he did accept a request to place in nomination the name of Michael Dukakis, the governor of Massachusetts, at the Democratic National Convention that summer.

Ironically, what was conceived as Bill's political debut on the national stage evolved into an unmitigated disaster. Before millions of TV viewers, he rattled on for thirty-three monotonous and rather boring minutes. At one point, TV cameras cut away from him and started depicting the restlessness among the delegates, many of whom booed him for his long-winded speech. Some of the more irate delegates shouted out for him to get off the stage.

In stunned silence, Hillary sat in disbelief, humiliated and ashamed at what she would later term "one of the most unbearable moments of my life."

The only applause Bill got was when he said, 'and, now, in conclusion...'"

Backstage, at the end of his speech, as he faced Hillary, Bill was fuming and began blaming Dukakis and his aides. "That god damn Greek motherfucker," he was overheard telling his wife. "He betrayed me. He stabbed me in the back. I'm finished in national politics."

She, too, blamed the Dukakis camp. During rehearsals, Bill had labored over the speech, going through nine different drafts trying to win the approval of Dukakis' advisers, who kept adding points to his speech, extending its length.

Before going on stage, Bill, along with Hillary, had dropped in for a visit to the Dukakis suite. During their meeting, Bill asked the candidate to read over the speech, telling him that it was "overbur-

From Mike Dukakis, Bill learned how not to run for president.

"He didn't help himself by allowing himself to be photographed in a tank, wearing a helmet that made him look more like MAD Magazine's Alfred E. Newman than a potential commander-in-chief of the armed forces," Bill said.

"The Republicans, led by Lee Atwater and Company, went after him like a pack of rabid dogs, saying Mike didn't believe in pledging allegiance to the flag or being tough on criminals."

dened with points and running too long."

After reading it quickly, Dukakis responded, "This is exactly the speech I want the delegates to hear. It's a great speech. Don't change a word of it." It was with those instructions that Bill exited from the suite.

Betsey Wright was there that night at the convention, and for a while, at least, she seemed to agree with Bill's assessment that "I've blown my chance to run for national office." She later told Hillary, "Your husband, my boss, has been annihilated. We'd better retreat back to Little Rock and never show our faces again."

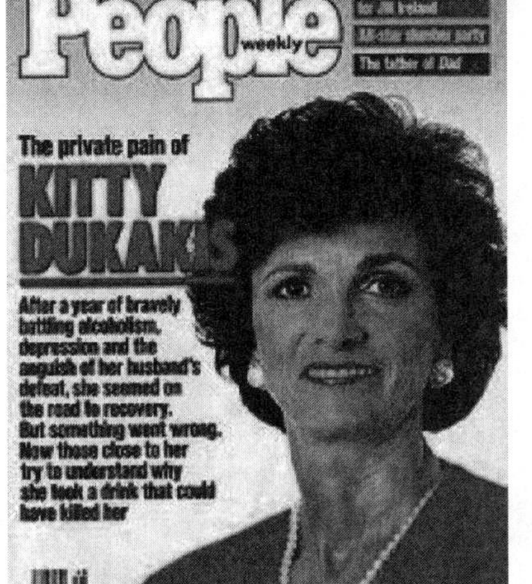

If Bill ever thought that Hillary as a political wife was a liability, he realized how strong she was when compared to Kitty Dukakis, wife of failed 1988 presidential candidate Mike Dukakis, whom Bill had supported.

A year after his 1988 defeat, she was hospitalized for drinking rubbing alcohol, which she candidly admitted in her memoir, *Now You Know*. She also wrote about her disappointment over her husband's defeat.

In 2006, she penned another book, *Shock*, in which she revealed she'd undergone electro-convulsive therapy treatment for her major depression.

After his speech, Hillary wanted Bill to return with her to their suite, but he was too keyed up, and told her he wanted to meet and talk with other Democratic power brokers.

She retreated, therefore, to the suite alone, and Bill reportedly was seen at around one o'clock that morning, entering the hotel room of an attractive, blonde-haired campaign worker. "The sex addict had a way of taking his mind off his public humiliation," a delegate from Arkansas later told his cronies.

Within eight days, Bill decided to make a comeback...well, a sort of comeback. He arranged for an appearance on Johnny Carson's *Tonight Show,* which he knew would reach a late night, relaxed and relatively permissive audience of millions.

On the previous night's broadcast, Carson had mocked him, claiming "Clinton's speech went over as big as a Velcro condom."

Then, on the air, Carson told Bill, "Your speech has just been approved by the government as a new sleeping aid."

Once on the show, however, Bill won over the audience with self-effacing jokes. To top them off, he performed "Summertime" as a saxophone solo.

***

On October 3, 1988, President Reagan invited Bill to the White House, along with other governors, for the signing of the long-anticipated Welfare Reform Bill.

Bill recalled their meeting: "I liked Reagan personally, and I enjoyed listening to his stories. He was something of a mystery to me, at once friendly and distant. I was never sure how much he knew about the human consequences of his harshest policies, or whether he was using the hard-core-Right or was being used by them."

Reportedly, Reagan asked Bill if he were indeed "considering a run for my job in 1992."

"It all depends on whether you'll endorse me, Mr. President," Bill said jokingly.

"I certainly want to, but I don't dare piss off Barbara Bush by not supporting her husband. She's an absolute terror if crossed."

"Reminds me of my own wife, Hillary."

"If you want to meet an equally strong woman, I'll take you over later to shake hands with Nancy. Can you imagine a day when a woman will run for president?"

"The possibility has occurred to me," Bill answered.

"Just think, Nancy as president, Barbara Bush as vice president," Reagan quipped. "Our enemies would tremble with fear. Russia would immediately surrender."

Bill Falls in Love with "The Beauty With Brains" & Wants to Divorce Hillary

During the course of her troubled marriage to Bill, Hillary had contemplated a divorce on more than one occasion. She often discussed her dilemma with her mother, Dorothy, who advised her to stay in the marriage for the sake of Bill's future as a politician and for the sake of their daughter, Chelsea. Dorothy reminded her daughter that she, herself, had endured a marriage to Hugh as part of a far from perfect union.

One night at 2AM, Hillary telephoned her mother in panic and insisted that she had to come over to see her, despite the impossibly late hour. "Something has struck me like a bolt of lightning," Hillary said. "I've got to see you right away."

Arriving at her mother's condo while Hugh was still asleep, Hillary was in tears. She told her mother that Bill had just stormed out of the Governor's Mansion after informing her that he wanted a divorce. His words were plain and very clear: "I've fallen in love with another woman, Marilyn Jo Jenkins, the woman I want to spend the rest of my life with."

Although he made no public comment, Vince Foster shared his concerns about this new romantic development in Bill's life. Reportedly, he told Webb Hubbell and a few select others, "Bill is both a food junkie and a sex junkie. He thrives on one-night stands. The last thing he wants is a greater commitment. And he always comes home to Hillary, and she always takes him back. She is the forever forgiving wife. At least that was the case until now. One night, Marilyn Jo Jenkins walked into his life, and Bill did the unthinkable: He fell in love."

As Betsey Wright supposedly put it: "I guess Bill figured that if his role model, JFK, had his Marilyn, so could Bill."

Bill had been introduced to Marilyn Jo at a party late in 1984, after she'd returned to Little Rock to establish a new life for herself. In her early forties, she had recently ended a fifteen-year marriage to James Norman Jenkins III, a junior military officer who had served in Vietnam as an Air Force pilot. The couple had two daughters, ages six and eight.

She was a strikingly beautiful blonde who looked far younger than her actual age. She stood tall and thin and was always beautifully dressed. Bill was once overheard saying to a state trooper, "Unlike Hillary, Marilyn has perfect taste in clothing and is always immaculately groomed. If I compared her to a movie star, it would be Grace Kelly in the 1950s."

Marilyn Jo's sister, Kay Denton, had married into the prestigious Bland family, one of the wealthiest in Arkansas and the owners of a major bottling company. It peddled, along with other consumer products, such soft drinks as RC Cola (Bill's favorite), Dr. Pepper, and 7-Up.

When Bill met her, Marilyn had been hired as an executive at a utilities company, the Entergy Corporation. She was praised for her intellect, her skill at organizing, and her acute business sense.

Biographer Gail Sheehy summed it up. "For Bill Clinton, Marilyn Jo must have been like a soft summer breeze. She had the honeyed voice of a small-town Southern woman. Yet she was an educated professional woman, who by the time they met, was surrounded by the gloss of a rich, politically active family. She didn't need a government job, and she was exceptionally discreet."

"In spite of Bill's affairs, there was only one he was really serious about, and that was Marilyn Jo Jenkins. He lost all sense of reason and his emotions went wild," claimed Betsey Wright. "Call it love."

By September of 1988, Marilyn Jo had become an obsession with Bill, and he called her as often as eighteen times a day. Some of his "after midnight" calls would last for almost two hours. During this time, he saw less and less of Hillary. Both of them had busy schedules and commitments, and often two or three days would pass before the two of them even spoke on the phone. Betsey noted that some of those calls lasted for only two or three minutes, and most of them were about Chelsea.

Somewhere along the line, Bill had begun to consider divorcing Hillary so he could marry Marilyn Jo. His main concern involved the consequences that a divorce would have on his eventual run for the presidency. He began to wonder if becoming president was just a distant dream, never to be realized. He kept asking himself and his aides, "Should I chase after the impossible dream and sacrifice all my personal happiness?"

When Paula Jones brought her sexual harassment lawsuit against President Clinton, her lawyers engaged in a bitter fight with Bill's attorney over whether to issue a subpoena to Marilyn Jo Jenkins. Bill was said to have fallen in love with her and had even gone so far as to ask Hillary for a divorce.

Arkansas State Trooper Danny Ferguson testified that early one morning in December of 1992, at 5:15AM, he had brought Marilyn to see Bill for a final rendezvous shortly before the governor left Little Rock to be inaugurated as President of the United States.

He even called in his consultant, Dick Morris, to discuss what possible affect a divorce might have on his future in politics. Morris apparently advised him that an immediate divorce would seriously damage his chances, not only of being president, but maybe even sabotaging his reelection as governor if he wanted to run again in 1990.

Bill countered that Ronald Reagan had shown that a divorced man could still be president.

"Yes, but Reagan divorced Jane Wyman in 1948, married Nancy Davis in 1952, and didn't win the presidency until 1980," Morris answered. "That's quite a long time line. You don't have a few decades for the memory of a first wife to fade like Reagan's did."

Bill paid almost daily visits to Marilyn Jo's luxurious condo in a building called Shadow Oaks. When his schedule didn't permit that, he made up for it with those marathon midnight phone calls. Some nights, when Hillary was asleep upstairs, Marilyn Jo slipped in through the rear entrance to the Governor's Mansion to be with Bill.

Danny Ferguson, an Arkansas State Trooper, claimed to have been a witness to the affair. "Bill told me he was in love with Marilyn Jo. He also said he still loved Hillary. That guy had a real problem. He claimed he was seriously considering divorcing Hillary, even though it would be painful. He also seemed deeply concerned about the effect that would have on Chelsea. I think he truly loved his daughter."

***

Although shrouded in secrecy during the late 1980s, Bill and Hillary's troubled marriage was seriously "on the rocks." No one knows for sure about the intricate dynamics that kept the relationship together. But the marriage was saved, perhaps at considerable cost to all three parties *[i.e., Hillary, Bill, and Marilyn Jo.]*

Over the years, however, insights have been gathered from what people, including Bill and Hillary themselves, have said.

In 1990, Bill told reporter Steve Korit, "If I had given up on our marriage months ago, if we'd gotten a divorce, I wouldn't be half the man I am today without the love of both Hillary and Chelsea."

"Hillary always likes to keep 'a zone of privacy' around her life, and she abhors discussing her personal marital situation in public," said Betsey Wright. "But she did survive a crisis in her life when divorce became a possibility."

She was rather candid at one point with a reporter from *Newsweek.* "What is important to us is that we have always dealt with each other. We haven't run away or walked away. We've been willing to work through all kinds of problems. You have hard times because people overwork and they get short-tempered. Marriages go through rough times because you have problems with family members like we've had. It's very stressful. There are all kinds of things that happen, and I think it's inappropriate to talk about it. I don't believe in all this confessional stuff, because from my perspective, you begin to undermine the relationship when you open it up to strangers. We don't talk about this kind of stuff in our marriages to family and friends. It's the way we are and how we live. And I think it's the way most people live."

Months later, Hillary was slightly more candid when she talked to another reporter, this one from *Glamour* magazine. "Bill and I have always been in love with each other," she claimed. "No marriage, including ours, is perfect. Just because it isn't perfect, doesn't mean that you can just get up and storm out the door. A marriage is always growing and changing. You can't just say, 'this is not ideal.' And walk away from it. I'm proud of my marriage. It's how I define my personhood—Bill and Chelsea."

When Hillary once appeared on TV with talk show host David Frost, he asked her if she and Bill had ever discussed divorce. "No! No!" she answered. "I never doubted our marriage, and I know Bill didn't either. Not only do we love each other, but we need each other. That love is so much a part of us that it was impossible to think of ending it or cutting it off or moving beyond it."

That was a lovely sentiment, but perhaps not consistent with the facts that were prevalent in her life during the late 1980s.

That period of her life is only briefly previewed, without any degree of detail or insight at all, in her long memoir, *Living History,* published in 2003 after she'd left the White House. In it, she quickly skipped over that period in her life, privately referring to it as "crossing a bridge over troubled waters."

But in some way, the challenges she faced in her marriage to Bill back in Little Rock during the late 1980s prepared her for her reign as First Lady of the United States, when those troubled waters rose into storm-tossed seas with hurricane force winds.

***

During this stormy period of Hillary's life, Betsey Wright was of great help to her...and to Bill, too. However, he later seemed to resent "the two Valkyries in my life who try to control my every move."

In the wake of his announcement that he would not seek the presidency, Hillary went through a serious re-evaluation of her marriage, telling Betsey, "I'm god damn tired of playing second fiddle to him. Maybe I should break loose and be my own woman, pursue my own political career without him."

She claimed that she'd long been the family's breadwinner, taking in as much as $200,000 a year to his puny $35,000 as governor. Many law firms had tried to lure her to New York, where she was told she could make at least $500,000 a year.

She bluntly told Bill in the presence of others, "I've made all the money to keep this family going. If you'd been able to keep your dick in your pants, you'd be running for president now, instead of that Dukakis who is sure to lose. You've fucked it up. If you're not going to run for governor again in 1990, then I will."

One close friend of the Clintons, who had known both of them for more than twenty years, discussed the problems of the warring couple. He did not want to be named—let's call him "Joe Smith"—but he did have a keen insight about what was going on at the time.

"In an ideal world, Hillary would have divorced Bill and married Vince Foster. He would have divorced Hillary and married Marilyn Jo. But that's not how it went. Hillary finally decided that divorce would harm both of them. They were deeply co-dependent on each other."

"Hillary told me that she finally decided that she'd invested too much of what she called 'my heart and soul' into the advancement of Bill's political career, and ultimately her own, to abandon it," Smith said. "'The Plan,' as she had named it, was still in effect, perhaps with some major changes. She was referring to their agreement, formulated years before, at Yale, whereby he would be president for eight years, followed by her assuming the presidency in 2001 for another eight years, a sixteen-year reign."

"She told me, 'There are worse things in a marriage than infidelity, and I'm going to stay with him under a new set of rules."

It was finally decided that both Bill and Hillary would go into therapy. In the summer of 1989, they attended sessions with a psychologist, Karen Ballard, who had also held previous family sessions with Bill, Virginia, and Roger in the wake of Roger's arrest on drug charges.

Dick Morris rejected the theory of co-dependence, taking a more cynical view. "He's not addicted to Hillary. I think he just uses her to help enable himself. To do good things and bad things, but to enable him. He sees the world in very functional terms."

"His goal is to get everybody to do what he wants them to do, and that includes Hillary," Morris said. "His relationship with his wife is largely functional. I've always believed it's shorthand: She loves Bill and Bill loves Bill, so they do indeed have something in common."

"It seems like a joke to me," Smith said, "but to save their marriage, Bill agreed to be faithful to Hillary in the future and quit chasing after the vixens. Of course, he had no intention of keeping his word. The first demand from Hillary was that he had to give up Marilyn Jo. He agreed never to see her again."

[The evidence indicates that Bill and Marilyn Jo continued to secretly see each other between 1989 and 1991 during his run for the presidency. During the course of various investigations, records later revealed that he placed fifty-nine phone calls to her during those three years.]

Ultimately, Hillary rejected F. Scott Fitzgerald's assertion that there are no second acts in American lives. "Ronald Reagan proved that Fitzgerald was wrong," Hillary said. "Reagan staged the greatest second act in American history by transforming himself from a fading B-list actor into a two-term President of the United States."

***

Betsey Wright's gloomy and pessimistic prediction that Bill would never be allowed to run for president ultimately damaged her position as his chief of staff in the Governor's Mansion.

She told her own aides, "Based on what happened to Gary Hart, Bill's womanizing is a time bomb waiting to explode. If that weren't enough, along comes Marilyn Jo Jenkins. The guy's in love."

The relationship between Betsey and Bill had turned sour after she began demanding that he confess to the number of affairs he'd had or was embroiled in at that point in time. "We can skip some of those quick blow-jobs in the bushes with whores during your morning jogs," Betsey had said to him one morning in his office. "I only need information about the red meat affairs."

Reportedly, the list of names he subsequently presented to her stunned her. Many of the women were known to her; others came as a complete surprise.

After that meeting, Bill conferred with Dick Morris, telling him, "I feel that her leash around my neck is tightening. Perhaps it's time to kick her upstairs and make her the chairman of the Arkansas Democratic Party."

As early as 1988, she'd "diagnosed" Bill as a man with "a severe midlife crisis. You're acting like a moron. You're not even trying to cover up your adultery. Your whole staff knows about it. God knows how many of your political enemies are arming themselves with ammunition. You and Hillary go about the mansion screaming at each other. How can anyone around this joint not know about it? You're even coming on to some of the women who work for us here. You're pulling the same kind of shit JFK did in the White House."

She later commented, "Bill went crazy in 1989. He was burning his bridge to Hillary. He ultimately ruined his relationship with me. I talked it over with Hillary, and then I decided to resign. I had no intention of becoming his warden."

In 1989, Betsey abruptly departed as Bill's chief aide. The real reason may never be known. There was speculation that she opposed Bill running for reelection as governor of Arkansas in 1990, since she knew he would never complete his term, as he planned to campaign for the presidency, perhaps beginning as early as 1991. Therefore, he would be in no position to serve the people of Arkansas as their governor for a four-year term.

Insiders in Little Rock speculated that Betsey wanted Hillary to seek the governorship, but that Bill was reluctant to surrender power.

After years of faithful and loyal service, Betsey was out.

***

One of the most compelling reasons for Hillary's consideration of a divorce from Bill had to do with the ever-growing menace of AIDS.

Ever since Hillary and Bill had visited San Francisco, she had been acutely aware of the toll AIDS was taking on part of the population. From the beginning, she was far too sophisticated to believe that AIDS could be dismissed as "merely a gay disease."

"Any fool should know that anybody with a blood stream is vulnerable to AIDS," she said. "During most of his administration, Reagan couldn't even bring himself to utter the word. If unchecked, I think AIDS will become a global epidemic. It will cause millions of deaths—men, women, and even children who may be born with the disease, passed on from their mothers."

Back in Arkansas, she demanded that Bill be tested for AIDS, since she knew he favored unprotected sex. At first reluctant to do so, he submitted to the test. Both of them anxiously awaited the results, and each of them were relieved to learn that he was not HIV-positive.

But down the line, a complication arose. It may be pure rumor, but word spread that at one point, that Bill had contracted syphilis from an unknown prostitute.

He underwent a successful treatment, and the matter was hushed up. However, his political enemies got wind of it and spread the rumor around Little Rock.

For years, it has been charged that Bill's refusal to release his medical records was primarily based on his concealment of two facets of his medical and psychological history: One involved speculation that he had undergone some psychiatric examinations; the other that he had at one time or another contracted a venereal disease.

***

In the wake of his uneasy marital reconciliation with Hillary, Bill pondered his own political future. Once again, he checked with master pollster, Dick Morris. His private polling revealed that the voters of Arkansas wanted to see new blood in the Governor's Mansion.

In spite of the difficulties, Bill's dream about running for president had never died. He perceived that 1992 might be his last chance, although he was aware that he'd have to unseat George H.W. Bush, who at that time was enjoying immense popularity. He also knew that if he did run again for governor, this time in 1990, and lost, his hope of running for U.S. President would fade forever.

Morris pointed out that although Richard Nixon had lost his bid for governor of California in 1962, he managed to bounce back and get elected as President of the United States in 1978.

That example was of little comfort to Bill.

It may have been Bill himself who proposed the daring plan that Hillary might run for governor of Arkansas. Privately, Morris conducted a poll as a gauge of her chances. All three of them were vividly aware that Lurleen Wallace of Alabama, wife of the notorious segregationist, George Wallace, had won the governorship of her state in 1966, after her husband was prevented by Alabama law from serving additional consecutive terms.

According to Morris' polling, Hillary had not sufficiently established an independent image of her own. At the very best, as Morris pointed out to her, she would garner only 42 percent of the vote, losing to her Republican challenger—that is, if she managed to get nominated for the state's Democratic primary. In the bid for the nomination, she would almost certainly face formidable competition from other Democratic contenders.

Max Brantley, the best-informed editor in Little Rock about all matters associated with Clinton, was asked what he thought of a Hillary candidacy. He expressed doubt that she could succeed in a macho-dominated Southern state like Arkansas. "She'd have a problem," he said, "especially among voters who consider her pushy, arrogant, and domineering. She's friendly and accessible, but she doesn't project that puppy dog warmth that Bill does. For some reason, a lot of people in the state consider her threatening."

What he didn't say was that many of her harshest critics, invariably Republicans, referred to her as "that bitch from Chicago."

Brantley also made a prediction: "At the last minute, Bill will probably go before his supporters and the press and announce that he is once again a candidate for re-election. I predict that if he's re-elected governor, he will not serve out the four-year term. *[Editor's note: Local election law in 1986 had prolonged the term of the Arkansas governership—previously defined as a two-year term— to four years.]* I think he's going to run for president in 1992. During his fifth term, the people around Little Rock won't see much of his hide. He'll be in some other state, campaigning for his chance to plop his ass down in the Oval Office."

Bill was asked by a reporter what he thought of his wife running for governor. "I think Hillary would make a wonderful governor," he said. "Unbelievably good, in fact. She'd be terrific. But I've not made up my mind yet if I plan to run for re-election. Also, I can't speak for Hillary. That's her job. If she really wants to be governor, her wish will have a great bearing on my own decision. If I step down and she takes my office, what will I become? First Gentleman?"

Meredith Oakley, writing in the *Arkansas Democrat,* said, "Hillary Clinton wouldn't be the first strong, capable, brilliant woman to stand aside for a weaker, less capable, less brilliant, husband."

Other writers have echoed more or less that same sentiment, suggesting that in many cases, U.S. governors were married to women far smarter than they were. Some have even speculated that Eleanor Roosevelt would have made a better president than her husband, Franklin.

During the weeks leading up to his decision to run or not to run for reelection as governor, Bill was characterized by Morris as "dithering and depressed. He was for the moment without a crusade, education and economic reform having been, until then, his favorite legislative pursuits. He didn't want to be a caretaker governor. He needed to be engaged in some important, valiant fight for the good of the world to lend coherence and structure to his life. When he didn't have those banners to carry, it would eat away at him. He'd become paranoid and surly, and, one suspects, escapist."

On March 1, 1990, time had run out for Bill. Hillary had forced that date upon him as a deadline. "You've got to tell the people what you're going to do," she had urged.

Up until the last minute, he seemed to be wavering, not entirely happy with any decision he might make. Hillary was more or less convinced that he would not seek a fifth term. She was even gearing up for her own campaign for governor.

Over breakfast that morning, she'd told him, "Bill this is your day. As they say in Arkansas, it's time to shit or get off the pot."

Without absolutely assuring her he was not going to run, he definitely left the impression with Hillary and his aides that he was ready to bow out of his state's gubernatorial race.

He walked out onto the stage and faced his most ardent supporters, along with many members of the press and TV crews. He later claimed, "In my announcement, I appeared ambivalent and a touch arrogant, but it was an honest expression of how I felt."

He told his stunned audience that "the fire of an election no longer burns in me." Hillary stood in the wings, waiting for his next line, certain that as planned, he would announce that he would not seek a fifth term. Suddenly, according to those who stood near her, a shock came over her face.

Contrary to what had been planned, Bill announced that he was going to seek re-election for a fifth term, explaining that he wanted to complete the work that he'd begun, that of bolstering the state's economy and improving its educational system. He asserted that as the state's g overnor, he had already made great leaps forward, but that there remained much work to be done.

Although he didn't exactly say so, he left the impression that he would remain in the office for the entire four-year term, and would not spend those years campaigning for president.

Later, he confessed to his aides: "So, I told a little white lie. In politics, you have to do that from time to time."

Bill's longtime friend, David Leopoulos, has stood adjacent to Hillary in the wings. "She practically passed out when Bill made his announcement. She was obviously shocked. I think Bill, backstage, had decided not to run, but once he faced the audience in those last thirty seconds, he changed his mind and threw his hat into the ring. That's good 'ol Bill for you!"

Chapter Eleven

"The Politics of Personal Destruction": His Enemies Accuse Bill Clinton of Cocaine Smuggling, Money Laundering, Gun Running, Maintaining Five Mistresses, & Paying for Sex from an Arkansas State Slush Fund

A Brief, Impersonal Encounter with Paula Jones (Labeled as "Trailer Trash" and/or "the Minnie Mouse of Arkansas") Almost Sabotages His Presidency

A former live-in boyfriend of Paula Jones sold the rights to about two dozen color photographs he'd snapped of her in various states of undress. The buyer was Bob Guccione of Penthouse magazine.

Bob Bennett, Bill Clinton's personal attorney, said. "This is simply a matter of a former boyfriend trying to make a fast buck."

Partly because of her squeaky voice, Paula Jones was nicknamed "The Minnie Mouse of Little Rock." She was hardly viewed as a *femme fatale*, although Bill told trooper Danny Ferguson that the young woman made his "knees knock."

He later paid her nearly a million dollars for a blow-job that never happened.

When Jones' allegations appeared against the president in Time, his defenders called her "a floozy, a tramp, and a slut."

Candice E. Jackson wrote: "Jones' detractors dismissed her as a big-haired trailer park queen and a money-grubbing opportunist, but her defenders described her as someone motivated only by 'an obsession to clear her name.'"

Hillary—seen here with Wal-Mart's Sam Walton—served on the company's board of directors from 1986 to 1992, praising and defending the retail giant. She became the head of the company's environmental committee.

Rob Walton, son of the founder, said, "She saved us from a false start on environmental policy."

Bill Clinton's political strategist, Dick Morris, recalled that during the governor's race in 1990, the candidate was "bored and restless." Even though he was neck-deep in commitments associated with his campaign for governor, he seemed preoccupied with nailing a bid for the presidency of the United States in the upcoming national elections of 1992, even though that would mean unseating George H.W. Bush, then at the height of his popularity.

Since she'd lost whatever chance she might have had to run for governor herself, Hillary devoted herself to earning money through the Rose Law Firm. Her efforts paid off. By the end of 1992, she and Bill had accumulated a net worth of a million dollars, making them the richest they'd ever been.

She had a seat on the boards of such marketing giants as Wal-Mart and TCBY, a major distributor of yogurt. She owned $80,000 of Wal-Mart stock herself. As a member of the board, she was concerned mainly with the company's recycling program and environmental concerns. TCBY had its headquarters in the tallest building in Little Rock. The corporation paid the Rose Law Firm $750,000 annually in legal fees, and its company executives were some of Bill's major campaign contributors.

Roy Drew, who handled some of Hillary's investments, later told *Business Week,* "She was doing what many other yuppies were during in the decade of greed. Money was very important to her."

Bill labeled what happened to him in the 1990s as "the politics of personal

The Most Famous Rock Band Groupie in Arkansas —"Sweet, Sweet Connie," Clad in a Teensy-Weensy Polka Dot Bikini— Gains Notoriety as an Installment in an Ongoing Series, "Bill's Bimbo Eruptions"

destruction," a name that, in retrospect, seemed remarkably appropriate. As reporters Joe Conason and Gene Lyons accurately concluded, "No President of the United States and no First Lady have ever been subject to the corrosive combination of personal scrutiny, published and broadcast vilification, and official investigation and prosecution endured by William Jefferson Clinton and Hillary Rodham Clinton. In historical terms, certain of the mechanisms necessary to inflict this kind of punishment—from the office of the Independent Counsel to the 24-hour news 'cycle' and the Internet—are quite recent innovations. All have been brought to bear against the Clintons with stunning effect."

Over the years, attack books on the Clintons would appear with dizzying frequency, each peppered with indictments never before leveled against a president and his First Lady. Accusations of money laundering and drug trafficking would morph into even more serious charges. These included revelations about the Clinton's links—all of them unproven, incidentally—to a series of murders.

Hillary would later be attacked for suggesting that she and her husband were the victims of a "right-wing conspiracy." She was telling the truth. Almost daily—before, during, and after their tenure at the White House—the Clintons faced a barrage of charges and "dirty assaults that would have "exceeded the excesses of Attila the Hun," according to one newsman.

The army of enemies working to overthrow them included a coven of private detectives, right-wing advocates, evangelicals, die hard George Wallace-type segregationists, rich eccentrics, angry office seekers who had been rejected, and politicians whom they had defeated.

The war against the Clintons on a major scale actually began in Little Rock during the summer of 1990. Four years later, Michael Kelly, in an article in *The New York Times Magazine*, summed it up:

> *"What threatens Bill Clinton seems much larger than mere partisanship. There is a level of mistrust and even dislike of him that is almost visceral in its intensity. In Washington, where power is generally treated with genuflecting reverence, it is no longer surprising to hear the president spoken of with open and dismissive contempt. Clinton is routinely depicted in the most unflattering terms: a liar, a fraud, a chronically indecisive man who cannot be trusted to stand for anything...or anyone."*

***

Lee Atwater, a Georgia boy from Atlanta and chairman of the Republican

National Committee, was one of the first *politicos* to believe that Bill would challenge President Bush in the 1992 elections.

To launch what evolved into a campaign of vilification against Bill, he summoned two political operatives, Rex Nelson and J. F. Vigneault, from Little Rock to Washington. Atwater wanted to destroy Bill before "his horse got out of the gate." Historically and arguably, Atwater's involvement might signal the beginning of that right-wing conspiracy Hillary would later refer to.

Two views of the meanest man in Southern politics, cigar-chomping Lee Atwater, Chairman of the Republican National Committee.

Atwater's shameless defamations and smear techniques enraged journalists and filmmakers from across the political spectrum.

Atwater also decided it would be wise to annihilate Hillary, too, since he feared that she one day might seek political office, too. He informed both Nelson and Vigneault that he wanted them to spread the word that "she likes pussy, even if it's not true. What is important is what others believe. Truth has nothing to do with politics. I think that in her heart, Hillary is a lesbian, even if she's too cowardly to admit it to herself."

Reportedly, during Atwater's meetings with Nelson and Vigneault, he issued instructions. "Throw everything you can against Bill Clinton—the women, the drugs, all that shit. Bring up what a redneck whore his mother is. Flaunt his little drug pusher brother at the voters. Why not claim, too, that Clinton is a secret agent of the KGB? After all, while at Oxford, he did make a secret visit to Moscow, where he may have been brainwashed. Play up those gay rumors that circulated when he first ran for Congress. Spice it up a bit. Claim that when he gets tired of licking pussy, he fucks virgin boy ass, since his cock isn't big enough to accommodate a real woman. You know, crap like that. What you don't know for a fact, make it up. The fiction is always better than the reality. We're out to win at all costs. That is my motto."

Atwater, as chairman of the RNC, described his smear tactics against Bill as "ratfucking." He was a total hypocrite in urging that Bill be exposed as a "whore-chasing womanizer." His own record of illicit conquests could have equaled Bill's. At one point, some aides to George Bush had urged him to drop Atwater, based on the perception that he was too vindictive and too dangerous.

His biographer, John Brady, wrote: "Atwater reveled in telling stories of his conquests, sharing details with office colleagues. Disposable sex without commitment was a huge piece of his ego, a badge of honor. He was also accused of using his RNC credit card to finance off-the-record weekends at a Virginia hotel with call girls."

Simultaneous with Atwater's own philandering, his wife, Sally Dunbar Atwater, was left at home to attend to their three children, Sally, Sarah, and Ashley.

Like Bill, Atwater—who was known as a hellraiser in school—began chasing after girls when he was fourteen. Also, like Bill, he had been a teenaged Southern boy who dreamed about becoming a musician. In time, he played the guitar for the rock band, the Upsetters Revue. One of his spicy recordings was the aptly named "Bad Boy."

He had entered politics by working on the campaign of that diehard segregationist, Senator Strom Thurmond, the notorious Dixiecrat from Right-Wing South Carolina.

In the Senate race in which Thurmond eventually triumphed, Atwater had smeared his opponent, Tom Turnipseed, spreading the word he was "a nigger lover, a communist, and a psychotic who'd undergone electroshock treatments to keep him from turning into a raving maniac."

"We threw everything against Turnipseed, as if his last name wasn't enough to defeat him," Atwater jokingly recalled. "Perhaps we left out that he

Earlier victims of Atwater's "ratfucking" smears included Democratic gubernatorial candidate for South Carolina, Tom Turnipseed; 1984 vice-presidential candidate Geraldine Ferraro; and Mike Dukakis.

molested eight-year-old gals. I didn't think of that at the time, though I should have. Change that to eight-year-old nigger gals."

After that successful campaign, Atwater drifted to Washington and to Ronald Reagan's "dirty tricks" campaign to smear Geraldine Ferraro, who was running for Vice President on the Democratic ticket. His campaign to tarnish her reputation was viewed by many Democrats as "driving one more stake into a political victim, even when she's already dead."

Dirty tricks: Democrats have cited the Willie Horton campaign strategy, as managed by Atwater, as proof that Republicans play "dirty" and rely upon "unfair attacks" to win presidential elections.

Willie Horton (*above, left*) was presented as every white conservative's nightmare.

In contrast, a feminized adaptation of Mike Dukakis depicted him as an "Arsenic and Old Lace" maiden aunt whose leniency allowed incarcerated criminals out of jails to create murder and mayhem like Horton did.

"Back in 1954, all you had to say to win votes was 'Nigger! Nigger! Nigger!'," Atwater said. "But in 1968, that was considered politically incorrect for some reason. So you bring up stuff like forced busing, states' rights, and all that shit. Speak in code. White people will get your meaning."

In the 1988 election, in which Bill had considered running, Atwater smeared Democratic candidate Mike Dukakis instead. He inflicted a lot of damage on Dukakis through infomercials about Willie Horton.

Politics makes VERY strange bedfellows, as evoked by right-winger Mary Matalin, Republican "apologist" who married the "Ragin' Cajun," James Carville, Bill Clinton's campaign manager.

Born in 1951 in South Carolina, Horton was a convicted felon serving a life sentence in Massachusetts for murder without possibility of parole. In June of 1986, he was granted a weekend furlough, from which he did not return. In April of 1987, still at large after ten months "on the lam," he committed assault, armed robbery, and rape.

Atwater picked up on the Horton issue after Dukakis clinched the Democratic nomination for president. Dukakis' Republican opponent, George H.W. Bush, referred to Willie Horton in his speech as a metaphor for lax enforcement of law and order. Triumphantly, Atwater predicted, "By the time we're finished, they're going to think Willie Horton is Dukakis' running mate."

Dukakis was blamed for the shortcomings of his state's furlough program, which had allowed a killer to run lose. Menacing mug shots of Horton, an African American, were flashed relentlessly across the nation's TV screens for weeks.

[On his death bed, in the spring of 1991, Atwater wrote Dukakis a letter, apologizing for "The naked cruelty" of the 1988 campaign.]

After a successful campaign, the then newly elected President H.W. Bush promoted Atwater to the Chairman of the Republican National Committee (RNC), defining him as "the best campaign manager ever."

Ironically, Atwater's chief deputy was Mary Matalin, who would later marry James Carville, "The Ragin' Cajun," and chief architect of Bill Clinton's own 1992 campaign for the presidency.

During the 1990 race for the governorship of Arkansas, Atwater decided to back the flamboyant Congressman Tommy Robinson, the former "tough-as-nails" sheriff (1981-1984) of Pulaski County. *[With a population of about 400,000, Pulaski County defines Little Rock, Arkansas's capital and largest city, as its county seat.*

Robinson had become notorious when he hauled a group of dangerous prisoners from the overcrowded Pulaski County Jail to the state prison in Pine Bluff. When the warden there refused to accept them, Robinson chained them to the prison's front gate before he, along with his deputies, drove off, leaving them there.]

From 1985 to '91, Robinson was one of the "boll weevil" Democrats in Congress, who voted with Reagan on most crucial issues. Politically, he was bankrolled by a consortium of fat cats who owned the utility companies, the natural gas works, or else were titans in the banking and timber industries.

After going on many a duck hunt with GOP power brokers, Robinson switched parties in July of 1989. He accused Bill of being "too far to the left," and won the praise of President Bush, who backed him as "a man of exceptional caliber."

Bill referred to the 1990 race for governor of Arkansas as "a real donnybrook." In the Democratic pri-

The Washington Post

TUESDAY, AUGUST 20, 1996

: The Rise

y Machine

le Diverse Support

a given that the campaign would be fully funded.

Now that he's become the Republican presidential nominee, Dole can turn to federal funds for support. After "running on fumes," as Dole aides put it, during the final months of the primary season, the campaign rushed to collect $62 million in federal money to run the general election campaign. A messenger was dispatched from the from the Republican convention in San Diego to fly to Washington and deliver the necessary paperwork.

"There's nothing that compares to him at the national level. No one has been at it as long, raised as much money from as many special interest groups," said Fred Wertheimer, who fought Dole on campaign finance for years as president of the public interest lobby group Common Cause.

Over the years, Dole has financed House and Senate races,

See DOLE INC., A12, Col. 1

Former Arkansas governor Jim Guy Tucker talks to reporters outside the federal courthouse in Little Rock.

Tucker Sentenced to 4 Years' Probation

Judge Cites Poor Health of Arkansas Ex-Governor, Whitewater Figure

Jim Guy Tucker, who had succeeded Bill as Governor of Arkansas, forcibly resigned his position in the wake of widely publicized scandals of his own. He was replaced by Mike Huckabee on July 16, 1996, after his conviction for fraud.

His conviction was not directly related to the investigation of Bill and Hillary Clinton's Whitewater real estate and related business dealings.

mary that May, he faced strong opposition within his own party, notably from Jim Guy Tucker, one of the state's best known politicians, and Arkansas' Attorney General Steve Clark, a politician who had taken over Bill's former office. Also challenging him was Tom McRae, the president of the Rockefeller Foundation, the philanthropy established and funded by former governor Winthrop Rockefeller.

Dick Morris was featured on the cover of the bona-fide September 2, 1992 edition of *Time* magazine.

Its unofficial, "underground" adaptation is depicted above.

Some readers cited it as an improvement over the original.

On the Republican side during that year's primary, the competition was between Robinson and Sheffield Nelson, former president of the Arkansas-Louisiana Gas Company. Each was a former Democrat who had switched sides and now defined himself as a Republican.

An early poll by Dick Morris produced a disastrous result, showing that voters had tired of Bill. It was shown that he might get only 43 percent of the vote. He was well aware that if he lost the race, his dream of occupying the Oval Office would be remote. "Hell, Democratic power brokers will see that I couldn't even win re-election in a primary in my home state. Some vote-getter I'd be on the national ticket."

Enraged, he needed someone to blame, and he targeted Morris, who had urged him to run for a fifth term. Morris told him that if he bowed out in 1990, and if it then looked hopeless in 1992, he wouldn't be able to run again until 1996. "By that time, you'd be out there in a forgotten political wilderness," Morris claimed. "Voters will say, 'Bill who?'"

Bill grew even more furious with Morris when he learned that he was also advising certain Republicans about how to get elected. He summoned Morris into his office, where, in front of others, he denounced him "as a fucking traitor. You've betrayed me. You're not really supporting me. For all I know, you're sabotaging my re-election. You're just in this to see how much money you can bleed from us."

One trooper said that Bill was so angry, he feared a violent confrontation between two enraged and very uptight men.

"I don't get anything but shit from you!" Bill yelled at Morris.

He returned the governor's rage and stormed toward the door, yelling back at Bill, "Go fuck yourself!"

Morris later recalled, "This was my own haunting exposure to Bill's violent side. He ran after me and tackled me, kneeling over my prone body. He was ready to start punching me when Hillary ran over and pulled him off me. She shrieked at Bill to control himself."

Then, relenting, Bill chased Morris into the main foyer of the Governor's Mansion, calling after him, "Dick, I'm sorry. I lost control. Please forgive me."

Morris left the building anyway, but Hillary ran after him, walking with him around the mansion's grounds. "Bill's overworked, stressed out," she said. "The poll numbers were just too much for him to take after all the work he's done for the people of Arkansas."

Morris returned, and although his friendship with Bill was never really repaired, he guided Bill through the tight race in the November election in which he defeated Sheffield Nelson. It was he who recommended to Bill that he hire James Carville as his campaign manager for the 1992 presidential race.

Hillary assured Morris that "Bill only attacks the people he loves,"

Somehow, she managed to calm his nerves. Eventually, she managed to persuade him to nurture the campaign through "to its bloody end. Bill won't attack you anymore. He needs you too much."

REVENGE PUBLISHING
(HOW DICK MORRIS GOT EVEN)

After his dismissal from the Clinton camp, Morris wrote a gossippy anti-Hillary book in which he claimed that the only person who could beat Hillary was Condoleezza ("Condi") Rice, an African American who had been the Secretary of State during the administration of George W. Bush.

Morris was correct on only one point: It would take an African-American to beat Hillary in the 2008 race for the White House.

A "Dirty Tricks" Cartoon Depicts Bill, Nude, as "The Emperor With No Clothes"

Developments unfolded quickly after Steve Clark withdrew from the governor's race. Jim Guy Tucker also withdrew as a candidate for governor, opting instead to run for lieutenant governor. He did this based on his belief that Bill would resign the post of governor sometime during the course of his elected tenure for the pursuit of the presidency itself. In his capacity as lieutenant governor, Tucker would thereby automatically be "promoted" to the governorship.

Bill still had to face a strong challenge from McCrae, who had opened his campaign by holding aloft a big broom, which he promised he'd use to "sweep Clinton and his cronies out of office and end corruption in Arkansas."

McRae was an honorable man, and had done many fine things during the course of his life, including serving in the Peace Corps. He was not really an attack dog, but he had been urged to become one if he wanted to beat Bill. He was the great-grandson of a well-known former governor of the state.

Bill had to fly to Washington to represent his state before the Delta Development Commission in Congress. During his absence, McRae seized upon this opportunity to hold a press conference on the steps of the Capitol Building in Little Rock. Standing before the audience, he unveiled a large-scale illustration of Bill, without clothes, discreetly covering his crotch with his hands. The cartoon's caption read—THE EMPEROR HAS NO CLOTHES.

In the middle of his attack, Hillary herself appeared, wearing a bold houndstooth-patterned suit, a pearl necklace, and a Clinton button on her lapel. Her presence disrupted the proceedings. She read a report written by McRae himself during his administration of the Rockefeller Foundation, in which he had praised Bill's accomplishments as governor. As one aide later said, "Poor Tom looked like a deer caught in the headlights."

Her appearance at that dramatic and contestatorial moment made front-page news across the state, winning both admiration and condemnation. Many conservative voters thought it unseemly for a First Lady to enter the political fray like that. In a column, Meredith Oakley wrote: "Bill Clinton not only lacks fire in his belly, but steel in his spine. He has to send Hillary out to do his dirty work."

Oakley did admit, however, that "Hillary set out to eat McRae's lunch and didn't stop until she'd finished off his dessert."

Whether her appearance contributed to McRae's loss in the primary cannot be determined. But Bill and Hillary celebrated in the Governor's Mansion when he emerged as the frontrunner, with Tucker elected as his lieutenant governor.

McRae wandered off into oblivion, eventually dying of Lou Gehrig's disease at the age of sixty-five after a long illness in his home town of Arkadelphia.

Bill and Hillary feared they would have to face Atwater's hand-picked candidate, Tommy Robinson, during the November election, but he lost to Sheffield Nelson. If Atwater had not succumbed to a brain tumor, Robinson's chances might have been greater.

Nelson, the former CEO of a gas company, was a formidable candidate armed with a roster of dirty campaign tricks. Born the son of a sharecropper, he was rather good looking, a blue-eyed blonde who had risen to the highest levels of the Arkansas business community. During his campaign against Bill, he became known for his sartorial elegance.

Nelson had once been a political ally of Bill's when he was a Democrat, and Bill in 1984 had appointed him as director of the Arkansas Industrial Development Commission.

Bill had promised to back him for governor in 1990. But when he'd announced that he was seeking a fifth term for himself, Nelson felt betrayed. When he'd bolted from the Democrats, Bill labeled him a turncoat.

"I got tired of waiting around in Bill's shadow to become governor," Nelson said.

Lawyer and businessman Sheffield Nelson was a "turncoat" who switched parties before challenging Bill for the governorship of Arkansas.

His extreme positions eventually destroyed his political career. One example included denying welfare benefits to "bastard babies."

Not only had Robinson lost, but in 1992, as a Congressman, he was involved in a banking scandal. He was found to have bounced 996 checks at the U.S. House of Representatives Bank, some of which were sixteen months overdue and had not been made good.

Based on what he'd seen about Nelson's tactics in the primary, Bill feared the smears he'd have to face in the general election. Nelson's aides had spread rumors about Robinson that he drank a pint of bourbon every day and that he was addicted to a sedative so powerful, it induced paranoia.

"My God," Bill had said. "What will Nelson's goons say about me?"

He was soon to find out.

"Paula Jones May Have Made Bill's 'Knees Knock,' But She Later Had Him by the Balls."

—James Carville

Taking time off from campaigning, Bill flew to Cleveland, where he delivered what many *politicos* later called "the greatest speech of his political career." He addressed the Democratic Leadership Council, which had its critics. The Rev. Jesse Jackson claimed that the initials DLC stood for "Democratic

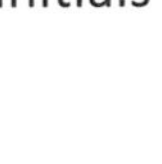

Leisure Class."

It was in Ohio that Bill launched his campaign for the Oval Office by articulating his chief goals. They included welfare reform, criminal justice reform, health care reform, protection of the environment, and sustained economic growth. He received a standing ovation, and there was a lot of discussion about his running for president.

His appeals had been directed at "mainstream Democratic voters," an attempt to woo back those who had deserted the party, becoming "Democrats for Reagan." He outlined his differences with the platforms endorsed by the Reagan/Bush people, "who seem to view government as the source of the nation's problems."

Thanking his supporters, he had to rush back to Little Rock to put out brush fires. Flying from Cleveland to Little Rock, Bill was greeted at the airport by Chelsea, who shared with him her secret ambition. "I want to be a great ballerina," she told him. "And my ballet classes are going great...just great."

Two days after his triumphant success in Cleveland, Bill made what he came to consider "the worst mistake of my life." He appeared at the Excelsior Hotel in Little Rock to address the Governor's Quality Conference.

Outside the ballroom sat a twenty-year-old secretary who was employed at the time by the Arkansas Development Commission for a modest salary of $10,270 a year.

THE GREAT AMERICAN TRAILER PARK

THE MUSICAL

The spotlight cast by Paula Jones and the charge that she was "trailer park trash" catalyzed the birth of a renewed interest in what journalist Stacy Davis defined as "The Crappy Caucasian craze."

In 2004, composer/lyricist David Nehls and playwright Betsy Kelso burst onto the national scene by intertwining stories about an agoraphobe, her tollbooth-collector husband, and the stripper who lives one trailer over into a hit musical.

For a man with a roving eye for beauty queens, Paula Corbin (later Jones) was an exception. In the view of many, she was described as "slight, somewhat mousy, with long dark hair and a high-pitched, voice." She was cheaply dressed and badly made up.

Born in an Arkansas backwater, the daughter of a garment factory worker and a holier-than-thou lay preacher of the Christian Fundamentalist Nazarene sect, Paula had grown up in a devout household where she was forbidden to even wear makeup.

After her father died of a heart attack when she was nineteen, she broke free of her restraints and dated a number of men. She also became addicted to short skirts. At one point, she even posed for seminude photos, which eventually found their way into Bob Guccione's *Penthouse.* When she went to work in Little Rock, her squeaky voice became the inspiration for her nickname, "Minnie Mouse."

At the time of her encounter with Bill, she was heavily dating a wannabe actor, Steve Jones. Employed as a ticket agent for Northwest Airlines, he bore a slight resemblance to Elvis Presley. She lived with him in a modest dwelling north of Little Rock. She would marry Jones in 1992 and move to California.

As *Newsweek* noted, Paula Jones, financed by the Clinton-hating right wingers with deep pockets, was willing to take her charges all the way to the Supreme Court, claiming that "Governor Clinton back in Little Rock dropped trou and told her to make like it was a lollipop."

The right-wing commentator, Ann Coulter, would later refer to Paula as "trailer park trash."

We have only Jones' much-disputed testimony as to what happened that afternoon in Little Rock. Even so, it almost, in time, toppled the leader of the Free World.

According to Paula's account, which Bill later denied, he sent state trooper Danny Ferguson over to Paula's desk. Once there, he delivered a message for her from the governor of her state. "Mr. Bill Clinton wanted you to know you make his knees knock."

Penthouse's British counterpart was quick to point out, on its cover, the political implications of what the fuss was about.

He also told her that the governor wanted her to go to his suite for a private meeting. He handed her a slip of paper with Bill's room number on it.

She would later claim that she had reservations about visiting his suite alone. But she was curious, as she anticipated that he might be ready to offer her a better and higher paying job in state government. Why she thought that, after the comment about making Bill's knees knock, was never explained.

Once she was in his room, and again, according to her testimony, there was little talk. "He grabbed me and tried to kiss me, and with one hand, he started to feel up my thigh, telling me he liked the curves of my body. I turned beet red and tried to pull away from him."

Still caught in his grip, he said, "I love the way your hair flows down your back."

"He tried to kiss me again, but I broke away. I went to sit down on the sofa close to the door."

"Are you married?" he asked.

"No, but I have a steady boyfriend."

According to Paula, he walked across the room and sat down on the sofa next to her. He then unzipped his trousers and slipped down his jockey shorts to reveal an erection. "He asked me to kiss his penis," she claimed.

At that point, she jumped up from the sofa and headed for the door. "I'm not that kind of girl," she told him. "Look...I've got to go."

He pulled up his trousers. "If you get into trouble for being away from your desk, check with Danny Ferguson, that trooper. We'll straighten everything out."

As she headed out the door, he called after her. "You're smart. Let's keep this between ourselves."

She recalled his voice as "being stern."

***

Just as the Clinton *vs.* Nelson race for the governor's seat entered its final days, a disgruntled former employee, Larry Nichols, exploded a legal bombshell.

Convening a press conference on the steps of the Capitol in Little Rock, Nichols announced to reporters that he was filing a $3 million libel suit against Bill. In it, he claimed that he'd been fired from his state government job and had been made a "scapegoat."

Reporters screamed to learn just who this Larry Nichols was. Later called a "right-wing malcontent," he had originally been hired by Bill as marketing director for the Arkansas Development Finance Authority (ADFA). A pale, slightly doughy man in his mid-forties, Nichols was a chain smoker fond of wearing Adidas track suits. A onetime football star from Conway, Arkansas, he had once made his living recording advertising jingles.

At the ADFA, he'd boasted to fellow employees that he was a CIA operative, working on behalf of the Nicaraguan Contras. He also claimed that he'd sided with President Ronald Reagan in wanting to give aid to this rebel group.

In September of 1988, an AP reporter heard these stories and began to investigate. He learned that during his tenure at the ADFA, Nichols had made 642 long-distance phone calls, at Arkansas' expense, to Contra leaders. This revelation led to Nichol's firing, at which time he denounced Bill as a "knee-jerk liberal."

Although Nichols had lost his job because of his link to the Contras, it was later alleged that it was Bill himself, who had developed and maintained sinister links to the Nicaraguan rebels. Allegedly, those links involved cocaine shipments, money laundering, and gunrunning. The headquarters and "nerve center" of these clandestine activities was said to have been Mena Airport, a sleepy and obscure backwater in the Ouachita Mountains along the remote western edge of Arkansas, near the Oklahoma border.

Larry Nichols. Called "a dangerous con artist," this employee, fired from the Arkansas Development Finance Authority (ADFA), filed a $3 million libel lawsuit against Bill Clinton.

"They may just kill me," he said, during an interview with *The New York Times*. "You'll read one day that I got drunk and ran into a moving bridge. Or that Larry Nichols got depressed over everything and blew his head off."

The charge was that with the full consent of Governor Clinton, the "Dixie Mafia" had funneled billions of dollars of cocaine, cash, and weapons through Mena. Profits from those transports allegedly helped to finance the illegal war in that embattled country of Central America. Congress had been unaware of this financing.

Whether the allegations were true or not, Bill's detractors alleged that Arkansas had degenerated into a "virtual Narco-state," with small backwoods banks within the state laundering more cash than some big financial institutions in New York City.

An aerial view of western Arkansas' Mena Airport and its landing strips. From 1981-1985, this controversial rural airport was a major center of international drug-smuggling traffic.

According to the Internal Revenue Service, thousands of kilos of cocaine and heroin, worth hundreds of millions of dollars, landed here from Central and South America.

The cocaine kingpin who was said to have orchestrated most of this was a man named Barry Seal, a notorious gunrunner and the largest importer of cocaine into the United States before his assassination in 1986.

Russell Welch, an Arkansas State Police investigator, later asserted that he believed that the Mena Airport was the nation's biggest point of entry for the importation of illegal drugs from Central America into the United States. Later, reports discovered that the otherwise insignificant airport at Mena was equipped with state-of-the-art equipment usually installed only at major-league international airports.

[In 1994, at a televised press conference in Washington, Bill, then president, denied any involvement in the illegal activities at the Mena Airport. He was pressed on the issue by Sarah McClendon, the doyenne of the White House Press Corp.

"The State of Arkansas had nothing to do with any illegal activity going on there," Bill claimed. "Zero, nothing. Zero. Everybody who's ever looked into this knows that."

Along with cocaine smuggling, gun-running, and money laundering, Bill and his cronies were also accused of instigating some fifty murders, although no smoking gun was ever revealed.

Later, the White House counsel's office released a report that castigated Nichols and others for spreading vicious rumors about Bill and his former associates.]

Nichol's lawsuit alleged that the governor maintained a "slush fund," regularly replenished with money from the ADFA that employed Nichols, for Bill to conduct adulterous romances with at least five mistresses. At the top of the list was Gennifer Flowers.

This represented the first public exposure of Bill's twelve-year affair with the singer. Flowers, then around forty years old, had also been given a job in state government.

Included on the lawsuit's list of Bill's conquests were two former Miss Arkansas title holders, Lencola Sullivan and Elizabeth Ward Gracen. Also named was Susie Whiteacre, a Clinton aide.

From the Rose Law Firm, Hillary launched a counter offensive with the help of Vince Foster and Webb Hubbell, her two closest associates at the com-pany. Her mission involved getting signed affidavits from all five of Bill's alleged mistresses. If one of them refused to sign such an affidavit, Hillary's policy involved discrediting the woman. Potentially, the most dangerous name on the list belonged to Gennifer Flowers.

Hillary told Hubbell, "Sheffield Nelson is so desperate to become governor, he may be behind the lawsuit from Nichols. We've got to go after these attack dogs of the Republican machine. We've got to hang tough. We can expose them. Let's face it: Everybody's closet is rattling with skeletons."

In Little Rock, in a last-ditch effort to sustain his allegations, Nichols met with Mike Gauldin, Bill's press secretary. It was reported that Nichols would agree to drop his claims against the governor for $150,000 in cash plus a payoff of the balance of his mortgage. Gauldin rejected the offer.

Even after he dropped the lawsuit, Nichols claimed that after that, he never went anywhere without a handgun. "I knew the Clintons may have wanted me dead. I was afraid that one day, a notice would appear in the paper that I got drunk and ran off a bridge. Or else that I got depressed and blew my head off with a gun. If you read it, don't believe it. Believe that I was murdered!"

Nichols later claimed, "Bill Clinton is nothing but a con man. If we ever could find a photograph of him sucking on a big ol' dick, you know what he'd say? 'Just because you suck one big ol' dick don't make you a fucking cocksucker. Let's forget that crap and talk about the economy.'"

In one of the genuinely consequential mistakes of his life, Bill began to place phone calls to Flowers, urging her to deny any sexual involvement with him. In the beginning, she agreed to do that.

But unknown to him, she began to secretly tape his calls to her, including one in which she compliments him on his oral skill for "eating good pussy."

At one point, he apologized to her for having to deny their long-lasting affair, but told her he had to do it for political expediency.

Even as part of his worst case scenarios, Bill probably never imagined that the woman for whom he'd professed love throughout those many years would almost derail his burning ambition to become the next President of the United States.

***

During the brutal final weeks of his 1990 campaign for governor of Arkansas, Sheffield Nelson's aides hired two impersonators. One was a lookalike for Gary Hart, the other evoked the image of Bill. Jointly, they recorded a satirical duet, warbling the Willie Nelson classic, "To All the Girls I Left Behind."

As their final campaign stop, Bill and Hillary arrived in Fort Smith, a Republican stronghold near Arkansas' western border. There, in a speech, Bill promised that he'd dance down Garrison Avenue, the town's main drag, if he won. He would keep that promise.

Just forty-eight hours after his re-election, he and Hillary returned to Fort Smith. Along with hundreds of their supporters, they danced in the rain. At first, they were tempted to perform to the blaring sounds of "Singin' in the Rain," but later, they switched their dance music to "Happy Days Are Here Again."

On election night in November, Bill and Hillary, along with their key supporters, gathered at the Governor's Mansion to tally the election results, county by county. Long before midnight, it became clear that Bill had been re-elected for a fifth term, having garnered fifty-seven percent of the vote.

Safe once again in the governor's seat, Bill devoted a lot of time to discussions with his better-informed supporters. Debating the issues, he repeatedly asked the same question: "Should I run for President of the United States?"

He just couldn't make up his mind. A turning point for him came when he flew to Los Angeles to deliver a speech. Sean Landres, a young Democratic supporter, volunteered to be his driver. He suggested that Bill run for president and use as his theme song Fleetwood Mac's "Don't Stop Thinkin' About Tomorrow."

Bill liked the idea a lot and thanked him. Indeed, in the months ahead, he'd follow that advice.

In his memoirs, Bill cited a phone call from Roger Porter, a White House aide to President Bush, as the motivation that finally helped him make the decision to run for president. He told Porter that he'd been thinking about running because he felt that his boss was not tackling the really big issues, many of them economic, facing the country.

At that point, Porter grew hostile. "Cut the crap, governor," he said. "If you run, we're prepared to destroy you. Members of the press are elitists. They'll believe any shit we spread about you in a backwater like Arkansas. We'll spend whatever we have to spend to take you out, and we'll do it early in the game."

"I tried to stay calm, but I was mad," Bill later wrote. Before hanging up, he informed Porter that threats from the Bush camp made it all the more likely that he'd announce his candidacy for the presidency.

Back in Little Rock, tensions mounted between Bill and Hillary, as both of them mulled over the pros and cons. Even though he had decided to run for president during his time in Los Angeles, by the time he returned to Little Rock, he was plagued by doubts once again.

His indecision began to make Hillary particularly tense, as noted early one morning by two state troopers. As she was driving away from the Governor's Mansion, she looked back. Braking her car, she jumped out and confronted them. "You haven't raised the goddamn American flag," she shouted at them. "I want the goddamn fucking flag raised every fucking morning at sunrise." Then, she got back into her car and drove off. After that, every sunrise over Arkansas was greeted with the raising of the Stars and Stripes.

To gauge the desirability of a possible electoral contest between Bill Clinton and George H.W. Bush, Dick Morris was summoned once again to poll voter preferences nationwide. The results of that poll were not particularly promising, showing that in a race against Bush, Bill would probably get only 39 percent of the vote, if that.

As governor of a small state like Arkansas, Bill was also aware that no man from a small state had ever been elected president since Franklin Pierce of New Hampshire had won the office in 1852.

After the Persian Gulf War against Iraq, in which U.S. forces routed Saddam Hussein's troops from their occupation of Kuwait, Bush's approval ratings had soared to 90 percent. Or, as Bill put it, "his popularity reached the stratosphere. At this point, Bush looks unbeatable."

But over a period of eighteen months, Bush's popularity began to fade. Bill and Hillary agreed that Bush's decline had to do with failed domestic policies. "I smell blood," Hillary told Morris.

By May of 1991, Bill was making speeches around the country. He generated thunderous applause with his calls for "opportunity, responsibility, community."

"We're on our way to the White House," he told Hillary, after returning from a flight in a six-seater plane provided by and paid for by the Democratic Leadership Council (DLC).

At the Governor's Mansion in Little Rock, Bill and Hillary had first conceived of the idea of promoting a co-presidency.

"If you vote for Bill, you also get me," Hillary told Morris, going on to propose, "We could promote the pair of us as a Blue Plate Special."

Word of this proposal spread far and wide, eventually reaching Richard Nixon in California. He didn't like the strategy at all, and publicly said so. "If a wife comes on too strong and too intelligent, it makes the husband look like a wimp," he told a reporter.

When Hillary heard this, she lashed back, "Tricky Dicky is a bitter old man who was forced out of the presidency because he was a liar. And a crook! He's trying to get back at me because he knows I was one of the people who helped end his presidency!"

Both Bill and Hillary plotted their upcoming attack on the sitting president. She promised she'd be an active, aggressive campaigner, and that she'd publicly refer to the Reagan-Bush era as a "Gilded Age of greed and selfishness, of irresponsibility and excess." She went on to promise that a Clinton administration would be "the most ethical in the history of the Republic."

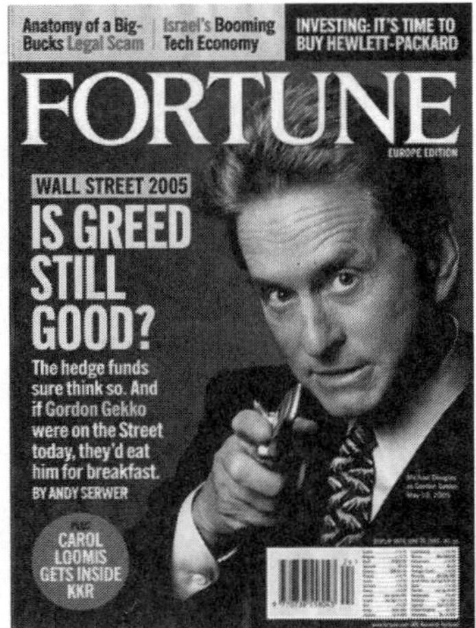

Bill plotted roughly equivalent attacks, planning to label the Reagan-Bush years "as an orgy of selfishness, a tragic interregnum."

He accused Bush of promoting a political climate where "Greed is good!" That was an echo of the words of Gordon Gekko, the crooked, scheming investment banker as portrayed by Michael Douglas in Oliver Stone's 1987 film, *Wall Street.*

***

Even before Bill's presidential campaign began, the first of what Betsey Wright labeled as "bimbo eruptions" exploded. It came about through publicity generated in *Penthouse* by Connie Hamzy, the most famous rock band groupie in Little Rock.

She was known as "Sweet, Sweet Connie," the name inspired by the lyrics in a song, "We're an American Band," released by the Grand Funk Railroad. Its lyrics went like this:

"Sweet, sweet Connie was doing her act,
Had the whole band, and that's a natural fact."

Sweet Connie was not shy about publicity, and in *Penthouse,* she had identified some of her lovers, even their penis sizes and copulative techniques. Her conquests had included Don Henley, Huey Lewis, and Mick Fleetwood.

In the *Penthouse* article (*"Confessions of a Rock 'n' Roll Groupie"),* she revealed details of her encounter with Bill Clinton in August of 1984 at the Riverfront Hilton in Little Rock.

Wearing a "teensy-weensy polka dot bikini," she was lounging by the pool when she noticed three suited men staring at her from a ground floor window within the hotel.

At one point, one of the men exited from the room and walked out onto the terrace beside the pool to confront her. He told her that Governor Clinton had spotted her and wanted to meet her.

She protested that she didn't have any clothes. But he told her, "That's all right with the governor."

She accompanied them from the pool area back into the hallway of the hotel, where she spotted Bill standing with two

Home Town Girl from Little Rock, "Sweet Connie Hamzy" was a local beauty who claimed to have had sex with numerous rock musicians. She's depicted above in a publicity photo.

Her alleged escapades as a groupie, wherein she revealed what specific rock stars are like "when they drop trou," were detailed in *Cosmopolitan* in 1974, on *The Howard Stern Show* in 1991, and again in a tell-all feature story in *Penthouse* in 1992.

Her allegations included the accusation that then-Governor Bill Clinton had propositioned her.

other men. Seeing her, he dismissed his companions. "I just had to meet you," he told her. "In that bikini, you really made my day. I'd love to see you in private. Do you have a room here?"

She told him she didn't, but that she lived nearby, and that they could go there for a rendezvous. "I hear you're pretty wild," she told him. "I'd love to get it on with you."

Allegedly, Bill then informed her that he had very little time. He took her hand and walked with her down the corridor, testing whether any of the doors would open. When it became clear that most of them were locked, he entered a laundry room. After checking it out, he decided it would not be safe because of the comings and goings of the hotel's housekeeping staff. Then he informed her that he was late for an appointment, but that he'd be back later, hoping to find her beside the pool.

She agreed, but their meeting never occurred.

Hamzy waited until 1991 to go public with revelations about this chance encounter. When Hillary heard about their appearance in *Penthouse* she confronted Bill. He claimed that she'd appeared before him and had dropped the top section of her bikini, exposing her breasts.

The Clintons worked to discredit Hamzy's assertions, which angered her. Counter-attacking, she submitted to a polygraph test, which she passed.

Hamzy included a rundown of her encounter with Clinton in her autobiography, which never reached the stores. Investors in Little Rock acquired the rights to the book, and it was never seen again. Presumably the copies were destroyed.

Bill and Hillary hoped to bury Hamzy's story—and those of others—when they attended a "Monitor Breakfast" in Washington, a ritual founded by Godfrey Sperling, Jr., a columnist for *The Christian Science Monitor.*

The program was a chance for potential politicians to be questioned by some of the top reporters in the nation. Toward the end of the breakfast, one nosy reporter asked Bill about the charges that he was a "serial womanizer."

At first, Bill's face flashed with anger, but he brought himself under control to deliver his response. In a modulated voice. "That's the sort of ridiculous charges that they were interested in in Rome at the time of that city's decline. My marriage has not been perfect or free of difficulties. But Hillary and I feel good about who we are, and we believe in our obligation to each other. We intend to be together thirty, even forty, years from now, whether I run for president or not. I think that ought to be enough said about that matter. Case Closed!"

"The case," as he'd called it, was hardly closed.

If anything, it was only the beginning.

***

The morning had dawned hot and stifling in Little Rock, as the sun sent its rays across the state's open fields to shine on the parasitic kudzu vine that was taking over vast acreage.

The night before, Bill had wavered again, fearing a run for the presidency and the damage it might cause.

"There's Chelsea to think of, too," he warned Hillary, who had grown impatient with his indecisive attitude about a run for the Oval Office.

At six that morning, she stormed into his bedroom. As she later told Morris, "If Bill didn't have the fire in his belly, I had enough in mine for the both of us."

The night before, she'd telephoned many of the major power brokers in the Democratic Party. In nearly every case, they urged her to get Bill to make the run. Except for him, the other candidates on the Democratic side didn't look good. "What are we going to do?" asked one *politico*. "Run Mike Dukakis again?"

She'd hardly slept through the early morning hours. In a bathrobe, she marched down the hallway to Bill's bedroom where she threw open the door and shouted at him. "Get the fuck up! We've got work to do. Hustle that fat ass out of the bed. You're going to run for President of the United States. No more wavering. I made the decision for you last night. You're heading for the history books. And don't forget that it was this red hot momma who put you there!"

Chapter Twelve

Maligned as "Cash for Trash" and "the Most Dangerous Woman in the United States" Gennifer Flowers Seeks to Hijack Bill Clinton From His Tortuous Road to the White House

Her Enemies Label Hillary as "The AntiChrist," "The Lady Macbeth of Little Rock," and as a "Radical, Militant, Feminist Lesbian"

BOUND FOR GLORY—Bill Clinton *(left)* and his new Vice President, Al Gore, represented a major shift in American politics as the new generation of Baby Boomer candidates took over leadership roles from the veterans of World War II.

Bill later had only praise for his selection of Gore, who immediately set about overhauling Federal operations. "He took to the job like a duck to water, bringing in outside experts," Bill said. "He eliminated hundreds of programs and 16,000 unnecessary regulations, reducing the Federal work force by 300,000 employees."

In this 1995 autobiography, Gennifer Flowers candidly confessed how she became the most famous "other woman" in America.

In it, she told readers about how "a freight train named Bill Clinton" entered her life with a roar eighteen years before the publication of her book, a scandal-soaked *exposé* that revealed graphic and steamy details of their torrid sex life.

"I was turned into an instant celebrity, entering a night of living hell with death threats."

Shortly after midnight on October 3, 1991, a brief but heavy rainstorm swept across Little Rock, but lasted only a few minutes. In a breakfast nook off the kitchen of the Governor's Mansion, Bill Clinton labored over a speech he'd deliver later that morning. At a rally, he would announce to the world at large that he was seeking the presidency of the United States.

Writing and rewriting, he struggled to get his speech right until around 4:30AM. Then he went to bed to get far too little sleep before he awakened early and headed out of the mansion for his ritual morning jog.

The day had dawned bright and clear, as he followed his usual route, just as trucks were dropping off their bundles of *The Arkansas Democrat-Gazette* at vending machines. That morning's banner headline read—HOUR ARRIVES FOR CLINTON.

He jogged by the Old State House, where American flags had been festooned for his appearance later that morning. Along the way, he encountered a number of early risers going about their day. Some of them called out to him, "Good luck, Governor!" A truck driver yelled to him, "Give Bush hell!"

He had a problem in that he was, in a way, betraying the people of Arkansas by announcing his race for the White House. In 1990, running for re-election, he had faithfully promised that he'd serve a full four-year term. Now, he was going against his word.

Webb Hubbell, Hillary's law firm partner, characterized Bill's situation as "a *Catch-22* dilemma. He had to be governor to run for president, but he couldn't be governor unless he promised *not* to run for president. He was torn as only he can be."

At 11PM the previous evening, Hillary had placed a secret call to Hubbell. She told him that after Bill made his announcement later that day, reporters from all over the country would be descending on Little Rock to dig up dirt on Bill and herself.

"Millions and millions of Americans have never heard of either of us, and they'll want all the lowdown," she claimed. "What they can't dig up, they'll

Bill—"A Draft Dodger, Womanizer, & Pothead"— Becomes the First Baby Boomer President of the United States

Aboard Their Campaign Bus, Bill & Hillary & Al & Tipper Are Accused of ORGIES and GROUP SEX

make up. There will be many questions about my work at the Rose Law Firm. There will also be the inevitable rumors about Vince (Foster) and me. I want you to deny that anything sexual was going on between us. And deny it emphatically. You *must* do that for me."

He promised that he'd faithfully adhere to her wishes.

Back from his morning jog, Bill sat in the breakfast nook, eating his favorite snack, a banana and peanut butter sandwich with lots of mayonnaise. It had had also been one of Elvis Presley's favorite.

The release of the autobiography of Orval Faubus, published in 1980, was a shallow literary event, the sad story of a man who set out to direct a "way behind" Southern state into the modern world. Along came the fight for integration at Central High in Little Rock that, to his regret, forever tarnished his name.

The book's claim is that Orval was "more victim than oppressor." Bill Clinton said, "Thank God I wasn't governor at the time."

After a shower, he dressed in a dark blue suit but delayed his departure because he could not make up his mind about which necktie to wear. He wanted one to make him look presidential in spite of his youth. An aide in the room with him advised, "Try not to wear one with a naked girl on it."

At that moment, Hillary stormed into the room to see what was causing the delay. When she saw him trying to choose among the ties, she selected a dark blue one with diagonal stripes. "For God's sake, wear this one and get on with it. How in hell are you going to make major decisions as president—perhaps launching a nuclear attack against Russia—if you can't decide on which god damn tie to wear?"

At Little Rock's Old State House, supporters, critics, TV cameramen, the press, and the idly curious had already assembled as Bill and Hillary drove up with some state troopers.

The saddest sight among the gathering was a former Arkansas governor, Orval Faubus, looking lonely, old, and dejected. He'd come not to cheer Bill on, but to sell copies of an autobiography in which he'd detailed his "valiant" stand against integrating a local high school. No one was buying it.

Another sad participant at the rally, although not looking it, was Virginia Kelley, Bill's mother. She was dressed in all her finery, which concealed what was really going on in her life. This was the day she'd dreamed about, the day her son announced his run for the U.S. Presidency.

Her overpainted face masked her darkest secret, which she would have to reveal to him later. Only the day before, her doctor had diagnosed that her breast cancer was spreading, and that she had only months to live.

Following an introduction by state treasurer Jimmie Lou Fisher, Bill delivered a thirty-minute speech, announcing his candidacy and pledging "new life for the American Dream."

As he finished his speech and moved away from the microphones, the first person he encountered was his daughter, Chelsea. "Good speech, Governor."

***

The days that followed Bill's announcement were frantic. Temporary headquarters had been set up In a former paint store in Little Rock. It became the nerve center of the Clinton-for-President campaign. Volunteers answered the constantly ringing phones, raising funds and enrolling workers in all fifty states, even as far away as Alaska and Hawaii.

Later, the staff would move into larger headquarters, commandeering the former offices of *The Arkansas Gazette,* which had been editorially favorable to Bill. It had recently been absorbed by the *Arkansas Democrat*, which was far more critical of him and his policies.

George Stephanopoulos, the son of a Greek Orthodox priest, signed on as Deputy Campaign Manager in charge of communications.

Despite his youth, during the next year of campaigning and for four years at the White House, he would evolve into Bill's Senior Adviser.

As Stephanopoulos would later say, "I saw it all—the arguments, the back-hall scheming, the last-minute flip-flops that somehow produced real accomplishments, but also set in motion an almost tragic series of events that placed the president's fate in the hands of the U.S. Senate."

Like Bill, George Stephanopoulos had been a Rhodes Scholar.

Raised within a strict Greek Orthodox home, he was young, rather short, good looking, and quite attractive to women who were not too tall.

James Carville—the forty-seven-year-old "Ragin' Cajun from Louisiana"—was designated as Bill's overall campaign manager. At the age of forty-seven, he had been broke and unemployed a few years earlier. He immediately took control of what Hillary had labeled "Our War Room."

Immediately, the *Clintonistas* assessed the strengths and weaknesses of the competitors they'd face in the upcoming Democratic Primary.

Major Democratic contenders included three senators: Bob Kerrey of Nebraska, Tom Harkin of Iowa, and Paul Tsongas of Massachusetts.

President Bush himself was facing a hard challenge from the Republican right in the form of Pat Buchanan, who had been a speech writer for the disgraced Richard Nixon. The wild card in the race, representing threats for both Bill and Bush, was the outspoken billionaire Ross Perot, who was mounting a third-party revolt against Bush, a fellow Texan.

Tom Harkin, who had served as a U.S. senator since 1985, had been an active military duty jet pilot (1962-1967) and had served five terms in the House of Representatives before winning a U.S. Senate seat from Iowa. He was an authentic Washington insider, having risen from a background of poverty, the son of an Irish American coalminer and a Slovene mother who had died when he was ten.

He had retired from the Naval Reserves in 1989 with the rank of commander, so his war credentials could be favorably compared to Bill's charges of draft dodging.

Like John F. Kennedy, Harkin was a Roman Catholic, but his religion was not expected to be an issue in the campaign the way it had been when JFK had run for office. Harkin was running for president as a Populist with strong backing from organized labor, and he attacked Bush for "being out of touch with working-class Americans." He was an early favorite for the Democratic nomination.

Like Harkin, Bob Kerrey, hailing from the plains of Nebraska, was also an early favorite. He had been governor of his state from 1983 to '87, and a U.S. senator since 1989. During the Vietnam War, he'd been awarded a Medal of Honor as a Navy SEAL for heroism in combat. During active duty, the lower part of one of his legs had been lost. His formidable military record was fully expected to be cited, in embarrassing contrast to Bill's draft-dodging charges.

Kerrey had announced his candidacy a

Stephanopoulos described Bill's campaign manager, James Carville *(depicted above)*, like this:

"He brought a combination of intuitive genius, intensity, and eccentricity—as if Machiavelli, a Marine drill sergeant, and an extra from the movie *Deliverance* had been morphed into a single Cajun creature."

Clinton with Paul Tsongas—A feud so pronounced it made the cover of TIME.

month earlier than Bill, but the Clinton campaign staff interpreted his early speeches as lackluster, no match for the charisma of Bill.

Senator Paul Tsongas of Massachusetts appeared as Bill's most serious challenger. He'd been a senator since 1979 and was strong on economic issues, opposing a tax cut for the middle class, but advocating one on capital gains as a means of sparking investment. *The New York Times* noted that, "Instead of fire-in-the-belly oratory, Mr. Tsongas offers a wry, self-deprecatory, and occasionally moralistic message about responsibility."

The *Clintonistas* referred to Jerry Brown as "Governor Moonbeam," a nickname that had originated in a 1978 interview that his singer girlfriend, Linda Ronstadt, had articulated to a reporter from *Rolling Stone.*

His most serious drawback involved his health, as he suffered from non-Hodgkin's lymphoma, a slow-growing cancer of the lymph system. He had submitted to a bone marrow transplant in 1986. Rumors spread that if elected president, he would die in office.

[*That rumor would have been true if he'd won in 1992, and then been re-elected in 1996. Tsongas would die in January of 1997, at the age of 55.*]

Of all the potential candidates Bill confronted, Jerry Brown was an enigma, The son of Edmund ("Pat") Brown (Governor of California from 1959-'67), Jerry himself held the same office from 1975 to January of 1983, having followed Ronald Reagan in that same position.

In a televised debate between Jerry Brown *(left)* and Bill Clinton, the tension between them became so raw that Brown announced he might not be able to support Bill if he won the Democratic nomination.

"The Boy has absolutely no sense of humor," Bill said.

As a campaigner, Brown promised "to take back America from the confederacy of corruption and careerism in Washington." Activists who included Jane Fonda and the Rev. Jesse Jackson were early supporters, but their endorsements might have been more of a detriment than an asset.

Regrettably for the Clinton campaign, the early caucuses were scheduled in the states of Iowa and New Hampshire. Bill's campaign staff wrote off Iowa, knowing that the results would swing in favor of that state's native son, Harkin. Likewise, results for the New Hampshire caucus were likely to go toward Tsongas of New Hampshire's neighboring state of Massachusetts. All that Carville could reasonably hope for was Bill's strong second place showing in New Hampshire.

Trudging through the February snows, Stephanopoulos criss-crossed the chilly state with Bill and Hillary, remembering "the cake donuts and the Greek pizzas, the Friday night boilermakers in dimly lit taverns in Manchester, and the bowling alleys on Saturday afternoons in which blue collar families rolled games of duckpins."

In spite of the competition, Bill's stand on health care, his calls for more and better jobs, and his promotion of easier terms for student loans, seemed to resonate with the state's Democratic voters.

Less encouragingly, rumors of Bill's womanizing had traveled northward to New England from Arkansas. At first, no one seemed to pay much attention, as they were limited mainly to rumors. But campaign aides noted that, to an increasing degree, Bill was being confronted with more personal questions than they'd seen with any other candidate for whom they'd worked.

Based on the lingering after-effects of Gary Hart's hubris, Bill and his personal life seemed to be undergoing intense scrutiny.

At one point, during a speech, he was asked by a young woman if he wore boxer shorts or briefs. He answered, "A combination of both—it varies."

Ms. Flowers Sends a Message to "Lover Boy Bill": "I Never Promised You a Rose Garden"

At 6:30AM on the morning of January 14, 1992, James Carville urgently placed a call to George Stephanopoulos, waking him up in a bleak motel room. Carville blurted out the bad news: "*The Star,* a supermarket tabloid, was about to headline an article in which Gennifer Flowers, a lounge singer from Little Rock, was claiming that she had had a twelve-year affair with Bill.

Later that day, copies of *The Star* were delivered to the Manchester Motel where the *Clintonistas* were staying in New Hampshire. Every member of the staff, including Hillary, avidly read the headline, *"MY 12-YEAR AFFAIR WITH BILL CLINTON,"* and the article that followed.

Reportedly, Flowers had been offered $150,000 by *The Star* to go public with her tawdry revelations. In need of cash, she agreed to expose her affair with Bill, knowing that it might greatly hamper, if not derail, his long-cultivated dream of becoming president.

Resentfully, she later charged that the Clintons and James Carville had tried "to paint me as a money-hungry bimbo."

A bimbo eruption from Gennifer Flowers threatened to derail Bill's quest for the presidency.

He denounced *The Star's* front page *exposé* as "trash journalism, old news. At least the tabloid isn't writing about the landing of space aliens from Mars or a man being born with the head of a cow."

Hillary likened the report to "the equivalent of those claims from people who've had a recent talk with Elvis."

At first, Bill tried to downplay the revelations: "I have more than Ms. Flowers' false claims to deal with. Some Democrats are labeling me a closet Republican."

He said, "I'm being accused of a draft I never dodged, and a woman I never slept with."

At first, both Carville and Stephanopoulos hoped to discredit *The Star's* revelations. Stephanopoulos thought it might have been "no more than a blow-job in the back seat of a car, or perhaps a one-night stand that morphed into a twelve-year alleged affair."

But the exposé wasn't going away. Flowers had promised a major press conference scheduled for Monday, in which she predicted, in advance of the event, that she'd explode a bombshell.

Both Hillary and Bill were huddling with their staffs when further tensions erupted. An offer had come in from *60 Minutes,* which was willing to grant them airtime immediately after their broadcast of that year's Super Bowl. The juxtapositioning of those two events would allow access to the largest audience of the year.

Stephanopoulos proposed that "*60 Minutes* is strong enough to cure us if it doesn't kill us first."

He urged Bill to go on TV and admit to having committed adultery, although not necessarily with Flowers. At that point, Bill was still denying an affair with the Little Rock *femme fatale.* He wanted to frame his bad boy image within the context of a plea that "Hillary and I have experienced some difficulties in our marriage."

"Both the Clintons were opposed to the use of the 'A' word," Stephanopoulos said.

"The word is too grating, too harsh, too in-your-face with viewers at home," Hillary had said.

It was finally decided that the Clintons would go on the air with *60 Minutes.* The venue would be within the Ritz-Carlton Hotel in Boston, with reporter Steve Kroft asking the hard questions.

Before the cameras rolled, Hillary confessed to her makeup man, "I'm afraid I might start to cry if the interview gets too personal. No woman wants to talk to millions of people about some of her worst pain. Imagine this: Millions of Americans will be witnessing the First Family of Arkansas airing their dirty linen in public."

The interview reached its highest moment of tension when Kroft suggested that Bill's marriage to Hillary was "an arrangement." Bill later admitted in a memoir, "I wanted to slug him."

As the camera rolled, Bill delivered his own version of their love and marriage: "You're looking at two people who love each other. This is not an arrangement or an understanding. This is a marriage!"

Hillary later wrote, "I wish I had let him have the last word, but now it was my turn to add my two cents, and I did."

"You know," she told Kroft, "I'm not sitting here, some little woman standing by my man like Tammy Wynette. I'm sitting here because I love him, and I respect him, and I honor what he's been through and what we've been through together. And you know, if that's not enough for people, then heck, don't vote for him."

Hillary and Bill appear on their famous *60 Minutes* interview.

"God damn it, mother-fucker, and son of a bitch," Bill shouted at his staff. "Here I am being introduced to millions of Americans for the first time, and I'm filmed denying an affair with an unknown lounge singer—and not a very good one at that."

How a Country-Western Diva's Anti-Hillary Rage Resuscitated a Tired Ode to Marital Fidelity

Here's an updated Tammy Wynette, *sans* the bouffante hair and cowgirl drag, still standing by her man.

[Hillary did not anticipate the venomous fallout that followed in the wake of her remarks, which were broadcast time and time again, from New England to the West Coast. She had not meant to single out Wynette personally, but was referencing her hit Country-Western song, "Stand by Your Man."

Enraged, or at least pretending to be, Wynette fired off a telegram to Hillary: "Mrs. Clinton, you have offended every woman and man who loves that song—several million in number. I believe you have offended every true country music fan and every person who had 'made it their own,' with no one to take them to the White House."

Hillary was forced to apologize.]

Wynette wasn't the only one angered by *60 Minutes.* After Flowers watched the show in Little Rock, she told reporters, "I thought Bill was a son of a bitch. What a crummy thing to do to me. I wasn't the one lying—he was. I hadn't asked to be in the public spotlight—Bill had. I had been unwillingly stripped naked for the world to examine, and dismissed as unworthy, and Bill was the catalyst for that dismissal. The emotional pain that resulted from seeing Bill on *60 Minutes* was some of the worst I had ever experienced."

At the end of their TV appearance, Hillary chatted with the CBS crew, who congratulated her on her performance. "Thanks," she said. "I hoped I came off better than a sleazily clad, cheaply made-up lounge singer."

One reporter contrasted Flower's "slot machine eyes and hydraulic lips with the First Lady of Arkansas' apple cheeks, pink skin, and moon eyes."

In time, Hillary would characterize the parade of women who alleged affairs with Bill as "mercenary rodeo queens."

Kroft later discussed his interview with the Clintons with *Vanity Fair:* "Hillary is tougher and more disciplined that Bill is, and she's more analytical. Among his faults, he had a tendency not to think of the consequences of things he says. I think she knows. She's got a ten-second delay. If something comes to her mind, and she doesn't think it will play right, she cuts it off before anybody knows what she is thinking."

***

Writing retrospectively about the Clinton's joint appearance on *60 Minutes*, many reporters concluded that Hillary "seemed to give weight to Bill's flimsy image."

The next day, a reporter asked Bill if he felt his wife should run for President.

"She should indeed," Bill said. "If she chooses to run, I'll withdraw and throw my support her way."

Little Rock's Femme Fatale Secretly Records Tapes of Clinton For Exposure to the World "Did He Use a Condom?" She's asked on CNN

That following Monday, some 350 reporters and TV cameramen showed up to attend Flowers' press conference. CNN decided to broadcast it live, in visible contrast to *60 Minutes'* previous decision to edit the Clinton's hour-long interview to just ten minutes of viewing time.

Flowers made her appearance before the press at New York's elegant Waldorf-Astoria Hotel.

The shocker of the press conference came when "Stuttering John," known for his appearances on *The Howard Stern Show,* asked Flowers if Bill had used a condom when he'd seduced her.

At that point in the press conference, Stephanopoulos, who was intensely watching Flowers' revelations, defined her televised interview as "a circus." She had publicly admitted that she had been approached by some Republicans eager for her to expose Bill. "I thought we could turn her appearance into an 'anatomy-of-a-smear' story, instead of a morality play about Clinton's character," Stephanopoulos said.

But the real bombshell that exploded during the course of her interview had nothing to do with condoms. Flowers revealed that she'd secretly recorded calls from Bill during conversations he'd made from within the Governor's Mansion.

When Bill's husky voice became audible, Stephanopoulos immediately recognized it, despite his suspicions that the sound tracks had been edited to portray his candidate in the worst possible light. Although the tape was scratchy, it revealed that Bill and Flowers had had some sort of very personal relationship, no doubt sexual in nature.

Stephanopoulos later confessed, "I was hit by a wave of nausea, doubt, embarrassment, and anger. Mostly anger. Bill lied to me. How could he have been so stupid? So arrogant? Did he want to get caught? How come he let me hang out there? I swore to reporters that Flowers' story was false."

He later theorized that in almost any political campaign, "the candidate you're promoting becomes your worst enemy."

During the months and years to come, Flowers did not stop with a mere press conference or tabloid *exposé*. She made personal appearances, posed for Bob Guccione's *Penthouse* magazine, and wrote two memoirs. They included *Passion and Betrayal,* published in 1995; and *Sleeping With the President,* which followed a year later. In the latter, she also hustled Clinton's "love tapes," for $19.95, plus $3 for postage and handling, with Visa, MasterCard, and personal checks accepted as payment.

She wrote: "So now we have this young, sexy, good-looking guy in the White House. He's obviously stuck in a crummy marriage and has an overactive sexual appetite. Why shouldn't we give the boy some slack? If he wants to go out and get his ashes hauled, why not let him?"

Stuttering John," depicted above on *The Howard Stern Show*, was John Melendez, an American writer and former radio personality, who became infamous for asking impertinent questions of celebrities—including Barbara Walters and Billy Crystal—on the red carpet.

Melendez claimed he began his stutter in the second grade as a result of abuse from his Puerto Rican father.

After Flowers' press conference, the "oxygen seemed to go out of Bill's message," said Carville. "At least temporarily. All that the sensation-seeking reporters wanted to know was the extent of Bill's relationship with this lounge singer. Then the story moved from tabloid fodder to the mainstream media."

A Boston TV poll showed that 80 percent of voters stated that Bill should remain in the presidential race. More ominously, another poll revealed that a large number of voters asserted that they would not support a candidate who was unfaithful to his wife.

As if adultery weren't enough to sabotage his campaign, the Republicans aggressively launched an even more devastating charge, which had first been aired during Bill's campaign for governor of Arkansas. He was accused of dodging an induction into the Army as a means of avoiding a sojourn in the rice fields of Vietnam.

Democrats Wanted to Know:
"If Daddy George Had His Jennifer, Why Can't Bill Have His Gennifer?"

During his 1992 presidential campaign, as revelations of Bill's pot-smoking and womanizing surfaced, spies from within the camp of President George H.W. Bush secretly supplied Bill, Hillary, Carville, and Stephanopoulos, with damaging information about both George Sr. and his son, George W.

To an increasing degree, and to their chagrin, the Clintons were repeatedly confronted with Karl Rove's "dirty tricks campaign." Calls from the GOP for a "Family Values ticket—good, clean, pure, with no pot-smoking, no marital infidelity," grew increasingly strident.

As Texas writer, Molly Ivins, put it, "Bill and Hillary faced an armada of Clinton-hating, Christian-right, gay-bashing gun toters."

In a 1992 interview with author Gail Sheehy, Hillary delivered a "toxic tidbit."

"Why does the press shy away from investigating rumors about George Bush's extramarital life?" She was referring to the first President Bush. "Bush and his carrying on outside marriage is well known in Washington circles," Hillary said. "I'm convinced that the silence about that is part of the Establishment—regardless of party—sticking together. Fitzgerald, Bush's mistress, and all these other people... Bill gets exposed for Gennifer Flowers, but Bush takes a pass on his Jennifer Fitzgerald. Gennifer and Jennifer spell their names differently, but the charges are the same."

As Sheehy explained it: "Most of us who write about politics have long been mystified by how Republicans seem to escape exposure of their personal peccadilloes, even in the era of 'gotcha journalism,' while Democrats always seem to get caught. My guess is simple: Republicans tend to sleep with their own kind. Democrats tend to sleep with women who kiss and tell."

Journalist Craig Unger in *Vanity Fair* defined Karl Rove (depicted above) as "Toxic. The *de facto* leader of the Republican party," "the brains of a disastrous (Republican) presidency tarred by scandal," and "an ugly stain on the GOP's reputation."

President George W. Bush called him "Turd Blossom," a name inspired by a wildflower that grows from piles of manure in the pastures of Texas.

Hillary claimed that she'd first heard of Bush's Jennifer at a tea with Anne Cox Chambers, the *doyenne* of a newspaper empire in Atlanta.

Later, after Sheehy encountered Hillary at a luncheon in Hollywood and asked her to confirm that revelation and its source, she wrote: "Hillary gave me the glittery lizard eye blink. Her voice went cold as a courtroom witness."

"I have no independent recollection of such a conversation as that between us," Hillary said.

In an article that appeared in *Vanity Fair,* Sheehy wrote about Bush's extramarital affair. The story was picked up by other publications and run under such headlines as HILLARY'S REVENGE, BILL'S WIFE DISHES THE DIRT, and HILLARY GOES TABLOID.

At the White House, Barbara Bush expressed outrage at Hillary for "stooping so low." *The New York Post* described the First Lady's fury under the headline, "BABS BITES BACK."

When asked to comment on Barbara's attack on her, Hillary responded diplomatically: "We're both very committed women. We care very deeply about our families, and we're supportive of our husbands."

As regard's George *père's* love interest, Hillary was referencing Jennifer Ann Isobel Patteson-Knight Fitzgerald. She was forty-two years old and divorced when she met Bush for the first time in 1974. She resembled Barbara Bush as "the First Lady used to be."

When news of the Bush/Fitzgerald liaison hit the media, reporters rushed to find out just who Jennifer Fitzgerald was.

"Poppy" marries "Bar" in Rye, New York, on January 6, 1945, during the closing months of World War II.

Those were their nicknames. They would later assume world power as George Herbert Walker Bush and Barbara Pierce Bush.

"How could such a lovely couple give birth to such a shit as George W. Bush?" Hillary once asked her aide, Betsey Wright.

She was the daughter of a prominent Boston family. Her mother had married Brig. Douglas Henry Patteson-Knight, a British military officer. After attending private schools in Virginia, Jennifer had married U.S. Army private Gerald FitzGerald. The marriage didn't work out, and she divorced him in 1959. *[Later, Jennifer formally changed the "G" in her surname from upper-case to lower-case.]*

In 1974, she was named as a personal assistant to Bush Sr., during his tenure as U.S. ambassador to Communist China, and based in Beijing. When he returned to Washington in 1975 to head the CIA, she came back with him.

When Bush became Ronald Reagan's vice president, based on the national elections of 1980, Jennifer was designated as his appointments secretary. Aides remembered her as a strong "guardian at the gate," turning down many who wished to meet with him in his capacity as vice president.

One close Bush aide, who didn't want to be named, asserted, "Jennifer makes Bush feel like he's God's gift to mankind. She exerts tremendous influence over him."

When too many rumors began circulating about Bush and his Jennifer, he transferred her to a position as his liaison to the Senate in 1985. After his election as president in 1988, he promoted her to Chief of Protocol at the State Department. Their affair was so widely known at the time that invitations to private parties in Washington often went out addressed to "President George H.W. Bush and Miss Fitzgerald."

As Chief of Protocol at the State Department, Jennifer often took trips with Bush aboard *Air Force One* when Barbara did not go along.

Jennifer arrived in Beijing on December 5, 1974. The very next day, she flew to Honolulu with Bush for a conference. After their business there was finished, Bush recorded in his diary that they flew back to Beijing together aboard an Iran Airlines flight wherein "Jennifer and I were alone in first class."

Somewhere along the way, Barbara must have learned the details of her husband's adultery. Pulling up stakes in Beijing, she returned to Washington and stayed away for three months until lured back to China by her husband.

Reportedly, Bill didn't gloat when he was informed that Bush had a Jennifer, too. He told aides, "I didn't like it when it was done to me, and I don't like it when it's done to Bush."

It was reported to the Clintons that in the wake of revelations about her husband's affair, Barbara entered "a state of depression." When Hillary heard of this, she told friends, "I understand her pain."

Reports reached the Clinton camp that Barbara "was wallowing in self-pity, especially when her husband became the head of the CIA and was often traveling most of the time in the company of Jennifer."

Barbara told her closest friends that, "I wonder why George doesn't leave me? Sometimes, I can't stand the pain of his desertion. I feel like speeding up my car and running into a tree, or else crashing into an oncoming car."

The allegation of an illicit Bush/Fitzgerald affair had first been attributed to Louis Fields, who had represented the United States as Ambassador to the 1984 Nuclear Disarmament talks in Geneva. In preparation for Bush-with-Jennifer's arrival in Geneva, Fields arranged for them to share a government guest house in which their adjoining bedrooms were directly interconnected.

"It was made absolutely clear to me that Vice President Bush and Miss Fitzgerald were romantically involved," Fields said. "It made me very uncomfortable."

Fields shared his revelation with Joseph Trento, a CNN investigative reporter. He, in turn, spilled the secret to his wife, Susan B. Trento, a former Congressional aide, who wrote *The Power House,* a book about influence peddling in Washington.

In 1980, during Ronald Reagan's campaign for president, with Bush on the same ticket as vice-president, it was reported that the Veep was "having an intense relationship with a young blonde photographer who worked for a photo agency assigned to cover the race for the White House from the Republican perspective.

During the course of that campaign, aides reported to Reagan about

Bush's affair. According to TV talk show host Merv Griffin, a close friend of Reagan and Nancy, Reagan laughed it off. Griffin told his friend, Eva Gabor, and others, "Ronnie admitted to me that he, too, had been partial to blondes during his Hollywood heyday.

"I married brunettes, but I had my share of blondes," Reagan told Griffin. "Lana Turner comes to mind, as do Betty Grable, Marilyn Monroe, and Doris Day. After Jane Wyman left me, I proposed marriage to Adele Jergens. I even gave her a diamond ring."

Other First Ladies have survived the infidelities of errant presidential husbands.

Depicted above is GOP *grande dame* Barbara Bush, as conceived by Herbert Abrams as her official White House portrait.

In 1981, during the first year of Reagan's presidency, his gossipy First Lady, Nancy, learned "the salacious details" of Bush's affair with Fitzgerald. She didn't keep it a secret. When the Veep (that is, Bush), learned that Nancy was spreading the news, he angrily dismissed it as "rumor mongering."

He wrote in his diary "I always knew that Nancy didn't like me very much, but there is nothing I can do about that. I feel sorry for her, but the main thing is, I feel sorry for President Reagan."

Back in the United States, Bush and Jennifer showed up together in unexpected places. On February 23, 1976, they attended a discreetly unpublicized rendezvous with Frank Sinatra in Manhattan. The singer offered to work for the CIA in some capacity, citing his many contacts around the world, and his previous encounters with such figures as the Shah of Iran and Prince Philip.

According to an aide, Bush jokingly suggested to Sinatra, "I might get Reagan to designate you as U.S. ambassador to Australia."

He was alluding to the singer's notorious concert tour "Down Under." In Australia, he had denounced members of the local press as a "bunch of bums and parasites," calling women reporters there "buck-and-a-half hookers," and referring to Australia's news corps as "a bunch of fags." After 114 Australian labor unions went on strike in protest of his remarks, Sinatra had to cancel his tour.

Almost daily, some disgruntled enemy of "The Bush Establishment" sent a gossipy bulletin to the Clinton camp. One of them alleged that Bush maintained "another wife" in Manhattan. The woman in question, though not officially married to George Sr., was identified as "Rosemarie" (last name not given), and described as a vivacious Italian beauty whose appearance rivaled that of the bombshell movie star and sex goddess, Gina Lollobrigida.

Adele Jergens (Ronald Reagan's off-the-record *inamorata* and playmate) with Marilyn Monroe in *Ladies of the Chorus* (1948).

Although Reagan had proposed marriage to Jergens, Monroe dated the future president behind her back.

When he suffered a sports injury and was confined, flat on his back, in a hospital bed, the sultry blonde goddess was a frequent visitor, offering Reagan various forms of physical therapy, including "lip service."

Bush had rented an apartment for her, and both of their names appeared on the apartment house directory. He never attended any public events with Rosemarie, limiting his outings with her to private parties hosted by his GOP cronies.

Their love affair transpired in the early to mid-1960s. When he dropped her in 1964, he agreed to pay her rent for another three months. In reaction, she consulted an attorney, mulling over the prospect of a breach-of-promise suit against the lover who had jilted her. During their consultation with her lawyer, she revealed that Bush had promised that he would divorce Barbara and marry her. She also stated that he changed his mind, based on his presidential ambitions. No suit was ever filed.

The jet age presented Bush with plenty of opportunities to fly from Houston to Washington and New York, leaving Barbara behind in Texas. As Rosemarie's attorney later stated, "In essence, Bush had two wives, one legal, the other common law."

***

Around the time of the 1980 Republican National Convention in Houston, Barbara and George Bush had changed their opinion of Bill Clinton. When they'd first heard that he might seek the presidency, they had dismissed him as "a pathetic hillbilly from the Ozarks." But after he'd survived so many scandals, and evolved into a battle-hardened *politico,* they came to respect the "growing menace of that whore-mongering Comeback Kid."

On the floor of the Republican Convention in 1992, delegates opposed to

Bush spread tales of his adulteries. To counter them, Barbara was hauled out into public view as a vehicle for the emphasis on the Bush clan's "family values." As if to hammer home the point, she appeared on the dais with her five children and twelve grandchildren.

in addition to disagreeing with her politically, one reporter from Los Angeles described Barbara as "bull-dyke tough, surviving her husband's infidelities, the alcoholism of George W., the sexual and banking scandal of her son, Neil, and the death of her little daughter, Robin, who came down with leukemia. No wonder Barbara smokes two packs of cigarettes a day. Call it 'high anxiety.'"

Whereas Bill Clinton faced hundreds of "Second Coming" tabloid headlines, an adulterous George H.W. Bush—also revealed as a philanderer—escaped relatively unscathed.

But on August 11, 1992, the *New York Post* published a front page story headlined THE BUSH AFFAIR.

Spy magazine did them one better, blatantly exposing President Bush and his cheating heart.

More than a decade before, at around the time of the 1980 convention in Houston, when Republican contender Ronald Reagan was campaigning with his vice presidential running mate, George H.W. Bush, *The New York Post* came out with a shocker, exposing Bush's affair with Jennifer.

Following the convention, from the Bush family compound in Kennebunkport, Maine, Bush convened a press conference, where it seemed inevitable that he would be questioned about the exposé in the *New York Post*. Bush had choreographed the press conference armed with family members behind him, including his strong-willed, 91-year-old mother, as he faced the press.

It fell onto reporter Mary Tillotson to ask the $64,000 question. In the words of one news reporter, "Her fellow newsmen seemed to lack the *cojones.*"

When questioned by Tillotson about his alleged affair with Jennifer Fitzgerald, Bush's face flashed with anger. Like Bill Clinton and Frank Sinatra, he had a violent temper, which he tried to conceal. "I'm not going to take any sleazy questions from CNN," he snapped. "I am very disappointed you would ask me such a question. I will not respond to it. I am outraged."

Later, Barbara defined the question as "a disgusting lie."

The press conference was held at the Kennebunkport compound where Brandon Gill, a writer for *The New Yorker*, had been a guest. "In the middle of the night, I got up to find a book to read," he recalled. "I couldn't sleep. After I searched and searched, I asked myself, 'Does any member of the Bush family ever read a book?' The only volume I could find was '*The Fart Book*.'"

Then-President George H.W. Bush with Jennifer Fitzgerald, his mistress. White House aides, years later, revealed that Jennifer was the president's "other wife."

The Clinton camp was also presented with shocking evidence against another Bush family member, the future U.S. president George W. Bush, and his wife, Laura. For access to its allegations, the general public would have to wait until Kitty Kelley, the best-selling and very controversial author, published her book, *The Family—the Real Story of the Bush Dynasty,* in 2004.

In it, she exposed the political clan's darkest secrets, some of them associated with drug abuse, alcohol addiction, womanizing, and nepotism.

Several months after the book's release, as it headed for sales in excess of a million hardcover copies, the Bush camp fought back, dismissing her as "a tabloid sleaze queen."

Kelley cited sources who charged that George W. snorted cocaine at Camp David when his father was president. One source for that revelation was Sharon Bush, the ex-wife of Neil Bush. Sharon later denied that she'd made that accusation, although the publicist who worked for Sharon at the time was present at the luncheon wherein that had been revealed. *[He admitted and confirmed that the revelation had, indeed, been made.]*

One reviewer of that book wrote, "The Bushes promote themselves as refugees from *The Donna Reed Show,* but they are really *The Sopranos."*

Kelley aired charges against both George W. and his wife, Laura, detailing their use of marijuana in the 1960s. Among the allegations were statements about how the couple made several trips to Tortola, capital of the British Virgin Islands. Laura wanted a reunion with her college roommate, Jane Clarke, who was living there at the time with her boyfriend, baseball great Sandy Koufax, a twelve-season survivor of a pitching career (1955-1966) with the Brooklyn/Los Angeles Dodgers.

Sources on Tortola, including a servant in their household, claimed that the Bushes used to enjoy pot-smoking parties.

This was not inconsistent with charges made against Laura when she attended Southern Methodist University in 1968. She had been known in her college days as a "go-to-girl who peddled dime bags of marijuana," according to Kelley's sources.

"Laura not only smoked dope," said Robert Nash, a public relations executive, "but she sold it, too."

When he was governor of Texas, George W. was repeatedly asked about his use of illegal drugs. His answers were so muddled that he became the butt of late-night jokes on TV, the same fate that had descended on Bill Clinton.

On *The Tonight Show,* Jay Leno mocked George W. "First, he claims that he hasn't done drugs in the past fifteen years. Then later, he changed that. He said, 'no, no, he hadn't done drugs in the past twenty-five years.' Then really, like an hour ago, what he really meant to say was, he hadn't done drugs since he was twenty-eight. And, then, finally, he admitted 'Look, I'm so high, I don't know what the hell I'm saying.'"

Later, when President George W. was asked by reporters about those pot-smoking parties, he flashed his famous temper like his father. "For god's sake, guys, it was the fucking Sixties."

Like equivalent charges facing Bill Clinton, George W. also faced his own "bimbo eruptions."

A woman in Midland, Texas, alleged that she'd had an affair with him during his oil wildcatting days. But when she announced she was about to "Kiss and Tell All" to the media, she claimed she was approached by "intelligence types," a reference to men from the CIA, who had worked for Bush Sr. when he was their boss.

"I was told to get out of Dodge," she claimed to reporters. "These guys made me realize that it was better to turn tricks in Midland than to stop breathing."

In Florida, Jeb Bush, George W.'s brother and competitor, was asked by reporters about his own possible infidelities within the context of his marriage.

In response, he told newsmen, "I've slept only with my wife."

But when his older brother, George W., was asked for comment about these claims, he told reporters, "Oh boy! Jeb said that? No comment. I mean, Jeb is setting a tough standard for the rest of our generation."

Although some aides in the Clinton campaign, when confronting the "dirty tricks" of GOP operatives in 1992, urged Bill and Hillary to air scandals about the Bush family, they opted not to. Obviously, that decision to suppress scandals as they pertained to the Bush camp as a means of countering ongoing attacks from Republicans had to originate at the very top—not from either Bill or Hillary, but from a united combination of both of them.

A source who worked for the Clintons, who preferred not to give his name, later revealed,

> *"The Clintons had a lot of dirt, far more than Ms. Kelley actually published in 2004. Some of the more tawdry secrets about the Bush dynasty ended up on her cutting-room floor.*
>
> *Somewhere along the way, in 1992, both Bill and Hillary agreed not to stoop to the level of their attackers and not go all out to expose the Bushes for the sleazeballs that they are.*
>
> *Perhaps it could be said that by holding back their attack dogs, Bill and Hillary created a context for their greatest moments. Maybe they made the right decision. I mean, let's face it—they won the fucking election based on the issues, and not based on airing charges of illicit sex and drug abuse. As James Carville reminded us, 'Keep on message. It's the economy, stupid.'"*

The Draft-Dodging Comeback Kid Promises New Hampshire, "I'll Stand By You Until the Last Dog Dies."

In New Hampshire, in the immediate aftermath of Gennifer Flowers' press conference, crowds in record numbers turned out to hear Bill at his rallies and, if possible, to get a look at "the betrayed wife."

"They're not coming to hear his message," Hillary told Carville. "They're turning out to see a freak show."

She flew to Colorado, which had a primary scheduled for March. She told a reporter for *The Daily Sentinel,* "You feel like you're standing in the middle of a firing range, and sometimes, they come close to hitting you on the top of the head."

"As Bill and I head out to campaign across the country, I say my favorite prayer every day. 'Dear Lord, be good to me. The sea is so wide, my boat so small.'"

Bill was still campaigning in New Hampshire, where he faced new charges. First aired in Arkansas during his race for governor, accusations about draft dodging arose in the South and drifted to New England and, ultimately, into the national press.

"You didn't have to be a war hero," Stephanopoulos said, "but you couldn't be seen as a draft dodger."

Two figures from Bill's past emerged to air charges against him. One was Colonel Eugene Holmes, who had been ROTC commander at the University of Arkansas in 1969. He charged that Bill failed to honor his pledge to join the ROTC. Cliff Jackson, an old foe from yesteryear, detailed how Bill pulled strings to avoid being sent to Vietnam.

Along with other conservatives, Jackson formed an anti-Clinton group, the Alliance for Rebirth of an Independent America. He was spearheading a movement to raise cash for radio and TV commercials, as well as newspaper ads, denouncing Clinton not only for having avoided the draft, but for his record as governor.

"The draft issue did all the damage that Flowers didn't do," Stephanopoulos said. "Or, as Bill put it, 'we dropped like a turd in the well,' as polls in New Hampshire showed him falling to third place."

As if that weren't enough, Arkansas itself came under attack. As author Judith Warner wrote, "The state was gaining renown as the poorest and, allegedly, the most corrupt in the Union, with a highly conservative, backroom-operating legislature, and a poorly educated, mostly rural, politically unsophisticated voting body."

As its governor, Bill was blamed for all these ills. In the face of mounting attacks, he bravely defended his progressive record as governor and even found praise for the state itself "trying to pull itself up by the bootstraps."

In spite of the gloom and doom within the Clinton camp, Stephanopoulos said, "No matter how hard you hit Bill, he popped up smiling."

In the final hours of the New Hampshire primary, Bill delivered one of his most famous speeches before a crowd in Dover. He addressed the character issue, making a solemn promise, "If you elect me, I won't be George Bush. I'll never forget who gave me a second chance, and I'll be there for you 'till the last dog dies."

That became his new rallying cry, as volunteers fanned out around the state to retain his status as a viable candidate. Election morning dawned cold and icy. Tension rose in the Clinton camp. "We wondered if we were still in the ball game," Carville said.

As anticipated, Paul Tsongas led with 35 percent of the vote, but Bill made a strong showing with 26 percent, well ahead of Jerry Brown, Tom Harkin, and Bob Kerrey. Carville dubbed Bill, "The Comeback Kid," and the label stuck throughout the rest of the campaign.

Tsongas said, "I'm not trying to play Santa Claus like Bill Clinton. To hear him tell it, you'll have Maine lobster on your plate every night."

As a fellow New Englander, Tsongas, as anticipated, won the Maine caucus with 30 percent of the vote, although Brown was almost neck and neck with him, getting 29 percent. Bill made a poor showing at 15 percent.

As anticipated, Kerrey won the South Dakota primary. As a native Nebraskan, he was viewed as "more understanding of our problems in this part of America."

During that primary, the press hounded Kerrey about his former involvement with the actress Debra Winger in the 1980s, when he'd been Governor of Nebraska. He had become enamored of the actress when she was in Lincoln filming *Terms of Endearment,* which became the Best Picture of the Year at Oscar time in 1983.

"What can I say?" Kerrey asked reporters. "She swept me off my feet." He might have been alluding to the fact that the lower part of one of his legs had been amputated following injuries suffered in Vietnam. He was one of the few candidates for major political office who, despite having described himself as agnostic, survived, according to *The New York Times.*

After winning the South Dakota Primary, Kerrey's campaign temporarily rebounded.

Bob Kerrey during the Vietnam era, training as a SEAL.

March loomed as a make-or-break month for Bill, because of primaries scheduled that month in Colorado, Maryland, and Georgia. Georgia was the first big primary in the South, and a loss there might have ended Bill's campaign.

He had strong support in Arkansas, especially among African Americans, He nonetheless lost Maryland to Tsongas. His support was much stronger in the Rocky Mountains, notably in Denver, and the Colorado primary ended up almost as a three-way tie: Brown winning at 29 percent, Bill getting 27 percent, with Tsongas edging close at 26 percent.

Actress Debra Winger dated Kerry.

"So he's missing one leg. It's the 'third leg' that matters."

He faced Georgia with a daunting challenge. He had yet to win a primary. The state had a large military presence, and Carville feared the draft-dodging charges would work against their campaign. Kerrey predicted that the voters of Georgia "will split Bill Clinton open like a soft peanut." *[He was referring to the fact that Georgia grew more peanuts than any other state—just ask Jimmy Carter.]*

Bill had powerful support in the state, including Governor Zell Miller. On election night, it was his first triumph, as he won 57 percent of the vote.

After his defeat, Kerrey withdrew. In spite of his "soft peanut" attack on Bill, he nevertheless was on Bill's "short list" as a possible vice presidential running mate.

Bill enjoyed strong support in South Carolina among white voters who had not been lured away by the Republicans. His main adversary there was Harkin, who traveled the state with native son, the Rev. Jesse Jackson, who urged voters to support his candidate. Although Jackson was highly critical of Bill, most of Bill's black support held steadfast, and he scored a win of 63 percent on election night, even better than his previous results in Georgia.

After that, Harkin dropped out of the race, throwing his support to Bill, a favor that led to their close relationship during Bill's presidency.

Bill now faced his greatest challenge so far. Super Tuesday was coming when he would have to face Brown and Tsongas in eight make-or-break primaries and three caucuses.

New England remained safe territory for Tsongas, as both Carville and Bill had anticipated. Tsongas carried his home state of Massachusetts and neighboring Rhode Island and also won the caucus in Delaware.

The Clinton campaign hoped to make its most impressive showings in the Southern and border states. Bill's dream came true, as he celebrated victories along the Southern tier, with wins in Louisiana (his strongest support coming from urban New Orleans), as well as Mississippi, Oklahoma, and Al Gore's home state of Tennessee. Gore had not yet been named as his vice-presidential running mate.

Based to some degree on the network he'd nurtured and maintained since his campaign in Texas for McGovern 1972, and bolstered by a heavy turnout by Mexican Americans, Bill also carried that state with 66 percent of the vote. He also shot to victory in the key state of Florida, winning 51 percent of the vote, with Tsongas getting only 34 percent. Victories continued to pile up, as far-ranging as Hawaii and Missouri.

With Super Tuesday behind him, Bill and Hillary turned to upcoming primaries in Michigan and her home state of Illinois. As he headed into the industrial belt, Tsongas announced that he would consider Bill as his Veep and running mate. Privately, Bill told Carville about Tsongas, "What an arrogant fucker!"

That same day, a nation-wide poll revealed that voters questioned Bill's honesty and character. In Michigan, he identified and subsequently courted "Democrats for Reagan" who had voted Republican in the 1980 and '84 elections, and who felt dissatisfied with his present competitors.

In Michigan, Bill discovered many voters from Arkansas, who had moved to Detroit, hoping to find employment in the auto industry. He also strongly appealed to African American and blue collar white voters.

In Illinois, with Hillary, he campaigned hard for the Hispanic and black vote, and for the support of the thousands of naturalized citizens from Eastern Europe (especially Poles and Albanians) who had settled in the state.

A key moment was defined during a debate in Chicago, where he faced off against Tsongas and Brown. Brown attacked Hillary, specifically for her role with the Rose Law Firm, which had attracted lots of Arkansas-derived business when Bill was governor.

"Hillary had defended me so nobly that I felt I could pay her back by denouncing the lies that Brown was spreading about my wife," Bill said. "Governor Moonbeam has some fucking nerve giving off his lunar blasts."

Right Wingers Denounce Bill as a Wimp Hiding Behind Hillary's Skirttails—"Stop, or My Wife Will Shoot You!"

Leaving the Busy Bee Coffee House in her native Chicago, Hillary, along with Bill, encountered a "gaggle of cameras and microphones." She was asked to respond to charges that she'd had a conflict of interest stemming from her dual capacity as both a lawyer for the Rose Law Firm and as First Lady of Arkansas.

She was overtired, annoyed, and stressed that morning, and she made comments that would later be used against her. "I thought Jerry Brown's remark was pathetic and desperate," she said. "This is the sort of charge that happens to women who have their own careers and their own lives. And I think it's a shame, but I guess it's something we have to live with."

"Those of us who have tried to have a career—tried to have an independent life and to make a difference—and certainly like myself, who has children...you know I've done the best I can to lead my life, but I suppose it'll be subject to attack. But it's not true, and I don't know what else to say except it's sad to me."

"Could you have avoided an appearance of conflict of interest?" asked another newsman.

"I wish that were true," she said. "You know, I suppose I could have stayed home and baked cookies and had teas, but what I decided to do was fulfill my profession, which I entered before my husband was in public life. And I've worked very, very hard to be as careful as possible, and that's all I can tell you."

Many members of the press, as well as "talking heads" on TV, amplified her remarks into an attack on stay-at-home mothers. And as the story spread, radical GOP pundits labeled her as "a foam-at-the-mouth radical feminist lawyer," suggesting that she was a militant Amazonian warrior who was stridently contemptuous of traditional American values.

Right-wing commentators even suggested that if she ever reached the White House, Hillary might pursue a lesbian agenda. The most evangelical of the Evangelicals labeled her "The Antichrist."

She later admitted, "I made a political error. I wasn't attacking housewives or mothers at home." Many newspapers linked her "tea and cookies" remarks to her previous criticism of archtypes implied by the Tammy Wynette song, "Stand by Your Man."

Her remarks led to such a frenzy of protests that she was forced to say, "I've done quite a lot of cookie baking in my life—and a lot of tea pouring as well."

The following day, after the "tea-and-cookies" scandal, Bill carried Illinois with 52 percent of the vote, double the number of votes delivered to Tsongas, with Brown trailing.

In Michigan, Bill won with a slightly less impressive 49 percent: Brown garnering 27 percent, with Tsongas trailing.

Later, aides reported to Carville that Brown was "seriously pissed off at Clinton, and might not support him if he gets the Democratic nomination."

In response, Bill claimed that Brown was "being both petty and a poor loser."

Bill also swept to victory in the Michigan primary, winning 49 percent of the vote, with 27 percent going to Brown, 18 to Tsongas.

In both Illinois and Michigan, President Bush easily beat his chief rival, Pat Buchanan, a victory which basically ended Bush's challenge from the far right fringe of the Republican Party.

Hillary's championing of women in the work force alienated many conservative voters, but won her millions of fans who defended working mothers. She was inundated with letters from all over the country, praising her stand. Many of them suggested that Bill should designate her as his vice presidential running mate, or at least assign her a cabinet post.

She told supporters that she didn't want the Veep spot, "because I don't want to spend the next four years attending funerals."

To an increasing degree, Hillary was viewed as a kind of Rorschach test for gauging the opinions of the American public, winning both supporters and detractors as she articulated and embodied (through the example of her own life) social changes in the modern woman.

In many respects, she became the symbol of the "modern liberated woman," an archetype which had first emerged during the dark days of World War II, and who had gone to work in defense plants while their husbands or boyfriends were fighting on the battlefields of Europe or on the war-torn islands of the Pacific. "I became a symbol for women of my generation," she said. "I was a hot-button issue."

Outrage engendered by her "tea-and-cookies" comment just wouldn't go away. It became an issue in the upcoming presidential campaign, even after Bill won the Democratic nomination and named Al Gore as his vice presidential running mate.

As if to counter the perception of Hillary as a feminist lion opposed to traditionally "feminine" pastimes, Hillary and Tipper Gore, Al's wife, were filmed pouring tea and nibbling cookies in New York's Waldorf Astoria Hotel.

This strategy didn't go over with a skeptical press. Republican strategist Roger Aiels asserted, "Hillary Clinton in an apron is about as convincing as Mike Dukakis in that military tank."

Another reporter attacked her new, "softer" image as being "as corny as Kansas in August. Her wide-eyed, down-home comments are so extraordinarily hokey they sound intentionally fake."

Writing in the *Arkansas Democrat-Gazette,* columnist Paul Greenberg claimed, "The first time I saw Hillary Rodham, she was angry about injustice and not fearful about saying so. She was more ideologically committed, less fashionably attractive. Now she's tough, controlled, less cosmetologized, intense with something contradictory under her surface. You have the idea she's holding back."

Presidential predecessors and role models: Eleanor and Franklin Roosevelt.

He had his girlfriends on the side and so did the First Lady. Even so, he was one of the greatest of all presidents, and she was unquestionably the greatest First Lady.

Some pundits credited Hillary with resurrecting Bill from the dead. Others noted that she'd paid a price for all this stress. Eleanor Clift, in *Newsweek,* wrote that she was "the lion of the past winter. Today, she's a burned-out, buttoned-up automaton compared with the vibrant woman who stormed purposefully onto the national scene."

Ann Lewis, a consultant for the Democratic Party, claimed that "Bill and Hillary symbolize a working partnership between a wife and her husband that we have not seen modeled before in the political arena, not even by Franklin and Eleanor. The lives of the Clintons are really more like the typical American family than the life led by George and Barbara Bush. The Bushes are an older model that no one could afford or choose to adopt anymore. Politics often lags behind reality."

Critic Naomi Wolf found Hillary "the embodiment of the feminist future: a woman who combines feminist values with worldly power in the form of her own sterling professional credentials and with her influence on her husband. To working women struggling to combine family and professional identities, this is an inspiring role model and a vision of a union among gender, idealism, and real power."

Ultimately, *Family Circle* entered the tea-and-cookie fray by challenging Barbara Bush and Hillary for a bake-off to see which of the wives made the better chocolate chip cookies. As part of its coverage, the magazine ran recipes from both the First Lady of the United States and the First Lady of Arkansas.

Hillary urged her supporters to vote for her cookies, even if they didn't think they were the best. "Be a good Democrat and vote for them anyway."

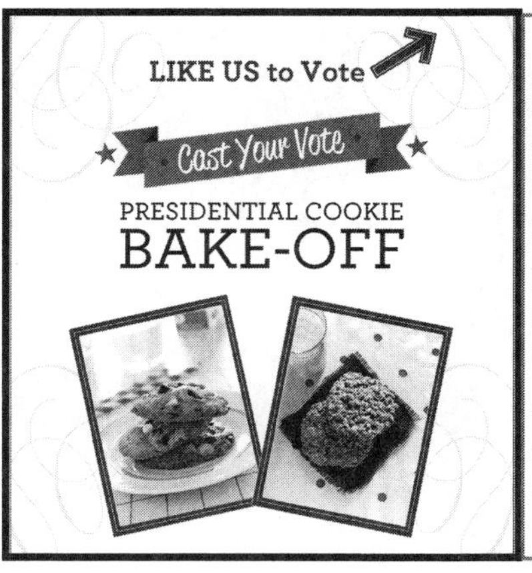

As the presidential race heated up, *Family Circle* entered the feud between two First Ladies, Barbara Bush and Hillary Clinton. Who had the best recipe for chocolate chip cookies?

The bake-off outcome was never quite determined, but Hillary claimed that her cookies were "more Democratic" because she used vegetable oil, in marked contrast to Barbara.

"Barbara uses so much butter fat in her recipe that it would almost guarantee a heart attack if you bit into one of her cookies."

In Jesse Jackson's "Hymie-Town" "A Redneck Bozo" Battles "Governor Moonbeam"

Confronted with a lack of campaign funds, Tsongas announced his withdrawal from the race. That left Bill, on a winning streak, face to face against his last major challenger, an embittered Jerry Brown himself.

Bill campaigned hard in the next primary (in Connecticut) on March 24 and expected to win because pollsters had indicated that he had strong support in that state. Unexpectedly, however, Bill encountered a backlash there from Tsongas supporters, who blamed him for forcing their candidate out of the race. In the aftermath, Brown won with 37 percent of the vote, with Bill "right on the fucker's trail" with 36 percent. Even though he had withdrawn from the race, Tsongas carried 20 percent of the vote.

The New York primary, "an animal following his own rules" (Bill's words), loomed next on the electoral calendar. Bill and Hillary had only about two weeks (until April 7) to convince the voters of one of the biggest, most powerful, and most sophisticated states in the Union, New York, that they should back them—two representatives from a rather backward Southern state. New York State, and, by association, the Big Apple of New York City, were up for grabs. For Bill, it was a "must win" state. Before his arrival there, James Carville had warned, "New York politics is not for sissies."

The Clintons set out to court the nation's most diverse urban population with almost every known ethnic group, including, for example, 600,000 from the Dominican Republic alone. Puerto Ricans and Jews also abounded in mass numbers, as did thousands upon thousands of members and/or supporters of the LGBT community. Also populated with Irish people and colonies from India, the Middle East, Pakistan, Albanians, and hundreds of other demographics, New York City had it all.

To many of these groups, President Bush seemed distant, elitist, remote, and disinterested in their problems and issues. Bush was interpreted as a "rich white man who had no regard for the poor and how they struggled to make a living." Playing on their fears, Bill promised remedies.

Fighting for his political life, Brown staged an epic battle to defeat Bill.

The Rev. Jesse Jackson had never been an admirer of Bill's. During Bill's campaign for the hearts and minds of New York, Jackson virtually camped out in New York City, urging African Americans and others to vote for Brown. As a means of returning the favor, Brown announced that, if nominated, he would name Jackson as his vice-presidential running mate. That turned out to be a huge mistake.

Because of that pledge by Brown, many members of the Jewish community threw their support to Bill. Jackson's close collaboration with the anti-Semitic and fiery Muslim leader Louis Farrakhan was well known (and much feared) among New York Jews. Jackson became even more loathed in 1984, when he poked fun at Jews, calling them "Hymies" and designating New York City as "Hymie-Town"

In retribution, Jackson was loudly denounced by such Jewish leaders as Nathan Perlmutter, executive director of the Anti-Defamation League of B'nai B'rith, who ridiculed his attempts to apologize and called him "a whore. He could light candles every Friday night and grow side curls, and it still wouldn't matter."

In an attempt to win the African American vote in New York City, Jerry Brown announced that he would name the Rev. Jesse Jackson as his vice presidential running mate.

That angered the Jews, who viewed Jackson as an anti-Semite.

In March of 1992, *The New York Times* ran unflattering articles on the involvement of the Clintons in the Whitewater investment in Arkansas. As media criticism of Bill's character continued churning itself out, he observed, "The press believed in shooting first, asking questions later."

Another issue emerged on March 29 in a face-off with Brown during a TV forum on WCBS. A newsman asked Bill if he'd ever smoked marijuana.

He admitted that he had at Oxford. "I experimented with marijuana a time or two, and I didn't like it. I didn't inhale, and I never tried it again."

Jerry Brown and his girlfriend, singer Linda Ronstadt, flew cross country, battling Bill for the Democratic nomination.

After Brown attacked Hillary, Bill told reporters, "I don't care what he says about me, but he ought to be ashamed of himself for jumping on my wife. He's not worthy of being on the same platform with Hillary. Jerry comes in with his family wealth and his $1,500 suits and makes a lying accusation about Hillary!"

The comment backfired and gave such late night TV hosts as Johnny Carson rich fodder for jokes at Bill's expense. Don Imus, the radio talk show host, called Bill "a redneck Bozo."

As if the pot issue weren't enough, when Bill appeared on *The Phil Donahue Show,* all that the TV host did for twenty minutes was pound him with questions about his "marital infidelity."

At the last minute, President Carter, who was never known for being an admirer of Bill's, announced his support for him in the crucial days before New Yorkers went to the polls.

That same day (April 2), when Brown tried to deliver a speech at the Jewish Community Relations Council in New York, he was booed and shouted down.

"Mr. Hymie-town"

At a midday rally on Wall Street, both Hillary and Bill were booed by stockbrokers. He had called them "a greedy bunch." At the last minute, In spite of its previous critical reviews, *The New York Times* endorsed Bill, as did *The Daily News,* even the *New York Post,* which had attacked him, perhaps with the most venom.

Before the polls opened, a last minute survey of Puerto Ricans revealed their 96 percent support for Bill.

A somewhat "battered and bloodied" Bill, with Hillary, awaited the election results on the night of April 7. Bill carried the state with 41 percent of the vote; Tsongas—even though he'd officially withdrawn from the campaign—finished second at 29 percent. Brown tagged along at 26 percent.

After hearing the results, Bill sang the old gospel song, "The Darker the Night, the Sweeter the Victory."

As returns came in that night from the primaries in other states, Bill learned that he'd also swept to victory in Minnesota, Kansas, and Wisconsin.

"I was a wreck, in spite of my victories," Bill lamented to Carville. "I'd gained weight, I'd lost my voice, and my reputation was forever damaged. I was exhausted. Not only that, but I came down with history's worst case of the flu and could hardly breathe. I looked like a balloon about to burst, thanks to those god damned donuts."

"What faced me?" he asked. "More primaries and a showdown at the Democratic Convention in New York. As Harry S Truman had warned future politicos, 'If you can't stand the heat, get out of the kitchen.' I was staying in the kitchen, keeping the iron skillets sizzling with red meat and the black pots boiling, giving off my steam."

***

Back in Little Rock and recovering his health, Bill won the Virginia caucus and received endorsements from the powerful unions, the AFL-CIO and the United Auto Workers.

Later, still on the campaign trail, this time in Pennsylvania, he faced brutal opposition from anti-abortion critics, yet swept nonetheless to victory with 57 percent of the vote.

He also carried his native state of Arkansas with 68 percent of the vote. Even better, the percentage of Democrats nationwide who now claimed that they'd vote for him rose to 60 percent.

Unexpectedly, a new challenger, posing more of a threat to President Bush than to him, had entered the presidential sweepstakes.

The challenger was H. Ross Perot, a billionaire and, like Bush himself, a fellow Texan. Perot had founded the Electronic Data Systems (EDA), which he had subsequently sold to General Motors. Later, in 1988, he founded Perot Systems, an enterprise later purchased by Dell for nearly $4 billion.

Perot had opposed the U.S.'s 1990 Persian Gulf War against Iraq. In his fiery and highly articulate campaign, he successfully tapped into Populist resentment of mainstream establishment politicians.

Stephanopoulos defined Perot as "the weird little man who is a ventriloquist's dummy for voter anger."

Unexpectedly, at the dawn of the crucial month of May, national polls suddenly defined Perot as "the top dog" (as Carville put it), beating Bush, as Bill lagged dangerously behind in third place.

In the meantime, riding out Perot's storm, Bill, in his words, "stuck to my knitting," picking up crucial "super delegates" before the upcoming convention. Senator Jay Rockefeller *[the influential Senator (1985-2015) from West Virginia, a rare Democrat in what had been a traditionally Republican dynasty]* joined Bill's bandwagon, despite Bill's previous opposition to his *[Republican]* relative, Winthrop Rockefeller, way back during Bill's political conflicts as an elected official in Arkansas.

On April 29, race relations became an issue in the campaign when riots broke out in California in the wake of the police beating of Rodney King, an African American who had tried to escape arrest after a prolonged high-speed chase through the streets of Los Angeles. Four white police officers from the LAPD had been acquitted by an all-white jury in Ventura County.

Before the riots ended, hundreds of people had been arrested. At the end of a three-day rampage through South Central Los Angeles, 2,300 people were injured and fifty were dead. In the aftermath of burnings and lootings, damage totaled more than $750 million.

In Los Angeles, Bill toured the devastation with Maxine Waters, an African American Democratic Congresswoman. Bill eagerly courted the support of the black community, some members of which viewed him skeptically in his capacity as the governor of a Southern state with a notorious civil rights record.

WAITING FOR PEROT

Bill Clinton feared Ross Perot as a candidate for president running as an Independent.

He told Hillary that Perot was going to take votes from him, not from President Bush. "This guy's coming on, and it's all going to come from me," Bill claimed.

He promised community development and called for reform. He spoke out against AIDS and promised Federal funding as a means of making schools safer. Despite the fact that it was Jerry Brown's home turf, Bill, with Hillary, fought hard for the all-important state of California.

Despite the efforts of both the Clinton and Bush campaigners, Perot continued to rise in the polls, Bill calling him "a Frankenstein monster of the Republican's own making."

"I was getting desperate, and I needed to get out the youth vote," Bill said. "Young people weren't watching the nightly news, but they were tuning to Arsenio Hall, so I decided to go on his show in sunglasses, playing my beloved saxophone. I think my strategy worked."

June 2 witnessed a string of important primaries in states across the nation. In the late hours of that day, Bill and Hillary celebrated as he carried California by 48%, as opposed to Brown's 40%.

That's not all: Bill also won other primaries from New Jersey to New Mexico, from Alabama to Montana. Former president Richard Nixon, retired, disgraced, and embittered, had predicted that Bush would triumph in the end, but polls contradicted him as Perot triumphantly continued his lead. "I was called 'dead meat' by most of the talking heads on TV," Bill said.

With Bill trailing in third place, Stephanopoulos summed things up: "Our campaign was broke in every way. We hadn't been paid in months, and our staff was split into two squabbling camps. To the general public, Clinton was a slick Southern yuppie educated at silver spoon schools such as Yale and Oxford who had dodged the draft, cheated on his wife, and lied about smoking pot."

In desperation, Bill agreed to appear on *The Arsenio Hall Show,* a late-night TV venue with demographics that included huge numbers of young people in their twenties. As the cameras rolled, Bill brought out his saxophone for renditions of "God Bless the Child," and one of his personal favorites, Elvis' "Heartbreak Hotel."

Bill's appearance before Jesse Jackson's Rainbow Coalition on June 13 became notorious. Originally conceived as a fence-mending reunion, it degenerated into just the opposite.

The night before Bill's appearance, Sister Souljah, a popular rap singer, had addressed the Coalition. She had gone on record making a racist rant: "If black people kill black people every day, why not have a week and kill white people? So if you're a gang member and you would normally be killing somebody, why not kill a white person?"

Two months after the Los Angeles riots over the Rodney King beating, Bill Clinton was watching the TV news when he heard the rap singer, Sister Souljah, make one of the most inflammatory statements uttered by a celebrity in the '90s. She said, "If black people kill black people every day, why not have a week and kill white people?"

Although she had the support of the Rev. Jesse Jackson, Bill—sending a signal to white voters—seized upon a political opening and denounced Souljah for having said it.

According to Dick Morris, "Clinton knew exactly what he was doing."

In his address to the Coalition, Bill said, "If you took the words 'white' and 'black' and reversed them, you might think David Duke (an avowed white racist) was giving that speech. We have an obligation, all of us, to call attention to prejudice whenever we see it."

Although Bill was praised by many as a voice of moderation, Jackson condemned him for attacking Sister Souljah, denouncing his speech as a "demagogic pitch to white voters." Then Jackson broadly hinted that he might cancel his endorsement and throw his support to Perot.

Bill later said, "I felt compelled to speak out about race-based violence."

At around the same time, George H.W. Bush's running mate, Danforth Quayle, also faced reporters. Ever since

Bush had designated him as Vice President, Bill had privately asserted, with more than a touch of ridicule, "He's not the brightest bulb in the chandelier."

The Trentonian

Quayle comes to Trenton

Dan can't spell 'potato'

He may be the vice president, but 'He's an idiot.'
– William Figueroa, 12, Mott School 6th grader

PAGE 3

When Quayle announced a public definition of his role as the anti-Clinton "pit bull," in the upcoming fall campaign, Bill responded, "Quayle's threat will strike terror in the heart of every fire hydrant in America."

The dynamics of the three-way race for the presidency was hugely influenced based on the bitter "for public consumption" feud between "the two Texans," Bush and Perot.

In July, Perot suddenly and unexpectedly announced his decision to abandon his campaign for president. In a convoluted explanation that evolved over a period of a few months, Perot said that a Bush operatives were "scheming to smear my daughter with a computer-altered photograph to disrupt her wedding."

Bush aides fought back, defining Perot's assertions as "all loony."

It was later revealed by Suzanne McGee, one of Perot's four daughters, that her father suspected that Bush was orchestrating a "dirty tricks" plot to expose Carolyn, his soon-to-be-married daughter, as a closeted lesbian.

Danforth Quayle became famous for his status as an attack dog aimed directly at the Clintons, and for visiting a classroom in which he told a young African American boy that he had misspelled "potato." The vice president told the kid that the correct spelling was POTATOE.

When not teaching spelling, the vice president and his wife, Marilyn, went on TV to attack homosexuals.

Wilbur Kristol, a historian, said, "Two great moments will stand out in American presidential history: The selection of Danforth Quayle as George H.W. Bush's running mate, and the choice by John McCain of Sarah Palin to run as his Veep."

***

Right before the convention, Bill's choice of a vice presidential running mate had narrowed down to Bob Graham, Governor of Florida, and Al Gore, a Senator from Tennessee. After mulling it over for days, Bill decided to link his future to Gore, even though that meant that both candidates on the Democratic ticket originated in the South.

Bill liked Gore and his intelligent, attractive wife, Tipper, although hardly endorsing her campaign against "vulgar and violent" lyrics in modern music.

Finally, July 11, the big day, had come as Bill, Hillary, and Chelsea flew into New York to attend the Democratic National Convention at Madison Square Garden. "After months of being told I was lower than a snake's belly, I was now being held up as a paragon of all things good and true," Bill said.

While the convention was still in progress, the latest nationwide poll put Bill in a double digit lead over Bush.

Hillary wasn't faring as well. By the time her feet hit the tarmac in New York, polls showed her public approval rating had sunk to a dismal 29 percent.

In New York, however, she would undergo a dramatic makeover before presenting herself to the convention. "I was like a kid in the candy store," she recalled, "trying out every style I could. Long hair, short hair, bangs, flips, braids, and buns."

At this point, nearly all of the former Democratic presidential hopefuls, including Tsongas and Harkin, were backing Bill. Only Brown held out, with Harkin criticizing Brown and asserting that he "was on an ego trip."

Wednesday, the second-to-last night of the convention, was a showdown night for Bill, as three of his former rivals, Bob Kerrey, Jerry Brown, and Paul Tsongas, delivered their speeches. Brown had withdrawn his previous threat and—in an about-face—delivered a speech endorsing Bill as the candidate he supported. Bill congratulated Brown for being "brave and classy."

Even Jesse Jackson forgave Bill for the Sister Souljah incident and endorsed him.

[As it happened, Teddy Kennedy swallowed his pride and endorsed Bill as well, despite the fact that on the Gennifer Flowers tape, Teddy had heard Bill say, "Senator Kennedy is so stupid he couldn't get a whore across a bridge," a sarcastic reference to Mary Jo Kopechne's tragic and messy death at Chappaquidick and Senator Kennedy's excruciating embarrassment during its aftermath.

Sixteen years later, in 2008, Teddy Kennedy, known for his tenacious, elephant-like memory, snubbed Hillary and forcefully endorsed Barack Obama, running at the time against Hillary as the Democratic Party's nominee for president.]

The highlight of the evening was the nominating speech delivered by Mario Cuomo, the governor of New York and one of the best orators in the Democratic Party. He had opted to forgive Bill who, in Gennifer Flowers' (no longer secret) tapes, had defined him as "a thug."

From the podium, Cuomo's stinging rhetoric rebuked Bush for his many failures and made a strong case for the Comeback Kid, calling him "a new voice in America, someone smart enough to know, strong enough to do, and sure enough to lead."

During the convention's roll call, after registering the presence of "the great state of Alabama," the public address system at Madison Square Garden tuned in to the voice of Bill's mother, Virginia Kelley, who announced that "Arkansas proudly casts our forty-eight electoral votes for our favorite son and my son, Bill Clinton."

The scales tipped in Bill's favor after Ohio announced the delivery of its votes to Bill. His victory in that key state meant that he had accumulated the 2,145 votes needed to make him the Democratic nominee. After his win, Bill broke precedence and appeared before the convention, as JFK had done in 1960. In the speech he delivered, he promised that, "Tomorrow night I will be The Comeback Kid."

$1.25 NYDailyNews.com SPORTS FINAL Friday, January 2, 2015

DAILY NEWS

NEW YORK'S HOMETOWN NEWSPAPER

Mario Cuomo
June 15, 1932 –
January 1, 2015

Liberal lion dead at 82 as son sworn in for 2nd term

SUPER MARIO

Former three-term Gov. Mario Cuomo passed away at home just hours after his son, Gov. Andrew Cuomo, took the oath for a second term Thursday.

PAGES 2,3,4,5,6,8

THE LIFE IMAGES COLLECTION/GETTY

Mario Cuomo, the former governor of New York, revered, post-mortem, on the front page of NYC's "home-town newspaper."

According to Bill Clinton, "I thought he was going to run against me for president. He was our finest orator, and he took some potshots at me. I fired back and later regretted the shitty things I said about him. But Mario and I made up, and he became one of my strongest defenders."

On a celebratory mood, Hillary grabbed Tipper Gore by the wrist, leading her into a dance. A reporter described it "like 1960s teenyboppers recovering their lost youth."

On stage at Madison Square Garden, Hillary made a stunning entrance. Wearing a yellow silk suit designed by Cliff Chally, her hair was dyed a honey blonde, compliments of Christophe. Even Virginia Kelley approved of Hillary's makeup, which had been conceived and applied by Charles Blackwell.

[Chally, who had previously designed clothes for the hit TV sitcom, Designing Women, *had been "steered" by Hillary's firm directive, "I'll wear anything except Nancy Reagan red."]*

The final day of the convention was Thursday, July 16. As the vice presidential nominee, Al Gore, handpicked by Bill himself, was nominated by acclamation.

Gore gave what was arguably the most "rip-roaring speech" (Bill's words) of his career. Contrary to the usual opinion, he showed that he had a sense of humor, claiming, "As a boy growing up in Tennessee, I always wanted to be a warm-up act for Elvis."

Appearing on stage to thunderous applause, "The Man from Hope" delivered an eloquent speech, championing the middle class, but also calling attention to minorities, including the poor, and those with disabilities. He also focused on the plight of the gays, the first reference to LGBT issues ever mentioned by a leading presidential associate at a national nominating convention. He ended his emotional oration with a call for national unity.

At the end of the convention, polls showed Bill with a twenty-point lead over Bush. But the candidate knew that his broad lead in the polls would probably not last.

As Bill later told Carville, "I fear there are many truckloads of shit we've got to wade through before my dream comes true."

Hillary used a less scatological reference, claiming, "We never know what land mines we'll stumble across."

***

The next day, the nominees, Bill and Al Gore, were joined by their wives, Hillary and Tipper, for the debut of a post-convention, 1,000 mile bus tour through states that included New Jersey, Pennsylvania, West Virginia, Ohio, Kentucky, and Illinois.

On this trip, the friendly quartet got to know each other. Maneuvering as a team in close proximity, they became privy to each others' flaws and strengths. As their bus tour progressed under the gaze of a national spotlight, their enemies spread the false rumor that these four relatively youthful candidates were engaged in "four-way sex at night."

The bus tour, passing waving crowds *en route*, made many unscheduled stops to greet the assembled crowds, a policy that invariably made them late, sometimes very late, for scheduled stops and speeches.

Their bus tour continued on through Missouri, Iowa, Wisconsin, and Minnesota. The Arkansas papers wondered in editorials, "Just who is running our state? Is Lieutenant Governor Jim Guy Tucker making all the decisions?"

Stopovers in other states would follow, including a swing through Georgia and ten hectic and exhausting days in North Carolina that incorporated scheduled events in ten separate towns and spontaneous stops and/or detours in several others as well.

Noting the success of the bus tour, the Bush attack dogs increased their ferocious barking. One of President Bush's chief aides, Mary Matalin, publicly referred to Bill as "a sniveling hypocrite." Ironically, Matalin was engaged at the time to James Carville, Bill's campaign manager.

Jokingly, Bill informed the Ragin' Cajun, "I hope you don't reveal all our campaign tactics during pillow talk."

Matalin earned the dubious distinction of introducing Stephanopoulos to his most vindictively ferocious media attack dog, the far right talk show mogul, Rush Limbaugh. On his TV shows, he frequently superimposed the face of Stephanopoulos onto the body of a baby.

"Don't you think it's time to get me out of diapers?" Stephanopoulos once asked the GOP talk-show attack dog.

"He must have listened," Stephanopoulos later said. "From then on, he pictured me as a toddler in short pants, riding a rocking horse."

Stephanopoulos kept abreast of how the Republicans were doing by gauging the changing nuances of Carville's reaction to his *fiancée*. "We Democrats knew we were doing well when James would come in and tell me that 'Mary's really ragging on me today.' On other days, he'd say, 'I'm scared. Mary's being too nice to me. You think they must have something on us?'"

During the bus tour, with Hillary, Al, and Tipper by his side, Bill kept suggesting the image and concept of a co-presidency: "Buy one *[President]*, get one free." He constantly extolled the virtues and administrative talents of his wife.

"If I get elected president, it will be an unprecedented partnership," he said, "far more than Franklin and Eleanor Roosevelt. They were two great people, but on different tracks from us. If I get elected, Hillary and I will do things together like we have done in Arkansas, but on a far broader national scope." He also continued his relentless attacks on Bush and his many economic failures.

President Bush, fighting for his political survival, launched a counter offensive to Bill's attacks on his administration. As part of the process, he threw discretion to the wind and insisted that Bill would launch the largest tax increases in American history and that his health care program would reflect "the compassion of the KGB." Also, as a dig at Bill's womanizing, Bush promised to set a "higher moral tone than Clinton would."

When Bill heard that, he said, "In Bush's case, that womanizer is such a god damn hypocrite," referring, of course, to Bush's own string of reported infidelities.

Despite the relentless attacks from the far right, Carville kept Bill's campaign on message by constantly reminding staffers, "It's the economy, stupid."

***

At the White House in August, Barbara and George Bush were getting ready to fly back to their home state of Texas to attend the Republican National Convention at the Astrodome in Houston. The most recent presidential poll had positioned Bill with a twenty-point lead over Bush.

As they boarded *Air Force One*, Barbara—jokingly or otherwise—told her husband, "Don't you think it's about time we started packing our bags to move out of the White House?"

He did not appreciate his wife's remark.

The GOP convention in Houston devolved into one of the most notorious in the history of the Republic, a blatant display of intolerance and bigotry, as best expressed by the dragon-fire rhetoric of Pat Buchanan, who had tried but failed to win his party's nomination, and the evangelical hysteria of Pat Robertson.

Both Bill and Hillary sat glued to their television sets, watching with dismay as one attack after another was leveled at them directly. Bill had to listen to repeated charges that he was a "skirt chaser" and a "draft dodger." Finally, he concluded, "Those fucking bastards threw everything at me, even the kitchen sink."

Among many low points at that year's GOP Convention, the deepest dungeon itself was reached when the crazed-looking Pat Buchanan appeared before the delegates for delivery of a fiery rant wherein he accused liberals and left-wing radicals of being "cross-dressers" and suggested that Woody Allen and Mia Farrow represented "family values" to the Democrats.

Buchanan went on to win sustained applause with his assertion that Bill's only experience in foreign affairs involved "stuffing himself at the International House of Pancakes."

"Hillary Clinton believes that twelve-year-olds should have the right to sue their parents," Buchanan charged, a refrain she'd heard many times before. "She compares marriage and the family as institutions tantamount to slavery or life on an Indian reservation."

Pamphlets depicting Hillary as "The Wicked Witch of the East" were distributed throughout the Astrodome. The caption read, *"I will get you, my pretty, and your little dog, too!"* a line ripped off from Margaret Hamilton's portrayal of the witch in Judy Garland's *The Wizard of Oz.*

Dozens of women in the audience wore badges that proclaimed, "ANOTHER COOKIE BAKER FOR BUSH."

Buchanan seemed to be attacking working mothers, articulating a policy that alienated millions of them, many of whom—in the absence of a supportive, resident male—had been forced into the job market as a means of paying their family's mounting debts. Although many of these women had voted Republican in the past, many were frustrated and even enraged by what they interpreted as a widening alienation from Buchanan's interpretation of Republican priorities.

It became obvious to many reporters that Buchanan seemed nostalgic for an America that had disappeared with the 1950s sitcom depicting Ozzie and Harriet and their sons, Ricky and David Nelson.

Barbara Bush, the most tolerant of all the Bushes, characterized Buchanan's bombast as "mean, hateful, and racist."

Another Pat, the venomously homophobic Pat Robertson, was also granted a platform at the GOP Convention. With beaming approval from "Moral Majority" leader Jerry Falwell, Robertson seemed to take his marching orders directly from God. He delivered fiery blasts at, among others, homosexuals. In the words of one reporter, "I don't think he considers gays as part of the human race." Despite the narrow and punitive nature of his overview, his words resounded powerfully among the far-right Evangelical fringe.

The GOP camp accused liberals of being baby killers, militant feminists, and "perverted homosexuals defacing the landscapes of America and its proud, traditional values."

One fiery delegate from Texas told a reporter at the convention in Houston that he had seen a document that insisted that if Bill Clinton is elected

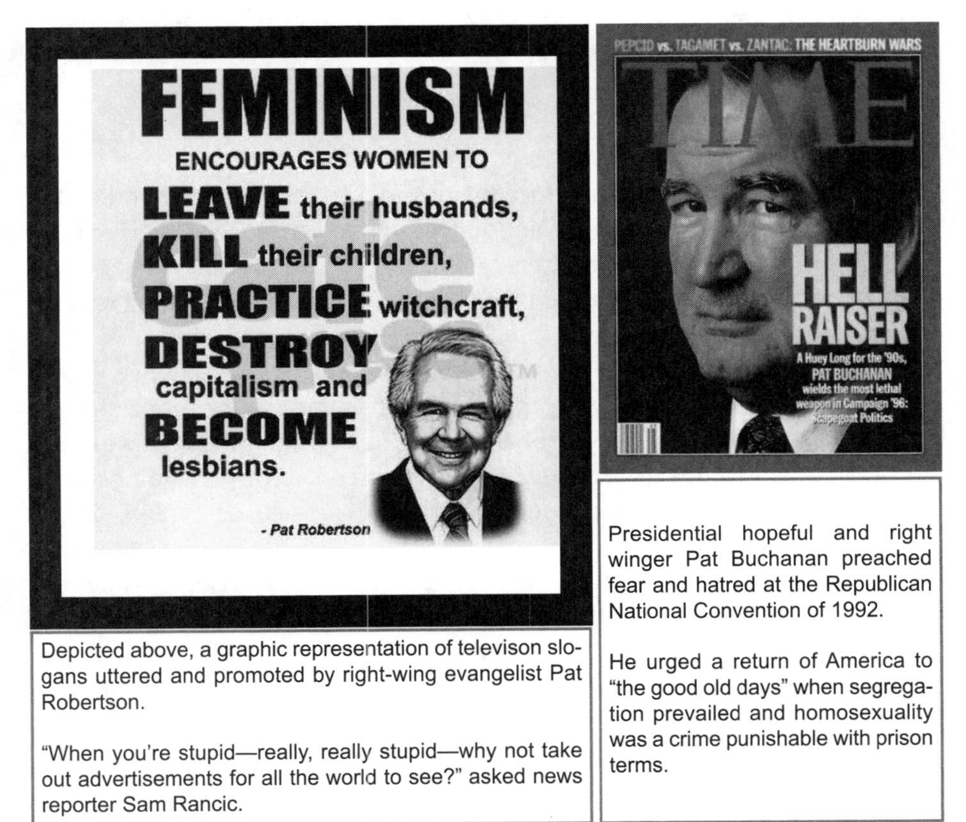

Depicted above, a graphic representation of televison slogans uttered and promoted by right-wing evangelist Pat Robertson.

"When you're stupid—really, really stupid—why not take out advertisements for all the world to see?" asked news reporter Sam Rancic.

Presidential hopeful and right winger Pat Buchanan preached fear and hatred at the Republican National Convention of 1992.

He urged a return of America to "the good old days" when segregation prevailed and homosexuality was a crime punishable with prison terms.

president, "He will legalize boy love, which will doom our nation."

As millions tuned in, Bill was ridiculed with the pejorative label "Slick Willie." That nickname became a rallying cry for Republicans during the final weeks leading up to the November election.

Rarely had a nominee for election to the American presidency appeared so undignified in his acceptance speech as did George H.W. Bush. His attack on Bill was likened to the "barking of a mad dog in August."

Bush claimed that "My dog Millie knows more about foreign policy than does that clown, Bill Clinton." The Clinton/Gore opposition team was dismissed as "Governor Taxes and the Ozone Man. If those two bozos are elected, every day in America will be Halloween, their favorite day." Bush drew loud applause after his public assertion that "Clinton's Elvis economics will lead to Heartbreak Hotel."

The sitting president also contrasted his own military record during World War II to "that draft-dodger who pulled strings to keep from going to Vietnam. While I bit the bullet, Clinton bit his nails."

At the end of the convention, "a feisty Bush" flew out of Texas, claiming, "I'm the real Comeback Kid. In 1948, they wrote off Harry Truman, claiming he'd lose to Thomas Dewey. *Harry showed 'em*. He gave them hell, and that's what I'm prepared to do to Clinton."

***

By September, just weeks before the presidential elections scheduled for November, Ross Perot suddenly announced his re-entrance into the presidential fray, despite the fact that his reputation had been badly damaged by his previous withdrawal from the race. Polls now reflected him in a less favorable light.

On October 1, he announced he was back seeking the presidency, defining his vice-presidential running mate as Vice Admiral James Stockdale, a highly decorated former prisoner of war in Vietnam. During the final weeks of the presidential campaign, Perot would visit sixteen states, spending about $13 million of his own money, a sum which in his capacity as a multi-billionaire, he could afford.

At long last, the moment arrived for the first of the televised presidential debates. Scheduled in St. Louis, on the campus of Washington University, it coincided with Bill and Hillary's 17th wedding anniversary.

Bush had strenuously objected to the admission of Perot into the debate. In contrast, Bill said, with enthusiasm, "Bring him on!"

The night of the debate, Bill was not in his greatest form, appearing a bit stiff as Bush drew attention to his familiar charges of draft dodging, his student involvement in anti-Vietnam protests, and his trip to Moscow many years before.

In contrast, Bill was more of a statesman during his discussion of America "drifting and worn down, needing to be re-energized and in need of a new direction."

It was never fully determined who "won" the debate, since opinions were split along party lines. Many pundits, however, asserted after the fact that the debate helped Perot more than either of his mainstream competitors.

During the debate, when Bush attacked Perot's inexperience, Perot shot back, "I don't have any experience in running up a $4 trillion debt." When Bush advocated his tax proposals, Perot joked, "I'm all ears," making fun of his prominent jug ears, their size emphasized by his crewcut.

A poll demonstrated that after the debate, more than 60 percent of the television audience asserted that they viewed Perot's viability as a candidate more favorably than they had before.

The second debate was in Richmond, Virginia, the seat of the Old Confederacy. Two days before he went on, Bill almost completely lost his voice, uttering sounds that came out as only whispers. His staff immediately summoned a voice coach, who taught him to make sounds through his sinus cavities.

"I might not have been in the best of voice that night, but Bush lost to both Perot and me by constantly looking at his watch, as if he were impatient to get off the stage."

A group of undecided voters had been designated to present their questions to the three candidates. Bill later claimed that he and Perot handled themselves adequately when asked, "How has the national debt personally affected you?"

Bush didn't seem to have an answer, wandering dangerously into such subjects as "teen pregnancy that he'd learned about in an African American Church." With touches of visible irritation, Bush finally stumbled and said, "It's not fair to say you can't know what a problem is unless you have it."

A poll later showed that 53 percent of the voters conceded victory to Bill.

The third and final debate took place on the campus of Michigan State University at East Lansing. It drew a spectacular televised audience of 90 million viewers.

Continuing his role as an attack dog, Bush accused Bill of acting "unpresidential," of being a "Jimmy Carter clone" and a "tax-and-spend liberal." He also accused Bill of being a waffler.

Bill shot back, scoring one of the major victories of the evening. "Talk about waffling! I can't believe you! You called trickle-down economics voodoo economics, and now you're its biggest practitioner!"

Both Bush and Perot went on to attack the "poor state" of Arkansas, Perot suggesting that if Bill were elected, "We'd all be plucking chickens for a living."

Bill shot back that in the past year, Arkansas was first in the nation in job growth.

Ultimately, whereas three of the post-debate polls designated Bill as the winner, *CNN/USA Today's* poll attributed victory to Perot.

Immediately, Bill hit the campaign trail again, now in the grueling, frenzied weeks that remained. His itinerary would include a 4,000-mile swing through eight states.

Although Bush might have lost the debate to Bill, but in one very personalized context, the sitting president won. One campaign worker *[the director of media relations for Bill's campaign in a Southern state, who didn't want his name used]* had the dubious privilege of standing beside both Bill and Bush—at different times, of course—as they urinated.

"Based on a ruler test, if dick size matters, Bush beat our candidate, 'Slick Willie,' a better name for whom might have been 'Wee Willie,' based on what I saw. As an ardent Democrat, I want to believe that we have bigger and better dicks than Republicans, but that wasn't the case in this particular presidential sweepstakes. Lyndon Johnson, an ardent Democrat, had perhaps the biggest dick of any candidate in the history of the Republic. He called it 'Jumbo.'"

Even though Bill's womanizing had the potential to possibly doom his candidacy, some aides later reported, perhaps with a sense of horror, his activities aboard his campaign's chartered Boeing 727, *Longhorn One.*

During the selection of the aircraft's (mostly blonde) flight attendants, someone had managed to include the most attractive of the applicants, and Bill was accused of "groping and fondling" some of them. "Bill turned *Longhorn* into a flying harem straight out of *The Arabian Nights,"* claimed a campaign aide.

***

In the weeks leading up to the election, as Hillary's critics increased their volume, so did the intensity of their attacks. Ironically, despite their venom, she began to attract millions of admirers. *The San Francisco Chronicle* defined her as a cross between Wonder Woman and Cinderella. Even *The Washington Post* noted that "a Hillary cult" was healthy, alive, and growing. There was talk that after Bill Clinton served for eight years, she should run for president herself.

During the last two weeks of October, Stephanopoulos revealed how he and his campaign chief, Carville, responded to the mounting pressures. "I gave up sleeping, and Carville never changed his underwear."

At one point, Bill barged into the room they were in, ranting, "That Bush, that god damn, mother-fucking son of a bitch!"

"What now?" Carville asked.

"He keeps portraying Arkansas as a fucking wasteland circled over by buzzards. Keep those TV ads running where the jerk says, 'Read my lips. No new taxes.' Remind voters how he betrayed them and raised taxes."

"Will do, general," Stephanopoulos promised.

***

On election day in November of 1992, after they voted, Bill and Hillary returned to the Governor's Mansion in Little Rock, where Chelsea joined them as they watched John Wayne's *The Searchers* (1956). After about thirty minutes, both of her totally exhausted parents fell asleep, and their daughter retreated upstairs.

At the War Room, Carville told Stephanopoulos, "We're going to win unless the Republicans come up with a last-minute scandal—say, something like Bill getting caught in bed with a nine-year-old boy or a dead girl."

That same day, in the late afternoon, Bill went jogging, stopping at McDonald's for a glass of water, not a juicy hamburger with fries.

He was back at the mansion by 6:30PM, when the returns started to come in from the Northeast. By 10:47PM, all three of the nation's major news networks had projected him as the winner.

Before dawn, after the final voting results had come in from the West Coast, the tallies were announced: He had won, with 43 percent of the popular vote. President Bush had garnered 37 percent; and Perot trailed in third place, with 19 percent of the popular vote. One percentage point was attributed to error.

In the Electoral College, Bill had won 372 to 168, carrying 32 states. *[States whose electoral votes had not gone to Clinton, but which, in contrast, had thrown them to Bush, included Florida, Arizona, Virginia, and North Carolina.]*

The Governor of Arkansas and his First Lady were now President-Elect and First Lady of the United States.

A new day had dawned in American politics: Voters had elected the nation's first Baby Boomer as the third youngest U.S. president in the history of the Republic. "They did that even though I carried more baggage than a god damn ocean liner," Bill said.

Addressing a rally at the Old State House in Little Rock, Bill spoke before TV cameras, calling for a "re-United States."

That night at the Governor's Mansion, his old friend from his days as a teenager, Carolyn Yeldell Staley, played the piano as the crowd sang "Amazing Grace." Suffering from allergies, his voice hoarse, Bill drowned out the others, as he was heard singing, "How sweet the sound, that saved a wretch like me. I once was lost, but now am found, was blind, but now I see."

That was the night Hillary announced to him that based on the new realities of her life, she was about to resign from the Rose Law Firm. "The question is, Mr. President, exactly what role am I going to play in the new Clinton Administration? My enemies don't call me Evita Perón for nothing!"

Long after midnight, after he had bid his many well-wishers goodbye, Bill dragged his weary body up the steps of the Governor's Mansion and to bed.

He would later recall his mood: "Instead of being elated, I was overcome with an ominous feeling. To borrow a phrase from Sir Winston Churchill, I felt 'The Gathering Storm.'"

Chapter Thirteen

Gays in the Military

Bill Is Accused of Contributing to the Collapse of Western Civilization

"Hillbillies from the Ozarks
Have Turned the White House Into a Rowdy Frat House."
—A White House Aide

Bill's Longtime Mistress Reveals That Although He's an Expert in the Oral Arts, He Has a Small Penis

Chief Justice William H. Rehnquist *(far right)* administers the presidential oath as Bill Clinton is sworn in as the 42nd President of the United States. Hillary, the new First Lady, looks on, barely managing to conceal her loathing of the head of the Supreme Court.

She chose a huge cadet-blue hat that stirred up controversy. A fashion critic later wrote, "A blue, unidentified object landed on the head of the First Lady."

As Carl Bernstein wrote: "Every opportunity was exploited to contrast the egalitarian values and youth of the Clintons with the privileged era of Reagan and Bush. The Clintons wanted to proclaim a transparency in government that would extinguish all vestiges of Nixonian secrecy and paranoia in the White House."

In November of 1992, after they'd won the presidential election, Bill and Hillary, beginning at the Little Rock Governor's Mansion, plunged into the busiest eleven weeks of their life. That period became known as "The Transition."

A staff had to be assembled and forged together at the White House; Cabinet members had to be appointed; meetings had to be set up; policies articulated, and thousands upon thousands of requests had to be answered. In addition, endless phone calls came in from around the world, including from such heads of state as Israeli Prime Minister Yitzhak Rabin and Egyptian President Hosni Mubarak.

Highs before the lows.
Bill as Man of the Year.

Breaking away from his duties in Little Rock, Bill flew to Washington for a meeting with lame duck president, George H.W. Bush. He found him courteous and "willing to share secrets that only a president should know."

"I thought he might be ready to spill the beans," Bill later told Vince Foster after his return to Little Rock. "I expected him to tell me that aliens from another planet had once landed on Earth and that the government had concealed it from the public. But nothing as dramatic as that."

Clintons Three on Inauguration Day

After his inauguration, Bill kissed Chelsea with more enthusiasm that he'd bestowed on Hillary. He was devoted to his daughter and always carried pictures of her to show to people on the road. Sometimes, when he talked about her, he became misty-eyed. Often when they were together, they held hands.

Bill also met with Robert Dole, the Republican leader of the Senate minority, a veteran who had been seriously injured in World War II by Nazi machine gun fire.

He huddled with this very dour

"If Hillary and I Don't Suceed at Reforming Health-Care, I'll Be Sorry I Ran for President."

—Bill Clinton

politician, a corn-fed boy who had grown up on the plains of Kansas and worked as a soda jerk.

"I was left with two impressions of him—one that he was going to oppose everything I proposed, and the other that he wanted my job and no doubt would run against me for president in '96."

Around Christmas of 1992, Bill was fed reports about Bush's final days at the White House. He was shocked and then angered when Bush pardoned several of his key aides, many of whom faced indictments based on their involvements in the Iran-Contra scandal. Bill told his staff, "Georgie boy is trying to save his own skin before his role in the scandal is exposed."

When Bill was in Los Angeles, he drove up to pay his final respects on former President Ronald Reagan. "He told me wonderful stories about his early days in Hollywood, and seemed to have perfect recall. But when I asked him about events in the White House, his mind would drift off, and he looked like he didn't know what I was talking about. He didn't remember Donald Regan, his former Treasury Secretary. After I left, I realized that he was coming down with Alzheimer's disease. He did present me with a glass jar of rainbow-hued jellybeans to eat on the plane back to Little Rock."

Gennifer Flowers did not like the Art Harris article about her in *Penthouse*.

He asked, "Are these real memories rushing back from a mistress scorned, sad, and bitter over what might have been? Or worse—the crocodile tears of, as many in the press have put it, 'a failed lounge singer' hell bent on hyping fantasy—self-promotion at all costs?"

"Or, as two former roommates suggest, has she pumped up a 'fling' to the level of a meaningful relationship, pouting publicly as she tattles all the way to the bank?"

Near the end of 1992, editors of *Time* magazine named Bill their "Man of the Year." The magazine suggested that he "might lead Americans to dig out of their deepest problems by reimagining themselves."

Shortly thereafter, the December "end of the year" edition of Bob Guccione's *Penthouse* skin magazine appeared for sale across the nation. To Bill and Hillary's horror, his former mistress, Gennifer Flowers, was featured on the front cover. Inside, she showed it all to the public. And in a feature story, she revealed the most intimate details ever associated, in the history of the Republic, with a Chief Executive's sexual proclivities and performances.

Bill's Mistress Dares Hillary to "Bare Her Butt, If She Can Find a Page Layout Big Enough"

It all began one morning when Gennifer Flower's agent, Blake Hendrix, called to inform her that Hugh Hefner of *Playboy* magazine might be willing to offer her a million dollars for a nude layout and a "tell-all" feature story—a blatant invasion of the most intimate bedtime details of the President-Elect.

Within days, Hefner's competitor, Bob Guccione of *Penthouse,* entered the bidding competition, with the almost too-good-to-be-true suggestion that if she posed for *Penthouse,* he might cut her in on the proceeds of the actual sales of the magazine. The tantalizing potentiality that she might make ten million dollars was dangled before her. She was broke at the time.

She realized that her endorsement of this *exposé* might "leave me fixed for life. I would never have to worry about getting a singing gig—or any other job." Of course, she found Guccione's offer more seductive than Hefner's. Consequently, her agent contacted Hefner, learning that he would not be willing to match the lucrative offer from his rival at *Penthouse.*

Art Harris, with "his shaved head and steely, penetrating eyes," showed up at Gennifer's apartment. In time, she began to distrust him after she discovered he was probing into her past life too deeply. As a writer for *Penthouse,* he had already been talking to, or planned to interview members of her family, a former roommate, and people who either knew her or had interacted with her. Although she feared a "hatchet job," she was reassured by Guccione's commitment to her final approval of the feature story before publication.

Lifestyle guru and *Penthouse* magazine's publisher, Bob Guccione:

PENTHOUSE: What makes a woman good in bed?
GUCCIONE: A man who is good in bed.

For Harris, Gennifer made "hot copy," revealing secrets that no president had ever aired before in public. Although asserting that he had a small penis, she nonetheless rated him nine on a scale of ten as a lover, mainly because of his skill at cunnilingus. She alleged that he would perform oral sex on her for fifteen minutes or more until she'd say, "Whoa, boy, come on up here."

She also revealed that once, when she was performing fellatio on him, "Bill came in my mouth, the first time that ever happened. He later apologized, claiming, 'Sorry, I thought you wanted me to.'"

She lamented that she had experienced very few orgasms with him. "There were times when he made me get those chills, but I've never had my head blown off. He was a predictable lover who favored the old-fashioned missionary position. No golden showers, no anal sex. I've had better lovers, but he was one of the best overall because of his combination of sweetness. All those caring features put him right up there."

In discussing the anatomy of the president-elect, she revealed that "even though his penis is on the small side, I never put him down for that. No matter what women say, size does matter. But with Bill, I knew that he'd be aggressive with oral sex."

For her nude photo layout, she flew to Los Angeles to be photographed by Earl Miller. Later, she revealed that he was a true professional and did not come on to her at all.

One of Gennifer's overriding concerns was that her mother would—within her *Penthouse* layout—see "The Precious," their nickname for her vagina. She had made a vow to her mother that she would not display "The Precious," but, according to her contract, it was clearly understood that she would have to expose far more than her breasts.

While posing for Miller, Gennifer told him, "I dare Hillary to bare her butt for any magazine. They don't have a page that broad."

Although Miller's photos made Gennifer—at the age of 42—appear at her most alluring, Guccione wanted her to fly to New York so that he, too, could snap pictures of her. With a swimming pool in the basement, and with Picassos and Renoirs hanging on the walls, she found his brownstone rather spooky, especially the all-black bedroom she'd been assigned upstairs.

When she met the publisher, she found him accessorized with the haircut and clothing of the 1970s, complete with lots of gold chains around his neck. At one point, he suggested that he use his mouth on her nipples to harden them, but she rejected his offer, telling him she could get the same effect just by pinching them, as she'd done for Miller in Los Angeles.

Weeks later, when a copy of *Penthouse* was delivered to her, she reacted in horror at the feature story. Guccione had reneged on the clause in her contract granting her final approval of the photos and text. After reading the article, she discovered that she had been portrayed, in the magazine's words, as a "gold-digging, no-talent, bleached blonde bimbo." She had also violated her promise to her mother. "There it was, 'The Precious,' on ample display."

As suggested by a writer for *The Village Voice* in Manhattan, "All of us got to see what drove the talented tongue of our president into ecstasy."

When Flowers began hustling the taped conversations she had secretly recorded of Bill, she wrote: "My motive for releasing the tapes was not to get rich from the proceeds of the sales, but to put the truth out to the American people and to let them hear Bill in his own words prove that he was willing to manipulate and lie."

In her memoir, she concluded: "I really loved Bill, and I believed he loved me, too. I thought what we had was a real relationship between two passionate, caring people, But I learned otherwise. In the end, he turned out to be nothing more than Cardboard Bill—a flat, two-dimensional piece of hardened paper, empty of all feelings."

***

Back in Little Rock, Hillary, Bill, and Chelsea packed up their possessions and prepared to have them shipped to Washington prior to their occupancy of the White House "as soon as George and Barbara vacated it." Since he could no longer fulfill his duties as governor, he violated his commitment to the voters of Arkansas, to whom he had promised that he would serve for the duration of his fifth term. Instead, Arkansas' duly elected lieutenant governor, Jim Guy Tucker, who had long lusted for the job, took over.

Bill left the office in December. "I fell twenty-four days short of breaking Orval Faubus' record as my state's longest-serving governor."

He later revealed some of the thoughts that raced through his mind during his plane ride to D.C. He was well aware that he represented a generational shift in American politics. No longer were veterans of World War II running the show, men such as Dwight D. Eisenhower, George H.W. Bush, even Ronald Reagan who had worked in the War Propaganda Office. Bill Clinton, a Baby Boomer, had assumed the most powerful position in the world.

"As Boomers, we were alternatively derided as spoiled and self-absorbed, but also lauded as idealistic and committed to the common good," Bill said. "Our politics were forged by Vietnam, civil rights, and the tumult of 1968, with its riots and assassinations of Robert F. Kennedy and Martin Luther King, Jr."

He was fully aware that Hillary would represent the "full force of the emerging women's movement." She planned to take an active role in government, and he knew that that decision would make her more controversial than she'd ever been in Arkansas. To his relief, however, a recent poll showed that her approval rating among the American people had gone from a "dismal depth" to a rating of 64 percent.

As Bill himself, her chief advocate, proclaimed, "Hillary would be the most professionally accomplished First Lady in the history of the United States."

Bill Forces an "Early Spring" on Washington

After His Inauguration, With Hillary, He Dances the Night Away

The morning of January 21, 1993 dawned over Blair House, where the Clintons had been lodged before their move later that day into the White House.

Bill awoke irritable, since he'd stayed up until 4AM laboring over his inauguration address, knowing that it would be perhaps the most important speech of his life.

As he dressed and had a skimpy breakfast, mostly black coffee, he found Hillary also irritable. They were both "raging with tension."

She paid more attention to her outfit that day, including her blue hat, than she had on any other day of her life, knowing that "it would be one for the history books."

Bill was the first member of his family out on the street in front of Blair House, where Secret Service men were already waiting for him with an official from the U.S. Parks Service. He glanced nervously at his watch, noticing that they were running thirty minutes late. A serviceman informed him that George H.W. Bush, as one of his final duties before his exit from public life, had been standing out on the North Portico of the White House waiting for the Clintons.

The Parks Service employee heard Bill say, "Where is that god damn bitch?" Would someone go in and tell her to haul her fat ass out here—and bring Chelsea, too!"

Within minutes, Hillary and Chelsea emerged. That same employee then heard Hillary call her husband, "a stupid motherfucker."

A new administration was dawning in Washington. It wasn't beginning on a happy note.

***

At the White House, Barbara Bush invited the Clintons in for coffee. As it was being served, the outgoing president made small talk with the incoming president. Also present were Al and Tipper Gore, chatting with the outgoing vice president, Danforth Quayle, and his wife, Marilyn. To Hillary, Marilyn seemed "downright hostile. "The bitch just glared at us. It was all too obvious that we'd destroyed her dream. She had wanted her retarded husband re-elected as vice president so that he might run successfully for president in 1996. Dreams die hard."

Pre-Inauguration headlines like this didn't make the Transition any easier.

At 10:45AM, the various parties departed for the West Front of the Capitol Building, with the two presidents sharing a limousine, followed with yet another limousine occupied by the outgoing and incoming First Ladies. Queried about what she and Barbara, two veteran adversaries, talked about, Hillary said, "I just don't remember. Nothing but chit-chat. I'll tell you one thing, we didn't exchange recipes for chocolate chip cookies."

Before Chief Justice William Rehnquist, Bill was sworn in as the forty-second President of the United States at the age of forty-six, making him one of the youngest in the history of the Republic. Ulysses S. Grant and Clinton were the same age when they took office; JFK had been forty-three. The youngest of them all had been Theodore Roosevelt at forty-two.

After the swearing in, Bill gave Hillary a brief kiss on the ear, then bestowed a bear hug on Chelsea. He then delivered his speech, an excerpt of which stated: "We force the spring. A spring reborn in the world's oldest democracy, that brings forth the vision and courage to reinvent America."

His speech was followed by words from the poet, Maya Angelou, a once traumatized mute girl born into a poverty-stricken black community in Stamps, Arkansas. She delivered a poem she'd written just for the occasion, "On the Pulse of Morning."

George Stephanopoulos later recalled the inaugural gala that followed as an event, "with a backstage scene straight out of a Robert Altman movie, with Elizabeth Taylor wrapped in an elaborate boa, Aretha Franklin leading her courtiers like a Nubian queen, and even Michael Jackson, wearing white gloves, dark glasses, military dress, and a pet monkey on his shoulder."

"The Gloved One" later led the room in a singing rendition of "We Are the World."

Bill was on his best behavior, except for one moment when a gossipy Secret Serviceman spotted him in the cloak room "with his presidential tongue down Ms. Taylor's throat."

That was followed by a round of nearly a dozen inaugural balls. Bill wanted to attend all of them. Hillary appeared at her most stunning, in a violet-blue lace gown. At each ball, Bill whirled her around the floor to the same theme song, Fleetwood Mac's "Don't Stop Thinkin' About Tomorrow."

Their favorite of the balls was the one staged by Arkansas, which drew family and friends. The Clintons entered to the collective sound of Razorback hog calls, "Sooooooo-ey!"

The final cost for the inaugural festivities came to $25 million, a tab fit for an oil-rich sheik.

Danced out, the Clintons returned to the White House at around 2AM that morning. Hillary was exhausted and went to bed, but Bill was too keyed up to sleep. Wandering about, he inspected his new living quarters.

With far too little sleep, he arose early the next morning and, after breakfast with them, bid his overnight guests goodbye.

The Bushes had long ago departed. Moving vans were already *en route* to Texas with their possessions.

Bill's first "non-official" duty involved accompanying his cancer-stricken mother, Virginia Kelley, to the Rose Garden. He pointed out the exact spot where he had shaken the hand of President John F. Kennedy when Bill was still a teenaged boy.

After that, Bill's first full day in office, January 21, 1993, included standing beside Hillary welcoming hundreds of visitors to the White House who were there to greet them and traipse through the Diplomatic Reception Room.

"The Eagle," in His Underwear, at the White House
Socks Throws Up; Chelsea Hates the Food;
"Evergreen" Warns the Secret Service to Back Off;
"Rasputin" Lurks Menacingly in the Shadows

The Secret Service assigned the Clintons code names—"Eagle" for Bill, "Evergreen" for Hillary, and "Energy" for Chelsea. Its members, as well as the White House staff, many of them faithful, long-time retainers, had to get used to what one of them called "this invading band of wild hillbillies from the backwoods of the Ozarks."

"The Clintons and all their cronies had no manners, no breeding, no class," an aide later revealed. "They were *gauche.*"

The executive mansion's former tenants, the Bushes, had led an orderly life, with breakfast served faithfully at 5:30AM. When the butler assumed that the Clintons would keep the same early hours, he entered their bedroom and woke them up. A sleepy, irritated Bill threw a shoe at him. "Get the hell out of here, you fool," Bill bellowed.

Within a week or two, the butler learned that the Clintons kept no set hours. Sometimes, Bill stayed up until two or three in the morning playing cards with his Arkansas bubbas.

An aide claimed, "The Clintons slopped all over the place, leaving take-out boxes, most often discarded pizzas, along with bags of popcorn thrown on the carpets. Some of these guys from Arkansas dressed like teenage rebels. They had no discipline, treating the private quarters of the president like some frat dormitory. On some occasions at night the president wandered around in his underwear."

Another aide claimed that the favorite word used by the Clintons was "fuck."

"It was fuck that, fuck this," he said. "Both Hillary and the president had violent tempers. On any given day, you could count on the president erupting in anger. His outbursts were as predictable as Old Faithful and twice as gaseous. He also farted a lot."

Political strategist Dick Morris, who had been labeled as "the Rasputin of the White House," later wrote about Bill's anger. "His face would become raw and red like a bloody steak. He railed at the press for reporting on his womanizing. 'How's Chelsea going to feel reading about all this bullshit?' he once asked me. It was frightening to watch his rage. He'd go on and on, pounding his fist and cursing."

Socks, the family's cat, did not like the new surroundings. The animal showed a disdain for the place by vomiting on the carpet in the West Hall before walking away in his red-jeweled collar "to take a piss," claimed an aide.

Chelsea also had a problem adjusting to the White House, especially to the cuisine the chef served. When Hillary heard this, she agreed to meet her after school and take her to a supermarket, where she could purchase the food she liked.

Once there, Hillary checked her wallet, discovering that she had only eleven dollars. She asked the manager if the store accepted credit cards. He responded that he wouldn't be accepting them until March and it was still only February.

She then asked if she could shop for groceries and if he could send the bill to 1600 Pennsylvania Avenue. He told her that it was against the store's policy to extend credit, even to the First Lady or the president. Both Hillary and her daughter left the store empty-handed. That night, Chelsea ordered take-out pizza, instructing that it be delivered to the White House.

The pitched battles between Hillary and Bill that had once resounded through the Governor's Mansion in Arkansas now also filled the corridors of the White House.

One morning was more violent than the others. An aide had informed Hillary that her husband had gone into the White House swimming pool sometime after midnight and that he'd been swimming in the nude with one of the more attractive young women from the White House staff.

Before breakfast, Hillary and Bill got into an argument that was heard by many members of the staff. At one point, she threw a lamp at him. A domestic worker leaked the story to *The Chicago Tribune,* which published it on February 19, 1993.

When Hillary was shown the story, she mocked the news account. "What does it matter? Another reporter claimed I threw the Bible at him. I'm sure there are other reports from the fucking press. I bet someone will claim I threw a Mercedes-Benz at him. The always reliable press!"

Hillary and Bill weren't always fighting, however. The White House counsel, Bernie Nussbaum, remembered walking in on them unexpectedly and "finding them in a clinch, really passionate with each other."

Both Bill and Hillary seemed to resent the Secret Service. The president felt that these men assigned to protect them invaded his privacy, especially when he wanted to slip around to seduce some willing subject.

Before moving into the White House, Hillary had visited Jacqueline Kennedy Onassis at her elegant Fifth Avenue residence in Manhattan. Both the former First Lady and the new First Lady discussed the problem of "living in that prison called the White House!"

Hillary was especially interested in what Jacqueline had to say about the difficulties of trying to bring up a child in the White House, where she had to be constantly alert, even to such horrors as kidnapping threats.

Hillary detested being trailed all the time by the Secret Service, especially when she wanted to escape for some privacy with her longtime lover, Vince Foster, whom she'd persuaded to come to Washington to work for them in the White House.

She seemed to feel that the Secret Service was "overbearing." On one occasion, she was heard yelling at two of the men, "Stay the fuck away from me! I don't want you coming within ten yards of me!"

At times, planning to escape from the confines of the White House, she concealed her hair with a baseball cap and wore large dark sunglasses. With the Secret Service trailing her, she rode her bicycle along a towpath beside the Potomac, her safekeepers maintaining a discreet distance behind her on White House bicycles.

At one point, two Japanese tourists flagged her down. "Oh, hell," she muttered. "I'm recognized."

That was not the case. The tourists wanted her to snap their picture. One of the most famous women on earth did just that, and they were none the wiser.

Almost daily, after going through the morning papers, Hillary was heard denouncing the latest press reports. "What have the assholes written about us now?" she asked Dee Dee Myers, Bill's Press Secretary.

Some of the First Lady's salty language seemed to eventually creep its way into Myers' workaday vocabulary. At one point during a press conference, she turned to confront some reporters, telling them to "eat shit and die!"

The Curious Tale of Bill's Medical Records

Did His Doctors Conceal a Long-ago STD from Public View?

For three decades, Dr. Burton Lee, a distinguished cancer specialist, had worked at Manhattan's Memorial Sloan-Kettering Hospital. When President George H.W. Bush moved into the White House, he requested that Dr. Lee become his chief physician, which put him in charge of the White House Medical Unit. It had been highly trained to supply emergency treatment to a president in the event of an assassination attempt.

Until Bill named his own choice as White House doctor, Dr. Lee had agreed to remain on duty during the transitional period.

On the morning of January 22, 1993, Lee was summoned to the office of Nancy Hernreich, the Deputy Appointments Secretary. There, he was handed a vial which had arrived from Little Rock. She instructed him to shoot its contents into the arm of the president, claiming that it was for his allergies, symptoms of which had become prominent during his governorship of Arkansas.

A discreet, cautionary physician, Dr. Lee told her that before he could or would do that, he wanted to examine Bill's medical records. "I didn't want to end my career by giving the president a shot and have him drop dead, particularly when I had been Bush's doctor," Dr. Lee said later during an interview. He placed a call to Dr. Susan Santa Cruz at her office in Little Rock, and requested the president's medical records.

In response, Dr. Santa Cruz informed him, "I can't turn them over to you unless I put through a call to Mrs. Clinton."

"I'll wait," Dr. Lee responded.

An hour later, he received notification that he'd been dismissed and was ordered to vacate the White House within two hours. "I had no doubt that the person who ordered me out was none other than Mrs. Clinton herself," Dr. Lee said.

Subsequently Hernreich summoned Dr. E. Connie Mariano, a retired naval admiral. As an internist, she administered the shot to Bill that Dr. Lee had resisted.

Dr. Mariano remained as the White House physician throughout the remainder of Bill's two terms as president. In fact, she was the doctor who drew the blood for the DNA test that later linked the president to Monica Lewinsky.

"We had a lot of controversy during my White House days," she said. "I was really the family doctor for the Clintons. To this day, I still keep in touch with them. We have remained friends."

***

It was usual for presidential candidates to turn over their medical records, along with their financial statements. But Bill resisted doing that when the question came up, as it did in 1992 and again in 1996 during his campaign for re-election.

By then, reporters were fully aware of his trail of womanizing, even during the peak of the AIDS era. Some newsmen speculated that he wanted to cover up his medical history because he might be HIV-positive.

Lawrence K. Altman, a reporter for *The New York Times,* asked Bill an embarrassing question: "Have you ever had a sexually transmitted disease?"

A smart lawyer, Bill knew how to escape a direct question by giving a "correct" but misleading response, thereby avoiding unpleasant repercussions.

"My press secretary, Michael D. McCurry, has already said that I never had a sexually transmitted disease," Bill said.

His new press secretary had, indeed, uttered that comment, repeating what he'd been told by Bill himself. That, however, did not make it truthful. But in answering the question the way he did, Bill was "correct" in that his press secretary had actually uttered those words.

Throughout the rest of his administration, including throughout the course of his second term, Bill stubbornly refused to submit his medical records for scrutiny by the press.

Suspicions were aroused. A rumor spread through the White House staff that the president might have a venereal disease. Such an incident was not unknown at the White House. Among U.S. presidents, in 1940, a very young John F. Kennedy was diagnosed with gonorrhea after a visit to a whorehouse in Harlem, accompanied by his homosexual best friend, Lem Billings. JFK had been successful in concealing his medical records, which were not made public until 1995, more than thirty years after his assassination.

ASK NOT!: Like Bill, his mentor, JFK, had a complicated history of sex and drugs

However, during his first month in office, Bill had asked to review the heretofore secret medical records of JFK, his hero and role model. He read that Dr. William P. Herbst, a urologist, had cleared up JFK's gonorrhea with Sulfide drugs. However, for the rest of his life, JFK suffered from post-gonnocal urethritis. [*Also called gonorrheal urethritis, its symptoms include painful urination and discharge, although approximately 25% of men are believed to have no symptoms.*] According to various doctors, JFK sometimes complained, "It's painful for me every time I have to take a piss." His penis would also become inflamed with an irritating skin rash.

After reviewing the records, Bill told Stephanopoulis that he had learned that JFK's sustained cortisone treatments acted in a way that greatly increased his sexual appetite, a factor that contributed to his reckless behavior with women.

Bill, too, was given cortisone treatments to ease his back pain, which was not as severe as that which JFK had suffered. Bill's knee injury continued to cause him acute pain, often interfering with his walk. "Do you think that god damn cortisone turns me into a raving sex maniac?" Bill asked his aides. "JFK and I should talk, if only he were around."

Hillary & Al Gore Battle Over "The Co-Presidency"

Before "The Warrior Queen" Commits Hari-Kari With the Press

The newly elected Vice President from Tennessee, Al Gore, wanted "to be the steel in Bill's spine." Actually, he'd wanted to be president himself, but was told to wait his turn until Bill served two full terms. *[Gore's tenure as vice president demonstrated his clear sense of prophecy for oncoming disasters based on issues that included global warming and overpopulation.]*

Professor William H. Chafe wrote: "Whatever Bill Clinton had promised

Gore, he had *[already]* committed three times to Hillary. She and Gore jousted each other, albeit with an atmosphere of civility."

Their silent feud began over which offices to occupy within the White House. Normally, First Ladies *[including Barbara Bush]* had been assigned to the East Wing. Hillary interpreted the East Wing as a politically irrelevant social center where First Ladies served tea and cookies to visiting ladies' clubs from Dubuque. Of course, she said that privately, not wanting to launch another "tea-and-cookies" press war.

In noted contrast to her predecessors, she demanded space in the overcrowded West Wing. "I want to be at the seat of power where the decisions about running the Free World are made, not assigned to Siberia. I want to be close to the Oval Office, where I can pop in on Bill at any time. Who knows what I might find going on there?"

According to political adviser Vernon Jordan, "Bill was playing it safe. He didn't want to step on Gore's toes, but he also wanted to please Hillary. Yet he didn't want to leave the impression that she was the Evil Queen behind the throne."

"Hillary definitely did not see herself as the Evil Queen," claimed Harold I. Ickes, the White House Deputy Chief of Staff and the son of the Secretary of the Interior under Franklin D. Roosevelt. "She saw Bill and herself as the White Knight and the Snow Queen."

Bill told Ickes that if it were up to him, he would knock down a wall and open up the Oval Office for direct access to his wife's office. "A completely open door policy fit for a co-president," he said. "But they won't let me knock down any walls in the White House."

Throughout the duration of the many behind-the-scenes struggles between Gore and Hillary, Ickes had a front-row seat. Privately, he voiced concern that Gore had come to view Hillary with suspicion and distrust. He also suspected that Hillary's plan involved running for president after Bill had served eight years, a role that Gore envisioned for himself.

During her first weeks as an unelected official, Hillary established a reputation for authoritarian rule. She had a strong will and even stronger opinions. Her temperament was directly contrasted with Bill's, which seemed to be indecisive and wavering on issues, wanting to please differing sides.

She was depicted as the commander in charge of the garrison, ordering her soldiers to man the machine guns against the attacking "Indians." She regarded their critics as mortal enemies with "zero tolerance."

In contrast, intimates saw two different Hillarys—the other caring and sensitive to the plights of others, especially children, women, and African Americans. It took much longer for her to endorse gay rights.

From the beginning, she launched a private war with the White House

Press Corps. She began by denying them access to the West Wing and to the office of the Press Secretary. She and Bill had suffered one leak after another when the press had access to the West Wing. Bill claimed, "We had more leaks than a tarpaper shack in Arkansas, with holes in the roof and large gaps in the walls. Day after day, one leak after another. It wasn't just raining, it was pouring."

Some members of the press viewed Hillary's barring them from the West Wing as "committing Hari-Kari." Carl Bernstein wrote: "After only two weeks in the White House, Hillary assumed the command as the first First Lady who was a warrior queen."

Helen Thomas, the veteran UPI correspondent who had covered the White House since the Kennedy era, said, "From the beginning, Hillary had a chip on her shoulder. We of the Press Corps never had a chance with her. She was aloof. I don't know why we got off on the wrong foot, but we did."

Sally Quinn, gossip columnist for *The Washington Post,* wrote: "The Clintons are creating hostility among the press. Imagine yourself on an airplane that crashes in some exotic, untamed location. You find yourself surrounded by a hostile crowd. Instead of giving them beads and eating their monkey tongues, you decide you don't need their help. Fine, but don't be surprised if you wind up with poison darts shot into your ass."

Quinn was right. Attacks on Hillary appeared daily.

In response to this armada of attack dogs, Hillary spoke to a reporter from *Newsweek:* "People can overlook and ignore a whole lot of stuff that is thrown out into the atmosphere if they view it as irrelevant, tangential, or just downright stupid and nasty. If you

All decked out in their finery *(from left to right)*, Bill, Tipper Gore, Al Gore, and Hillary.

To some pundits, the picture looked like "a wife-swapping" submission on an internet dating site.

Reportedly, Gore impishly knew how to frighten Bill with a castration fear. During the Lorena and John Wayne Bobbitt saga, when an angered wife cut off her philandering husband's penis, Gore kept Bill appraised with daily briefings about the penis re-attachment surgery and whether Bobbit would be able to achieve an erection in the wake of the surgery.

Months later, when Bobbit was cast as the male lead in a porn film, Gore smuggled a copy into the White House so that Bill could see a post-operative man in action. Gore assured Bill that he didn't think Hillary, in a fit of anger, would ever inflict such an indignity onto him, but reportedly, the president—at least to some degree—remained unconvinced.

don't have a view of the world that is bigger than yourself, if the only reason that you're doing something just to fulfill your own personal ambition, then you can't sustain a campaign against that kind of concerted attack."

When she wasn't battling with the press, Hillary was said to have operated a "secret police," silencing potential information emerging from witnesses who had much to report on what was going on behind the scenes at the White House.

Dick Morris, an adviser to Bill since 1977, was seen popping up at the White House. He was called "a symbol of a mercenary politician, even a force of evil."

Later, Morris turned on the Clintons and wrote a series of books that were critical of them, in the opinion of some, even vengeful. On October 1, 1998, he wrote in *The New York Post:* "The secret police of the Clintons cover up scandal by silencing potential witnesses. Both Clintons have mounted a campaign to intimidate, frighten, threaten, discredit, and punish innocent Americans whose only misdeed is their desire to tell the truth in public."

Richard Poe, a *New York Times* bestselling author, claimed: "Long before Morris testified before Ken Starr's grand jury or penned his *New York Post* column, Congressional investigators knew of Hillary's role as White House enforcer and of the cast of shady characters who surrounded the First Lady—people whose sinister connections ranged from the criminal underworld and foreign intelligence agencies to the darkest of the CIA's black operations."

A Hostile Press Explodes with News of Nannygate, There's no Political Honeymoon for Bill & Hillary

As Attorney General, Bill Nominates a Former Playboy Bunny

George Stephanopoulos said that it was customary for the Washington Press Corps to grant an incoming president a hundred-day honeymoon, time enough to learn where the light switches are located within the White House, and perhaps get used to running the Free World. "Bill Clinton was granted a honeymoon all right—a honeymoon in hell."

Author Gail Sheehy characterized the 23 months between Clinton's inauguration (in January of 1993) till November 8, 1994 (when the Democrats lost control of Congress), as an administration "rocked by revelations, humiliations, shame, smears, and personal tragedies."

Even before assuming office, the president-elect ran into trouble over the names he put forth for attorney general.

As a result of the candidates he proposed, the Nannygate scandal became the first of many "-gate" scandals, the suffix, of course, inspired by the Watergate scandal which eventually demolished the Nixon administration.

Hillary had insisted that Bill nominate a woman for the post of attorney general. Many of her more ardent supporters had actually wanted her to take over the post herself.

As Bill's nominee, which required Senate approval, he named Zoë Baird, a forty-year-old senior vice president and general counsel at Aetna Life and Casualty Company. Baird had previously worked in the Justice Department of the Carter Administration. Baird and her husband, Paul Gewirtz, a law professor at Yale, had a three-year-old son.

After her name was put forth, *The New York Times,* on January 14, 1993, broke the news on page one that the Bairds had employed a married pair of illegal aliens from Peru, Victor and Lillian Cordero, between 1990 and 1992. The husband worked for the couple as a chauffeur, and his wife functioned as a nanny for their son. Baird had not paid Social Security taxes for the couple, but her husband eventually made a lump sum (retroactive) payment early in 1993. During her background vetting, Baird had revealed this potential problem to the White House. At the time, Hillary reportedly did not interpret it as "a big deal."

Zoë Baird, of Nannygate notoriety, on the cover of *Time*.

She seemed to blame her husband for the failure to pay income taxes on the illegal aliens she'd hired.

Big mouth Rush Limbaugh broadcast that "her blame-it-on-her-husband defense was a Femi-Nazi ploy."

After the article appeared in *The New York Times,* it became a very big deal. Generating headlines across the country and providing fodder for talking heads on TV news programs to chew on, it was revealed that the Bairds made combined annual salaries of $600,000, yet that they paid the Corderos a combined salary of only $250 a month, well below the minimum requirement. In the press, the Bairds were portrayed as "overpaid rich Yuppies" and found no sympathy.

Joe Biden, head of the Senate Judiciary Committee, compared the Baird controversy to "a freeway crash," and he recommended that her name be withdrawn. Baird was seen leaving Biden's office twice, each time in tears.

Calls for the withdrawal of her nomination

flooded the switchboards of members of Congress and the White House. Headlined as "Nannygate," the controversy generated a firestorm of chatter on conservative talk radio.

On January 22, in the middle of the night, Bill withdrew Baird's nomination. The Corderos, by then divorced, fled back to Peru.

In a cover story, *Time* magazine, whose editors had recently named Bill their "Man of the Year," did another cover piece, this time labeling the Nannygate scandal as "CLINTON'S FIRST BLUNDER." The scandal had far-reaching implication, exposing a nationwide propensity for hiring undocumented workers as household helpers, child-minders, and gardeners. Nannygate-type controversies and *exposés* would continue to plague politicians as America moved relentlessly into the 21st Century.

Hillary continued to insist that Bill name a woman to the post, and he came up with Kimba Wood, a Federal judge for the U.S. District Court for the Southern District of New York. Wood had been named to that post by President Ronald Reagan in 1988, her nomination winning unanimous approval in the U.S. Senate at the time.

As amazing as it seems, it was discovered that during her vetting process, Wood also revealed a Nannygate problem. She, too, had hired an undocumented alien, although at the time that was not illegal. Unlike Baird, she had paid the required taxes on her employee.

Although no official announcement had been made, the press went after her, too, again in an attack dog mood. Reporters rushed to dig up any "dirt," discovering that during her long-ago tenure as a student in London, she had trained for five days as a Playboy bunny.

In 1999, she had married Frank E. Richardson, the Wall Street financier. Before that, in 1995, she had been named as "the other woman" in a notorious divorce case inaugurated by Richardson's estranged socialite wife, Nancy.

Bill's second choice for Attorney General, Kimba Wood, also had a Nannygate problem. She had other scandals, too.

She was named as "the other woman" when the wife of the millionaire financier, Frank Richardson, sued for divorce. Also, to everyone's horror, it was revealed that during college, Wood had once auditioned for a job as a Playboy Bunny.

In the wake of these revelations, her name was hastily withdrawn as a candidate for Attorney General.

Janet Reno: Unlike Kimba, her opponents never exposed her as a former *Playboy* bunny.

After hearing the latest news, Stephanopoulos claimed that he went apoplectic. "Our failure to ferret out all the information earlier, and the media's insatiable appetite for bad news, and our uncanny ability to provide it, amounted to another debacle."

The fear of another Nannygate contributed to Wood's hasty withdrawal from consideration as attorney general.

Still, Hillary insisted that Bill name a woman as attorney general. Once again, he acquiesced to her request, eventually locating a qualified female candidate without any Nannygate (or equivalent) complications.

Janet Reno had become State Attorney for Dade County (Miami) in 1978. She had never married and had no children. A woman of modest means, she had worked with Attorney Hughie Rodham, Hillary's brother, and he recommended her highly. She mowed her own lawn and did her own housework, driving around in a pickup truck. All this suggested a rather macho image which led to speculation that she was a lesbian.

She was the daughter of two well-known journalists in the Miami area. Her mother, Jane, worked at *The Miami News,* and her father, an emigrant from Denmark, Henry Reno, was a police reporter for *The Miami Herald.* The Renos had sent their daughter, Janet, to Harvard Law School.

Bill said, "Janet was a very down-to-earth person, the salt of the earth, a fine and noble woman. Instead of marrying and raising a family, she has devoted her life to public service."

On March 11, 1993, Janet Reno was unanimously confirmed by the Senate, making her the first female attorney general in U.S. history.

The World's Most Publicized Haircut

Amazingly, Bill Clinton's haircut on May 23, 1993, made headlines around the world. *The New York Times* erroneously reported that two runways at the Los Angeles International Airport were shut down for nearly an hour and that some incoming flights were delayed, being forced to circle overhead while *Air Force One* delayed its departure on the tarmac, with its engines running, so that the president could get a razorcut, onboard, from the celebrated Beverly Hills hairdresser, "Christophe."

A Parisian, Christophe Jouenne, was one of Hollywood's most talented and sought-after hairdressers to the stars. He had styled Hillary's appearance before the National Democratic Convention that previous May.

The inaccurate report, it was later discovered, came from the Federal Aviation Administration. When Bill read the escalating dramas associated with his haircut, he told Stephanopoulos, "I had the Secret Service check. There were no delays at the airport. It's a lie. The way it's being reported, I shut down the whole god damn city of Los Angeles! What motherfuckers!"

A later investigation revealed that the Secret Service was correct. There had been no delays at LAX, no airplanes circling overhead. The only people who had to wait were angry reporters who spent twenty minutes complaining about the delay in the rear seats of *Air Force One*.

The bill for the razorcut was calculated at $200, although some sources reported the cost as $400.

Once again, as he had so many times before, Stephanopoulos lamented the incident. "The perception was more powerful than the reality, and the underlying truth—that Clinton had been self-indulgent and insensitive to the image of having a Hollywood hairstylist cut his hair on a busy airport runway, and that his staff had been too stupid to stop it from happening, was bad enough."

The incident was made worse when news reporters wrote follow-up stories. Who paid for the haircut? Did the government pick up the check?

Hillary later claimed that the Clintons had a "personal service contract" with Christophe, which they did not.

Stephanopoulos could hardly contain himself. "Oh, that'll help!" he later exclaimed. "Talk about a populist president who didn't want to appear elitist!

Christophe Jouenne was the most famous hair stylist in Hollywood, catering to movie stars. When Bill Clinton called him to come aboard Air Force One, waiting on the tarmac at LAX, for a razorcut, it became an example of the president's over-indulgence and, consequently, a national scandal.

The press falsely claimed that Bill virtually shut down the airport, forcing planes to circle overhead.

Ultimately, Bill's haircut came to rank up there with Nixon's plumed guards at the White House, or Nancy Reagan's new china.

Hillary as "Czarina of Health Care Reform" Seeks Universal Coverage for Americans as Republicans Vow to "Shoot Her Down"

After only a month in the White House, Bill appointed Hillary as head of a major initiative to bring about health-care reform. Affected by whatever reforms she'd manage to inaugurate would be the medical professions, an industry that represented one-seventh of the U.S. economy. Both Hillary and the newly elected president sought universal coverage for all American citizens. Even at the beginning of their involvement, they were well aware that when Harry S Truman had advocated such reform in 1948, it almost cost him his presidency.

In such a powerful role, Hillary became the first First Lady ever assigned such a major responsibility that would affect millions of Americans, notably the uninsured. She knew from the beginning that the Republicans, including the likes of Senator Bob Dole, would adamantly line up to oppose her. He sent word that he had the use of only one arm because of an injury he suffered during World War II, "but I'll use it like a three-fisted hand to strike down her ridiculous plan."

Privately, key members of Bill's own team lined up behind Hillary's back to oppose her being offered the position. Lloyd Bentsen was a tall, patrician Texan who had run for Vice President against Danforth Quayle on the Mike Dukakis ticket in 1988 that had opposed George H.W. Bush. Bill had appointed Bentsen as his new treasury secretary.

Bentsen feared that Hillary's new role would stir up more resentment in Congress than she already faced. Other aides whispered in Bill's ear that appointing his wife to such a post "was a dangerous idea." However, each of them wanted their objection to Hillary kept a secret, fearing retaliation from her.

Dick Morris feared that Hillary was surrounding herself with ultra-liberals. James Carville, another Clinton adviser, expressed somewhat the same idea. "These fucking liberals are all over the place, even hanging from the chandeliers."

Within days, Hillary had been nicknamed "The Czarina of Health Care Reform," with comparisons to Catherine the Great of Russia. Almost daily, she advanced forward with meetings on health care. She was made aware of the rapid growth of the GOP's opposition. "We'll turn the Iron Lady of the White House into a Paper Tiger," a coven of right-wingers in Congress threatened in a secret meeting.

Ira Magaziner, who had been a classmate of Bill's at Oxford, and a fellow Rhodes Scholar, was named as Hillary's chief of staff, supervising her assembled health-care task force. Tall, angular, and intense, he had been a successful business consultant and would be in charge of day-to-day operations, trying to get her health plan implemented.

Hillary received a call from Mario Cuomo, governor of New York. "Your husband must really have been pissed off at you when he put in in charge of such a thankless job."

When word eventually reached Hillary that one of Bill's own staff was ardently opposed to health-care reform, considering it impractical because of the skyrocketing budget deficit, she would often storm into the Oval Office, where she could be heard denouncing his "shithouse staff."

Her cramped quarters in the West Wing could not accommodate her burgeoning staff, so she was assigned offices for them in the ornate Executive Office Building (EOB) across from the White House. It had been constructed in 1871 as housing for the Departments of State, War, and the Navy. Now its interior was filled with as many as 500 people: secretaries, committee members, researchers, schedulers, and personal assistants, each of whom worked for her.

These active "War Rooms" were collectively nicknamed "Hillaryland." Others labeled them as "Hillary's Intensive Care Unit."

Initially, when members of Hillary's team announced parts of her health care plan, the public seemed to approve. She met constantly with members of Congress, both Democrats and Republicans, as well as with special interest groups, including doctors and leaders of the insurance industry. For a while, her popularity soared, but there were ominous sounds on the horizon as attacks on her plan mounted.

Her most vociferous opponents even hired investigators to probe her past, especially her work at the Rose Law Firm. That old bugaboo of the failed real estate development in the Ozarks, "Whitewatergate," reared its dragon-like head again. Rumors swept through Congress that she might face a Federal indictment.

Stephanopoulos observed that "Her health-care plan was both idealistic and terribly ambitious. It was logical yet inflexible, overly complex, susceptible to misinterpretation."

The intensity of the debate over health care had its lighter moments, as she remembered. Once, during a difficult, tension-filled meeting, an aide asked her if she'd like something to drink. She requested a diet Dr. Pepper.

"For the rest of my life, wherever I would go, someone was there to present me with a diet Dr. Pepper. I felt like the sorcerer's apprentice, the Mickey Mouse character in the classic animated film *Fantasia.* I couldn't turn off the Dr. Pepper machine."

It would not be until September 28 that Hillary would appear before the House Ways and Means Committee. This marked the first time a First Lady was the lead witness in a major administrative legislative initiative. Over the course of the subsequent few days, she would appear before other House committees plus two Senate committees. She showed a sharp sense and mastery of the issues and dazzled some Congressmen, even her enemies.

Later, she reflected on her appearance. "I thought of a quote from Dr. Samuel Johnson. He once said that a woman preaching was like a dog walking on its hind legs. It is not done well, but you are surprised to find it done at all."

"After I left the Hill, I was told that the Republicans were going to take a pound of flesh out of me, if not a whole lot more. Some of my worst enemies were even talking about a jail term for me in a Federal prison, where I would be locked in a small bleak cell and allowed out for one hour out of every twenty-four for a little exercise."

In the Lincoln Bedroom, "Queen Nefertiti Has a Rendezvous With a Bubba Boy from Hope

A Femme Fatale in a Peekaboo Power Suit Gets Locked into a Bear Hug With the Leader of the Free World.

Barbra Streisand is the diva of divas.

This ugly duckling from Brooklyn, hailed as the greatest singer who ever lived, became an elegant modern-day Queen Nefertiti, but with slightly crossed eyes.

The Oscar-winning actress was a political dilettante, who enjoyed power behind the throne not seen since Frank Sinatra during the early days of the Kennedy administration.

A global icon, she was an ardent Democrat and supporter of Bill Clinton. With fifty gold albums, she was also rich and sought after for fund-raisers.

Her greatest attribute was summed up in a word: *CHUTZPAH*. Director Martin Ritt put it another way: "She has the balls of a Russian infantryman." In her own evaluation, the diva said, "I'm a liberal, opinionated Jewish feminist, and I push a lot of buttons."

In 1992, she was at first rather lukewarm to Bill Clinton's candidacy, throwing her support to Mario Cuomo, the Governor of New York, whom she knew and understood. "We spoke the same language," she said. "I don't know about this jumbo hamburger-eating Bubba from some backwoods in Arkansas. Sounds like white trash to me." But when Cuomo bowed out of the presidential race, she shifted her support to Bill, beginning with a fund-raiser she hosted for him in Beverly Hills.

The gala event, attracting *tout* Hollywood, was held at the estate of Freddie Fields of Creative Management Associates. Guests included Senator Al Gore, running at the time for vice president. Some 1,200 donors showed up for the event, which was broadcast to New York City and Washington.

The comedy team of Mike Nichols and Elaine May reunited to provide entertainment, with songs by Tammy Wynette—who by now had supposedly forgiven Hillary for the previous offense she had taken—and Dionne Warwick. Dressed in black, Streisand sang such hits as "People" and "Happy Days Are Here Again," followed with "God Bless America."

At the event, Hillary was overheard saying, "Streisand is worth all the rest of the entertainers. She can raise major dough, and I hear she's worth at least $500 million herself."

James Spada in his book, *Streisand, Her Life,* wrote: "Barbara used to be controversial because of her emotional singing, her idiosyncratic acting, her bluntness, her perfectionism, her occasional rudeness, and her choice of lovers. Now, she was controversial because of her political beliefs, the controversies that surrounded her mushroomed now that she was an F.O.B.—Friend of Bill, one of the president's extended circle of intimates and advisers. *People* magazine, in contrast, called the president the first F.O.B "Friend of Barbra."

"How things change," she said in her first huddle with Bill. "Now I'm a friend of a U.S. president. Before that, I was among the Top Ten on Richard Nixon's enemies list. I felt that if Tricky Dickie stomped on democracy and proclaimed himself king, I would be among the first to go to the gallows."

Beginning the night of that fund-raiser and during the months and years ahead, through both the '92 and the '96 campaigns, Streisand became Bill's *über-Democrat* in Hollywood.

When Bill won the election, it came as no surprise when Streisand was designated as a headliner at the inauguration in January of 1993. CBS paid $8 million for broadcast rights mainly because Streisand had agreed to sing.

She made a dazzling appearance in a Donna Karan pin-striped power suit with a peekaboo slit up the leg. There, before going onstage, she mingled with such fellow guests as Michael Jackson , Elizabeth Taylor, and Bob Dylan. At the end of her performance, Bill came forward and locked Streisand in one of his Arkansas style bear hugs.

Of all the inauguration balls, the Arkansas ball was the biggest and most spectacular, and Streisand was there as a guest of honor to dance the night away.

It was at this ball that Streisand met Virginia Kelley, Bill's flamboyant, matronly, and very Southern mother. In garish makeup with too-loud colors and weird hair, and with a history of playing the horses and chasing after men, she was letting the good times roll.

As unlikely as it seemed, they formed an "odd couple friendship" that evolved into a kind of mother-daughter relationship. From that night on, Virginia and Barbra called each other at least once a week.

Before some 12,000 guests, Ben F. King handed the just-inaugurated president a saxophone so that he could entertain the crowd. In a party mood, the president performed the saxophone solo against the background of the Coasters' Golden Oldie, "Yakety Yak."

***

Hillary was notified on March 19, 1993 that Hugh Rodham, Sr., her father, had suffered a heart attack and had drifted into a coma in a hospital in Little Rock. Although she had planned to attend the annual Gridiron Dinner with Bill, she canceled and took a plane to Arkansas, where she would sit on and off at his bedside for the next sixteen days, awaiting his predictable death, which occurred on April 7.

Bill, who had remained behind in Washington, wanted to honor Streisand and thank her. There were those who were saying that she, along with other Hollywood money, had put him into the White House by raising millions for his campaign.

She had become the subject of late night jokes among the nation's talk show hosts, David Letterman joked that Streisand's ranking was so powerful that "she could take home nuclear secrets overnight, but had to return them the next morning."

As a polarizing figure, she was denounced in the press, some reporters dismissing her as "an empty-headed Hollywood wannabe." Bill himself was attacked for his "panting dog" expression every time he met a Hollywood actor.

As his "dates" for the Gridiron Dinner, Bill showed up with Streisand on one arm, his mother, Virginia, with her "Minnie Mouse eyelashes," on the other.

Streisand was even asked if she planned to run for the Senate seat from California. "Do you want to become Senator Yentl?"

She dismissed the idea, saying,

In *The Owl & the Pussycat*, released in 1970, Barbra Streisand ("La Divinissima") managed to look simultaneously trashy and divine.

"No way. Going around shaking hands and having babies pee on me?"

That night, Virginia and Streisand cemented their relationship, later described as "very close, almost maternal." The two women were a study in contrasts, Streisand elegantly groomed in *haute couture,* whereas Virginia appeared with her hot pink lipstick overly applied, her bouffant dyed black hair with a white skunk strip in the middle.

Along with Elvis Presley, Streisand had long been Virginia's favorite singer.

That night, Streisand was invited for a "sleepover" in the luxurious Lincoln Bedroom, which gave rise to rumors that persist to this day.

Many accounts state that Hillary did not learn of this invitation until she returned to Washington. Actually, that was not true. At least three top staffers in the White House were assigned the task of "telling me everything the president does, even taking a leak."

Armed with that information, she flew back to Washington from her father's sickbed in a state of rage, suspecting Bill of having seduced Streisand.

As one White House aide later said, "Hillary must have been sharpening her nails during that flight back from Little Rock." Staffers on the midnight shift at the White House reported a screaming match and slamming doors, the sound of objects being thrown.

"Here I was in a sterile hospital room grieving over my dying father, while you're here at the White House escorting Streisand into the Lincoln Bedroom," a White House staffer could hear Hillary yelling at her errant husband.

Bill emerged the next day with "claw marks" on his face. His then Press Secretary Dee Dee Myers claimed that the scars were a result of a shaving accident. Seeming not aware of that claim, Bill later that day said that the scratch marks had resulted from time spent "wrestling with Chelsea" which made the incident bizarre, considering his daughter's age. Neither of these explanations seemed to explain the injury to his face, which was a two-inch-long gash that began at his right earlobe and ran down his jawline to his "clawed" neck.

Later, Stephanopoulos was queried more intensively. Was it true that a thirteen-year-old girl would be "rolling around" on the floor with her daddy, and that she would have inflicted such a deep wound to his face?

Later, Bill tried to explain his way out of his earlier explanation. "I'm ashamed. I was like a kid again, playing with my daughter, just goofing off. I reaffirm that I'm not a kid, and nothing like that will happen again."

The word went out: Streisand was banned from sleepovers in the White House. However, she was such an important fund-raiser for the Clintons, that Hillary feared alienating her.

[Streisand didn't go over with many of Bill's future girlfriends, including Monica Lewinsky. Informer Linda Tripp taped her saying, "I hate Barbra Streisand. She's just sooooooo annoying."]

Either in Washington, New York, or Los Angeles, Streisand had chances to meet privately with Bill. Rumors of an affair spread rapidly. If those rumors were true, Bill would be added to a distinguished list of notables to have experienced the intimate charms of pop music's most durable diva.

[Streisand's name, during the course of her eventful career, was romantically linked to Prince Charles, Sydney (son of Charlie) Chaplin, hairdresser Jon Peters, Jon Voight, Ryan O'Neal, Anthony Newley, Liam Neeson, Clint Eastwood, Richard Gere, Kris Kristofferson, Robert Redford, Tommy Smathers, and inevitably, Elvis Presley. Streisand's affair with Canadian Prime Minister Pierre Trudeau catalyzed rumors of an impending marriage and what would have resulted in Streisand's consequent elevation to First Lady of Canada.]

At one point, the press was reporting that she was set to marry Miami Vice's Don Johnson, the tall, blonde, and boyishly handsome actor. Streisand claimed, "He could have charmed Hitler." Reports surfaced that before she'd agree to marry him, she was urging him to become circumsized.

Had presidential events occurred differently, Streisand might have been invited for a sleepover at the White House long before Clinton extended his invitation. In 1963, at a reception at the White House, she was introduced to John F. Kennedy, telling him, "You're a doll!"

He was polite, but didn't pick up on her flirtation.

In spite of Hillary's attack on him, Bill defiantly invited Streisand back to Washington in April when his wife once again was out of town. She presented him with a copy of her new album, *Back to Broadway.*

Later that same month, Streisand must have decided it was time to "do some suck-up" with the alienated Hillary.

In New York, accompanied by her old flame, Pierre Trudeau, she attended a glittering dinner at the New York Public Library honoring Hillary. Before the elegant audience, Streisand said, "There is no one in the country who would deny the competence of Hillary Clinton. Her intellect, her stamina, her warmth, and her courage. The criticism of her has again demonstrated that the strong, competent woman is still a threatening figure in our culture."

If there were any bad blood between Hillary and Streisand, the singer tried to make up for it by contributing to Hillary's Senate campaign.

Later, taking time out from one of her concert tours, Streisand attended a dinner at the White House honoring Japanese Emperor Akihito and his wife, Empress Michiko. This time, she was escorted by ABC news anchor Peter Jennings, the dazzling couple almost stealing the show from the emperor and empress, in the opinion of some commentators.

Months later, Bill flew to California. There, the Commander-in-Chief invited Streisand to visit him at his hotel suite. David Gergen, White House adviser, later said, "Hollywood was a world Bill enjoyed very much. All the glitz and glamor." However, he refused to speculate on a possible Clinton/Streisand affair.

But one Secret Service agent later made the claim that he walked in on Bill as he was "chasing Barbra around a piano."

In May of 1993, Streisand received an invitation to attend the annual White House correspondent's dinner. Her former beau, Richard Baskin, the film composer and producer, was her escort that night. She looked dazzling in an off-the-shoulder white satin gown and diamonds.

Back in 1983, she'd begun her romance with Baskin by telling him, "I just love your coffee ice cream." He would soon become her lover, her confidant, and sometimes collaborator.

Barbra was a great success at the dinner. According to *The New York Times,* "On a clear day in Washington, you could see Barbra Streisand forever." At the time, Bill was said to be thinking about naming her as his administration's new Ambassador to Israel.

The year swept by quickly and in December of 1993, Virginia, in ill health and suffering from cancer, arrived at the White House. She was growing weaker and required regular transfusions.

In her autobiography, *Living History,* Hillary said, "The indomitable Mrs. Kelley was determined to live every last minute of her life to the hilt, and Bill and I wanted her to spend as much time as possible with us. But she insisted on attending Streisand's New Year's Eve concert in Las Vegas."

The singer had invited her to sit in a front-row seat at her long-awaited return to the concert stage. Of course, Virginia, inveterate gambler, as she was, planned to make a swing through the casinos as well.

After bidding farewell to Streisand, Virginia flew back to Little Rock and was driven to Hope, where she died in her sleep on January 6, 1994. Streisand attended the funeral, greeting both Bill and Hillary in the town where Bill had grown up. At the funeral, Streisand heard a rendition of "On Holy Ground," a hymn that would later inspire her album, *Higher Ground,* released in 1997. After Virginia died, Streisand endowed a breast cancer research program in her name at the University of Arkansas' Medical School.

In May of 1994, Streisand launched her USAir American Tour in the USAir Arena in Washington. Bill and Hillary, along with power brokers from both parties, attended the event. The show included a medley of songs from Streisand's 1983 film, *Yentl.*

During her concert, she rendered the joyful and triumphant "Happy Days Are Here Again." The footage of her performing that song, coupled with the inspiration conveyed by its lyrics, became part of the archival legacy of a bold new administration, whose implications were at the time being widely publicized throughout Washington and the world.

Shortly before Bill left the White House on December 20, 2000, he bestowed on Streisand the National Medal of Arts. After his departure, she would be banished from the White House throughout the subsequent eight-year (January 2001-January 2009) administration of George W. Bush.

Daniel Halper, the online editor of *The Weekly Standard,* in his book *Clinton, Inc.,* met with a close friend of Bill's who did not want to be named. He told Halper, "Everybody you think he fucked, he did—and the more dangerous, the better." The aide went on to mention celebrities who included Streisand and Sharon Stone. "All genius is flawed," the former Clinton aide said. "The great artists are addicted, if not to alcohol, they're drug addicts, or whatever. Bill's addiction is pussy."

Facing Hysterical Opposition to Gays in the Military, Bill Clinton is Forced to "Cave In" —Hence, the Notorious "Don't Ask, Don't Tell"

During his 1992 run for the White House, Bill had appealed to gay and lesbian voters, promising them that, if elected, he would allow them to serve openly and proudly in the military.

But from the first week he took office, he realized he would face stiff opposition, especially from old political relics of yesterday, like Senator Robert Dole, who wanted to use the issue of gays in the military as a weapon to destroy Bill's chance for re-election in 1996 when Dole himself wanted to run.

Bill set up a meeting with Colin Powell, the chairman of the Joint Chiefs of Staff, hoping to encounter a more enlightened view. He was seriously disappointed.

Born in Harlem in 1937, Powell was the son of immigrants from Jamaica, a Caribbean island not known for its tolerance of homosexuals. He had worked closely with Reagan, a president widely despised at the time by gays, who referred to him as a homophobe.

Bill didn't know if Powell were as homophobic as he appeared to be when it came to gays serving openly in the military. Many commentators suspected that Powell was taking a hard line against gays as a means of appealing to the far right of the Republican base, with perhaps the intention of seeking the presidency himself in 1996, in a campaign that would pit him directly against Bill.

"Clinton was apoplectic on the subject of Powell," claimed Dick Morris.

"He was terrified of him. He felt the press was giving him a free ride, promoting him as a future candidate for president. An initial poll we took showed that Powell could defeat Clinton."

In a tense meeting with Bill, Powell candidly admitted that he had allowed hundreds of gays to serve America during the recent Gulf War, because dozens of them were skilled in translating Arabic, an understanding of which was vital to deciphering messages from the enemy. However, once the gays had served the military's needs, they were booted from the Army with dishonorable discharges, despite having served their country honorably and well.

A Bigoted Four-Star General Discredited

Colin Powell's reputation as the quintessentially objective military man remained intact until he soiled himself during Congressional DADT testimonies

"That seemed like a callow, even cruel way to treat loyal American soldiers," Bill lamented.

In his confrontational meeting with Powell, the president reminded him that the United States military had spent $500 million on the logistics of discharging well-trained homosexuals, many of them well qualified because of their higher educations and knowledge of foreign tongues.

"Such a waste of manpower, such a waste of millions," Bill pointed out to Powell. The four-star general remained unconvinced, informing Bill that he would testify against gays in the military when called before Congress.

When the results of the meeting were reported to Stephanopoulos, he summed up the White House's position. "Impassioned testimony from the highest-ranking black man in America denying the parallels between skin color and sexual orientation would trump our strongest civil rights argument for ending the ban, and legislation overturning an executive order would fly through both houses of Congress by veto-proof margins. Gays serving in the military would be denied new protection, and the president would have another embarrassing defeat during his first week on the job."

American homosexuals would eventually feel that they had been "sold down the river" by the candidate they had backed so fervently and to whose campaign they had contributed so heavily.

In 2010, Senator Robert Byrd of West Virginia died at the age of 92.

Although many Americans, including Presidents Obama and Carter, praised his role as the longest serving senator in U.S. history, it is unlikely that any gay American or any African-American mourned his passing. He was a venomous, aggressively outspoken homophobe and racist.

In 1944 he had joined the KKK, an organization that not only lynched and shot black men, women, and children, but used brutal forms of sadism to suppress them, including dismemberments and castrations.

In the Senate, Byrd's rants against gays were so violent that he seemed to want to do the same to them.

The strongest opposition came from Senator Robert Byrd, Democrat from West Virginia, an aging relic of yesterday who had carried his decades of prejudice to Washington. He had been elected to Congress in 1953, becoming a Senator in 1959. Byrd was described as "an elegant popinjay in his three-piece suits and his gray hair which tapered to a widow's peak." He had never been known for his tolerance. Right after World War II, in 1946, he issued a statement: "I shall never fight in the armed forces with a negro by my side. Rather, I should die a thousand times, and see Old Glory trampled in the dirt never to rise again, than to see our beloved land become degraded by race mongrels, a throwback to the blackest specimen from the wilds. The Klan is needed today as never before, and I am anxious to see its rebirth in West Virginia and in every state of the nation."

In 1993, Byrd turned his racist rants into some of the most violent homophobic attacks ever presented in the Senate. He even managed to introduce the Roman emperor Tiberius, citing his use of young male prostitutes as sex slaves.

In 1964, Byrd had filibustered the Civil Rights Act for fourteen hours. In an ironic statement in 1993, he said that if gays were allowed to serve in the military, the next thing on the gay agenda would involve pleas for something "unthinkable"—that is, same-sex marriage and the "affrontery" of actually being able to join the Boy Scouts of America." He claimed that American civilization, as he knew it, would collapse.

"Dealing with Byrd," Hillary said, "was like climbing a steep mountain. He wants to create a permanent second class for millions of Americans, African

Americans and gays in particular."

Dee Dee Myers was one of the first of the *Clintonistas* to realize how deep the prejudice against gays ran. "In politics, perception is everything," she said. "Word got out that our populist president had gotten drunk with power and was moving ahead and not sensitive to the wishes of the majority of the American people on the gay issue. In politics, you have to be careful that certain things don't become metaphors. For example, when it was discovered that George H.W. Bush didn't know that grocery stores had food scanners at checkout counters, that become the symbol for his out-of-touch presidency."

In 1991, a Republican, Dick Cheney, the Secretary of Defense, was far more enlightened than most people in his party on the gay issue. He called the idea that gays were a security risk "an old chestnut." Later, when he was George W. Bush's vice president, he admitted that he was in favor of same-sex marriage, a lot of his philosophy based on his having a lesbian daughter.

As millions of Americans attacked gays, they picked up some surprising support. The most famous example came from a right-wing Republican, Senator Barry Goldwater, who had sought the presidency when he ran unsuccessfully against Lyndon B. Johnson in 1964. Goldwater told *The Washington Post* in June of 1993, "You don't have to be straight to shoot straight."

Republicans weren't the only ones objecting to gays serving openly in the military. The most prominent Democrat among the attack dogs was Sam Nunn. A senator from Georgia (1972-1997), he was also the chairman of the powerful U.S. Senate Committee on Armed Services.

Born in the bowels of redneck Georgia (Macon, in 1937), he brought the prejudices of his boyhood to the floor of the U.S. Senate. He remains today a despised figure within the GLBT community.

Rear Admiral Craig Quigley, a spokesman for the U.S. Navy, strongly opposed Bill's advocacy. He claimed, "Homosexuals are notoriously promiscuous. In shared shower situations, heterosexuals would have an uncomfortable feeling of someone watching."

Quigley, of course, blindly ignored the fact that gays and straights, in both military and in civilian locker rooms, have been showering together and/or collaborating side by side since the days of the Revolutionary War, and that millions of straight men were also "notoriously promiscuous."

At one point, he posed for photographs, along with Senator John Warner of Virginia, aboard a submarine to show that straight men would have to sleep close to gay men in cramped conditions, and presumably become the victims of unwanted sexual advances. Nunn seemed blind to the fact that such a situation already existed throughout the military.

Elizabeth Taylor, who was married to Warner from 1976 to 1982, was inundated with letters from her loyal fans, who wondered how she could have married such a "bigoted hayseed."

Opposition continued to mount, with the majority of public opinion turning against gay servicemen. Faced with attacks from the Joint Chiefs of Staff and from members of Congress, Bill admitted, "I was forced to cave in."

On December 21, 1993, the Clinton administration issued a defense directive, commanding that military applicants were not to be asked about their sexual orientation. The policy came to be known as "Don't Ask, Don't Tell."

One of her fans wrote to Elizabeth Taylor with the following message: "Elizabeth, we love you, but how could you marry such a homosexual hater as Senator John Warner of Virginia?" As one newsman described him, "Warner was a conservative Southerner, a 'fag-hating' Republican."

In December of 1999, while she was still First Lady, Hillary issued a statement: "Gays and lesbians already serve with distinction and should not face discrimination. Fitness to serve should be based on an individual's conduct, not their sexual orientation."

She cited a story from her own life, showing how a person's prejudice could give way when someone got to know gay people and worked with them or befriended them. She claimed that her father, Hugh Rodham, Sr., had grown up with the usual prejudices of his day, not only against homosexuals, but against Catholics, Democrats, Jews, and blacks, too.

In December of 1976, Elizabeth Taylor married Senator John Warner of Virginia. The years (1976-1982) she spent in that marriage were relatively unhappy.

After her divorce, she said, "You never get over men like the flu. Every divorce is like a little death." She'd previously divorced Nicky Hilton, Michael Wilding, Eddie Fisher, and Richard Burton.

In Little Rock, his best friends had become Larry Curbo, a nurse, and Dr. Dillard Denson, a neurologist. The Rodhams lived in a condo next to Denson and Curbo's.

The two couples became the best of friends. One night after watching a TV show, when Hugh criticized homosexuals, his wife, Dorothy, asked, "But what about

Dillard and Larry?"

As amazing as it seemed, Hugh didn't know that his two best friends were gay and that they had lived together, unofficially, as husband and husband for years.

"One of my father's last stereotypes melted," Hillary said. "He cared a lot for Larry and Dillard, and he meant a lot to them. In fact, it was Larry who was sitting beside Hugh in the hospital holding onto his hand at the very moment my father died."

"After Dad's death, both Larry and Dillard proved to be Dorothy's most valued friends, helping her adjust to widowhood and remaining her trusted companion until her own death."

The moment the repeal took effect, at midnight, U.S. Navy Lt. Gary C. Ross, taking Dan Swezy into his arms, married his same-sex partner of 11½ years.

As a couple, they became the first same-sex military couple to legally marry in the United States.

***

Gays scored a major victory in 2007 when twenty-eight retired generals and admirals urged Congress to repeal DADT, citing evidence that at least 65,000 gay men and lesbians were already serving honorably in the U.S. Armed Forces, and there were perhaps thousands more. The men also cited that there were at least a million GLBT veterans who had been retired honorably from the various branches of the armed services.

The Ross-Swezy nuptials were followed by an announcement from Retired Rear Admiral Alan S. Steinman *(depicted above)*, who self-identified as Out and proud. That made him the highest-ranking military person to publicly define him or herself as gay in the immediate aftermath of the defeat of DADT.

In 2008, 104 retired generals and admirals released a similar endorsement of gays in the military. The tide was turning. Even Colin Powell himself, in July of 2009, suggested that the U.S. military's policy banning self-identifying gays, in lieu of changing times, needed to be reviewed.

When Barack Obama ran for president in 2008, he promised that he would work to repeal the ban on gays in the military. He was opposed by the Senate's leading homophobe, John McCain of Arizona.

The Senate, by a tally of 65 to 31, voted to lift the ban on December 28, 2010. On December 22, President Obama signed the repeal of the ban into law. The end of DADT was set for September 20,

2011.

Unknown to most Americans, homosexuals had already achieved ranks in the highest tiers of government. Voters had already elected some gay presidents, albeit ones forced during their eras to live deep in the closet. "James Buchanan and Abraham Lincoln come to mind," claimed gay activist Larry Kramer.

Bloody Altercations Near "Whacked-Out Waco," Texas Involve the Clintons in a Religious War

The U.S. Government's Siege Against "Christ Re-Incarnate"

Attorney General Janet Reno's most controversial order came early in her administration. It was the notorious "Waco Siege" of April, 1993.

A religious compound of the Branch Davidians, a zealous religious sect that had broken off from the Seventh Day Adventist Church, was led by David Koresh—"The Messiah"—on a hilltop in the community of Elk, Texas, nine miles northeast of Waco. The sect believed in the imminent Apocalypse, an event that would signal the end of the world as we know it, the "Second Coming" of Jesus Christ and the defeat of the wicked armies of Babylon.

The group was suspected of weapons violations, and Reno ordered that a search warrant be obtained. Agents of the Bureau of Alcohol, Tobacco, Firearms, and Explosives, along with Texas state law enforcement and members of the US military attempted to raid the Branch Davidians' heavily armed ranch compound. During their effort, four agents were killed and twenty injured.

Reno met with Bill in the Oval Office, seeking his approval to have Federal agents storm the compound using tear gas to force them out and surrender.

"Janet told me that she'd received reliable reports that Koresh was sexually abusing some of the children, and that he was planning a mass suicide."

Ordered to move ahead, the FBI launched a massive armored raid on the compound. Koresh ordered his followers to set a fire. When the windows were opened to ventilate away the tear gas, winds on the hilltop fanned the flames, setting off a massive fire that resembled a holocaust. Whereas only eleven of the zealots escaped, seventy-six of Koresh's followers, including "Christ Incarnate himself," were killed. The list of casualties included twenty-one children and two pregnant women.

The eleven survivors, each of whom had left the compound, were arrested. The Waco Siege remains controversial to this day, even though a government investigation concluded that the Branch Davidians themselves had started the raging fire. In the aftermath, it was determined that some 80 members of the cult had died of burns, asphyxiation, wounds suffered from collapsing buildings, or gunfire.

The nation was left reeling from the ghastly outcome of this standoff," Hillary wrote. "All of us felt the regret over the violence and death caused by a perversion of religion."

***

"Another misuse of religious differences for purposes of political power was occurring during the Bosnian War," Hillary claimed.

At the end of his first hundred days in office, Bill said, "We were nowhere near a satisfactory solution to the Bosnian crisis."

The war in the Balkans followed the breakup of Yugoslavia, which had been held together since the end of World War II by the iron-fisted regime of Marshal Tito. A frenzy of "ethnic cleansing" swept this war-torn country, the most devastating conflict in Europe since World War II. The crisis would eventually engulf the Clinton administration.

A Prominent Clinton Adviser (Dick Morris) Evaluates Bill as "an Emotional Albino," and Hillary as "More Like Reagan & Nixon than Eleanor Roosevelt"

Carl Bernstein wrote that during his first months in office, Bill learned to maneuver politically by trial and error. "But in terms of his character, he remained basically unchanged: Ambitious, narcissistic, charming, brilliant, roguish, undisciplined, incredibly able—and often personally disappointing."

Later, Dick Morris became a Clinton basher in articles, comments, and books. At one point, he called Bill "an emotional albino."

As for Hillary, he found her "bright, but not *very* bright." According to Morris, "She is not supple, flexible, or terribly skillful politically. She's brittle and rigid. The fragility of iron that cracks when you drop it, as opposed to steel, which doesn't. She likes to play the role of Eleanor Roosevelt, her supposed role model, but in reality, she's more like Reagan. She's also like Nixon in that she definitely has a streak of ruthlessness and paranoia in her political style. She has a very long shit list, comparable to Nixon's enemies list."

The Clintons' first one-hundred days in office were coming to an end. It had been a time of turbulence and strong opposition, even blatant attacks on their character and motivations. Her health care plan appeared to be facing more and more formidable obstacles, and his fundamental economic stimulus plan had been shot down in the Senate, where Dole and others wanted him to fail.

At a press conference on April 23, Bill proclaimed, "In our first hundred days, we have already fundamentally changed the direction of the American government." A bold statement, but not really true.

As the month of April came to an end, Hillary gave each key member of the White House staff a long-stemmed pink rose. Her card read: "I want to thank you for all the work you've done since the inauguration in January. We've had a historic opportunity to make great things happen in our nation." That was true in a sense, but those great things had not happened and didn't appear to be coming to fruition any time soon. Instead, a sense of gloom and doom had fallen over the White House.

"What will the summer bring?" Hillary asked Bill, Webb Hubbell, and Vince Foster. "What new pile of shit will we sink into? Time will tell soon enough."

As she later recalled, "That summer, fall, and winter were nightmares."

Chapter Fourteen

"The Gates of Hell"

Open to Consume the Clintons

Gomorrah on the Potomac:

Travelgate, Troopergate, & Whitewater-gate

Fostergate

Though Ruled a Suicide, Critics Insist that Hillary's Lover (Vince Foster) Was Murdered, Most Foul

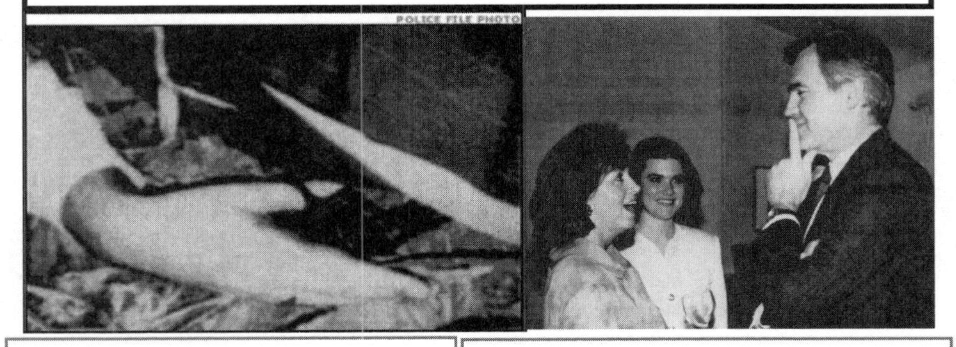

This is a detail from a police file photo of Vince Foster's right hand, with gun, as discovered after his suicide.

His body was found at Fort Marcy, one of a ring of fortifications constructed during the Civil War to defend the U.S. capital against a Confederate attack.

Emergency Medical Services rushed to this park at 6:09PM. In their wake came John Rolla, an investigator for the park police. He touched Vince's body, finding that it was still relatively warm. There was no sign of rigor mortis. Some of the blood on the dead man's face was still wet, but starting to dry.

Foster, enigmatic and bemused, with fans.

A lot of women staffers at the White House informally voted Vince Foster as "the sexiest man in the White House." He was tall, very handsome, a real Southern gentleman who had a quiet but commanding charisma.

In the photo above, Kaki Mehlburger *(left)* and Helen Dickey stand by, entranced. As yet another secretary said, "I practically had an orgasm every time he came near me."

Clinton-hating Linda Tripp, the last person to see him before he left the White House, said, "Vince wasn't like the Clintons. He wasn't ruthless."

"Vince did it. He really did it. It's my fault. It's all my fault."

—Hillary to Harry Thomason,
Hollywood Producer

Back in Little Rock, Hillary's two best friends, Vince Foster and Webb Hubbell, had lunch by themselves, minus their usual companion, Hillary Rodham Clinton.

Her former partners at the Rose Law Firm missed their comrade. Hubbell had already been working for the Clinton administration, and he and Hillary wanted Vince to join them. "Bill and Hillary are already in serious trouble, and they need you. I, too, need you close at hand," Hubbell told Vince.

"Will wonders never cease?" Vince said to Hubbell. "I thought Bill's trail of womanizing would disqualify him from higher office outside Arkansas. But President of the United States! My prediction was wrong. He made it. He's truly the Comeback Kid!"

Then Hubbell added an ominous afterthought: "As president, his troubles are only beginning. Past scandals will return to haunt him. Now I'm being prophetic. And I'm sure that now that they're in a bigger arena, they're creating fresh scandals. Let's face it: Scandal just seems to follow the Clintons wherever they go."

"As you know, I care for Hillary very much," Vince said, "but I have repeatedly rejected her offer to move to Washington as White House

The suicide of Vince Foster was official Washington's highest-ranking suicide since James Forrestal, Secretary of Defense, committed suicide in 1949 during the administration of Harry S Truman.

Almost immediately, Vince's suicide became a political scandal. "If this could happen to Vince—the 'Rock of Gibraltar' to the Clintons—maybe it could happen to anyone," claimed George Stephanopoulos.

President Clinton said, "What happened to Vince is a mystery about something inside of him. All of us are people, with our strengths and weaknesses, and maybe we have to pay a little more attention to our friends, families, and co-workers."

Stephanopoulos told *The Washington Post,* "The fundamental truth is that no one can know what drives a person to do something like this. Since you can't ever know, it's impossible to speculate on it."

Rumors: Enquiring Minds Want to Know

Did Bill Clinton Attempt to Rape Jacqueline Kennedy Onassis?

counsel," Vince said. "My wife, Lisa, doesn't want me to go either. Frankly, I think she's relieved to have gotten rid of Hillary here in Little Rock."

Two days later, again over lunch, Hubbell stopped eating his spaghetti to comment on the twinkle in Vince's eyes.

"Guess what?" he said. "I talked to Hillary last night. She's a persuasive woman. I'm temporarily leaving my family behind until the kids finish school in Little Rock. As a lone blackbird, I'm flying to Washington to serve as a White House counsel to Hillary. I'm invading Gomorrah on the Potomac. May God have mercy on my soul."

This picture of Webb Hubbell and First Lady Hillary Clinton was taken in the Spring of 1993, shortly after the Clintons moved into the White House. Hillary had just appeared before the press in the Rose Garden.

Their intimacy added fuel to rumors that had begun back at the Rose Law Firm in Little Rock.

"Great!" Hubbell said. "I'm returning to Washington tomorrow. We'll work together with Hillary as a team. Call us The Three Musketeers."

After Bill was inaugurated, Hubbell was designated as White House liaison to the Justice Department. Bill had wanted to appoint him Attorney General, but Hillary kept insisting on a woman. Finally, on April 2, 1993, after the nominations of both Zoë Baird and Kimba Wood were shot down, and after Janet Reno was named as Attorney General, Hubbell was formally nominated as Associate Attorney General. Reno designated him as the Justice Department's chief operating Officer charged with oversight of its 100,000 employees and its $10 billion annual budget.

In his memoir, *Friends in High Places,* published in 1997, Hubbell recalled those heady early days in Washington "where the town almost swallowed us whole. The president was busy fighting the furor over gays in the military. The First Lady was caught up in health-care reform. My old buddy, Vince, now the Deputy White House Counsel, was holed up with his boss, Bernie Nussbaum, trying to find an Attorney General who didn't have a 'Nanny problem,' and I was trying to get up to speed on all sorts of strange new subjects, such as HIV-infected Haitians at the Guantanamo base in Cuba."

As part of the Arkansas "coven" that Bill brought to the White House, Vince was the most appealing of the faces of the "New South." Newly installed at 1600 Pennsylvania Avenue, he didn't seek the spotlight, but was discreetly powerful in a self-effacing way.

Within the first few weeks, an informal caucus from within the secretarial pool decided that Vince, not Bill, was "the man we'd most like to have an affair with."

Corridor gossip later spread the word that romantic hopefuls would probably not succeed at snaring the amorous attentions of Vince. Not only was he married (although his wife, Lisa, was still in Arkansas, discreetly out of sight), but that Hillary had already claimed Vince as her "Main Man No. 2."

During his second week on the job, a Secret Service agent privately claimed that he'd walked into Vince's office without knocking. There, he discovered "the First Lady and Foster in deep embrace. One of her breasts was exposed."

Although he was on the White House payroll, most of Vince's duties centered on the personal affairs of the Clintons, including taxes and financial disclosure forms. Vince was the agent who arranged for their holdings to be incorporated into a blind trust. He privately told Nussbaum, chief counsel to the president, "Their records, I fear, are a potential time bomb. We live in a town of 'gotcha' journalism. I dread reading the morning papers. At times, I feel like a guppy plopped into a goldfish bowl."

["Bernie," as he was called, had known Hillary ever since they'd served together on President Nixon's Watergate Impeachment Committee. Nussbaum would later resign, disgraced over his mishandling of both the Whitewater and the Foster investigations.]

Vince talked to his boss daily, Nussbaum lending a sympathetic ear. "Who's being exposed today?" Vince asked.

An outgoing White House attorney said, "The more deeply Foster was drawn into mopping up behind Hillary's political messes, the less he pleased her and the more he implicated himself. Refusing her requests, sometimes outrageous, might alienate her, the one person he so desperately wanted to please."

Fellow staffers quickly noted, "Vince hated Washington. The brutality of the place shocked this Southern gentleman. He was out of his league, and the only person who could comfort him was Hillary herself. His wife was still in Arkansas, and Bill was always somewhere else, so Hillary and Vince were able to spend many evenings together."

As reporter Carl Bernstein wrote, "Vince Foster shared a side of himself with Hillary that he did not share with his wife, and she shared a piece of her own life that she could not share with Bill."

It was later revealed in *The New York Post* that Vince and Hillary shared a "love nest" in northern Virginia, a short drive from D.C., where they could retreat from the fetid politics of the Potomac. There, presumably they enjoyed quiet times similar to those they'd experienced in the Governor's Mansion in Little Rock when Bill was away.

But, regrettably, as pressures on her as First Lady intensified, she began to see less and less of Vince. Sometimes, she was so rushed, she'd storm into his office and plop papers on his desk with orders to "Handle this shit."

Nussbaum felt that Vince missed his wife, Lisa, and his family, and that he was homesick for Arkansas. He noted that Bill had brought along "some Arkansas comfort to handle his lonely nights."

Apparently, he was referring to Marsha Scott, an attractive blonde who was rumored to have been Bill's "hottie" back in Little Rock. Vince suspected that she was still carrying on an affair with the president.

Reporter Phillip Weiss described Scott as "a fox in fox's clothing. Ms. Scott is a slack-jawed blonde with a hippie past, a Dyan Cannon type who knows how to play the California ditz whenever anyone asks her what she's been up to."

Bill had arranged for his "hippie girlfriend" to be hired as director of White House correspondence, a job that paid almost $100,000 annually. Almost immediately after her arrival, she fired twenty longtime staffers. Millions of letters piled up before replacements were found.

For the first time in his life, Vince, the Golden Boy of Arkansas' legal hierarchies, was coming under sustained fire, especially from the press. *The Wall Street Journal* came down especially hard on him. One article suggested that the Clintons had brought him to Washington only as a means of concealing their misdeeds. Another insultingly labeled him as "one of the good ol' Bubba Boys from way down South in Dixie."

Travelgate

The Clinton Administration's First Ethics Controversy Erupts in the White House. What Was Hillary's Role?

The first major ethics scandal of the Clinton administration was the Travel Office Controversy, dubbed in the press as "Travelgate." With a name, and associations, that evoked Richard Nixon's infinitely more serious "Watergate" crisis, it would become the first use of the suffix "-gate". It was later applied to many of the Clinton's future scandals, including "Monicagate," "Filegate," and "Whitewater-gate."

It erupted in May of 1993, after seven employees of the White House Travel Office were abruptly fired. As justification for the shakeup, the White House cited "financial improprieties." Critics immediately charged that the firings were not warranted, that the FBI was needlessly involved, and that the real reason behind the dismissals was to allow cronies of the Clintons to commandeer the White House's travel business.

NEW YORK POST

HILLARY DID IT

Travelgate headlines, each as lurid and accusatory as possible

Since the era of Andrew Jackson *[U.S. President from 1829-1837]*, there had been a White House Travel Office. In 1993, it operated on an annual budget of $7 million, its job involving the coordination of travel for representatives of participating news organizations and billing them later.

The Clintons had received reports of irregularities in the Travel Office and accusations of possible kickbacks from a charter airline company. Billy Ray Dale, the Travel Office's director, with a work history that went back to 1982 and the Reagan era, came under suspicion.

Hillary's first links to the travel office scandal did not originate through Vince, but from Harry Thomason, a Hollywood producer working in the White House with the goal of sharpening the Clinton's favorable public image. Vince privately referred to Thomason as "The Meddler."

Thomason approached Hillary, charging that "the people who run the travel office are a bunch of crooks. We've got to get our people in there!"

Armed with that accusation, Hillary then pressured Vince and also David Watkins, the White House's Operations Director, to "clean house."

The FBI was summoned to find some instance of wrongdoing. In the end, it was Watkins and Vince who would become the fall guys.

Before members of the "old guard" were fired, Hillary called Vince almost daily, demanding to know, "What's being done? He preferred a "wait-and-see" attitude, which made her impatient and frustrated. Travelgate caused a rift in their formerly close bond. It would never be mended.

Using Vince as her frontman, Hillary played a large backseat role in the firings. When later called upon to testify, she claimed, "I do not remember certain conversations."

A series of investigations into the firings would extend over a period of nearly eight years. Although she was never officially charged with any crime, Hillary was alleged to have played a central role in the firings and for making false statements during an investigation.

Somehow, a lot of the blame for this murky and messy affair fell on an increasingly depressed Foster. He was accused of being the muscle behind the "slapdash firings, and the air of cronyism" associated with them. The fallout was immense, singeing and burning him as well as his friend and *protégé*, William Kennedy.

In time, Vince became obsessed with Travelgate, especially with Hillary's disapproval of the way he'd handled his role in what had by now blossomed into a full-blown scandal. He feared a Congressional hearing and although he considered resigning, he did not want to return, humiliated, to Arkansas.

Hillary's romance with Vince ended abruptly in the wake of Travelgate. During the final two weeks of his life, she refused to take his calls. In turn, he began to refer to her sarcastically as "The Client." He feared that he'd handled Travelgate badly, and he had an even greater fear that he might end up in jail.

Dick Morris, formerly a highly positioned Clinton adviser and confidant, later claimed, "When Hillary is upset, she reacts viscerally and closes the door. There is no colder feeling on the planet. Vince found that out for himself."

In her 2003 autobiography, Hillary said, "Travelgate was perhaps worth a two-or three-week life span. Instead, in a partisan political climate, it became the first manifestation of an obsession for investigation that persisted into the next millennium."

White House counselor William H. Kennedy III called it "pure, palpable hatred of the Clintons. It started and it never quit."

In December of 1994, a Federal Grand Jury indicted the Travel Office's director, Billy Ray Dale, on two counts of "embezzlement and criminal conversion." Consequently, he faced up to twenty years in prison if convicted. Eleven months later, in November of 1995, he was acquitted of both charges.

***

During the final weeks of Vince's increasingly tense relationship with Hillary, "I think both of them ended up broken-hearted," a White House staffer said. "I'm sure they longed for those better days back in Arkansas, their long lunches, and their private dinners at the Governor's Mansion without Bill."

"But as their troubles mounted, it seemed that there was no way that he could do enough for her," Hubbell said. "She became almost hysterical with demands that he extinguish various brushfires. She just wasn't her old self any more, at least that's what Vince told me. I felt sorry for him. In some ways, he reminded me of a jilted lover."

During the final days of his life, Vince sometimes didn't rise from his bed, but spent his time working on papers, alone and with the shades drawn to shut out all daylight. He was reported to be in a deep depression, or, in the words of Nussbaum, "heading down that stairway to a dark gulf."

At the time, he was taking a prescribed anti-depressant, a medication called Trazedone.

During his last day at the White House, Hillary was in Arkansas, visiting her mother, Dorothy Howell Rodham.

July 20, 1993, the last day Vince was reported alive, was a bright, sunny day. He was seen wandering aimlessly in the Rose Garden, which was in full bloom, the air heady with the scent of roses.

The last staffer who saw him was the soon-to-be notorious, Clinton-hating Linda Tripp, an ex-Army wife and single mother who later broke news that led to the Monica Lewinsky scandal.

[Five years later, on July 28, 1998, before Kenneth Starr's grand jury investigation, Tripp said, "I have reason to believe that the Vince Foster tragedy was not depicted accurately under oath by members of the administration, which is why I am afraid. They were lying under oath. None of the behavior in the White House following Foster's death was just of people mourning him. It was far more ominous than that. I felt endangered."]

Vince Foster's Suicide Becomes a Cause Célèbre. Hillary is Fingered as the Culprit

Without telling anyone where he was going, Vince had disappeared from the White House. He had driven to Fort Marcy Park, a Federal Park outside Washington in suburban Virginia, with views opening onto the Potomac.

At around 6PM that evening, July 20, 1993, a jogger came across his body, sprawled out near a Civil War cannon.

Two U.S. Park Police Investigators were summoned to the scene. In Vince's hand was an antique .38 caliber revolver, which had belonged to his father. It appeared that he'd fired a bullet into his mouth, and that it had exited through the back of his neck.

When the Park Officers found Vince's jacket in his gray Honda Accord, and that it displayed a gold White House badge, an urgent call was placed to the Secret Service. In response, agents were summoned to the scene of the apparent suicide.

Bill's White House Chief of Staff, Mack McLarty, was the first to hear of Vince's death from the Secret Service. At the time, Bill was in the West Wing, taping a TV show with talk show host Larry King.

McLarty's immediate response was to place a call to Hillary in Arkansas, where she was at the condo of her mother, Dorothy.

He did not hold back the news. "Vince is gone," he blurted out. "He killed himself."

On the other end of the phone, he heard a startled gasp followed by what sounded like a hysterical *cri de coeur.*

Lisa Caputo, Hillary's press secretary, was nearby, later asserting, "From her reaction, I thought Bill had been assassinated."

After speaking to her and offering whatever comfort he could, McLarty rushed to deliver the news to Bill. He had just finished his segment for the TV show, and since it had gone so well, he had volunteered to stick around for another thirty-minute interview.

McLarty signaled to Bill to follow him into the corridor, where he told him the news. The White House communications director, George Stephanopoulos, witnessed what happened next: "Bill's head dropped. He seemed to steady himself on Mack's arm as he was put on an elevator to the private rooms upstairs."

Bill turned to Stephanopoulos. "I have to go to Vince's Lisa. We have lost our Rock of Gibraltar."

The president went on to say: "I'm devastated. I've known Vince since we were kids. He was my boyhood friend next door when we were growing up in Hope. His loss is like a stab in my heart."

Within the hour, Bill was seen getting into an unmarked Chevy Suburban with two Secret Service agents, who drove him to the Foster home in Georgetown. Details about the exchange between the president and Foster's newly widowed wife, Lisa, aren't known.

Soon, various friends arrived, including writer Sally Quinn, David Gergen, Vernon Jordan, and Ben Bradlee, former editor of *The Washington Post.* Marsha Scott, Bill's alleged *amoretta,* also appeared on the scene.

Deeply troubled over Vince's suicide, Bill reportedly spent the night with Scott, as she would later confide to David Watkin's wife, Ileene. *[There are no secrets in Washington, especially if you tell somebody something in confidence. Ileene's husband, David, was an old Clinton aide from Arkansas, who had actually fired White House staffers during the Travelgate scandal.]*

Back in Arkansas, Hillary recovered quickly and was soon on the phone to the White House, speaking to Nussbaum. There was an immediate fear that Vince had left a suicide note, perhaps professing a politically awkward "undying love for her."

Because Vince had operated to some degree as Hillary's personal lawyer, she seemed concerned about removing her personal documents from his office. Based on Hillary's orders, several boxes were taken away, despite the objections of Deputy Attorney General Philip Heymann.

One of the files transferred from Vince's office was marked "WHITEWA-

TER."

Later, Hillary claimed, "This spawned an industry of conspiracy theorists and investigators trying to prove that Vince was murdered to cover up what he knew about Whitewater."

"The rest is history, or so the saying goes," Nussbaum said. "Obviously, the last thing Vince would ever want was to contribute in any way to those right-wing conspirators who set out to destroy the Clintons over Whitewater."

Six days went by before Steve Neuwirth, a White House counsel, fished out twenty-eight scraps of torn-up yellow paper from Vince's briefcase. They hadn't been noticed before. Later interpreted as the draft of a letter of resignation, it was the closest thing anyone ever found to a suicide note—something he had hastily scribbled and then decided to tear up.

It revealed that Vince's scribbled and later torn-up document, as part of his *adieu,* attacked the FBI for "lying in their reports." He accused *The Wall Street Journal,* claiming "they lie without consequence."

He also wrote that he was not meant for his job in the spotlight, or for public life in Washington at all. "Here, ruining people is a blood sport. The public will never believe the innocence of the Clintons and their loyal staff."

"I made mistakes from ignorance, inexperience, and overwork. I did not knowingly violate any law or standard of conduct, including any action in the Travel Office. There was no intent to benefit any individual or specific group."

News of the existence of the tattered note was delayed for thirty hours before its contents were made public.

When Hillary returned to the White House, a friend who did not want to be named said, "She was destroyed by Vince's suicide. She may never get over it. I think she's suffering internal bleeding, at least where her heart is."

As she later admitted in an autobiography, "For months after Vince's death, I drifted along on automatic pilot."

In the wake of Vince's death, the White House staff buzzed with rumors. One of the most outrageous comments came from a homosexual aide, who told friends, "I once stood next to Vince at a urinal. I must say, Hillary lost a great friend. I could only envy her. There was meat there for the poor."

Both Bill and Hillary flew into Little Rock to attend Vince's funeral. After the service, the funeral *cortège* made its way to Hope, where Vince was buried on the outskirts of the town where he grew up. Later, friends reported that Hillary seemed alienated from Lisa and the Foster family, although Bill was sympathetic.

Later, Vince's widow reportedly told friends, "I can't stand to see the Clintons on TV. I hate everything about them."

Did Vince Foster's Death Result from Foul Play?

A Firestorm of Controversy Engulfs the Nation

What happened later that summer would evoke a scandal with unanswered questions and conspiracy theories that continue deep into the 21st Century.

On July 21, the day after Foster's death, a police report was released. It stated that "Foster's injury was not inconsistent with that of a self-inflicted wound." Their final conclusion, issued on August 11, was that "Vince Foster shot himself in Fort Marcy on July 20, 1993."

In the days and weeks ahead, a firestorm erupted that some critics referred to as "Fostergate."

Conspiracy theorist and Clinton hater, William Safire.

Bill claimed, "Safire set out to prove that Hillary and I were as bad as they come. He tried to tie Vince's death to some illegal link of misconduct by Hillary and myself. He speculated that Vince had illegally kept records that were incriminating to us."

Emmett R. Tyrell, in *The American Spectator*—a publication funded by Clinton-hating billionaire Richard Mellon Scaife—called the Clinton presidency "the weirdest ever," suggesting that Vince might have "met with foul play."

The press relentlessly savaged both Bill and Hillary. William Safire, a right-wing columnist for *The New York Times,* accused her of being "a congenital liar." *[He had previously worked as a speech writer for two disgraced politicians, Richard Nixon and Spiro Agnew.]*

Safire set out to make Vince's suicide a *cause célèbre.*

The wildest and most irresponsible of the murder theorists could be easily dismissed, but those occupying powerful posts in the government were harder to ignore. Some of them questioned whether Vince had committed suicide. None was more notable than the Republican Speaker of the House of Representatives (1995-99), the fiery and abrasively rough-edged Congressman from Georgia, Newt Gingrich. He added gasoline to the Foster suicide fire by saying, "I believe there are plausible grounds to wonder what happened to Vincent Foster. There is reason to question whether or not it was suicide."

William H. Chafe, a professor of history at Duke University, wrote: "If Bill Clinton had believed that there was a way out of the demonization that flourished in the nation's capital, he now had to realize that the forces of polarization were growing stronger, not weaker, and that any victories he could secure would come at great cost." The professor could have included Hillary in that dire assessment.

Televangelist Pat Robertson of *The 700 Club* told The Faithful: "Suicide or murder? That's the ominous question surfacing in the Whitewater swell of controversy concerning Vince Foster's mysterious death."

Bill responded in anger. "I heard a lot of right-wing talk show people. All that sleazy stuff they said. They didn't give a rip that he had killed himself or that his family was miserable, or that they could break the hearts of his friends and Lisa. It was just another weapon to slug us with, to demonize us with."

Rush Limbaugh claimed that Vince was murdered in an apartment owned by Hillary and that his body was then transported to Fort Marcy.

Larry Nichols, a former close aide to the Clintons during Bill's governorship of Arkansas *[and later, one of his most implacable enemies]* claimed, "Vince's body was wrapped in a long shag multi-colored carpet and the 6'4", 200-pound corpse was placed in a waiting government car." The suggestion was that Vince had been shot in the White House and then, as part of an extended conspiracy, that he was then thrown into the trunk of a car for delivery to Fort Marcy, where the suicide scenario played out after having been carefully choreographed in advance.

POSTER BOY: Newt Gingrich became Bill & Hillary's "Nightmare on Pennsylvania Avenue."

One of the more bizarre aftereffects revolved around Dan Burton, the Republican Representative to the House of Representatives from Indiana, the Chairman of the House Government Reform and Oversight Committee. He became Capitol Hill's leading conspiracy theorist, creating a media blitz by firing a .38 caliber pistol into a watermelon in his back yard. The melon, supposedly, replicated the shape and density of Foster's skull and brain during what Burton tried to justify as a simulated re-enactment of the alleged murder. Thoroughly discredited as makeshift, unscientific, and sensationalist, the comparison "backfired."

In 1994, Burton sent a five-page investigative report to Kenneth Starr during his "Watergate and more" investigation of the Clintons.

In it, Burton cited several points, including that "carpet fibers of various colors were found on Mr. Foster's jacket." He also cited that "blonde to light brown hairs of Caucasian origin were discovered on Vince's T-shirt, pants, belt, shoes, and socks. No fingerprints were discovered on the revolver and the fatal bullet was never found. In most self-inflicted gunshot wounds through the mouth, teeth are broken. Foster had all his teeth intact."

[Even as late as 1998, Burton was still spreading and publicizing his charges of murder. "If I could prove ten percent of what I believed happened to Vince Foster, Bill Clinton would be exposed. The guy's a scumbag. That's why I went after him."

In 1997, Burton organized an investigation into alleged financial abuse during recent Democratic Party campaigns, with special focus on the Clintons and their 1996 election to the presidency. His committee's investigation ran for several years, during the course of which it issued more than 1,000 subpoenas of Clinton administration officials and cost over $7 million. The committee, and more pointedly, Burton's leadership of it, were described as a "farce" by The Los Angeles Times*; a "travesty" and a "parody" by* The New York Times, *and "its own cartoon, a joke, and a deserved embarrassment" by* The Washington Post.

As a Republican, Burton served as the U.S. Representative from Indiana's Fifth Congressional district from 1983 to 2013. At the end of his elected terms in office, he remained a devoted member of the Tea Party Caucus.]

A reason often cited for the alleged "assassination" of Vince, or so it was speculated, was that, "He was the man who knew too much about the Clintons."

Only the wildest of conspiracy theorists suggested that Hillary herself had actually pulled the trigger. Others, more "reasonable" in their scope and tone, claimed that the murder had been committed by Bill's "favorite member" (not named) of the Secret Service, the one who allegedly accompanied him on his most personal of sexual trysts.

A Sensationalist Author Demands Hillary's Imprisonment "For the Murder of Vince Foster"

Marinka Peschmann, author of *Following Orders: The Death of Vince Foster,* was more outrageous than virtually any other commentator during her published attack on Hillary. ("Hillary should not be in the White House. She should be in jail!")

Very shortly after Hillary announced her run for the presidency in the spring of 2015, rumors and allegations of Vince Foster's possible murder within the White House resurfaced. *The National Enquirer* led off the tabloids, with revelations from investigator Robert Morrow and the (deeply estranged) former Clinton aide, Larry Nichols. They claimed that Vince Foster was shot to death in his White House office.

Morrow wrote, "The dirty secret haunting Hillary to this day is that it was her instruction to move Foster's body so that it was no longer under the jurisdiction of the Washington, D.C. police. By having the body dumped in Fort Marcy Park, the investigation fell under a different jurisdiction—that is, the *[supposedly more lenient]* U.S. Park Police."

Both Morrow and Nichols charged that Hillary herself "orchestrated" the plot to smuggle the corpse out of the White House in a government car.

"To My Knowledge, Laura Bush Is the Only First Lady Who Ever Murdered Someone."

—Hillary Clinton

It was in the oil-producing city of Midland, on the night of November 6, 1963, when the stars were big and bright over Texas. Even though it was a school night, Laura Welch (later Bush), had been given the keys to the family car, a 1963 Chevrolet, to drive to a birthday party. At the age of seventeen, she was in her senior year of high school.

Already an inveterate smoker (outside the house), she was puffing on a cigarette and chatting with her girlfriend, Judy Dykes, who was riding in the Chevrolet's front passenger seat.

At 8:08PM, Laura, as driver, was speeding toward an intersection on Farm Road 868. Distracted, she ran through a stop sign. Regrettably, heading south along La Mesa Highway in a 1962 Corvair sedan was the school's star athlete, Michael Douglas, "The Golden Boy of Midland." Reportedly, he had just "dumped" Laura that afternoon as his girlfriend.

Her car plowed into his driver's side door, killing him instantly. He was DOA upon arrival, by ambulance, at the Midland Memorial Hospital. In "the shock of my life," Michael's father had been riding in the car behind him, and had witnessed his son's brutalizing death.

Laura and Dykes escaped from the havoc she had wreaked with only minor injuries.

The police arrived on the scene, but did not even give Laura a ticket for running a stop sign. Her blood was not tested for alcohol.

At Michael's funeral, most of the high school turned out to pay their respects. Locked alone in her room, Laura did not attend.

It was six weeks before Laura returned to school. Fortunately for her, no one confronted her with the charge of killing Michael, the boyfriend who had rejected her a few hours before his death, with her reckless driving.

When Laura's future husband, George W. Bush, entered politics in his race for the governorship of Texas, two reporters visited police headquarters at Midland. There, they were told that the file on Michael Douglas' death had been removed and couldn't be found.

During the eight years that Bush was president, the death of Michael Douglas caused by his First Lady was considered "off limits" to much of the press. Details were hard to come by, since the Midland City Attorney and the police department blocked information. Lawyers for *The Globe* finally forced them to issue a report.

Star-Crossed Sweethearts of Midland, Texas

Laura Bush *(left)* the high school senior who smokes (and allegedly sells) dope, drives recklessly, and kills her victim, the late Michael Douglas *(right)*.

Local resident Billie Ruppe had lived across the street from Laura's family for twenty-five years. Ruppe told the press, "She was a nice girl but I'll never forget her wild driving. I'd call it 'two-wheeling.' She seemed to go around every curve on two wheels."

Accountant Richard Pendleton said that he used to be the paper boy and lawn mower for the Welch family.

"Around four o'clock was Happy Hour. Her Mom and Dad were real lushes. They were nice people but drank a lot. Laura herself was a party girl. I was a party boy, too, so I knew. In those days, when you were invited to a party, it was bring your own bottle."

In her memoir, *Spoken From the Heart,* Laura finally talked about the night she killed Douglas. "In those awful seconds, my car door must have been flown open by the impact, and my body rose in the air until gravity took over, and I was pulled, hard and fast, back to earth. The whole time, I was praying that the person in the other car was alive."

He wasn't. The collision hurled Douglas' car fifty feet off the road. He died instantly of a broken neck and spinal column.

In the aftermath of Douglas' death, Laura said that she and Dykes were rushing to get to a drive-in movie. That could have been true. What she never mentioned was that they were coming from a party that had begun in the late afternoon, and where liquor was flowing.

Inquiring Minds Want to Know: Did Sharon Stone Uncross Her "Basic Instinct Legs" for Bill Clinton?

It wasn't all sorrow, pain, and humiliation at the White House. Bill Clinton had moments of pleasure. He was a movie fan, and, as president, he would be shipped any first-run feature he wanted to see before it was released nationwide.

His alltime favorite was the 1992 neo-*noir* erotic thriller, *Basic Instinct,* starring Sharon Stone and Michael Douglas. As detective Nick Curran, Douglas investigates the brutal murder of a rich rock star. In doing so, he becomes involved in torrid sex with its prime suspect, Catherine Tramell (Stone), an enigmatic crime novelist.

What made the movie infamous, and what led to Bill sitting through six different showings of it at various times, was Stone's infamous leg-crossing scene, which exposed her vulva. The actress later claimed that her most secret organ was allegedly filmed without her knowledge, although it was never explained how the director, Paul Verhoeven, had managed to do that.

After its release, *Basic Instinct* generated heated controversy because of its overt sexuality and graphic depiction of violence. Gay activists protested its skewed depiction of homosexual relationships and its portrayal of a bisexual woman as a "murderous narcissistic psychopath."

The film grossed $352 million worldwide, becoming one of the biggest money makers of the 1990s.

[HOLLYWOOD TRIVIA: Many actors and actresses were considered for the roles. Some were actually offered the parts but turned them down after reading the script. Up for the part of the detective were Chuck Norris, Al Pacino, Harrison Ford, Wesley Snipes, Robert De Niro, Mel Gibson, Bruce Willis, Sylvester Stallone, Jack Nicholson, Charlie Sheen, Richard Gere, John Travolta, Nicholas Cage, Denzel Washington, and Kevin Costner. After Kim Basinger turned down the female lead, it was offered to Julia Roberts, Greta Scacchi, Meg Ryan, Michel Pfeiffer, Geena Davis, Kathleen Turner, Ellen Barkin, Mariel Hemingway, and Demi Moore.

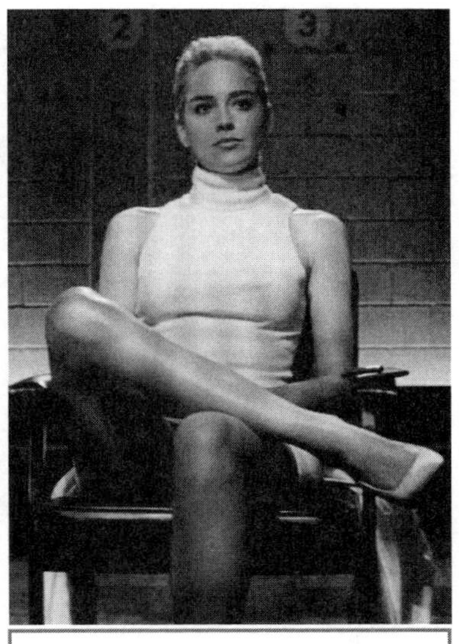

Sharon Stone, as author Catherine Trammell, positions herself indiscreetly in a still shot from *Basic Instinct* (1992).

Born in Pennsylvania in 1958, Stone had previously appeared in the 1990s with such stars as James Caan, Ryan O'Neal, and Tom Selleck. Although she first garnered attention when she appeared opposite Arnold Schwarzenegger in Total Recall *(1990), it was* Basic Instinct *that made her an international star.*

After the release of Total Recall, *she had posed nude for* Playboy. *By 1999, that magazine had named her among the "25 Sexiest Stars of the Century."]*

In early March of 1993, Bill agreed to meet with Soviet leader Boris Yeltsin in Vancouver, Canada. On April 3, the president flew to Canada for a summit. ""In Russia, Yeltsin was up to his ears in alligators, and I wanted to help him," Bill said. "I didn't want to look weak like my hero, JFK, did when he met Khrushchev in Vienna in 1961," Bill said. "Unlike Nikita, Yeltsin was on weak ground when we came together. One week before our meeting, the Duma in Moscow had failed to impeach him, but the motion had gotten a lot of votes."

"Ultimately, I couldn't write the $500 million aid check he wanted, " Bill said, "but I promised this big bear of a man that a lot of Yankee dollars were on the way. The only thing that really shocked me about Boris was that when he wanted to take a piss, he took it, regardless of where he was and who was watching. Actually, I understood his need to take a piss. For a man who consumes bottles of vodka every day, there is a need to get rid of some of the liquid."

Bill later told a reporter that Yeltsin was "full of piss and vinegar." He more accurately could have said "full of piss and vodka."

Stephanopoulos later said he understood what people meant when they called a drunk "tight. Yeltsin's skin was stretched across his cheeks in a way that nearly obliterated his features. With his slicked back white hair, he looked like a boiled potato lathered in sour cream."

Later, when Yeltsin was asked if he were happy at how the summit had ended, he said, "One can't be happy unless he's in bed with a beautiful woman. But I'm satisfied."

Sharon Stone's perceived allure and notoriety inevitably led to satirical kickbacks.

Here's a spoof on her role in *Basic Instinct* in the form of an ad for Itambé yogurt. Everyone knew it was a reference to Sharon.

"The summit was a success, marred only by a mistake on our part," Stephanopoulos claimed. "Richard Gere, Cindy Crawford, Sharon Stone, and Richard Dreyfuss were all in Vancouver making movies. Dreyfuss had been a campaign supporter, and he invited the president over to his hotel suite for a late-night drink, which inevitably and justifiably led to clucks in the press for hobnobbing with Hollywood stars at a Superpower Summit."

Stephanopoulos described the meeting: "It was in the suite, and all of us were sweating. What was Sharon Stone wearing? A blouse and slacks or something—I'm not sure. I was too busy watching Cindy."

Yeltsin and Clinton, each dealing with their respective revolutions at home, appear together, each with crutches, on the cover of *Time.*

As far as it is known, that would be Bill's first introduction to Stone.

It would not be his last.

Columnist Maureen Dowd filed a dispatch for *The New York Times.* "The president and his staff clearly enjoyed the *badinage* during the couple of hours he spent with Sharon Stone and a handful of other Hollywood nabobs, after talking policy all day with the Russians."

In her book, *The Clintons at the White House,* Sally Bedell Smith revealed a story about Stone being invited to a Clinton fund-raising dinner. Smith pointed out that Hillary was no fool and was well aware that her husband was a serial philanderer.

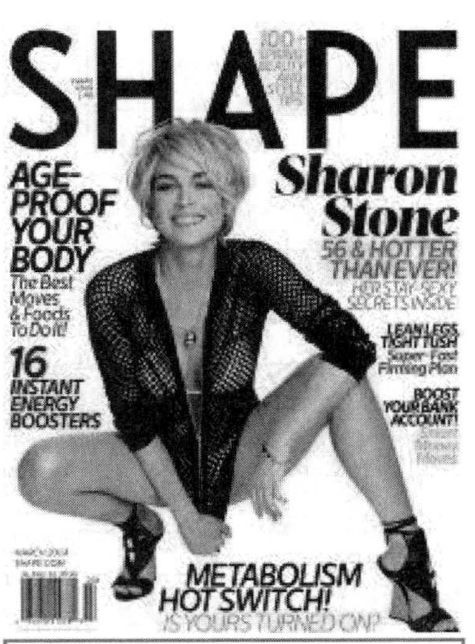

Positioning herself indiscreetly for photographers seemed to become something of an industry: Here's Sharon Stone at 56 and, according to the magazine, "Hotter Than Ever."

According to Smith, Hillary learned that the sexy blonde Hollywood goddess was to be seated next to the president at a dinner in 1995. The First Lady seemed aware that there had been something going on between her husband and Stone, or else that Bill might have an "obsession" with Stone ever since his first screening of *Basic Instinct.*

Hillary instructed the person responsible for the dinner's seating chart to remove Stone from her cozy spot next to the president and to reposition her some distance away. The seating charge was reconfigured, but when Bill arrived at the dinner, he ordered that the original seating arrangement be put back into place. Consequently, Stone was seated next to him, and throughout the dinner, they were a cozy duo.

Smith wrote, "Unless evidence of Clinton's affairs proved incontrovertible, Hillary simply preferred to turn a blind eye. To keep her marriage going, she had, years ago, devised a 'don't ask, don't tell' approach."

"What Hillary found harder to tolerate was public humiliation," Smith claimed. "Time and time again, she rose to Bill's defense, even when the facts overwhelmingly suggested that he was lying."

"Tolerating Bill's weakness," said Susan Thomases, Hillary's close friend, "has always been part of her relationship with Bill."

Whereas it has been revealed in various books and articles that Bill arranged to "get together" with Barbra Streisand during his visits to California, author Christopher Andersen also alleged that, "Bill arranged similar hotel rendezvous with the stunning blonde star Sharon Stone when he was in California. During one trip to the West Coast, Clinton changed his schedule so that he and Stone could both be in San Francisco at the same time. Clinton often gushes to friends about his favorite Sharon Stone scene—predictably, the graphic leg-crossing shot in *Basic Instinct."*

According to Dick Morris, "Bill Clinton was really, really hot for Sharon Stone. He has it bad for her."

"I Wish I Hadn't Invited the Clintons"

—Jacqueline Kennedy Onassis

For an August, 1993, vacation, a former First Lady, Jacqueline Kennedy Onassis, extended an invitation to the sitting First Lady, Hillary Rodham Clinton, for her, with Bill, to spend some time with her on Martha's Vineyard.

Only hours before their arrival, Jacqueline told her secretary, "I wish I hadn't invited them. I'm sorry they're coming. It's nothing personal against Bill and Hillary. But the place will be overrun with the press, with the Secret Service, with sightseers. I'd rather go canoeing."

Jacqueline found much to admire about the Clintons. "She felt an affinity with Bill and his wife," wrote biographer Sarah Bradford. "Of course, she knew of the photograph of the young William Jefferson Clinton taken in the Rose Garden with Jack. There were many things about Bill that reminded her of Jack, his famous charm and intellectual curiosity, as well, no doubt, the rumors of his sexual peccadilloes."

Teddy Kennedy told his sister-in-law, "I've talked to Bill and Hillary on several occasions, and both of them worship at Jack's altar."

When Bill was seeking the Democratic Party's nomination for president in the May, 1992, primary, Jacqueline threw her support to him. It meant she'd have to go against Paul Tsongas, who was a favorite son of Massachusetts. She liked the fact that Bill had frequently cited her former husband as one of the main reasons that he'd entered politics. She and her son, John Kennedy, Jr., had contributed heavily to Bill's political war chest.

The Clintons would be arriving on Martha's Vineyard aboard the yacht, *Relemar,* which was owned by Jacqueline's companion and oc-

Beginning with her debut in Newport, Rhode Island, Jackie Kennedy Onassis became one of the most alluring women in the world, with more magazine covers devoted to her than to almost any other celebrity in America.

She not only married two of the most famous and powerful men on earth—John F. Kennedy and Aristotle Onassis—but she captured the hearts of movie stars, including Marlon Brando, Warren Beatty, Paul Newman, William Holden, Gregory Peck, and Frank Sinatra.

Bill Clinton also came under her alluring spell.

casional lover, Maurice Tempelsman.

"Who would have thought that the very patrician Jacqueline would end up with a diamond merchant born to Orthodox Jews in Belgium?" Hillary was overheard saying to Bill and two aides before she boarded Maurice's yacht.

Of course, the Tempelsman yacht wasn't as luxurious as the super-size *Christina,* on which Jacqueline had sailed the Grecian seas with her late husband, Aristotle Onassis.

Ironically, Tempelsman was sometimes called "the poor man's Aristotle Onassis." Both of them were somewhat portly, and both had an affection for Dunhill cigars and collected rare art. Each of them, in his separate way, was a financial wizard.

Hillary had told friends, "I heard Maurice gives Jacqueline a lot of presents, and I also hear that she likes lots of presents, especially valuable ones. I understand JFK was very stingy with her. She got more money, I'm told, from old man Kennedy."

Waiting on Martha's Vineyard for the arrival of the Clintons, Jacqueline had coffee with Teddy Kennedy, who had always adored her. Showing her political savvy, she suggested to him that he should go down to the pier to greet the Clintons when they arrived aboard Maurice's yacht.

"But Maurice is there," Teddy said.

"Maurice isn't running for re-election," she reminded him. "The place will be swarming with reporters and photographers."

During her stay, Hillary had an opportunity for several long talks with Jacqueline. She even revealed to the former First Lady her intention of eventually becoming the first serious female presidential candidate in U.S. history.

"But I'll have to wait until the 21st Century

Diamond merchant Maurice Tempelsman was an unlikely beau for Jackie in her declining years, but he won her over with his financial savvy and his loving support of her. "Other husbands and lovers have betrayed me," she told Ted Sorensen. "But Maurice will always be there for me."

Caroline and John Jr. were at first suspicious of him, but he won them over, too, by showing his love and devotion to their mother.

Maurice recalled that one of his most painful experiences involved the compilation of Jackie's final will and testament, a long, complex document that left most of her estate to her son and daughter. After Jackie's funeral, John Jr. told Maurice that he'd like to have his mother's apartment for himself to live in during the renovation of his loft in Tri-Be-Ca. The older man moved into the Sherry Netherland.

Later, with Caroline, John sold Jackie's apartment at 1040 Fifth Avenue to oil tycoon David Koch for $9.5 million, and John and Caroline, over Maurice's protests, auctioned off their mother's possessions at Sotheby's.

tury," Hillary said. "We shared our hopes, our dreams, our disappointments. We even talked of the possible fear of assassination that every president and his First Lady have to deal with in the White House. In all, our time together was magical."

Sometimes, Katherine Graham, publisher of *The Washington Post,* sat in on discussions with Jacqueline and Hillary. She heard Jacqueline say to Hillary, "You and I grew up in different times. In my day, no woman really thought she might ever be president. Our greatest dream was to grow up and marry a powerful man, preferably a rich one. That was what we were taught in Newport."

"When I decided to attach myself to a handsome young senator from Massachusetts, I seriously thought he might be president one day, even though he was Catholic," Jacqueline said. "I was prepared to overlook a lot to become a small part of history, if only a footnote. You, on the other hand, might end up making history all on your own."

"One difference in our situations," Hillary said, "is that you suffered in silence if Jack let you down. I have to read about Bill's shortcomings on the front page."

Jacqueline was discreet in referring to the womanizing of both Bill and JFK. She then issued a warning, commenting on "the peculiar and dangerous attraction evoked by charismatic politicians. Bill's personal magnetism might evoke strong feelings in women. He might become a target. He has to be careful, so very, very careful."

Graham, with her keen eye, noted that Jacqueline seemed slightly awkward around Bill and when they

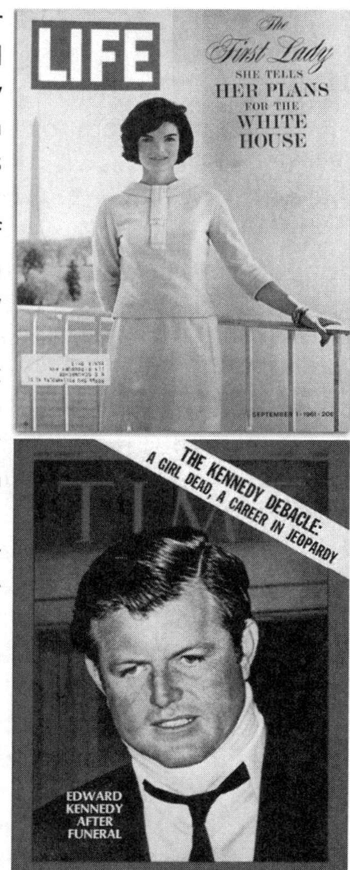

Although their love affair usually escaped press attention, Jackie and her brother-in-law, Teddy Kennedy, shared many intimate moments.

Long after her departure from the White House, they stood each other though one crisis after another.

She supported him during the disastrous aftermath of his drunken car accident at Chappaquidick, in which Kennedy "groupie," Mary Jo Kopechne, a secretarial assistant, was drowned, unleashing a hornet's nest of accusations about sexual improprieties associated with his election campaign.

And during her financial negotiations with the (hostile) estate of her just-deceased husband, Artistotle Onassis, Teddy was the man who came to her rescue.

were alone, she asked Jacqueline about that.

In a rare moment of indiscretion, Jacqueline revealed to her that for several years, Bill had pursued her.

Graham already knew about Bill's affair with her friend, Pamela Harriman, and she just assumed that Bill wanted "another feather in his cap" through the seduction of the second *grande dame* of the Democratic Party.

Jacqueline, according to the source noted below, confessed that one afternoon, Bill had visited her Fifth Avenue apartment and had almost forcibly tried to seduce her, even though she protested his sexual advances. "We almost indulged in a wrestling match," she described to Graham. "It was most embarrassing. I mean, I was flattered that I turned him on so much at my age, but Bill was just like Jack in the sense that neither of them wanted to take 'no' for an answer."

"Ever since that day, I prefer not to be alone in the same room with Bill. I fear he's a man who never gives up."

When Graham returned to Washington, she found Jacqueline's story so tantalizing, she wanted to share it. Obviously, she couldn't print it in *The Washington Post,* but she relayed the story over dinner one night to author Truman Capote.

That turned out to be a big mistake. Capote was drinking heavily at the time. Although he was sworn to secrecy by Graham, he nonetheless spread the story of Bill's

In her memoirs, Hillary referred to her friend, Katherine Graham, the publisher of The Washington Post, as "always gracious." When Bill confessed his fling with Monica Lewinsky, Hillary turned to Graham for support and sympathy.

The publisher had had her own experience "with the agony of infidelity" based on her own cheating husband, Philip Graham, who had committed suicide in 1963.

Perhaps Hillary never learned that Graham, in a rare moment of indiscretion, betrayed her confidence to a gossipy author by the name of Truman Capote.

Author Truman Capote is seen escorting Katherine Graham, his guest of honor, to his "Party of the Century" at the Plaza Hotel in New York in November of 1966. In the wake of the gossipy turmoil unleased by that event, Capote observed, "I invited 500 guests, and made 15,000 enemies."

Graham was a veteran hostess herself, entertaining the power elite of Washington. An invitation to her mansion in Georgetown was as desirable as an invitation to the White House.

She confided to Capote, "In Washington, there is always a dilemma: Too much booze combined with conflicting ideologies can be lethal."

attempted rape of Jacqueline throughout Washington and New York. The rumor even made it to Hollywood.

When confronted with his gossipy indiscretion, Capote became defensive: "I'm just a born storyteller," he said. "And an imp."

***

In October of 1993, Jacqueline stood next to Bill at the re-dedication of the John F. Kennedy Library.

He later told friends, "I'd heard reports that she was ill, but she appeared quite hearty the last time we talked. She gave no inkling of settling down and cutting back on her workload. She told me that she planned to continue working as an editor for at least another twenty years."

Nine months later, in May of 1994, Jacqueline died at the age of sixty-four, succumbing to non-Hodgkin's lymphoma

"I wept," Hillary said. "She was too young to die."

After Jacqueline's death, Bill wrote: "Jackie is the most private of great public icons. To most people, she is an indelible image of elegance, grace, and grieving. To those lucky enough to know her, she was what she was and much more—a bright woman full of life, a fine mother, and a good friend. I know Hillary will miss her, too. She had been a source of constant encouragement, sound advice, and genuine friendship to my wife."

***

September of 1993 represented one of the high points in Hillary's career. She had to appear before committees from both the House and the Senate. She was forced to testify before one of her most avowed enemies, Dick Armey, a tall, blunt, booted Texan who originally came from the cold winds of North Dakota. He had been elected to the House of Representatives, as a Republican from Texas, in 1984.

[Armey would later become closely associated with Minority Whip Newt Gingrich in drafting the very conservative Republican Manifesto known as the "Contract with America," many of whose proposals were later vetoed by Clinton.]

At last, Armey and Hillary came face to face at a hearing. Before it began, he said Hillary's health care reform bill was a "Kevorkian prescription for the jobs of American men and women."

[Dr. Jack Kevorkian was a leading advocate of legalized assisted suicide.]

As the cameras began rolling, Armey promised representatives of the networks that he'd make the inquiry "as exciting as possible."

"I'm sure you'll do that," Hillary shot back at him.

"We'll do the best we can," he responded.

"You and Dr. Kevorkian," she said with a smirk, eliciting laughter from the audience.

"I have been told about your charm and wit," Armey said to her. "Let me say this: Reports of your charm are overstated and reports of your wit are understated."

Texas Congressman and House Majority leader Dick Armey *(depicted above in 1997)* had no admiration for Hillary—in fact, he detested what he called "America's Evita Péron."

"Her thoughts sound like Karl Marx. She hangs around a lot of Marxists. All her friends are Marxists."

Historians later concluded that Hillary's appearance was the highlight of the Clinton Administration's first term. The press, in an "about face," actually praised her for a change. "It's a long way to Tipperary on getting health care reform through Congress," claimed *The Washington Post,* "but Mrs. Clinton has made a brilliant beginning. She is a super star."

Writing in *The New York Times,* Maureen Dowd asserted, "It was, in a way, the official end of the era in which presidential wives pretended to know less than they did and to be advising less than they were."

In the end, however, Hillary's health reform bill became a rallying cry for her enemies, especially the most ardent of anti-Clinton zealots. Powerful interests lined up against her, including the medical profession, small businesses, and all Republicans, who planned to use her advocacy of it to defeat the Democrats in the 1996 fall elections.

"Bill Clinton Placed My Hand On His Aroused Penis."

—Kathleen Willey

On March 15, 1998, Kathleen Willey, a former White House volunteer who had been described as "a widow with Junior League looks," appeared on the TV news program, *60 Minutes.*

She alleged that on November 29, 1993, President Clinton had sexually assaulted her in the Oval Office. She claimed that "he had groped her and placed her hand on his aroused penis."

She gave her reason for appearing on the show and for going public with her revelations as: "Too many lies are being told, too many lives are being ruined."

Willey's name had surfaced when she had been called upon to testify in the Paula Jones sexual harassment case against the president.

The White House immediately denied the assault charges made by Willey. To fight back, they released details contained within about a dozen letters, and an equivalent number of phone messages she'd placed to the president through the White House switchboard after the harassment was alleged to have taken place. In each of these, she appeared "friendly and eager for more contact with Bill Clinton." At one point, she referred to herself as his "Number One Fan."

With a certain glee, Bill's enemies were fast to trumpet Willey's accusations, immediately conspiring to broadcast them to a wider audience.

House Speaker Newt Gingrich and Congressman Henry Hyde petitioned the office of Kenneth Starr, the independent counsel investigating the president. Starr was asked if his special prosecutors had compiled enough incriminating evidence against the president to justify the debut by the House of Representatives of an impeachment process.

Democratic activist Kathleen Willey charged that President Clinton sexually assaulted her in the Oval Office.

"Clinton never seemed to understand where he lived and worked—and had sex—in the White House," she claimed.

"He treated the people's house as if it were a 'cool pad' back in Hot Springs, Arkansas, or a frat house at a college."

When Bill learned what Hyde was trying to do, he said, "My mother raised me to look for good in everybody. When I watched the vituperative Mr. Hyde, I was sure there must be a Dr. Jekyll in there somewhere, but I was having a hard time finding it."

Willey's accusations were met with immediate skepticism from the media. Gene Lyons, the Arkansas journalist and author, wrote: "Here's a woman who said that her husband came home one day and told her that he had bankrupted the family, and would have to sell everything to keep himself out of jail. So they had a big fight, her husband ran away, and the first thing she did was run to the White House, where the president put his hands on her body, and then came home and, *whoops!,* her husband is dead. How much of a coincidence is that?"

After the alleged groping incident, Willey

went home, only to learn that her husband had committed suicide that afternoon, leaving her with a monstrous debt, including long overdue payments to the Internal Revenue Service.

Her husband, Ed Willey, Jr., had gone to a remote, forested part of King and Queen County, Virginia, northeast of Richmond, and had put a pistol in his mouth and pulled the trigger, presumably dying instantly.

As Willey later stated, "It did not escape my notice that five months after Vince Foster drove to a wooded area in in Virginia and put a pistol to his mouth, so did my husband."

In his memoirs, Bill wrote: "Willey's story was not true. We had evidence that cast doubt on her story, including the affidavit of her friend, Julie Hiatt Steele, who claimed that Willey had asked her to lie by saying, under oath, that she had described the alleged episode to Steele shortly after it happened, when in fact, she hadn't."

Bill noted that Starr had granted Willey immunity, even after she was caught falsifying information about her involvement—in an episode otherwise unrelated to her allegations about Bill—with a married man.

In outrageous contrast, Steele, a registered Republican, was indicted, the legal charges against her ruining her financially. Starr's office even went so far as to question the legality of her adoption of a child from Romania.

Linda Tripp, the former White House aide who was a key figure in the Monica Lewinsky hearings, testified about Willey before a grand jury. She claimed that Willey had pursued a romance with Clinton and that she routinely attended events at which the president would appear. "She wore a black dress she thought he liked," Tripp claimed.

According to Robert Ray, who was appointed as a replacement for Kenneth Starr in 1999, "Willey's deposition testimony differed from her grand jury testimony on material aspects of the alleged incident." Ray had wanted to prosecute Willey for perjury, but by that time, she was protected by the immunity agreement Starr had granted her.

Bill said that the Willey claims just faded away when it was revealed that she had sought $300,000 from a tabloid in an attempt to sell her story.

But instead of fading away, in 2007, despite the inconsistencies in her story, Willey published a tell-all book entitled *Target—Caught in the Crosshairs of Bill and Hillary Clinton,* releasing it at the time Hillary was gearing up to run for president in 2008.

Willey was luridly graphic in describing the incident that she alleged had taken place in the Oval Office:

> *"Clinton kissed me on the mouth, and, before I knew it, I was backed up into the corner, against the closed bathroom door. His hands were*

all over me. I tried to twist away. He was too powerful. Then he took my hand and put it on his erect penis. I was shocked. I yanked my hand away, but he was forceful. He ran his hands all over me, touching me everywhere, up my skirt, over my blouse, my breasts. My mind raced. His face had turned beet red."

She went on to claim that after that, she managed to escape his clutches and fled from his office.

In that memoir, she vengefully editorialized:

"Make no mistake. Bill Clinton is not a feminist. He raped Juanita Broaddrick. He assaulted me. He promised young Monica Lewinsky a future with him. He objectifies women, treats them like trash, and calls them names worse than 'bimbo.' He holds all women in contempt, except those who tell him what to do, who guide him, and discipline him and mother him, as Hillary does."

"She enabled her husband to degrade, abuse, and assault women for more than thirty years. She condoned his behavior, facilitated it, and swept up after it. In doing so, she stopped at nothing, while Bill victimized women. She kicked us when we were down—smearing us in the media, digging into our backgrounds, humiliating and terrorizing us."

***

Halloween of 1993 arrived at the White House like a poisonous brew blended by a cackling witch.

Although she'd presumed that the failed Whitewater real estate development was behind Bill and her, Hillary read in *The Washington Post* that a criminal investigation of the Madison Guaranty Savings & Loan had been launched: The bank had been run by their former partners, Jim and Susan McDougal, and it was an entity separate from the Whitewater development deal. Nonetheless, by implication, the Clintons were still being pulled into the quagmire.

"Bill and I never deposited money in the Savings & Loan, and we never borrowed from it," Hillary maintained. "The name Whitewater came to represent a limitless investigation of our lives that cost the taxpayers more than $70 million for the Independent Counsel's investigation alone."

Whitewater signaled a new tactic in political warfare: Investigation as a weapon for political destruction. In the wake of *The Washington Post's* article,

The New York Times followed soonafter with an *exposé* of sorts of its own to protect themselves.

Hillary hired David Kendall to represent them in the Whitewater case. He immediately commandeered the files that had been removed, because of her instructions, from Vince Foster's office in the wake of his suicide. Kendall then told the Clintons that trying to re-create McDougal's bizarre paper trail was "like shoveling smoke."

Then he flew to Arkansas to visit the site of the Whitewater Development. There, he discovered prominent signs announcing that it was FOR SALE. Soon, another sign went up as a warning to reporters flocking there: "GO HOME, IDIOTS!"

The media's obsession with Whitewater continued though the Christmas holidays, when cancer-stricken Virginia Kelley flew in from Arkansas for a final visit to the White House.

Senate Minority leader Bob Dole called for Attorney General Janet Reno to appoint an Independent Counsel to investigate Whitewater.

In an attempt to deflect Dole's demands for an Independent Counsel, White House aides such as David Gergen and Stephanopoulos urged Bill and Hillary to turn over the Whitewater documents to *The Washington Post,* since they had done no wrong.

But Hillary stridently vetoed the idea. She had been intimately involved in the deal, especially because of her close association with the Rose Law Firm in Little Rock.

"Her strategy failed," Stephanopoulos said later, in an analysis of her decision. "The story did not die as she wanted it to. Most media attacks, including one from *Newsweek,* suggested a cover-up."

Through all the trials and tribulations of both Bill and Hillary, tight-lipped, slender, fastidious, and camera-shy David Kendall (*depicted above)* has been their dogged lawyer, fighting their battles on the front lines.

Whether it involved an Arkansas land deal, a blue dress with semen stains, mysterious files reported missing, or litigation linked to investigators like Kenneth Starr, he was always there defending his clients. He was still on the scene in 2015, defending Hillary during "all that insane" e-mail furor.

Reared in a Quaker family in Indiana, Kendall is the son of a grain elevator manager and a schoolteacher mother. As a lawyer, he is not known as a pit bull, but he enjoys the complete trust of both Bill and Hillary.

The New York Times, on December 20, 1993, rather accurately stated, "Based on what's publicly known, there's probably not a crippling scandal here. But the White House is behaving as if there were."

In Congress and in the media, there were calls for a full-scale investigation into Whitewater. Horrified, Clinton aide David Gergen proclaimed, "The White

House was in free fall."

Looking back, Stephanopoulos recalled, "If a genie offered me the chance to turn back time and undo a single decision from my White House tenure, I'd head straight to the Oval Office Dining Room on December 11, 1993, and get Hillary and Bill to change their minds about denying *The Washington Post* access to the Whitewater documents. It was a moment—and a decision—that changed history."

Carl Bernstein wrote, "For the first time in history, a president's wife sent her husband' presidency off the rails."

Historian William H. Chafe said: "Had David Gergen and Stephanopoulos prevailed, there would have been no Independent Counsel, no Kenneth Starr, no Monica Lewinsky, no impeachment. Instead, Hillary made the call to say 'no.' And the results were catastrophic."

***

As if that wasn't enough, Hillary received a frightening "Doomsday call," as she characterized it later, from David Kendall, their personal lawyer charged with all legalities associated with Whitewater.

Kendall quickly summarized an article by David Brock that had appeared in the right-wing monthly, *The American Spectator.*

According to Hillary, "Our attorney, David, summarized the article for me. Brock's main sources were four Arkansas troopers from Bill's former bodyguard detail. The stories were worse than the most salacious garbage in supermarket tabloids. The troopers claimed that they had procured women for Bill when he was governor of Arkansas."

At the White House, in horror, Hillary watched the story unfold on CNN's nightly news, noting that they led off the broadcast by airing charges of Bill's illicit sex romps. Other *exposés* were on the way, including a devastating one that appeared in the *Los Angeles Times.*

"All of this was going on during our first Christmas at the White House," Hillary said. "It was our worst Christmas in memory."

After Christmas, Hillary summoned Stephanopoulos and some of her chief White House aides for an emergency meeting. The question before them was whether to create an Independent Counsel's office to investigate Whitewater and other charges. The Independent Counsel's office was scheduled to expire in January of 1994. For it to continue, it would need new authorization from the government.

Stephanopoulos warned that if she didn't agree to submit evaluation of the affair to an Independent Counsel, the Republicans might use that against her and sabotage her health-care reform plan.

Hillary seemed to become ballistic after hearing that. For the first time, her staff noticed tears forming in her eyes. "Bill and I were out there alone during the campaign, and I'm feeling very lonely right now," she said. "Nobody is fighting for me."

Suddenly, regaining her composure, and as part of what appeared to be an abrupt shift in her mood, she turned to Stephanopoulos. "I don't want to hear anything more! I want us to fight! I want a campaign *NOW!* If you don't believe us, you should leave!"

Then she stormed out of the conference.

He was shocked that she would dare to question his loyalty. He went into a rage. After all, he'd seen them through all the battles—gays in the military, Gennifer Flowers, Whitewater, and many others.

"I couldn't believe I was being attacked for being disloyal, for abandoning the Clintons," he said. "Fuck her! I'm arguing for what's best—for her, for him, for all of us and everything we're fighting for. *Fuck her!*"

Only one bright note emerged from what looked like *Götterdammerung.* Soonafter, Maggie Williams, Hillary's Chief of Staff, appeared with an issue of *USA Today.* From it, she read aloud that Bill and Hillary had been voted "The World's Most Admired Couple."

***

On her last day of her final visit to the White House, before her departure for Las Vegas, Virginia Kelley read the Troopergate revelations in *The American Spectator.* Then she turned to her son: "Mr. President, these Arkansas boys aren't the brightest bulbs in the chandelier. I just wish they could find another way to make a living."

TROOPERGATE

As if there weren't enough "gate" scandals plaguing Bill Clinton,as president, his enemies soon dredged up yet another from his political past.

It involved the spread of stories about his womanizing years before, during his terms as governor of Arkansas. They were largely promulgated by Cliff Jackson, his enemy from the bad old days of partisan politics in the Deep South.

Exposed and amplified with right wing money, Bill was "tarred and feathered" as "the Son of the Devil."

Allegations were made that he used state funds to launch and maintain a series of affairs with young women with the collusion and assistance of State Troopers.

"All of these guys were pissed off at me because I didn't give the fuckers government jobs," Bill asserted.

David Brock of *The American Spectator*, an on-again, off-again Clinton hater, broke the revelations. He later said, "I hit the president like a ton of bricks. I threw in every titillating morsel the troopers claimed."

Chapter Fifteen

"Dogpatch Madonna"

Paula Jones Sues

for Sexual Harassment & Claims She Can Reveal "Distinguishing Marks" on the Presidential Penis

Bill's Lawyers Work Frantically to Suppress Photos of His "Johnny Reb" Being Made Public

Special Prosecutor Kenneth Starr Arrives Not to "Investigate" Bill & Hillary, but to Orchestrate an Impeachment

"I looked up from my desk and saw Bill Clinton staring at me," said Paula Jones. "The rest is history."

Bill Clinton told Kenneth Starr, "I do not consider fellatio, fondling, mutual masturbation, to fall under the court's definition of sex."

The day after Chelsea's 17th birthday, Monica Lewinsky put on a navy blue dress from the GAP before visiting Bill Clinton.

What followed almost ruined him.

Bill and Hillary had survived the first year of his presidency. But now, they were plunged into 1994. He would later write, "The year was one of the hardest in my life, one in which important successes in foreign and domestic policy were overshadowed by the demise of health-care reform and an obsession with bogus scandal. It began with personal heartbreak and ended in political disaster."

Author David Brock, who sounded Troopergate's first call to arms, later came to question the testimonies and veracity of "these bubba boys from Arkansas."

He was referring to the death of his mother in January and the end-of-the-year election losses the Democrats later suffered, one of the most painful in recent memory.

When George Stephanopoulos dropped into the Oval Office, he found Bill enraged. "I'm getting god damn tired about all these assholes, including these state troopers from Little Rock, claiming how they had to procure women for me. I may be a fat old man these days, but back in Arkansas, I didn't need any fucking bastard to procure gals for me. I could get my own."

After reading daily reports of new accusations against his boss, Stephanopoulos said, "No other president had ever put up with as much crap as they tossed at Bill."

Author David Brock, who had exposed the Troopergate scandal, later claimed, "I threw in every titillating morsel and dirty quote the troopers from Arkansas served up."

Almost daily, aides, and especially Hillary, had to deal with Bill's frustrations. He told Dick Morris, "Here I am trying to bring about world peace with the Russians, and help Hillary establish health-care reform, but all the god damn press wants to talk about is Whitewater, or perhaps an alleged mole on my dick."

As Bill and Hillary made plans to head to Moscow, Republicans in Wash-

Hillary's Health-Care Reform is Destroyed by the GOP After Democrats are Bloodied & Defeated, and Republicans Commandeer Both the House and the Senate

ington were screaming for an Independent Counsel to investigate not only Whitewater, but Vince Foster's suicide, which was to an increasing degree being gossiped about as a murder.

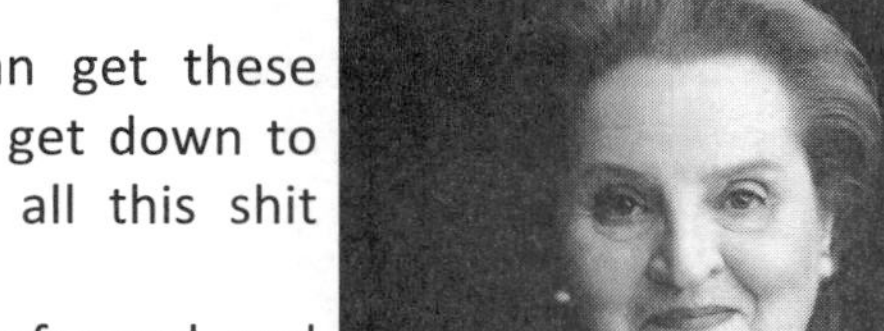

Above, a trio of mug shots snapped during the incarceration for civil disobedience of former dissident and, arguably, Central Europe's hippest politician, Václav Havel, first president (1993-2003) of the Czech Republic.

During their nightlife crawls through Prague, he and Bill bonded effortlessly.

Treasury Secretary Lloyd Bentsen advised Bill, "It's time to lance the boil, perhaps appoint an Independent Counsel, so we can get these investigations over with and get down to some serious business—not all this shit being thrown at us!"

Communications were enhanced by the presence and collaboration of Madeleine Albright, Bill's Czech-born, diplomatically savvy Secretary of State, Madeleine Albright.

Fluent in English, French, Russian, and Czech; she speaks and reads Polish and Serbo-Croatian as well. Like Hillary, she's an alumnus of Wellesley College.

In the wake of his mother's funeral, and perhaps as a means of escaping calls for his resignation as president, Bill flew to Europe, a diplomatic mission whose highlights included a visit to Moscow. Before that, in the Czech Republic, he met with Václav Havel, its president. Accompanying him was Bill's Ambassador to the United Nations, Madeleine Albright, who would converse with Havel in his own language.

Havel took Bill on a tour of Prague's "hot jazzclubs," where young people had supported his "Velvet Revolution." At one of them, Bill played "Summertime" and "My Funny Valentine" on a gift from Havel, a specially made saxophone.

He also made a brief stop in Kiev to meet with Leonid Kravchuk, president of Ukraine, before continuing on to Moscow. He supported Kravchuk in his program to disarm and remove nuclear missiles in his country still in place from the Soviet Cold War.

Hillary and Chelsea caught up with Bill in Moscow, where they lodged in guest quarters at the Kremlin. In the dead of a Russian winter, they met with Boris Yeltsin, president of the Russian Federation, who thanked Clinton for recent American aid.

In calls to Washington, Bill was told, "The whole town, including the press, has only one thing on its mind: Whitewater." He was informed that even former President Carter had joined the Republicans in calling for the appointment of an Independent Counsel.

Chief aides David Gergen, David Kendall, and Bernie Nussbaum were still loudly articulate about the dangers of appointing an Independent Counsel. After endless debates, and sometimes heated arguments with Hillary, Bill agreed at last to have Janet Reno appoint one.

When Nussbaum heard that Bill might allow a special prosecutor, he asked him, "Are you going to put your head in that noose?"

In March, Nussbaum submitted his resignation as White House Counsel, based partly on his perception that he saw only "gloom and doom" ahead for Hillary and Bill. As the president later admitted, "Bernie was among the first to see the handwriting on the wall. If only we'd listened to him."

Bill later wrote: "Though I had said I could live with a special prosecutor, I almost didn't live through it. It was the worst presidential decision I ever made, wrong on the facts, wrong on the law, wrong on politics, wrong for the presidency and the Constitution. Perhaps I did it because I was completely exhausted and grieving over mother."

While Bill was still in Moscow, Janet Reno appointed Robert B. Fiske as special prosecutor. He'd been a prominent trial lawyer in Manhattan and a former U.S. Attorney General for the Southern District of New York. He immediately launched an investigation into Whitewater and the lingering controversy over the death of Vince Foster. Fiske announced to reporters that he wanted to resolve questions about Whitewater as "quickly as I can, consistent with doing the job right." He also announced that he planned to question, under oath, both the President and the First Lady.

Before their departure from Europe, the Clintons flew to Belarus and then on to Geneva, where Bill met with President Hafez Al-Assad of Syria. *[President of Syria from 1971-2000, Hafez Al-Assad was replaced by his authoritarian son, Bashar Al-Assad, in 2000. Both father and son described their regimes as secular, although foreign commentators have contended that their regimes exploited and continue to exploit ethnic and sectarian tensions as a reinforcement of their power.]*

Clinton referred to Hafez as "a ruthless but brilliant man, who had once wiped out a whole village as a lesson to his opponents." Although Hafez Al-Assad had been a known supporter of terrorist groups, he left the meeting promising Bill that he would make peace with Israel.

***

Back in Washington, Bill faced a hurricane. "Everything seemed to happen at once."

Los Angeles had recently suffered through one of its worst earthquakes, requiring $16 billion in Federal aid for repairs and rebuilding of 600,000 businesses and homes.

Bill's State of the Union address was delivered on January 25, as he called for welfare reform and a health-care overhaul. But Newt Gingrich in the House and Bob Dole in the Senate vowed to work to destroy all of his proposals.

Disaster lay ahead, as Bill moved into February, hosting the third National Prayer Breakfast. Mother Theresa was its guest speaker.

By the second week of that month, Bosnian Serbs bombed the market place at Sarajevo, killing dozens of innocents. NATO threatened to retaliate against the Serbs with bombing raids. The Serbs violated an agreement, and on the 28th of the month, NATO fighters shot down four of their planes after they flew into the no-fly zone. This was the first military action NATO had taken in its forty-year history.

"Another Eruption on Mount Bimbo"

—The Washington Post

As the new year of 1994 deepened, the White House was reeling from ongoing anti-Clinton attacks on radio, TV, and in newspapers, magazines, and books. A whole new crop—seemingly an industry until itself—witnessed the publication of at least a dozen vituperative books condemning the Clintons.

Many of Bill's enemies were reading *Slick Willie: Why America Cannot Trust Bill Clinton,* by Floyd G. Brown. In this indictment, Bill was labeled as a criminal, a liar, and a man dangerous to America. Allegations laid out in the book focused on bimbo eruptions, charges of laundering of campaign contributions, and alleged "deals" with foreign governments to benefit one man: Bill Clinton himself.

With her recent husband, Steve Jones, Paula Corbin Jones had moved to California, where he could pursue an acting career. On a visit back to Little Rock, a so-called friend had handed her a copy of David Brock's pejorative-laced article in *The American Spectator.* In it, she was identified only as "Paula."

"Oh, my God," she said, after reading the article. "That's complete bullshit. It's a lie!"

In her search for an apology from the president, Paula somehow managed to end up in the Little Rock office of one of Bill's most dangerous political enemies, Cliff Jackson. He had been a classmate of Bill's at Oxford and was one of the most aggressive persons on record in his exposure and condemnation of Bill's draft-dodging.

Jackson came up with the idea of "piggybacking' Paula's sexual harassment charges onto the Troopergate revelations at a joint press conference in February, within the context of the right-wing Conservative Political Action Conference.

Paula's decision to present her accusations alongside those of the former State Troopers from Arkansas was viewed as an "odd marriage" by reporters, since each of the groups was touting a different version of her brief encounter with Bill.

"This Paula Jones has fallen in with the Clinton haters," Hillary privately told her aides. "I don't think she knows the difference between a Republican and a Democrat."

Despite the scandals articulated at the press conference, a lot of the mainstream media seemed reluctant to air Paula's sensational charges, as she had no actual proof of an encounter with Bill other than an allegation by a state trooper.

One trooper claimed that he had personally escorted Paula to Bill's hotel room, from which she emerged an hour later. The trooper suggested that she'd had a satisfying sexual encounter and that she'd make herself available to become the governor's regular girlfriend.

Having flown in from Long Beach, California, Paula, with her husband, Steve, introduced herself to America at the Omni Shoreham Hotel in Washington, D.C. State troopers Roger Perry and Larry Patterson were the press conference's other star attractions.

Clinton haters were provided with a toll-free number that would accept contributions for the "Troopergate Fund," whose purpose seemed to be to line the pockets of Perry, Patterson, and their lawyers.

It was hoped that Jones' allegations would bring new life to Troopergate, which, during February of 1994, was "losing steam" and getting rather stale in newsrooms across the country

To pay for Paula's expenses, including the cost of her trip from California, funds were provided by the right-wing Legal Affairs Council, which had previously raised $300,000 in support of Oliver North's Iran-Contra defense.

Newt Gingrich, who would become Speaker of the House later that year, showed up to shake the hands of the troopers.

Any reluctance in the media to write about Paula Jones changed on May 6, 1994, when she filed a $700,000 sexual harassment lawsuit. She was just two days before the state of limitations ran out for the filing of such a case. When she did, however, mainstream media picked it up, often headlining her allegations on the frontpages of America's hometown newspapers.

Paula's husband, Steve Jones, announced to the press, "Bill Clinton is the scum of the earth."

Her lawyers informed Bill that they would drop the case if he would sign the following statement:

> *"I do not deny meeting Paula Jones on May 8, 1991, in a room at the Excelsior Hotel in Little Rock. She did not engage in any improper or sexual conduct. I believe her to be a truthful and moral person."*

The hostelry in Little Rock previously known as the Excelsior Hotel will live in infamy.

It was here that Governor Clinton was alleged to have dropped his trousers, exposed his erection, and invited Paula Jones to perform fellatio.

Like Jones herself, the hotel has undergone a complete makeover and is today identified as the Peabody Hotel Little Rock.

Many guests at check-in request the room where the Jones/Clinton encounter was said to have occurred.

When Hillary read the statement, she exploded, warning him that signing it was as good as admitting that her allegations were true. Her refusal to allow him to sign that document was viewed as one of the biggest mistakes of her life. It would lead to untold horrors for them, including millions of dollars in legal fees and revelations that would ultimately build a case for Bill's impeachment.

In a bizarre twist, unknown in the history of any other U.S. President, Paula claimed she could describe "distinguishing characteristics" on the presidential penis.

Talking to his chief aides, Bill said he would agree to have a urologist visit the Oval Office "and examine my Johnny Reb to prove she's lying." It was speculated, perhaps wrongly, that he had a rather obvious mole on his penis. Other reporters in their stories placed the mole in a position right above the ginger-colored hairs on his crotch.

With the understanding that Paula's allegations by now had spread throughout the nation, comics and talk show hosts turned the event into a carnival, mocking both Paula and Bill. The Las Vegas late-night comedy circuits produced the roughest jokes of all. There, one of the comics asked, "Is it a Federal offense for a guy to try to get some pussy?"

James Carville suggested that an investigator might turn up anything if he flashed a hundred dollar bill in a redneck trailer camp.

Reporters from all over the country flocked to Paula's hometown, Lonoke, Arkansas. One journalist filed his opinion of the town, calling it "a place of big hair and tight jeans and girls whose dreams rarely go farther than a stint at a hairdresser's school, an early marriage, and a baby named Brittany, Tiffany, or Brooke."

Reporters from *Newsweek* visited Little Rock for an *exposé* in its issue of May 29, 1994. They revealed that many persons who knew Paula scoffed at her claims.

In their book, *The Hunting of the President,* Joe Conason and Gene Lyons wrote: "Paula Jones' former coworkers said that although Paula kept them entertained with detailed soap opera accounts of her love life, she had never mentioned her encounter with Clinton. Describing her as a 'Dogpatch Madonna,' associates portrayed her as an unreliable, self-dramatizing person who had made a pest of herself hanging around the reception desk outside the governor's office for months following the allegedly horrifying incident at the Excelsior Hotel, prattling like a starstruck teenager about Clinton's sex appeal and his hair."

Mike Gauldin, a former press aide to Bill when he was governor, said, "I remember Paula Corbin. I had to listen to hours and hours of beauty shop inane conversation—she was a groupie."

James D. Retter, in his book, *Anatomy of a Scandal,* said that Paula described her encounter with Bill as having taken place at around 2:30PM. However, reporters learned that Bill, on the day of the alleged incident, had delivered a breakfast speech at the Excelsior at 8:30AM, and that his activities throughout the rest of that afternoon were well documented. They included an active involvement at a function at the Governor's Mansion where his presence was attested to by at least a hundred eyewitnesses.

To prepare for the upcoming lawsuit, Bill and Hillary hired Robert Bennett, the relatively liberal older brother of the arch conservative, right-winger William (Bill) Bennett.

[According to Clark Clifford, "Bennett is usually hired not because he is a bulldog but because he has a reputation for working out settlements. Bennett himself says that when you have to go to trial, you have already lost."]

Betsey Wright was already at work, "digging for dirt" associated in any way with Paula. Her aides privately claimed that their goal was to brand Paula as "a lying slut."

Politicos later claimed that it was a tactical mistake to have hired Bennett as a lawyer just a few days before Paula Jones' lawyers faced a deadline for her to file her sexual harassment lawsuit. His engagement by the Clintons provided the heretofore reluctant *Washington Post* with the "news item" and excuse it needed to go public with a story, which many reporters on the *Post* had otherwise found "too repulsive for a family newspaper."

At one point, Bennett compared Paula "to a mongrel dog." It was later revealed that Bennett and his fellow lawyers worked over the next few years "battling to prevent candid snapshots of Clinton's sexual organs entered as evidence." This startling claim was not corroborated with any explanation of how Paula's lawyers had obtained photographs of "President Erectus."

In an attempt to block the lawsuit, Bennett filed a claim in court, alleging a "presidential immunity defense." In his brief, he stated that a sitting president should not have to face such a lawsuit until he was out of office, mainly because it would seriously interfere with the business of running the government of the United States.

His argument received mixed reviews. One reporter wrote, "It seems that the White House response is based mainly on the claim that Paula Jones is white trash. She does need a new wardrobe, new makeup, and a different hairdo. I'm sure the Republicans will soon bring in a stylist for her."

"In case you didn't read between the lines, the Clinton camp is trying to depict this backwoods girl as a floozy, a tramp, and a slut," the newsman charged. "Of course, that doesn't mean there is any evidence to prove she is either. Maybe she's just a girl who feels she's been wronged."

Another journalist asked, "What are all these charges and countercharges? Do they mean that Bill Clinton did not proposition this young woman in a hotel room in Little Rock? Or might they mean that he hit on her in so crude a manner because he thought she was a tramp? Had he thought she were a lady, he might have been more subtle in his approach instead of whipping it out and ordering her 'to suck it, bitch.'"

Author Candice E. Jackson noted, "The

Pudgy, right-wing blabbermouth, Jerry Falwell, evangelical Southern Baptist pastor, televangelist, and a conservative political commentator known for his stance against homosexuality, was the co-founder (in 1979) of the so-called Moral Majority. Publicly, he doubted Bill Clinton's Christianity.

Famous quotes attributed to Falwell include the following: 1) Christians, like slaves and soldiers, ask no questions. 2) The whole global warming thing is created to destroy America's free enterprise system and our economic stability. 3) Any sex outside of the marriage bond between a man and a woman is a violation of God's law, and 4) Bill Clinton took his marching orders directly from Satan.

Appearing on CNN a day after Falwell's death in 2007, journalist and social commentator Christopher Hitchens said, "The empty life of this ugly little charlatan proves only one thing: that you can get away with the most extraordinary offenses to morality and to truth in this country if you will just get yourself called 'reverend'."

Later, on C-SPAN, Hitchens said that "if Falwell had been given an enema, he could have been buried in a matchbox".

brief introduction of Paula Corbin (Jones) led to a five-and-a-half year court battle racking up millions of dollars in legal bills, a Supreme Court ruling that binds future presidents, bitter family relations, and the end of a marriage for Paula Jones. It also compelled Clinton to make disclosures about his personal life that he'd rather have taken to his grave."

Half of American Voters Brand Bill & Hillary as "Liars" And Many Others Believe They Are Murderers

One of Bill's major achievements during the first term of his presidency was the designation of Stephen Breyer in March to a seat on the Supreme Court, thereby replacing the retiring Henry Blackmun. Known for his pragmatic approach to Constitutional law, Breyer would generally be associated with the more liberal wing of the court. A former lecturer at Harvard Law School, starting in 1967, he later became assistant prosecutor on the Watergate Special Prosecution Force in 1973.

Also in March, a nationwide poll found that more than fifty percent of Americans believed that Bill and Hillary were lying about their involvement in Whitewater.

Taking advantage of that discontent, Jerry Falwell, leader of the so-called "Moral Majority," released a popular video, *Circle of Power,* that attracted thousands of viewers. A violent and impassioned indictment, the film accused the Clintons of major crimes that included plotting a plane crash in Alaska, and the smuggling of cocaine into the U.S. via a remote airport in Arkansas. The Clintons were even accused of murdering eyewitnesses who might have exposed their alleged crimes.

Events in April moved forward quickly both on the foreign and domestic fronts. Forces from NATO dropped bombs on Bosnia again, as the war there escalated.

On April 22, Richard M. Nixon, one of the most notorious presidents in the history of the Republic, died. To Bill's astonishment, he was asked to speak at his funeral. He was later heavily criticized by the most progressive members of his own party for finding some kind words to say about Nixon within the context of his eulogy.

Before the end of April, Bill was consoling Hillary, who feared—with good reason—that her health-care reform bill would collapse in fiery defeat. Misinformation was rampant, as exemplified by the American Council for Health Reform. It ridiculously claimed that under the Clinton proposal, a citizen would be jailed for five years for purchasing a health plan other than the one sanctioned and administered by the government.

Above, a disgraced former president, Richard Nixon, comes face to face with a disgraced sitting president, Bill Clinton.

Bill later claimed, with a sense of irony, "Compared to the Republicans who took over the party in the 80s and 90s, Nixon was a wild-eyed liberal."

Based on the roiling passions still evoked by Whitewater and all those "bimbo eruptions," Republican Congressman Newt Gingrich seized the moment. He released a rather unworkable "Contract With America," demanding a return to the country's greatness, which he said had been profoundly damaged during the short months of the Clinton Administration. He called for a balanced budget, welfare reform, congressional term limits, and other challenges—in essence, a return to Ronald Reagan's "Morning in America."

In 2010, Baylor University, a private Baptist University in Waco, Texas, disgraced itself by naming the notorious Kenneth Winston Starr as its 14th president.

Ironically, the swearing-in ceremony was held on Constitution Day, an event meant to honor a document that Bill Clinton charged Starr with repeatedly violating.

At his inauguration, Starr—outfitted with all the trappings, and regalia of *haute* academia—was falsely praised as exemplifying "great virtues of democracy, tolerance, patience, and respect for others" during his obsessive attempts to destroy Bill Clinton.

Both Bill and Hillary agreed that June, July, and August of 1994 was "The Summer of Our Discontent." Special Prosecutor Robert Fiske concluded that Vince Foster's death was, indeed, a suicide. This angered Republicans who wanted him to have ruled it as an unsolved murder. Fiske also concluded after a careful, rather intrusive investigation, that the Clintons had committed no crime based on their involvement in any aspect of the Whitewater development project.

Yet through a series of maneuvers, engineered by the Republicans, a three-judge Federal Appeals Court ruled that it would replace Fiske with a new Independent Counsel, Kenneth Starr. According to reports, Starr would reopen the entire investigation, beginning at ground zero. That meant that Whitewater as well as the "murder" of Vince Foster would each be meticulously, even obsessively, revisited and re-investigated yet again.

The lilywhite, sanctimonious, and rather pasty-looking Starr reminded many of a stern and judgmental Presbyterian deacon. Based on massive coverage in the press, he would soon become a household name, one that would live in infamy. Millions of dollars of taxpayer monies would be tossed away in his endless investigations, probing into the deepest secrets of Bill's private life.

A right-wing extremist, Starr had been a former solicitor general during the presidency of George H.W. Bush. As one journalist noted, "Starr came to Washington not to investigate the Clintons, but to bury them in an unmarked grave."

At the 1992 Republican National Convention, the Rev. Pat Robertson ridiculed and diminished presidential candidate Bill Clinton by mockingly referring to him as "Slick Willie."

Actually, Robertson wanted to be president himself, reigning over a nation that he hoped to reconfigure into an American theocracy.

Presenting absolutely no evidence, Robertson charged that Bill was committed to a radical plan to destroy the American family.

"He more or less suggested that God was a right wing Republican," wrote Roy Richardson. "Robertson should know. God gets him on the phone at frequent intervals to give him directions. God told Robertson that gays and lesbians are responsible for the most devastating of hurricanes and tornadoes. That would be laughable were it not for the fact that morons believe that crap."

A onetime Nixon operative, right-winger Roger Ailes created the most profitable propaganda machine in history, Fox News, an organization even Donald Trump has attacked.

Rolling Stone claimed, "The network deals in anger and bombast, with a virulent paranoid streak, and unending appeals to white resentment."

The magazine went on to assert, "Ailes repackaged Nixon for TV in 1968, papered over Reagan's budding Alzheimer's in 1984, and shamelessly stoked racial fears to re-elect the first president Bush, then waged a secret campaign on behalf of Big Tobacco to derail health care reform."

To their dismay, the Clintons also learned that Starr, as a "working attorney," had filed an anti-Clinton brief during the orchestration of Paula Jones' lawsuit. Astonishingly, a three-judge panel, when confronted with what many observers interpreted as a monumental conflict of interest, did not agree that that Starr's involvement prevented him from conducting a fair and reasonable investigation into charges against both Clintons.

Accusations against the Clintons came fast and furious. "The Rottweiler," Roger Ailes, the staunchly Republican president of CNBC, accused the Clintons of a "Whitewater cover-up, real-estate fraud, illegal contributions, abuse of power, and murder," a reference, of course, to the suicide of Vince Foster.

Clinton-hating, a new and ever-enraged American industry, had been born. One of its by-products was an unprecedented series of anti-Clinton books, many of which made charges so outrageous that only the mentally deficient would take them seriously.

An especially popular title that emerged from the poisonous stew was entitled, *Slick Willie: Why America Cannot Trust Bill Clinton* by Floyd G. Brown. It catalogued the usual charges—draft-dodging, drug dealing, Gennifer Flowers, and a lot more. The author labeled Bill as a "criminal and liar," and outlined "life-threatening" experiences" he suffered during the research of his book.

The first of the new crop of rabidly anti-Hillary books had appeared in 1993. Entitled *Big Sister Is Watching You,* it was written by Texe Marrs. In it, he accused Hillary of leading a coven of "the Fourth Reich of Femi-Nazis." She was accused of heading a "Marxist-Terrorist Network" and of "promoting a cruelly deceitful lesbian/homosexual agenda."

Marrs alleged that Hillary had used "awesome Gestapo powers, a coven of brutally corrupt women, a regiment of hardened militant feminists that included lesbians, sex perverts, child molester advocates, Christian haters, and the most doctrinaire of communists."

After her tenure as attorney general, Janet Reno went on to become an inspired spokesperson for the destructive effects of domestic violence.

Among the guilty parties cited was the poet who had been commissioned to read her poetry at Bill's Inauguration, Maya Angelou, a friend of Malcolm X who had referred to Caucasians as "white devils." Marrs claimed that Angelou was a former prostitute, stripper, and flag-burner. Other "Femi-Nazis" cited in the book included Dr. Joycelyn Elders, whom Marrs denounced as "The Condom Queen" based on sex education programs she had inaugurated or endorsed during her tenure as Surgeon General.

The relatively liberal Supreme Court Justice, Ruth Bader Ginsburg, whom Marrs labeled as 'the Scarlet Judge of the Supreme Court," was accused of advocating that children have sex with adults. He went on to designate Janet Reno as "the Duchess of Doom."

Reno came in for the harshest criticisms. Marrs wrote: "Janet Reno is a "queer choice for Attorney General." According to Florida Attorney Jack Thompson, "She is a hardened, closeted lesbian, who is so wickedly, sexually corrupt that she has frequently used call girls for sex and, as Dade County, Florida, attorney, she sexually harassed female county employees."

Both Bill and Hillary were attacked daily on the Rush Limbaugh Show. At one point, he claimed that Vince Foster was mysteriously murdered in an

Writer Texe Marrs, a former officer in the U.S. Air Force and faculty member at the University of Texas, runs a Christian ministry near Austin. He has received news coverage for his belief that the Oklahoma City bombing was planned and executed by the U.S. government; that the Holocaust never happened; and that Bill and Hillary Clinton are practitioners of Masonic magic and the occult mysticism of ancient Egypt.

His book, *Big Sister Is Watching You*, in his words, "provides convincing evidence that in the 60s, 'Hippie Hillary' aided the cop-killing, radical Black Panthers."

"Now she believes that God wants her to kill babies."

"Is Hillary—as rumored—a lesbian? Why did her female friends in the White House present her with a most unusual gift: a witch's hat?"

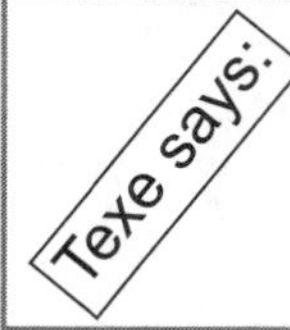

Femi-Nazis from the Fourth Reich

As defined by ultra-conservative radical, Texe Marrs

Surgeon General Jocelyn Elders, is "The Condom Queen"

Supreme Court Justice Ruth Bader Ginsburg,..."Favors legalizing child sex with adults."

Poet Laureate Maya Angelou, shown here reading a poem at Bill's inauguration, was "a former prostitute."

apartment owned by Hillary, and that she ordered that his body be removed and subsequently dumped in that park location in Virginia.

Mobs Attack Hillary's Bus Tour With Placards Alleging that She's "A Commie Bitch" and Urging Her to Return to Russia

As Hillary set out on a bus tour to win support for her health-care reform bill, she learned that cardboard cutouts of her were being used for target practice around the country. In every state in the Union, strong forces of opposition, usually operating on misinformation, a lot of it vengeful, attacked her. One printed handout, distributed nationwide, accused the Clintons of being "immoral communist homosexuals."

Betsey Wright claimed that Hillary put up a brave front. "She looked hard and tough, but this brittle exterior concealed a more vulnerable core."

"Hillary suffered a lot in silence," said Lisa Caputo, her press secretary. "Her greatest 'sin' was trying to bring affordable health care to those suffering or facing death for lack of money. For that, she was pilloried."

Hillary's send-off bus tour, evocative of the Freedom Rides through Southern states during the Civil Rights conflicts of the 1960s, was launched in Portland, Oregon. Immediately, her caravan's route was blocked by another bus wrapped in red tape, suggesting the government-sanctioned red tape that would proliferate if Hillary's health care reforms were passed by Congress. Overhead, a low-flying plane buzzed her caravan with a red banner proclaiming, "BEWARE THE PHONY EXPRESS."

Hillary's tour was labeled the "Health Security Express." She encountered unyielding hostility when she drove through Oregon and

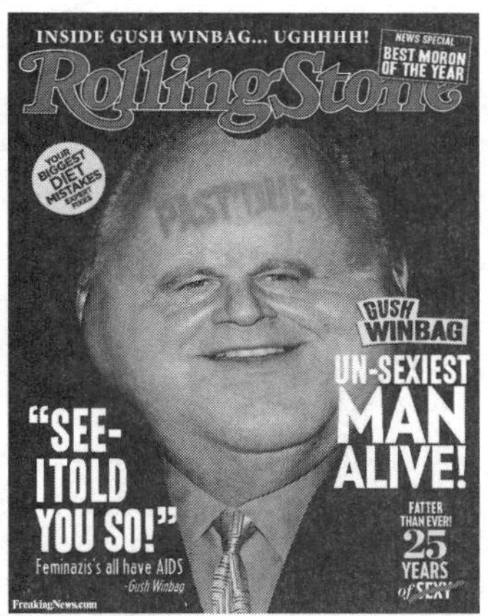

Michale Wolff, writing in *Vanity Fair*, documented Rush Limbaugh's jaunty, rapid-fire manner in an article, "The Man Who Ate the G.O.P."

In it, he described Limbaugh as "post-pill-popping, post-cochlear-implant (to correct his deafness), post-fat-and-sloppy. In a public appearance, he looked like Johnny Cash in a black suit and black shirt, two buttons open, hair slicked back. In the ailing radio industry, his audience is graying, the average age of his listeners is 67 and rising."

Wolff could have added, "His audience consists mostly of alienated white men born during an era that no longer exists."

Washington State. "I had not seen such faces of hate since the segregation battles of the 1960s," she said.

Before she set out on her tour, Dick Morris showed her one of his latest polls, which revealed that a preponderance of Americans thought she had "too much influence over the president." As some of the anti-Hillary forces so crudely put it, "Bill Clinton is pussy-whipped!"

Wherever she went seeking grassroots support, Hillary's bus tour encountered hundreds upon hundreds of protesters, many of these rallies carefully engineered by her worst enemies. Often, she looked out from her tinted window on the bus to see a familiar placard that read, "FUCK YOU, BITCH!" Never in her life had she faced such violence and condemnation.

At one point during the tour, on the outskirts of Seattle, demonstrators swarmed her motorcade. At that time, she was riding in a limousine. Fists pounded on her window as obscenities were screamed at her. About twelve young men attempted to overturn her car until Secret Service men, at gunpoint, forced them to retreat. After that assault, members of her security guard ordered her to wear a bulletproof vest throughout the remainder of the tour.

In her nightly calls to Bill, she poured out her anguish. "We've been trying to do something good for the American people, something that would save human lives. All I get are catcalls and charges of being a lesbian bitch. At one point, this horrible creature, a large woman, rose up from the audience and called out, 'Mrs. Clinton, how many pussies did you lick today?'"

On radio talk shows throughout the Northwest, hosts urged protesters to run out *en masse* to attack her bus tour. The loudest protesters, and the most potentially dangerous, were anti-abortion militants. Many of them would be arrested for their violence.

During the first months of becoming First Lady, Hillary launched a vigorous nationwide campaign for health care reform, suffering through the fractious, hot summer of 1993.

Ridiculed as a caricature of a power-hungry, radical feminist, she faced overpowering forces obsessed with undermining what she had hoped would be "the achievement of my lifetime."

Wherever she went, Hillary faced "BABY KILLER" signs.

When she tried to make her first address at a rally, she was shouted down. Someone had rigged up an audio system to drown her out. "Mrs. Clinton," a woman's voice boomed out during the debut of one of her addresses. "You must stop killing babies. God's hand of judgment will fall upon our nation. Until it does, killing babies must stop. Until that great day, the voice of unborn babies cry out for justice from their graves." The voice was suddenly silenced as the loudspeaker went dead.

As Hillary tried to leave the rally, three Secret Service agents arrested a trio of men, one armed with a gun, the other two with hunting knives. Under interrogation, the young men revealed that one of them had volunteered to shoot a bullet into Hillary's brain, with the understanding that the other two would lunge at her with knives aimed at her heart. All three of them admitted that although they were aware that they might be shot down by Secret Service men, but were prepared to sacrifice their lives for the unborn babies of the world.

The clarion call from most of the protesters claimed that the Clintons "wanted to ban firearms, protect homosexuals, open more abortion clinics, and mandate socialized medicine."

Hillary's tour organizers had to cancel several of her appearances, citing security concerns, and re-route parts of her itinerary to avoid violent attacks.

By the time her caravan returned to Washington (DC), Newt Gingrich delightedly announced to the press that Hillary's health-care reform "was on life support."

George Mitchell, the Senate Majority Leader, suggested her plan had as much chance of surviving a vote as "a nine-year-old girl thrown into a pool of hungry sharks who hadn't had any food in a week."

"Health care was once Bill's poster child," claimed William Kristol, a GOP spokesman. "Now, it's his tar baby."

Bill Clinton's "Flying Harem"

While Hillary was on her bus tour, Bill, back at the White House, adopted what he called "a theory based on the oft-repeated slogan, 'when the cat's away, the mice will play.'"

As biographer Christopher Andersen wrote, "Even as the Paula Jones case grew exponentially, Bill continued his ongoing extramarital relationships with several women inside and outside the White House, and was actively on the hunt for more."

One typical story of the president having a sexual encounter was later related by Mike McGrath, the master White House steward. He recalled working in the pantry rounding up food products for the upcoming weekend in the White House.

He claimed that a former flight attendant, by now a presidential aide, approached him. He remembered her as a "real stunner in high heels and a short hemline." She told him to stay in the pantry for the next twenty minutes.

Bill had met her when he flew on *Longhorn One* that chartered Boeing 727 that he used during his 1992 presidential campaign. One of his campaign staffers later alleged, "Bill routinely fondled, groped, and sexually harassed flight attendants during his entire race for the White House. All of them had been hired because they were real good lookers. Bill showed a distinct preference for hot blondes, the Sharon Stone types."

Reporters at the time referred to *Longhorn One* as "Bill Clinton's Flying Harem," although they didn't print that.

The White House pantry was positioned a few steps from the Oval Office's study. The door was usually left open between the pantry and the study, but the aide had blocked it shut with a doorstop. When she emerged twenty minutes later, McGrath admitted he was shocked. "I soon learned that she had her twenty minutes every morning with the president," he later alleged.

"The Clintons are Destined to Fade Into the Dusty Archives of History"
—Historian Barbara Michaels

In August of 1994, George Mitchell, then the Senate's Majority Leader, and a Democrat from Maine, privately said that Hillary's health care plan was "dead as stillborn." He came up with a compromise that would delay requirements of employers and exempt small businesses from insuring their employees. But not enough Democratic senators backed his proposal. Health-care reform would have to wait until another day.

Sometimes, perhaps as part of attempts to forget about Paula Jones and Whitewater, Bill entertained aspiring young politicians, both men and women, visiting Washington. He was often asked the best way to break into politics. He shared his experience of how he did it. "I learned my trade in tiny Ozark churches where they charmed poisonous snakes and spoke in tongues."

As if 1994 hadn't been horrendous enough, the Clintons, from their perch within the White House, had to listen to the fall election returns that November. "The voters knocked their fists down my throat," Bill proclaimed, as he sat hearing the projected winners.

In the aftermath of these elections, the Democrats suffered crushing defeats, rejections mainly of Bill's administration and of Hillary's attempts at health-care reform. The Democrats lost eight seats in the Senate, fifty-four in the House, and eight governorships. This was the worst defeat since Harry S Truman lost Democratic congressional seats in the post-war autumn of 1946.

In the White House library, Hillary looked at the TV set in disgust as George

W. Bush defeated her friend, Ann Richards, for the governorship of Texas. "What a jackass!" she proclaimed. Earlier in the evening, she'd watched the TV in disbelief as Mario Cuomo lost his bid for re-election as Governor of New York.

David Gergen noted the gloom and doom that had descended over the White House. "If you just spoke to Bill, he would lash back at you. At times, he seemed incoherent."

Bill admitted in a memoir, "I was profoundly distressed by the election. I had tried to do too much to help people. We made too many enemies. There were too many scandals."

Gergen also noted that Hillary was devastated, not only because of the defeat of her health-care plan, but because of her father's death, the never-ending scandals circling over Bill's head, and the ongoing accusations of murder.

Reporter Joe Klein blamed Hillary for her unwillingness to listen to different points of view. Dick Morris said, "The more Hillary seemed strong, the weaker the president looked. There was sharp tension between the president and his First Lady."

In the days and weeks ahead, for the most part, Hillary retreated to her room, wanting to be alone. She even mulled over the temptation to retreat completely from public life. One afternoon, an aide brought a tea tray to her room and found her in reported "conversation" with Eleanor Roosevelt.

Hillary *(depicted above, right, addressing Families, USA, in 2005)* shocked some supporters and provided "fodder" to her enemies when she admitted that on occasion, she spoke to the "ghost" or "spirit" or "memory" of Eleanor Roosevelt. Eleanor's voice "from the other side," according to Hillary, came through clearly and forcefully.

"The former First Lady *(depicted above, left)* helped me get through the traumatic campaign year of 1992. Talking to her was one of the saving graces I have hung on to for dear life."

Right-wing evangelists were quick to cite a passage in the Old Testament's book of Deuteronomy that identifies necromancy (communication with familiar spirits from the dead) as an "abomination to God."

She later told her aides, "Eleanor told me to pick up the pieces and put them together again. Brace up and go out into the world and try to accomplish something good in spite of the personal attacks on me. I decided that was what I must do."

The White House staff noted that as 1994 came to an end, Bill and Hillary rarely spoke to each other, although both parents continued to dote on Chelsea. They wanted to shield her from the press, as some reporters had launched cruel attacks on her physical appearance.

"Their co-presidency had become schizophrenic," Morris reportedly said. Or was it Mary Matalin who uttered that remark?

Most newspeople agreed that Hillary's bus tour had run off a deep cliff and then sunk into the murky depths of the ocean. At a private Democratic caucus, one Senator bluntly told his colleagues, "Hillary Clinton has destroyed our party."

"A culture of concealment caused the White House to come down with a virus," claimed reporter Mike Isikoff, who seemed to have developed an obsession with Bill's sex life.

A former member of Hillary's health-care force (who did not want to be named) told *The New York Times,* "I find Hillary to be among the most self-righteous people I've ever known in my life. It's her one great flaw. It's what killed health care."

***

By December, Whitewater had claimed its first victim, Webb Hubbell, Hillary's longtime partner at the Rose Law Firm in Little Rock and the rumored father of Chelsea. He pleaded guilty that month to Federal charges for over-billing clients. Judge George Howard sentenced him to twenty-one months in jail.

"Webb became dinosaur meat for the right wing," Hillary lamented.

In addition to his jail term, Hubbell was ordered to pay $400,000 in fines. He didn't have the money. Hillary arranged for him to earn it by assigning him work as a consultant. Critics called it "hush money."

Not only that, but Jim Guy Tucker, the governor of Arkansas who had replaced Bill, was also indicted and later convicted of conspiracy and one count of mail fraud as part of Kenneth Starr's investigation of the Whitewater scandal. His conviction had nothing to do with the Clintons,

On July 16, he resigned as governor, and was replaced with Mike Huckabee, until then, the lieutenant governor.

Based on his ill health, Tucker received a lenient sentence consisting for the most part of house detention and four years probation. Later, he suffered through a liver transplant at the Mayo Clinic in Rochester, Minnesota.

In the aftermath of the defeat of the Democrats at the polls, Hillary granted an interview with Author Gail Sheehy. "I know I'm the projection for many wounded men. I'm the boss they never wanted to have. I'm the wife who went back to school and got a degree and a job as good as theirs. I'm the daughter who they never wanted to turn out to be independent. It's not me, personally, they hate--it's the change I represent."

As she wrote in *Living History,* "Bill talked about social change. I embodied it."

A friend of the Clintons, who did not want to be named, gave a dim portrait of their marriage in 1994. "They were trapped in a marriage in which both sides, at times, wanted to escape. Yet they knew they needed each other, and they had to hold together to fight off various demons."

"Winning the presidency again in 1996 and dealing with their scandals and lawsuits were reasons enough to stay together," he said. "When called upon, and when absolutely necessary, they made public appearances together, putting on their smiling faces, but it was obvious to me that their hearts weren't in it. I suspected both of them were very unhappy in their marriage."

"She had her ups and downs as First Lady of Arkansas. She had faced hostility down South, but nothing like she had to deal with in Washington. This was the bigtime, not some Southern backwater. The big bad boys in the capital were questioning her past law practice, her marriage, even her sexual preference. Nothing seemed off the table when it came to her. That certainly went for Bill, too."

Meanwhile, back in Arkansas, a bitter debate arose over whether the romanticized portrait of the state's former governor, Jim Guy Tucker, should continue to be exhibited in the seat of the Arkansas State Government.

Tucker had ascended from lieutenant governor to governor after Bill Clinton resigned to assume the presidency in December of 1992. He was the first sitting governor of Arkansas to be convicted of criminal charges during his time in office.

President?
Hillary defined Clinton-hater and presidential hopeful Mike Huckabee, 44th Governor of Arkansas (1996-2007) as "a hayseed, marred in the prejudices and stupidity of the discarded Old South of yesterday, a grits-and-gravy type politician."

Right photo above, cover of Huckabee's 2015 memoir in praise of conservative values.

To chase away the clouds over the White House, Hillary, for Chelsea's sake, decided to choreograph an old-fashioned Christmas. She invited art students from Georgetown University to create and install the Executive Mansion's Yuletide decorations. She was too busy to supervise their work, but when she asked, she was told that it was progressing beautifully.

When she finally came downstairs to see the giant tree decorated and lit, she thought it was spectacular. But then she studied it more carefully. The ornaments were beautifully fashioned, but provocative, many of them depicting crack pipes and condoms. The most prominent ornament was a depiction of the Three Wise Men, each of them showing off a gigantic erection.

As one year ended and another was about to begin, Bill and Hillary, along with their aides, were talking about the upcoming presidential elections of 1996. To adequately prepare for it, they'd have to begin organizing their re-election campaign early in 1995.

In December of 1995, although trouble lay ahead for him, Newt Gingrich was the happiest man in Washington after *Time* magazine named him "Man of the Year" for his role in demolishing the four-decades-long Democratic majority in the House of Representatives. After the honor bestowed on him by *Time,* he allegedly sent Hillary a note: "Call me your worst nightmare. I have changed the center of gravity in the nation's capital. Sorry you got blown away by my hurricane winds."

After Christmas, she popped into the Oval Office unannounced. She found Bill reading the latest poll about the voters' reactions to the candidates associated with the race for the presidency in 1996. Assuming that he'd be re-nominated, he would have to face such challengers as Bob Dole. The poll suggested that Bill would get less than forty percent of the vote.

As she entered, Bill ripped the polling results into shreds. "These asshole pollsters have me losing my bid for re-election. Apparently, the jerks have never heard of 'The Comeback Kid.'"

Bill & Hillary Battle the GOP's "Crybaby Rottweiler," Who Orchestrates a Shutdown of the U.S. Government

January of 1995, like every other month in their administration of the White House, loomed with what Bill called "good and bad news." Unemployment had dropped to 5.4 percent, but, on the other hand, Kenneth Starr was working around the clock re-investigating Vince Foster's suicide, seemingly obsessed with the idea that he had been murdered, and probing financial dealings from years before in Arkansas, hoping to find the "smoking gun" that would lead to the president's impeachment and an indictment based on financial irregularities associated with the First Lady.

On January 24, Bill delivered his State of the Union address to a hostile Congress, the first assembly in forty years dominated by Republicans. He vainly called upon them to "put aside partisanship, pettiness, and pride."

In the House, Newt Gingrich remained stony and indifferent to Bill's plea for cooperation. Privately, Bill referred to him as "the buffoon from Georgia. He thinks he's prime minister running the country. He demotes me to minister of foreign affairs. And, before I forget, he's one dingleberry-coated asshole."

Gingrich denounced President Lyndon B. Johnson's Great Society as "a counterculture value system."

Back at the White House, Bill faced a financial crisis threatening Mexico, which could not repay its debts. He realized that an economic collapse in Mexico would have dire effects on the U.S. economy, since Mexico was America's third largest trading partner.

As president, he managed to choreograph a Mexican loan guarantee, which *The New York Times* described as "the least popular, least understood, but most important foreign policy decision of the Clinton presidency."

Since the year had begun, Bill and Hillary were preoccupied with working out a strategy for his re-election in November of 1996. Once again, he relied on the political savvy of Dick Morris.

Leon Panetta, a "deficit hawk," had become Bill's Chief of Staff in June of 1994, having replaced Mack McLarty. Panetta seemed to hold Morris in contempt. So did George Stephanopoulos, who described Morris as "a short, stocky, man with a dark, blow-dried pompadour, crowning a small sausage of a man encased in a green suit with wide lapels, a wide floral tie, and a white collared shirt carrying a briefcase that gave him the look of a B-movie mob lawyer, circa 1975—the kind of guy who gets brained with a baseball bat for double-crossing the boss."

Most of Bill's aides seemed to view Morris as a political turncoat, since he also worked for such controversial figures as the notorious Senator Jesse Helms of North Carolina, who seemed to think that homosexuals were secretly plotting to overthrow the U.S. government.

Hillary admitted, "Bill and I viewed Morris' opinions with a pound of salt and overlooked his histrionics and self-aggrandizing."

Morris constantly presented the results of his latest political polls to the Oval Office. Another media consultant, Robert Squier, labeled Morris as "the Julia Child of cooked polls," suggesting that his opinion samplings always seemed to match up with advice he'd previously delivered.

"The Arkansas country boy and the street-smart New York Jew were known around the White House as "The Odd Couple,'" said Stephanopoulos.

Morris was a collateral relative of the notorious gay attorney, Roy Cohn, the vindictive *enfant terrible* of the Joseph McCarthy era. Both the commie-hunting senator and his boy wonder had a fondness for male hustlers.

On April 22, both Bill and Hillary came face to face with their nemesis, Kenneth Starr. He arrived at the White House to interrogate each of them, under oath, about Whitewater. Later, she expressed disgust for her Inquisitor. "The idea of a hard-core Republican partisan rummaging through our lives, looking at every check we had written for twenty years, and harassing our friends on the flimsiest of excuses infuriated me."

After Starr's interrogation of Bill, the president politely invited him to inspect the Lincoln Bedroom. "I was trying to be courteous to him, believing at the time that he would act reasonably and legitimately, conclude this utterly ridiculous probe that was going nowhere. Boy, did I soon change my mind. I think Hillary resented my being so nice to this creep."

The next day, April 19, 1995, Bill woke up to hear the news that a truck bomb had exploded in a Federal Building in Oklahoma City, killing 168 people, including 19 children who at the time were under the supervision of the building's Daycare Division. Timothy McVeigh, an alienated U.S. military veteran, was arrested for setting off the bomb, an act he described as an attempt to avenge the FBI's siege of the

SPORTS ★ ★ ★ FINAL

DAILY NEWS

NEW YORK'S HOMETOWN NEWSPAPER

TERROR STRIKES AMERICA'S HEART

THEY BLEW UP THE BABIES

- 12 tots die as car bomb shatters Oklahoma City
- Death toll at 31, 200 missing in America's worst terror outrage
- Clinton vows vengeance

12-PAGE SPECIAL REPORT

LATE NEWS BULLETIN: SUSPECTS SPOTTED NEAR SAN ANTONIO

"The images from Oklahoma City were disturbingly intimate: A little girl, limp as a rag doll, carried out of the smoking rubble by a heart-broken fireman; a terrified office worker being lifted onto a stretcher," Hillary said.

"The familiarity of the setting and the number of casualties brought the tragedy home to America in ways that other atrocities up until then could not. That was the point of the attack."

THE DAILY OKLAHOMAN

MORNING OF TERROR

City Struggles With Shock of Deadly Bombing

Branch Davidian compound near Waco between February and April of 1993. Riveted and heartbroken by the tragedy, Bill and Hillary flew to Oklahoma for a memorial service honoring the victims.

[The Oklahoma City bombing had occurred almost two years after the February, 1993 underground bombing of the World Trade Center in New York, when terrorists drove a van filled with explosives into the underground parking facilities beneath the North Tower of the World Trade Center, a building which—although badly damaged—nonetheless managed to survive until September 11, 2001.]

The United States had officially entered the world of terrorism on the homefront, and Bill vowed to fight this rising threat "for as many tomorrows as it takes."

"As if one Rottweiler (Starr) wasn't enough, Bill and I had to face off against that Maddog (Republican) Senator from New York, Al D'Amato," Hillary said. "He was the chairman of the Senate Banking Committee, and he decided to open up a second front against us."

Replicating (fruitlessly) most of the work of Starr's committee, he, too, launched an investigation into the suicide of Vince Foster, having already convinced himself that he had been murdered.

Hillary stood by helplessly as she watched her closest aides, including her press secretary, Maggie Williams, paraded before the committee. "It was unbearable to see Maggie raked over the coals again and again and to know that her legal bills were mounting daily," Hillary said.

For Hillary, the most painful sight was when her friend, Susan Thomases, was called before the Senate committee. She was the wife of the Hollywood producer, Harry Thomases, who was a close adviser of the Clintons.

"Susan's decades-long struggle with multiple sclerosis had impaired her memory, and she tried as hard as she could to respond to D'Amato's bullying interrogation," Hillary said. "It was heartbreaking for me to watch his treatment of this poor woman. The Senator inflicted great emotional and monetary damage on innocent people."

Of all the White House aides, Betsey Wright faced the most horrendous legal bills, totaling $650,000.

Newsweek columnist Joe Klein, who wrote *Primary Colors,* criticized Bill and Hillary for not coming to the aid of their beleaguered staff members. "The Clintons leave them out there to dangle in the wind," he claimed. He called the president and his First Lady, "The Tom and Daisy Buchanan of the Baby Boom Political Elite."

[His reference, of course, was to the extravagant, reckless lives of the fictional characters created by F. Scott Fitzgerald in his classic novel, The Great Gatsby, *first published in 1925.]*

Oblivious to any conflict of interest, D'Amato was also the chairman of Bob Dole's presidential campaign, a position that made it in his interest to sabotage or circumvent any possibility of Bill getting re-elected to a second term. D'Amato's hearings would drag on endlessly for eleven months, as he summoned witness after witness, most of whom had no first-hand knowledge of the events being probed. By October 26, 1995, the Senate Whitewater Committee had issued some fifty summonses to employees of various Federal agencies.

"Republican Senator Al D'Amato of New York was like a direct descendant of the rat which brought the bubonic plague of the Middle Ages into England," Hillary said.

For purely political reasons, the argumentative New Yorker decided to intervene in, and amplify, the investigations of both the death of Vince Foster and the Whitewater allegations.

"Instead of pursuing his job to help the people of New York, he spent days, weeks, months, attacking us—and got nowhere," Hillary claimed.

Bill continued to be baffled by all these continuing Whitewater investigations. At one point, he met with Alan Simpson, the Republican Senator from Wyoming. "Of course, we know you did nothing wrong about Whitewater," Simpson said. "That's not what the probe is about. It is about making the public *think* you did something wrong."

April 14, 1995 was a key moment in the history of the Clinton presidency, as he announced his decision to seek re-election. His public statement came just four days after the terminally dour and usually humorless Senator Bob Dole said that he would seek the presidential nomination of the Republican Party.

June witnessed bitter fights between the president and Congress over the Federal budget. Bill tried to counter Republican cuts that would cause hardship for millions of Americans, including children. "These right-wing boys care more about protecting big business than they care for the hard-working average American family," he claimed.

In September, Bill's head was spinning with events in Bosnia and the Middle East, but he also faced a serious run-in on the homefront with the Republican-dominated Congress. Gingrich was leading the assault on the budget, wanting to make gigantic cuts in food stamps, student loans, Medicare, and Medicaid.

To block Bill's protests, Gingrich threatened to get his fellow Republican Congressmen to refuse to raise the debt limit, which would cause the United States to default on its debts. A showdown emerged, with Bill warning about the dangers of default, which would plunge the government, as well as the country itself, into chaos. International currency markets would suffer, as if by a whirlwind.

At the end of October, Bill and Hillary celebrated twenty tumultuous years of married life, marred by multiple betrayals and adulteries. In spite of that, they remained loyal to each other. She had (to a very minor degree) disparaged the lyrics and title of, "Stand by Your Man," but, as witnessed by the survival of her marriage, she had, indeed, stood by Bill nonetheless. For the occasion, he gave her an upgraded diamond ring, since at the time of their marriage, he had not been able to afford a good one.

Senator Robert Dole—one of the last veterans of World War II to seek the highest office in the land—was a humorless and bitter symbol from yesteryear when he ran against Bill Clinton for president in 1996.

"He was a sad figure who ended up hawking Viagra on TV," Bill said.

In a last-ditch effort to prevent a government shutdown, Bill confronted Gingrich and Dick Armey, as well as others within the GOP elite. Armey threatened him, telling him that if he did not acquiesce to Republican demands, it would mark the end of his presidency. Bill retaliated by telling him that he would never approve the GOP budget "even if I drop to five percent in the polls."

After Bill vetoed their spending bill, the Republicans, led by Gingrich, shut down the government as part of a fiscal crisis lasting from November 14 to November 19, 1995. Some 800,000 government workers were sent home. Only essential services remained open, causing hardships for millions of Americans. In a climate of brinksmanship where all parties refused to back down, another shutdown occurred between December 16 and January 6, 1996.

Then the unthinkable happened:

THE GOVERNMENT SHUT DOWN

Gingrich came in for harsh attacks from the press. He was ridiculed when he flew to Israel aboard *Air Force One*, along with Bill and former Presidents Jimmy Carter and George H.W. Bush.

Their entourage had been assembled for the funeral of the Israeli then-Prime Minister Yitzhak Rabin, who had been assassinated on November 4 by a fanatical right-wing Israeli extremist opposed to his having negotiated with the Palestinians.

Gingrich was assigned to a seat in the back of the plane, and he "raged and ranted" at such treatment. A famous cartoon of him as a spoiled infant, wailing in diapers, appeared on the frontpage of the *New York Daily News* under the headline, "CRY BABY."

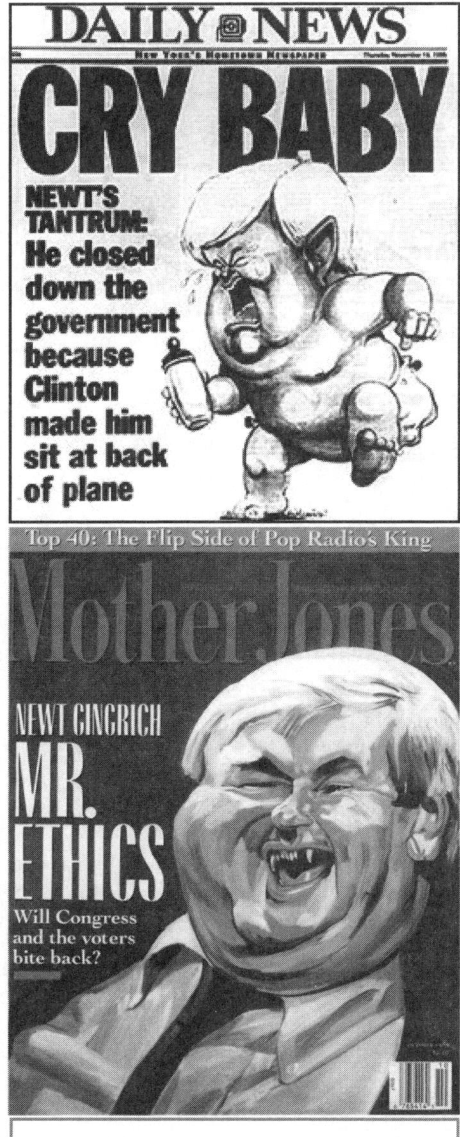

Naughty Newt
(The Man Who Would Be King)
The most despised politician in America.

Despite the troubles it brought to the Clintons, November wasn't a complete disaster for them. On November 12, the presidents of Serbia, Croatia, and Bosnia reached a peace agreement, ending a four-year conflict that cost a quarter of a million lives with two million people made homeless.

"These government shutdowns were heart-breaking," Hillary said. "Programs like Meals on Wheels were shut down, cutting off food for some 600,000 senior citizens who depended on it for their entire food intake. Ultimately, Gingrich's strategy of playing chicken with Bill failed. That Georgia boy brought hardships to millions of Americans, including working mothers and underfed children. I felt such a great relief when we could reopen our government and put workers back on the payroll, now that Bill had prevailed."

The battle over the budget finally came to an end in January of 1996, when Bill and Congress agreed to a seven-year balanced budget plan that included modest spending cuts and tax increases.

***

As another dreadful year (1995) came to an end, there was more trouble on the Whitewater front. William H. Kennedy III, who had worked with Hillary at the Rose Law Firm in Little Rock, had joined the White House staff as Associate Counsel. On December 12, he refused to release subpoenaed notes of a 1993 meeting between Bill's attorneys and White House officials about Whitewater.

However, on December 20, in a vote that followed party lines and loyalties, the Senate voted that the White House was required to answer the subpoena.

After that, Bill agreed to drop his claim of attorney/client privilege and release the notes. In spite of all the turmoil the subpoena had catalyzed, the notes, in the end, were quite vague and of no value, providing no proof of any illegal activity by the Clintons, to the disappointment of the Republicans.

Hot & Steamy Meetings With a Thong-Wearing Intern, Whom He Doesn't Trust Enough to Ejaculate

In early July of 1995, twenty-two-year-old Monica Samille Lewinsky, born in San Francisco, began an internship in the office of the White House's Chief of Staff. It would be beyond her wildest dreams to know that one day, she would live in the pages of history for giving the world's most famous blow-jobs.

She came from a relatively prosperous family, her father, Bernard Lewinsky, an oncologist, was the son of German Jews who had fled from Nazi Germany. Her mother was an author who wrote under the name of Marcia Lewis. Her parents had divorced in 1987, and each of them had remarried.

Significantly, Monica had learned to talk before she could walk. Her critics later claimed that she talked too much and had too good a memory. Perhaps it would have been better, both for her and the president, if she had forgotten just a few of the tantalizing, Bill-related details unfit for publication in a family newspaper.

She had previously worked in the drama department at the Beverly Hills (California) High School, dreaming of becoming a movie star. It was at this time that she began a five-year affair with the married Andy Bleiler, a drama teacher.

It was during that hot, sultry summer of '95 that Monica caught the roving eye of the President of the United States. She was twenty-two. Bill was old enough to be her father.

Long before she actually met him, she'd heard other female interns at the White House rave about Bill. Many of them seemed to have a crush on him. She judged him from his pictures, finding, in her view, that "he was rather ugly, with a big nose and coarse, wiry-looking hair." To her, he was "an old guy," and he no sex appeal for her at all. She decided that her fellow interns had "very bad taste in men."

She first saw Bill in the flesh one sultry July day when she attended an arrival ceremony on the South Lawn of the White House, during which Bill extended greetings to the president of South Korea. From her position behind gold ropes that marked the VIP section, she wore a sundress, her head shielded by a wide-brimmed straw hat.

She recalled that moment to author Andrew Morton, who wrote her memoir, *Monica's Story.*

"There was an intense flirtation, an intense chemistry between us," she recalled. "But I don't think it was that much different from other women he'd flirted with, or had been attracted to."

"When I first saw him," Monica wrote, "my heart skipped a beat, my breathing became a little faster, and there were butterflies fluttering in my tummy. He had a glow about him that was magnetic. He exuded sexual energy. Now I saw what all the girls were talking about."

But on her second encounter with him, she was disappointed. She found him operating on autopilot as he moved along a line of greeters. "He looked straight through me this time, as if I weren't even there." The White House staff had lined up for a departure ceremony, as he boarded a plane to fly with Chelsea and Hillary to Camp David.

She wanted to give a flirtation with him another chance, so she attended the next departure ceremony, this one on August 9. From J. Crew, her mother had purchased a sage green suit for her, and she decided to wear that for the event. During this occasion, she claimed, "He gave me *The Look.* Our exchange was intense but brief. He undressed me with his eyes."

Later, he recalled that day to her, claiming, "I knew that one day I would kiss you."

The very next day (August 10), she attended a celebration for his forty-ninth birthday. *[His actual birthday was August 19.]* Thinking he might recognize her, she chose to wear the same sage-green suit. The event was cowboy themed, and the president showed up looking a bit like Roy Rogers. "That afternoon, he looked deeply into my eyes, and I was hooked. His arm brushed against my breast."

A romance didn't develop until November, when she took a salaried position handling correspondence in the White House office that dealt with legislative matters.

On November 15, during the government shutdown, White House office workers were celebrating the birthday of Jennifer Palmieri, who had gotten Monica her present job. At the last minute, the president opted to attend the event.

Monica remembered that during the party, she had what she termed "a lot of presidential face time."

When the president stepped into the inner office of the White House Chief of Staff, she decided to seize the moment. Clad in a navy blue pantsuit, she trailed him. As she confessed, "I put my hands on my hips and with my thumbs, lifted the back of my jacket, allowing him a fleeting glimpse of my thong underwear, where it showed above the waistline of my pantsuit." It was a daring move on her part, and it definitely attracted the president's roving eye.

Later in the day, as she passed the office of George Stephanopoulos, she noticed that inside, Bill was standing alone. *[Stephanopoulos was no longer the communications representative for the president, but had been appointed Senior Adviser for Policy and Strategy.]*

Spotting her, Bill gestured for her to enter the room. In their first real involvement, she blurted out that she had a crush on him.

Laughing, he invited her into the back office. Alone with him, he was no longer that old guy, but "gorgeous, with a softness and tenderness to him." He asked her if he could kiss her, and she gave her permission, finding him "an incredible, sensual kisser."

About two hours later, at around 10PM, she had another rendezvous with him in the darkened office of Stephanopoulos.

During her testimony with Kenneth Starr, she claimed, "I unbuttoned my jacket, and he unhooked my bra. He touched my breasts with his hands and mouth. He put his hand down my pants and stimulated me manually in the genital area. While he was talking on the phone with a Congressman or a Senator, I performed oral sex on him."

When he finished his phone dialogue, she told him she wanted to complete the act, but he claimed that he needed to wait to ejaculate in her mouth until he trusted her more.

Their next sexual encounter occurred two days later. Working late at the White House during the government shutdown, she came face to face with Bill again. Pizza was ordered for the staff, and the president suggested she bring him some.

Instead of eating it, he lured her into a bathroom, where she unbuttoned his shirt. She found it "very sweet when he sucked in his stomach," and then assured him that there was no need for him to do that. "I love your tummy," she said.

"He unzipped his pants and exposed himself," she said. "Once again, I performed oral sex on him, but he did not ejaculate."

Their last sexual encounter of 1995 occurred on the afternoon of December 31. When he didn't seem to remember her name, he called her "Kiddo."

"It's Monica Lewinsky, President Kiddo," she said, jokingly.

"We moved to his private study, where he kissed me and lifted my sweater, exposing my breasts. He fondled them with his hands and sucked on my nipples. I then performed oral sex. Again, before he blasted off, he stopped, using that same line that he didn't know me well enough to trust me."

"He was so cute," she said. Before sending me on my way and into another year, he gave me a long, lingering kiss."

After wishing him a Happy New Year, she left his office study in a state of "high elation."

That night, as revelers along the east coast were drinking and singing *Auld Lang Syne,* she knew that a hot romance had just begun with the President of the United States.

"But," she speculated. "Will he divorce Hillary and marry me and make me First Lady?"

Chapter Sixteen

Reporter Joe Klein Defines 1996 as a Replay of the Salem Witch Trials

"There's Madness, a New Poison, in the Political Air"

As His Enemies Rage, Bill (Defined by Robert Dole as "the Baby Boomer Who Never Grew Up") Is Re-elected President

Bathroom Summit: Monica Lewinsky & Bill Clinton Exchange Cunnilingus & Fellatio

President Bill Clinton shakes the hand of a White House intern, Monica Lewinsky. As "skin met skin," it would lead to an affair that almost cost him his presidency.

Author Candice E. Jackson claimed, "As a man, Bill Clinton seduced a young woman and left her in the dust. You can't blame him entirely for the disappointment and despair Monica experienced when the results of their affair fell short of his promises. In her search for a hero, she was willing to turn herself over to the care of a 'femivore' who ensnared her."

After eight years in the White House, facing a battlefield of right-wing warlords, Bill Clinton's hair turned gray.

Scandals followed him even during his departure from the White House, based on his having issued 140 controversial pardons, including one for his drug-dealing brother, Roger.

"I experienced more than my fair share of controversy," Bill said. "When I ran for a congressional seat in 1974 in Arkansas, rumors spread that I was a homosexual. But by the time I vacated the presidency, no one—not even my worst enemies—accused me of being a homosexual."

As the New Year of 1996 arrived at the White House, as Bill Clinton was trying to get on with the business of running the Free World, he was increasingly drawn back to those heady days in Arkansas when he was its governor.

He had wanted to leave that world far behind him. "I wanted to regard it like Elvis did that day when he sang, 'Yesterday is dead and gone.' But my enemies would not let me bury yesterday and its memories."

Early in January, Bill met with his nemesis, Newt Gingrich, the Speaker of the House of Representatives. The chubby Georgia boy admitted to Bill that, "We made a mistake in shutting down the government. We thought you'd cave in, bubba, but you didn't."

It was already obvious that Gingrich might have difficulties fulfilling his "Contract with America" during the upcoming budget wars of 1996.

After he'd gone, Bill contemptuously referred to him as "Leroy McPherson." *[Gingrich had been born in Yankee country (Harrisburg, Pennsylvania) to a sixteen-year-old mother and a nineteen-year-old father. The marriage lasted only long enough for him to impregnate his bride, and then he was gone. When the fat little baby was born, his mother named him Newton Leroy McPherson.]*

In 1956, Gingrich's mother, Kathleen (Kit) Daugherty, married Army officer Robert Gingrich, who adopted "Newt," as he had been nicknamed.

As he grew up, he shared some things in common with his sworn enemy, Bill, including draft dodging during the Vietnam war and adultery.

In 1962, while still a teenager, Newt married 26-year-old Jacqueline (Jackie) Battley, his high school geometry teacher. The couple had two daughters. In the spring of 1980, he abandoned his wife to take up with Marianne Ginther. He came to the hospital, where Jackie was recovering from surgery associated with cancer, to inform her he was divorcing her.

He had already decided he wanted to be president one day. In reference to the news he had delivered to his then-wife, he told his campaign treasurer, L.H. Carter, that "Jackie is not young enough or pretty enough to be the wife of a president. And besides, she has cancer."

After divorcing Jackie, he married Ginther, who helped him to control his finances, since he was deeply in debt. She later revealed on *ABC's Nightline* that he had wanted them to have an "open marriage."

While still married, he launched yet another affair in Washington, D.C.,

During a Whitewater Trial in Little Rock, "A Thief and a Con Artist" (Hillary's Words) Implicates the President

this one with a staffer, Callista Bisek, at the House of Representatives. She was twenty-three years his junior. After divorcing Marianne, he married Callista, a bottle blonde.

Ignoring his own hypocrisies, he became one of Bill's most vociferous critics, attacking his womanizing. Appearing on *Meet the Press,* he claimed the Clintons were "counterculture McGovernites." Jesse Helms, the Senator from North Carolina and an outspoken (some say relentless) foe of the Clintons, went even farther, claiming "Bill Clinton is unfit to be commander-in-chief."

A longtime Senator from North Carolina, Jesse Helms, Jr., often used racially charged and homophobic language in his campaigns and editorials. He was once called "rotgut Southern mush, a relic of a time when it was commonplace to denounce Jews, niggers, and faggots."

Ridiculed as "Senator No," he hated the Clintons, but was also opposed to civil rights, disability rights, feminism, gay rights, affirmative action, abortion, and the National Endowment for the Arts. ("They cater to perverts.")

When Bill's infidelities were exposed, Gingrich claimed, "This pattern of indiscretion disqualifies Clinton from being president."

Later on, when Gingrich's own adulteries were exposed, he said, "There's no question that at times in my life, partially driven by how passionately I felt about my country, I worked too hard and things happened in my life that were not appropriate."

Missing Whitewater Documents Mysteriously Reappear

The New Year had hardly begun when, on January 4, 1996, Carolyn Huber, a longtime Clinton aide and White House assistant, announced that she'd found Hillary's long-subpoenaed Rose Law Firm Whitewater billing records. They reflected her work representing Madison Guaranty Savings & Loan between the late autumn of 1985 until the spring of 1986.

On hearing of the discovery, Bill said, "Just when I thought things couldn't get any weirder in Whitewater world, they did."

At that point, 50,000 pages of Whitewater documents had already been turned over to Kenneth Starr, but he demanded more. He had become relentless in his demands.

Huber claimed that she thought the box had been moved to her office from a storage area on the third floor of the White House in August of 1995, but she had not noticed it until now. She also revealed that the billing records in some cases contained hand-scribbled notes that Vince Foster had made only weeks before his suicide (or murder, as some critics continued to maintain without any real proof). One of these notations from Vince stated, "Whitewater is a can of worms you shouldn't open."

Even Bill admitted, "On the surface, the discovery of these long-sought after documents looked suspicious."

Not only Starr, but the leading Republican attack dog in the Senate, Alphonse ("Al") D'Amato of New York claimed that there was definitely a cover-up involved. On the Senate floor, he delivered fierce attacks on Hillary. Reportedly, he told his aides, "If only we could give her the Marie Antoinette treatment."

The right-wing columnist for the otherwise liberal *New York Times,* William Safire, continued his assaults on the First Lady, infuriating Bill. Privately, he told aides, "If I weren't president, Safire would end up with the bloodiest nose in recorded history."

A distant possibility emerged that Hillary might be indicted for obstruction of justice, which would have been a first for the wife of an American president. The recently discovered documents revealed to Starr's investigators that Hillary, as an attorney for the Rose Law Firm, had billed sixty hours of legal work, including thirty conferences and phone calls over a period that totaled fifty-three different days.

The documents also revealed that she was linked to another sham real estate deal—the Castle Grande project—which had been orchestrated by Jim McDougal when he was president of Madison Guaranty.

Jim had made fraudulent loans to the Castle Grande project, funneling money into an undeveloped 1,050-acre site positioned within a ten-minute drive south of Little Rock. The loans had been associated with plans for the construction of a shopping center, a trailer park, and, among others, a microbrewery. None of them ever got built. The question the prosecutors kept asking was, "Where did the money go, and how, if at all, were Bill and Hillary implicated?" The records showed that Hillary had fourteen meetings with Seth Ward, the father-in-law of Jim, concerning the ill-fated Castle Grande. Even with all this new evidence, there was still no conclusive "smoking gun." Senator D'Amato faced extreme disappointment.

However, Starr wouldn't give up. On January 22, he issued a subpoena to Hillary for a "criminal probe" into her records, hoping to discover illegal acts she'd tried to conceal during all the months he'd been calling for delivery of pertinent records to his offices. His demand to summon her before a Grand Jury represented the first time the wife of a sitting president had ever been subpoenaed.

She knew she would have to face hours of intense, hostile questions.

Starr's actions enraged Bill, who called it "a cheap, tawdry publicity stunt. I had to stand helplessly by as my wife came under attack. All I could do was tell the press that if everybody in this country had the fine character of my wife, America would be a better place."

"Boys like Starr and D'Amato took real pleasure—a real big kick—beating up on my wife," Bill said. "They were hell bent on a personal vendetta against America's First Lady. Thank God she was a lot tougher and stronger than these nellies. That was one of the reasons I loved her."

As Hillary Faces a Grand Jury Indictment, She's Also Accused of Adopting An Alien Baby from Outer Space

Before facing Starr on the witness stand, Hillary met with Dick Morris. "You are going to be indicted on something as yet undefined," he warned her. "A source of mine leaked the news to me. I've talked to people close to Starr,

Established as a sister to *The National Enquirer*, The *Weekly World News* was a campy, largely fictional news tabloid published from 1979 to 2007, and noted for its outlandish cover stories. The presidency was often the victim of political satire. Revelations claimed that all the founding fathers were gay, and that George Washington and Abraham Lincoln were actually women.

Hillary was a frequent target. The tabloid followed (or invented) the adventures of P'lod, a horny extraterrestrial who, in the White House, had an affair with Hillary, leading to a violent confrontation with Bill.

WWN also revealed that many prominent Americans were still alive, including Elvis Presley, John F. Kennedy, Michael Jackson, and Marilyn Monroe. Of course, to hear *WWN* tell it, Adolf Hitler, although decrepit and very old at this point, is still alive and living in luxury somewhere in Brazil.

and he has something on you. What he has, I'm not sure, but it's something, some dark secret heretofore not exposed."

"It doesn't take much to indict," she responded. "In the words of Edward Bennett Williams, 'a prosecutor can indict a ham sandwich if he chooses.'"

"When you're indicted, tried, and convicted," Morris told her, "there is a way out. A presidential pardon."

"I'll never ask Bill for a pardon," she said. "I'll go on trial and expose Starr as the shit that he really is."

On the day that Morris confronted her with his assertions and warnings, she faced yet another charge. On the shelves of grocery stores across America, there appeared a picture of a grotesque and horrible little creature from Outer Space. Evoking the plight of the character played by Mia Farrow in *Rosemary's Baby,* the tabloid charged that within the White House, Hillary had adopted a malevolent, hideous, and pint-sized Baby Satan.

Aides close to Hillary reported that at around this time, she was hovering on the verge of a nervous breakdown. Shaken to her core, she said, "I can't go on like this. I can't take much more of Starr's shit." She lost her appetite, along with ten pounds, and she walked the lonely corridors of the White House at night unable to sleep.

As a means of amplifying his orchestrated humiliation of her, Starr ordered that the venue for her cross-examination would be within a centrally positioned District of Columbia courthouse, where she would face maximum exposure. Secret Service agents offered to drive her into an underground parking section where she could take an elevator to the courtroom. She rejected

Things to laugh at when you're high:
MORE WEIRD TABLOIDS BASHING the CLINTONS

As time went by, they got even more *stoooopid*.

the plan.

"I'll go in through the front entrance and face all the cameras and onlookers," she said. "I'll stand tall and proud in spite of my inner turmoil. I'll answer all the questions thrown at me with authority and style."

Before entering the courtroom, Hillary had told reporters, "Cheerio! I'm off to face the firing squad!" Inside, she confronted Starr's firing squad, eight of his male deputies. "All of whom," in her words, "looked like the pasty-faced Starr himself."

In the words of author Gail Sheehy, "Hillary came to look upon Starr as a modern day Inspector Javert from *Les Misérables,* a fictional villain who would pursue his miscreant into the sewers of Paris. She was up against a prissy prosecutor who had challenged her integrity, had found her fingerprints on every alleged Clinton misdeed, and had forced her to face a 'clusterfuck' of cameras staked out to record her appearance before a grand jury. She demonized Starr, transforming him into a gruesome, re-creation of cross-dressing J. Edgar Hoover." Over the coming months, she came to interpret Starr as the skunk at her garden party.

Outside the courtroom, she faced "an armada of people, including reporters and TV cameras. They did not discover a broken woman, but a rather defiant one. "I tried to be as helpful as I could," she said at the end of the hearing.

Many of the jurors later expressed praise for her gracious demeanor under fire. Starr did not succeed in breaking her down on the stand. Later, he reportedly told his deputies, "There's not enough evidence to indict the bitch."

A longtime friend of Bill's, Taylor Branch, visited the White House at this time, and later expressed his dismay at the president's condition. "He went through peaks and valleys, which were very close together. It was jarring and painful to see him this overwrought."

Later, that friend indulged in some speculation. "Was Bill's real fear that Starr had some evidence that might lead to a jail term for his wife?"

[Back at the White House, after her testimony, Bill, Hillary, and Chelsea read the afternoon newspapers and watched the early evening news roundup on TV. As expected, she made all the headlines and led off the TV news.

At first, she was puzzled by one headline—"DRAGON LADY TESTIFIES." It seemed the so-called "dragon" derived from how the embroidered black wool coat she'd worn to the courthouse had been perceived by a reporter, who viewed the design as the emulation of a dragon. Actually, its design—an art deco rendering of seashells, not a dragon—had been conceived as a series of appliquéd swirls by Connie Fails, her designer in Little Rock.]

Hillary as "The National Nanny" Urges Teenagers Not to Have Sex

During all the turmoil whirling around her head, Hillary had managed to write a book, *It Takes a Village,* and planned an eleven-city publicity tour to promote sales. It eventually became a bestseller, earning a million dollars, which was turned over to a children's charity. Her book would spend eighteen weeks on *The New York Times* bestseller list, including three weeks as number one. It sold 450,000 copies in hardcover alone.

It focused on the impact individuals in a community, as well as groups, have on the growth of a child outside the family. She advocated a society which met all the needs of a child—in other words, it takes a village to rear a child. She claimed that children should be surrounded by "caring, nurturing, and informed adults."

(Left image above) The cover of one of many editions of a worthwhile and well-intentioned book whose release was scheduled to offset the damages of the Starr Report.

Without reading it, Robert Dole attacked it at the Republican National Convention that August. "It doesn't take a village to raise a child," he said. "It takes a family."

The first media attack *[it appeared even before publication]* was launched by the loud mouth of Rush Limbaugh, who never needed an excuse to condemn anything Hillary did, or whatever he thought she might have done. He was her worst enemy over the air waves.

Barbara Walters was selected as the host of Hillary's first TV interview. The Green Room of the White House was set up to film the exchange between these two strong-willed women.

As the interview opened,

Televised book talk (*It Takes a Village)* with Hillary and talk show host Phil Donahue.

Walters ignored the book and made their talk political. "Instead of your book, you have become the hot button issue of the day," the TV host charged. "How did you get into all this?"

"I ask myself that every day, Barbara," Hillary answered. "Eventually, the questions are answered and they go away and more questions come up and we'll just keep doing our best to answer them."

She told Walters that she got "distressed—a little sad, a little angry and irritated at all this probing. But I know that's part of the territory, and we'll just keep plowing through and trying to get to the end of this."

In 1996, Hillary, who had an aversion to the national press, appeared in a televised interview with Barbara Walters, ostensibly to promote her book, *It Takes a Village*. Walters asked hard-core political questions instead.

Hillary, who was making a concrete effort to soften her image, never looked more glamorous, relaxed, and self-confident.

Before the cameras were switched on, an adviser talked to her about style: "Be careful, be real, look for opportunities for humor, and make it a point to appear in movie star hair and makeup."

As for the previously missing and then suddenly found records, she explained that all of the Clinton files from Arkansas had been dumped into the upper rooms of the White House "since we do not have a home of our own at this point. Not all of the boxes had been examined. Our records are a mess." She even got Walters to confess that her records, like those of most Americans, were also a mess.

After their interview, Hillary launched her book tour. At every stop, she was asked

Even though her book, *It Takes a Village*, was meant to show her concern for children growing up in America, her promotion of it invariably turned political, to judge by the Newsweek cover above.

And despite her good intentions, at the Republican National Convention, her views were attacked as "anti-family." She was falsely accused of proposing that kids be separated from their parents if they were born out of wedlock or to poor mothers.

about the Whitewater investigation. But, unlike her health-care bus tour, she met supportive, positive audiences for the most part, women who were interested in her message about how to bring up children.

With sarcasm, some critics referred to her as "America's National Nanny," asserting that in her book, she sounded like everyone's maiden aunt, urging the country's teenagers not to engage in sexual activity. She advocated abstinence instead, claiming that teenagers were not able to cope with the drawbacks of a sexual relationship—pregnancy, venereal disease, abortion.

Newsweek had planned to put her book on its front cover. When she eventually saw the cover of the edition that contained the story about her book, its frontispiece was an unflattering photograph of her run under the banner head—"SAINT OR SINNER?" The article was more of a review of her political problems than of her views on the care and rearing of children.

The book got her embroiled in yet another controversy. Barbara Feinman, a professor of journalism at Georgetown University, claimed that she had ghostwritten the book for Hillary, and that it had been understood that she would eventually be paid $120,000 from Simon and Schuster. Hillary had not given her credit in the book. When confronted by reporters, she claimed, "Many people helped me write this book, including my own mother. I wrote the book myself."

Perhaps if she had specifically acknowledged Feinman for her contribution to the manuscript, the controversy could have been avoided.

As He Navigates the Waters of the River Styx "President Potholes" Addresses Congress

In his State of the Union address on January 23, 1996, Bill announced that "the era of big government is over." In addition to commandeering the Republicans' rallying cry, in his words, "I defanged the rattlesnake."

As Bob Dole, who would challenge him that year for the presidency itself, said, "We Republicans had to sit through a long speech at the banquet table, only to have our meal snatched from our hungry mouths. We were left only with bitter gruel. The president advocated welfare reform, more police on the streets, and a balanced budget. That left us to talk what? Abortion? Gay Rights? Single Mothers?"

Maureen Dowd, columnist for *The New York Times,* pejoratively labeled Bill "President Pothole, a fixer of tiny things."

Bill countered her charge, claiming "that little things had amounted to big changes." He said that nearly eight million new jobs had been created and that for the first time in years, U.S. automakers were outselling their Japanese rivals. He later flew to Bosnia to lend moral support to the American troops bogged down in an ethnic conflict.

Old scores and partisan hatreds die hard in D.C.

Back in Washington, he was gratified by the passing of the START II treaty, which eliminated two-thirds of the nuclear arsenals of both the United States and the former Soviet Republic.

"After all that, *The Times* calls my achievements 'potholes,'" he said in anger. "There are days you can't win. Maybe if I could become an alchemist, turning rocks into gold, I'd get some respect around here."

Despite his historic achievements, both Bill and Hillary kept getting caught up in the poisonous tidewaters of Whitewater, which he had come to compare to the dark, gloomy, murky, and forbidding waters of the River Styx.

When Bill encountered Alan Simpson—the crusty old senator from Wyoming, who was retiring--he told the president: "We're paying you guys back for Watergate."

To his own frustration, Dole couldn't benefit from broadcasting information about Bill's womanizing, based on fears that his opponents would dredge up charges of his own extramarital affair (or affairs).

Polls showed that Bill had a sixty percent approval rating among the American public. Yet half of those polled felt he "lacked personal and moral standards." Yet they were willing to re-elect him in spite of these personal flaws.

More "Dirt" on the World's Most Famous Office Romance

Burdened with the complex problems of the Free World, and with his *scandal du jour* at the White House, Bill nonetheless managed to launch the New Year with the pursuit of the black thong of one Monica Lewinsky. "I'll go to my grave regretting that," he later confided to friends.

On January 7, a deep snowstorm had paralyzed Washington, D.C., and many offices were closed. In its immediate aftermath, even the White House operated with only a skeletal staff.

Monica was reading a book in bed at the Watergate apartment owned by her mother. On that windy, snowy afternoon, a call came in for her. "To my surprise and shock, it was the President of the United States himself," she recalled. He wanted her to hazard the blizzard and pay him a visit at the Oval Office. After she'd dressed enticingly, she asked her brother to drive her to the White House, without telling her sibling what she was up to.

There, the president and Monica arranged to meet through the simulation of a "chance encounter" as a device to avoid suspicion among other staff members who had managed to navigate their way to work despite the snowstorms.

Inside the Oval Office, Bill maneuvered her into the bathroom. During the Clinton years, Monica, so far as it is known, is the only visitor who ever accompanied Bill to the toilet as part of a "Bathroom Summit."

This was the same bathroom where President Johnson had conducted very different types of summits during the 1960s. He would invite staff members, or even a visiting dignitary or two, into the bathroom "to keep talking while I take a big Texas style crap!"

On that icy day, Monica remembered sensing "a little boy quality" in Bill, something she found very attractive. She told him, "You are like a ray of sunshine, but sunshine that makes plants grow faster and makes their colors more vibrant."

He aroused an insecurity in her, as she later confessed: "I saw two sides of him—one a needy man who was not getting the sensitive, loving tenderness he wanted fulfilled. It was obvious that he just wasn't receiving nurturing he so desperately desired. Yet there was that other side of him, his reputation as a philanderer requiring a different woman every day."

To the Starr committee, Monica delivered more vivid *[and more pornographic]* details of her "Bathroom Summit" with the president: "He deep kissed me and unhooked my bra to fondle my breasts to which he applied his mouth."

He also wanted to perform cunnilingus on her, but she told him that she was menstruating so that would have to wait until another day. However, she did admit to performing fellatio on him.

Their next sexual encounter came about through a chance meeting one Sunday, January 21, near a White House elevator. He spotted her and invited her once again into the Oval Office.

She later said that he started kissing her and unbuttoned her dress to suck on her nipples. "He then unzipped his pants and exposed his erection." At this point, she performed fellatio on him again.

At the time, they were in the hallway leading from the Oval Office to his study. However, both of them heard someone enter the Oval Office.

"The president zipped up real quick and went out to deal with business before coming back later. I just remember when he walked out after zipping up, he was still visibly aroused. I just thought it was funny."

On February 4, Bill took time out from his duties to call Monica at her desk in the White House. He asked her to revisit the Oval Office for their sixth sexual encounter.

Later, in testimony delivered to Starr and his deputies, she would go into detail about what happened next: "I was wearing a long dress that buttoned from the neck to the ankles. Bill unbuttoned it and unhooked my bra. He was looking at me and touching me and telling me how beautiful I was. He touched my breasts with his hands and his mouth. He also touched my genitals, first through my underwear and then directly. I performed oral sex on him."

Later, she talked with him at his desk in the Oval Office for forty-five minutes, the only real conversation they'd ever had up to that point. "That was the start of our friendship which had begun to blossom."

That friendship was short-lived. On President's Day, February 19, he called her at her mother's Watergate apartment and once again invited her to visit him in the Oval Office.

This time, she sensed something was wrong that he wasn't telling her over the phone. She went to the White House and was allowed into the Oval Office by a tall, slender, Hispanic plainclothes agent.

Bill got right to the point. "I no longer feel right about our intimacy," he told her. "We've got to put a stop to it."

"He hugged me, but did not kiss me," she later claimed. "In tears, I left the office while he took a phone call from some sugar grower in Florida."

During March and April of 1996, there would be other contacts between the president and Monica.

On March 29, Monica was walking down the corridor of the White House when she encountered the president, who was wearing one of the neckties she'd presented to him. Later that afternoon, he phoned her at her desk and asked her if she'd like to attend a movie that night in the White House screening room. Hillary was in Athens at the time. She declined, telling him, "I don't want it to appear that I'm hanging out in the West Wing uninvited."

Two days later, on a Sunday, he asked her to revisit the Oval Office on the pretext of delivering some important papers. She agreed and presented him with another Hugo Boss necktie as a present. In California, she had once sold neckties, and was clever at selecting (her words) "tasteful and presidential ones."

This time, they were interrupted by a call from Hillary, who was visiting Ireland at the time.

Again sneaking away to a position in the hallway beside the presidential study, Monica testified that he "kissed my bare breasts and fondled my genitals."

In what became her most notorious and highly publicized claim, she said he inserted a cigar into her vagina before putting it into his mouth, claiming, "It tastes good."

After that sexual encounter, they walked together through the Rose Garden. During their brief time, she thought to herself, "I dared not think the unthinkable: That he really cared for me."

When news of this encounter was later revealed to America, it led to a "monstrous increase" in cigar sales throughout the land.

Many of the president's aides were aware of his sexual liaisons with Monica, and some of them wanted to protect Bill from his own impulses, fearing that his affair with Monica would lead to public exposure and humiliation. "Let's hope Hillary doesn't find out," one aide said to another.

Evelyn Lieberman, the Deputy Chief of Staff for White House Operations, considered Monica "a nuisance, always hanging out in the West Wing." She called her a "clutch," meaning someone who is always in some place where she should not be.

"Everybody seemed to think my encounters with the president were all my fault," Monica lamented. "They felt I was stalking him or else I was making unwanted advances toward him."

Monica's boss, Timothy Keating, Staff Director for Legislative Affairs, notified her that she would have to leave her job at the White House. He was transferring her to a new post at the Pentagon. "He told me that I was too sexy to be working in the White House, and that my new job at the Pentagon, where I would be writing press releases, was a far sexier job."

She burst into tears, fearing she'd never see Bill again. "My relationship with him would be gone forever."

On Easter Sunday, April 7, Monica had another sexual encounter with the president when she told him of her dismissal. He talked to her over the phone and found her crying. He asked her if she could come and see him, and she agreed to do that.

In his private study, off the Oval Office, he told her he, too, was upset over her dismissal, and that he promised to bring her back to the White House after the November elections.

Once again, they had a sexual encounter, where he unzipped his pants to expose an erection. He invited her to perform oral sex on him.

But in the middle of the act, Dick Morris placed a call to him. He asked her to continue to fellate him in the hallway while he talked to Morris.

When Harold Ickes, one of his chief aides, entered the Oval Office and called out for Bill, the president heeded the summons. She fled, exiting through another door.

Although she and the president had occasional phone sex and chance encounters, their sexual episodes didn't resume until February of 1997.

The Defiant Susan McDougal—
What Happens When You "Diss Upon a Starr"

March 4 marked the debut, in Little Rock, of the Watergate trial of Jim and Susan McDougal. Hundreds of reporters and TV newspeople, along with satellite trucks and klieg lights, descended on the courthouse there. U.S. Federal Judge George Howard presided. In his mid-60s, he was a bantam weight, the deeply religious African American son of a dirt-poor sharecropper.

In the beginning, Jim McDougal seemed to like the media attention until the case went against him. He liked to banter with the reporters, telling them stories of politics from the old days in Arkansas. An eccentric, Jim showed up in white suits and Panama hats, evoking the Big Daddy character in Tennessee Williams' *Cat on a Hot Tin Roof.*

The Whitewater investigations and trials would set off a series of events worthy of a 1,500-page volume. It was the story of lies, betrayals, jail terms, heart attacks, wrecked lives, and financial disasters whose main goal was "to get the Clintons."

Other lives, including innocent ones, were destroyed in the aftermath of the multi-million dollar probe, at taxpayer expense, which was merely a sideshow to the main attraction, the President of the United States and his First Lady.

Witnesses popped up on the scene to become, almost overnight, household names. One such person was a shady Arkansas financial figure, David Hale, who had run a government-funded lending agency dispensing loans to small businesses. He had already pleaded guilty to two felonies, and he presented questionable testimony at the McDougal trial, obviously hoping to get a lighter sentence for his crimes. In a memoir, Hillary labeled him "an accomplished thief and con artist."

His accusations against Bill had never surfaced before the McDougal trial. He charged that Bill, then governor of Arkansas, had pressured him to make a fraudulent $300,000 loan to Susan McDougal. He also claimed that Bill had asked him to keep his name out of the transaction.

During Starr's Whitewater probe, "Hale overnight went from being an indicted scam artist to the government's pampered witness," Susan later charged.

On April 28 at the White House, Bill videotaped sworn testimony for around four hours, denying Hale's charges, calling his claims "absurd and untrue."

This tape was played to the grand jury on May 9.

After his interrogation at the White House by Starr and his deputies, Bill later recalled, "They were the sleaziest, filthiest people you could imagine. I wanted to take a shower after it was over."

Instead of looking at the Lincoln Bedroom, Starr demanded a full search of the Clinton's living quarters, even a thorough probe of Chelsea's room and a detailed search of the lingerie drawers of the First Lady in case "she's hidden something among her bras and bloomers" as Bill later referred to it. "These boys merely confirmed my worst suspicions about them: All of them were panty sniffers."

Jim McDougal, the flamboyant savings and loan manipulator, had been one of Bill Clinton's staunchest supporters, frequently asserting, under oath, that he had done nothing wrong in the financial maneuverings that had prefaced the Whitewater scandal.

But after his 1996 conviction on charges of fraud, he became a cooperating witness for the prosecution, turned on the Clintons, and made serious allegations against them, many published in a memoir which was widely debunked for its contradictions and lack of evidence.

Before his death in jail in 1998, deeply embittered and after years of failing health, he told Susan, his former wife, "Fuck the Clintons! Fuck 'em! What the fuck have they ever done for us? At the first sign of trouble, they ran like dogs."

As president of Capital Management Services, Hale had defrauded the U.S. Government's Small Business Administration for $3.4 million. As Bill himself charged, "Hale gave money to himself through a series of dummy corporations."

It was later revealed that Hale had also benefitted from payments made by the agents of the "Arkansas Project," a $2.4 million campaign set up to investigate Bill's activities as governor. The project was financed by Clinton-hating billionaire Richard Mellon Scaife of Pittsburgh.

Hale did escape with a relatively light sentence of only two years. On the stand, he was filled with tears and remorse for any wrongdoing. As Susan later wrote, "It was like trying to punch the Pillsbury Dough Boy. You were never going to deal any real damage."

Susan watched in horror and disgust as her former husband was treated by Starr "like a rich widower at a church social." In her opinion, Jim delivered false testimony against the Clintons, hoping that like David Hale, he, too, would get a lighter sentence.

She claimed that she didn't feel any great loyalty to the Clintons—in fact, she had never gotten along with Hillary. "But I knew beyond a shadow of doubt this was a witch hunt. I also knew that Bill and Hillary had done nothing wrong, but were being implicated by Jim and that Hale fellow trying to save their own skins."

She later discussed her turbulent marriage to Jim. "It was like going to a movie, *The Sound of Music,* but ending up watching *The Exorcist."*

On April 14, Jim McDougal was convicted of eighteen felony accounts of fraud and conspiracy in regard to questionable loans made by his savings and loan. Since the loans had been federally guaranteed, taxpayers were out $68 million. Starr tried to get Jim a reduced sentence, since he had cooperated with his investigation of the Clintons.

[In 1998, at the age of fifty-seven, while locked in solitary confinement at a Federal prison in Fort Worth, Texas, Jim died of a heart attack.]

On May 28, Susan appeared before Judge Howard, sobbing. "If not for Whitewater, I would be married and have children. I just ask you please for your mercy and to tell you how sorry I am." She had been found guilty in connection with a $300,000 "business loan" made in 1986.

She was convicted of four counts of fraud and conspiracy related to the Whitewater Development scheme. But because of other ongoing court proceedings, her jail time would not begin until March 7, 1998.

It was determined that she would serve two years in a Federal prison. But, as she was leaving the courthouse, Starr served her with a subpoena to make yet another appearance before yet another Whitewater Grand Jury, that trial scheduled to begin in two weeks.

After her sentencing, a broke, broken, and despondent Susan said, "I was filled with an uncontrollable rage. It's impossible to understand what it feels like to be convicted of a crime you didn't commit. The anger is beyond control."

Her defense attorney, Bobby McDaniel, blasted Starr's prosecutors, claiming that Susan was a "political prisoner," because

A Nest of Vipers

Many of the allegations that mushroomed into the Whitewater scandal originated with David Hale *(depicted above)*, a former Arkansas municipal judge and banker. Based on charges unrelated to the Whitewater deal, he pled guilty and went to jail for conspiring to defraud the Small Business Administration by looting money from a dummy business he established. He was sentenced to two years and four months in prison.

As part of his guilty plea, he agreed to provide testimony to Kenneth Starr and the investigators of the Whitewater scandal. Although he had testified in 1989 against the McDougals about the bankruptcy of the Madison Guaranty Savings and Loan, he never mentioned Bill Clinton in his detailed account of the $300,000 loan at that time. It was not until Hale came under Indictment on other charges that—as part of his plea bargain, he alleged any crime by Clinton.

Consequently, in testimony damning to the Clintons, Hale testified in U.S. District Court that then-Governor Bill Clinton urged him to make a fraudulent $300,000 loan and that he not be named in the loan.

On June 23, 1994, Eugene Fitzhugh, another Arkansas lawyer and businessman linked to "anti-Clinton forces cooperating with the Independent Counsel," pleaded guilty to trying to bribe David Hale.

she refused to cooperate in the Independent Counsel's investigation of the Clintons. He told reporters that he was appealing Susan's conviction.

Before a Grand Jury, at the debut of what was supposed to be a re-opening of the Whitewater case, aspects for which she had already been convicted, Susan gave her full name for the record, but then refused to answer any more questions. She told the Grand Jury, "Get another Independent Counsel, and I'll answer every question." Judge Susan Webber Wright, no friend of Bill's, sentenced Susan for civil contempt of court. She was ordered to report to the U.S. Marshal's office in Little Rock on September 9, at which time she would be transported to the Faulkner County Jail in Conway, Arkansas.

There, she was placed in a holding cell ten feet by five feet, with a dirty concrete floor, a single bench, and a toilet with no seat.

Susan McDougal is pictured here in waist chains and leg irons, a photo that enraged much of America, even Republicans.

The American Civil Liberties Union filed a lawsuit on her behalf, alleging that she was being held in barbaric conditions in a politically motivated, unethical attempt by Kenneth Starr to force her to testify.

After several hours, two marshals came for her with waist chains and leg irons. She was handcuffed and then her hands were chained to her waist. She was to be escorted to the jail's van for transport to prison. But because of the leg irons, she could take only baby steps. She feared she'd fall, landing on her face.

The Independent Counsel, Kenneth Starr, became a despised figure to millions of Americans. Susan McDougal said, "I was offered a deal—relief from legal jeopardy that included Whitewater charges in exchange for damaging information about Bill and Hillary."

"I didn't possess such information, and I wouldn't repeat the lies Starr's deputies wanted to put in my mouth."

She hoped no one would see her in this position, but as she stepped outside, a bevy of reporters and cameramen were there to record the event. They stormed around her, screaming questions at her. One of the chained prisoners behind her called out to her, "Gal, what in the fuck did you do?"

"He no doubt thought I was a madwoman, a serial killer, a cannibal, whomever, to be so severely chained like this."

"I knew I was going to lead off the evening's TV news," she said. "The entire world could see that Starr had beaten me and humiliated me. I mustered what dignity I could and hobbled to the van."

From September 9, 1996 until March 6, 1998, she would spend eighteen months in prison, eight of them in solitary confinement, where she was allowed out only one hour a day.

During that lockdown, she was caged in a Plexiglas-enclosed, soundproofed cell.

She was also subjected to "diesel therapy"—that is, the penal system's practice of hauling a prisoner around to various jails, perhaps in an attempt to break his or her spirit. She logged time in jails in such cities as Los Angeles and Oklahoma City before ending up back in Little Rock.

"Susan just wouldn't lie and tell Starr and his men what they wanted to hear—not the truth, but what they wanted the 'truth' to be," Bill claimed.

In the days, weeks, and months ahead, she was inundated with letters from all over the country, many of them written by Republicans. Much of America was outraged after having seen her walking in shackles to a police van before being forcibly hauled off to prison. That seemed to show "the insanity of Starr's never-ending investigation."

As she was transported in police vans from one prison to another, Susan found that they all had something in common—"They were overcrowded, filthy, loud, often filled with raving lunatics, hardened murderers, and designed for the greatest discomfort to break your spirit and humiliate you." She was forced to shower in front of "lesbian guards and other female inmates who wanted to rape me."

In March of 1998, after she'd served her time for civil contempt of court, she had to begin serving a two-year sentence for her 1996 conviction in the Whitewater trial. She served four months before she was released for medical reasons.

Even so (also in 1988), she had to face an embezzlement trial in California where she was acquitted on all twelve counts.

To top it off, Starr's Office of Independent Counsel then brought yet another criminal contempt-of-court charge against her, alleging obstruction of justice. The trial began in March of 1999. It ended with a hung jury of 7-5 in favor of acquittal. The judge ruled her not guilty.

In January of 2001, during the final hours of the Clinton presidency, Bill issued a presidential pardon for Susan. She was a free woman at last, albeit one of the most tragic victims of the Kenneth Starr investigation.

In 2003, Susan penned her harrowing ordeal instigated by Starr in a memoir called *The Woman Who Wouldn't Talk.* She relayed in gruesome detail the conditions to which she had been subjected. It was revealed how a small-town

Arkansas woman became a nationally known felon in one of the most fascinating and unexamined legacies of the Clinton presidency.

Launching More Trials, & Demanding Additional Testimony from Bill, Starr Refuses to Give Up

On June 17, Starr launched yet another Whitewater trial, this one aimed at two Arkansas bankers, Robert Hill and Herby Branscum, Jr.

They were accused of illegally using bank funds to reimburse themselves for political contributions they had made, including funds given to aid Bill during his race for the governorship of Arkansas in 1990.

Once again at the White House, Starr's "goons" (Bill's words) descended on him for another videotaped testimony. "I got even with these fuckers this time by telling them all the bathrooms were out of order, and they'd have to go piss on the lawn in front of cameramen."

The president called Starr's latest charges "absurd." Bill's testimony and lack of evidence led to the bankers being cleared.

Bill denounced Starr's latest attempt to "get me like this. I am sickened by the abuse of prosecutorial power," he claimed. "The enormous legal costs my friends have been forced to bear. The staggering costs to the taxpayers of this unwarranted prosecution. How many more millions of dollars of taxpayer money will Starr spend to try to remove me from office? Nixon's Watergate crimes were real. Whitewater was a failed real estate investment. I never set foot on the property."

Senator Robert Dole *(left)*, nominated at the Republican National Convention in 1996, picked Jack Kemp as his vice presidential running mate.

Together, they launched a mean-spirited and uninspired campaign that failed to unseat the sitting president.

"I'll be here for another four years," Bill Clinton so accurately predicted, to the dismay of Dole and Kemp.

***

The summer of 1996 droned on, as night after night, the talking heads of TV asked one question: "Will Bill Clinton be re-elected?"

During the hot, sultry month of August, Republicans convened in San Diego, a city filled with more illegal immigrants than GOP delegates to the Convention. Delegates had seemingly determined that it was Senator Bob Dole's "time at bat," and that the prevailing state of American affairs demanded the election of a conservative. Some GOP operatives feared that Dole lacked the charisma of Bill Clinton and might lose the debates.

Actor Christopher Reeve, famous for his screen impersonation of Superman, had become paralyzed after falling from a horse.

As part of his advocacy for increased medical research for the regeneration of spinal cord tissue, he made a "heart-warming but heart-breaking" appearance before the Democratic National Convention in 1996.

Dole selected Jack Kemp, a former quarterback for the Buffalo Bills, as his vice presidential running mate. Kemp had been Secretary of Housing and Urban Development.

Unlike the right-wing extremism of the notorious 1992 Republican convention, the San Diego crowd was more moderate this year in its tone. At the podium, the convention featured such popular moderates as Colin Powell, a military hero who had opted not to seek the presidency itself.

When he accepted the GOP nomination for the upcoming presidential race, Dole told his fellow right wingers, "Bill Clinton is the Baby Boomer who never grew up."

***

The Democratic delegates, on the other hand, convened at the end of August in Hillary's hometown of Chicago. *Politicos* predicted that Bill, as part of his nomination for re-election, would experience "a coronation instead of a nomination," and they were on target.

An unusual array of speakers preceded his acceptance speech. They included former movie star, Christopher Reeve (Superman), who had been paralyzed in a fall from a horse. Jim and Sarah Brady also appeared, thanking Democrats for their support of anti-gun legislation.

During his acceptance speech, Bill presented an optimistic portrait of America to the Democratic convention and to millions watching him on television. He contrasted Dole's speech at the Republican convention to his own: "Senator Dole wanted to build a bridge to the past. I come before you wanting to build a bridge to the 21st Century!" His words generated a standing ovation.

Jim Brady and his wife, Sarah, became poignant symbols for the horrors of gun violence, and leading advocates of gun control.

Jim had been paralyzed for life in 1981 when he was shot by John Hinckley during an assassination attempt on the life of then-President Ronald Reagan.

One reporter contrasted Dole's speech with Clinton's. "Dole reminded me of my philosophy professor who put me to sleep. On the other hand, Bill could sell Fords to Chevrolet dealers."

At the end of the convention, Bill's approval rating, despite his many scandals, had soared to sixty percent. He knew however, that he'd never be popular in redneck America where voters continued to attack him for policies that they negatively associated with "guns, gays, and abortions."

After his re-nomination at the Democratic convention, Bill reportedly made an agreement with his wife. "If you help me fulfill my dream of getting re-elected, and ignore some of the scandal around me, along with my many faults, I will help you achieve your dream of becoming the first woman President of the United States."

"You've got yourself a deal, Big Boy," she answered.

The Texas billionaire, Ross Perot, as feisty as ever, once again announced himself as a candidate for president, as he had done in 1992. But his popularity would never rise to its previous heights, due in large part to his withdrawal

Dick Morris and his wife and frequent co-author, Eilene McGann, depicted together on the cover of *Time,* developed a flourishing cottage industry based on the publication and sale of their anti-Clinton books.

Sherry Rowlands was the prostitute, based on her revelations to the tabloids, who made Morris famous outside the Beltway. She claimed that he had a foot fetish and that he allowed her to listen in to his (presumably privileged and confidential) telephone conversations with Bill Clinton.

Rowlands, whose dislike for Morris was obvious, told reporters, "I believe in destiny. Public exposure was his destiny. You can only get so big in the head. If you're doing things behind their backs, stabbing people, it's only a matter of time before destiny catches up with you."

from the race in '92, with the justification that he didn't want fraudulently doctored [i.e., photoshopped] images of his daughter in a "lesbian situation" to be made public.

In 1996, Perot once again threw himself into the presidential race, repeating his 1992 refrain urging voters to cast their ballots for him. "If you vote for Clinton, he won't be able to serve you. He'll spend at least two years of his administration in jail."

Media organized fast against DOMA. Their message?

Gay People Aren't Politically Passive.

Piss them off at your own risk.

On Sept 21, 1996 Bill signed DOMA, a move most of his gay constituents defined as a betrayal. The hue and cry that followed was loud and long.

Before leaving Chicago, Bill faced yet another scandal, this one not of his own making. His political adviser, Dick Morris, had been exposed for his a long-term affair with a prostitute, Sherry Rowland. It was revealed that in Morris' suite within Washington's Mayflower Hotel, he would sometimes let Rowland listen as he talked to Bill in the Oval Office.

Erskine Bowles, Bill's new Chief of Staff, went to Morris's suite and, as part of a face-to-face confrontation, demanded his resignation from Bill's presidential campaign.

One of Morris' comments during his exit was quoted as: "The trouble in the White House is that Hillary is not satisfied with being the junior partner. She wants to be the commander-in-chief."

An Insulting Directive to American Gays & Lesbians: "It's Illegal to Marry the Person You Love"

Bill perhaps was ashamed that for political reasons, he had signed the Defense of Marriage Act (DOMA) in September of 1996. During one of the presidential debates, his rival, the homophobic Senator Dole, made it clear to millions of TV viewers that the president had signed his endorsement of DOMA at midnight when there were no reporters around and when photographers had been barred.

DOMA defined marriage for Federal purposes as the union of one man with one woman. It also granted states the right to refuse to recognize a same-sex marriage performed under the laws of other states.

First introduced by the Republicans in 1996, DOMA passed both houses of Congress by large, veto-proof majorities. Even though he signed it, Bill would later advocate DOMA's repeal. In his memoirs, he did not even mention the legislation, perhaps because he did not want his endorsement of it to become part of his legacy.

Authored by Bob Barr, a Congressman from Georgia, the bill had been reviewed by the House Judiciary Committee. Some of its members had said that enactment of DOMA would demonstrate the government's "moral disapproval of homosexuality."

A hero to gay and lesbian America, Ted Kennedy denounced DOMA "as a mean-spirited form of legislative gay-bashing designed to inflame the public four months before the November elections."

The sole independent in the Senate, Bernie Sanders of Vermont, voted against the bill. *[In 2015, Sanders would compete against Hillary for the Democratic nomination for the presidency.]*

Most of gay America were "shocked and angered" over Bill's signing of the legislation. *[Even though he'd signed it, he denounced it as "unnecessary and divisive."]* It was viewed as a great betrayal of the gays and lesbians who had so ardently supported him in his race for the presidency. Although he did

The sole independent in the Senate, Bernie Sanders of Vermont, voted against DOMA.

In 2015, Sanders would compete against Hillary for the Democratic nomination for president.

A hero to gay and lesbian America, Senator Ted Kennedy denounced DOMA "as a mean-spirited form of legislative gay-bashing, designed to inflame the public four months before the November election."

Bob Barr, the mean-spirited, ultra-right-wing Congressman from Georgia, was the author of DOMA. He was described as "the idol of the gun-toting, abortion-fighting, IRS-hating right wing of American politics."

However, he later changed his mind about same-sex marriage.

sign it, Bill, as president, had been an advocate of Gay Rights and had pushed for AIDS funding, and he'd also appointed LGBT people to his administration.

On July 10, 2009, Bill officially endorsed same-sex marriage and urged that the Supreme Court reject DOMA, as "discriminatory and unconstitutional." The court acquiesced in 2015, based on a narrow 5-4 vote.

"This Is the Last Time I'll Ever Again Seek Political Office"

—Bill Clinton

Although Bill's re-election was almost assured, he nonetheless campaigned arduously across the nation, fearing that Democrats, thinking he'd already won, might stay home on election day.

For the most part, he met ardent supporters who hailed his candidacy. Of course, there were vulgar people along the route. In one town hall, some fool in the rear called out, "Bill, tell us, are you still lapping Gennifer Flowers' pussy?"

The catcaller was thrown out of the rally.

Near the end of the campaign, Bill faced the largest number of hecklers in Denver. But he handled them with humor. "Mark Twain said that every dog needs a few fleas. Now, I'll admit, I'd had a few more than I wanted. But Twain said that fleas keep every dog from worrying so much about being a dog."

In his last stop on the campaign trail, before flying to Little Rock for the election, Bill paid a midnight call at Sioux Falls, South Dakota. Even at that hour, the eager crowds were still up and awake, wanting to get a look at him. "This is the last rally of the last campaign I will ever run," he told his supporters.

After he placed his vote on election day in Little Rock, Bill was dismayed that early reports on TV indicated low voter turnout. Apparently, many Democrats were staying at home, thinking their support would not be necessary for a Clinton re-election.

The Texas billionaire, Ross Perot, had lost confidence and prestige with voters during his bid for the presidency back in 1992. Now, in 1996, he might nevertheless still be a spoiler.

When the results were announced, Bill carried forty-nine percent of the vote. Perot's entry into the race had prevented Bill from getting the symbolic fifty percent he had wanted. Dole limped in with forty-one percent. In the Electoral College, Bill swept to victory with a 379 to 159 vote.

When the results were tallied, Bill had won Arizona and Florida, which had not voted for him in '92. In contrast, he'd lost three states which had carried him in '92: Georgia, Montana, and Colorado.

Historically, Bill became the first Democratic president to win a second term since Franklin D. Roosevelt's 1936 victory during the depths of the Great Depression.

***

After a year of scandal, defeats, and ultimate victory, Bill sat in the Oval Office on the final day of 1996. With tremors of regret, he mused to Hillary and his closest aides, "I've come to the point in my life where I have more yesterdays than tomorrows."

Despite the relentless attacks, Bill Clinton remains one of America's most popular presidents. His charm and charisma seemed to win out over his weakness for chasing after women.

My Life, his long, bestselling autobiography, describes the day-to-day bombardments of his presidency, the venomous attacks, his loyal aides and the "raging maniacs" on the other side, the heartbreaking setbacks, and the sometimes breathtaking achievements.

As First Lady, with dreams about becoming president herself one day, Hillary was placed in the unenviable position of having to deal with the public exposure of her husband's philandering.

"He screwed up in more ways than one," she told her aides. "That Bill didn't have the decency to conceal his adultery made it worse."

"Of course, it was humiliating for me. It threatened not only his presidency, but my future dream of becoming the first woman president of the United States."

Chapter Seventeen

The Most Explosive Sex Scandal in the History of the White House.

Lewinsky Blabbed Too Much, Remembered Too Much. Bill Wonders "If Any Man on the Planet Should Suffer Lewinsky, Jones, and Tripp In a Single Lifetime"

Clinton's Lawyer Assures the Nation that Bill's Penis, "In Terms of Size, Shape, and Direction, is That of a Normal Man"

Those happy faces in the Oval Office, President Clinton and Monica Lewinsky, would within months turn sad and depressed.

Monica's lifestyle, appearance, values, and morality would be denigrated, although she did receive some sympathy and support from well wishers who viewed her as "a girl wronged."

"In the eyes of many Americans, I was this sad, pathetic loser who loved the limelight and made up a relationship with the president," Monica said.

In spite of pressures the Clintons survived in the 90s, Hillary, Bill, and daughter Chelsea faced the 21st century with renewed hope and courage. "We're still together," Chelsea said, "Now and forever."

The Clintons' comeback in the 21st Century has become a phenomenon. Leaving the White House under a cloud and penniless, they have bounced back to become a major force in the world.

Bill today is a global humanitarian; Hillary the *duenna* of the Democratic Party, and Chelsea has emerged as a formidable public figure in her own right.

"Stand by your man."

George Stephanopoulos is shown in the Oval Office offering aid and support to the embattled President Clinton.

"The hoofbeats were closing in on us," his aide said. "Whitewater became the catchall term for any allegation of unseemliness and impropriety against anyone anywhere near the Clintons or the White House."

By 1997, both Bill and Hillary had grown, strengthened, and evolved. They were no longer the wide-eyed innocents who had arrived on the doorstep of the White House in 1993. As she admitted herself, "My life was like steel tempered in fire, a bit harder on the edges, but more durable and more flexible."

She said that although her husband, at fifty, was showing his age, and that his hair was almost completely white, she was still his best friend. Four years in the Oval Office had aged him, but "he still had that boyish smile, sharp wit, and infectious optimism that I'd fallen in love with twenty-five years before," she claimed.

As for her controversial hair styles, she was blonder than ever. Her hairdos had improved, and her sense of fashion had sharpened. That was evident when she showed up in 1997 at the post re-election round of Inaugural Balls wearing a fabulously embroidered gold tulle gown with a matching satin cape, both of which were designed by Oscar de la Renta.

Their second term in office had gotten off to a bad start when Hillary had a dispute with Bill over which Supreme Court Justice would swear him in. Tradition called for the ceremony to be spearheaded by Chief Justice William Rehnquist. She objected violently, claiming that he was a racist.

[In 1952, Rehnquist had written that "white people in the South don't like colored people." He'd also once stated that he strongly favored the court's key pro-segregation decision from 1896.]

"I detest Rehnquist, and he loathes us," she told her husband. She wanted

Bill & Hillary On the World Stage

At Dinner In Russia, Boris Yeltsin Serves a Pig's Ear to Bill, & Moose Lips to Hillary

the oath delivered by either Ruth Bader Ginsburg or Stephen Breyer. In the end, Bill decided to go with Rehnquist, feeling tradition called for it. "Like you, though, I hate the fucker's guts," he told her.

Chief Justice William Rehnquist donated that ridiculous, chevron-striped judicial robe—the garb he had designed and worn while presiding over the impeachment trial of President Clinton in the Senate—to the Smithsonian Institution.

His critics had ridiculed it as *schmaltz* and scandalous *schmatte* appropriate to a Gilbert & Sullivan operetta.

He had Sotheby's appraise the value of the robe at $30,000, an amount he subsequently deducted from his income tax.

When the two men came together for the swearing in, the hostility between them was barely concealed. "It was as frosty as the cold temperature that winter day," Bill said.

At the end of the ceremony, Rehnquist, in a sort of mocking voice, told Bill, "Good luck! You'll need it!"

Hillary also questioned "the joker" who had arranged the seating. She was placed on the dias for the swearing-In ceremony beside her number one enemy in Washington, Newt Gingrich, Speaker of the House of Representatives, who was on an impassioned campaign to remove her husband from office.

Supreme Court Justice William Rehnquist—vain, egotistical, self-important, and unfunny—a Bill Clinton hater.

During a later encounter with the president, he told Bill, "The Senate should have removed you from office."

She noted with a certain glee that he had run into trouble with the House Ethics Committee for setting up his own tax-exempt group to finance his public speaking, a violation of tax laws. The day after Bill's inauguration, she read with delight that Gingrich had not only received a reprimand, but that he'd been ordered to pay a $300,000 fine.

Surely that "joker" Hillary had referred to, the one who had arranged the seating, could not have come up with a more odd combination than positioning Chelsea (who wore a miniskirt) immediately beside the ninety-five-year old Strom Thurmond, the frisky nonagenarian Senator from South Carolina. He told her, "I do believe you're prettier than your mother. Yes, you are, and if I was seventy years younger, I'd court you."

Soon, Chelsea would be far removed from Washington's political circus, as she'd enrolled at

Stanford University in California. Later, Hillary reported that she was suffering from "empty nest syndrome—disoriented, teary, nostalgic, and proud, all at the same time."

Bill Clinton, Innkeeper of the Fat Cat Hotel

During Bill's second term, Erskine B. Bowles, a North Carolina investment banker and millionaire, became the new Chief of Staff at the White House. He had little tolerance for political scandal and partisan warfare.

Bowles had met Bill in 1992 when he became a fund-raiser for him. Almost from the beginning, the two men formed a strong bond. At one point, Bill referred to him as "my brother" or at least the brother I wished I'd had."

Bowles once told friends, "Bill has more personal magnetism than anybody I've ever met. I want to organize the White House along more businesslike lines—no more midnight conferences. My first major job is to negotiate with the GOP majority and strike a deal on the budget."

Privately, Bowles told his aides, "We've got to keep Bill out of all talks. He'll agree to anything."

The New York Times applauded Bowles' new businesslike approach to running the government, hailing the deficit reduction as a milestone, "the equivalent of the fall of the Berlin Wall."

As he began his second term, Bill's political enemies were ready

Socks, the cat associated with the Clintons during their White House years, became the most celebrated feline in the world. He spent most of his days just outside the Oval Office, on the desk of Betty Currie, the president's private secretary. When Bill brought Buddy, his Labrador, to meet Socks, the cat detested him instantly, a feud that later caused pet-related tension in the White House.

When their administration ended, the Clintons took Buddy with them, but left Socks in the care of Currie. The cat lived with her at her home in Hollywood, Maryland, dying at the age of eighteen in 2009.

During the Whitewater trials, Currie was dragged before Kenneth Starr's investigating committee for information about the relationship between the president and the intern.

Although Currie was a deeply religious woman who would not lie to protect Bill, she was not a hostile witness.

to pounce on anything he did, including taking very close looks at the people he invited for sleepovers at the White House.

In all, the Clintons had entertained and housed, usually for very short stays, more than a thousand guests in the Executive Mansion, many of them in either the Lincoln Bedroom or the Queen's Bedroom directly across the hall. Many were celebrities—Chevy Chase, Tom Hanks, or Steven Spielberg, but others were just friends from Arkansas or contributors to his campaign. His enemies called Bill's White House the "Fat Cat Hotel."

Bill denied this until a note surfaced from him, directing a member of his staff to "Give me the top list, the $50,000 or more donors."

The parade of Bill's house guests appalled right-wing commentator Charles Krauthammer. "Has there ever been a president so lacking in discrimination in his choice of friends, associates, liaisons, partners? So willing to embrace, engage, exploit, transact with anyone? So ready to start overnights right away?"

Still plagued with Kenneth Starr's ongoing and relentless probes into his private life, Bill managed to begin his second term in office with a record for having generated noteworthy accomplishments during his first term. He had balanced the budget, increased investment in education, cut wasteful spending, offered tax relief for middle class Americans, saved Medicare from going broke, and offered health-care to some five million uninsured children.

Unlike Ronald Reagan, who seemingly did not want to admit that AIDS even existed, Bill pushed forward with programs not only to aid victims, but to seek a possible cure. Although the death rate was going down in the United States, the disease was exploding throughout Africa, which Hillary had recently visited.

In spite of all these accomplishments, Whitewater and Starr would simply not go away. Onlookers were shocked when Starr announced that he would resign as Independent Counsel on August 1 to accept a position as Dean of Pepperdine Law School in Malibu, California. Bill was relieved, claiming that "Starr had obviously come to believe that Whitewater was a dry hole." The position endowed for Starr at Pepperdine was financed by Clinton-hater and billionaire, Richard Mellon Scaife.

As news of Starr's retreat spread, the anti-Clinton brigade refused to accept Starr's resignation, and he was pressured to "hang in there" and keep looking for wrongdoing.

"What has Starr accomplished?" Bill asked. "He deeply damaged a lot of good people's reputations, and saddled them with crippling legal bills. He wasted millions of dollars in taxpayer money."

Acquiescing to right-wing pressure, Starr relented, and agreed to stay and continue looking for something he could use against Bill and Hillary.

In February, Bill continued to receive foreign visitors, including Prime Minister "Bibi" Netanyahu of Israel, followed by a visit in early March from Yasser Arafat of Palestine.

On March 13, Bill paid a visit to the Hobe Sound, Florida home of golf pro Greg Norman. An Australian nicknamed "The Great White Shark," Norman, winner of more than eighty-five international golf tournaments, had been the world's number one-ranking golfer in the 1980s and '90s. Bill's visit with the golf star had gone pleasantly, lasting late into the night. But as he was leaving, the steps outside Norman's home were not well lit. Missing the last step, the president took a bone-wrenching fall.

Rushed to the nearest hospital, he was X-rayed, the doctors finding that he'd torn some ninety percent of his right quadriceps. *[In Bill's case, "quadriceps" referred to the large muscle of his thigh, the one that extended from his femur (the bone of the upper leg), stretched over his patella (the kneecap) and anchored into the top of his tibia.]*

Golf pro Greg Norman was called "The Great White Shark."

He entertained the president until late at night, but was later partially responsible for crippling him.

Flown back to Washington aboard *Air Force One,* he had to endure several hours of surgery, followed by six months of sometimes agonizing rehabilitation. He could no longer jog or play golf and would have to spend at least two months on crutches.

Against the advice of his doctors, Bill flew to Helsinki, the capital of Finland, to meet with Boris Yeltsin. It was a tense time. NATO was set to admit Poland, Hungary, and the Czech Republic, each of them uncomfortably close to the Russia's western border.

President Clinton called the British prime minister, Tony Blair, "My little brother."

A poll taken in Britain found that voters thought their own prime minister was "much sexier" than President Clinton. At a White House dinner, Hillary, for reasons of her own, decided to seat Blair on her left and her worst enemy, Newt Gingrich, on her right.

Neither of the two world leaders was in the best of health at the time of their summit, Yeltsin having just recovered from open-heart surgery. When his aircraft landed at Helsinki, Bill had to be unceremoniously lowered, from his seat in a wheelchair perched atop a Finnair catering platform, to the tarmac.

"Yeltsin is still the Russian bear, but a benign one," Bill said.

Hillary had her own problems with Yeltsin. Once, at dinner, he had his chef prepare moose lips for her. He also cut off the ear of a roasted pig displayed on a serving platter and gave it to Bill while he devoured the other one. Hillary later commented, "I was glad that a pig had only two ears."

By the time both leaders flew back to Washington or Moscow, although Bill faced attacks from Henry Kissinger and other GOP leaders, many Russians claimed in headlines, "Bill Clinton kicked Boris in the ass."

As part of other diplomatic strategies, the president also met with other world leaders, becoming, as one reporter called it, "the big brother" of Tony Blair in London.

Even Helmut Kohl, the German Chancellor, was evaluated, in the words of author John F. Harris, as something akin to Bill's "gruff great uncle, watching over a talented but wayward nephew."

Rumors Have It that Paula Jones Compares Bill's Penis to the Leaning Tower of Pisa

Starr's probe into Bill's sex life intensified in late May, when the Supreme Court ruled 9-0 that Paula Jones would not have to wait to seek "justice" until Bill was out of office, and that she could proceed immediately with her sexual harassment suit against him. The majority of Supreme Court justices naïvely asserted that such a lawsuit would not be "unduly burdensome or time-consuming" for Bill.

How wrong they were.

It was announced in the press that Paula's case had been taken over by a law firm in Dallas that was closely linked to the right wing Rutherford Institute.

As tales from the Jones camp intensified, there was more focus on what "identifying characteristics" Paula had seen when Bill exposed himself to her that day back in Little Rock.

Word leaked out that it was not a large mole on his penis, but that he was a victim of Peyronie's disease. Named for the French physician, François Gigot de Peyronie, in 1743, this problem with a penis is characterized by a curvature in the penile shaft that is often associated with painful erections and a growing mass of scar tissue.

Even though allegedly, she had only briefly glimpsed the governor's penis,

Paula apparently had complete recall. With her lawyers, she revealed that "it seemed to hang downward like the Leaning Tower of Pisa," of which she had seen a photograph. To her sister, Lydia Cathay, she described Bill's penis as "gross and crooked."

In reference to his state of tumescence at the time, she did admit, however, that she had "only a split-second glance," and "It could have been no more than a partial erection."

To contradict the testimony, Bob Bennett, Bill's lawyer, issued a statement, assuring the nation that the presidential penis "in terms of size, shape, direction, whatever the devious mind wants to concoct, is that of a normal man."

It was later reported that when urologists at the National Medical Center in Bethesda, Maryland, examined the president, they found no curvature of the penis. A medical reporter for *The Washington Times,* however, claimed that "a definitive diagnosis is possible only when an erection is induced." The *Post* reporter wrote that the president did not produce an erection for his medical examiners.

Major trouble was on the way, as an article in *The Washington Post* revealed. The report claimed that Starr's deputies were interviewing more than a dozen women who might, at one point or another in the past, have been intimately involved with Bill. Starr falsely asserted that he had "no interest in Bill's sex life, and that he wanted to interview these women to see if Bill had "said anything about Whitewater."

Most of the press ridiculed that statement. As one reporter claimed, "From the moment he gets up, to his last thought before falling asleep, Starr does nothing but think about President Clinton's sex life. He's obsessed with it."

Wasting millions of dollars of taxpayer money, Starr got the cooperation of the FBI for probes into Bill's past. Private investigators were also hired.

Bill summed up his dilemma: "The country was in good shape and getting better, and we were advancing peace and prosperity around the world. Yet the mindless search for scandal continued."

In August, Bill reported to the nation that unemployment had fallen to 4.8 percent, the lowest since 1973. Yet Starr's deputies wanted to know during interrogations of various women, "Did Clinton penetrate your vagina, or did he put his penis into your mouth and proceed to ejaculate?"

Throughout the course of 1997, Hillary's disgust with Starr continued unabated. Formally accusing him of illegally leaking testimonies from a grand jury to the media, she wrote a letter charging him with a "leak-and-smear" campaign against her husband.

As Their Enemies Plot their Downfall, The Clintons' Move Deep into September

"I, myself, deeply regret what happened between me and President Clinton. Let me say it again: I, Myself. Deeply. Regret. What Happened. At the time—at least from my point of view—it was an authentic connection, with emotional intimacy, frequent visits, plans made, phone calls and gifts exchanged. In my early 20s, I was too young to understand the real-life consequences, and too young to see that I would be sacrificed for political expediency. I look back now, shake my head in disbelief, and wonder: What was I—what were we—thinking? I would give anything to go back and rewind the tape."

—Monica Lewinsky

Although other serious scandals were on the way, Bill and Hillary faced September of 1997 seemingly more committed to each other than ever before. White House staffers noted that their shouting matches had virtually ended.

When Hillary, America's most famous female Baby Boomer, turned fifty, *Time* devoted a cover story to her, and she appeared on *The Oprah Winfrey Show.* The TV host complimented her on her looks, even her hairdo. "I finally found a haircut that suits me," Hillary told TV audiences. For the first time in four years, her approval rating with the public had shot up to sixty percent.

By the autumn of 1997, Bill, perhaps trying to escape "what I had done with my dick" (his words), flew on his first trip to South America, visiting Brazil, Argentina, and Venezuela.

Back in the United States, he learned that in Little Rock, Judge Susan Webber Wright had dismissed with prejudice two of the four counts in the Paula Jones lawsuit. That meant that they could not be refiled.

Bill's lawyers offered to settle on the other two counts, although he said paying it would take all the monies that he and Hillary had saved during the course of two decades. He believed that he could win the case if it went to trial, but he didn't want to "waste three more years in office" fighting off Paula and her many right-wing backers.

Her lawyers notified Bill that they would not accept a financial settlement and that they would continue to pursue her claims of sexual harassment. They demanded a public apology. He notified her attorneys, "I cannot do that because her charges against me are false."

On February 12, *The Washington Post* published an anonymous ad paid for by Monica Lewinsky and addressed to "Handsome."

> *HANDSOME*
> *With love's light wings did*
> *I o'er perch these walls*
> *For stony limits cannot hold love out,*
> *And what love can do that dares love attempt.*
> *—Romeo and Juliet 2:2*
>
> *Happy Valentine's Day*
> *M.*

Monica Lewinsky and her affair with the president became tabloid fodder. Whereas Democrats lambasted her as a threat to the presidency, Republicans branded her an adulteress, lampooning her style, her weight, her taste, and her "Beverly Hills morals."

Her very name, Monica, became a symbol for runaway sexuality. Stand-up comedians across the nation, the "talking heads" on TV, and literally hundreds of scandal-mongering Internet sites attacked her mercilessly, often with touches of mysogyny, driving her to the brink of suicide.

[She called him "Handsome" when she was feeling good about him. Otherwise, depending on her mood, she referred to him as "Big Creep" or "Butthead." It was later revealed that Monica also had a nickname for Hillary. She called the First Lady "Baba," a short version of the Russian word, Babushka.]

On February 28, 1997, for the first time in eleven months, Monica returned to the Oval Office where they engaged in yet another sexual encounter. It began when she attended a taping of his weekly radio address in the Roosevelt Room. Bill spotted her and whispered to his personal secretary, Betty Currie, that he wanted to meet with her in the Oval Office.

That night, she wore a navy blue dress from GAP, little knowing that it would become the most famous blue dress in recorded history.

Despite the financial problems that led to its temporary shutdown in 2014, Harry Mohney's Erotic Heritage Museum in Las Vegas allegedly offered Monica Lewinsky between $250,000 and $1 million (reports varied) for the DNA-stained dress she'd purchased at the GAP and worn during her affair with President Clinton.

Like Lewinsky's sexual relations with Clinton, the deal was never consummated.

In July of 1998, Lewinsky relinquished her uncleaned dress, a garment roughly similar to the one depicted above, to Kenneth Starr's investigators after signing an immunity agreement based on her delivery of testimonies unfavorable (and embarassing) to Bill.

Currie escorted Monica to the Oval Office, and waited outside for fifteen to twenty minutes while Bill led Monica into the presidential study.

Sexually, Monica would later claim that they shared another "bathroom summit" as she performed oral sex on him. But before climaxing, to avoid ejaculating in her mouth, he pulled out, telling her, "I don't want to get addicted to you, and I don't want you to get addicted to me."

She confessed that the president, for the first time, reached a climax with her, but that although the bulk of his semen squirted onto the floor, some drops landed on her blue dress.

As a belated Christmas gift, he presented her with a beautifully bound volume of Walt Whitman's *Leaves of*

Grass and a blue glass hat pin.

Before leaving, she complained to him about his not having climaxed directly into her mouth. "I care about you so much," she told him. "I don't understand why you won't let me swallow. It's important to me. I mean, it just doesn't feel complete, it doesn't seem right."

He later lamented their encounter: "I never should have started it, and I certainly should not have started it back after I resolved not to in 1996."

After that liaison, quick though it was (and unsatisfying to her), she hoped he would arrange another rendezvous soon. But nothing happened until Saturday, March 29, when she came together for her final sexual encounter with the president.

At the White House, Monica met Currie once again, who escorted into the study, where she was told to wait for the president.

Although she'd read of the accident he'd had in Florida, she was nonetheless shocked when he hobbled in on crutches. "I was babbling on about something, and he shut me up by suddenly kissing me," she said. "He unbuttoned my blouse and touched my breasts without removing my bra. He then put his hands down my pants. I wasn't wearing any panties. He manually stimulated me. I wanted him to touch my genitals with his genitals, and he did, lightly and without penetration. Then I performed oral sex on him, and he ejaculated."

For a time, Linda Tripp *(left)* and Monica Lewinsky were the best of friends—or at least Lewinsky thought so.

But whereas Lewinsky fell in love with Bill Clinton, Tripp harbored a venomous hostility toward him.

Tripp belonged to a small cabal of anti-Clinton White House staffers held over from the administration of George H.W. Bush. As such, Tripp was a virtual spy, learning all "the dirt" she could, and reporting it to right-wing sources.

Later, in grand jury testimony, the president would deny that he met her that Saturday.

During the weeks that followed, Monica continued to pester the president about getting her old job back at the White House, from which she had been dismissed. He put her off, claiming that a member of his staff member, Marsha Scott, Deputy Assistant for Presidential Personnel, might look into it to see if something were available.

Later, during complaints she articulated to Linda Tripp, Monica said, "All I heard from him is 'I'll do, I'll do,' but he doesn't, he doesn't. I feel he's just stringing me along."

Saturday, May 24, 1997—the day

Bill ended their sexual relationship—was pivotal to the trajectory of Bill's affair with Monica. She had brought him a shirt from Banana Republic, and he invited her into his private study.

Instead of inaugurating another sexual encounter, he told her that he'd had hundreds of affairs, but "after turning forty, I'm making an effort to be faithful to my wife. I want to end our private relationship, thought I hope we can remain friends."

She begged him to continue it, but he appeared adamant, though he still held out the prospect he could help her find a good job.

On July 3, rebuffed in her attempts to solicit a job, she wrote the president an infamous letter. In it, she threatened him that if he did not keep his promise to return her to the White House, she might have to "explain the situation to my parents." She also suggested that if he would not allow her to return to the White House, perhaps he might get her a good job in New York at the United Nations.

The next day, after his receipt of the threatening letter, Bill invited Monica to confer with him privately. She described it as "a very emotional visit" that occurred at 9AM. Immediately, he scolded her, telling her, "It's illegal to threaten the President of the United States."

In spite of her threat, she later testified that the president was "the most affectionate with me he'd ever been. He stroked my arm, toyed with my hair, kissed me on my neck, and praised my intellect and beauty."

Trying to hold onto him, she held out the possibility of a relationship with

Actor/comedians Molly Shannon and John Goodman satirizing Monica Lewinsky and Linda Tripp on *Saturday Night Live*.

Many viewers thought the impersonators came off better than the originals.

him after his tenure as president. "What would we do when I'm seventy-five and have to pee twenty-five times a day?" he responded.

She admitted she left his office that day "emotionally stunned, knowing he was still in love with me."

During a subsequent, very tense meeting at 9:30PM on July 14, the president met Monica in the Oval Office again. She found him "very cold and distant" and sensed trouble.

This was the first time he brought up the subject of Linda Tripp. Apparently, he had learned of Monica's close friendship with her. "Can you trust this woman?" he asked.

"Most definitely. I can trust her completely."

The president wasn't so sure. He'd heard that Tripp had recently leaked news about his alleged involvement with Kathleen Willey.

Their meeting was interrupted by a near hour-long call with his attorney, Bob Bennett. When he returned, the president asked Monica if she'd ever told Tripp any details about their intimate relationship."

"I have never spoken one word about it to her," she lied.

On August 11, *Newsweek* carried the story that the president had made sexual advances toward Willey, quoting Tripp as one of the sources. Obviously, the president grew alarmed when he learned that Tripp was Monica's best friend. If Tripp were willing to expose the Willey incident to *Newsweek,* she surely would be eager to reveal the far more explosive charges of the president's affair with Monica. Bill and Bennett huddled together in private in the Oval Office to review the ramifications of a possible threat looming from Tripp.

Five days later, based in part on the implications of the article in *Newsweek*, Monica, on August 16, arranged another meeting with the president, during which she tried unsuccessfully to resume their sexual relationship.

He was heading for Martha's Vineyard to celebrate his birthday on August 19, and she brought along gifts for him. "I wanted to give him a birthday kiss, and he agreed to that," she later claimed. "But when he did, I felt his genitals through his pants and tried to perform fellatio on him, but he declined."

"I'm trying not to do this, and I'm trying to be good," he told her.

She reported that he seemed visibly upset, and that he quickly ended the meeting. She followed up with a letter to him. "It was awful when I saw you for your birthday. You were so distant, I missed you even though I was holding you in my arms."

In the days and months ahead, Monica continued to complain about Bill's failure to line up a position for her. She told Tripp, "He doesn't have the balls to tell me the truth."

She continued relentlessly in her campaign to get him to find her a good job, but he either ignored her messages, or took no action. Finally, on October 6, she received a call from Tripp, who informed her that she'd heard from a good source that "You'll never work at the White House again."

With the collapse of her dream about continuing a career within the White House, she continued to press the president to recommend her for a job at the United Nations. She wrote, and sent him, bitter letters. She left a recorded message for him on October 6. In it, she asked that he acknowledge "that you fucked up my life. I also want you to get me a job. I don't want to work for this position. I just want it to be given to me."

Then she sent yet another letter to the president, claiming "You don't want to bring me back to the White House because you just plain don't care for me enough. I just loved you—wanted to spend time with you, kiss you, listen to you laugh—and I wanted you to love me back. I've waited long enough. I give up. You let me down, but I shouldn't have trusted you in the first place."

In an October 10 call from the president, she said, "He got so mad at me, he must have turned purple."

Angrily, he blasted her. "If I had known the kind of person you really are, I wouldn't have gotten involved with you."

At the White House, the heat was on and more intense than ever. On November 4, the president was called upon to answer Paula Jones' set of Interrogatories. One of them called for him to list any woman "other than your wife with whom you've had, proposed having, or sought to have sexual relationships, beginning when you first became Attorney General of Arkansas and going up through your administration as President of the United States.

Bill went into a rage. No political candidate in the history of the Republic had ever been called upon with a demand of such an invasion of privacy. Hillary was also livid. Bill immediately filed an objection through his lawyers to the "scope and relevance of these Interrogatories."

On Thursday, November 13, 1997, after days and weeks of unanswered phone calls and notes delivered to Currie, Monica had a brief encounter with Bill that was not scheduled. Ernest Zedillo, President of Mexico, was visiting the White House at the time. She later described her meeting with Bill as a "hysterical escapade."

It evolved into a study in frustration for Monica, and at one point, she was fuming mad. When Currie finally informed her that the president had gone to play golf, Monica in her own words, "went ballistic."

When the president returned, Monica continued to press Currie, claiming she had more gifts for the president. The secretary suggested that Monica wait in Currie's car in the White House parking lot. Once there, Monica found the doors of Currie's car locked, so she had to wait in the rain.

Currie finally arrived in the parking lot to escort Monica in through a rear door of the White House in advance of slipping her into the presidential study.

Anxiously, she waited and waited. Finally, Bill came into the study. She presented him with an antique paperweight in the shape of the White House. She also showed him an e-mail that reported on the desirous effect of chewing Altoids breath mints while performing fellatio.

"I'm chewing Altoids right now," she said.

Again, he rebuffed her sexual overtures, claiming, "I don't have enough time for oral sex." He gave her a quick kiss before rushing off to dine with Zedillo.

***

As presidential adviser, Vernon Jordan so colorfully put it, "The shit hit the fan on December 5."

Paula Jones' lawyers had assembled a list of potential witnesses to testify in her behalf, and Monica's name was on that list. Jordan warned Monica that—as part of the Jones case—she might have to testify under oath about her affair with the president.

On the night of Friday, December 5, at a Christmas party at the White House, to which Monica had somehow been invited—she was able to exchange a few polite words with the president as part of a dialogue that lasted no more than about forty-five seconds. Back home, she described her anguish in a letter she sent to him. "You want me out of your life. I guess the signs have been made clear for a while. I have several gifts for you, and I had wanted to give them to you in person. But that obviously is not going to happen."

On the morning of Saturday, December 6, confused and quietly enraged, Monica arrived unannounced at the Northwest Gate of the White House with Christmas gifts for the president, including a "Hugs & Kisses" box. For admittance inside, she needed permission from Currie, who could not be located by the security guards. When she finally learned that the president was unavailable because he was meeting privately with Eleanor Mondale, Monica turned in anger and, in tears, fled.

When the president spoke to her the next morning by phone, he chastised her for "making such a stink at the gate," and for her frequent attempts to gain access to the Oval Office.

At the end of his angry tone, he surprised her by inviting her to visit him. He told her she'd be cleared to enter the White House at 12:52PM that same day.

In the Oval Office, she "bitched" about Vernon Jordan for doing nothing to find her a job. There was no sex during this visit. She later sent an e-mail to a friend. "Things have been crazy with The Creep. But I did have a wonderful visit with him. When he doesn't put his walls up, it is always heavenly."

On December 11, Monica had a meeting with Jordan, who promised that he'd make calls on her behalf to such private companies a Young & Rubicam. He asked her why she got angry at the president.

"He doesn't call me enough or see me enough," she said.

"You're in love, that's your problem," he said.

On December 15, Paula Jones' attorneys served Bill with a set of demands, asking that he "produce all documents related to any communications between him and Monica Lewisky *(sic).*"

Two days later, he called Monica at around 2:30AM. They spoke for half an hour. He told her it "broke my heart to see you on the list of potential witnesses."

When Monica was served with a subpoena in the *Paula Jones vs. Bill Clinton* case, she called Vernon Jordan, an aide to the president.

She sobbed so loudly over the phone, however, that he couldn't understand her. Later, she met with him in his office, defining him as "brusque and unsympathetic."

During her meeting, when she learned that Jordan was scheduled to meet with President Clinton later that evening, she asked, "Give him a hug for me, will you?"

He patted her on the back as part of his farewell gesture, saying, "I don't hug guys."

He suggested that she might sign an affidavit denying an affair with him. "That might be enough to satisfy the bastards so you will not have to be deposed on a witness stand." He also told her to claim that she visited the White House to see Betty Currie, and that she, on occasion, brought the president letters when no one else was around to deliver them.

Weeks later, before Starr's inquisitors, Bill claimed that he did not remember speaking to Monica on December 17. In the context of the Jones case, he stated, "I never asked her to lie."

After she returned from two job interviews in New York, Monica flew back to Washington on December 19, where she was served with a subpoena in the Jones case. She burst into tears.

A process server had been provided with information by Tripp about how to gain entrance to the Pentagon and how, once inside, he could find his way through the labyrinthine defense complex to serve the subpoena on Monica. "She'll be a sitting duck," Tripp said.

One of the subpoena's demands involved turning over any gifts the president had given her, a mandate that later greatly upset Bill.

Later that day, Currie arrived at Monica's lodging within her mother's apartment at the Watergate complex and took whatever subpoenaed gifts Monica chose to turn over. Currie then drove home and hid them in a box under her bed.

In addition to those gifts, Monica was ordered to turn over all letters, cards, notes, memoranda, and all phone records associated with her links to the president.

She immediately set up a meeting with Jordan to discuss getting her a lawyer. At this confab, he asked her if she had ever had a sexual relationship with the president.

She denied it, although later claiming that "with a wink and a nod, I just knew he knew I was having something with the president."

According to testimony, she even, in front of Jordan, brought up the issue of the president divorcing Hillary at the end of his second term.

When he later conferred with Bill, Jordan bluntly asked him, "Mr. President, have you had sexual relations with Monica Lewinsky?"

"No, never!" Bill said. "And that's a definite answer."

On December 22, Monica again met privately with Jordan, since he had arranged a possible lawyer for her, Francis Carter. At this meeting, she was slightly more revelatory, concerned that someone might have been eavesdropping on her conversations with Bill. "Why would that be of concern?" Jordan asked her. "You told me you didn't have sex."

"But we've had phone sex," she admitted for the first time.

Jordan drove her to Carter's office. He signed on as her lawyer, promising "to get Jones' mad dogs from chasing after you."

After her meeting with Carter, Monica then went to the Pentagon and had a "back alley" talk with Tripp. "If Paula Jones' lawyers subpoena me, I'm telling the truth," Tripp told a stunned Monica. "I will not commit perjury and place myself in harm's way. I'm sorry, but that's my bottom line."

Sunday, December 28, 1997, was a key moment in the explosive and embarrassing saga. A meeting with Bill had been arranged in the Oval Office. It began innocently enough, with Monica and Bill playing with "Buddy," the president's chocolate-colored Labrador.

During their time together, he presented her with some Christmas gifts, including a marble bear's head, a small box of chocolates, a pair of joke sunglasses, and even a stuffed toy replica of a black dog from Martha's Vineyard. In retrospect, this exchange of gifts appears reckless, since gifts from him were being subpoenaed.

Although there was no sex during their final hours together, she later admitted that he "kissed me passionately."

Before she left, the president assured her that they were involved in a "political vendetta. The bastards want to get whatever dirt that's damaging to me."

Before she left the Oval Office for her final time, Bill told her, "Thank god you never revealed anything to that number one blabbermouth in Washington, that Linda Tripp girl. They have no evidence of any relationship between the two of us. I'll thank you forever for keeping that a secret."

As author Joe Conason wrote, "If, during the last hour she spent with Clinton, Lewinsky had alerted him to the obvious danger posed by Tripp, everything might have turned out differently. But she couldn't bring herself to do that. It would have meant admitting that she had betrayed their secret and thereby jeopardized him."

On the last day of the year, Wednesday, December 31, 1997, Monica had breakfast with Jordan at the Park Hyatt Hotel in Washington. It was at that point that she admitted for the first time that Linda Tripp was involved in the Jones case, and might also have private information—dates, activities, and places—associated with Monica's trysts with the president. Monica went on to confess that Tripp might even have read some of her notes and correspondence associated with those trysts within her mother's apartment at Watergate.

Reportedly, Jordan told her to, "Go home and make sure that they're not there."

She later testified that she understood that Jordan was telling her to "throw away any copies or drafts of notes she'd sent or contemplated sending to the White House."

When she returned home, as the year was coming to an end, she wasn't singing *Auld Lang Syne.* Instead, she burned the drafts of more than fifty notes, memos, or letters she had contemplated sending to Bill but never mailed.

Linda Tripp
"A Spy in the House of Love"

"With a friend like that Jersey gal, you don't need an enemy."

So spoke Monica Lewinsky about her former best friend, Linda Tripp, a civil servant who secretly recorded Monica's phone calls in which she described in minute detail her sexual relationship with Bill Clinton.

Tripp, never a winner of any beauty contest, had worked in the administration of George H.W. Bush. "In one of my major mistakes, I kept her on the job when I took over," lamented Bill.

In the summer of 1994, during Bill's first term in office, White House aides wanted to get rid of Tripp, and as a means of accomplishing that, they arranged a position for her in the public affairs office at the Pentagon, which came with a whopping $22,000-a-year raise.

In spite of an age difference, Tripp and Monica bonded when both of them found themselves working at the Pentagon after they each had more or less been booted from the White House for their indiscretions. Even though they received more pay, their positions at the Pentagon were far less glamorous and exciting than their previous postings within the White House.

During the previous months, Tripp had written copious notes as Monica had confessed—"not leaving out one detail"—her sexual encounters with the president. Tripp began to envision publication of a tell-all book about what she'd learned during her time in the White House before her (enforced) transfer to the Pentagon.

To accomplish this, she needed to repair her relationship with the Manhattan literary agent, the tall, husky-voiced blonde, Lucianne Goldberg.

During the Watergate hearing of the 1970s, it was learned that for $1,000 a week, Goldberg had been a spy in George McGovern's campaign trail for the presidency. At the time, she was hired by, and reported to, forces backing Richard Nixon.

She reported on "all the dirty stuff," associated with McGovern, his associates, and his campaign, but found no smoking gun to use against him. Nixon read her reports, mainly, as he confided, "for the dirty jokes told by members of the Fourth Estate."

Lucianne Goldberg in the '90s was America's most notorious literary agent, urging Linda Tripp to reveal all the "dirty secrets" of the Clinton administration. "I'm the gypsy cab of agents," she claimed.

A tall woman given to flowing black shawls, she is a maverick who also hawked racy novels, including one in which a character called "Baby" could unzip a man's fly with her toes.

This pit bull of the publishing world said, "It's horrible that a married president was having sex with a kid at taxpayer expense in the Oval Office. It's scummy, scandalous, and wrong."

Goldberg had become moderately notorious in 1970 when, along with Jeannie Sakol, she'd founded "The Pussycat League," a group of women opposed to the presuppositions of the Women's Liberation Movement. Her anti-feminist tract was entitled *Purr, Baby, Purr.*

As a literary agent, Goldberg became known for her shocking *exposés,* including one about Senator Ted Kennedy. Entitled *Teddy Bare,* it exposed what "really happened" that night en route to Chappaquiddick. She'd also published policeman Mark Fuhrman's book about the O. J. Simpson murder trial and investigation.

Goldberg had been the agent for Kitty Kelley's book, *The Last Star,* an *exposé* of the life of Elizabeth Taylor. Kelley sued Goldberg for concealment of, and non-payment of, foreign royalties—and won the case in 1983.

Goldberg had met Tripp in 1993 and discussed a tell-all book about the late Vince Foster, suggesting that his death resulted from murder, not suicide. But at some point, Tripp backed out, fearing for her Federal job.

"Who do you think you are, the Queen of England?" Goldberg had asked Tripp before slamming down the phone.

On hearing Tripp's new revelations about the president and the intern, Goldberg said, "My tabloid heart beats loud."

Although Tripp had not specifically named Monica during her inaugural proposals for the project, Goldberg thought it could be a sensational book, holding out the possibility of a $500,000 advance. She could even arrange a ghost writer for Tripp, Maggie Gallagher, a conservative Yale graduate. Goldberg even came up with a working title—*Behind Closed Doors: What I Saw at the Clinton White House.*

"I love dish," Goldberg said. "And *bubeleh*, if you're going to go after the big *kahuna*, you better kill him!"

What Tripp didn't know at the time was that Goldberg was taping their phone conversations. In an ironic twist, Goldberg instructed Tripp to begin taping all of "this intern's phone confessions," assuring Tripp that the procedure was legal in the State of Maryland. *[Actually, it was illegal in that state.]*

Tripp revealed to Goldberg that she found the president "disgusting. He's sickening, having sex with this young intern. I find it appalling. It's time he got his comeuppance, and I'm the one to do it."

On October 3, Tripp purchased a $100 tape recorder at Radio Shack and recorded the first of many of Monica's conversations on the phone. As Monica's biographer wrote, "Whatever Tripp's motivation, when she pressed the 'record' button of her tape machine, she began a process of entrapment that would lead to the humbling of a president, and the near destruction of his lover."

Tripp wanted to record every confession that came from Monica's oral-sex performing lips. Author Gene Lyons wrote: "The divorced Tripp had a reputation as a snoop and a busybody, and if Clinton's aides had examined her background carefully, they might have worried about her far sooner than they did. After marrying Budd Tripp, a military officer, she followed him around from one Army base to another, occasionally accepting some secretarial job to help supplement his Army pay.

Marcia Lewis, Monica's mother, claimed, "Tripp sought out my daughter, a vulnerable, easy target. Tripp had an obsession with Clinton—at one point, she claimed that Hillary was jealous of her because she suspected that she was having an affair with her husband. This woman is delusional and pops up everywhere Clinton has trouble. She seemed to insinuate herself in every situation that had a whiff of scandal. She is like a meddlesome witch, a praying mantis."

In one of the most insincere comments ever made, Tripp, on December 12, told Monica, "The problem I have with you, frankly, is I feel entirely maternal toward you. And it's almost like—it's like me yelling at my kids, not that that ever has any effect. When I yell at you, it's out of love."

Marcia Lewis *(left)* stood by her daughter, Monica Lewinsky, throughout the massive media interest, vilifications, and overzealous prosecutions.

As stated by Marcia: "Kenneth Starr found my daughter's Achilles' heel—and that was me. What better way to force someone to do what they don't want than to threaten those they love?"

"My own family saw that technique used very effectively by Josef Stalin, which is why we left Russia."

Once, when Tripp visited Monica in her (mother's) Watergate apartment, she was shown the blue dress with the semen stains. Monica was considering having it dry cleaned, but Tripp told her not to. She claimed if there were an investigation, Monica might have to produce the dress as evidence of her having had a fling with the president. Bill's DNA was on that dress.

Fearing that Monica might have the dress dry cleaned in spite of her warning, Tripp reportedly considered stealing the dress before she left the apartment that night.

After that meeting with Monica at the Watergate complex, Tripp continued to record everything Monica said, even her allegation about Bill's having inserted his cigar into her vagina. In time, Tripp would share those tapes with Jackie Bennett, the chief aide to Kenneth Starr.

Deep in December Our Hearts Will Remember, But Our Minds Will "Forget"

As 1997 was coming to an end, Bill, on December 6, met with Bob Bennett in the Oval Office. There, he learned that Paula's attorneys had come up with a possible witness in her behalf.

"They are alleging you've had an affair with her, even in this office," Bennett said. "They're going to call on her to testify."

Bill responded in anger. "Bob, do you think I'm fucking crazy? I know the press is watching me every minute. I'd be a fool to carry on with what's her face here in the White House. No, it did not happen. I flatly deny it. I'm retired from my war games of yesterday."

Bennett responded, "The only thing you have to worry about is if you lie when interrogated by the Starr people. If you do, the crazies will come after you. They will try to impeach you if you lie. That's the only thing you have to worry about."

"Then I've got nothing to worry about," Bill said, "because the Lewinsky girl and I did nothing inappropriate, and I'm sure she'll swear to that."

When Bill's lawyer eventually learned that, indeed, his client had lied to him, he asked, "How could anyone so smart be so dumb?"

Right before Christmas, Hillary, Bill, and Chelsea flew to Sarajevo to encourage the people of Bosnia to stay on a pathway to peace.

As he flew back to the U.S., he told reporters that during the upcoming year, he hoped that "the worst of the partisan wars with the Republicans would come to an end."

That wish would not be granted. "If anything," he lamented, "the ideological divide between us and the GOP would grow wider than the Grand Canyon itself."

On March 3, 1999, Monica Lewinsky agreed to appear with Barbara Walters on her investagative TV show, *20/20*.

Monica owed some $800,000 in legal bills and could have gotten money for such an appearance, but she wanted to appear with Walters for free, because she resented charges that she was cashing in on her notoriety.

This was Monica's first big chance to introduce herself to what she hoped would be a forgiving public.

Chapter Eighteen

The Baby Boomer President Comes Under Fire From Characters as Immoral as He Is

(It's Nixon's Watergate, Replayed as Political Farce)

Tacky Bathroom Trysts with an Oral Artist Morph Into a Nationwide Impeachment Crisis

"Babbitt With a Badge" (Kenneth Starr) Is Denounced for His "Predilection for Canine Zeal & Prosecutorial Misjudgments"

Bill Clinton became the tabloid headliner of America.
Even legal genius Alan Dershowitz weighed in with his opinion.

Bill Clinton Emerges as the Chief Protagonist In a Sordid Saga Bereft of Heroes and Riddled with Crackpots

His Enemies Denouce Bill's Administration As "A Cancer of Cynicism, Narcissism, & Deceit"

"Regardless of what happens to Bill, the nation will be exposed to Hillary Clinton, and Hillary could—and should—be our first woman president."

—Dorothy Stuck, Little Rock newswoman

That awful year—1998—descended like a nightmare on the Clintons at their embattled fortress, the White House. He wrote: "When the year began, I had no idea that it would be the strangest year of my presidency, full of personal humiliation and disgrace, policy struggles at home and triumphs abroad, and, against all odds, a stunning demonstration of the common sense and fundamental decency of the American people. During that dreadful year, the darkest part of my inner life was in full view."

At the start of the year, Kenneth Starr, the Independent Counsel, had gone to Attorney General Janet Reno to request that his mandate to investigate Whitewater be extended to embrace potential charges of obstruction of justice and perjury. Although she had been appointed by Bill, she gave Starr this sweeping new authority, obviously having no idea that his ultimate goal in-

Linda Tripp and Lucianne Goldberg Are Ridiculed as "Patrons of the Bar Scene in Star Wars"

French Leaders Chuckle at "How Silly Americans Can Be"

volved entrapping the president in perjury.

On November 11, 1997, Linda Tripp had called David Pyke, one of the lawyers working on the Paula Jones case. She revealed that she'd recorded, at her home in Maryland, Monica's confession and description of her affair with the president. When he learned of this, Pyke defined the possession of such tapes as "The Holy Grail." However, as a lawyer, he was concerned that the tapes had been recorded in Maryland, a state in which the submission of such evidence was against the law.

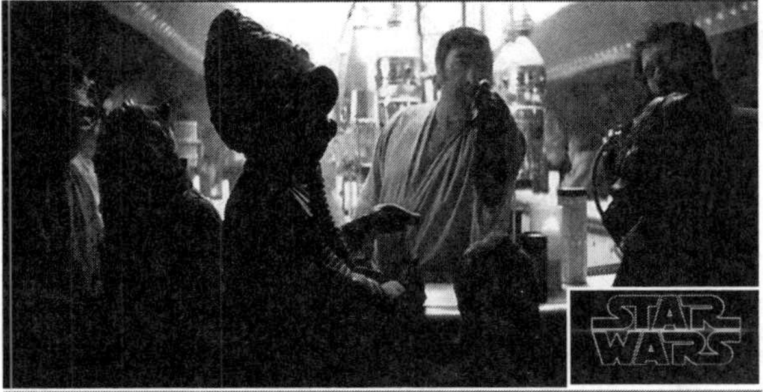

In director George Lucas' first installment of *Star Wars* (1977), a movie that expanded into a franchise generating unimaginable profits, the directors devoted enormous attention to special effects and costumes. Collectively, they defined the population groups of a fictional, "alternative" galaxy. They included Siths, Wookiees, humanoids, robotic droids, Force-sensitives, and assorted aliens with varying degrees of repugnancy.

Here, in a scene from the film, is a scattering of a cross-section, gathered together at a watering hole of the distant, starry-galactic future.

Political insiders compared the witnesses subpoenaed or coerced by Ken Starr's Independent Counsel (including Lucianne Goldberg, Linda Tripp, and Paula Jones) to the "alternative galaxy" characters developed during the production of the Lucas film.

However, he decided that it was too early to spring news of the existence of the tapes onto Bill and Monica. "Let them go ahead and perjure themselves first," Pyke advised.

On January 12, five days before Bill was to testify in his hours-long deposition, the lawyers for Paula Jones received Linda Tripp at their offices. With her, she carried her secret tapes. Each had been recorded during the time she pretended to be a friend of Monica Lewinsky and had listened to her lengthy "confessions" of her affair with the president.

When Bill was scheduled to appear, he still had no clue that such tapes existed. Therefore, the stage was set for him to deny the affair with the intern and, thus, commit perjury, which Starr and his deputies so hopefully wished he'd do.

At his deposition, Bill had not been alerted that during the previous day, FBI agents and Starr's deputies had more or less house arrested Monica and had interrogated her after issuing heavy threats of jail time. As Bill later claimed, "The cards were stacked against me, and, like a little lamb, I wandered into the slaughterhouse."

His deposition was conducted in front of his former law student at the

University of Arkansas, Judge Susan Webber Wright. She had flown in from Little Rock since she had been the judge in the Paula Jones case there.

Bill was interrogated by Paula's lawyers, each of whom had listened to Tripp's illegal recordings. That put them in a strong position not only to entrap Bill in a perjury charge, but to implicate him in an obstruction of justice accusation.

Before taking the stand, Bill and his lawyer, Bob Bennett, were given a list of criteria that stipulated what constituted sexual relations. The lawyers claimed that it covered "contact with the genitals, anus, groin, breast, or inner thigh, with the intent of arousal or to gratify the sexual desire of any person."

Although the case was supposed to be about Paula and her sexual harassment charge, the president was interrogated for only fifteen minutes on that. The other remaining hours were devoted solely to Monica Lewinsky.

The first question was, "Have you ever had an extramarital affair with Monica Lewinsky?"

Since he and the intern had never actually engaged in sexual intercourse, he felt justified in denying an affair. Fortunately, he was not asked if she had ever performed fellatio on him.

Although Bill told his aides he felt he had survived the interrogation, he left the confrontation deeply troubled, fearing the potential danger he might be facing. Back at the White House, he canceled dinner plans for the evening and locked himself into the presidential study, where he brooded until around 4AM.

Even though unaware of the Tripp tapes, he, as a smart lawyer, sensed that Jones' lawyers possessed evidence of which he was unaware, and that they were waiting to entrap him with it at the last moment. He feared that their information might be lethal enough to force him to resign, in the way that the Watergate tapes sent Richard Nixon flying back to California.

In a memoir, Bill wrote: "What I had done with Monica Lewinsky was immoral and foolish. I was deeply ashamed of it and didn't want it to come out. In the deposition, I was trying to protect my family and myself from my selfish stupidity. I believed that the contorted definition of sexual relations enabled me to do so, though I was worried enough about it to invite the lawyer interrogating me to ask specific questions. I didn't have to wait long to find out why he declined to do so."

In his despair, he called his old political adviser, Dick Morris, who had recently faced an embarrassing sexual *exposé* of his tryst with a prostitute. "You poor son of a bitch," Morris said. He could sympathize with his plight, although later, he turned on both Bill and Hillary, attacking them in televised media and in his books.

Bill told him, "I didn't do what they said I did, but I may have done enough so that I don't know if I can prove my innocence. There may be gifts, and there may have been messages left on her answering machine. You know, ever since the election, I've tried to shut myself down sexually, but sometimes I slipped up, and with this girl, I just slipped up."

Bill feared that when the American people learned of his sordid affair, he would be forced to resign. He wanted Morris to choreograph a new poll to determine if the public would forgive him if he confessed to wrongdoing.

A few days later, Morris called with the results of his latest poll. The public might accept a confession that he'd had an adulterous relationship, but they would not forgive him lying under oath.

Bill told Morris, "In that case, fuck it all, we'll just have to beat this thing."

After reporter Joe Klein heard of the poll and its conclusions, he commented, "This nauseating revelation seemed to encapsulate all the worst aspects of the Clinton administration: The president was a man who would actually poll whether or not he should tell the truth."

In his desperation, the president made a foolish decision. He phoned his personal secretary, Betty Currie, summoning her to the White House for a Sunday meeting. In the Oval Office, he coached her in what she might say during a deposition if she were called upon to give one.

He suggested she might claim that she had never known him to be in the Oval Office alone with Monica. He also wanted her to say: "There was nothing wrong in his relationship with this White House intern." He made these suggestions to her as a lawyer, and fully aware that he was asking her to commit perjury on his behalf.

The day after his deposition, Bill had to face one of the most humiliating experiences in his marriage. He decided to go and wake Hillary up at 7AM and inform her what was going on. Not the truth, but a reassuring lie.

Awakening her, he said that he had been deposed by Paula Jones' attorneys over an alleged affair with a White House intern, Monica Lewinsky. He called her "a needy person who came to me for advice. Nothing improper ever took place between us. I spoke to her only a few times, and every time I did, Betty Currie was in the office with us. It's just another one of those invented affairs that our enemies keep concocting to use against me."

Sitting on her bed, he told her, "There are news reports on the Internet and airwaves as well as a story coming out in the *Post.* They're claiming I had an affair with this intern and that I asked her to lie to Jones' lawyers."

Hillary listened carefully and told him she believed him.

After that fateful morning, and after the president had left her room, she rose from her bed, heading for the shower. When she later met with aides, she was reported to have a steely determination on her face. It was obvious that regardless of what had happened, she was preparing to go into battle to save his presidency.

Later in the day, Hillary confided to their lawyer, David Kendall, "I've got to believe him. He's done lots of lousy things, but he has never lied to me. Sometimes it's painful for him to confess the truth, but he does. I'm not mad at him as much as I'm mad at his psychotic accusers, a bunch of crazies. The press doesn't help the situation very much either."

George Stephanopoulos later wrote, "How could she not believe him? She had to believe that he wouldn't risk their life's work for a fling with an intern only a few years older than Chelsea. She had to believe that he loved her enough not to humiliate her. She had to do what she had always done before: Swallow her doubts, stand by her man, and savage his enemies."

As Carl Bernstein put it: "Her investment in the truthfulness of her husband's explanation was nothing less than a lifetime's savings."

The first time she had to face the public, a woman bombarded her with a question. "How can you rise out of bed every day let alone go out and face the world?"

"Sometimes, I ask myself that same question," Hillary answered. "But I follow Eleanor Roosevelt's advice. She said that every woman in political life 'must develop skin as tough as rhinoceros hide.'"

Hillary later wrote of her learning of the Lewinsky scandal. "I had little trouble believing accusations against Bill were groundless. By that time, I had endured more than six years of groundless claims fomented by some of the same people and groups associated with the Jones case and the Starr investigations."

"For me, the Lewinsky imbroglio seemed like just another vicious scandal manufactured by political opponents: After all, since he had started in public office, he had been accused of everything from drug-running to fathering a child with a Little Rock prostitute, and I had been called a thief and a murderer."

It is not known if Bill ever told Hillary some shocking news, but as the controversy continued to blossom, he'd confided to his lawyer, Bob Bennett, that if enough Democrats broke ranks and sided with the Republicans, he doubted if his presidency would last a week.

"It's not just the presidency at stake," Bill also told Bennett, "but my marriage. The Gennifer Flowers/Paula Jones was one thing. This is quite another pile of shit. It's more than a pile. Call it a dinosaur dump."

The Most Dangerous Journalist in America

The first media exposure came when *The Drudge Report* hit the internet, revealing that the president had had an affair with a White House intern. In March of 1995, the report had only 1,000 subscribers, but when it began to reveal details about the president and his intern, its circulation rose to 85,000.

The report was the creation of Matt Drudge, who had once worked as a telemarketer for *Time-Life* books. When he had started *The Drudge Report,* he had relied on part gossip *[often wrong]* and part opinion.

The year he broke Bill's scandal, as an ardent pro-lifer, he was hosting a Saturday night TV News and Opinion show on the Fox News Channel. As part of that broadcast, he aired a picture of a tiny hand reaching out from a womb to dramatize his arguments against abortion. Fox discovered that the picture had actually been snapped during an emergency pre-natal, *in utero* operation on a fetus for *spina bifida [a birth defect where there is incomplete closing of the backbone and membranes around the spinal cord]*. In the aftermath of that, Fox and Drudge parted company.

A great deal of attention focused on Matt Drudge himself for breaking the news. Many *politicos,* especially those he had exposed, called him a scavenger, patrolling the night for scandalous tidbits. Labeled "the most dangerous journalist in America," he was said to have patterned himself after the popular columnist, Walter Winchell.

Writing in *Newsweek,* Michael Isikoff said, "Drudge is a menace to honest, responsible journalism. To the extent he's read and people believe him, he's lethal."

David McClintick called him a "modern day Tom Paine, a possible precursor to millions of town criers using the Internet to invade turf of bigfoot journalists."

Privately, Bill had his own opinion, referring to Drudge as "The Big Asshole, emitting daily farts the equivalent of the blast at Hiroshima."

Drudge soon took his place among what the press dubbed "The Three Evils," a reference to the squealer, Linda Tripp ("Hear Evil") and her literary agent, Lucianne Goldberg ("See Evil"). Drudge became known as their closely associated counterpart, "Speak Evil."

The Drudge Report shocked Washington with its revelations. It also broke the story that *Newsweek* was about to expose a sexual relationship between the president and the intern.

The *Washington Post* was one of the first newspapers to hit the streets with a banner headline—*CLINTON ACCUSED OF URGING AIDE TO LIE: STARR PROBES WHETHER PRESIDENT TOLD WOMAN TO DENY ALLEGED AFFAIR TO JONES LAWYERS.*

On a morning talk show, *Good Morning America,* Sam Donaldson said, "If sufficient evidence exists, there should be an immediate demand for the pres-

British-born Andrew Sullivan, a pioneer of the political blog, is openly gay and a practicing Roman Catholic. In 2001, it was revealed that he'd posted anonymous ads for unprotected anal sex, preferably with "other HIV-positive men."

That led to criticism of him in the media for his attacks on Bill Clinton's "incautious behavior."

The very opinionated and very controversial Matt Drudge drew fire, but also praise from many defenders. Mark Halperin defined him as "the Walter Cronkite of his era."

Todd Purdum in *The New York Times* begrudgingly hailed him as "America's reigning mischief-maker."

The wicked, often cringe-inducing comedian, Joan Rivers, the Queen of Comedy, incorporated the Bill Clinton/Monica Lewinsky affair into her satirical repertoire.

Rivers was quoted as saying, "Monica Lewinky gave Clinton 'The Godfather,' an offer he couldn't refuse. In this case, it involved her vagina and a Cohiba. That's too much for any man!"

A native of El Paso, Sam Donaldson, Jr., was a reporter and news anchor who served with ABC News beginning in 1967. He has known many American presidents, and, of course, had strong opinions about all of them.

"People ask me about my relationship with Ronald Reagan," he said. "I say it's a case of two 'hams' discovering each other. Only I played the 'straight man,' and he always had the last world."

"I told Bill Clinton that the only way to avoid being seen as a partisan reporter was to be equally vicious to every president, including him."

ident's resignation."

In reference to *The Drudge Report's* appearance on January 19, naming Monica, she later said, "That was the day I became radioactive."

In the wake of its exposure in *The Washington Post,* the story of the president's affair went mainstream. It was reported that Starr was investigating charges of a massive cover-up. There were immediate calls for Bill to resign. He told Bob Bennett, "I feel under siege. Like some of those settlers in the wilds of Texas, their wagons circled by hostile Indians ready to scalp them."

White House press secretary Mike McCurry was Bill Clinton's embattled spokesperson throughout the Whitewater and Lewinsky scandals, but his honesty was not always appreciated by his administrators. In 1988, he expressed doubts about Bill Clinton's fitness to remain in office.

Long after the departure of the Clintons, he resurfaced in 2014 as a teacher of politics and religion at a Methodist theological seminary, an event that changed his image from a hyper-politicized spin doctor to a supporter of the faith-based values that, in his words, might melt the "frozen tundra" of today's politics.

"Mike had taken some pretty hard shots at me," Bill said. "I didn't care about that. He was also against me in the primary season, but had done a good job at (the) State (Department) explaining and defending our foreign policy. So I gave him the job. Boy, did he get some hard questions about me."

George Will, a commentator for ABC-TV News, pronounced the Clinton presidency "deader than Woodrow Wilson's after he had a stroke."

In a vicious assault, Andrew Sullivan in *The New Republic,* characterized the Clinton reign as "a cancer of cynicism, narcissism, and deceit. At some point, not even the most stellar of economic records, not even the most prosperous of decades, are worth the price of such a cancer metastasizing even further. It's time to get rid of it."

In the White House, Erskine Bowles, the president's Chief of Staff, watched an ABC news broadcast in total disgust. Months later, he finally heard the report of a semen-stained blue dress, he left the room, telling aides, "I'm about to vomit." Later on, he reportedly said to aides, "I can't stand to be in the same room with Bill." He didn't plan to resign right away, because it would look terrible for the president, but he knew he would, as soon as he felt the timing appropriate.

After the scandal broke, Bowles refused to get involved in any way with "that Lewinsky mess. For the time I have left in the White House, I plan to stick only to the running of the country's affairs."

Bowles had been a frequent golf partner of Bill's, but after revelations associated with the Lewinsky affair, he never hit the links with Bill again.

Bill's press secretary, Mike McCurry, also found himself in embarrassing positions. He constantly had to face the media, making denials that he knew weren't true. He also knew that the press was aware that he wasn't telling the truth.

As one newsman put it, "Mike had a nudge-nudge, wink-wink relationship with us. I mean, he's really telling us, 'you guys realize I'm forced to say this, but all of you know it's crap.'"

At least on the surface, the Vice President, Al Gore, stood by Bill. Gore wanted to run for president in the next election (2000), and had been counting on Bill's support. However, many of his backers felt that Gore might have a better chance if he ran for president and "distanced yourself from the skirtchaser."

Gore's wife, Tipper, remained leery of Bill's professed innocence. "Knowing him as little as I do, but from what I've heard, I'm very skeptical."

In a joint appearance with Bill and Gore at the University of Illinois, the president told his Veep, "They're staging a fucking *coup d'état.*"

Gore didn't need to be told who "they" were.

Bill was greatly disappointed with and felt somewhat abandoned by some of his key staff members, who wanted to distance themselves from him. But the cruelest blow of all was when he heard from Hillary that Chelsea "did not want him to set foot on the campus grounds of Stanford if invited to give a speech." It was humiliating enough for her to attend classes with Carolyn Starr, the daughter of the dreaded Independent Counsel seeking to destroy her father.

By now, every newspaper in the country, every radio and TV broadcaster, were carrying news of the president and the intern.

Some stories compared Monica to fellator Linda Lovelace, the porno queen who had starred in the top-grossing flick, *Deep Throat* (1972), demonstrating her oral skills.

It seemed for a while that all of America was talking about Monica's stained blue dress. ABC and most other TV stations referred to the dress as containing "bodily fluids" from the president. For some reason the word "semen" was taboo.

As one Las Vegas comic asked, "What are the president's bodily fluids? Instead of shooting off in her mouth with semen, did he actually piss in her mouth? Urine is a bodily fluid."

Many comedians even poked fun at the alleged sexual habits within Bill's home state of Arkansas. Appearing in her one-woman show in Chicago, Joan Rivers said, "What does an Arkansas woman say after making love? 'Daddy get up, you're crushing my cigarettes.'"

Wolf Blitzer on CNN speculated that "presidential aides, fearing for their jobs, figure that their boss is going to resign like Nixon, so they are sending out *resumés*."

Bob Woodward, who had exposed Nixon and Watergate, claimed that "President Clinton might have been wiser to have learned from the lesson of Watergate. That is, the cover-up can be worse than the crime."

On right-wing talk radio, Americans were urged to assemble at the gates of the White House, invade it, and forcibly drag Bill and Hillary into the street. Hosts proclaimed that the United States "is now a banana republic."

Bill watched "with despair in my heart," as Stephanopoulos—who had resigned from the White House staff back in November of 1996—discussed, as part of an appearance on *The Today Show,* his possible impeachment.

Hillary defined Carville as "our most contentious, in-your-face, don't-give-'em-an-inch friend that we have."

Carville denounced the charges, saying "All this god damn shit boils down to is that the president may have gotten a couple of blow jobs, and Starr and his shitheads want to make a Federal case out of it."

During the first weeks of 1998, Bill continued to stonewall revelations about his affair "That time in my life was like living in a nightmare," he later said.

During his State of the Union address in January, he did not mention the scandal, but presented an optimistic view of the American economy.

In a moment of near-despair, during the darkest moments of the political frenzy generated by the excesses of the Independent Counsel, Bill Clinton made some rueful comparisons to the conflicts and conundrums discussed in *Darkness at Noon* (German: *Sonnenfinsternis*).

First published in German in 1940 and in English early in 1941, it's a novel that expressed its author's sense of betrayal by the Soviet Union's version of Communism at the onset of World War II. Set in 1938 during the Moscow show trials amid Josef Stalin's great purge, it was written by the Hungarian-born British novelist Arthur Koestler.

It focuses on an old-school Bolshevik who is arrested, imprisoned, and tried for crimes against the government that he helped to create. Literary critic Kingsley Martin described the novel as "one of the few books written in this epoch which will survive it".

In a surprise, a *Chicago Tribune* poll taken of public opinion after his address revealed that his approval rating had shot up to 72%. Only 26% felt that Starr was conducting a fair investigation. Two days later, he heard even better news: CNN's poll showed that he had an approval rating of 79%, an astonishing figure for a president so mired in scandal.

Both Bill and Hillary summoned one of their best friends and advisers, Sidney Blumenthal, to the White House. In a huddle with Hillary, Blumenthal compared the latest attack on Bill to the "Catilinarian Conspiracy," a reference to ancient Roman times when the orator and politician Cicero had exposed a rebellion by Catiline, who was trying to overthrow the Roman Republic. In 63BC, Catiline was exposed and had to flee from Rome to escape execution.

Hollywood producer Harry Thomason turned out to be one of Bill Clinton's most enduring and supportive friends. As Bill was leaving the White House, he thanked Thomason as one of the men "who had brought me to the dance," meaning his eight years in the White House.

Harry and his wife, Linda, were among the close friends Bill and Hillary invited to sleep over on the night of his inauguration in January of 1993.

Hillary told Blumenthal "If Bill doesn't have the backbone to fight this, I'll be the steel plate in his spine."

Later that day, Blumenthal met with Bill in the Oval Office. "I saw a man, the president, who was beside himself."

Bill told his friend, "I feel like a character in the novel, *Darkness at Noon.* I am someone who is surrounded by an oppressive force that is creating a lie about me, and I can't get the truth out."

Blumenthal compared the probe into Bill's private life to a "right-wing *putsch.* Starr's investigation was helping to destroy the role of the United States in world affairs—all for some silly blow-job."

Later, Blumenthal watched in dismay as Bill made a previously scheduled appearance on public television in a program hosted by Jim Lehrer. His close friend, Hollywood producer Harry Thomason, also watched in dismay as Bill was grilled about the Lewinsky affair. The producer knew a lot about performance, and he found Bill's appearance, "Like a man on the hot seat—uneasy, nervous, tentative in his responses."

"There is not a sexual relationship," Bill claimed when asked about Monica. He was trying to be clever in avoiding the question. Technically, there was no ongoing sexual relationship with Monica at the time he appeared on the show. But he failed to mention that there had ever been a sexual relationship.

After seeing the show, Thomason flew to Washington, where he stayed for a month or so, hoping to help Bill in his hour of need.

CNN Legal Analyst, Jeffrey Toobin, claimed that the president "marinated in his sense of victimhood."

Hillary also appeared on TV, on NBC's *Today Show,* hosted by Matt Lauer. Unlike Bill, she was viewed as far more "poised, primed, and confident," in the words of one reviewer. She denied charges of her husband's infidelity, claiming that, "We keep no secrets from each other."

It was at this time she uttered her famous line, "There is this vast right-wing conspiracy that has been conspiring against my husband since the day he announced for president."

On Monday, January 26, 1998, Bill appeared in the Roosevelt Room of the White House. As he faced TV cameras, he was ostensibly there to promote after-school health care. But all that reporters wanted to know were details about his alleged affair with Monica Lewinsky.

He faced the cameras and said, "I want to say one thing to the American people. I want you to listen to me. I'm going to say this again: I did not have sexual relations with *that woman,* Miss Lewinsky. I never told anybody to lie, not a single time. Never! These allegations are false."

Monica Lewinsky, Paula Jones, & Kenneth Starr Tighten the Noose Around Bill's Neck

"The Clinton White House branded me the unstable stalker, the dimwit floozy, the Poor Innocent who didn't know any better."

—Monica Lewinsky

On January 4, 1998, Monica Lewinsky's lawyer, Frank Carter, drafted an affidavit for her as part of a maneuver to prevent her from being deposed. In it, she denied having had a sexual relationship with the president. Two days later, she went to Carter's office and picked up a copy of the draft. She read it, but didn't sign it, telling Carter that she needed to think it over.

Then, she phoned Vernon Jordan and discussed the affidavit with him, claiming that she found two or three sentences troubling. She went on to say that she was worried about one sentence that declared that she had never been alone with the president. She decided to rewrite it, claiming that there were other people present at any time she met with Bill.

Within less than an hour after speaking to Monica, Jordan called the president and spoke to him for thirteen minutes, records reveal.

Monica had recently seen the movie *Titanic* (1997), which dealt with not only a doomed ship, but a doomed love affair. She later admitted, "I cried my eyes out." The film reminded her of her own bittersweet affair with the president. After she returned home, she wrote him a "mushy love note."

In it, she decried the fact that she'd never spent a night of passion with him, and lamented that they had never been lovers in the true sense. She was particularly upset when newspapers published pictures of the president and his First Lady in bathing suits, dancing together on a beach in St. Thomas, one of the U.S. Virgin Islands.

On January 4, Monica asked Betty Currie if she could visit her at home to drop off something for the president. Her parcel included not only her love note, but a copy of a book called *The Presidents of the United States,* which she had purchased at an antiquarian bookstore.

Before leaving, she asked the president's secretary to have Bill call her, which he did the following day. When he spoke to Monica, he thanked her for the book, but admonished her for writing such a mushy note, fearing that it might fall into the wrong hands and subsequently be used against them.

She discussed the affidavit with him, and asked him if he'd like to go over it. He said he did not, as he had seen about fifteen other affidavits from other potential witnesses. She did not attempt to cover up the slightly angry, even jealous, tone in her voice. She said she was troubled about her transfer from the White House to the Pentagon. "People at the White House who don't like me might contradict me and get me in real trouble."

Her voice seemed to have an accusatory tone to it, as if blaming him for all her current troubles. As she remembered it, he seemed anxious to get her off the phone. Unaware of it at the time, she could not imagine that this would be the last time she ever spoke "to the man I love."

Monica phoned Tripp before deciding to sign the affidavit. "Don't sign it," Tripp advised, "until the bastards have gotten you a good job in New York."

At this point, Monica appeared unaware that with this advice, Tripp was trying to entrap her. If Monica had held out signing the affidavit until Jordan came through with the job, it would be a form of blackmail—that is, she was willing to lie to get a good job, a reward for her silence. And that would implicate both Jordan and the president in an attempt to obstruct justice, thereby falling under Starr's recently obtained new guidelines for "expanded jurisdiction." Inevitably, this evidence could form one of the justifications for the president's possible impeachment.

It was later claimed that Tripp also wanted to tape Monica "recanting" her previous confessions about limited sex with the president and finally admitting that "she had full intercourse with the president." Monica wasn't willing to go that far.

On January 7, at Carter's office, she signed the affidavit, knowing that it contained false statements. She then took the affidavit to Jordan's office. After she left, records show that he phoned the president, informing him that the affidavit had been signed, and that indeed, in it, she had denied a sexual relationship. According to later testimony, the president ended the call quickly, just saying, "Fine, good."

In reference to her signing the affidavit, Monica later recalled, "I was, in effect, putting on my team jersey, to be on the president's side."

The bridge that would link Monica Lewinsky to Paula Jones—two women from very different worlds—seemed like a long span to cross over troubled waters. But Paula's lawyers were determined to do it, as they moved forward with their sexual harassment suit against the president.

In the aftermath of revelations that much of the drama surrounding Linda Tripp and Monica Lewinsky had taken place here, the Ritz-Carlton at Pentagon City, in Arlington, Virginia, just outside Washington, became a tourist attraction.

Monica was brutally interrogated in room 1012. It immediately became the most requested accommodation in the hotel.

A pre-trial hearing was held in front of Judge Susan Webber Wright, in which the attorneys were ordered to name all the witnesses they planned to subpoena. Monica's name was on that list. The reason, or so the lawyers stated, that motivated the call for this former White House intern, was to reveal that the president had a pattern of rewarding women with good jobs based on their willingness to have sexual relations with him.

Unknown to Monica, on January 12, Tripp called Starr's office to let his deputies know that the president had had an affair with a White House intern, and that the young woman had been issued a subpoena in the Paula Jones case.

Tripp also charged that both the president and Jordan had urged the woman to commit perjury, and she also revealed that she had twenty hours of tape in which Monica discussed the details of her affair with Bill. Tripp also alleged that Monica had refused to sign the affidavit until Jordan used his influence to get her a good job in New York, perhaps at Revlon.

The OIC responded immediately. In just

two hours, an FBI agent and six Federal prosecutors were at Tripp's home in Maryland going over her evidence. At this debriefing, Tripp was told to set up a luncheon with Monica at the Ritz Carlton. It was clearly understood that Tripp would be body wired, and that agents in a room upstairs would be listening to and recording every word.

Tripp turned her tapes over to Jackie Bennett, one of Starr's deputies. Bennett had been called "a hard-core conservative without nuance or diplomatic skill," by the *New York Post.*

When Starr was informed of Tripp's evidence he reportedly said, "Within weeks, Al Gore will be President of the United States, a post he's always wanted, and he'll have me to thank for that. I have been delivered manna from heaven. Clinton will be kicked out of the White House, landing on his fat ass on Pennsylvania Avenue."

At long last, a job offer had come through from Revlon, which would pay Monica $40,000 a year (less that she earned at the Pentagon) in the Communications Department. She accepted the offer, later recalling, "I was Cinderella off to the ball, heading for New York and a new life without 'Handsome.'"

What she didn't know at the time was that "the two ugly sisters" *[Linda Tripp and Lucianne Goldberg]* would ensure that she would never make it to that fairytale ball.

Monica Lewinsky used a biblical reference, the archetype of Judas, depicted above during a key moment in his betrayal of Jesus, in her description of the actions of her former friend, Linda Tripp.

Monica went on to describe Tripp as "a disgusting, despicable, venomous, and evil human being. She betrayed me for no other reason than malice and spite."

On January 14, Monica had a face-to-face meeting with Tripp in which she presented her with a three-page document, regarding points to make in Tripp's own affidavit if she had to face a subpoena.

"This is what my lawyers have taught me. You don't very often say 'no' unless you really need to. The best answer is to say 'Not that I recall' or 'not that I really remember.' The trick is to be evasive without actually committing perjury if called upon to testify."

The following day, Monica's lawyer, Carter, filed a motion to quash the subpoena issued by Jones' attorneys.

A luncheon meeting was arranged between Tripp and Monica at the Ritz Carlton in Pentagon City. Tripp arrived body-wired, with Federal agents listening in from within Room 1012 at the hotel.

Monica's lunch with Tripp would last for

three hours. By now, Monica had become suspicious, mainly because of the "incriminating" questions Tripp shot at her. When Tripp got up to go to the women's room, she left her purse on the table. Monica opened it to see if there was a recording device inside. But the microphone and its transmitter had gone to the toilet with Tripp.

During their tense luncheon, Monica lied to Tripp, telling her that she had not yet signed an affidavit, when, in fact, she had. Tripp, or so it seemed to Monica, was trying to lead her down a corridor to a prison cell. For both parties, the luncheon ended inconclusively. Neither side got what she wanted. The date of the luncheon was a Tuesday. On Friday, January 16, a trap was set for Monica.

She was still wearing her gym gear after a workout, when FBI agents, directed by Tripp, followed Monica to a food stall in Pentagon City, where she was trying to get something to eat. The agents descended on an unsuspecting Monica, ordering her to Room 1012 of the Ritz Carlton. In a brown pants suit, Tripp followed behind.

Monica also learned that Tripp not only had betrayed her, but that she had been in negotiations with a New York literary agent, Lucianne Goldberg, to write a tell-all book about Monica's affair with the president, in which she planned to publish details of all of Monica's confessions. In his book, *A Vast Conspiracy,* Jeffrey Toobin also vented his spleen on Tripp and Goldberg. He wrote that Goldberg emerged "from a virtual space somewhere between the Republican National Convention and the bar scene in *Star Wars,* like Norma Desmond in *Sunset Blvd.,* her heart full of murder and longing."

In Room 1012, Monica encountered more FBI agents and "the cold-eyed prosecutors" from Starr's office. She particularly recalled the stone face of Mike Emmick, who had been personally selected by Starr to interrogate her. She later referred to Starr's deputy as "a revolting specimen of humanity."

Also in the room sat "my Judas," Monica's reference to Tripp. She had a look of triumph on her face, as Monica referred to her as a "treacherous bitch."

By now, Monica knew that she had been the victim of a "sting," but how serious would this be for her and the president? She was soon to find out.

In a voice evocative of a cold winter's night in the Arctic, Emmick moved in on her, outlining the case against her, which included obstruction of justice, subordination of perjury, witness tampering, and conspiracy. "In all, you could face up to twenty-seven years in jail when we get through with you."

After hearing this, she later recalled, "It was like my stomach had been cut open and someone had poured acid into the wound. I felt an intense, stinging pain, and overwhelming feeling of abject terror."

Within the hour, she learned that her testimony might ultimately lead to impeachment proceedings against the president. Emmick revealed to her for the first time that Tripp for the past few months had recorded all of her phone conversations. Not only that, but she learned that during their Tuesday lunch, Tripp had been outfitted with a body wire by FBI agents.

As Monica told her biographer, Andrew Morton, "I realized I could be sent to jail, where I would come out an old lady. No one would ever want to marry me then. My life would be over. So I thought there was no way out, other than killing myself." Since the hotel had sliding windows, she briefly considered jumping to her death.

She kept glancing at Tripp, who remained stone faced. "I wanted to hurt her. I felt like an animal wanting to claw her skin."

Monica begged her brutal interrogators to let her put through a call to her lawyer, but they refused. The interrogation continued as she grew more frightened and intimidated.

She was told to cooperate—or else. It was even suggested that she might also be body wired for a meeting she'd set up with Betty Currie and Vernon Jordan, perhaps even with the president himself. At one point, Emmick told her that if she would cooperate, he might get Starr to have her jail term reduced from twenty-seven years to just five years.

Suddenly, Jackie Bennett entered the room. He was the deputy who had traveled to Maryland to retrieve Tripp's tapes. As Morton wrote, "Bennett, like a pit bull terrier with a kitten, made short order of his reluctant witness."

In legal circles, Bennett was known as "The Thug." During his interrogation of Monica, he threatened to round up her mother and force her to testify, warning that if she didn't cooperate, she, too might face jail time, like Susan McDougal in the Whitewater investigation. "Who do you want to protect?" Bennett asked Monica. "The president, your lover boy, or your own mother? It's your decision, girlie."

Finally, she was allowed to call her mother, Marcia Lewis, who was in New York at the time. At that point, she could only assure her mother that she was all right, as Marcia had been repeatedly trying to get in touch with her. An FBI agent stood by the phone, ready to cut off the call if Monica revealed that she was being held a prison in a hotel room in Pentagon City.

For ten hours that Monday, with an occasional break, Monica was held prisoner by FBI agents and Starr's relentless interrogators. Bill Clinton would later claim that "she was treated like a serious felon."

Finally, she was allowed to get through to Marcia, again in New York, to tell her what was happening. Her mother agreed to go to Grand Central at once and board the next train to Washington to come to the aid of her daughter.

During the course of that afternoon, Monica heard some alarming news:

The president was slated to testify the following day, giving his deposition. She feared he'd be ambushed by Jones' attorneys, who possessed incriminating information, of which she assumed Bill was unaware. It seemed like he'd be walking into a perjury entrapment.

At the time she was kidnapped by FBI agents, Carter had not yet filed her sworn affidavit. Therefore, technically, she was not guilty of perjury.

She protested, "This was supposed to be a Whitewater investigation. Your linking me to that real estate development is ridiculous. I've never set foot in Arkansas."

Finally, at around 10PM, her mother arrived. She was defiant. Telling her daughter, "There's no way in hell you're going to spend twenty-seven years in jail, not even twenty-seven minutes."

***

That night, Monica's father, Bernie Lewinsky, in Beverly Hills, was apprised by telephone of his daughter's predicament. For the first time, he was made aware of the scandal, not only Monica's kidnapping by the FBI, but her affair with President Clinton. He claimed he'd get a good lawyer onto the case at once.

Bernie had a close friend, William Ginsburg. Although he was best known for defending medical malpractice cases, he was willing to take on Monica's case.

Bearded and bespectacled, he'd represent her from January to June of 1998. He became famous for his appearances on television defending Monica, wearing bow ties. He had a deep voice. As one reporter wrote, "Imagine a sober W.C. Fields." Although during the course of his long career, he would try some 300 cases in 21 states, his name would forever after be linked to that of Monica Lewinsky and her plight.

The attorney's name even became part of the English language. Today "The Full Ginsburg" means appearing on a lot of talk shows.

William H. Ginsburg, a seasoned malpractice lawyer, bolted to fame when he was hired by Monica Lewinsky's father, a noted California oncologist, to defend her. Before that, Ginsburg had been best known for defending the doctor accused of covering up the cause of Liberace's death. (The gay entertainer had died of AIDS.)

To his critics, Ginsburg, at times, seemed more intrigued by appearing on TV talk shows than he did in defending Monica. Some of his statements were controversial and in some cases appeared to undermine Monica's credibility.

Ginsburg later said he would have relished the chance to cross-examine Kenneth Starr in a courtroom, but he withdrew from the case. In later years, he admitted to a few personal friends the reason why:

"To tell the truth, I came to despise both Monica and Clinton."

The term originated on February 1, 1998, when he appeared on all five of television's major Sunday morning talk shows, the first person who had ever accomplished this amazing feat. He became an instant celebrity.

From the beginning, Ginsburg came under fire for having failed to secure an immunity deal for Monica with Starr. Starr's deputy, Robert J. Bittman, nicknamed "Bulldog," finally got Ginsburg to agree to have Monica sign a ten-page document, exposing her sexual relationship with the president in exchange for immunity. Even so, Starr refused to grant it.

Although she continued to claim that "He is still the man I love," she agreed that she would testify against him in exchange for immunity. But despite that attempt at a strategic compromise, Starr stubbornly refused to grant her immunity.

"His refusal marked the precise moment when Bill Clinton's survival in office was assured," wrote legal analyst Jeffrey Toobin. "If Starr had agreed to the immunity deal that day, he would have had the ammunition—in testimony and in conclusive genetic evidence—to prove that Clinton had lied. He could have had an impeachment report for Congress in a month or less. Instead, Starr's obsession with toughness led him into disaster."

Writing in *The New York Times,* Murray Kakutnai said: "Starr's office bungled its investigation of Clinton through a combination of zealotry, infighting, and ineptitude."

By the time Starr finally granted Monica immunity, it was July 28. "The political and legal terrain had been transformed since those frenzied first days of the scandal in January. The delay of nearly six months had allowed the country to come to terms with the fact that the president had probably lied about his affair with the intern," wrote Toobin. "But the public by now knew he had managed to do a pretty good job as president anyway."

Although she had avoided prosecution, Monica still had to testify before Starr's interrogators. Her date in court was August 6, to be followed by Bill's testimony on August 17. She'd already learned that the president had been forced to take a blood test at the White House to determine if, indeed, that was his DNA in the semen on her blue dress.

Starr's deputies had spent weeks gearing up, writing a series of questions for both Monica and the president. Some questions were struck down as too provocative. One question that was killed was, "What does the president's semen taste like?" Like Paula Jones, Monica was to be asked about the shape and size of Bill's penis. Neither of those questions was asked.

To Monica, it seemed that every cameraman and reporter in the world turned out for her day in court as she made her way into the courthouse In Washington, D.C., on Pennsylvania Avenue. She recalled it "as the most degrading day of my life."

On the stand, she was asked about the cigar inserted into her vagina. She had to reveal intimate details of oral sex with Bill, and she also was queried about the blue dress from GAP. She later labeled her interrogation as "fundamentally misogynistic." She was also asked, "Who unzipped whose zipper? Did he put his mouth on your breasts? Did he suck on your nipples?"

Two months before her grand jury appearance, Ginsburg had bowed out of the case and flown back to California. Before his departure, he wrote a note to Starr which was later made public: "Congratulations. As a result of your callous disregard for cherished Constitutional rights, you may have succeeded in unmasking a sexual relationship between two consenting adults at the cost of millions of dollars in taxpayer money."

Feeling "emotionally raped," Monica, at the end of the day, fled from her inquisitors. But her ordeal wasn't over yet.

On September 3, accompanied by her new attorney, Sydney Hoffman, she had to report to the office of the Independent Counsel to listen to twenty hours of "tortuous" testimony as recorded by Tripp. It took three full days. She described it "as humiliating and painful. More bullshit than substance."

Toobin heard the tapes and wasn't impressed with Monica's chatter. He later wrote: "The president's first 45-minute conversation with Ms. Lewinsky must have cured him of his infatuation. There were few better measures of Tripp's dedication to her book research and Clinton-hating than the simple fact that she tolerated Lewinsky's inane chatter for so long."

In Toobin's book about the case, *A Vast Conspiracy,* he claimed that Starr's deputies had "a predilection for canine zeal and prosecutorial misjudgments." He also called the entire case "shabby but not illegal. The whole impeachment crisis was never anything more than it appeared to be—that of a humiliated middle-aged husband who lied when he was caught having an affair with a young woman."

He accused Starr and the president's other adversaries of being "literally consumed with hatred for him. They were willing to trample all standards of fairness—not to mention the Constitution—in their effort to drive him from office." Toobin also said that Bill dealt with the crisis "not with candor and grace, but rather with the dishonesty and self-pity that are among the touchstones of his character."

***

In 2015, Monica summed up her life for *Vanity Fair:* "In my own case, each click of that YouTube link reinforces the archetype, despite my efforts to parry it away. Me! America's B.J. Queen! That intern! That vixen! Or, in the inescapable phrase for our 42nd president, 'That woman!'"

"Bill Clinton Has a 5-inch (or 5½-inch) Circumcized Penis"

—Paula Jones

On April 1, 1998, Bill and Hillary were on the final leg of a presidential trip to Africa, when both of them breathed a sigh of relief. He'd talked to his lawyer, Bob Bennett, in Washington.

He had just learned that Judge Susan Webber Wright, Bill's former student in Little Rock, had thrown out the Paula Jones sexual harassment lawsuit against him. The judge granted the president's motion for a summary judgment, ruling that Paula had not shown where she'd suffered any damages. And whereas Paula had also claimed that Bill had intentionally inflicted emotional distress on her, the judge ruled that she had failed to show that the president's action constituted "outrageous conduct."

In her ruling, Wright said that even though Governor Clinton's actions "were boorish and offensive," they were not severe enough to constitute sexual harassment under the law.

Facing a press conference, Bill was asked what he thought of the judge's ruling. "When I am out of office, I will have a lot to say about this. Until then, I'm going to honor my commitment to all of you and go back to work. I haven't challenged anything, including things I consider questionable, because I think it is wrong. The American people have been through enough."

Appearing before Larry King on his TV talk show, Paula claimed that she feared for her life. "I am not suicidal. I love my life and my children. I drive very well. If I'm run off the road, it was someone deliberately trying to kill me."

Then, backed by a seemingly endless supply of right-wing money, Jones' legal team announced that they were going to appeal the dismissal of her case to the U.S. Court of Appeals for the Eighth District. During an oral argument, two of the three judges on the panel appeared sympathetic to the arguments of her team.

Bob Bennett had failed in his effort to get the case postponed until the president was no longer in office, the justices voting 9 to zero that the case could move forward.

John W. Whitehead, president of the Rutherford Institute, Paula's financial backer, claimed that Paula should win the case because it "would draw attention to the importance of protecting powerless women from embarrassment in the work place. The rule of law should extend to the highest office in the nation."

"For all she's been through for so many years, Paula should get some money," said one of her lawyers, Joseph Cammarata. "In Clinton-speak, it depends on your definition of 'some.'"

Since the case was still ongoing, reporters continued to probe. Tantalizing, even salacious, details were revealed when Paula's sworn affidavit of September 29, 1997 was revealed. She had been quizzed extensively about the size and shape of the presidential penis, a first for an American president.

In her testimony, she said, "I briefly observed the penis of William Jefferson Clinton in a hotel suite at the Excelsior on May 8, 1991. That is the only time I have seen his genital area, and I have never had it described to me by anyone, nor have I read anything on the subject."

"Mr. Clinton's penis was circumcised and seemed to me to be rather short and thin. I would describe its appearance as seeming to be five to five and one-half inches, or less, in length, and having a circumference of the approximate size of a quarter, or slightly larger."

On a face-off, Bill Bristow, one of Bill's defense lawyers, questioned Paula.

BRISTOW: You made the statement that you are not a bimbo. Would you tell me your definition of the word bimbo?

PAULA: Trailer Park Trash.

BRISTOW: Now, Mrs. Jones, when you make a statement that the president's penis looks small to you, that implies a certain familiarity with the male anatomy—in other words, that you were in a position to make comparative studies. Have you ever taken any anatomy classes?

PAULA: No.

BRISTOW: So I gather that your ability to discern distinctive characteristics about the male penis would be based on experience you have had in your life where you have had the opportunity to view other male penises, is that correct?

PAULA: It—very few, if there were. Yeah, I made it probably on that assumption and plus he was a really big man and really overweight and it seemed like it was real little compared to his weight.

Bristow also confronted Paula with a list of her previous affairs, including Mike Turner, who had sold seminude photographs of her to *Penthouse*.

Bristow read from notes that Turner had received from Paula. He quoted certain remarks she had scribbled:

"Mike, gorgeous, I love to snuggle up to your sexy, soft body and wonderful butt."

"Mike, Thanks for letting me sleep off my drunk."

"Mike, thanks for the wonderful time I had last time. Your (sic) *great in bed."*

"Mike, your (sic) *a real sweetheart. Let's do something soon, okay? Love you babe, Paula."*

During this round of questioning, Paula's lawyer, Donovan Campbell, was seen sitting in the courtroom, suffering in silence.

***

The Paula Jones case never went to court. On November 13, Bill's lawyers settled $850,000 on her to drop the case. However, he would make no apology. The settlement took half of his and Hillary's life savings, and they were already deeply in debt because of their legal bills.

"I wanted to get back to work and forget all about this horrid girl and all her right-wing backers goading her on—each of them trying to put a noose around my neck."

The case seemed to have no end. In March of 1999, after Bill had survived impeachment, Judge Wright ruled that Paula would get only $200,000 of the settlement, the rest of the money going to pay legal fees.

Even though she lost most of the money, Paula made an appearance on TV to show off her new nose job, compliments of Dr. Daniel C. DiCriscio. The plastic surgeon's image-enhancing work was paid for by a Republican donor.

On April 12, 1999, Judge Wright ruled that Bill was in civil contempt of court because his conduct was deemed "contumacious" *[i.e., stubbornly disobedient].* She claimed that he had given evasive and misleading answers designed to obstruct the judicial process.

This was the same judge who had sent Susan McDougal to prison for eighteen months on a contempt-of-court charge. At least she wasn't sending the president to jail.

Wright ruled that Bill had to pay the court $1,202, plus an additional $90,000 to Jones' lawyers for expenses. That was a disappointment to them, since they had requested nearly half a million dollars.

Even with all these rulings and a settlement, the case didn't seem to go away. On January 19, 2001, the day before the president left the White House, the Arkansas Bar took disciplinary action against Bill, stripping him of his license to practice law in Arkansas for the next five years. Of course, he never had any intention of ever practicing law in that state again. "I have far bigger fish to fry," he was overheard telling two of his aides.

"I Hate Your Guts, You Filthy, Slimy, Son of a Bitch"

—*Hillary Clinton to her husband*

As dawn broke over the White House on August 15, 1998, Bill had been awake all night, dreading his testimony before a grand jury later that morning. The time had come for him to confess the truth to Hillary about his affair with Monica Lewinsky.

He woke her up to relate to her the bad news. Although reportedly he gave a "rather vanilla" description of his involvement with the intern, he did confess to oral sex.

"Hillary looked at me as if I had punched her in the gut, almost as angry at me for lying to her in January as for what I had done. All I could do was tell her that I was sorry and that I had felt I couldn't tell anyone, even her, what had happened. I told her that I loved her, and I didn't want to hurt her or Chelsea, that I was ashamed of what I had done."

In her own memoir, *Living History,* the First Lady gave her reaction to Bill's confession: "I could hardly breathe. Gulping for air, I started crying at him and yelling at him. 'What do you mean? What are you saying? Why did you lie to me?' I was furious and getting more so by the second. I was dumbfounded, heartbroken, and outraged that I'd believed him at all."

The White House staff outside the door leaked some of what she'd said to her unfaithful husband. *"YOU STUPID, STUPID ASSHOLE! YOU FUCKING BASTARD! I HATE YOUR GUTS, YOU FILTHY, SLIMY, SON OF A BITCH!"*

His confession to Hillary was followed by a chilly weekend at the White House. One staffer noted that downstairs, when Bill went to take his wife's hand, she "shrank from him with a certain loathing, like he was extending the hand of a contagious leper."

He later admitted that telling Chelsea was even harder, because "I was afraid I would lose not only my marriage, but my daughter's love and respect as well."

Hillary's close friend, Sidney Blumenthal, later commented on the aftermath of Bill's confession. "She had hoped that her husband had reformed himself, that whatever agony she had gone through earlier in her marriage had been resolved. Now, she was discovering that it was not over. In a way, this blow to her pride made her, in the eyes of many, a more accessible and sympathetic figure."

His confession to Hillary had occurred on a Saturday morning. The following Monday, in the Map Room of the White House, he appeared for his videotaped testimony before the grand jury. Members of the jury, back at the courthouse, watched his testimony via closed circuit television.

Facing the camera, the president was vaguely aware that Starr had an extensive body of evidence to use against him. By now, he knew that Monica had been granted immunity and that she had already testified. On August 3, a blood sample, drawn from one of his veins in the White House, had shown, after its analysis in a laboratory, that his DNA matched the stain on her blue dress.

Representing the prosecution, Robert ("Bulldog") Bittman confronted Bill. He asked him how his admission of "inappropriate intimate contact" could be reconciled with the previous testimony of his lawyer. Representing Bill, Bob Bennett had gone on record as saying, "There is no sex of any kind in any manner, shape, or form."

The president replied with what was considered a comic literalism. "It depends on what the meaning of the word 'is' is. If 'is' means 'is and never has been,' that's one thing. If it means 'there is none,' that was a completely true statement."

Bill's answer spread through the media, some historians comparing the "fame quotient" of its labyrinthine phraseologies "to the presidential locution of Lincoln's 'Fourscore and seven years ago...'"

The testimony would take an agonizing four hours as the President of the United States sat on the hot seat, as dramatic events were about to explode, worldwide, each of which would require all of his attention.

He later claimed, "Starr was trying to turn my interrogation into a pornographic home movie, asking questions designed to humiliate me and to disgust Congress and the American people *[to the point where]* they'd demand my resignation, after which he might be able to indict me."

During his testimony, he did admit that "on certain occasions, he had engaged in wrong conduct with Miss Lewinsky. While morally wrong, it did not constitute sexual relations as I understood the definition of the term. But I will say no more about the specifics of what happened between that woman and myself."

He finished his testimony at 6:30PM. He had been scheduled to address the nation at 10PM that evening. During his broadcast, watched by millions, he took sole responsibility for his personal failure and for misleading everyone, but he also used the occasion to attack Starr and the other witch hunters. He held out a plea that his enemies would stop "the pursuit of personal destruction and the prying into private lives."

In her apartment, Monica stayed glued to her TV set. She later claimed, "I was very hurt and angered by his speech. It made me feel like a piece of trash. I wondered how I could have ever cared about this man. He was so self-righteous, so self-centered."

The next day, Bill, Chelsea, Hillary, and Buddy (his chocolate Labrador) headed for a working vacation on Martha's Vineyard. Perhaps the saddest photograph ever taken of this troubled family was when they walked across the South Lawn of the White House to board a helicopter.

Only Buddy remained loyal to his master. Hillary was clearly alienated, and Chelsea would take a long time to forgive her father for his lies and sexual indiscretions. As one reporter wrote, "For the president, the adage held true: A dog is man's best friend."

***

In August of 1998, the American embassies of Tanzania and Kenya were bombed, killing 257 people, including twelve Americans. A total of 5,000 people were seriously injured. The attacks were engineered by the terrorist group Al Qaeda, led by the crazed Osama bin Laden, who obsessively threatened "death to all Americans."

While at Martha's Vineyard, Bill had been up all night. By 3AM, he ordered U.S. Navy destroyers in the northern Arabian Sea to launch Cruise missile attacks against targets in Afghanistan. It was later learned that the attack occurred too late to kill bin Laden. As Bill later put it, "Elvis had left the building."

The president's critics denounced the missile attack, claiming that the move was lifted from the plot of the 1997 Dustin Hoffman/Robert De Niro black comedy film, *Wag the Dog.* The plot centered on a fictional president ordering bombing raids over an enemy state to distract his fellow countrymen from his other difficulties.

It was later learned that Bill feared criticism of his launching a military attack in the middle of all his sex scandals. He was aware that millions of Americans might view this missile assault as his attempt to distract the public from his own per-

As president, Bill Clinton was confronted with horrors from Al Qaeda years before President George W. Bush, in the words of his critics, "fell asleep and allowed the terrorist bombings of New York and Washington,"

This WANTED FOR MURDER poster was issued by the U.S. State Department after the terror bombings, less than four minutes apart on August 7, 1998, of the U.S. embassies in Kenya and Tanzania. Hundreds of people were killed, almost 5000 were injured, and the blow to U.S. prestige was insufferable.

sonal problems.

He delayed ordering the assault on Afghanistan for three long months. This delay allowed bin Laden to escape with his men into the mountains. As Senator Bob Kerrey said, "We had a round in our chamber, and we didn't use it."

Bin Laden's escape from American missiles allowed him to sneak away to plot his attack on America on 9/11.

"Just think," James Carville reportedly said. "Were it not for a couple of blow jobs, the World Trade Center might still be standing, the Pentagon not bombed, and all those people still alive. Imagine!"

Back at the White House, a rumor went around Washington that Hillary was seen tossing Bill's clothing over the Truman Balcony.

***

Novelist William Styron visited Hillary at Martha's Vineyard, later reporting that she looked "shell-shocked. She was devastated. It was all she could do to keep her composure. To everyone who saw her, it was obvious the strain she was going through."

Years later, on looking back, Hillary reflected on her contrasting feelings about her husband. "He had violated my trust, hurt me deeply, and given his enemies something real to exploit after years of enduring their false charges, partisan investigations, and lawsuits."

"As his wife, I wanted to wring his neck. But he was not only my husband, he was also the President of the United States. I thought that, in spite of everything, he led America and the world in a way that I continued to support. His failing was not a betrayal of his country. My marriage hung in the balance. Life moved on, and I moved with it."

In September, she and Bill visited Moscow and also flew to Ireland, occupying separate bedrooms. Unless called upon, they seemed distant from each other, although friendly and gracious to their hosts.

In the autumn, hoping to save their marriage, Bill and Hillary went to a marriage counselor. He later wrote: "I got reacquainted with my wife again. I had always loved her very much, but not very well. We were still each other's best friend. I hoped we could save our marriage."

However, in the White House, he was still assigned to the couch in the small living room adjoining their bedroom. He likened it to the equivalent of being in the doghouse. For two months, he slept alone.

Hillary Calls in an Adulterous "God Squad" To Persuade Bill to Repent His Sins

Hillary decided to stage "an act of redemption" by inviting ministers (not Billy Graham) to the White House for prayer and more counseling. She called these men her "God Squad."

The Rev. Jesse Jackson was the first to accept the invitation. He told both of them that Biblical figures had also succumbed to temptation. "Take David and Bathsheba or Samson and Delilah," he said.

Bill told Jackson that he'd seen the movie versions, with David played by Gregory Peck, Bathsheba by Susan Hayward; Samson by Victor Mature; and with Hedy Lamarr featured as Delilah.

To conclude the evening, Jackson noted that "Starr is playing God with the government's millions."

Jackson left the White House after assuring the First Couple that "God forgives men of their sins." Presumably, he included himself in that. At the time, he was carrying on an extramarital affair with Karin Stanford, a young woman he later impregnated. She gave birth to his child. Like Bill himself, the preacher would later have to apologize to his followers.

As another member of the "God Squad," Hillary summoned the controversial Gordon MacDonald, who later wrote a book called *Rebuilding Your Broken World.*

Summoned to the White House as a spiritual adviser to Bill Clinton, the Rev. Gordon MacDonald, depicted here, was a "pastor with a past."

After a spectacular evangelical rise, in 1987, before he met Bill, MacDonald was exposed and humiliated for his involvement in an adulterous affair. He quickly and publicly admitted, "I have sinned."

In the words of MacDonald, "Throughout history, many of the greatest leaders have been those who fought their way back from 'broken worlds.'"

"Most outstanding men and women in the Bible seem to have had some sort of experience with brokenness," he wrote. "We would likely disqualify from office King David, an adulterer and murderer; Joseph, a convicted rapist; and Jacob, a habitual liar."

When asked about why he had selected MacDonald, Bill reportedly said, "It takes a sinner to help a sinner."

Like Bill, the preacher later experienced disgrace, when he was exposed for having an adulterous affair with a young woman in his congregation. He was removed from his ministry after his affair was made public.

Marc Fisher, writing in *The New York Times,* claimed, "The minister accepted the task of counseling Bill Clinton's broken spirit. He shares with the president a life that has risen and plunged with dizzying speed. He had been one of the shining lights of the evangelical world until his affair was exposed."

Later, MacDonald appeared on ABC's 20/20, a TV show. "I spent several hours with a deeply broken man," he claimed. "A deeply sorrowful man. We didn't talk politics. We talked about man and his deeply personal walk with God."

Although Margaret Thatcher Calls the U.S. President "a Pervert," & Although "Froggie Chirac" Wants to Know "How Many Inches?" Other World Leaders, *(including Tony Blair and Nelson Mandela)* Defend and Support Bill

As would be expected, every world leader had a different opinion of Bill's dilemma and his alleged misconduct. "Iron Lady" Margaret Thatcher privately called him "Randy Willie" to her friends. "The man's a pervert. Can't control his zipper."

French President Jacques Chirac had something else on his mind. "How do you convert 5½ inches into centimeters?"

Although news of Bill's affair often led off the nightly news in Paris, much of the French press viewed the charges as ridiculous. One Paris reporter wrote, "Oh, those Americans. They can be so silly when it comes to sex. Imagine trying to overthrow the leader of the Free World for a little indulgence in fellatio! The president could have advanced major causes in the world and saved the taxpayers millions of dollars had he merely gone into the bathroom by himself when he was overcome with those urges. A tight fist would have solved his problem very quickly, and any DNA evidence could have been flushed down the toilet and not splashed on that infamous blue dress. Thank

God it wasn't one of our Chanels."

In his memoirs, Bill said he was greatly moved and touched by the world leaders who backed him. Nelson Mandela in South Africa let him know that "nobody's perfect. I'm all for you and your policies."

"After getting that message, I knew I could not be all that bad," Bill said.

"He also received support from Tony Blair ("my little brother"), Václav Havel, Crown Prince Abdulla of Jordan, Fernando Cardoso ("Greetings from Brazil"), Mexico's Ernesto Zedillo, and Kim Dae Jung, a longtime democracy activist in South Korea. Jung had been sentenced to execution in the late 1970s until President Carter intervened on his behalf.

FAST FORWARD: On December 15, 2011, almost a dozen years after Bill's impeachment trials, a Paris court declared Jacques Chirac *[Mayor of Paris 1977-95 and President of France 1995-2007]* guilty of diverting public funds and abusing public confidence. He received a two-year suspended prison sentence.

Bill sent a message to the leader who had mocked him during the most embarrassing depths of his anxiety:

"You have my back, monsieur, and my sympathy. How many inches do you have? Tell me in centimeters if you wish. I'll get Hillary to convert for me. Congratulations on missing the bullet."

The Baroness Margaret Hilda Thatcher ("The Iron Lady") was Prime Minister of the United Kingdom from 1979 to 1990, the longest serving British prime minister of the 20th Century, and a revered icon of many conservatives in the U.S.

According to the Baroness: "One of the things being in politics has taught is that men are not a reasoned or reasonable sex."

Whereas she had adored Ronald Reagan in the 1980s, she had left office when Bill Clinton took over. Nevertheless, she had plenty of opinions about his new leader, none of them favorable. The one most frequently savored by liberals within the U.K. was: "Had Mr. Clinton been a resident of London, I'm sure his girlfriends would have included Christine Keeler and Mandy Rice-Davies."

[In 1961, party girls Christine Keeler and Mandy Rice-Davies were deeply "embedded" within Britain's notorious Profumo Scandal. Because of security breaches based on their intimacies with both Britain's Secretary of State for War and also with Naval attachés from the Soviet embassy, they were at the center of what some historians define as the most damaging British sex scandal since Henry VIII.]

On the home front, former president, George H.W. Bush, reportedly had a different reaction. "Clinton is a womanizing, Elvis-loving, non-inhaling, truth-shading, war protesting, draft-dodging, abortion protecting, gay-promoting, gun-hating Baby Boomer from Hell. He was too much of a devil for hell to accept him, so they sent him back, to us."

Nelson Mandela, the South African anti-apartheid revolutionary and politician, was president of his country from 1994 to 1999, an era that more or less paralleled the presidency of Bill Clinton.

Hillary admitted, "I loved listening to him speak in that slow, dignified manner that manages to be both formal and alive with good humor."

"His generosity of spirit was inspiring and humbling. He told me that as a young man, he had a quick temper, but learned to control it as a means of surviving in prison."

Amazingly, the two former presidents, in later years, became friends....of a sort.

Billy Graham sent word: "Christ the Lord is a forgiving savior." Ann Richards, former governor of Texas, sent her message—"Just like a man, but I love you still."

Roger Clinton called: "Time to kick ass, Big Brother!"

From Elizabeth Taylor came this message "Even I have wandered on occasion down the primrose path—but then, who in hell hasn't?"

Jimmy Carter noted, "When I admitted that I lusted after the Statue of Liberty, I didn't get into so much trouble. Good luck."

One message raised a presidential eyebrow. "You showed those fuckers!—from Mother Theresa."

"Do you think Mother Teresa has gotten a new secretary?" Bill asked, jokingly.

"Mr. President, I'm sure that's a prank," said his own secretary.

"I'd like to think not," he said. "Perhaps for once or twice in her pristine life, the Holy Mother got down and dirty like the rest of us."

After Embracing Raquel Welch as a Role Model Hillary Hits the Campaign Trail With a New Look

Early every morning, Hillary could be seen working out at the White House gym. Like an Olympic athlete in training, she successfully began to drop pounds. "I've always been worried about my fat ass," she told aides. "I want a dramatic change in my image."

During discussions with her favorite hairdresser, Christophe, he suggested that she employ a young woman named Isabelle Goetz. "She doesn't know a damn thing about politics—and that's what you want. But she knows a hell of a lot about style!"

A small, polite, and rather sweet woman, with a mixed French and Swiss ancestry, she arrived at the White House to help Hillary with her makeover. She put both hands on each of Hillary's cheeks. "You have a lovely face," Goetz told her. "But it's a bit broad. To distract from it, I see you with a very feminine hair style, short and sexy."

She reached into her file and pulled out three pictures of the movie actress, Raquel Welch. "My suggestion is that Miss Welch should be your role model."

The First Lady seemed to trust the demure girl, viewing her as a "budding Audrey Hepburn," who knew a lot about style. She ordered a new wardrobe from Oscar de la Renta, and spoke on occasion with *Vogue* editor Anna Wintour about new styles in fashion.

As author Gail Sheehy wrote: "Gone were the dark dominatrix eyebrows and the barrel-bottomed suit jackets and treacly pastels. More often, she appeared in New York black. For evening events at the White House, she began to look noticeably sexy. At one governor's dinner, she turned heads in a Bill Blass number with a thigh-high slit."

As the First Lady moved closer and closer to the dreaded age of fifty, she was viewed as "a woman in a surge of postmenopausal zest."

A beautiful, chic style-setter, Isabelle Goetz, fashion maven, was summoned to the White House to give Hillary a complete makeover. "I work with the shape of a client's face, and look at the way she wears her hair, the way it falls. I want a client to enjoy their style and not fight their hair," said Goetz.

Her clients have included royalty, even Secretary of State John Kerry.

As a presidential contender in 2004, Kerry paid $1,000 to Goetz and flew her to Pittsburgh for a last minute touch-up before appearing on *Meet the Press*.

Goetz advised Hillary to develop a new look, one inspired by the allure of movie goddess Raquel Welch.

A mature, secure, and very attractive Raquel is seen here modeling one of her wigs.

"When you like the way you look, you radiate the beauty you are feeling," was Raquel's advice to the First Lady.

"My wig collection makes life easier. They're so natural looking, people will never know you're wearing one."

***

On September 18, 1998, the House Judiciary Committee convened. It was comprised of a rather bizarre group of congressmen, including Mary Bono, widow of the singer Sonny Bono, former husband of Cher and former mayor of Palm Springs, California who had died in a skiing accident. The panel also included a gay male, three other women, six Jews, and five members of the Black Caucus.

Meeting in executive session, and to Bill's profound embarrassment, this committee voted to release the videotape of Bill's grand jury testimony. Consequently, the public was allowed to see the president grilled without mercy for four hours, without any side shots of his interrogators. Upon its release, millions of Americans were revolted by the Independent Counsel's excess, including Hillary, who watched the screening in private.

Surveys later revealed that much of the anger was directed not at her husband, but at Starr himself. Except for the Clinton haters, who were enthralled, many viewers were offended by Starr's coven of prurient prosecutors, who had embarrassed not just the president, but the United States, subjecting America to ridicule, especially in the Middle East.

When Bill made it clear to Richard Gephardt (depicted above) that he was not going to resign the presidency, the Democratic leader came up with another strategy, and effectively publicized and "sold" it to his colleagues in Congress.

"We will win by losing."

In other words, Gephardt believed that Republicans, for having launched and amplified a supremely embarrassing partisan vendetta, would eventually alienate and offend the majority of voters.

After watching the tapes, Democratic Congressman James Moran of Virginia phoned Hillary. "If you were my sister, I think I'd just grab Bill, your philandering and lying husband, and pull him out behind the woodshed, where I would break his nose."

The last day of September was a great occasion for the country. It was also the last day of the fiscal year for the Federal government, and the president announced to the nation that it had a budget surplus of $70 billion, a first in nearly three decades.

"But in spite of this remarkable achievement," Hillary said, "the god damn press still seemed obsessed with Starr's fucking porno."

Controversial Starr Report Makes Bill Out to Be "A Diseased Pervert & Sex-Obsessed Degenerate" Starr Is Denounced as "A Dirty Old Man"

On September 9, 1998, Kenneth Starr delivered bound copies of his 445-page report, plus 36 boxes of supporting documents and testimony, to the office of the Sergeant-of-Arms at the House of Representatives. Two vans under heavy guard arrived to make the delivery, calling for the impeachment of the president.

A former law clerk in the Supreme Court, Brett Kavanaugh, wrote most of the Starr Report. He was one of Starr's young *protégées.* He was criticized for including too many sexual details in his document. Several deputies asked him why he found it necessary to include such lines as "after another sexual encounter with Ms. Lewinsky, she watched as the president masturbated in the sink."

Clinton's avowed antagonist, then-President George W. Bush, appears prominently in this White House press photo depicting the June 1, 2006, swearing in by Justice Kennedy of Brett Kavanaugh as a Federal judge. Kavanaugh's wife, Ashley, looks on. Kavanaugh had worked for Bush during the notoriously controversial Florida recount that gave him the presidency.

Bush had nominated Kavanaugh three years before, in 2003, to the D.C. Appeals Court, but his confirmation was contentious and stalled for three years based on his partisanship.

Prior to his elevation to the rank of a Federal judge, Kavanaugh had spearheaded the investigation into the suicide of Vince Foster. Later, he had been labeled a pornographer based on his authorship of the infamous Starr Report, in which he detailed the Lewinsky/Clinton affair in graphic lips-on-penis detail.

Every sexual encounter, regardless of how perfunctory, between Monica and Bill, was vividly replicated in Starr's report—not just once, but twice, and in a few cases, a total of four times.

Whitewater, the subject of the original investigation, was hardly mentioned in the report. However, the word "sex" was used 581 times.

Even though he seemed to dwell on pornographic details, he nonetheless seemed to oppose impeachment, as recommended by Starr. "The president needs therapy, not removal from office," Kavanaugh said.

Starr presented eleven grounds for impeachment, including perjury, obstruction of justice, and abuse of office. However, he wisely concluded that some members of Congress wouldn't bother to read all the charges, so he presented a summary:

> *"In this case, the president made and caused to be made false statements to the American people about his relationship with Ms. Lewinsky. He also made false statements about whether he had lied under oath or otherwise obstructed justice in his civil case. By publicly and emphatically stating in January 1998 that 'I did not have sexual relations with that woman' and these 'allegations are false,' the president also effectively delayed a possible congressional inquiry, and then he further delayed it by asserting Executive Privilege and refusing to testify for six months during the Independent Counsel investigation. This represents substantial and credible information that may constitute grounds for an impeachment."*

Allegedly, Starr had told his deputies, "I want the nation to be repulsed by Clinton and what he did, so much so they will demand his resignation regardless of what Congress does. I want them to know Clinton for what he is, a diseased pervert and a sex-obsessed degenerate."

Even after filing the report, Starr falsely continued to maintain that he had been fair. But as more reports leaked out, few believed him, even the more partisan Congressmen on the Hill.

One member of his legal team claimed that it had been suggested that the president should have been forced to drop his trousers and underwear and expose his penis to see if it matched the description supplied by Paula Jones. Such had been the case when authorities forced Michael Jackson to expose his penis to the cameraman during his child molestation case. Many critics viewed such an action against the president "as far too humiliating for the leader of the Free World to endure."

Some members of Congress, including a few Republicans who actually read the report, denounced Starr as "a dirty old man." One delegate from Missouri called him "a frustrated porno writer at heart."

When attacked, Starr rather smugly responded, "But I love the narrative."

Overcome with joy, Newt Gingrich, still Speaker of the House, wanted the report released immediately even before he read it.

The Republicans, led by Gingrich, were not the only ones wanting the report released. A Democrat, and a powerful force on the House Rules Committee, Richard Gephardt, wanted the report to go public just as soon as possible. He might have been in the same party as the president, but he was no fan of Bill's. After reading the report, he asked, "Is that cigar thing real?"

Before any impeachment, many Democrats, including Gephardt, urged Bill to resign the office and put "an end to this mess." It was constantly put before Bill that Nixon had resigned over Watergate to avoid impeachment.

On September 18, the House Judiciary Committee convened. The Democrats, and many Republicans, agreed that some of Starr's material was just too graphic. Interpreted as particularly objectionable was "a description of

It took a hip, gay, and articulate congressman, Massacusetts Democrat Barney Frank, to pour some non-hysterical rationality onto the psychotic context of the Bill Clinton Sex War.

The aggressive congressman challenged the Republicans, claiming that they had embarrassed themselves with attempts to unseat a twice-elected president with trivia and by masking their intent with "obfuscatory language."

With irony and a touch of sarcasm, Bill Clinton praised Frank for "capturing the hypocrisy of those conservatives who act as if they believed that 'life for a working class person begins at conception and ends at birth.'"

In 1991, Elizabeth Taylor launched White Diamonds perfume.

In 1993, when Hillary became First Lady, she sent her a year's supply.

Meeting in New York, the Queen of *Décolletage* met Hillary again when the gown she wore displayed a reasonable view of "The First Bosom." At their meeting, both women complained about how they'd been depicted in the press.

"The fuckers keep calling me a scarlet woman," Dame Elizabeth said. "I'm way more than scarlet. After the life I've led, I'm positively purple."

oral-anal sexual contact between the president and the intern. That was voted for "redaction." Some of the Congressmen left the meeting in laughter.

Later, when Senator Strom Thurmond of South Carolina heard that sodomy may have been involved, he stood up on the Senate floor and asserted that sodomy was practiced only by homosexuals, not by heterosexuals. The chamber burst into derisive laughter.

Finally, the question of whether to release Starr's report reached the floor of the House. The most loyal defenders of the president were twenty-nine members of the Black Caucus.

Gephardt lobbied for full disclosure. He told fellow Democrats that by dumping Bill and putting this sad episode behind was the best remedy, "like cutting out a cancer. Otherwise, we might end up damaging the Democratic Party for the next generation."

The final vote in the House was 363 to 63. Starr's report would be made public.

Upon its release, the news went around the world, some newspapers publishing the entire 112,000-word report. America's enemies took special delight, gloating over the humiliation of an American president. Bill Clinton was mocked around the world and became "the hit man" of comedians.

On November 19, the eyes of the nation were trained on Starr when he arrived on the Hill to testify before Congress. For days, his deputies had rehearsed him. Aware of the high stakes involved in his testimony, he set out to remedy his battered reputation as a partisan warrior. As anticipated, the Republicans asked him polite questions, each of them aimed at embarrassing the president. But when it came time for grilling by the Democrats, Starr's seat got hotter. He was even exposed for having a conflict of interest. Before taking his post, he, as a lawyer, had filed a brief for Paula Jones in her harassment suit against the president.

Based on her poisonous relationship with Republican NY Senator Alphonse D'Amato, Hillary vastly preferred Democratic contender Charles Schumer, whose "official photo" is positioned above.

Liberals in the predominantly liberal state loved Hillary.

With a certain aplomb, he denied all charges of any wrongdoing or any conflict of interest.

He came under fire from Barney Frank, the gay congressman from Massachusetts. He got Starr to admit that he had found no impeachable offenses in either the Travelgate or Filegate charges he'd investigated. Both Hillary and Bill had been cleared, but Starr was forced to confess that he held back news of their innocence until after the November elections.

He was also accused of violating Monica Lewinsky's civil rights by holding her a virtual captive without her lawyer at the Ritz Carlton Hotel in Pentagon City. He was also charged with leaking grand jury testimony, an indictable offense.

It was a day of homages from the Republicans and harangues from the Democrats. Starr didn't come out very well. According to the next polling, his popularity continued to fall. In the end, he was viewed as just another partisan attack dog, a Republican lackey who had cost the American taxpayers millions of wasted dollars.

In a Mammilary Encounter, Hillary, With Half Her Breasts Exposed, Meets "the Queen of Décolletage," Elizabeth Taylor

As the winds of autumn blew across the Potomac, wafting toward the White House, Bill, with a heavy heart, plodded along at 1600 Pennsylvania Avenue. He told his aides, "I feel under House Arrest."

Wondering if Bill and Hillary had reconciled, post Monica Lewinsky, the press, with sharpened pens, waited to record details associated with their October 11 wedding anniversary. As it turned out, Hillary showed up without him in Sofia, Bulgaria.

Increasingly, Hillary was on the move, looking more and more like the independent woman she was. That was emphasized by her new look and fashionable wardrobe. On several occasions, she flew from Washington to New York to attend certain galas, such as one at Carnegie Hall or the National Endowment of the Arts and Humanities.

At the latter, she showed up in a stunning gown with plunging *décolletage.* It was the public's first view of the "First Bosom"

"With knockers like that waiting for him, why does Bill Clinton need a blow job from some fat little Jewish girl?" one reporter asked another.

At one of the galas, she encountered Elizabeth Taylor, the reigning "Queen of *Décollétage*." Richard Burton had claimed that her breasts, before they withered, would topple empires.

The dazzling movie star suggested that Hillary should consider a move to New York City. "No one in Manhattan gives a damn who you fuck—or in any combination."

"A home in New York would surely beat where I'm living now," Hillary joked. "Public housing."

Later, over a drink with Taylor, Hillary told the star that some calls were coming in that she should run for the Senate from the State of New York after she became a resident.

"That would follow the example of this politician with whom I had a brief fling," Taylor confessed.

"Let me guess," Hillary said. "Was his name Robert?" And had he lived previously in Massachusetts and had a famous brother?"

"You got that right," Taylor answered.

"As a senator, I would make only $136,000 a year," Hillary said. "Bill and I owe millions."

"Why don't you let your philandering husband get off his ass and go out and earn some money?" Taylor suggested. "From what I'm told, you've been the chief breadwinner of the family. Tell the fucker it's his turn."

"Great idea, Liz," she said.

"I love you, darling, but for god's sake, don't call me Liz. It's Elizabeth to you."

After publicly vilifying Bill Clinton for committing adultery, Henry Hyde of Illinois, chairman of the House Judiciary Committee, was exposed as an adulterer himself.

Chastened, Hyde warned his fellow Congressmen, "especially those with skeletons in their closets," that Bill and Hillary would retaliate as part of a scorched earth policy against their attackers.

"They plan to reveal any indiscretions, including several cases of homosexual attachments, some dating from the college days of certain GOP members of the House."

***

In spite of her new looks and popularity, Hillary never could escape her critics. Some of them blamed her for her husband's infidelity, calling her a "cold, sexless, depriving wife."

She later flew to Bolivia, where rumors spread that she was "shacked up" with an exceedingly handsome, tall, dark, and well-built young man, who had been her tour guide leading her to the site of archeological digs.

Back in America, she hit the campaign trail as the November midterm elections were coming up. Touring through twenty states, she proved to be an effective fundraiser for Democratic candidates.

She put up a brave front, and for the most part, she faced enthusiastic audiences. Occasionally, some heckler would call out, "Why don't you leave the cheating bastard?"

Democratic Senator Robert Byrd of Virginia claimed that "Hillary Clinton is defending Bill, but not really engaged."

She was especially interested in backing California Senator Barbara Boxer, and she also campaigned hard in New York for Charles Schumer. She had a special reason for wanting him to win. He was running against her nemesis, Senator Al D'Amato, who had led the Senate's Whitewater hearings.

The most recent polls listed her as the most popular woman in America, her approval rating soaring to seventy percent. It seemed that her husband's sex scandals had made her even more sympathetic. However, right before the election, her doctor diagnosed a blood clot in her leg and advised her to curtail such a heavy campaign schedule.

As Betsey Wright observed, "Perhaps the media didn't pick up on it. Hillary was not just helping out Democratic candidates in the midterms. She was actually beginning her campaign for public office, even though she hadn't quite determined what that office would be. Perhaps the Senate seat from New York, although she was not a resident as of yet."

"With her determination, I predict one day she'll make it to the White House, except this time, she'd be running the Free World from the Oval Office. Who knows? Perhaps she'd have her own scandal one day giving blow jobs to a handsome young male intern."

***

The crucial midterm elections were approaching, as threats of impeachment hung in the air. Bill spent many a sleepless night at the White House, wandering the lonely corridors as a skeletal number of Secret Service agents hawkeyed him.

He feared the midterm elections on November 3. "The Republicans had a big financial gain over us in fat cat money," he said. "All the talking heads on TV were predicting disaster for us, mainly because of me."

He had his defenders, including a fellow Democrat, John Conyers, Jr. of Michigan. He maintained that even if all the charges leveled against Clinton were true, they hardly constituted "high crimes and misdemeanors."

In contrast, Henry Hyde of Illinois, who had chaired the House Judiciary Committee since 1995

Chief of Staff to Bill Clinton and Counselor to President Obama, Chicago-born John Podesta has been an advocate for many causes, perhaps none so strange as defending believers in UFOs. He has urged the government to release secret files related to alien spacecraft which may (or may not) have landed on earth.

"It is time for the government to declassify records that are more than 25 years old and to provide scientists with data that will assist in determining the real nature of this phenomenon."

claimed, "By November, we will have strung Clinton up by the balls."

Every night at the White House, Bill sat alone in front of the TV set, as one talking head after another continued to predict his demise.

Many Democrats up for re-election campaigned hard, trying to divert attention away from the president and onto political issues such as programs to save Social Security and the elimination of tax cuts for the rich.

In addition to attacks on Bill, the Republicans launched anti-gay ads in key states. These ads falsely claimed that if the president were re-elected, every state would be forced to recognize same-sex marriage, a ridiculous, fraudulent claim, of course, but millions of voters fell for that propaganda. In the words of one of the ad campaign's creators, "We decided to make our ads as revolting as we possibly could. We filmed two men kissing. It made me want to vomit."

However, some surveys showed that many of these ads backfired. In the middle of the campaign, in October 6, Matthew Shepard, a gay 21-year-old student at the University of Wyoming, was beaten and tortured, then hung out on a fence near Laramie, Wyoming, in a style that evoked a crucifixion.

His friends, parents, and supporters rallied around his death at the hands of two psychopaths, generating massive public sympathy. This did much to tone down homophobia. Many of the antigay ads were yanked during this period, which was almost a national mourning at such a brutal death.

Radical conservatives pulled many anti-gay "infomercials" from TV broadcasts when it was revealed that on the night of October 6, 1998, young Matthew Shepard was singled out for being gay and then brutally assaulted by psychotic homophobes near Laramie, Wyoming.

Six days later, after hanging from a fence in a style that evoked a crucifixion, he died from his injuries.

In the aftermath, widely reviewed by international news organizations, his parents, Dennis and Judy Shepard, organized the Matthew Shepard Foundation and became nationally televised spokespersons against violence aimed at homosexuals.

At long last, the results of the November 3 midterms came over the TV sets across the country. By the end of the night, it appeared that the Democrats were scoring an upset victory.

It had been predicted that in the Senate, the party would lose five to six seats. In fact, they lost none, each of the Senators up for re-election holding onto their posts.

In the House, the Democrats

took back five seats. This marked the first time the president's party in power had pulled off such a feat in the sixth year of a presidency since 1822.

At the White House, Erskine Bowles, Bill's chief of Staff, resigned. He was replaced by John Podesta, whom Bill had known for three decades. Previously, he'd served as White House staff secretary and the Deputy Chief of Staff. Like Al Gore, the vice president, Podesta was a dedicated environmentalist.

Bill said, "Podesta has a fine mind, a tough hide, a dry wit, and is a better hearts player than Bowles."

An Adulterous Bill Clinton Faces Off Against Adulterous Republican Leaders in the House, Including "Hot Tub Tom"

Although Newt Gingrich, Speaker of the House, had worked tirelessly to unseat Bill Clinton, the Georgia politician was having trouble of his own. Once, Bill's chief of Staff, Erskine Bowles, had asked Gingrich why the Republicans were pursuing Bill with such ferocity.

Gingrich delivered a smart-ass answer: "Because we can!"

A day after Bill's inauguration in 1997, the House had voted to reprimand Gingrich and fine him $300,000 for campaign violations arising from his use of tax-exempt funds for political purposes.

After the midterm elections, Gingrich faced GOP opposition in the House. The pressure was so strong that he resigned the Speakership on November 6, which would be followed by his outright resignation from Congress on January 3, 1999.

While pursuing Bill for adultery, demanding his impeachment, it was later revealed that he, too, was involved in an adulterous relationship.

When Bill learned of this, he told an aide, "So we two boys from Dixie have something in common after all: A cheating heart."

Gingrich's scandals and disgrace brought an end to what was called his pipe dream—that of becoming President of the United States. Elizabeth Drew, a journalist, exposed his secret desire: He wanted Bill out of office, with Al Gore taking over. It was then assumed that Gore would pardon Bill, after which Gingrich would seek Gore's own impeachment for doing so.

With both Bill and Gore removed from office, Gingrich, as Speaker of the House, would then be in line for the presidency. Like most dreams, that, of course, never happened.

Other than Starr and Gingrich, "that Chicago creep," (Bill's words), Henry

Hyde of Illinois became Bill's next Number One enemy. Hyde was the Republican leader of the House Judiciary Committee. Before taking on Bill, he had been one of the most vocal critics in Congress opposed to abortion.

Forgetting momentarily about abortion, he turned the full power of his position into removing Bill from office. He told America that it was "the Constitutional and civic duty of the House to impeach Clinton for perjury."

"The flag of our Founder Fathers is falling!" Hyde screeched. "I ask you to catch the falling flag as we keep our appointment with history."

Hyde served as chief prosecutor in the House when Bill was charged with perjury and obstruction of justice. In his closing statement to the House, Hyde claimed that, "A failure to convict will make the statement that lying under oath is not all that serious."

Hyde, at the age of seventy-four, was defined by *Time* magazine as "a man of courtliness and character," although Bill referred to him privately as "the biggest turd in hell." In an almost laughable assertion, *USA Today* wrote that "Hyde is too intellectually honest to throw his weight around for partisan reasons." Ironically, as events unfolded, it became clear that the opposite of that claim was true. As Hyde's choice for chief counsel, he made a poor selection in naming David Schippers, a sixty-eight-year-old prosecutor and former Chicago defense lawyer. Schippers was a Democrat in name only. Actually, he was called a "ferocious conservative" and would later write a book, *Sellout,* in which he would lament that the president had not been impeached.

Hyde pushed ahead, urging impeachment, even though many moderate Republicans were against it, favoring a censure instead. *[Previously, both James Polk and Andrew Jackson had been censured by the House during their respective tenures as president.]* Surveys showed that three-quarters of voters did not want to see the president impeached.

In the middle of Hyde's impeachment hearings, the news website, *Salon.com,* published an *exposé* with the headline *THIS HYPOCRITE BROKE UP MY FAMILY.* In it, it was alleged that Hyde had indulged in an extramarital affair himself with one Cherie Snodgrass, a married woman with three children. Forced to admit to the truth of the affair, Hyde called it "a youthful indiscretion."

News of Hyde's affair soon became a political flashpoint. House majority whip Tom DeLay, Republican of Texas, called the *exposé* "a disgusting piece of rumor-mongering."

Norm Sommer, a Florida retiree and friend of Fred Snodgrass, Cherie's cuckolded husband, called Hyde "the biggest phony in Washington. Why should this guy be a *de facto* judge on whether there should be an impeachment when he's also guilty of an adulterous affair?"

Fred Snodgrass, a former Chicago furniture salesman, also denounced

Hyde as "a super hypocrite. At least the president picked a single woman, not a wife with a husband and three kids at home."

Even though exposed, Hyde continued on his quest, which Bill likened to "Don Quixote chasing windmills across the plains of La Mancha." Hyde sent Bill eighty personal, invasive questions, demanding answers, a sort of "admit-or-deny" testimony. To cause even more embarrassment to the president, he released two hours of Linda Tripp/Monica Lewinsky inane chatter. On one tape, Monica can be heard lamenting that Tripp needs to get laid.

***

Late in 1998, Bob Livingston of Louisiana was named Speaker-Elect of the House, as a replacement for the disgraced Newt Gingrich. Regrettably for him, Larry Flynt, the controversial publisher of *Hustler* magazine, took out a full-page advertisement in *The Washington Post.* In it, he offered to pay a million dollars to any woman willing to go public about an affair with a high-ranking government official.

He was inundated with calls to his 800 number. Overwhelmed with women claiming affairs, Flynt and his investigators narrowed

The publisher of Hustler magazine, Larry Flynt, depicted above, has long been known for exposing the "sex, lies, and crooked politics" of Washington. In fact, in 2004, he published a tell-all book about it, *The Naked Truth*.

Flynt's exposé of Bob Livingston's adultery during the peak of Monicagate led to his (forced) resignation as Speaker-elect of the U.S. House of Representatives.

According to Flynt, "Livingston tried to gain points by saying that his affairs were never with anyone who worked for him. I knew better. He was screwing a judge in his home state of Louisiana, fucking a lobbyist on Capitol Hill, and also making it with an intern on his staff."

Flynt claimed to know a lot more he could have exposed about Livingston's sex life, including his "particular fetishes."

the list down to some fifty possibilities. Finally, he chopped the list down to just twelve women. Several had claimed affairs with Livingston.

When news of this reached other members of the House, many Republicans interpreted the new (and adulterous) leader as an obstacle to Bill's possible impeachment. Furious, many of them demanded Livingston step down.

Faced with few other choices, Livingston appeared before his colleagues, informing them of what they already knew: "I have been outed by Larry Flynt. During my thirty-three year marriage to my wife, Bonnie, I have on occasion strayed from my marriage. I want to assure everyone that these indiscretions were not with employees on my staff." *[This was an obvious reference to Bill and Monica.]* "I have never been asked to testify under oath about them"

Then, after calling on the president to also step down from his office, Livingston received a standing ovation.

Finally, the Republicans came up with a candidate they considered "clean as a hound's tooth," to borrow a phrase from Dwight D. Eisenhower. He was Dennis Hastert, a sort of compromise candidate who, so far as it was known, had not been involved in any sex scandal. No one had come forward to claim an adulterous affair with him. No woman, that is...

Unlike the speakers who had preceded him, it took many years for Hastert to be exposed. In 2015, he pleaded NOT GUILTY to Federal charges that he had illegally made massive bank withdrawals and lied to authorities in association with promises he

Bob Livingston of Louisiana calling for Bill Clinton's destruction during the impeachment debate.

Majority Whip Tom DeLay *(depicted after his arrest, above)* was one of the major forces seeking to oust Bill Clinton. "He held prayer meetings in his office to seek God's support for his divine mission," Bill claimed. "His efforts to get rid of me were not about morality, not about the rule of law, but about power."

DeLay's own legal problems lay ahead. In 2005, he was indicted by a Travis County Grand Jury based on criminal charges of violating election laws.

Under pressure from the party he had disgraced, he resigned his position as Republican House Majority leader. Convicted in January of 2011, he was sentenced to three years in jail.

In 2012, after lengthy infighting and calling in of favors, he was acquitted by the Texas Court of Appeals in a decision that raised a lot of eyebrows.

had made to pay off a young man who had been a teenaged wrestler on the team Hastert had coached decades ago. He had been a coach in Yorkville, about fifty miles southwest of Chicago, from 1965 to 1981, when he was alleged to have become sexually involved with one of his young athletes.

At last, a Speaker of the House opposing Bill Clinton whose adultery was with someone other than a biological female!

Dennis Hastert is seen as he appeared as a Social Studies teacher in a 1975 high school yearbook in Yorkville, Illinois, decades before he became Speaker of the U.S. House of Representatives.

In 2015, years after Monicagate, this former high school wrestling coach was exposed for sustaining a sexual relationship with one of his then-teenaged male students. Hastert was charged with paying this unidentified "victim from his past" staggering sums in blackmail, for decades, as a means of concealing his "prior misconduct."

Hastert's family and friends asserted that the indictment was intended as part of a "political witch hunt."

In the House, the leading attack dog was the Republican Majority Whip, Tom DeLay of Texas. He was the real power in the House, and he'd helped Gingrich lead "the Republican Revolution" of 1994.

DeLay had been accused of having led a notorious private life during his time in the Texas Legislature. He was considered a drunkard and a playboy, earning the nickname of "Hot Tub Tom." When elected to Congress, he was consuming from eight to a dozen gin martinis most evenings at various fundraisers and receptions. By 1985, he professed that he'd become a "Born Again Christian" and had given up drinking and, presumably, "alleycatting" too.

DeLay not only denounced Clinton's morals, but those of Gingrich, too. "I don't think that Newt could set a high moral standard, a high moral tone. You can't do that if you're keeping secrets about your own adulterous affairs."

But when confronted with charges of his own adultery, DeLay countered, "I was no longer committing adultery by the time of Clinton's impeachment train. There's a big difference here. I had returned to Christ and repented my sins by that time."

Due in part to DeLay's tough guy arm-twisting, he was known on the floor of the House as "The Hammer." As revealed by legal analyst Jeffrey Toobin, "DeLay browbeat Republicans into voting YES for impeachment, even though many of them may have preferred censure instead. He threatened to take away their subcommittee chairmanships if they did not. With everything from his slicked-back hair to his well-cultivated air of menace, DeLay practically encouraged the legend of his own ferocity."

As everyone else seemingly was involved in adultery, Bill's own affair led to a vote on impeachment on Friday, December 18. "Tis the season to be jolly at the White House," Bill remarked with gallows humor.

On December 19, the House passed two of the four articles of impeachment as presented by the Hyde committee. In a vote of 228 to 206, members endorsed the charge that Bill had lied to a Grand Jury. On the second charge, alleging obstruction of justice and hiding gifts, the house voted to impeach 221 to 212, with five Republicans voting no.

"The vote was the culmination of years of unconscionable conduct by Kenneth Starr and his cohorts," Bill charged.

The impeachment trial of the president would take place in the Senate in the early part of 1999.

Hillary Plots a Renaissance in the Big Apple
"If I run against JFK Jr., He's Likely to Beat My Ass."

One friend of the Clintons, who did not want to be named, appraised their lives as 1998 drifted to its dreadful end:

> *"Hillary knew that by spring, Bill might be out of a job. But she didn't want to go down into defeat with him. She was playing by her own rules in this House of Cards. In November and December, she seemed to have the winning hand."*
>
> *"Almost daily, she was getting calls from New York, urging her to change her residence and run for the Senate. One of her strongest supporters was Charles Rangel, the Democratic congressman from Harlem."*
>
> *"She had long contemplated running for the Senate from somewhere, even Arkansas, before making her quest for the presidency. Her most daring ambition was to seek the presidency in 2000, although that would have her butting heads with Vice President Al Gore."*
>
> *"If Bill were kicked out of office, she did not want to walk off into the*

sunset of oblivion with him," the source claimed. "She was inspired by the example of Eleanor Roosevelt. That greatest of First Ladies achieved even greater fame after burying her cheating spouse (FDR). After all, she helped draft the first Declaration of Human Rights world-wide at the United Nations, and became the most admired woman on earth."

[Ironically, Eleanor, too, had faced strong pressure to run for public office after she left the White House. She was urged to run for vice president on a ticket with Harry S Truman in 1948. She, too, was urged to run for the Senate, representing New York State.

The most daring suggestion was that Eleanor should battle Truman for the Democratic nomination at the National Convention.]

From her White House phone, Hillary was in almost daily touch with *politicos* in New York. She was told that if she decided to run, it was highly likely that her opponent would be Rudolph Giuliani on the Republican ticket.

She also heard some disconcerting news from New York City Mayor Ed Koch. He warned that supporters were urging the popular John F. Kennedy, Jr., to run for the Senate.

"People love Jackie's son more than they like me," she told Koch. "I fear if I ran against him, he'd kick my ass."

Three weeks later, Koch called again, reporting on a meeting he'd had "with young John-John. He's not going to go for the Senate. He's considering a run for governor instead."

The New York Senate seat had come up for grabs following the announcement that Pat Moynihan would not seek re-election.

Hillary, or so it was said, found the atmosphere at the White House too depressing, so she escaped to the Dominican Republic to be the guest of one of her favorite designers, Oscar de la Renta.

Hillary feared that John F. Kennedy, Jr. would be a formidable rival if he decided to oppose her for the Democratic nomination for Senator from the State of New York. Politicos speculated the John wanted to become the Senator from New York, or perhaps its governor, as a prelude to his running for the presidency of the United States.

"He was gorgeous, and I knew he'd get the female vote," Hillary said. "All he has to do is strip down and show off his physique. I also hear his endowment matched that of his college. What advantages he had. He starts out with one of the most famous names on the planet. Oh, did I mention? He had a charismatic father, and a mother who was one of the most stunning women of the 20th Century."

Her designer host reportedly claimed that her visit was the first step in winning over the votes of the 600,000 or so Dominicans who had emigrated to New York City.

One reporter, covering her visit, reported seeing her walking along the beach with a handsome young Dominican, "wearing a bikini that looked as if stuffed with a foot-long salami."

There were rumors, probably untrue, of an affair. Perhaps it was no more than a harmless flirtation. "After all," De la Renta said. "Hillary is a woman, not a saint."

***

With impeachment looming over Bill's head, that year's Christmas festivities at the White House were not particularly joyful or carefree.

"The Valkyrie who was always ready to lift her wounded barefoot boy from the battlefield and fly him to Valhalla had at long last withdrawn her approval and support" wrote Gail Sheehy.

Bill was reported to be on the verge of a nervous breakdown, wandering the corridors of the White House in the pre-dawn hours in his underwear.

A Secret Service agent revealed, "At one point during the last days of the Nixon presidency, he ran jaybird naked down the corridor one night. Two of our guys had to restrain him and carry him back to his bedroom, where a guard was placed outside his door. At least Bill wore his panties."

The designers of the cover of this edition of *US News & World Report* chose to feature Monica Lewinsky's blabbering mouth as background for this image of the humiliated president.

Almost daily, Bill asked his aides, "Where have all the FOBs gone?" He was referring, of course, to the clique known as "Friends of Bill."

"The FOBs seemed to have been replaced by the SOBs," Bill said.

Author Gore Vidal visited Washington. Hillary had called on him at his home in Ravello, Italy, along the Amalfi Coast. He told a friend, "I really should drop in and visit Bill and Hillary. No one is calling on them anymore."

***

It came as a real surprise to Hillary

Hillary admitted she was flattered when the English Editor-in-Chief of American *Vogue*, Anna Wintour *(depicted above)*, telephoned to propose a cover shot and an article in the upcoming issue of her celebrated magazine.

Said Hillary: "It was gutsy of her to offer, and counterintuitive [i.e., contrary to common sense expectations] for me to accept. In fact, the experience did wonders for my spirits."

With her trademark pageboy haircut and dark sunglasses, Wintour was a towering figure in the world of commerce and fashion. Her aloof personality contributed to her reputation as hostile, and she was so demanding, she became closely associated with her nickname, "Nuclear Wintour."

Annie Leibovitz, one of the most celebrated portrait photographers in the world, came to the White House to photograph Hillary for the cover of *Vogue*. The First Lady later said, "The photographs were great, giving me a chance to look good when I had been feeling so low."

Prior to working with Hillary, Leibowitz had crafted photographic portraits of The Rolling Stones and John Lennon, and developed "a close relationship" with the acclaimed feminist writer and essayist Susan Sontag, a friendship which endured until Sontag's death in 2004.

when she received a call requesting that she pose for a picture to run on the cover of *Vogue.* "That's the last magazine I expected to grace," she said. "Usually, I make the front page of *The National Enquirer* about my so-called 'lesbian romps.'"

For the occasion, Oscar de la Renta designed a stunning burgundy-colored gown for her. The venues for the shot included, among others, the Truman Balcony at the White House. The scene would be directed by fashion maven Anna Wintour, with photography by Annie Leibowitz, arguably the greatest photographer in America.

The fashion director, Paul Cavaco, presented Hillary with a choice of jewelry, including pearl-and-diamond earrings from Cartier. He later pronounced the shot as "one of a woman who's got it all goin' on."

Later, as the year ended, Hillary was asked what her legacy as First Lady would be.

"Legacy?" she repeated. "I was on the cover of *Vogue.* That's my fucking legacy."

An Embattled President Survives His Impeachment Trial
As His Wife Begins Her Quest to Rule the Free World

The New Year of 1999 dawned with uncertainty over the White House. On January 7, Clinton hater William Rehnquist, Chief Justice of the Supreme Court, opened the Clinton impeachment trial in the Senate. He didn't appear in the type of plain black robe usually worn by a Supreme Court Justice. He paraded in wearing a robe he'd designed himself, with chevrons of gold braid on the sleeves. He'd gotten the idea from the costumes from a production of the Gilbert & Sullivan comic opera, *Iolanthe.*

Hillary later said, "How fitting that he should wear a theatrical costume to preside over a political farce."

On the eve of the impeachment trial, Hillary donned her Amazonian armor, standing on the battlefield, proclaiming, "Bill Clinton will serve until the last day, the last hour, the last minute of his presidency."

For the first time in months, she took her husband's hand as they stood together welcoming Democrats from the Hill for a sort of pep rally in the Rose Garden.

As the Senate proceeded with its impeachment trial, it was interrupted for Bill to give his annual State of the Union speech before Congress. Polls showed his approval rating reaching an alltime high. In his speech, he honored Hillary for representing America so well all over the world. She was wildly applauded by Democrats.

Bill noted that his address was "the last State of the Union address of the 20th Century." In closing, he said that, "Perhaps, in the daily press of events, in the clash of controversy, we don't see our own time for what it truly is, a new dawn for America."

On that occasion, he greeted the new Speaker of the House, Dennis Hastert, whose own sexual disgrace would not come until years later. "We shook hands and talked as if nothing in the world was going on, especially his attempt to take away my presidency," Bill said.

Much of the business of running the Free World came to a glaring halt, as Bill became absorbed in the daily charges and countercharges coming from the Senate floor. He was especially grateful for the support of the Black Caucus. "Black people all over America knew that the drive to impeach me was being led by right-wing white Southerners who had never lifted a finger for civil rights."

At the trial, thirteen House Republicans from the judiciary Committee served as "managers," another word for prosecutors. These included Chairman Henry Hyde of Illinois and Lindsey Graham of South Carolina.

One of the unsung heroes of Bill's defense team was "Clinton's Consigliere," attorney Bruce Lindsey, an assistant to the President during both of his terms in office. The closest of Bill's advisers, he had been at the center of the White House efforts to contain investigations of the President.

The New York Times described Lindsey *(depicted with Clinton in photo above)* as "a thin, grim, and gray fixture who can usually be spotted at the periphery of Clinton's field of vision with a cellphone at his ear."

Dale Bumpers had been the 38th governor of, and later a Senator from, Arkansas

Drawing on his years of experience, he operated as a defense attorney for Bill Clinton during his impeachment trial.

It was he who delivered its articulate, impassioned, and ultimately successful closing argument.

Clinton's defense team featured Dale Bumpers, who had served as the 38th Governor of Arkansas from 1971 to 1975, and then in the United States Senate from 1975 till 1999.

One of Bill's most devoted defenders was Bruce Lindsey, often called "Clinton's *consigliere*." After Vince Foster died, Lindsey stepped in to take charge of the growing Whitewater affair. He fought all the battles, standing by Clinton through all the bimbo eruptions, always defending his man.

After six years, the little Rock Native was battered, bruised, and awash in legal bills incurred during his trips before grand juries. Although he had endured many attacks on his reputation, he soldiered on for Bill, sublimating both himself and his career for his friend of three decades.

As *The New York Times* concluded, "But for all Lindsey's complaints about Washington had done to him, he remains unable—perhaps unwilling—to cut his ties with the man who brought him to Washington. As Clinton enters the final stages of his presidency, it seems increasingly obvious that when the president finally leaves the White House, it will be with Lindsey at his side, no doubt lingering for a moment to shut out the lights one last time."

Indeed, Lindsey today is Chairman of the Board of the Clinton Foundation.

After hearing arguments on both sides, Democratic Senator Robert Byrd of West Virginia moved, on January 25, for dismissals of both articles of impeachment for lack of merit. The motion to dismiss failed on a party line vote of 56 to 44.

the weekly Standard

ACQUITTED

For three days, from February 1 to 3, House managers presented videotaped closed door depositions from Monica Lewinsky, Bill's friend, Vernon Jordan, and White House aide Sidney Blumenthal.

On February 4, Senators voted 70 to 30 that excerpting these videotapes would suffice as testimony, and that live witnesses need not appear before them. A total of thirty videotaped excerpts from Monica were shown, as she delivered testimony about the small gifts the president had given her and his attempt to find her a good job.

The Washington Post

Clinton Acquitted

2 Impeachment Articles Fail to Win Senate Majority

PHILADELPHIA DAILY NEWS

THE PEOPLE PAPER

LATE SPORTS

PRESIDENT'S DAY

Acquitted, Clinton says it's time to move on

On February 8, closing arguments were presented from each side. Speaking for the president, White House counsel Charles Ruff declared: "There is only one question before you, albeit a difficult one, one that is a question of fact and law and Constitutional theory. Would it put at risk the liberties of the people to retain the president in office? Putting aside partisan *animus,* if you honestly say that it would not, that those liberties are safe in his hands. You must vote to acquit."

Bumpers made the closing argument in Bill's defense. The president would later define it as "a magnificent speech, by turns erudite and emotional, earthy, and profound."

He attacked House managers for their lack of compassion, claiming that Bill had been punished enough already "for a terrible moral lapse. After all these years, the

In 2015, a reporter looked back on Bill Clinton's February 12, 1999 acquittal in the Senate:

"He is a Southern man born and bred. If his natural charm, charisma, and Arkansas twang attract younger women to his junk, then so be it. It's a law of nature. You can't keep a hound from howlin' at the moon, and you can't keep a Clinton from keepin' it in his pants. There's just too much 'Arky' in him."

" Sure, Clinton lied about getting his Razorback pig 'sooied' in the Oval Office. But looking back today, with 10% unemployment and a deficit as bloated as Monica Lewinsky, who really cares?"

president was found guilty of nothing official or personal."

Bumpers said, "When you hear somebody say 'This is not about money,' it is about money. And when you hear someone say, 'This is not about sex,' it's about sex. The American people are now and for some time have been asking to be allowed a good night's sleep. They're asking for an end to this nightmare. It's a legitimate request."

In his concluding remarks, Bumpers asked, "Where were the elements of forgiveness and redemption, the very foundation of Christianity?"

Following every day of the trial, Hillary later said that it reminded her of an old saying from Sunday school. "Faith is like stepping off a cliff and experiencing one of the outcomes--you will either land on solid ground or you will be taught to fly."

On the date of the final vote to impeach or not, Bill woke up at the White House "feeling like Eisenhower must have felt when he gave the order to launch the D-Day landings on the beaches of Normandy in June of 1944." He would pace the floor throughout the vote, waiting for "that call" from his trusted lawyer, David Kendall.

Later that day, the Senate emerged from its closed deliberations to vote on the Articles of Impeachment. A two-thirds majority, 67 votes, would be necessary to convict and remove the president from office. The perjury charge against Bill failed. Whereas 45 senators (all of them Republican) voted guilty, 55 senators (45 Democrats and 10 Republicans) voted not guilty.

As for the obstruction of justice charge, whereas 50 Republicans voted guilty, 45 Democrats and 5 Republicans voted not guilty. Thus, the senators failed to remove the president, since they did not muster a two-thirds majority.

Chief Justice Rehnquist had hoped to preside over the successful impeachment of the president. But that was not going to happen. In his final words, he said, "It is therefore ordered and adjudged that the said William Jefferson Clinton be, and hereby is, acquitted of the charges in the said articles." Barely concealing his disappointment, Rehnquist gaveled the impeachment proceedings to a close at 12:30PM.

One newsman later reported, "I just sat through the lowest moment in the history of the U.S. presidency."

Bill commented on the vote. "I was just glad the ordeal was over for my family and my country. After the vote, I was profoundly sorry for what I had done to trigger the events and the great burden they imposed on the American people, and that I was rededicating myself to a 'time of reconciliation and renewal' for America."

The biggest question put to him was, "How did you keep from going out of your mind?"

In looking back at this sordid episode in American history, Bill said, "Chelsea still loved me and, most important, Hillary stood with me and loved me through it all. I almost wound up being grateful to my tormentors: They were probably the only people who could have made me look good to Hillary again. I even got off the couch and was allowed to return to my cozy bed...and to Hillary, the woman I loved."

"As I faced the final months of my administration, I admitted to myself that I would never be a perfect person, but Hillary was laughing again, and Chelsea was still doing well at Stanford. I was still doing a job I loved, and spring was on the way."

A Lawyer for the Prosecution Is Seriously Pissed Off

"Lies, Cowardice, Hypocrisy, Cynicism, Butt-Covering, Amorality"

David Schippers, a lawyer and a Democrat, became famous when he was promoted to the role of Chief Investigative Counsel for the US House Judiciary Committee during the president's impeachment trial. To commemorate his involvement, he wrote *Sellout: The Inside Story of President Clinton's Impeachment*, which attacked the Clinton White House and the verdict that kept him in office. It depicted some members of the Senate as incompetent and/or corrupt. It was his moment in history.

Ironically, Schippers would appear on the world stage a few years later, again as part of a scathing historical footnote.

Just two days after 9/11, he went public with the explosive charge that he had been told by FBI agents from Minnesota and Illinois that they were aware of a massive oncoming attack from terrorists that would target the financial district of lower Manhattan, including the World Trade Center.

According to Schippers, these agents also told him that they knew the location and the date (September 11, 2001) of the impending attacks, as well as the names of the airline hijackers and the sources of their funding.

Schippers claimed he tried to contact the office of John Ashcroft, U.S. Attorney General, but his calls were not returned. Neither were his calls to other Federal officials.

David Schippers

Other than Kenneth Starr, the one man most angered by the Senate failure to impeach was David P. Schippers, Chief Investigative Counsel for the Clinton impeachment. He even wrote a book about his disappointment called *Sellout,* published in 2000.

This former Chicago prosecutor, who had convicted such Mafia bosses as Sam Giancana, thought he had seen everything—"treachery, double crosses, sellouts. But what I saw behind the scenes at the Clinton impeachment shocked me to my core." In *Sellout,* he maintained that many Democrats didn't even examine the evidence—"They didn't want to know."

He went on to reveal that one Republican senator told him, "I don't care if you prove that Clinton raped a woman and then stood up and shot her dead. You are not going to get sixty-seven votes."

Schippers also accused both Republicans and Democrats of conspiring to conceal "the most damning evidence of impeachable, even criminal, offenses."

"What I saw during the trial was not a pretty sight," Schippers said. "Lies, cowardice, hypocrisy, cynicism, butt-covering, amorality—all these combined to make a mockery of the impeachment process."

"Democrats in both Houses sold out basic principles of law and decency for the sake of protecting one of their own," Schippers claimed. "The president and the White House waterboys sold out the American people—not just a one-time spasm of political experience, but in a deliberate snarl of sophistry and cynical manipulation of public opinion, in the singular aim of which was political self-preservation. In the process, Clinton soiled not just himself, but the Constitution, the public trust, and the presidency itself."

Reviewers ridiculed many of Schipper's claims. In one segment, Schippers had written that when the president finally appeared before a grand jury, he was treated with extraordinary dignity and respect by the jurors and prosecutors. "Judge Starr bent over backwards to be fair to the president."

As critic Michael Foreman wrote: "If you believe that, then you also believe in Santa Claus, the Tooth Fairy, and that Hitler was a kind and gentle soul who wanted to bring good will and peace on earth."

New York, New York
If You Can Make It Here, You Can Make It Anywhere

—Hillary Clinton

As the world trained its eye on Hillary, the First Lady made her first public appearance, post impeachment, at a fundraising gala in the Grand Ballroom of Manhattan's Plaza Hotel.

Ironically, this occurred at the same time Monica Lewinsky was appearing on television in a controversial interview hosted by Barbara Walters.

Hillary had no intention of watching Barbara and Monica in a replay of that TV event.

The First Lady had moved on, and within her sight was the possibility of running in the State of New York for the U.S. Senate. On this night she was more or less "becoming a New Yorker."

She wore a high-buttoned pants suit and was introduced by Senator Chuck Schumer, whom she'd helped put into office.

As one reporter summed up her appearance, "Hillary Rodham Clinton declared her independence from a faithless husband. Bill Clinton may retire in disgrace, but she will be around to have an impact on the 21st Century. More future history books will be written about her—and not her husband."

Epilogue

At last, the time had come for the Clintons to pack up and leave the White House to make room for new occupants, George W. Bush and his wife, Laura. The previous eight years had been a time of achievement and triumph, but also of disappointments, betrayal, and scandal.

For their final night in the White House, Bill and Hillary did not want to go to bed, wandering from room to room for strolls down memory lane. All day had been spent packing boxes to be shipped to Little Rock or New York.

Earlier in the day, Bill had pre-recorded his farewell address to the nation. Until the final hour of his presidency, he would continue to perform duties, including freeing $100 million to support more police on the streets.

On her last full day in the White House, Hillary spent some time just lounging in her favorite armchair in the West Sitting Room or visiting Chelsea's bedroom, where her daughter had grown up.

When morning came, Bill talked to Mark Knoller of CBS Radio. "I'm going to miss being president. I enjoyed the job, even on the bad days, and I had more than my share of those damn times. I'm sorry I can't run for a third or fourth term, like FDR."

He also expressed regret that George W. Bush and his Veep, Dick Cheney, "will try to undo many of my achievements. They will work to sabotage my finest programs. Those bastards, especially that Cheney fellow, see the world as a very different place from the way I look at it."

For his final duty in office, he headed to the Oval Office for one last time. He sat down at his desk and performed a presidential ritual: By hand he drafted a note to the incoming president, following in the footsteps of George W. Bush's father, who had written such a letter to Bill.

After that, Bill left the office, saying a farewell to it, before going to thank the loyal White House staff. Hillary joined him, also thanking them for "all the good years and all the bad times we survived."

Buddy Carter, the veteran White House butler, embraced Hillary warmly and, to the sound of a marine combo band, they turned the moment "into a joyous dance," in her words. "We skipped and twirled across the marble floor. My husband cut in, taking me in his arms as we waltzed together down the long hall. Then I said goodbye to the staff where we had spent eight years of living history."

Then they went in to greet the Bushes and Cheneys for a cup of coffee. The new president didn't like the coffee, claiming that "Laura Bush will have to teach the kitchen staff how to make coffee like I like it."

Limousines were waiting outside to take the Clintons and the Bushes along Pennsylvania Avenue to the Capitol.

Outside the White House, Bill paused for a moment of reflection, telling Hillary, "I didn't achieve my dream, my impossible dream."

"And what was that?" she asked.

"I had wanted to rule over the Second Coming of Camelot with my beloved Queen Guenevere."

She gave him a kiss and headed for a limousine to join Laura. She paused and looked back for a final glance.

"We'll be back," she promised the White House.

After Bush's Swearing In Ceremony, she and Bill headed for Andrews Air Force Base, where *Air Force One* was waiting to take them on their final trip.

Before Bill boarded, he turned to Hillary. "Guess what's running through my mind? You know our old campaign song? I'm still thinkin' about tomorrow, and I'm sure you are, too."

"Hell, yes, I am," she said. "The motherfuckers who wanted to destroy us have not heard the last of

Hillary Rodham Clinton."

THE AUTHORS

DARWIN PORTER

As an intense and precocious nine-year-old, **Darwin Porter** began meeting movie stars, TV personalities, politicians, and singers through his vivacious and attractive mother, Hazel, a somewhat eccentric Southern girl who had lost her husband in World War II. Migrating from the depression-ravaged valleys of western North Carolina to Miami Beach during its most ebullient heyday, Hazel became a stylist, wardrobe mistress, and personal assistant to the vaudeville comedienne Sophie Tucker, the bawdy and irrepressible "Last of the Red Hot Mamas."

Virtually every show-biz celebrity who visited Miami Beach paid a call on "Miss Sophie," and Darwin as a pre-teen loosely and indulgently supervised by his mother, was regularly dazzled by the likes of Judy Garland, Dinah Shore, Veronica Lake, Linda Darnell, Martha Raye, and Ronald Reagan, who arrived to pay his respects to Miss Sophie with a young blonde starlet on the rise—Marilyn Monroe.

Hazel's work for Sophie Tucker did not preclude an active dating life: Her *beaux* included Richard Widmark, Victor Mature, Frank Sinatra (who "tipped" teenaged Darwin the then-astronomical sum of ten dollars for getting out of the way), and that alltime "second lead," Wendell Corey, when he wasn't emoting with Barbara Stanwyck and Joan Crawford.

As a late teenager, Darwin edited *The Miami Hurricane* at the University of Miami, where he interviewed Eleanor Roosevelt, Tab Hunter, Lucille Ball, and Adlai Stevenson. He also worked for Florida's then-Senator George Smathers, one of John F. Kennedy's best friends, establishing an ongoing pattern of picking up "Jack and Jackie" lore while still a student.

After graduation, as a journalist, he was commissioned with the opening of a bureau of *The Miami Herald* in Key West (Florida), where he took frequent morning walks with retired U.S. president Harry S Truman during his vacations in what had functioned as his "Winter White House." He also got to know, sometimes very well, various celebrities "slumming" their way through off-the-record holidays in the orbit of then-resident Tennessee Williams. Celebrities hanging out in the permissive arts environment of Key West during those days included Tallulah Bankhead, Cary Grant, Tony Curtis, the stepfather of Richard Burton, a gaggle of show-biz and publishing moguls, and the once-notorious stripper, Bettie Page.

For about a decade in New York, Darwin worked in television journalism and advertising with his long-time partner, the journalist, art director, and distinguished arts-industry socialite Stanley Mills Haggart. Jointly, they produced TV commercials starring such high-powered stars as Joan Crawford (then feverishly promoting Pepsi-Cola), Ronald Reagan (General Electric), and Debbie Reynolds (selling Singer Sewing Machines), along with such other entertainers as Louis Armstrong, Lena Horne, Arlene Dahl, and countless other show-biz personalities hawking commercial products.

During his youth, Stanley had flourished as an insider in early Hollywood as a "leg man" and source of information for Hedda Hopper, the fabled gossip columnist. On his nightly rounds, Stanley was most often accompanied by Hedda's son, William Hopper, a close friend of Ronald Reagan's.

When Stanley wasn't dishing newsy revelations with Hedda, he had worked as a Powers model; a romantic lead opposite Silent-era film star Mae Murray; the intimate companion of superstar Randolph Scott before Scott became emotionally involved with Cary Grant; and a man-about-town who archived gossip from everybody who mattered back when the movie colony was small, accessible, and confident that details about their tribal rites would absolutely never be reported in the press. Over the years, Stanley's vast cornucopia of inside Hollywood information was passed on to Darwin, who amplified it with copious interviews and research of his own.

After Stanley's death in 1980, Darwin inherited a treasure trove of memoirs, notes, and interviews detailing Stanley's early adventures in Hollywood, including in-depth recitations of scandals that even Hopper during her heyday was afraid to publish. Most legal and journalistic standards back then interpreted those oral histories as "unprintable." Times, of course, changed.

Beginning in the early 1960s, Darwin joined forces with the then-fledgling Arthur Frommer organization, playing a key role in researching and writing more than 50 titles and defining the style and values that later emerged as the world's leading travel accessories, ***The Frommer Guides,*** with particular emphasis on Europe, California, New England, and the Caribbean. Between the creation and updating of hundreds of editions of detailed travel guides to

England, France, Italy, Spain, Portugal, Austria, Germany, California, and Switzerland, he continued to interview and discuss the triumphs, feuds, and frustrations of celebrities, many by then reclusive, whom he either sought out or encountered randomly as part of his extensive travels. Ava Gardner and Lana Turner were particularly insightful.

One day when Darwin lived in Tangier, he walked into an opium den to discover Marlene Dietrich sitting alone in a corner.

Darwin has also ghost written books for celebrities (who shall go nameless!) as well as a series of novels. His first, *Butterflies in Heat,* became a cult classic and was adapted into a film, *Tropic of Desire,* starring Eartha Kitt, among others. Other books included *Razzle-Dazzle,* about an errant female movie star of questionable morals; and an erotic thriller, *Blood Moon,* hailed as "pure novelistic Viagra, an American interpretation of Arthur Schnitzler's *La Ronde."*

Darwin's novel, *Marika,* published by Arbor House, evoked Marlene Dietrich for many readers.

His controversial novel, *Venus,* was suggested by the life of the fabled eroticist and diarist, Anaïs Nin. His novel, *Midnight in Savannah,* was a brutal saga of corruption, greed, and sexual tension exploring the eccentricities of Georgia's most notorious city.

His novel, *Rhinestone Country,* catalyzed a guessing game. Which male star was the inspiration for its lovable rogue, Pete Riddle? Mississippi Pearl praised it as "like a scalding gulp of rotgut whiskey on a snowy night in a bowjacks honky-tonk."

Darwin also transformed into literary format the details which he and Stanley Haggart had compiled about the relatively underpublicized scandals of the Silent Screen, releasing them in 2001 as *Hollywood's Silent Closet,* "an uncensored, underground history of Pre-Code Hollywood, loaded with facts and rumors from generations past."

Since then, Darwin has penned more than twenty uncensored Hollywood biographies, many of them award-winners, on subjects who have included Peter O'Toole, Marlon Brando; Merv Griffin; Katharine Hepburn; Howard Hughes; Humphrey Bogart; Michael Jackson; Paul Newman; Steve McQueen; Marilyn Monroe; Elizabeth Taylor; Frank Sinatra; John F. Kennedy; Vivien Leigh; Laurence Olivier; the well known porn star, Linda Lovelace; Anne Bancroft; Sophie Tucker; Veronica Lake; Lucille Lortel; Greta Keller; Tamara Geva; all three of the fabulous Gabor sisters; plus Tennessee Williams, Gore Vidal, Truman Capote, Jacqueline Kennedy Onassis, Jane Wyman, and Ronald and Nancy Reagan.

As a departure from his usual repertoire, Darwin also wrote the controversial *J. Edgar Hoover & Clyde Tolson: Investigating the Sexual Secrets of America's Most Famous Men and Women,* a book about celebrity, voyeurism, political and sexual repression, and blackmail within the highest circles of the U.S. government.

He has also co-authored, in league with Danforth Prince, four *Hollywood Babylon* anthologies, plus four separate volumes of film critiques, reviews, and commentary.

His biographies, over the years, have won more than 30 First Prize or runner-up awards at literary festivals in cities which include Boston, New York, Los Angeles, Hollywood, San Francisco, and Paris.

Darwin can be heard at regular intervals as a radio commentator (and occasionally on television), "dishing" celebrities, pop culture, politics, and scandal.

A resident of New York City, Darwin is currently at work on two biographies slated for release in 2016. These include *James Dean—Tomorrow Never Comes* and *Donald Trump, The Man Who Would Be King.*

DANFORTH PRINCE

The publisher and co-author of this book**, Danforth Prince** is a "Young Turk" within the post-millennium publishing industry. He's president and founder of Blood Moon Productions, a firm devoted to researching, salvaging, compiling, and marketing the oral histories of America's entertainment industry.

One of Prince's famous predecessors, the late Lyle Stuart (self-described as "the last publisher in America with guts") once defined Prince as "one of my natural successors." In 1956, that then-novice maverick launched himself with $8,000 he'd won in a libel judgment against gossip columnist Walter Winchell. It was Stuart who published Linda Lovelace's two authentic memoirs—*Ordeal* and *Out of Bondage.*

"I like to see someone following in my footsteps in the 21st Century," Stuart told Prince. "You publish scandalous biographies. I did, too. My books on J. Edgar Hoover, Jacqueline Kennedy Onassis, and Barbara Hutton stirred up the natives. You do, too."

Prince launched his career in journalism in the 1970s at the Paris Bureau of *The New York Times.* In the early '80s, he resigned to join Darwin Porter in researching, developing and publishing various titles within *The Frommer Guides,* jointly reviewing the travel scenes of more than 50 nations for Simon & Schuster. Authoritative and comprehensive, they were perceived as best-selling "travel bibles" for millions of readers, with recommendations and travel advice about the major nations of Western Europe, the Caribbean, Bermuda, The Bahamas, Georgia and the Carolinas, and California.

Prince, along with Porter, is also the co-author of several award-winning celebrity biographies, each configured as a title within Blood Moon's Babylon series. These have included *Hollywood Babylon—It's Back!; Hollywood Babylon Strikes Again; The Kennedys: All the Gossip Unfit to Print;* and *Frank Sinatra, The Boudoir Singer.*

Prince, with Porter, has co-authored such provocative biographies as *Elizabeth Taylor: There is Nothing Like a Dame.*

With respect and a sense of irony about "When Divas Clash," Prince and Porter also co-authored *Pink Triangle: The Feuds and Private Lives of Tennessee Williams, Gore Vidal, Truman Capote, and Members of their Entourages,* as well as *Jacqueline Kennedy Onassis: A Life Beyond Her Wildest Dreams.* A more recent effort is *Peter O'Toole—Hellraiser, Sexual Outlaw, Irish Rebel.*

Prince is also the co-author, with Darwin Porter, of four books on film criticism, three of which won honors at regional bookfests across America, including Los Angeles and San Francisco. Special features within these guides included the cinematic legacy of Tennessee Wiliams; the implications associated with strolling down *Sunset Blvd.,* that "Boulevard of Broken Dreams"; behind-the-scenes revelations about the making of *Ben-Hur,* starring Charlton Heston. From *Flesh* to *Trash,* he previewed many of Andy Warhol's films and "unzipped" Marlon Brando. He also took a cinematic look at the legacy of Greta Garbo in the re-release of her movies of long ago, revisiting *Mata Hari, Anna Christie, Queen Christina, Anna Karenina, Camille,* and *Ninotchka,* among many others.

Prince, a graduate of Hamilton College and a native of Easton and Bethlehem, Pennsylvania, is the president and founder (in 1996) of the Georgia Literary Association, and of the Porter and Prince Corporation, founded in 1983, which has produced dozens of titles for both Prentice Hall and John Wiley & Sons. In 2011, he was named "Publisher of the Year" by a consortium of literary critics and marketers spearheaded by the J.M. Northern Media Group.

According to Prince, "Blood Moon provides the luxurious illusion that a reader is a perpetual guest at some gossippy dinner party populated with brilliant but occasionally self-delusional figures from bygone eras of The American Experience. Blood Moon's success at salvaging, documenting, and articulating the (till now) orally transmitted histories of the Entertainment Industry, in ways that have never been seen before, is one of the most distinctive aspects of our backlist."

Publishing in collaboration with the National Book Network (www.NBN-Books.com), he has electronically documented some of the controversies associated with his stewardship of Blood Moon in more than 50 videotaped documentaries, book trailers, public speeches, and TV or radio interviews. Any of these can be watched, without charge, by performing a search for "Danforth Prince" on **YouTube.com**, checking him out on **Facebook** (either "Danforth Prince" or "Blood Moon Productions"), on **Twitter** (#BloodyandLunar) or by clicking on **BloodMoonProductions.com**.

During the rare moments when he isn't writing, editing, neurosing about, or promoting Blood Moon, he works out at a New York City gym, rescues stray animals, talks to strangers, runs an *AirBnB.com* Bed and Breakfast (historic **Magnolia House**, on the Manhattan-facing north shore of Staten Island) and regularly attends Episcopal Mass early every Sunday.

INDEX

BLOOD
MOON
Productions, Ltd.

Blood Moon Productions

Entertainment About How America Interprets Its Celebrities

As described by *The Huffington Post*, "Blood Moon, in case you don't know, is a small publishing house on Staten Island that cranks out Hollywood gossip books, about two or three a year, usually of five-, six-, or 700-page length, chocked with stories and pictures about people who used to consume the imaginations of the American public, back when we actually had a public imagination. That is, when people were really interested in each other, rather than in Apple 'devices.' In other words, back when we had vices, not devices."

Reorganized with its present name in 2004, Blood Moon originated in 1997 as the Georgia Literary Association, a vehicle for the promotion of obscure writers from America's Deep South. For several decades, Blood Moon and its key players (Darwin Porter and Danforth Prince) spearheaded the research, writing, and editorial functions of dozens of titles, and hundreds of editions, of THE FROMMER GUIDES, the most respected (and best selling) name in travel publishing.

Blood Moon maintains a back list of more than 30 critically acclaimed biographies, film guides, and novels. Its titles are distributed by the National Book Network (www.NBNBooks.com), and through secondary wholesalers and retailers everywhere.

Since 2004, Blood Moon has been awarded dozens of nationally recognized literary prizes. They've included both silver and bronze medals from the IPPY (Independent Publishers Association) Awards; four nominations and two Honorable Mentions for BOOK OF THE YEAR from Foreword Reviews; nominations from The Ben Franklin Awards; and Awards and Honorable Mentions from the New England, the Los Angeles, the Paris, the Hollywood, the New York, and the San Francisco Book Festivals. Two of its titles have been Grand Prize Winners for Best Summer Reading, as defined by The Beach Book Awards, and in 2013, its triple-play overview of the Gabor sisters was designated as Biography of the Year by the Hollywood Book Festival.

For more about us, including access to a growing number of videotaped book trailers, TV and radio interviews, and public addresses, each accessible via **YouTube.com,** search for key words "Danforth Prince" or "Blood Moon Productions." Or click on **www.BloodMoonProductions.com;** visit our page on Facebook; subscribe to us on Twitter (#BloodyandLunar); or refer to the pages which immediately follow.

Thanks for your interest, best wishes, and happy reading. Literacy matters! Read a book!

Coming soon, in time for the 2016 elections,

another proud and presidential addition to
Blood Moon's Babylon Series

From the same biographers who crafted this love story about ***Bill & Hillary***; an award-winning overview of **Ronald Reagan's *Love Triangle*** *(described on the next page)*; and an *exposé* of everything you ever wondered about ***THE KENNEDYS,***

this will be a breathlessly irreverent overview of the Republican Party's most controversial candidate since John McCain joined forces with roguish Sarah Palin.

DONALD TRUMP

THE MAN WHO WOULD BE KING

An artfully lurid overview of the presidential ambitions of America's Most Fascinating Republican

Softcover, 500 pages, with photos, available everywhere in August, 2016.

ISBN 978-1-936003-51-8

LOVE TRIANGLE

RONALD REAGAN, JANE WYMAN, & NANCY DAVIS

Unique in the history of publishing, this scandalous triple biography focuses on the Hollywood indiscretions of former U.S. president Ronald Reagan and his two wives. A proud and Presidential addition to Blood Moon's Babylon series, it digs deep into what these three young and attractive movie stars were doing decades before two of them took over the Free World.

***

As reviewed by Diane Donovan, Senior Reviewer at the California Bookwatch section of the Midwest Book Review: ***"Love Triangle: Ronald Reagan, Jane Wyman & Nancy Davis may find its way onto many a Republican Reagan fan's reading shelf; but those who expect another Reagan celebration will be surprised: this is lurid Hollywood exposé writing at its best, and outlines the truths surrounding one of the most provocative industry scandals in the world.***

"There are already so many biographies of the Reagans on the market that one might expect similar mile-markers from this: be prepared for shock and awe; because Love Triangle doesn't take your ordinary approach to biography and describes a love triangle that eventually bumped a major Hollywood movie star from the possibility of being First Lady and replaced her with a lesser-known Grade B actress (Nancy Davis).

"From politics and betrayal to romance, infidelity, and sordid affairs, Love Triangle is a steamy, eye-opening story that blows the lid off of the Reagan illusion to raise eyebrows on both sides of the big screen.

"Black and white photos liberally pepper an account of the careers of all three and the lasting shock of their stormy relationships in a delightful pursuit especially recommended for any who relish Hollywood gossip."

***

In 2015, LOVE TRIANGLE, Blood Moon Productions' overview of the early dramas associated with Ronald Reagan's scandal-soaked career in Hollywood, was designated by the Awards Committee of the **HOLLYWOOD BOOK FESTIVAL** as Runner-Up to Best Biography of the Year.

LOVE TRIANGLE: Ronald Reagan, Jane Wyman, & Nancy Davis

Darwin Porter & Danforth Prince

Hot, scandalous, and loaded with information the Reagans never wanted you to know.

Softcover, 6" x 9", with hundreds of photos. ISBN 978-1-936003-41-9

THE KENNEDYS

ALL THE GOSSIP UNFIT TO PRINT

A Staggering Compendium of Indiscretions Associated With Seven Key Players in the Kennedy Clan

Darwin Porter & Danforth Prince

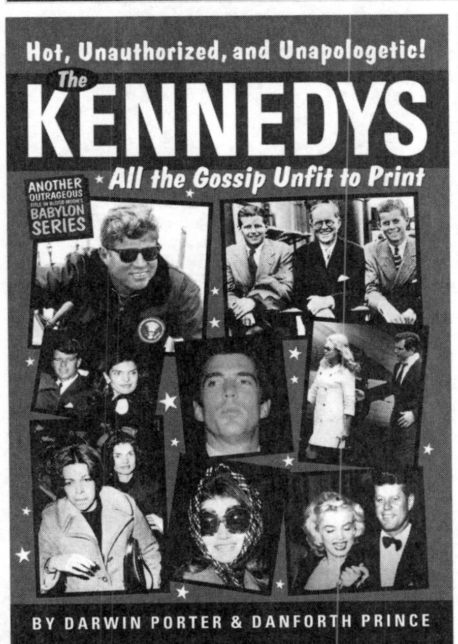

The great enemy of truth is very often not the lie—deliberate, contrived, and dishonest, but the myth—persistent, persuasive, and unrealistic."
—John F. Kennedy

A Cornucopia of Relatively Unknown but Carefully Documented Scandals from the Golden Age of Camelot

"Pick this book up, and you'll be hard-pressed to put it down"
—Richard Labonté, *Q-Syndicate*

The Kennedys were the first true movie stars to occupy the White House. They were also Washington's horniest political tribe, and although America loved their humor, their style, and their panache, we took delight in this tabloid-style documentation of their hundreds of staggering indiscretions.

Keepers of the dying embers of Camelot won't like it, but Kennedy historians and aficionados will interpret it as required reading.

Hardcover, with hundreds of photos and 450 meticulously researched, highly detailed, and very gossipy pages with more outrageous scandal than 90% of American voters during the heyday of Camelot could possibly have imagined.

ISBN 978-1-936003-17-4. Temporarily sold out of hard copies, but available for e-readers

JACQUELINE KENNEDY ONASSIS

A Life Beyond Her Wildest Dreams

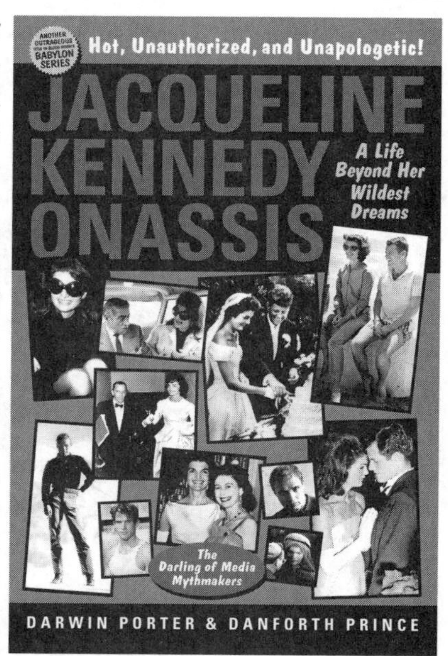

After floods of analysis and commentary in tabloid and mainstream newspapers worldwide, this has emerged as the world's most comprehensive testimonial to the flimsier side of Camelot, the most comprehensive compendium of gossip ever published about America's unofficial, uncrowned queen, **Jacqueline Kennedy Onassis**. Its publication coincided with the 20-year anniversary of the death of one of the most famous, revered, and talked-about women who ever lived.

During her tumultuous life, Mrs. Onassis zealously guarded her privacy and her secrets. But in the wake of her death, more and more revelations have emerged about her frustrations, her rage, her passions, her towering strengths, and her delicate fragility, which she hid from the glare of the world behind oversized sunglasses. Within this posthumous biography, a three-dimensional woman emerges through the compilation of some 1,000 eyewitness testimonials from men and women who knew her over a period of decades.

An overview of the life of Mrs. Onassis is a natural fit for Blood Moon, a publishing enterprise that's increasingly known, worldwide, as one of the most provocative and scandalous in the history of publishing.

"References to this American icon appear with almost rhythmic regularity to anyone researching the cultural landscape of America during the last half of The American Century," said Danforth Prince. "Based on what we'd uncovered about Jackie during the research of many of our earlier titles, we're positioning ourselves as a more or less solitary outpost of irreverence within a landscape that's otherwise flooded with fawning, over-reverential testimonials. Therein lies this book's appeal—albeit with a constant respect and affection for a woman we admired and adored."

Based on decades of research by writers who define themselves as "voraciously attentive Kennedyphiles," it supplements the half-dozen other titles within Blood Moon's Babylon series.

JACQUELINE KENNEDY ONASSIS—A LIFE BEYOND HER WILDEST DREAMS

Darwin Porter and Danforth Prince

Biography/Entertainment 6" x 9" 700 pages with hundreds of photos

ISBN 978-1-936003-39-6 Also available for E-readers.

America's most enduring and legendary symbol of young, enraged rebellion, James Dean continues into the 21st Century to capture the imagination of the world.

After one of his many flirtations with Death, which caught up with him when he was a celebrity-soaked 24-year-old, he said, "If a man can live after he dies, then maybe he's a great man." Today, bars from Nigeria to Patagonia are named in honor of this international, spectacularly self-destructive movie star icon.

Migrating from the dusty backroads of Indiana to center stage in the most formidable boudoirs of Hollywood, his saga is electrifying.

A strikingly handsome heart-throb, Dean is a study in contrasts: Tough but tender, brutal but remarkably sensitive; he was a reckless hellraiser badass who could revert to a little boy in bed.

A rampant bisexual, he claimed that he didn't want to go through life "with one hand tied behind my back." He demonstrated that during bedroom trysts with Marilyn Monroe, Rock Hudson, Elizabeth Taylor, Paul Newman, Natalie Wood, Shelley Winters, Marlon Brando, Steve McQueen, Ursula Andress, Montgomery Clift, Pier Angeli, Tennessee Williams, Susan Strasberg, Tallulah Bankhead, and FBI director J. Edgar Hoover.

Woolworth heiress Barbara Hutton, one of the richest and most dissipated women of her era, wanted to make him her toy boy.

Tomorrow Never Comes is the most penetrating look at James Dean to have emerged from the wreckage of his Porsche Spyder in 1955.

Before setting out on his last ride, he said, "I feel life too intensely to bear living it."

Tomorrow Never Comes presents a damaged but beautiful soul.

Coming Soon! Available Everywhere Early in 2016

JAMES DEAN—TOMORROW NEVER COMES

Softcover, with photos. ISBN 978-1-936003-49-5

PETER O'TOOLE

Hellraiser, Sexual Outlaw, Irish Rebel

At the time of its publication early in 2015, this book was widely publicized in the *Daily Mail, the NY Daily News, the NY Post, the Midwest Book Review, The Express (London), The Globe, the National Enquirer,* and in equivalent publications worldwide

One of the world's most admired (and brilliant) actors, Peter O'Toole wined and wenched his way through a labyrinth of sexual and interpersonal betrayals, sometimes with disastrous results. Away from the stage and screen, where such films as *Becket* and *Lawrence of Arabia*, made film history, his life was filled with drunken, debauched nights and edgy sexual experimentations, most of which were never openly examined in the press. A hellraiser, he shared wild times with his "best blokes" Richard Burton and Richard Harris. Peter Finch, also his close friend, once invited him to join him in sharing the pleasures of his mistress, Vivien Leigh.

"My father, a bookie, moved us to the Mick community of Leeds," O'Toole once told a reporter. "We were very poor, but I was born an Irishman, which accounts for my gift of gab, my unruly behavior, my passionate devotion to women and the bottle, and my loathing of any authority figure."

Author Robert Sellers described O'Toole's boyhood neighborhood. "Three of his playmates went on to be hanged for murder; one strangled a girl in a lovers' quarrel; one killed a man during a robbery; another cut up a warden in South Africa with a pair of shears. It was a heavy bunch."

Peter O'Toole's hell-raising life story has never been told, until now. Hot and uncensored, from a writing team which, even prior to O'Toole's death in 2013, had been collecting under-the-radar info about him for years, this book has everything you ever wanted to know about how THE LION navigated his way through the boudoirs of the Entertainment Industry IN WINTER, Spring, Summer, and a dissipated Autumn as well.

Blood Moon has ripped away the imperial robe, scepter, and crown usually associated with this quixotic problem child of the British Midlands. Provocatively uncensored, this illusion-shattering overview of Peter O'Toole's hellraising (or at least very naughty) and demented life is unique in the history of publishing.

PETER O'TOOLE: Hellraiser, Sexual Outlaw, Irish Rebel
Softcover, with photos. ISBN 978-1-936003-45-7

This book illustrates why *Gentlemen Prefer Blondes*, and why Marilyn Monroe was too dangerous to be allowed to go on living.

Less than an hour after the discovery of Marilyn Monroe's corpse in Brentwood, a flood of theories, tainted evidence, and conflicting testimonies began pouring out into the public landscape.

Filled with rage, hysteria, and depression, "and fed up with Jack's lies, Bobby's lies," Marilyn sought revenge and mass vindication. Her revelations at an imminent press conference could have toppled political dynasties and destroyed criminal empires. Marilyn had to be stopped…

Into this steamy cauldron of deceit, Marilyn herself emerges as a most unreliable witness during the weeks leading up to her murder. Her own deceptions, vanities, and self-delusion poured toxic accelerants on an already raging fire.

"This is the best book about Marilyn Monroe ever published." —**David Hartnell,** Recipient, in 2011, of New Zealand's Order of Merit (MNZM) for services to the entertainment industry, as defined by Her Majesty, Queen Elizabeth II.

Winner of literary awards from the New York, Hollywood, and San Francisco Book Festivals

MARILYN AT RAINBOW'S END

SEX, LIES, MURDER, AND THE GREAT COVER-UP, BY DARWIN PORTER

ISBN 978-1-936003-29-7

Temporarily sold out of hard copies, but available for E-Readers

"Darwin Porter is fearless, honest and a great read. He minces no words. If the truth makes you wince and honesty offends your sensibility, stay away. It's been said that he deals in muck because he can't libel the dead. Well, it's about time someone started telling the truth about the dead and being honest about just what happened to get us in the mess in which we're in. If libel is lying, then Porter is so completely innocent as to deserve an award. In all of his works he speaks only to the truth, and although he is a hard teacher and task master, he's one we ignore at our peril. To quote Gore Vidal, power is not a toy we give to someone for being good. If we all don't begin to investigate where power and money really are in the here and now, we deserve what we get. Yes, Porter names names. The reader will come away from the book knowing just who killed Monroe. Porter rather brilliantly points to a number of motives, but leaves it to the reader to surmise exactly what happened at the rainbow's end, just why Marilyn was killed. And, of course, why we should be careful of getting exactly what we want. It's a very long tumble from the top."

—ALAN PETRUCELLI, Examiner.com, May 13, 2012

ELIZABETH TAYLOR

There is Nothing Like a Dame

All the Gossip Unfit to Print from the Glory Days of Hollywood

For more than 60 years, Elizabeth Taylor dazzled generations of movie-goers with her glamor and her all-consuming passion for life. She was the last of the great stars of Golden Age Hollywood, coming to a sad end at the age of 79 in 2011.

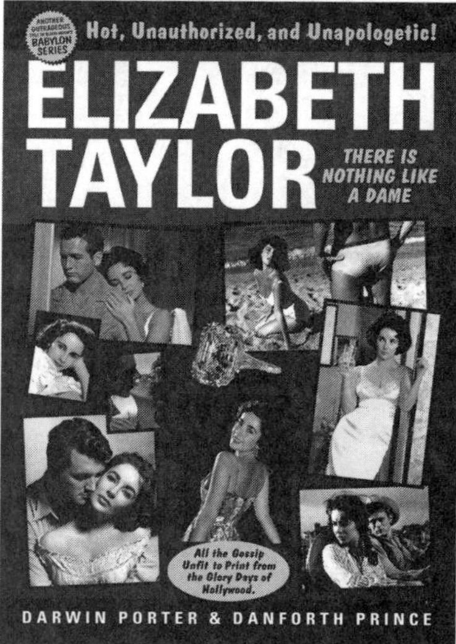

But before she died, appearing on the Larry King show, she claimed that her biographers had revealed "only half of my story, but I can't tell the other half in a memoir because I'd get sued."

Now, Blood Moon presents for the first time a comprehensive compilation of most of the secrets from the mercurial Dame Elizabeth, whose hedonism helped define the jet set of the tumultuous 60s and beyond.

Throughout the many decades of her life, she consistently generated hysteria among her fans. Here, her story is told with brutal honesty in rich, juicy detail and illustrated, with a new revelation on every page.

It's all here, and a lot more, in an exposé that's both sympathetic and shocking, with a candor and attention to detail that brings the *femme fatale* of the 20th century back to life.

"What has never been denied about Elizabeth Taylor is that the young actress, though small for her age, was mature beyond her years, deeply ambitious, and sexually precocious...Insiders agreed she always had a strong rebellious streak. Could the studio system's vice-like grip on publicity have stopped scandals about their most valuable child star from leaking out?

"A recent biography of Taylor claims that as a teenager, she lost her virginity at 15 to British actor Peter Lawford, had flings with Ronald Reagan and Errol Flynn, was roughly seduced by Orson Welles, and even enjoyed a threesome involving John F. Kennedy.

The authors—Darwin Porter and Danforth Prince—also allege Taylor was just 11 when she was taught by her close friend, the gay British actor, Roddy McDowall, the star of Lassie Come Home, *how to satisfy men without sleeping with them."*

Tom Leonard in THE DAILY MAIL, October 19, 2015

***

"I'm called a scarlet woman. That's wrong. I'm positively purple."

—Elizabeth Taylor

"Before they wither, Elizabeth Taylor's breasts will topple empires."

—Richard Burton

Softcover, 460 pages, with photos ISBN 978-1-936003-31-0.
Temporarily sold out of hard copies, but available as an E-book.

THOSE GLAMOROUS GABORS

Bombshells from Budapest, by Darwin Porter

Zsa Zsa, Eva, and Magda Gabor transferred their glittery dreams and gold-digging ambitions from the twilight of the Austro-Hungarian Empire to Hollywood. There, more effectively than any army, these Bombshells from Budapest broke hearts, amassed fortunes, lovers, and A-list husbands, and amused millions of *voyeurs* through the medium of television, movies, and the social registers. In this astonishing "triple-play" biography, designated "Best Biography of the Year" by the Hollywood Book Festival, Blood Moon lifts the "mink-and-diamond" curtain on this amazing trio of blood-related sisters, whose complicated intrigues have never been fully explored before.

"You will never be Ga-bored...this book gives new meaning to the term compelling. Be warned, *Those Glamorous Gabors* is both an epic and a pip. Not since *Gone With the Wind* have so many characters on the printed page been forced to run for their lives for one reason or another. And Scarlett making a dress out of the curtains is nothing compared to what a Gabor will do when she needs to scrap together an outfit for a movie premiere or late-night outing.

"For those not up to speed, Jolie Tilleman came from a family of jewelers and therefore came by her love for the shiny stones honestly, perhaps genetically. She married Vilmos Gabor somewhere around World War 1 (exact dates, especially birth dates, are always somewhat vague in order to establish plausible deniability later on) and they were soon blessed with three daughters: **Magda**, the oldest, whose hair, sadly, was naturally brown, although it would turn quite red in America; **Zsa Zsa** (born 'Sari') a natural blond who at a very young age exhibited the desire for fame with none of the talents usually associated with achievement, excepting beauty and a natural wit; and **Eva**, the youngest and blondest of the girls, who after seeing Grace Moore perform at the National Theater, decided that she wanted to be an actress and that she would one day move to Hollywood to become a star.

"Given that the Gabor family at that time lived in Budapest, Hungary, at the period of time between the World Wars, that Hollywood dream seemed a distant one indeed. The story—the riches to rags to riches to rags to riches again myth of survival against all odds as the four women, because of their Jewish heritage, flee Europe with only the minks on their backs and what jewels they could smuggle along with them in their *decolletage*, only to have to battle afresh for their places in the vicious Hollywood pecking order—gives new meaning to the term 'compelling.' The reader, as if he were witnessing a particularly gore-drenched traffic accident, is incapable of looking away."

—New York Review of Books

Softcover, 730 pages, with hundreds of photos ISBN 978-1-936003-35-8

PINK TRIANGLE

The Feuds and Private Lives of Tennessee Williams, Gore Vidal, Truman Capote, and Famous Members of their Entourages

Darwin Porter & Danforth Prince

The *enfants terribles* of America at mid-20th century challenged the sexual censors of their day while indulging in "bitch-fests" for love & glory.

This book exposes their literary slugfests and offers an intimate look at their relationships with the *glitterati*—MM, Brando, the Oliviers, the Paleys, U.S. Presidents, a gaggle of other movie stars, millionaires, and dozens of others.

This is for anyone who's interested in the formerly concealed scandals of Hollywood and Broadway, and the values and pretentions of both the literary world and the entertainment industry.

"A banquet... If *PINK TRIANGLE* had not been written for us, we would have had to research and type it all up for ourselves...Pink Triangle is nearly seven hundred pages of the most entertaining histrionics ever sliced, spiced, heated, and serviced up to the reading public. Everything that Blood Moon has done before pales in comparison.

"Given the fact that the subjects of the book themselves were nearly delusional on the subject of themselves (to say nothing of each other) it is hard to find fault. Add to this the intertwined jungle that was the relationship among Williams, Capote, and Vidal, of the times they vied for things they loved most—especially attention—and the times they enthralled each other and the world, [*Pink Triangle* is] the perfect antidote to the Polar Vortex."

—Vinton McCabe in the NY JOURNAL OF BOOKS

"Full disclosure: I have been a friend and follower of Blood Moon Productions' tomes for years, and always marveled at the amount of information in their books—it's staggering. The index alone to *Pink Triangle* runs to 21 pages—and the scale of names in it runs like a *Who's Who* of American social, cultural and political life through much of the 20th century."

—Perry Brass in THE HUFFINGTON POST

"We Brits are not spared the Porter/Prince silken lash either. PINK TRIANGLE's research is, quite frankly, breathtaking. PINK TRIANGLE will fascinate you for many weeks to come. Once you have made the initial titillating dip, the day will seem dull without it."

—Jeffery Tayor in THE SUNDAY EXPRESS (UK)

PINK TRIANGLE—The Feuds and Private Lives of Tennessee Williams, Gore Vidal, Truman Capote, and Famous Members of their Entourages
Darwin Porter & Danforth Prince

Softcover, 700 pages, with photos ISBN 978-1-936003-37-2 Also Available for E-Readers

INSIDE LINDA LOVELACE'S DEEP THROAT

DEGRADATION, PORNO CHIC, AND THE RISE OF FEMINISM

DARWIN PORTER

An insider's view of the unlikely heroine who changed the world's perceptions about pornography, censorship, and sexual behavior patterns

The Most Comprehensive Biography Ever Written of an Adult Entertainment Star and Her Relationship with the Underbelly of Hollywood

***Darwin Porter**, author of some twenty critically acclaimed celebrity exposés of behind-the-scenes intrigue in the entertainment industry, was deeply involved in the Linda Lovelace saga as it unfolded in the 70s, interviewing many of the players, and raising money for the legal defense of the film's co-star, Harry Reems. In this book, emphasizing her role as a celebrity interacting with other celebrities, he brings inside information and a never-before-published revelation to almost every page.*

The Beach Book Festival's Grand Prize Winner: "Best Summer Reading of 2013"

Runner-Up to "Best Biography of 2013" *The Los Angeles Book Festival*

Winner of a Sybarite Award from HedoOnline.com

"This book drew me in..How could it not?" Coco Papy, *Bookslut.*

the Award-Winning overview of a story that changed America and the Entertainment Industry forever:

INSIDE LINDA LOVELACE'S DEEP THROAT
Degradation, Porno Chic,
& the Rise of Feminism

Another hot and insightful commentary about major and sometimes violently controversial conflicts of the American Century by

Darwin Porter

Softcover, 640 pages, 6"x9" with photos.
ISBN 978-1-936003-33-4

PAUL NEWMAN

The Man Behind the Baby Blues, His Secret Life Exposed

Darwin Porter

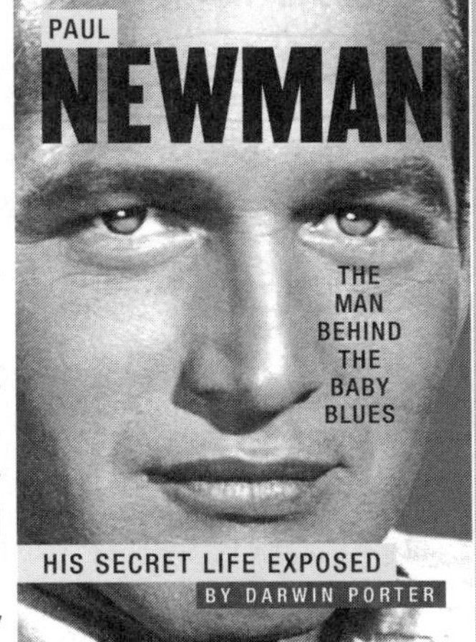

Drawn from firsthand interviews with insiders who knew Paul Newman intimately, and compiled over a period of nearly a half-century, this is the world's most honest and most revelatory biography about Hollywood's pre-eminent male sex symbol.

This is a respectful but candid cornucopia of once-concealed information about the sexual and emotional adventures of an affable, impossibly good-looking workaday actor, a former sailor from Shaker Heights, Ohio, who parlayed his ambisexual charm and extraordinary good looks into one of the most successful careers in Hollywood.

Whereas the situations it exposes were widely known within Hollywood's inner circles, they've never before been revealed to the general public.

But now, the full story has been published—the giddy heights and agonizing crashes of a great American star, with revelations and insights never before published in any other biography.

"Paul Newman had just as many on-location affairs as the rest of us, and he was just as bisexual as I was. But whereas I was always getting caught with my pants down, he managed to do it in the dark with not a paparazzo in sight. He might have bedded Marilyn Monroe or Elizabeth Taylor the night before, but he always managed to show up for breakfast with Joanne Woodward, with those baby blues, looking as innocent as a Botticelli angel. He never fooled me. It takes an alleycat to know another one. Did I ever tell you what really happened between Newman and me? If that doesn't grab you, what about what went on between James Dean and Newman? Let me tell you about this co-called model husband if you want to look behind those famous peepers."

—Marlon Brando

Paul Newman, The Man Behind the Baby Blues, His Secret Life Exposed

Recipient of an Honorable Mention from the New England Book Festival

Hardcover, 520 pages, with dozens of photos. **ISBN 978-0-9786465-1-6**

Also available for e-readers

FRANK SINATRA, THE BOUDOIR SINGER

All the Gossip Unfit to Print from the Glory Days of Ol' Blue Eyes

Darwin Porter & Danforth Prince

Even If You Thought You'd Heard It All Already,You'll Be Amazed At How Much This Book Contains That Never Got Published Before.

Vendettas and high-octane indiscretions, fast and furious women, deep sensitivities and sporadic psychoses, Presidential pimping, FBI coverups, Mobster mambos, and a pantload of hushed-up scandals about **FABULOUS FRANK AND HIS MIND-BLOWING COHORTS**

"Womanizer Sinatra's Shocking Secret Sins are revealed in a blockbuster new book, including his raunchy romps with Liz Taylor, Marilyn Monroe, Jackie-O, and Nancy Reagan. Every time the leader of the Free World would join him in Palm Springs, the place was a sun-kissed brothel, with Kennedy as the main customer." **— THE GLOBE**

Frank Sinatra, The Boudoir Singer
Hardcover, 465 pages with hundreds of photos ISBN 978-1-936003-19-8
Also available for E-readers

J. EDGAR HOOVER AND CLYDE TOLSON

Investigating the Sexual Secrets of America's Most Famous Men & Women

Darwin Porter
How the FBI Investigated Hollywood

This epic saga of power and corruption has a revelation on every page—cross dressing, gay parties, sexual indiscretions, hustlers for sale, alliances with the Mafia, and criminal activity by the nation's chief law enforcer.

It's all here, with chilling details about the abuse of power on the dark side of the American saga. But mostly it's the decades-long love story of America's two most powerful men who could tell presidents "how to skip rope." (Hoover's words.)

"Everyone's dredging up J. Edgar Hoover. Leonardo DiCaprio just immortalized him, and now comes Darwin Porter's paperback, *J. Edgar Hoover & Clyde Tolson: Investigating the Sexual Secrets of America's Most Famous Men and Women.* It shovels Hoover's darkest secrets dragged kicking and screaming from the closet. It's filth on every VIP who's safely dead and some who are still above ground."

—Cindy Adams, The New York Post

"This book is important, because it destroys what's left of Hoover's reputation. Did you know he had intel on the bombing of Pearl Harbor, but he sat on it, making him more or less responsible for thousands of deaths? Or that he had almost nothing to do with the arrests or killings of any of the 1930s gangsters that he took credit for catching?

"A lot of people are angry with its author, Darwin Porter. They say that his outing of celebrities is just cheap gossip about dead people who can't defend themselves. I suppose it's because Porter is destroying carefully constructed myths that are comforting to most people. As gay men, we benefit the most from Porter's work, because we know that except for AIDS, the closet was the most terrible thing about the 20th century. If the closet never existed, neither would Hoover. The fact that he got away with such duplicity under eight presidents makes you think that every one of them was a complete fool for tolerating it."

—Paul Bellini, FAB Magazine (Toronto)

Winner of Literary Awards from the Los Angeles & the Hollywood Book Festivals
Temporarily sold out of hard copies, but available for E-Readers. ISBN 978-1-936003-25-9

WHAT does a man really have to do to make it in Show Biz?

Finally—A COOL biography that was too HOT to be published during the lifetime of its subject. TALES OF A LURID LIFE!

The drama of Steve McQueen's personal life far exceeded any role he ever played on screen. Born to a prostitute, he was brutally molested by some of his mother's "johns," and endured gang rape in reform school. His drift into prostitution began when he was hired as a towel boy in the most notorious bordello in the Dominican Republic, where he starred in a string of cheap porno films. Returning to New York before migrating to Hollywood, he hustled men on Times Square and, as a "gentleman escort" in a borrowed tux, rich older women.

And then, sudden stardom as he became the world's top box office attraction. The abused became the abuser. "I live for myself, and I answer to nobody," he proclaimed. "The last thing I want to do is fall in love with a broad."

Thus began a string of seductions that included hundreds of overnight pickups--both male and female. Topping his A-list conquests were James Dean, Paul Newman, Marilyn Monroe, and Barbra Streisand. Finally, this pioneering biography explores the mysterious death of Steve McQueen. Were those salacious rumors really true?

Steve McQueen King of Cool Tales of a Lurid Life

Darwin Porter

A carefully researched, 466-page hardcover with dozens of photos
Temporarily sold out of hard copies, but available now for e-readers

ISBN 978-1-936003-05-1

Humphrey Bogart

The Making of a Legend

Darwin Porter

A "cradle-to-grave" hardcover about the rise to fame of an obscure, unlikely, and frequently unemployed Broadway actor

Whereas **Humphrey Bogart** is always at the top of any list of the Entertainment Industry's most famous actors, very little is known about how he clawed his way from Broadway to Hollywood during Prohibition and the Jazz Age.

This pioneering biography begins with Bogart's origins as the child of wealthy (morphine-addicted) parents in New York City, then examines the love affairs, scandals, failures, and breakthroughs that launched him as an American icon.

It includes details about behind-the-scenes dramas associated with three mysterious marriages, and films such as *The Petrified Forest, The Maltese Falcon, High Sierra,* and *Casablanca.* Read all about the debut and formative years of the actor who influenced many generations of filmgoers, laying Bogie's life bare in a style you've come to expect from Darwin Porter. Exposed with all their juicy details is what Bogie never told his fourth wife, Lauren Bacall, herself a screen legend.

Drawn from original interviews with friends and foes who knew a lot about what lay beneath his trenchcoat, this exposé covers Bogart's remarkable life as it helped define movie-making, Hollywood's portrayal of macho, and America's evolving concept of Entertainment itself.

This revelatory book is based on dusty unpublished memoirs, letters, diaries, and often personal interviews from the women—and the men—who adored him.

There are also shocking allegations from colleagues, former friends, and jilted lovers who wanted the screen icon to burn in hell.

All this and more, much more, in Darwin Porter's exposé of Bogie's startling secret life.

WITH STARTLING NEW INFORMATION YOU'VE NEVER SEEN BEFORE
about Bogart, the movies, and Golden Age Hollywood

542 pages, with hundreds of photos **ISBN 978-1-936003-14-3**

Also available for E-Readers

BRANDO UNZIPPED

An Uncensored *Exposé* of America's Most Visible Method Actor and Sexual Outlaw

by Darwin Porter

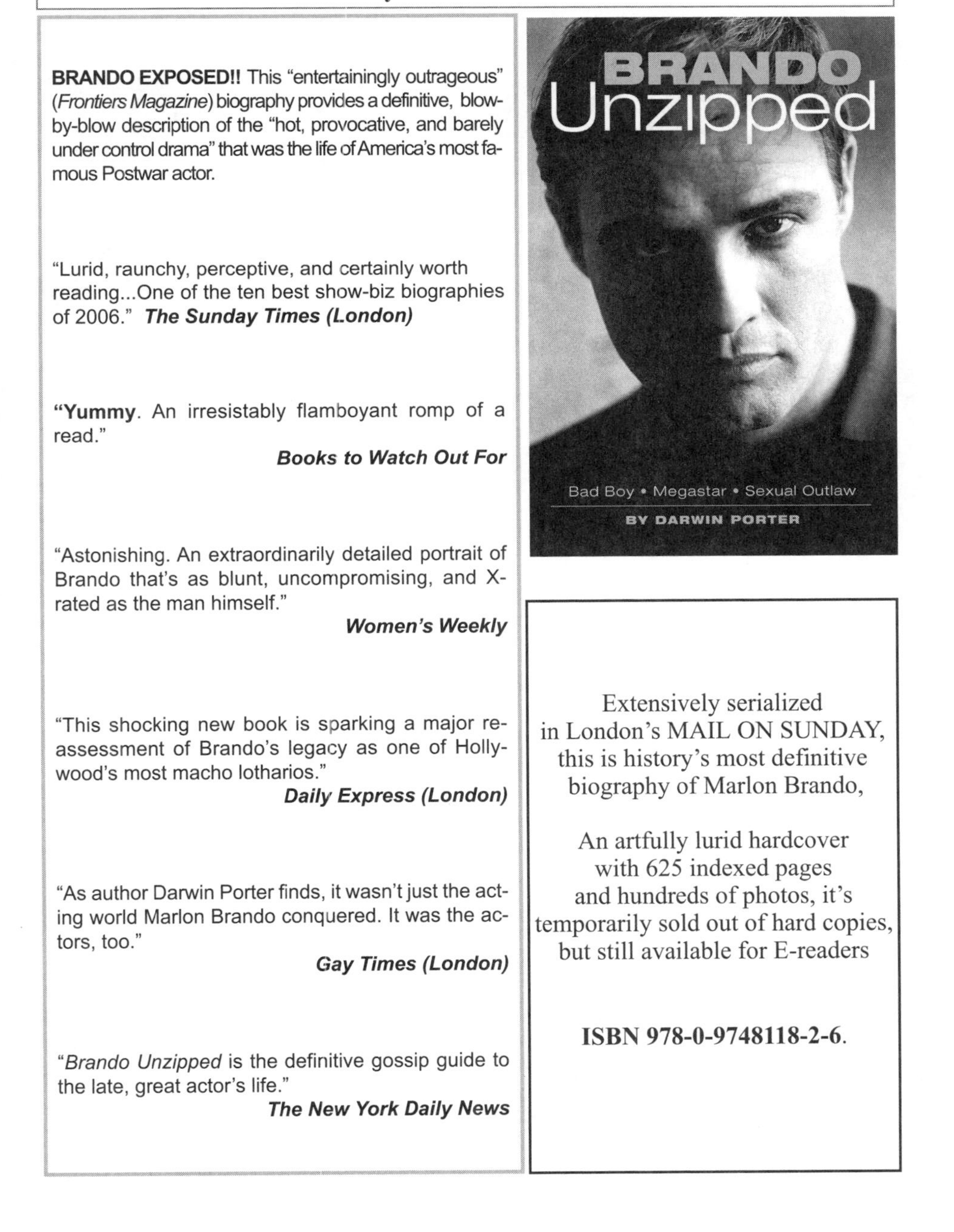

BRANDO EXPOSED!! This "entertainingly outrageous" (*Frontiers Magazine*) biography provides a definitive, blow-by-blow description of the "hot, provocative, and barely under control drama" that was the life of America's most famous Postwar actor.

"Lurid, raunchy, perceptive, and certainly worth reading...One of the ten best show-biz biographies of 2006." ***The Sunday Times (London)***

"**Yummy**. An irresistably flamboyant romp of a read."

Books to Watch Out For

"Astonishing. An extraordinarily detailed portrait of Brando that's as blunt, uncompromising, and X-rated as the man himself."

Women's Weekly

"This shocking new book is sparking a major re-assessment of Brando's legacy as one of Hollywood's most macho lotharios."

Daily Express (London)

"As author Darwin Porter finds, it wasn't just the acting world Marlon Brando conquered. It was the actors, too."

Gay Times (London)

"*Brando Unzipped* is the definitive gossip guide to the late, great actor's life."

The New York Daily News

Extensively serialized
in London's MAIL ON SUNDAY,
this is history's most definitive
biography of Marlon Brando,

An artfully lurid hardcover
with 625 indexed pages
and hundreds of photos, it's
temporarily sold out of hard copies,
but still available for E-readers

ISBN 978-0-9748118-2-6.

Jacko
His Rise and Fall

The Social and Sexual History of Michael Jackson

Darwin Porter

He rewrote the rules of America's entertainment industry, and he led a life of notoriety. Even his death was the occasion for scandals which continue to this day.

This is the world's most comprehensive historical overview of a pop star's rise, fall, and to some extent, rebirth as an American Icon. Read it for the real story of the circumstances and players who created the icon which the world will forever remember as "the gloved one," Michael Jackson.

"This is the story of Peter Pan gone rotten. Don't stop till you get enough. Darwin Porter's biography of Michael Jackson is dangerously addictive."

The Sunday Observer (London)

"In this compelling glimpse of Jackson's life, Porter provides what many journalists have failed to produce in their writings about the pop star: A real person behind the headlines."

Foreword Magazine

"I'd have thought that there wasn't one single gossippy rock yet to be overturned in the microscopically scrutinized life of Michael Jackson, but Darwin Porter has proven me wrong. Definitely a page-turner. But don't turn the pages too quickly. Almost every one holds a fascinating revelation."

Books to Watch Out For

This book, a winner of literary awards from both *Foreword Magazine* and the Hollywood Book Festival, was originally published during the lifetime of Michael Jackson. This, the revised, post-mortem edition, with extra analysis and commentary, was released after his death.

Hardcover 600 indexed pages with about a hundred photos

ISBN 978-0-936003-10-5. Also available for E-readers

This is What Happens When A Demented Billionaire Hits Hollywood

HOWARD HUGHES
HELL'S ANGEL
BY DARWIN PORTER

From his reckless pursuit of love as a rich teenager to his final days as a demented fossil, Howard Hughes tasted the best and worst of the century he occupied. Along the way, he changed the worlds of aviation and entertainment forever.

This biography reveals inside details about his destructive and usually scandalous associations with other Hollywood players.

"The Aviator flew both ways. Porter's biography presents new allegations about Hughes' shady dealings with some of the biggest names of the 20th century"
—New York Daily News

"Darwin Porter's access to film industry insiders and other Hughes confidants supplied him with the resources he needed to create a portrait of Hughes that both corroborates what other Hughes biographies have divulged, and go them one better."
—Foreword Magazine

"Thanks to this bio of Howard Hughes, we'll never be able to look at the old pinups in quite the same way again."
—The Times (London)

Winner of a respected literary award from the Los Angeles Book Festival, this book gives an insider's perspective about what money can buy—and what it can't

814 pages, with photos. Also available for E-Readers

ISBN 978-1-936003-13-6

HOLLYWOOD BABYLON STRIKES AGAIN!

THE PROFOUNDLY OUTRAGEOUS VOLUME TWO OF BLOOD MOON'S BABYLON SERIES

"These books will set the graves of Hollywood's cemeteries spinning" **Daily Express**

Hollywood Babylon Strikes Again!

Darwin Porter and Danforth Prince
Hardcover, 380 outrageous pages, with hundreds of photos

ISBN 978-1-936003-12-9

OUT OF THE CELLULOID CLOSET, A HALF-CENTURY REVIEW OF

HOMOSEXUALITY IN THE MOVIES

A Book of Record, Reference Source, and Gossip Guide to 50 Years of Queer Cinema

Out, outrageous, provocative, and proud, this comprehensive anthology and library resource reviews 500 of the best of Hollywood's output of gay, bisexual, lesbian, transgendered, and queer questioning films, with a special emphasis on how gays changed the movies we know and love.

Conceived as a working guide to what viewers should stock within their DVD queues, it reviews everything from blockbusters to indie sleepers, with about a dozen special features discussing the ironies, betrayals, subterfuge, and gossip of who, what, and how it happened when the film world's closet doors slowly creaked open beginning in 1960.

***

"In the Internet age, where every movie, queer or otherwise, is blogged about somewhere, a hefty print compendium of film facts and pointed opinion might seem anachronistic. But flipping through well-reasoned pages of commentary is so satisfying. Add to that physical thrill the charm of analysis that is sometimes sassy and always smart, and this filtered survey of short reviews is a must for queer-film fans.

"Essays on Derek Jarman, Tennessee Williams, Andy Warhol, Jack Wrangler, Joe Gage and others—and on how The Front Runner *never got made—round out this indispensable survey of gay-interest cinema."*

RICHARD LABONTÉ
BOOK MARKS/QSYNDICATE

Winner of the New England Book Festival's
Best GLBT Title of 2010

50 YEARS OF QUEER CINEMA
500 of the Best GLBT Films Ever Made

Softcover, 400 pages, with photos. ISBN 978-1-936003-09-9

BLOOD
MOON
Productions, Ltd.